Adult Development

Custom Edition for Ashford University

Taken from:

Lifespan Development, Fourth Edition by Denise Boyd and Helen Bee

ASHFORD
UNIVERSITY
FOUNDED 1918

PEARSON
Custom
Publishing

PEARSON

Excerpts taken from:

Lifespan Development, Fourth Edition
by Denise Boyd and Helen Bee
Copyright © 2006, 2003 by Pearson Education, Inc.
Published by Allyn and Bacon.
Boston, Massachusetts, 02116

Printed in the United States of America

10   9   8   7   6   5   4

ISBN 0-536-16988-8

2005240500

DG

Please visit our web site at *www.pearsoncustom.com*

PEARSON CUSTOM PUBLISHING
75 Arlington Street, Suite 300, Boston, MA 02116
A Pearson Education Company

FOREWORD

WELCOME TO ASHFORD UNIVERSITY!

I applaud you for making the decision to return to school and finish your degree. A college education is critical in today's workplace—but more importantly, learning is a lifelong endeavor that enriches your journey.

We at Ashford University are committed to helping you achieve your personal and professional goals. This course, *Adult Development and Life Assessment,* is a perfect way to jump back into the educational arena. In this course, you will study the psychology of adult development, but learning is more powerful when it is applied and reflective. We encourage you to use this course as an opportunity to reflect on your life thus far and plan for the future you desire.

Reflecting on life's complexities and dilemmas, a character in Arthur Miller's, *All My Sons* observed that his life experiences could be thought of as "a tapestry hung on four or five hooks." He concluded that his experiences were important because they shaped the tapestry uniquely, but the hooks on which the tapestry hung were *essential.* Your value-based decision to finish your bachelor's degree can be one of those essential hooks—on which so much of what lies ahead depends.

Enjoy the journey.

Warmly,

Elizabeth T. Tice, Ph.D.
Provost

BRIEF CONTENTS

CONTENTS

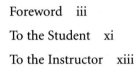

7 Physical and Cognitive Development in Late Adulthood   164

8 Social and Personality Development in Late Adulthood   193

TO THE STUDENT

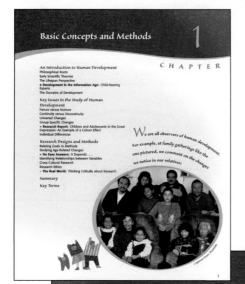

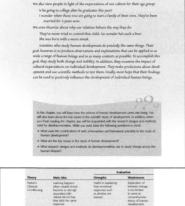

Before you begin your study of human development across the lifespan, it is important that you know what an incredibly complex field it is. To convey this complexity, textbooks must include a great deal of information. Thus, studying human development may be one of the most information-intensive learning experiences of your academic career. Fortunately, this book includes a number of features that will help you manage and sort out all this information.

HOW TO WORK WITH THIS BOOK

A textbook isn't like a magazine or a novel. You should keep in mind that the goal of working with a textbook is to understand and remember the information in it. To work with this book most effectively, take advantage of its structural and pedagogical features.

- *Chapter Outlines.* Before you read each chapter, read over the outline at its beginning. More information will stick in your mind if you have an idea of what to expect.

- *Preview Questions.* The introduction to each chapter ends with a list of questions to keep in mind as you read. Be sure to read the questions before continuing with the rest of the chapter. Like the chapter outline, the questions create a set of mental "hooks" on which to hang the information in the chapter.

- *Headings and Subheadings.* The preview questions correspond to the chapter's major headings. Think of these headings and their subheadings as a way of dividing the information that follows them into categories. Thinking of the information in this way will create a network in your mind that will make it easier to recall information when you are tested. Taking notes on your reading and arranging them according to the book's headings will help even more. To give yourself the best chance of creating these information networks, stop reading between major sections, reflect back on what you have read, and review your written notes.

- *Before Going On.* To help you review, the book includes a feature called Before Going On at the end of each major section. You should stop reading and try to answer the questions in this feature when you come to it. If you can't answer the questions, go back and review the section. You will know what parts of the text to review because each question corresponds to a subheading. Once you've completed this process, take a break before you begin another major section.

- *Marginal Glossary.* Key terms are defined in the margin near where they are first used in the text. As you come to each boldface term in the text, stop and read its definition in the margin. Then go back and reread the sentence that introduced the key term.

- *Critical Thinking Questions.* These questions encourage you to relate material in the book to your own experiences. They can also help you remember the information in the text, because linking new information to things you already know is a highly effective memory strategy.

- *Make the Connection.* Each chapter includes a question titled Make the Connection. Thinking about these questions will help you integrate information across chapters.

- *Themed Essays.* There are four kinds of themed essays throughout the book. **No Easy Answers** help you understand the complexities involved in trying to apply developmental theories and research to real life problems. **Development in the Information Age** essays will inform you about how various information media have affected perceptions of development and how such media may influence the developmental process itself. **Research Reports** recount the findings of important studies, and essays entitled **The Real World** offer practical advice on parenting, teaching, caregiving, and other aspects of daily life to which developmental psychology is relevant.

- *Policy Questions.* Discussions of social policy issues relevant to human development appear at the end of each part. For example, the Policy Question at the end of Part 1 addresses proposals to prosecute women for using drugs during pregnancy. These discussions will provide you with insight into how the findings of developmental research may be used to influence policy changes in the real world. They may also serve as starting points for group discussions and research projects.

- *Key Terms.* Key terms are listed alphabetically at the end of each chapter, in addition to being defined in the margin. When you finish a chapter, try to recall the definition of each term. Page numbers are listed for all the terms, so you can easily look back in the chapter if you can't remember a definition.

- *Chapter Summaries.* Looking over the chapter summary can also help you assess how much of the information you remember.

- *Practice Tests.* You'll find multiple-choice and fill-in-the-blank questions for every chapter, organized by the major chapter sections, right at the back of your textbook. When you finish reading a chapter, take the practice test and find out what you've mastered and what you need to review. You can check your understanding of the major concepts in each chapter by referring to the answer key provided at the end of the book.

The task of understanding and remembering the information in a developmental psychology textbook may seem overwhelming. However, when you finish reading this book, you will have a better understanding of yourself and of other people. So, all your hard work will be well worth the effort.

Denise Boyd

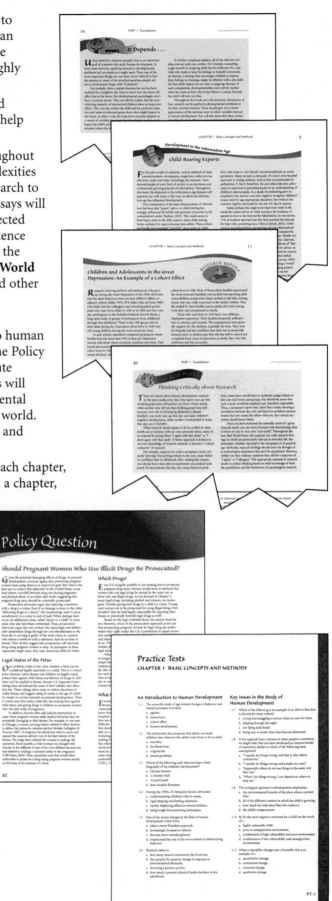

TO THE INSTRUCTOR

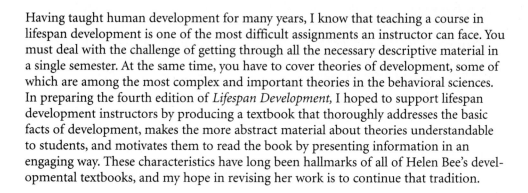

Having taught human development for many years, I know that teaching a course in lifespan development is one of the most difficult assignments an instructor can face. You must deal with the challenge of getting through all the necessary descriptive material in a single semester. At the same time, you have to cover theories of development, some of which are among the most complex and important theories in the behavioral sciences. In preparing the fourth edition of *Lifespan Development*, I hoped to support lifespan development instructors by producing a textbook that thoroughly addresses the basic facts of development, makes the more abstract material about theories understandable to students, and motivates them to read the book by presenting information in an engaging way. These characteristics have long been hallmarks of all of Helen Bee's developmental textbooks, and my hope in revising her work is to continue that tradition.

GOALS

The goals of the fourth edition are as follows:

- To find that difficult but essential balance of theory, research, and practical application
- To make the study of human development relevant not just for psychologists but also for students in the many other fields in which this information is needed, including nursing, medicine, social work, education, and home economics
- To keep all discussions as current as humanly possible, so that students encounter the very latest thinking and the most recent research
- To write in as personal and direct a way as possible, so that the book is more like a conversation than a traditional text, without sacrificing either theoretical clarity or rigor of research

NEW TO THE FOURTH EDITION

The fourth edition has been thoroughly revised and updated to reflect the latest research in the field of human development. Following are some highlights of the new edition:

- *MyDevelopmentLab,* a state-of-the-art, interactive and instructive solution for developmental psychology. Designed to be used as a supplement to a traditional lecture course or to completely administer an online course, MyDevelopmentLab combines multimedia, tutorials, video, audio, simulations, animations, and controlled assessments to engage students.

- *New organization.* Separate chapters on physical, sensory, and perceptual development in infancy (Chapter 4) and cognitive development in infancy (Chapter 5) provide for a fuller and more detailed discussion of these important topics.

- *Updated research.* Approximately 800 of the most recent findings from the field are featured. The fourth edition includes the latest on brain development; the developmental effects of television viewing; the homeschooling movement; teenage pregnancy, sex, drug and tobacco use, and suicide; advances in assisted reproductive technologies; same-sex marriage; singlehood and cohabitation; hormone replacement therapy; Alzheimer's; living arrangements among the elderly; stem cell research; and much more!

- *Expanded coverage* of a number of critical topics in human development. These include heredity and environment, sensory and perceptual development in infancy, conditioning and modeling in infancy, schematic learning and memory in infancy, fine and gross motor skills in infancy and early childhood, emotional development in early childhood, health and wellness in middle childhood, friendships in middle childhood, bullying, culture and self-esteem, adolescent egocentrism, adolescent identity development, intimate relationships in early adulthood, and the empty nest and its refilling.
- *New Policy Question section* examining the social policy issues surrounding the controversial stem cell research debate.
- *Practice tests at the end of the book.* From 20 to 25 multiple-choice questions per chapter give students the chance to gauge their knowledge about the material in the text and to prepare for exams.

PEDAGOGY

The fourth edition of *Lifespan Development* includes several important pedagogical features.

- *Marginal Glossary.* Each boldface term mentioned in the text is defined in the margin.
- *Before Going On.* At the end of each major section, Before Going On encourages students to stop reading and test their recall of various pieces of information before moving on.
- *Make the Connection.* These questions encourage students to look back at previously discussed theories or data and relate them to information in the current chapter.
- *Critical Thinking.* Critical Thinking questions throughout each chapter focus on relationships between the information in the text and students' personal experiences.
- *Key Terms.* All boldface terms in a chapter are also listed at the end of the chapter in alphabetical order with page references.
- *Chapter Summaries.* Each chapter ends with a summary organized by major chapter headings, with each point under each heading corresponding to a specific subheading in the chapter. This organization allows students to assess systematically how well they remember the chapter material and to know exactly where to look back in the chapter for information they want to review.

THEMED ESSAYS AND POLICY QUESTIONS

The fourth edition of *Lifespan Development* includes four kinds of thought-provoking themed essays, plus six special social policy sections.

No Easy Answers   The *No Easy Answers* essays introduce students to the idea that there are many questions for which developmental psychologists cannot provide definitive answers. For example, the essay in Chapter 3 deals with the issue of pregnancy in women with epilepsy. A woman with epilepsy must decide between two risks: possible birth defects in her baby caused by her anticonvulsant medication and the many complications that can accompany epileptic seizures during pregnancy. Either path she chooses carries risk. Developmentalists can't tell a woman with epilepsy that if she does *x*, *y*, or *z*, her baby will turn out fine.

I developed these discussions in response to my own students' continuing difficulty in understanding that psychology is not a science that can offer straightforward recipes for perfect behavioral outcomes. My hope is that, by reading these discussions, students will become more sensitive to the complexity of human development and more tolerant of the ambiguities inherent in the behavioral and social sciences.

Development in the Information Age
In the first three chapters, these discussions focus students' attention on how various information media have shaped the public's understanding of development. For example, *Development in the Information Age* in Chapter 3 discusses how the news media sensationalize multiple births and, as a result, often obscure the real risks inherent in multiple pregnancies. In subsequent chapters, *Development in the Information Age* essays present ideas and research about how information technology may shape development itself. For example, the essay in Chapter 4 considers whether television harms the developing brain, and the one in Chapter 15 deals with Internet addiction.

Research Report
Research Reports provide detailed accounts of specific research studies. For example, Chapter 17 discusses research on mild cognitive impairment and Alzheimer's disease.

The Real World
The Real World essays explore practical applications of developmental theory and research, in such areas as parenting, teaching, caregiving, aging, and working. For example, the essay in Chapter 2 suggests how a parent might use learning principles to shape a child's behavior.

Policy Question
A *Policy Question* feature is found at the end of each part in the fourth edition; an additional feature appears after Chapter 18. The features discuss the following questions:

Part 1:   *Should Pregnant Women Who Use Illicit Drugs Be Prosecuted?*
Part 2:   *"Deadbeat Dads": Irresponsible Parents or Political Scapegoats?*
Part 3:   *Has Test-Based Reform Improved Schools in the United States?*
Part 4:   *What Types of Couples Should be Sanctioned by Society?*
Part 5:   *How Should Stem Cell Research Be Funded and Regulated?*
            Do People Have a Right to Die?

The first goal of these discussions is to acquaint students with a few social and political issues related to topics discussed in the text. The second goal is to encourage students to find out how these issues are being dealt with where they live. Each *Policy Question* feature ends with a list of suggestions that should help students find out more about the issue. My hope is that students will gain an understanding of the implications of developmental psychology for social policy as well as of the impact of social policies on human development.

SUPPLEMENTS FOR THE INSTRUCTOR

- *Instructor's Manual.* The Instructor's Manual has been thoroughly revised by Karen Saenz of Houston Community College. Each chapter includes the following sections:
  - What's New, highlighting the changes to the fourth edition
  - "At-a-Glance" grids, showcasing the resources available for instructors and students by chapter
  - Chapter Preview
  - Learning Goals
  - Extensive and detailed Teaching Notes, which include the Learning Objectives, cross-referenced in the Grade Aid Study Guide, critical thinking questions, and classroom activities
  - Lecture Launchers

- Instructor Resources, including suggested videos, Transparency and Handout Masters, and references to the full-color transparency acetates found in the Allyn & Bacon Human Development Transparency Set

Detailed chapter outlines will be available for download with the Instructor's Manual on our Supplements Central website.

- *Test Bank.* Prepared by Phyllis A. Marley, Texarkana College, the Test Bank is composed of approximately 2,000 fully referenced multiple-choice, true/false, short-answer, and essay questions. This supplement is also available in TestGen computerized version, for use in creating tests in the classroom.

- *Video.* A completely new Allyn & Bacon "Insights into Developmental Psychology" Video is available to accompany the fourth edition of *Lifespan Development.* The video highlights important high-interest topics across the lifespan. Ask your local sales representative how to obtain a copy.

- *Allyn and Bacon Human Development Transparency Package.* An extensive set of full-color transparencies is available through your sales representative.

- *PowerPoint Presentation.* Prepared by Edward Brady, Southwestern Illinois College, this multi-media resource contains key points covered in the textbook, images from the textbook, and a link to the Companion Website for corresponding activities.

- *Digital Media Archive for Human Development.* This comprehensive source for images includes charts, graphs, maps, tables, and figures, with audio clips and related Web links.

SUPPLEMENTS FOR THE STUDENT

- *Grade Aid Study Guide.* The Grade Aid Study Guide for the fourth edition of *Lifespan Development* has been revised by Karen Saenz. It offers students a rich and highly structured learning tool. Each chapter of the Grade Aid Study Guide includes the following sections:

  - "Before You Read," containing a brief chapter summary and learning objectives
  - "As You Read," offering a collection of demonstrations, activities, and exercises
  - "After You Read," consisting of three short practice quizzes and one comprehensive practice test
  - "When You Have Finished," presenting web links for further information and a crossword puzzle using key terms from the text

- *MyDevelopmentLab.* This state-of-the-art, interactive and instructive solution for developmental psychology is designed to be used as a supplement to a traditional lecture course or to completely administer an online course. MyDevelopmentLab combines multimedia, tutorials, video, audio, simulations, animations, and controlled assessments to engage students.

- *Practice tests at the end of the book.* From 20 to 25 multiple-choice questions per chapter give the students the chance to gauge their knowledge about the material in the text and to prepare for exams.

- *Companion Website.* Connecting the textbook to the Internet, this website includes learning objectives, flashcard glossary terms, and online practice tests, organized by chapter. Visit this site at www.ablongman.com/boydbee4e.

ACKNOWLEDGMENTS

No one ever accomplishes much of anything alone. Therefore, I would like to thank a number of people for providing me with the support I needed to complete this project. First and foremost, my husband Jerry Boyd, my sons Matt and Chris Boyd, my daughter Marianne Meece, my son-in-law Michael Meece, and my mother Bobbie Roberts have served as my most important cheerleaders. Likewise, a number of people in my church and neighborhood "families" were instrumental in helping me accomplish this goal.

My colleagues at Houston Community College–Central (Madeleine Wright, Genevieve Stevens, David Gersh, and Saundra Boyd) acted as sounding boards for various ideas and supported me through some personally challenging events that happened to coincide with the writing of this book.

I also must thank several people at Allyn & Bacon for their help. First, I am indebted to Rebecca Dudley Pascal for encouraging me to get involved in textbook writing. Thanks also to Carolyn Merrill, who was instrumental in my being offered the opportunity to prepare the third edition of this book. The fourth edition was supervised by Karon Bowers, who provided many ideas and words of encouragement. To all three, I express my thanks for educating me about the process of turning an idea into a textbook. The knowledge I acquired from them about textbook writing and marketing has resulted in a book far better than I ever could have produced on my own.

Of course, developmental editors are essential to the process. I am indebted to Lisa McLellan for pointing out digressions, improving the logical order of the topics in several chapters, and correcting numerous typos and grammatical errors. I also deeply appreciate her cogent summaries of reviewers' comments.

Finally, I would like to thank the many colleagues who served as reviewers for their thought-provoking comments and criticisms as well as their willingness to take time out of their busy schedules to help me improve this book.

Jeffrey Arnett
University of Maryland

Cynthia Avens
Daytona Beach Community College

Barbara E. Baker
Nashville State Tech

Troy E. Beckert
Utah State University

Laura Hess Brown
State University of New York at Oswego

Barbara DeFilippo
Lane Community College

Julie Felender
Fullerton College

Tina Footen
Boise State University

Loren Ford
Clackamas Community College

Kathleen V. Fox
Salisbury State University

Lynn Haller
Morehead State University

Debra L. Hollister
Valencia Community College

Scott L. Horton
University of Southern Maine

Suzy Horton
Mesa Community College

Shabana Kausar
Minnesota State University

John S. Klein
Castleton State College

David D. Kurz
Delmar College

Billie Laney
Central Texas Community College

Kathryn Levit
George Mason University

Susan Magun-Jackson
University of Memphis

April Mansfield
Long Beach City College

Carrie M. Margolin
The Evergreen State College

Joseph A. Mayo
Gordon College

Alan C. Miller
Santa Fe Community College

James E. Oliver
Henry Ford Community College

Regina K. Peters
Hawkeye Community College

Joe E. Price
San Diego State University

Celinda Reese
Oklahoma State University

Paul Roodin
State University of New York at Oswego

Jonathan Schwartz
Yeshiva University

Lynn Shelley
Westfield State College

Rosalind Shorter
Jefferson Community College

Stephanie Stein
Central Washington University

Kevin Sumrall
Montgomery College

Stephen Truhon
Winston-Salem State University

Bradley M. Waite
Central Connecticut State University

Eugene H. Wong
*California State University–
San Bernardino*

Virginia V. Wood
University of Texas–Brownsville

Denise Boyd

Basic Concepts and Methods

We are all observers of human development. For example, at family gatherings like the one pictured, we comment on the changes we notice in our relatives:

© Spencer Grant, PhotoEdit

He's grown so much since the last time I saw him.

She's turned into such a beautiful young lady.

His hair's turning gray—the hair he has left, that is.

Grandma seems more frail than last year.

At the same time, we notice the things about people that appear to remain the same:

Aunt Frieda's as bossy as ever.

I don't understand how someone could go through so much and still be so cheerful, but he's always had a lot of faith.

We also view people in light of the expectations of our culture for their age group:

Is he going to college after he graduates this year?

I wonder when those two are going to start a family of their own. They've been married for 3 years now.

We even theorize about why our relatives behave the way they do:

They've never tried to control that child. No wonder he's such a brat.

She was born with a mean streak.

Scientists who study human development do precisely the same things. Their goal, however, is to produce observations and explanations that can be applied to as wide a range of human beings and in as many contexts as possible. To accomplish this goal, they study both change and stability. In addition, they examine the impact of cultural expectations on individual development. They make predictions about development and use scientific methods to test them. Finally, most hope that their findings can be used to positively influence the development of individual human beings.

In this chapter, you will learn how the science of human development came into being. You will also learn about the key issues in the scientific study of development. In addition, when you finish reading the chapter, you will be acquainted with the research designs and methods used by developmentalists. While you read, keep the following questions in mind:

● What were the contributions of early philosophers and behavioral scientists to the study of human development?

● What are the key issues in the study of human development?

● What research designs and methods do developmentalists use to study change across the human lifespan?

An Introduction to Human Development

The field of **human development** is the scientific study of age-related changes in behavior, thinking, emotion, and personality. Long before the scientific method was used to study development, though, philosophers offered a variety of explanations for differences they observed in individuals of different ages. Their ideas continue to influence the field today, and many Western beliefs about human development are based on them.

PHILOSOPHICAL ROOTS

Philosophers who attempted to explain human development were especially interested in understanding why babies, who seem to start life so similarly, grow up to be adults who differ widely in intelligence, personality, and other characteristics. Of particular concern to most was the problem of explaining how and why some people grow up to be productive citizens while others become threats to the community. Expressed more simply, why do some of us grow up to be "good" and others "bad"?

In one way or another, most philosophers have approached this question by trying to determine whether factors inside people (such as intelligence) or outside of them (such as family environment) make them good or bad. Three ideas about the interaction of internal and external factors have been especially important in Western thinking about human development.

Original Sin For centuries, the Christian doctrine of *original sin* has influenced European and American views on human development. This doctrine teaches that all humans are born with a selfish nature because of the sin of Adam and Eve in the Garden of Eden. Even when people do good works, this doctrine says, they do so for selfish reasons. For example, a man may give money to charity so that others will admire him. According to this doctrine, to become capable of doing good works for pure motives, people must experience spiritual rebirth. After rebirth, individuals are in touch with the Holy Spirit, which helps them learn how to behave morally through prayer and Bible study. However, throughout life, even those who have experienced rebirth must confront the continual temptation to follow the inclinations of their sinful nature. Thus, from this perspective, differences in "goodness" and "badness" are the result of different degrees of success in overcoming one's sinful nature. In other words, interactions between an inborn, internal characteristic—the original sin nature—and an external influence—the Holy Spirit—produce differences in development.

Innate Goodness The ideas of 18th-century Swiss philosopher Jean-Jacques Rousseau have also influenced Western views of human development. Rousseau claimed that all humans have *innate goodness*. This view asserts that all human beings are naturally good and seek out experiences that help them grow (Ozman & Craver, 1986). Rousseau believed that just as an acorn contains everything necessary to make an oak tree, children have within themselves everything they need to grow up to be competent and moral adults. Like acorns, children need only nutrition and protection to reach their full potential. For Rousseau, the goal of human development is to achieve one's inborn potential. "Good" behavior results from growing up in an environment that doesn't interfere with the individual's attempts to do so. In contrast, "bad" behavior is learned from others or happens when a person experiences frustration in his efforts to express the innate goodness with which he was born. Therefore, like the original sin view, the innate goodness perspective suggests that development involves a struggle between internal and external factors.

human development the scientific study of age-related changes in behavior, thinking, emotion, and personality

CRITICAL THINKING ?

Other cultures and religions have different ways of viewing the process of development. How do the original sin, innate goodness, and blank slate views compare to your own beliefs? How do you think your own culture and religion have contributed to these beliefs?

The Blank Slate   In contrast to both of these perspectives, 17th-century English philosopher John Locke proposed that the mind of a child is a *blank slate*. Locke said, "I imagine the minds of children as easily turned, this or that way, as water" (Ozman & Craver, 1986, p. 62). The blank slate view suggests that adults can mold children into whatever they want them to be. Therefore, differences among adults can be explained in terms of differences in their childhood environments. Thus, from this perspective, development—whether its results are good or bad—takes place because of external, environmental factors acting on a person, whose only relevant internal characteristic is the capacity to respond.

EARLY SCIENTIFIC THEORIES

Philosophy can provide a framework for ideas about human development. However, in the 19th century, people who wanted to better understand development began to turn to science. Charles Darwin and other evolutionists believed they could understand the development of the human species by studying child development. Many, including Darwin, kept detailed records of their own children's early development (called *baby biographies*), in the hope of finding evidence to support the theory of evolution (Charlesworth, 1992). These were the first organized studies of human development.

Darwin's theory of evolution is the source of many important ideas in the study of human development. For example, the concept of developmental stages comes from evolutionary theory. However, critics of baby biographies claimed that studying children for the purpose of proving a theory might cause observers to misinterpret or ignore important information.

G. Stanley Hall of Clark University wanted to find more objective ways to study development. He used questionnaires and interviews to study large numbers of children. His 1891 article entitled "The Contents of Children's Minds on Entering School" represented the first scientific study of child development (White, 1992).

Hall agreed with Darwin that the milestones of childhood were similar to those that had taken place in the development of the human species. He thought that developmentalists should identify **norms,** or average ages at which developmental milestones are reached. Norms, Hall said, could be used to learn about the evolution of the species as well as to track the development of individual children. In 1904, Hall published *Adolescence: Its Psychology and Its Relations to Physiology, Anthropology, Sociology, Sex, Crime, Religion and Education.* This book introduced the idea that adolescence is a unique developmental period.

Arnold Gesell's research suggested the existence of a genetically programmed sequential pattern of change (Gesell, 1925; Thelen & Adolph, 1992). Gesell used the term **maturation** to describe such a pattern of change. He thought that maturationally determined development occurred regardless of practice, training, or effort. For example, infants don't have to be taught how to walk—they begin to do so on their own once they reach a certain age. Because of his strong belief that many important developmental changes are determined by maturation, Gesell spent decades studying children and developing norms. He pioneered the use of movie cameras and one-way observation devices to study children's behavior. Gesell's findings became the basis for many tests that are used today to determine whether individual children are developing normally.

MAKE THE CONNECTION

Review philosopher Jean-Jacques Rousseau's innate goodness idea. How does Gesell's view compare to it?

THE LIFESPAN PERSPECTIVE

Until quite recently, psychologists thought of adulthood as a long period of stability followed by a short span of unstable years immediately preceding death. This view has changed because, for one thing, it has become common for adults to go through major life changes, such as divorce and career shifts. As a result, several theorists whose ideas you will encounter later in this book have proposed stage models of development that include adult phases.

norms average ages at which developmental milestones are reached

maturation the gradual unfolding of a genetically programmed sequential pattern of change

Development in the Information Age

Child-Rearing Experts

For the past couple of centuries, various methods of mass communication—newspapers, magazines, radio, movies, television, audio and video recordings, the Internet—have exposed people at every level of society to an enormous and continuously growing amount of information. Throughout this book, Development in the Information Age features will acquaint you with many of the ways in which the information age has influenced development.

One consequence of the mass dissemination of information has been that "expert" advice on child-rearing has strongly influenced the beliefs and practices of parents in the industrialized world (Hulbert, 2003). This trend seems to have begun early in the 20th century, when child-rearing books authored by experts became best-sellers. These articles and books recommended "scientific" approaches to child-rearing. No longer were grandparents or other older adults to be viewed as experts on bringing up children. Instead, young parents were encouraged to turn to pediatricians and psychologists. Most physician-experts advocated rigid feeding and sleeping schedules for children and advocated formula feeding. Their recommendations were often motivated by the belief that sterilized formulas provided more protection against infant mortality than breastfeeding. Such advice was in harmony with the recommendations of many psychologists of that era, such as John B. Watson (you'll learn more about Watson in Chapter 2), who suggested that too much physical affection would "spoil" children.

In sharp contrast, during the 1950s, the ideas of Dr. Benjamin Spock, author of the classic book *Baby and Child Care,* became predominant. Spock urged parents to openly display affection toward children and warned against engaging in too much conflict. However, by the end of the century, most parents, along with professionals who work with children, had come to view Spock's recommendations as overly permissive. Many turned to advocates of a more even-handed approach to raising children, such as that recommended by pediatrician T. Berry Brazelton. He and others like him advocated an approach to parenting based on an understanding of children's inborn needs. As a result, breastfeeding grew in popularity, but parents were also urged to recognize children's innate need for age-appropriate discipline, but without the excessive rigidity advocated by the pre–Dr. Spock experts.

Today, perhaps the single most important trend in the search for expert advice on child-rearing is the tendency of parents to turn to the Internet for information. In one survey, 71% of mothers reported that they had searched the Internet for help with a parenting issue (Allen & Rainie, 2002). Child-rearing recommendations representing diverse philosophical orientations abound on the World Wide Web. Consequently, there is no single expert "voice" that predominates. Health-oriented sites, such as kidshealth.org, are very popular. Likewise, sites sponsored by child psychologists receive millions of "hits" each day. But parents are also turning to the Net for advice on their children's spiritual development and to search for nontraditional treatments for conditions such as attention-deficit hyperactivity disorder (Bussing, Zima, Gary, & Garvan, 2002).

Perhaps the most revolutionary aspect of being a "wired" parent, though, is the Internet's potential for helping parents build social networks with other parents. Parents use the Internet to make connections via chatrooms, discussion boards, and email with others who face similar parenting challenges, such as those associated with being a single parent or with raising a child with a disability. Thus, the Internet may be facilitating a return to an approach to parenting that was considered old-fashioned a century ago, one that assumes that real-life experience is the best way to become a child-rearing expert.

Another important factor that has affected developmental perspectives on adulthood is the significant increase in life expectancy that has occurred in the industrialized world. At the beginning of the 20th century, Americans' life expectancy at birth was only 49 years. By the century's end, the expected lifespan of someone born in the United States was about 76 years. As a result, older adults now constitute a larger proportion of the U.S. population than ever before. In fact, adults over the age of 100 are one of the most rapidly growing age groups in the industrialized world. Thus, the characteristics and needs of older adults are increasingly influencing many disciplines.

As interest in the entire lifespan has grown, the scientific study of human development has become more interdisciplinary. Psychologists, who are primarily interested in individuals, have learned that research in other sciences can greatly enhance their understanding of human development. Anthropologists provide information about culture, and sociologists explain the influence of race, socioeconomic status, and other social factors on individual development. Advances in biology are especially critical to an understanding of the physiological foundations of human behavior.

The changes outlined above have led to the adoption of a lifespan perspective. The **lifespan perspective** maintains that important changes occur during every period of development and that these changes must be interpreted in terms of the culture and context in which they occur (Baltes, Reese, & Lipsitt, 1980). Thus, understanding change in adulthood has become just as important as understanding change in childhood, and input from many disciplines is necessary to fully explain human development.

Paul Baltes has been a leader in the development of a comprehensive theory of lifespan human development (Baltes, Staudinger, & Lindenberger, 1999). Baltes has proposed that the capacity for positive change, or *plasticity,* in response to environmental demands is possible throughout the entire lifespan. Consequently, one of Baltes's most important contributions to the study of human development is his emphasis on the positive aspects of advanced age. He points out that, as human beings age, they adopt strategies that help them maximize gains and compensate for losses. For instance, one of Baltes's most often quoted examples is that of concert pianist Arthur Rubinstein, who was able to outperform much younger musicians well into his 80s (Cavanaugh & Whitbourne, 1999). Rubinstein reported that he maintained his performance capacity by carefully choosing pieces that he knew very well (maximizing gain) and by practicing these pieces more frequently than he had at earlier ages (compensating for the physical losses associated with age). You will read more about Baltes's theories and his research later, in the chapters devoted to late adulthood.

THE DOMAINS OF DEVELOPMENT

Scientists who study age-related changes across the lifespan often use three broad categories, called *domains of development,* to classify these changes. The **physical domain** includes changes in the size, shape, and characteristics of the body. For example, developmentalists study the physiological processes associated with puberty. Also included in this domain are changes in how individuals sense and perceive the physical world, such as the gradual development of depth perception over the first year of life.

Changes in thinking, memory, problem-solving, and other intellectual skills are included in the **cognitive domain.** Researchers working in the cognitive domain study topics as diverse as how children learn to read and why some memory functions deteriorate in old age. They also examine the ways in which individual differences among children and adults, such as intelligence test scores, are related to other variables within this domain.

The **social domain** includes changes in variables that are associated with the relationship of an individual to others. For instance, studies of children's social skills fall into the social domain, as does research on individual differences in personality. Individuals' beliefs about themselves are also usually classified within the social domain.

Using domain classifications helps to organize discussions of human development. However, it is always important to remember that the three domains do not function independently of one another. For instance, when a girl goes through puberty, a change in the physical domain, her ability to think abstractly (cognitive domain) and her feelings about potential romantic partners (social domain) change as well. Likewise, older adults who suffer from Alzheimer's disease demonstrate obvious changes in the cognitive domain. But these changes both result from and lead to others in the remaining two domains. Physical changes in the brain are the most likely cause of Alzheimer's disease. The experience of living with the disease may cause a sufferer to be unable to maintain a regular eating and exercise schedule, thus leading to deterioration in physical health. Moreover, individuals who have such severe memory impairments often forget important things about the people with whom they associate, such as their names and relationships. As a result, social relationships are disrupted or may even be impossible.

Before going on . . .

- Summarize the original sin, innate goodness, and blank slate views of human development.

- What were the contributions of Darwin and Hall to the scientific study of human development?

- What is the lifespan perspective?

- What are the three domains of development?

Key Issues in the Study of Human Development

The study of human development has changed considerably since the early days. For one thing, developmentalists have come to understand that inborn characteristics interact with environmental factors in complex ways. For another, the pioneers thought of change almost exclusively in terms of norms, whereas today's developmentalists view norms as representing only one way to measure change. Finally, the term *development* now encompasses the entire human lifespan rather than just childhood and adolescence.

NATURE VERSUS NURTURE

Some early developmentalists thought of change as resulting from *either* forces outside the person *or* forces inside the person. The debate about the relative contributions of biological processes and experiential factors to development is known as the **nature-nurture controversy.** In struggling with this important issue, psychologists have moved away from either/or approaches toward more subtle ways of looking at both types of influences.

Inborn Biases One of the newer ideas on the nature side is the concept of *inborn biases.* The basic notion is that children are born with tendencies to respond in certain ways. Some of these inborn biases are shared by virtually all children. For instance, from the earliest days of life, babies seem to listen more to the beginning and end of sentences than to the middle (Slobin, 1985). Babies also come equipped with a set of apparently instinctive behaviors that entice others to care for them, including crying, snuggling, and, very soon after birth, smiling.

Other inborn biases may vary from one individual to another. Even in the early days of life, for example, some infants are relatively easy to soothe when they become distressed, while others are more difficult to manage. Whether these inborn patterns are coded in the genes, are created by variations in the prenatal environment, or arise through some combination of the two, the basic point is that a baby is not a blank slate at birth. Babies seem to start life prepared to seek out and react to particular kinds of experiences.

Internal Models of Experience Thinking on the nurture side of the issue is also more complex than in the past. For example, modern developmentalists have accepted the concept of *internal models of experience.* There are two key elements to this concept. The first is the idea that the effect of some experience depends not on any objective properties of the experience but rather on the individual's *interpretation* of it, the meaning the individual attaches to that experience. For instance, suppose a friend says to you, "Your new haircut looks great; it's a lot nicer when it's short like that." Your friend intends to pay you a compliment, but you also hear an implied criticism ("Your hair used to look awful"), so your reactions, your feelings, and even your relationship with your friend are affected by how you interpret the comment—not by what your friend meant or by the objective qualities of the remark.

The second key element of the internal models concept is that interpretations of experience are not random or governed by temporary moods but rather are organized into *models,* which can be thought of as organized sets of assumptions or expectations about oneself or others. For example, if you regularly hear criticism in other people's comments, you may have an internal model whose basic assumption is something like this: "I usually do things wrong, so other people criticize me."

lifespan perspective the current view of developmentalists that important changes occur throughout the entire human lifespan and that these changes must be interpreted in terms of the culture and context in which they occur; thus, interdisciplinary research is critical to understanding human development

physical domain changes in the size, shape, and characteristics of the body

cognitive domain changes in thinking, memory, problem-solving, and other intellectual skills

social domain change in variables that are associated with the relationship of an individual to others

nature-nurture controversy the debate about the relative contributions of biological processes and experiential factors to development

If the concept of internal models is correct, then what matters about this team's victory is not the experience of success itself but rather how each girl interprets it.

The Ecological Approach Another important facet of current thinking about environmental influences is a growing emphasis on the importance of looking beyond a child's immediate family for explanations of development. According to this view, we must understand the *ecology*, or the *context*, in which the child is growing: the neighborhood and school, the occupations of the parents and their level of satisfaction in these occupations, the parents' relationships with each other and their own families, and so on (e.g., Bronfenbrenner, 1979, 1989). For example, a child growing up in a poverty-stricken, inner-city neighborhood, where drugs and violence are a part of everyday life, is coping with a set of problems radically different from those of a child in a relatively safe and more affluent neighborhood.

A good example of research that examines such a larger system of influences is Gerald Patterson's work on the origins of delinquency (Patterson, Capaldi, & Bank, 1991; Patterson, DeBarsyshe, & Ramsey, 1989). His studies show that parents who use poor discipline techniques and poor monitoring are more likely to have noncompliant children. Once established, such a behavior pattern has repercussions in other areas of the child's life, leading to both rejection by peers and difficulty in school. These problems, in turn, are likely to push the young person toward delinquency (Dishion, Patterson, Stoolmiller, & Skinner, 1991; Vuchinich, Bank, & Patterson, 1992). So a pattern that began in the family is maintained and exacerbated by interactions with peers and with the school system. Figure 1.1 shows Patterson's conception of how these various components fit together. Clearly, such models enhance our understanding of how the environment influences development.

A similarly interactionist model is implicit in the ideas of *vulnerability* and *resilience* (Garmezy, 1993; Garmezy & Rutter, 1983; Masten, Best, & Garmezy, 1990; Moen & Erickson, 1995; Rutter, 1987; Werner, 1995). According to this view, each child is born with certain vulnerabilities, such as a tendency toward emotional irritability or alcoholism, a physical abnormality, an allergy, or whatever. Each child is also born with some protective factors, such as high intelligence, good physical coordination, an easy temperament, or a lovely smile, that tend to make her more resilient in the face of stress. These vulnerabilities and protective factors then interact with the child's environment, so the same environment can have quite different effects, depending on the qualities the child brings to the interaction.

The combination of a highly vulnerable child and a poor or unsupportive environment produces by far the most negative outcomes (Horowitz, 1990). Either of these two negative conditions alone—a vulnerable child or a poor environment—can be overcome. A resilient child in a poor environment may do quite well, since she can find and take advantage of all the stimulation and opportunities available; similarly, a vulnerable child may do quite well in a highly supportive environment in which parents help the child overcome or cope with her vulnerabilities. The "double whammy"—being a vulnerable child in a poor environment—leads to really poor outcomes for the child.

CONTINUITY VERSUS DISCONTINUITY

Another key issue in the study of human development is the *continuity-discontinuity* issue. The question is whether age-related change is primarily a matter of amount or degree (the *continuity* side of the debate) or more commonly involves changes in type or kind (the *discontinuity* side). For example, a 2-year-old is likely to have no individual friends among her playmates, while an 8-year-old is likely to have several. We could think of this as a **quantitative change** (a change in amount) from zero friends to some friends. This view implies that the qualitative aspects of friendship are the same at every age—or, as developmentalists would express it, changes in friendship are *continu-*

quantitative change a change in amount

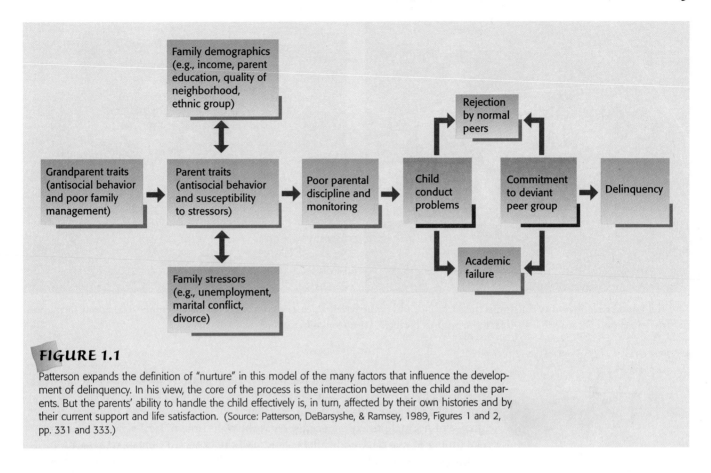

FIGURE 1.1

Patterson expands the definition of "nurture" in this model of the many factors that influence the development of delinquency. In his view, the core of the process is the interaction between the child and the parents. But the parents' ability to handle the child effectively is, in turn, affected by their own histories and by their current support and life satisfaction. (Source: Patterson, DeBarsyshe, & Ramsey, 1989, Figures 1 and 2, pp. 331 and 333.)

ous in nature. Alternatively, we could think of the difference in friendships from one age to another as a **qualitative change** (a change in kind or type)—from disinterest in peers to interest or from one sort of peer relationship to another. In other words, from this perspective, changes in friendships are *discontinuous*, in that each change represents a change in the quality of a child's relationships with peers. Thus, friendships at 2 are quite different from friendships at 8 and differ in ways that cannot be captured by describing them solely in terms of the number of friends a child has.

Of particular significance is the idea that, if development consists only of additions (quantitative change), then the concept of stages is not needed to explain it. However, if development involves reorganization or the emergence of wholly new strategies, qualities, or skills (qualitative change), then the concept of stages may be useful. As you'll learn in Chapter 2, one of the important differences among theories of development is whether they assume development occurs in stages or is primarily continuous in nature. Nevertheless, most human development theorists and researchers would agree that age-related changes can be classified using three categories: *universal changes, group-specific changes, and individual differences.*

UNIVERSAL CHANGES

Universal changes are common to every individual in a species and are linked to specific ages. Some universal changes happen because we are all biological organisms subject to a genetically programmed maturing process. The infant who shifts from crawling to walking and the older adult whose skin becomes progressively more wrinkled are following a plan that is an intrinsic part of the physical body, most likely something in the genetic code itself.

qualitative change a change in kind or type

The biological clock obviously constrains the social clock to some extent at least. Virtually every culture emphasizes family formation in early adulthood because that is, in fact, the optimal biological time for child rearing.

However, some changes are universal because of shared experiences. A social clock also shapes all (or most) lives into shared patterns of change (Helson, Mitchell, & Moane, 1984). In each culture, the **social clock,** or a set of *age norms,* defines a sequence of normal life experiences, such as the right time to start school, the appropriate timing of marriage and childbearing, and the expected time of retirement.

Age norms can lead to **ageism**—a set of prejudicial attitudes about older adults, analogous to sexism or racism (Palmore, 1990). In U.S. culture, for example, older adults are very often perceived as incompetent. As a result, many are denied opportunities to work because employers believe that they are incapable of carrying out required job functions. Thus, social expectations about the appropriate age for retirement work together with ageism to shape individual lives, resulting in a pattern in which most people retire or significantly reduce their working hours in later adulthood.

GROUP-SPECIFIC CHANGES

Group-specific changes are shared by all individuals who grow up together in a particular group. One of the most important groups to which we all belong is our culture.

Cultural Context The term *culture* has no commonly agreed-on definition, but in essence it describes some system of meanings and customs, including values, attitudes, goals, laws, beliefs, moral guidelines, and physical artifacts of various kinds, such as tools, forms of dwellings, and the like. Furthermore, to be called a culture, a system of meanings and customs must be shared by some identifiable group, whether that group is a subsection of some population or a larger unit, and must be transmitted from one generation of that group to the next (Betancourt & Lopez, 1993; Cole, 1992). Culture shapes not only the development of individuals, but also ideas about what normal development is.

For example, researchers interested in middle and late adulthood often study retirement: why people retire, how retirement affects their health, and so on. But their findings do not apply to older adults in nonindustrialized cultures, where adults gradually shift from one kind of work to another as they get older rather than giving up work altogether and entering a new phase of life called "retirement." Consequently, developmentalists must be aware that retirement-related phenomena do not constitute universal changes. Instead, they represent developmental experiences that are culturally specific.

social clock a set of age norms defining a sequence of life experiences that is considered normal in a given culture and that all individuals in that culture are expected to follow

ageism a prejudicial view of older adults that characterizes them in negative ways

Children and Adolescents in the Great Depression: An Example of a Cohort Effect

Research involving children and adolescents who grew up during the Great Depression of the 1930s illustrates that the same historical event can have different effects on adjacent cohorts (Elder, 1974; 1978; Elder, Liker, & Cross, 1984). Glen Elder and his colleagues used several hundred participants who were born either in 1920 or in 1928 and who were also participants in the Berkeley/Oakland Growth Study, a long-term study of groups of participants from childhood through late adulthood. Those in the 1920 group were in their teens during the Depression; those born in 1928 were still young children during the worst economic times.

In each cohort, researchers compared participants whose families had lost more than 35% of their pre-Depression income with those whose economic condition was better. They found that economic hardship was largely beneficial to the cohort born in 1920, who were teenagers when the Depression struck full force, while it was generally detrimental to the cohort born in 1928. Most of those whose families experienced the worst economic hardship were pushed into assuming adult responsibilities prematurely. Many worked at odd jobs, earning money that was vitally important to the family's welfare. They felt needed by their families, and as adults, they had a strong work ethic and commitment to family.

Those who were born in 1928 had a very different Depression experience. Their families frequently suffered a loss of cohesion and warmth. The consequences were generally negative for the children, especially the boys. They were less hopeful and less confident than their less economically stressed peers; in adolescence, they did less well in school and completed fewer years of education; as adults, they were less ambitious and less successful.

These two cohorts were only 8 years apart, yet their experiences were strikingly different because of the timing of a key environmental event in their lives.

Historical Context Equally important as a source of variation in life experience are historical forces, which affect each generation somewhat differently. Social scientists use the word **cohort** to describe a group of individuals who are born within some fairly narrow span of years and thus share the same historical experiences at the same times in their lives. Within any given culture, successive cohorts may have quite different life experiences (see Research Report).

CRITICAL THINKING

How do your culture's behavioral expectations for 20-year-olds differ from those for 70-year-olds?

INDIVIDUAL DIFFERENCES

Individual differences are changes resulting from unique, unshared events. One clearly unshared event in each person's life is conception; the combination of genes each individual receives at conception is unique. Thus, genetic differences—including physical characteristics such as body type and hair color as well as genetic disorders—represent one category of individual differences. Characteristics influenced by both heredity and environment, such as intelligence and personality, constitute another class of individual differences.

Other individual differences are the result of the timing of a developmental event. Child development theorists have adopted the concept of a **critical period.** The idea is that there may be specific periods in development when an organism is especially sensitive to the presence (or absence) of some particular kind of experience.

Most knowledge about critical periods comes from animal research. For baby ducks, for instance, the first 15 hours or so after hatching is a critical period for the development of a following response. Newly hatched ducklings will follow any duck or any other moving object that happens to be around them at that critical time. If nothing is moving at that critical point, they don't develop any following response at all (Hess, 1972).

cohort a group of individuals who share the same historical experiences at the same times in their lives

critical period a specific period in development when an organism is especially sensitive to the presence (or absence) of some particular kind of experience

The broader concept of a sensitive period is more common in the study of human development. A **sensitive period** is a span of months or years during which a child may be particularly responsive to specific forms of experience or particularly influenced by their absence. For example, the period from 6 to 12 months of age may be a sensitive period for the formation of parent-infant attachment.

In studies of adults, one important concept related to timing has been the idea of *on-time* and *off-time* events (Neugarten, 1979). The idea is that experiences occurring at the expected times for an individual's culture or cohort will pose fewer difficulties for the individual than will off-time experiences. Thus, being widowed at 30 is more likely to produce serious life disruption or forms of pathology such as depression than would being widowed at 70.

Atypical development is another kind of individual change. **Atypical development** (also known as *abnormal behavior, psychopathology,* or *maladaptive development*) refers to deviation from a typical, or "normal," developmental pathway in a direction that is harmful to an individual. Examples of atypical development include mental retardation, mental illness, and behavioral problems such as extreme aggressiveness in children and compulsive gambling in adults.

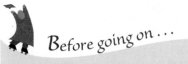

Before going on · · ·

- How do developmentalists view the two sides of the nature-nurture controversy?

- What is the continuity-discontinuity issue?

- What kinds of changes are universal?

- What are the three contexts associated with group-specific changes?

- How do genetic differences and the timing of experiences contribute to individual differences?

Research Designs and Methods

The easiest way to understand research methods is to look at a specific question and the alternative ways we might answer it. For example, older adults frequently complain that they have more trouble remembering people's names than they did when they were younger. Suppose we wanted to find out whether memory really declines with age. How would we go about answering this question?

RELATING GOALS TO METHODS

Researchers who study human development use the scientific method to achieve four goals: to describe, to explain, to predict, and to influence human development from conception to death. To describe development is simply to state what happens. A descriptive statement such as "Older adults make more memory errors than young and middle-aged adults" is an example of this first goal of human development. To meet this goal, all we would have to do is measure memory function in adults of various ages.

Explaining development involves telling why a particular event occurs. To generate explanations, developmentalists rely on *theories*—sets of statements that propose general principles of development. Students often say that they hate reading about theories; what they want are the facts. However, theories are important because they help us look at facts from different perspectives. For example, "Older adults make more memory mistakes because of changes in the brain that happen as people get older" is a statement that attempts to explain the fact of age-related memory decline from a biological perspective. Alternatively, we could explain memory decline from an experiential perspective and hypothesize that memory function declines with age because older adults don't get as much memory practice as younger adults do.

Useful theories produce predictions, or *hypotheses,* that researchers can test, such as "If changes in the brain cause declines in memory function, then elderly adults whose brains show the most change should also make the greatest number of memory errors." To test this hypothesis about changes in the brain and memory, we would have to measure some aspects of brain structure or function as well as memory function. Then we would have to find a way to relate one to the other. Alternatively, we could test the expe-

sensitive period a span of months or years during which a child may be particularly responsive to specific forms of experience or particularly influenced by their absence

atypical development development that deviates from the typical developmental pathway in a direction that is harmful to the individual

riential explanation by comparing the memories of older adults who presumably get the most memory practice, such as those who are still working, to the memories of those who get less practice. If the working adults do better on tests of memory, the experiential perspective gains support. Moreover, if both the biological and the experiential hypotheses are supported by research, we have far more insight into age-related memory decline than we would have from either kind of hypothesis alone. In this way, theories add tremendous depth to psychologists' understanding of the facts of human development and provide them with information they can use to influence development.

Let's say, for example, that an older adult is diagnosed with a condition that can affect the brain, such as high blood pressure. If we know that brain function and memory are related, we can use tests of memory to make judgments about how much the person's medical condition may have already influenced his brain. At the same time, because we know that experience affects memory as well, we may be able to provide him with training that will help prevent memory problems from developing or worsening (see No Easy Answers on page 14).

STUDYING AGE-RELATED CHANGES

A researcher who sets out to study age-related change has basically three choices: (1) Study different groups of people of different ages, using what is called a **cross-sectional design;** (2) study the same people over a period of time, using a **longitudinal design;** (3) combine cross-sectional and longitudinal designs in some fashion, in a **sequential design.**

Cross-Sectional Designs To study memory cross-sectionally, we might select groups of people of various ages, such as groups of 25-, 35-, 45-, 55-, 65-, 75-, and 85-year-olds. Figure 1.2 shows the results of just such a study, in which adults of different ages listened to a list of letters being read to them, one letter per second, and then had to repeat the letters back in the order given. You can see that performance was distinctly worse for the 60- and 70-year-olds, a pattern found in a great many memory studies (Salthouse, 1991).

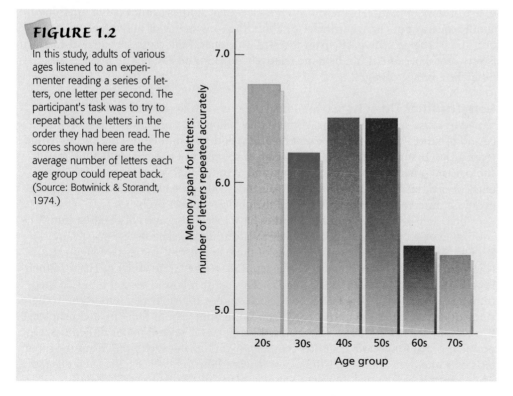

FIGURE 1.2

In this study, adults of various ages listened to an experimenter reading a series of letters, one letter per second. The participant's task was to try to repeat back the letters in the order they had been read. The scores shown here are the average number of letters each age group could repeat back. (Source: Botwinick & Storandt, 1974.)

Memory span for letters: number of letters repeated accurately

Age group

cross-sectional design a research design in which groups of people of different ages are compared

longitudinal design a research design in which people in a single group are studied at different times in their lives

sequential design a research design that combines cross-sectional and longitudinal examinations of development

It Depends . . .

Using research to improve people's lives is an important goal of scientists who study human development. In most cases, however, applying research to developmental problems isn't as simple as it might seem. Thus, one of the most important things you can learn about research is that the answers to many of the practical questions people ask about development begin with "It depends."

For example, when a parent discovers her son has been molested by a neighbor, she wants to know how the abuse will affect him in the future. But developmental psychologists don't have a concrete answer. They can tell the mother that the overwhelming majority of traumatized children show no long-term effects. They can also analyze the child and his particular situation and make an educated guess about what might happen in the future. In other words, the long-term outcomes depend on a variety of variables: how long the abuse lasted, at what age it began, the child's personality, the way the parents handled the situation when they learned of the abuse, and so on.

To further complicate matters, all of the relevant variables interact with one another. For example, counseling might benefit an outgoing child but be ineffective for a shy child who tends to keep his feelings to himself. Conversely, art therapy, a strategy that encourages children to express their feelings in drawings, might be effective with a shy child but have little impact on one who is outgoing. Because of such complexities, developmentalists can't tell the mother what she wants to hear: that if she follows a certain formula, her child will turn out fine.

Throughout this book, you will encounter discussions of how research can be applied to developmental problems in No Easy Answers features. These should give you a better appreciation of the intricate ways in which variables interact in human development. You will also learn that these intricacies often frustrate efforts to use psychology to find solutions to everyday problems.

CRITICAL THINKING ?

Suppose a cross-sectional study of sex-role attitudes reveals that adults between the ages of 20 and 50 have the most egalitarian attitudes, while teenagers and adults over 50 have more traditional attitudes. How might cohort differences influence your interpretation of these results?

Because these findings fit our hypothesis, it is tempting to conclude that memory ability declines with age. But we cannot say this conclusively based on the cross-sectional data, because these adults differ not only in age, but also in cohort. The differences in memory might reflect, for example, differences in education and not changes linked to age or development. Furthermore, cross-sectional studies cannot tell us anything about sequences of change with age or about the consistency of individual behavior over time, because each participant is tested only once. Still, cross-sectional research is very useful because it can be done relatively quickly and can reveal possible age differences or age changes.

Longitudinal Designs   Longitudinal designs seem to solve the problems presented by cross-sectional designs, because they follow the same individuals over a period of time. For example, to examine our hypothesis on memory decline, we could test a group first at age 25, then at 35, again at 45, and so on. Such studies allow psychologists to look at sequences of change and at individual consistency or inconsistency over time. And because longitudinal studies compare performance by the same people at different ages, they get around the obvious cohort problem.

A few well-known longitudinal studies have followed groups of children into adulthood or groups of adults from early to late adult life. The Berkeley/Oakland Growth Study is one of the most famous of these long-term studies (see Figure 1.3) (Eichorn, Clausen, Haan, Honzik, & Mussen, 1981). The Grant study of Harvard men is perhaps equally famous (Vaillant, 1977). This study followed several hundred men from age 18 until they were in their 60s. Such studies are extremely important in the study of human development, so you'll be reading more about them in later chapters.

Despite their importance, longitudinal designs have several major difficulties. One problem is that longitudinal studies typically involve giving each participant the same tests over and over again. Over time, people learn how to take the tests. Such *practice effects* may distort the measurement of any underlying developmental changes.

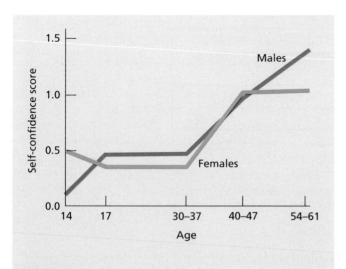

FIGURE 1.3

These results are from a famous study in Berkeley and Oakland, California, of a group of participants born either in 1920 or in 1928. They were tested frequently in childhood and adolescence, as well as three times in adulthood. Here you can see the sharp rise in self-confidence that occurred for both men and women in this group in their 30s—a pattern that may reflect a shared personality change, triggered by the common experiences of the social clock. (Source: Haan, Millsap, & Hartka, 1986, Figure 1, p. 228.)

Another significant problem is that not everyone sticks with the program. Some participants drop out; others die or move away. As a general rule, the healthiest and best educated are most likely to stick it out, and that fact biases the results, particularly if the study covers the final decades of life. Each succeeding set of test results comes from proportionately more and more healthy adults, which may make it look as if there were less change or less decline than actually exists.

Longitudinal studies also don't really get around the cohort problem. For example, both the Grant study and the Berkeley/Oakland Growth Study observed and tested participants born in the same decade (1918–1928). Even if both studies showed the same pattern of change with age, we wouldn't know whether the pattern was unique to that cohort or reflected more basic developmental changes that would be observed in other cultures and other cohorts.

Sequential Designs   One way to avoid the shortcomings of both cross-sectional and longitudinal designs is to use a sequential design. To study our memory hypothesis using a sequential design, we would begin with at least two age groups. One group might include 25- to 30-year-olds, and the other 30- to 35-year-olds. We would then test each group several times over a number of years, as illustrated in Figure 1.4 (page 16). In a sequential study, each testing point beyond the initial one allows researchers to make two types of comparisons. Age-group comparisons provide them with the same kind of information as a cross-sectional study. Comparison of each group to itself at an earlier testing point allows the researchers to collect longitudinal evidence at the same time.

Sequential designs also allow for comparisons of cohorts. For example, notice in Figure 1.4 that Group A is 30 to 35 years old at testing point 1, and Group B is 30 to 35 years old at testing point 2. Likewise, Group A is 35 to 40 at point 2, and their counterparts in Group B are this age at point 3. If same-age comparisons of the two groups reveal that their memory performance is different, researchers have evidence

	Age at testing point 1	Age at testing point 2	Age at testing point 3
Group A	30 to 35	35 to 40	40 to 45
Group B	25 to 30	30 to 35	35 to 40

FIGURE 1.4

This grid represents a design for a sequential study of memory function.

that, for some reason, the two cohorts differ. Conversely, if the groups perform similarly, investigators can conclude that their respective performances represent developmental characteristics rather than cohort effects. Moreover, if both groups demonstrate similar age-related patterns of change over time, researchers can conclude that the developmental pattern is not specific to any particular cohort. Finding the same developmental pattern in two cohorts provides psychologists with stronger evidence than either cross-sectional or longitudinal data alone.

IDENTIFYING RELATIONSHIPS BETWEEN VARIABLES

After deciding what design to use, the researcher interested in age and memory ability must decide how to go about finding relationships between *variables*. To developmentalists, variables are characteristics that vary from person to person, such as physical size, intelligence, and personality. When two or more variables vary together, there is some kind of relationship between them. The hypothesis that memory declines with age involves two variables, memory and age, and suggests a relationship between them. There are several ways of identifying such relationships.

Case Studies and Naturalistic Observation   **Case studies** are in-depth examinations of single individuals. To test the hypothesis about memory and age, we could use a case study comparing one individual's scores on tests of memory in early and late adulthood. Such a study might tell us a lot about the stability or instability of memory in the individual studied, but we wouldn't know if our findings applied to others.

Still, case studies are extremely useful in making decisions about individuals. For example, to find out whether a child is mentally retarded, a psychologist would conduct an extensive case study involving tests, interviews of the child's parents, behavioral observations, and so on. Case studies are also frequently the basis of important hypotheses about unusual developmental events, such as head injuries and strokes.

When psychologists use **naturalistic observation** as a research method, they observe people in their normal environments. For instance, to find out more about memory in older adults, a researcher could observe them in their homes or workplaces. Such studies provide developmentalists with information about psychological processes in everyday contexts.

The weakness of naturalistic observation, however, is *observer bias*. For example, if the researcher who is observing older adults is convinced that most of them have poor memories, he is likely to ignore any behavior that goes against this view. Because of observer bias, naturalistic observation studies often use "blind" observers who don't know what the research is about. In most cases, for the sake of accuracy, researchers use two or more observers so that the observations of each observer can be checked against those of the other(s).

case study an in-depth examination of a single individual

naturalistic observation the process of studying people in their normal environments

Like case studies, naturalistic observation studies are limited in the extent to which the results can be generalized. In addition, naturalistic observation studies are very time-consuming. They must be repeated in a variety of settings so that researchers can be sure people's behavior reflects development and not the influences of a specific environment.

Correlations A **correlation** is a relationship between two variables that can be expressed as a number ranging from −1.00 to +1.00. A zero correlation indicates that there is no relationship between the two variables. A positive correlation means that high scores on one variable are usually accompanied by high scores on the other. The closer a positive correlation is to +1.00, the stronger the relationship between the variables. Two variables that change in opposite directions have a negative correlation, and the nearer the correlation is to −1.00, the more strongly the two are connected.

To understand positive and negative correlations, think about the relationship between temperature and the use of air conditioners and heaters. Temperature and air conditioner use are positively correlated. As the temperature climbs, the number of air conditioners in use goes up. Conversely, temperature and heater use are negatively correlated. As the temperature decreases, the number of heaters in use goes up.

If we wanted to know whether age was related to memory, we could use a correlation. All that would be necessary would be to administer memory tests to adults of varying ages and calculate the correlation between test scores and ages. If there was a positive correlation between age and the number of memory errors people made—if older people made more errors—then we could say that our hypothesis had been supported. Conversely, if there was a negative correlation—if older people made fewer errors—then we would have to conclude that our hypothesis had not been supported.

Useful as they are, though, correlations have a major limitation: They do not indicate *causal* relationships. For example, even a high positive correlation between memory errors and age would tell us only that memory performance and age were connected in some way. It wouldn't tell us what caused the connection. It might be that younger adults understand the test instructions better. In order to identify a cause, we have to carry out experiments.

Experiments An **experiment** is a study that tests a causal hypothesis. Suppose, for example, that we think age differences in memory are caused by older adults' failure to use memory techniques such as repeating a list mentally in order to remember it. We could test this hypothesis by providing memory technique training to one group of older adults and no training to another group. If the trained adults got higher scores on memory tests than they did before training and the no-training group showed no change, we could claim support for our hypothesis.

A key feature of an experiment is that participants are assigned *randomly* to one of two or more groups. In other words, chance determines which group each participant is placed in. When participants are randomly assigned to groups, the groups have equal amounts of variation with respect to characteristics such as intelligence, personality traits, height, weight, and health status. Consequently, none of these variables can affect the outcome of the experiment.

Participants in the **experimental group** receive the treatment the experimenter thinks will produce a particular effect, while those in the **control group** receive either no special treatment or a neutral treatment. The presumed causal element in the experiment is called the **independent variable,** and the characteristic or behavior that the independent variable is expected to affect is called the **dependent variable.**

In a memory technique training experiment like the one suggested above, the group that receives the memory training is the experimental group, and the one that receives no instruction is the control group. Memory technique training is the variable that we, the experimenters, think will cause differences in memory function, so it is the independent variable. Performance on memory tests is the variable we are using to measure the effect of the memory technique training. Therefore, performance on memory tests is the dependent variable.

CRITICAL THINKING ?

Researchers have found a positive correlation between a mother's age at the birth of her child and the child's later IQ: Very young mothers have children with lower IQs. How many different explanations of this correlation can you think of?

correlation a relationship between two variables that can be expressed as a number ranging from −1.00 to +1.00

experiment a study that tests a causal hypothesis

experimental group the group in an experiment that receives the treatment the experimenter thinks will produce a particular effect

control group the group in an experiment that receives either no special treatment or a neutral treatment

independent variable the presumed causal element in an experiment

dependent variable the characteristic or behavior that is expected to be affected by the independent variable

Experiments are essential for understanding many aspects of development. But two special problems in studying child or adult development limit the use of experiments. First, many of the questions researchers want to answer have to do with the effects of particular unpleasant or stressful experiences on individuals—abuse, prenatal influences of alcohol or tobacco, low birth weight, poverty, unemployment, widowhood. For obvious ethical reasons, researchers cannot manipulate these variables. For example, they cannot ask one set of pregnant women to have two alcoholic drinks a day and others to have none. To study the effects of such experiences, they must rely on nonexperimental methods, such as correlations.

Second, the independent variable developmentalists are often most interested in is age itself, and researchers cannot assign participants randomly to age groups. They can compare 4-year-olds and 6-year-olds in their approach to some particular task, such as searching for a lost object, but the children differ in a host of ways other than their ages. Older children have had more and different experiences. Thus, unlike psychologists studying other aspects of behavior, developmental psychologists cannot systematically manipulate many of the variables they are most interested in.

To get around this problem, researchers can use any one of a series of strategies, sometimes called *quasi-experiments,* in which they compare groups without assigning the participants randomly. Cross-sectional studies are a form of quasi-experiment. So are studies in which researchers compare members of naturally occurring groups that differ in some dimension of interest, such as children whose parents choose to place them in day-care programs and children whose parents keep them at home.

Such comparisons have built-in problems, because groups that differ in one way are likely to differ in other ways as well. Compared with parents who keep their children at home, parents who place their children in day care are generally poorer, are more likely to be single parents, and tend to have different values or religious backgrounds. If researchers find that the two groups of children differ in some fashion, is it because they have spent their days in different environments or because of these other differences in their families? Researchers can make such comparisons a bit easier if they select comparison groups that are matched on those variables the researchers think might matter, such as income, marital status, or religion. But a quasi-experiment, by its very nature, will always yield more ambiguous results than will a fully controlled experiment.

CROSS-CULTURAL RESEARCH

Increasingly common in human development are studies comparing cultures or contexts, a task that researchers approach in several ways. One method of study, borrowed from the field of anthropology, is the ethnographic method. An **ethnography** is a detailed description of a single culture or context based on extensive observation. Often the observer lives in the culture or context for a period of time, perhaps as long as several years. Each ethnographic study is intended to stand alone, although it is sometimes possible to combine information from several different studies to see whether similar developmental patterns exist in the various cultures or contexts.

Alternatively, investigators may attempt to compare two or more cultures directly, by testing children or adults in each of the cultures with the same or comparable measures. Sometimes this involves comparing groups from different countries. Sometimes the comparisons are between subcultures within the same country; for example, increasingly common in the United States is research involving comparisons of children or adults living in different ethnic groups or communities, such as African Americans, Hispanic Americans, Asian Americans, and European Americans.

Cross-cultural research is important to the study of human development for two reasons. First, developmentalists want to identify universal changes—that is, predictable events or processes experienced by individuals in all cultures. Developmentalists don't want to make a general statement about development—such as "Memory declines with age"—if the phenomenon in question happens only in certain cultures. Without cross-

ethnography a detailed description of a single culture or context

cultural research, it is impossible to know whether studies involving North Americans and Europeans apply to people in other parts of the world.

Second, one of the goals of developmentalists is to produce findings that can be used to improve people's lives. Cross-cultural research is critical to this goal as well. For example, developmentalists know that children in cultures that emphasize the community more than the individual are more cooperative than children in more individualistic cultures. However, to use this information to help all children learn to cooperate, they need to know exactly how adults in such cultures teach their children to be cooperative. Cross-cultural research helps developmentalists identify specific variables that explain cultural differences.

Ethnographers often interact in everyday settings with members of the cultures they study.

RESEARCH ETHICS

Research ethics are the guidelines researchers follow to protect the rights of animals used in research and humans who participate in studies. Ethical guidelines are published by professional organizations such as the American Psychological Association, the American Educational Research Association, and the Society for Research in Child Development. Universities, private foundations, and government agencies have review committees that make sure all research sponsored by the institution is ethical. Guidelines for animal research include the requirement that animals be protected from unnecessary pain and suffering. Further, researchers must demonstrate that the potential benefits of their studies to either human or animal populations will be greater than any potential harm to animal subjects.

Ethical standards for research involving human participants address the following major concerns:

Protection from Harm It is unethical to do research that may cause participants permanent physical or psychological harm. Moreover, if the possibility of temporary harm exists, researchers must provide participants with some way of repairing the damage. For example, if the study will remind subjects of unpleasant experiences, like rape, researchers must provide them with counseling.

Informed Consent Researchers must inform participants of any possible harm and have them sign a consent form stating that they are aware of the risks of participating. In order for children to participate in studies, their parents must give permission after the researcher has informed them of possible risks. Children older than 7 must also give their own consent. If the research takes place in a school or day-care center, an administrator representing the institution must consent. In addition, both children and adults have the right to discontinue participation in a study at any time. Researchers are obligated to explain this right to children in language they can understand.

Confidentiality Participants have the right to confidentiality. Researchers must keep the identities of participants confidential and must report their data in such a way that no particular piece of information can be associated with any specific participant. The exception to confidentiality is when children reveal to researchers that they have been abused in any way by an adult. In most states, all citizens are required to report suspected cases of child abuse.

Knowledge of Results Participants, their parents, and the administrators of institutions in which research takes place have a right to a written summary of a study's results.

Deception If deception has been a necessary part of a study, participants have the right to be informed about the deception as soon as the study is over.

research ethics the guidelines researchers follow to protect the rights of animals used in research and humans who participate in studies

Before going on . . .

■ Discuss the pros and cons of cross-sectional, longitudinal, and sequential research designs.

■ How do developmentalists use case studies, naturalistic observation, correlations, and experiments to identify relationships between variables?

■ Why is cross-cultural research important to the study of human development?

■ List the ethical standards used by researchers to protect the rights of research participants.

The Real World

Thinking Critically about Research

There are reports about human development research in the news media every day. One report may say that drinking grape juice will protect you from a heart attack, while another may tell you that drinking grape juice will increase your risk of developing Alzheimer's disease. Similarly, one study may say that day care helps children's cognitive development, while another is interpreted to mean that day care is harmful.

When research results appear to be in conflict or when results are at variance with our own personal values, many of us respond by saying either "I agree with that study" or "I don't agree with that study." A better approach is to learn to use your knowledge of research methods to become a "critical consumer" of research.

For example, suppose you read a newspaper report of a study "proving" that putting infants in day care causes behavior problems later in childhood. After reading this chapter, you should know that only an experiment can produce such proof. To demonstrate that day care causes behavior prob-

lems, researchers would have to randomly assign infants to day-care and home-care groups. You should be aware that such a study would be unethical and, therefore, impossible. Thus, a newspaper report may claim that a study showing a correlation between day care and behavior problems demonstrates that one causes the other—but you, the critical consumer, should know better.

Once you have evaluated the scientific merit of a given research result, you can move forward with determining what it means to you in your own "real world." Throughout the text, Real World boxes will acquaint you with research findings we think are particularly relevant to everyday life. But remember, whether reported in the newspaper or in psychology textbooks, research findings should never be thought of as authoritative statements that can't be questioned. However, neither are they ordinary opinions that call for a response of "I agree" or "I disagree." The appropriate response to research results is critical thinking based on solid knowledge of both the possibilities and the limitations of psychological research.

Summary

An Introduction to Human Development

- The philosophical concepts of original sin, innate goodness, and the blank slate have influenced Western ideas about human development.
- Darwin studied child development to gain insight into evolution. G. Stanley Hall published the first scientific study of children and introduced the concepts of norms and adolescence.
- Today's developmentalists recognize that change happens throughout the lifespan.
- Theorists and researchers classify age-related change according to three broad categories: the physical, cognitive, and social domains.

Key Issues in the Study of Human Development

- Historically, developmentalists have argued about nature versus nurture, but now they believe that every developmental change is a product of both.
- Developmentalists also differ with regard to the continuity-discontinuity issue. Some emphasize qualitative changes, while others focus on quantitative changes.

- Universal age-related changes are those that are experienced by all human beings.
- Group-specific changes are common to individuals who have similar cultural and historical experiences.
- Genetic factors and the timing of experiences are two important causes of individual differences in development.

Research Designs and Methods

- Developmental psychologists use scientific methods to describe, explain, and predict age-related changes and individual differences. Most also want to use research results to improve people's lives.
- In cross-sectional studies, separate age groups are each tested once. In longitudinal designs, the same individuals are tested repeatedly over time. Sequential designs combine cross-sectional and longitudinal comparisons.
- Case studies and naturalistic observation provide a lot of important information, but it usually isn't generalizable to other individuals or groups. Correlational studies measure relationships between variables. They can be done quickly, and the information they yield is more generalizable than that from case studies or naturalistic observation. To test causal hypotheses, it is necessary to use experimental

designs in which participants are assigned randomly to experimental or control groups.

● Cross-cultural research helps developmentalists identify universal factors and cultural variables that affect development.

● Ethical principles governing psychological research include protection from harm, informed consent, confidentiality, knowledge of results, and protection from deception.

Key Terms

ageism (p. 10)

atypical development (p. 12)

case study (p. 16)

cognitive domain (p. 6)

cohort (p. 11)

control group (p. 17)

correlation (p. 17)

critical period (p. 11)

cross-sectional design (p. 13)

dependent variable (p. 17)

ethnography (p. 18)

experiment (p. 17)

experimental group (p. 17)

human development (p. 3)

independent variable (p. 17)

lifespan perspective (p. 6)

longitudinal design (p. 13)

maturation (p. 4)

naturalistic observation (p. 16)

nature-nurture controversy (p. 7)

norms (p. 4)

physical domain (p. 6)

qualitative change (p. 9)

quantitative change (p. 8)

research ethics (p. 19)

sensitive period (p. 12)

sequential design (p. 13)

social clock (p. 10)

social domain (p. 6)

Theories of Development

2

C H A P T E R

Every parent knows it's a constant struggle to keep babies from putting everything in their mouths.

© David J. Sams/Stock Boston, LLC.

Whether it's an attractive toy or a dead insect they encounter while crawling across the living room floor, infants seem to be driven to use their mouths to explore. Have you ever wondered why? An inborn drive to explore the environment may be responsible, or babies may find the physical sensation of mouthing an object highly pleasurable. Perhaps babies use their mouths more than toddlers and preschoolers do because they don't yet have the ability to fully control other parts of their bodies. Clearly, there are many possible explanations.

As you learned in Chapter 1, developmental psychologists use theories to formulate hypotheses, or testable answers, to such "why" questions. However, there are many types or layers of theories. At the broadest level are three very broad families of theories—psychoanalytic theory, learning theory, and cognitive-developmental theory. Theories within each of these families attempt to provide developmentalists with comprehensive explanations of just about every facet of human development. At the opposite end of the spectrum are minitheories, which explain very narrow and specific aspects of development.

Most minitheories have their roots in the major families. Ultimately, too, developmentalists hope to be able to integrate minitheories into more comprehensive explanations of human development. Thus, developmental scientists continue to search for an overarching, comprehensive explanation of human development, but today's theorists often take the more modest minitheoretical approach.

This chapter will introduce you to the three major families of theories. These theories will come up again and again as you make your way through this book. This chapter will also acquaint you with a few current theoretical trends in the field of human development, and you will learn how developmental psychologists compare theories. As you read, keep the following questions in mind:

- How do the theories of Freud and Erikson explain developmental change?
- How do the theories of Pavlov, Skinner, and Bandura explain developmental change?
- How do Piaget's theory and the information-processing approach explain developmental change?
- What kinds of theories have recently captured the attention of developmental psychologists?
- What criteria do psychologists use to compare one theory to another?

Psychoanalytic Theories

...oretical approach to explaining babies' fascination with mouthing objects
...uggest that infants derive more physical pleasure from mouthing objects
...ipulating them with other parts of their bodies. Such an approach
... belong to the family of **psychoanalytic theories,** a school of thought
...ith Viennese physician Sigmund Freud (1856–1939). Psychoanalytic
...elieve that developmental change happens because internal drives and
...ions influence behavior.

FREUD'S PSYCHOSEXUAL THEORY

Freud developed his psychoanalytic theory while working with mental patients, particularly those with *hysterical disorders.* Hysterical disorders are physical problems, like blindness, for which doctors can't find a medical cause. Freud thought that these problems were caused by experiences patients couldn't remember. He hypnotized patients to help them remember, and he studied the dreams they reported. He also asked patients to tell him everything they could remember about specific periods of their lives, without censoring anything. These methods led to the development of modern psychotherapy.

One of Freud's most distinctive concepts is the idea that behavior is governed by both conscious and unconscious processes. The most basic of these unconscious processes is an internal drive for physical pleasure that Freud called the **libido.** He believed the libido to be the motivating force behind most behavior.

Freud also argued that personality has three parts. The **id** contains the libido and operates at an unconscious level; the id is a person's basic sexual and aggressive impulses, which are present at birth. The **ego,** the conscious, thinking part of personality, develops in the first 2 to 3 years of life. One of the ego's jobs is to keep the needs of the id satisfied. For instance, when a person is hungry, it is the id that demands food immediately, and the ego is supposed to find a way to obtain it. The **superego,** the portion of the personality that acts as a moral judge, contains the rules of society and develops near the end of early childhood, at about age 6. Once the superego develops, the ego's task becomes more complex. It must satisfy the id without violating the superego's rules.

The ego is responsible for keeping the three components of personality in balance. According to Freud, a person experiences tension when any of the three components is in conflict with another. For example, if a person is hungry, the id may motivate her to do anything to find food, but the ego—her conscious self—may be unable to find any. Alternatively, food may be available, but the ego may have to violate one of the superego's moral rules to get it. In such cases, the ego may generate **defense mechanisms,** ways of thinking about a situation that reduce anxiety (see Table 2.1 and No Easy Answers). Without defense mechanisms, Freud thought, the degree of tension within the personality would become intolerable, leading to mental illness or suicide.

Many of Freud's patients had memories of sexual feelings and behavior in childhood. This led Freud to believe that sexual feelings are important to personality development. Based on his patients' childhood memories, Freud proposed a series of **psychosexual stages** through which a child moves in a fixed sequence determined by maturation (see Table 2.2, page 26). In each stage, the libido is centered on a different part of the body. In the infant, the mouth is the focus of the drive for physical pleasure; the stage is therefore called the *oral stage.* As maturation progresses, the libido becomes focused on the anus (hence, the *anal stage*), and later on the genitals (the *phallic stage* and eventually the *genital stage*).

psychoanalytic theories theories proposing that developmental change happens because of the influence of internal drives and emotions on behavior

libido in Freud's theory, an instinctual drive for physical pleasure present at birth and forming the motivating force behind virtually all human behavior

id in Freud's theory, the part of the personality that comprises a person's basic sexual and aggressive impulses; it contains the libido and motivates a person to seek pleasure and avoid pain

ego according to Freud, the thinking element of personality

superego Freud's term for the part of personality that is the moral judge

defense mechanisms strategies for reducing anxiety, such as repression, denial, or projection, proposed by Freud

psychosexual stages Freud's five stages of personality development through which children move in a fixed sequence determined by maturation; the libido is centered in a different body part in each stage

The Repressed Memory Controversy

no EASY answers

Though they are removed from consciousness by the defense mechanisms of denial and repression, Freud claimed, traumatic events suffered in childhood, such as sexual abuse, lie smoldering in the unconscious. While hidden away, they cause distress in the personality and may even lead to serious mental illness. Consequently, Freud thought that the goal of psychotherapy was to uncover such events and help individuals learn to cope with them.

Memory researchers have investigated Freud's claim that childhood trauma is often forgotten in this way. It turns out that a few people who were crime victims or who were abused by their parents as children do forget the events for long periods of time, just as Freud predicted. However, most victims have vivid memories of traumatic events, even though they may forget minor details (Baddeley, 1998; Lindsay & Read, 1994). Moreover, those who commit crimes or abuse children are more likely to forget the incidents than are the victims (Taylor & Kopelman, 1984).

Memory experts also point out that therapists who directly suggest the possibility of repressed memories risk creating false memories in their clients' minds (Ceci & Bruck, 1993). However, repression does sometimes occur, and discovery of a repressed memory does sometimes improve a person's mental health. Thus, mental health professionals face a dilemma. Should they ignore the possibility of a repressed memory or risk creating a false one?

Therapists address the dilemma by obtaining training in techniques that can bring out repressed memories but don't directly suggest that such memories exist. For example, when clients believe they have recalled a repressed event, therapists help them look for concrete evidence. In the end, however, both therapist and client should recognize that they must often rely on flawed human judgment to decide whether a "recovered" memory was really repressed or was invented in the client's mind.

Optimum development, according to Freud, requires an environment that will satisfy the unique needs of each period. For example, the infant needs sufficient opportunity for oral stimulation. An inadequate early environment will result in *fixation,* characterized by behaviors that reflect unresolved problems and unmet needs. Thus, as you might guess from looking at the list of stages in Table 2.2, emphasis on the formative role of early experiences is a hallmark of psychoanalytic theories.

Freud's most controversial idea about early childhood is his assertion that children experience sexual attraction to the opposite-sex parent during the phallic stage (ages 3 to 6). Freud borrowed names for this conflict from Greek literature. Oedipus was a

TABLE 2.1	Common Defense Mechanisms	
Mechanism	**Definition**	**Example**
Denial	Behaving as if a problem didn't exist	A pregnant woman fails to get prenatal care because she convinces herself she can't possibly be pregnant, even though she has all the symptoms.
Repression	Pushing the memory of something unpleasant into the unconscious	A child "forgets" about a troublesome bully on the bus as soon as he gets safely home from school every day.
Projection	Seeing one's own behavior or beliefs in others, whether they are actually present or not	A woman complains about her boss to a co-worker and comes away from the conversation believing that the co-worker shares her dislike of the boss, even though the co-worker made no comment on what she said.
Regression	Behaving in a way that is inappropriate for one's age	A toilet-trained 2-year-old starts wetting the bed every night after a new baby arrives.
Displacement	Directing emotion to an object (or a person) other than the one that provoked it	An elderly adult suffers a stroke, becomes physically impaired, and expresses her frustration through verbal abuse of the hospital staff.
Rationalization	Creating an explanation to justify an action or to deal with a disappointment	A man stealing money from his employer says to himself, "They won't give me a raise, so I deserve whatever I can take."

TABLE 2.2	Freud's Psychosexual Stages			
Stage	**Approximate Ages**	**Focus of Libido**	**Major Developmental Task**	**Some Characteristics of Adults Fixated at This Stage**
Oral	Birth to 1 year	Mouth, lips, tongue	Weaning	Oral behavior, such as smoking and overeating; passivity and gullibility
Anal	1 to 3 years	Anus	Toilet training	Orderliness, obstinacy or messiness, disorganization
Phallic	3 to 6 years	Genitals	Resolving Oedipus/ Electra complex	Vanity, recklessness, sexual dysfunction or deviancy
Latency*	6 to 12 years	None	Developing defense mechanisms; identifying with same-sex peers	None
Genital	12+	Genitals	Achieving mature sexual intimacy	Adults who have successfully integrated earlier stages should emerge with sincere interest in others and mature sexuality.

*Freud thought that the latency period is not really a psychosexual stage, because libido is not focused on the body during this period; therefore, fixation is impossible.

male character who was involved in a romantic relationship with his mother. Electra was a female character who had a similar relationship with her father. During the phallic stage boys are supposed to have such an intense desire to possess their mothers that they often fantasize about killing their fathers. Freud referred to these feelings as the *Oedipus complex*. In Freud's view, the boy responds to the anxiety generated by these conflicting feelings with a defense mechanism called *identification*. In other words, he attempts to match his own behavior to that of his father. According to Freud, by trying to make himself as much like his father as possible, the boy not only reduces what he perceives as the chance of an attack from the father, but also acquires masculine behavior patterns.

A parallel process is supposed to occur in girls; Freud named it the *Electra complex*. A girl experiences the same kind of attraction to her father as a boy does toward his mother. Likewise, she sees her mother as a rival for her father's attentions and has some fear of her mother. Like the boy, she resolves the problem by identifying with the same-sex parent.

ERIKSON'S PSYCHOSOCIAL THEORY

Freud's views were criticized by many of his contemporaries. Many of Freud's critics accepted his assertion that unconscious forces influence development, but they questioned his rather gloomy view that childhood trauma nearly always leads to emotional instability in adulthood. Later theorists, known as *neo-Freudians*, proposed ideas that built on the strengths of Freud's theory but tried to avoid its weaknesses.

Erik Erikson (1902–1994) is the neo-Freudian theorist who has had the greatest influence on the study of development (Erikson, 1950, 1959, 1980b, 1982; Erikson, Erikson, & Kivnick, 1986; Evans, 1969). Erikson thought development resulted from the interaction between internal drives and cultural demands; thus, his theory refers to **psychosocial** stages rather than to psycho*sexual* ones. Furthermore, Erikson thought that development continued through the entire lifespan.

In Erikson's view, to achieve a healthy personality, an individual must successfully resolve a crisis at each of the eight stages of development, as summarized in Table 2.3. Each crisis is defined by a pair of opposing possibilities, such as trust versus mistrust or integrity versus despair. Successful resolution of a crisis results in the development of the characteristic on the positive side of the dichotomy. A healthy resolution, however, does not mean moving totally to the positive side. For example, an infant needs to have experienced some mistrust in order to learn to identify people who are not trustworthy.

psychosocial stages Erikson's eight stages, or crises, of personality development in which inner instincts interact with outer cultural and social demands to shape personality

TABLE 2.3	Erikson's Psychosocial Stages	

Approximate Ages	Stage	Positive Characteristics Gained and Typical Activities
Birth to 1 year	Trust versus mistrust	Hope; trust in primary caregiver and in one's own ability to make things happen (secure attachment to caregiver is key)
1 to 3	Autonomy versus shame and doubt	Will; new physical skills lead to demand for more choices, most often seen as saying "no" to caregivers; child learns self-care skills such as toileting
3 to 6	Initiative versus guilt	Purpose; ability to organize activities around some goal; more assertiveness and aggressiveness (Oedipus conflict with parent of same sex may lead to guilt)
6 to 12	Industry versus inferiority	Competence; cultural skills and norms, including school skills and tool use (failure to master these leads to sense of inferiority)
12 to 18	Identity versus role confusion	Fidelity; adaptation of sense of self to pubertal changes, consideration of future choices, achievement of a more mature sexual identity, and search for new values
18 to 30	Intimacy versus isolation	Love; person develops intimate relationships beyond adolescent love; many become parents
30 to late adulthood	Generativity versus stagnation	Care; people rear children, focus on occupational achievement or creativity, and train the next generation; turn outward from the self toward others
Late adulthood	Integrity versus despair	Wisdom; person conducts a life review, integrates earlier stages and comes to terms with basic identity; develops self-acceptance

But healthy development requires a favorable ratio of positive to negative. Of the eight stages described in Table 2.3, four have been the focus of the greatest amount of theorizing and research: trust in infancy, identity in adolescence, intimacy in early adulthood, and generativity in middle adulthood.

Erikson believed that the behavior of the major caregiver (usually the mother) is critical to the child's resolution of the first life crisis: *trust versus mistrust.* To ensure successful resolution of this crisis, the caregiver must be consistently loving and must respond to the child predictably and reliably. Infants whose early care has been erratic or harsh may develop mistrust. In either case, the child carries this aspect of personality throughout her development, and it affects the resolution of later tasks.

Erikson's description of the central adolescent dilemma, *identity versus role confusion,* has been particularly influential. He argued that, in order to arrive at a mature sexual and occupational identity, every adolescent must examine his identity and the roles he must occupy. He must achieve an integrated sense of self, of what he wants to do and be, and of his appropriate sexual role. The risk is that the adolescent will suffer from confusion arising from the profusion of roles opening up to him at this age.

In the first of the three adult stages, the young adult builds on the identity established in adolescence to confront the crisis of *intimacy versus isolation.* Erikson defined intimacy as "the ability to fuse your identity with someone else's without fear that you're going to lose something yourself" (Erikson, in Evans, 1969). Many young people, Erikson thought, make the mistake of thinking they will find their identity in a relationship, but in his view it is only those who have already formed (or are well on the way to forming) a clear identity who can successfully enter this fusion of identities that he called *intimacy.* Young adults whose identities are weak or unformed will remain in shallow relationships and will experience a sense of isolation or loneliness.

CRITICAL THINKING ❓

In which of Erikson's psychosocial stages would you place yourself? Does Erikson's description of it correspond to the challenges and concerns you are confronting?

The middle adulthood crisis is *generativity versus stagnation,* which is "primarily the concern in establishing and guiding the next generation" (Erikson, 1963, p. 267). The rearing of children is the most obvious way to achieve a sense of generativity, but it is not the only way. Doing creative work, giving service to an organization or to society, or serving as a mentor to younger colleagues can help the midlife adult achieve a sense of generativity. Failing that, the self-absorbed, nongenerative adult may feel a sense of stagnation.

The key idea underlying Erikson's theory is that each new crisis is thrust on the developing person because of changes in social demands that accompany changes in age. The fourth stage of industry versus inferiority, for example, begins when the child starts school and must learn to read and write. The child can't stay in elementary school until she does so. Even if she doesn't learn to read and write, she is pushed forward into middle school and high school, carrying the unresolved crisis with her as excess baggage. Thus, the childhood crises set the stage for those of adolescence and adulthood.

EVALUATION OF PSYCHOANALYTIC THEORIES

Psychoanalytic theories such as Freud's and Erikson's, summarized in Table 2.4, have several attractive aspects. Most centrally, they highlight the importance of the child's earliest relationships with caregivers. Furthermore, they suggest that the child's needs change with age, so parents and other caregivers must continually adapt to the changing child. One of the implications of this is that we should not think of "good parenting" as an unchanging quality. Some people may be very good at meeting the needs of an infant but less capable of dealing with teenagers' identity struggles. The child's eventual personality and her overall mental health thus depend on the interaction pattern that develops in a particular family. The idea of changing needs is an extremely attractive element of these theories, because more and more of the research in developmental psychology is moving developmentalists toward just such a conception of the process.

TABLE 2.4	**Psychoanalytic Theories**		
		Evaluation	
Theory	**Main Idea**	**Strengths**	**Weaknesses**
Freud's Psychosexual Theory	Personality develops in five stages from birth to adolescence; in each stage, the need for physical pleasure is focused on a different part of the body.	Emphasizes importance of experiences in infancy and early childhood; provides psychological explanations for mental illness	Sexual feelings are not as important in personality development as Freud claimed.
Erikson's Psychosocial Theory	Personality develops through eight life crises across the entire lifespan; a person finishes each crisis with either a good or a poor resolution.	Helps explain the role of culture in personality development; important in lifespan psychology; useful description of major themes of personality development at different ages	Describing each period in terms of a single crisis is probably an oversimplification.

Psychoanalytic theory has also given psychologists a number of helpful concepts, such as the unconscious, the ego, and identity, which have become a part of everyday language as well as theory. Moreover, psychologists are taking a fresh look at Freud's ideas about the importance of defense mechanisms in coping with anxiety (Cramer, 2000). Freud is also usually credited with the invention of psychotherapy, which is still practiced today. An additional strength of the psychoanalytic perspective is the emphasis on continued development during adulthood found in Erikson's theory. His ideas have provided a framework for a great deal of new research and theorizing about adult development.

The major weakness of psychoanalytic theories is the fuzziness of many of their concepts. For example, how could researchers detect the presence of the id, ego, superego, and so on? Without more precise definitions, it is extremely difficult to test these theories, despite their provocative explanations of development.

Before going on . . .

- In Freud's view, how do the id, ego, and superego work together to keep the personality functioning?

- How do Erikson's stages differ from Freud's?

- Name at least two strengths and two weaknesses of psychoanalytic theory.

Learning Theories

Psychologist John Watson (1878–1958) offered ideas about human development that were very different from those of Freud and other psychoanalysts. Watson believed that, through manipulation of the environment, children could be trained to be or do anything (Jones, 1924; Watson, 1930). To refer to this point of view, Watson coined the term **behaviorism,** which defines development in terms of behavior changes caused by environment influences. As Watson put it,

> Give me a dozen healthy infants, well-formed, and my own specified world to bring them up in and I'll guarantee to take any one at random and train him to become any type of specialist I might select—doctor, lawyer, merchant, chief, and yes, even beggerman and thief, regardless of his talents, penchants, abilities, vocations, and race of his ancestors. (1930, p. 104)

Watson's views were based in the theoretical family that includes the **learning theories,** which assert that development results from an accumulation of experiences. Thus, in contrast to psychoanalysts, learning theorists would say that infants repeat the behavior of putting objects in their mouths because they find the sensations it produces rewarding. Alternatively, when they put something in their mouths that tastes bad, infants learn not to mouth such an object again.

PAVLOV'S CLASSICAL CONDITIONING

Russian medical researcher and Nobel prize winner Ivan Pavlov (1849–1936) discovered an important learning principle: Organisms can acquire new signals for existing responses (behaviors). The term **classical conditioning** refers to this principle. Each incidence of learning begins with a biologically programmed stimulus-response connection, or *reflex.* For example, salivation happens naturally when you put food in your mouth. In classical conditioning terms, the food is the *unconditioned (unlearned, natural) stimulus;* salivating is an *unconditioned (unlearned, natural) response.*

Stimuli presented just before or at the same time as the unconditioned stimulus are those that are likely to be associated with it. For example, most foods have odors, and to get to your mouth, food has to pass near your nose. Thus, you usually smell food before you taste it. Food odors eventually become *conditioned (learned) stimuli* that elicit salivation. In effect, they act as a signal to your salivary glands that food is coming. Once the connection between food odors and salivation has been established,

behaviorism the view that defines development in terms of behavior changes caused by environmental influences

learning theories theories that assert that development results from an accumulation of experiences

classical conditioning learning that results from the association of stimuli

smelling food triggers the salivation response even when you do not actually eat the food. When a response occurs reliably in connection with a conditioned stimulus in this way, it is known as a *conditioned (learned) response.*

Classical conditioning is of interest in the study of development because of the role it plays in the acquisition of emotional responses. For example, things or people present when you feel good will become conditioned stimuli for pleasant feelings, while those associated with uncomfortable feelings may become conditioned stimuli for a sense of unease. Classical conditioning is especially important in infancy. Because a child's mother or father is present so often when nice things happen, such as when the child feels warm, comfortable, and cuddled, the mother and father usually serve as conditioned stimuli for pleasant feelings, a fact that makes it possible for the parents' presence to comfort a child.

SKINNER'S OPERANT CONDITIONING

Another type of learning is **operant conditioning,** a term coined by B. F. Skinner (1904–1990), the most famous proponent of this theory (Skinner, 1953, 1980). Operant conditioning involves learning to repeat or stop behaviors because of the consequences they bring about. **Reinforcement** is anything that follows a behavior and causes it to be repeated. **Punishment** is anything that follows a behavior and causes it to stop.

A *positive reinforcement* is a consequence (usually involving something pleasant) that follows a behavior and increases the chances that the behavior will occur again. Some kinds of pleasant consequences, such as attention, serve as reinforcers for most people most of the time. But strictly speaking, a reinforcement is defined by its effect; we don't know something is reinforcing unless we see that its presence increases the probability of some behavior.

Negative reinforcement occurs when an individual learns to perform a specific behavior in order to cause something unpleasant to stop. For example, coughing is an unpleasant experience for most of us, and taking a dose of cough medicine usually stops it. As a result, when we begin coughing, we reach for the cough syrup. The behavior of swallowing a spoonful of cough syrup is reinforced by the cessation of coughing. In other words, we make the unpleasant experience of coughing go away when we engage in the behavior of swallowing cough syrup. Thus, the behavior of taking cough syrup is learned through negative reinforcement.

Definitions and simple examples of positive and negative reinforcement may be misleading when it comes to understanding how the two operate in real-life contexts. For example, most people understand that paying attention to a preschooler's whining is likely to increase it, an example of positive reinforcement. However, parents learn to attend to whining preschoolers because whining is irritating, and responding to it usually makes it stop. In other words, like taking cough syrup for an annoying cough, the parents' behavior of responding to whining is negatively reinforced by its consequence— namely, that the child *stops* whining.

In contrast to both kinds of reinforcement, punishment stops a behavior. Sometimes punishments involve eliminating nice things—taking away TV privileges, for example. However, punishment may also involve unpleasant things such as scolding. Like reinforcement, however, punishment is defined by its effect. Consequences that do not stop behavior can't be properly called punishments.

An alternative way to stop an unwanted behavior is **extinction,** which is the gradual elimination of a behavior through repeated nonreinforcement. If a teacher succeeds in eliminating a student's undesirable behavior by ignoring it, the behavior is said to have been *extinguished.*

operant conditioning learning to repeat or stop behaviors because of their consequences

reinforcement anything that follows a behavior and causes it to be repeated

punishment anything that follows a behavior and causes it to stop

extinction the gradual elimination of a behavior through repeated nonreinforcement

(Photo: © Ken Hayman/Black Star)

Laboratory research involving animals was important in the development of Skinner's operant conditioning theory.

Such examples illustrate the complex manner in which reinforcements and punishments operate in the real world. In laboratory settings, operant conditioning researchers usually work with only one participant or animal subject at a time; they needn't worry about the social consequences of behaviors or consequences. They can also control the situation so that a particular behavior is reinforced every time it occurs. In the real world, *partial reinforcement*—reinforcement of a behavior on some occasions but not others—is more common (see The Real World, page 32). Studies of partial reinforcement show that people take longer to learn a new behavior under partial reinforcement conditions; once established, however, such behaviors are very resistant to extinction.

Shaping is the reinforcement of intermediate steps until an individual learns a complex behavior. For example, you wouldn't start learning to play tennis by challenging a skilled player to a match. Instead, you would first learn to hold the racquet properly. Next, you would learn the basic strokes and practice hitting balls hit or thrown to you by an instructor. Next, you would learn to serve. Finally, you would put all your skills together and play an actual match. All along the way, you would be encouraged by the sense of satisfaction gained from accomplishing each step toward the goal.

BANDURA'S SOCIAL-LEARNING THEORY

Learning theorist Albert Bandura (b. 1925), whose ideas are more influential among developmental psychologists than those of the conditioning theorists, argues that learning does not always require reinforcement (1977a, 1982a, 1989). Learning may also occur as a result of watching someone else perform some action and experience reinforcement or punishment. Learning of this type, called **observational learning,** or **modeling,** is involved in a wide range of behaviors. Children learn to hit by watching other people in real life and on television. Adults learn job skills by observing or being shown them by others.

However, learning from modeling is not an entirely automatic process. Bandura points out that what an observer learns from watching someone else will depend on four things: what she pays attention to and what she is able to remember (both cognitive processes), what she is physically able to copy, and what she is motivated to imitate. Because attentional abilities, memory, and physical capabilities change with age, what a

CRITICAL THINKING 9

Describe instances in your everyday life when your behavior is affected by classical or operant conditioning or when you use these principles to affect others' behavior.

shaping the reinforcement of intermediate steps until an individual learns a complex behavior

observational learning, or **modeling** learning that results from seeing a model reinforced or punished for a behavior

Modeling is an important source of learning for both children and adults. What behaviors have you learned by watching and copying others?

The Real World

Learning Principles in Real Life

Virtually all parents try to reinforce some behaviors in their children by praising them or giving them attention. And most try to discourage unwanted behaviors through punishment. But it is easy to misapply learning principles or to create unintended consequences if you have not fully understood all the mechanisms involved.

For example, you want your children to stop climbing on a chair, so you scold them. You are conscientious and knowledgeable, and you carefully time your scolding and stop scolding when they stop climbing, so that the scolding operates as a negative reinforcer—but nothing works. They keep on leaving muddy footprints on your favorite chair. Why? Perhaps the children enjoy climbing on the chair, so the climbing is intrinsically reinforcing to them and outweighs the unpleasantness of your scolding. One way to deal with this might be to provide something else for them to climb on.

Another example: Suppose your 3-year-old son repeatedly demands your attention while you are fixing dinner.

Because you don't want to reinforce this behavior, you ignore him the first six or eight times he calls you or tugs at your clothes. But after the ninth or tenth repetition, with his voice getting whinier each time, you can't stand it any longer and finally say something like "All right! What do you want?" Since you have ignored most of his demands, you might think you have not been reinforcing them. But what you have actually done is create a partial reinforcement schedule. You have rewarded only every tenth demand, and psychologists have established that this pattern of reinforcement helps create behavior that is very hard to extinguish. So your son may continue to be overly demanding for a very long time.

If such situations are familiar to you, it may pay to keep careful records for a while, noting each incident and your response. Then see whether you can figure out which principles are really at work and how you might change the pattern.

child learns from any given modeled event may be quite different from what an adult learns from an identical event (Grusec, 1992).

As children, according to Bandura, we learn not only overt behavior, but also ideas, expectations, internal standards, and self-concepts, from models. At the same time, we acquire expectancies about what we can and cannot do—which Bandura (1997) calls *self-efficacy*. Once those standards and those expectancies or beliefs have been established, they affect the child's behavior in consistent and enduring ways. For example, self-efficacy beliefs influence our overall sense of well-being and even our physical health.

EVALUATION OF LEARNING THEORIES

Several implications of learning theories, summarized in Table 2.5, are worth emphasizing. First, learning theories can explain both consistency and change in behavior. If a child is friendly and smiling both at home and at school, learning theorists would explain the child's behavior by saying that the child is being reinforced for that behavior in both settings. It is equally possible to explain why a child is happy at home but miserable at school. We need only hypothesize that the home environment reinforces cheerful behavior but the school setting does not.

Learning theorists also tend to be optimistic about the possibility of change. Children's behavior can change if the reinforcement system—or their beliefs about themselves—change. So, problem behavior can be modified.

The great strength of learning theories is that they seem to give an accurate picture of the way in which many behaviors are learned. It is clear that both children and adults learn through conditioning and modeling. Furthermore, Bandura's addition of mental elements to learning theory adds further strength, since it allows an integration of learning models and other approaches.

TABLE 2.5	Learning Theories		
		Evaluation	
Theory	**Main Idea**	**Strengths**	**Weaknesses**
Pavlov's Classical Conditioning	Learning happens when neutral stimuli become so strongly associated with natural stimuli that they elicit the same response.	Useful in explaining how emotional responses such as phobias are learned	Explanation of behavior change is too limited to serve as comprehensive theory of human development.
Skinner's Operant Conditioning Theory	Development involves behavior changes that are shaped by reinforcement and punishment.	Basis of many useful strategies for managing and changing human behavior	Humans are not as passive as Skinner claimed; the theory ignores hereditary and cognitive, emotional, and social factors in development.
Bandura's Social-Learning Theory	People learn from models; what they learn from a model depends on how they interpret the situation cognitively and emotionally.	Helps explain how models influence behavior; explains more about development than other learning theories do because of addition of cognitive and emotional factors	Does not provide an overall picture of development

However, the learning theorists' approach is not really developmental; it doesn't tell us much about change with age, either in childhood or in adulthood. Even Bandura's variation on learning theory does not tell us whether there are any changes with age in what a child can learn from modeling. Thus, learning theories help developmentalists understand how specific behaviors are acquired but do not contribute to an understanding of age-related change.

Before going on . . .

■ What is classical conditioning?

■ How does operant conditioning cause learning?

■ What concepts does Bandura add to learning theories to make them more useful?

■ What are the strengths and weaknesses of learning theories as an explanation of human development?

Cognitive Theories

The group of theories known as **cognitive theories** emphasizes mental aspects of development such as logic and memory. A cognitive theorist might propose that babies use their senses, including the sense of taste, to build mental pictures of the world around them. Thus, infants mouth everything in their environment until they have learned all they can from this behavior; then they move on to a more mature way of interacting with the world.

cognitive theories theories that emphasize mental processes in development, such as logic and memory

Piaget based many of his ideas on naturalistic observations of children of different ages on playgrounds and in schools.

(Photo: © Bill Anderson/Photo Researchers, Inc.)

CRITICAL THINKING ❓

Describe three or four examples of assimilation and accommodation in your everyday life.

(Photo: Stone)

Using Piaget's terminology, we would say this infant is assimilating the object to her grasping scheme. What scheme is being accommodated at the same time as she adapts her grasping scheme?

PIAGET'S COGNITIVE-DEVELOPMENTAL THEORY

One of the most influential theories in the history of developmental psychology is that of Swiss developmentalist Jean Piaget (1896–1980). Originally educated as a natural scientist, Piaget spent six decades studying the development of logical thinking in children. Because of the popularity of Watson's views, psychologists in the United States paid little attention to Piaget's work. During the late 1950s, however, American developmentalists "discovered" Piaget. From then on, developmental psychologists in the United States began to focus on children's thinking more than on how environmental stimuli influenced their behavior.

Piaget was struck by the fact that all children seem to go through the same sequence of discoveries about their world, making the same mistakes and arriving at the same solutions (Piaget, 1952, 1970, 1977; Piaget & Inhelder, 1969). For example, all 3- and 4-year-olds seem to think that if water is poured from a short, wide glass into a taller, narrower one, there is then more water, because the water level is higher in the narrow glass than it was in the wide glass. In contrast, most 7-year-olds realize that the amount of water has not changed. To explain such age differences, Piaget proposed several concepts that continue to guide developmental research.

A pivotal idea in Piaget's model is that of a **scheme,** an internal cognitive structure that provides an individual with a procedure to follow in a specific circumstance. For example, when you pick up a ball, you use your picking-up scheme. To throw it to someone, you use your looking scheme, your aiming scheme, and your throwing scheme. Piaget proposed that each of us begins life with a small repertoire of sensory and motor schemes, such as looking, tasting, touching, hearing, and reaching. As we use each scheme, it becomes better adapted to the world; in other words, it works better.

We possess mental schemes as well, most of which develop in childhood and adolescence. Mental schemes allow us to use symbols and think logically. Piaget proposed three processes to explain how children get from built-in schemes such as looking and touching to the complex mental schemes used in childhood, adolescence, and adulthood.

Assimilation is the process of using schemes to make sense of experiences. Piaget would say that a baby who grasps a toy is *assimilating* it to his grasping scheme. The complementary process is **accommodation,** which involves changing the scheme as a result of some new information acquired through assimilation. When the baby grasps a square object for the first time, he will accommodate his grasping scheme; so the next time he reaches for a square object, his hand will be more appropriately bent to grasp it. Thus, the process of accommodation is the key to developmental change. Through accommodation, we improve our skills and reorganize our ways of thinking.

Equilibration is the process of balancing assimilation and accommodation to create schemes that fit the environment. To illustrate, think about infants' tendency to put things in their mouths. In Piaget's terms, they assimilate objects to their mouthing scheme. As they mouth each one, their mouthing scheme changes to include the instructions "*Do* mouth this" or "*Don't* mouth this." The accommodation is based on mouthing experiences. A pacifier feels good in the mouth, but a dead insect has an unpleasant texture. So, eventually, the mouthing scheme says it's okay to put a pacifier in the mouth, but it's not okay to mouth a dead insect. In this way, an infant's mouthing scheme attains a better fit with the real world.

Piaget's research suggested to him that logical thinking evolves in four stages. During the *sensorimotor stage,* from birth to 18 months, infants use their sensory and motor schemes to act on the world around them. In the *preoperational stage,* from 18 months to about age 6, youngsters acquire symbolic schemes, such as language and fantasy, that they use in thinking and communicating. Next comes the *concrete operational stage*, during which 6- to 12-year-olds begin to think logically and become capable of solving problems such as the one illustrated in Figure 2.1.

The last phase is the *formal operational stage*, in which adolescents learn to think logically about abstract ideas and hypothetical situations.

Table 2.6 describes these stages more fully; you will read about each of them in detail later in the book. For now, it is important to understand that in Piaget's view, each stage grows out of the one that precedes it, and each involves a major restructuring of the child's way of thinking. It's also important to know that research has confirmed Piaget's belief that the sequence of the stages is fixed. However, children progress through them at different rates. In addition, some individuals do not attain the formal operational stage in adolescence or even in adulthood. Consequently, the ages associated with the stages are approximations.

INFORMATION-PROCESSING THEORY

The goal of **information-processing theory** is to explain how the mind manages information (Klahr, 1992). Information-processing theorists use the computer as a model of human thinking. Consequently, they often use computer terms, like *hardware* and *software*, to talk about human cognitive processes. In addition, they experiment with programs designed to enable computers to think as humans do.

Theorizing about and studying memory processes are central to information-processing theory. This theory breaks memory down into subprocesses of encoding, storage, and retrieval. *Encoding* is organizing information to be stored in memory. For example, you may be encoding the information in this chapter by relating it to your own childhood. *Storage* is keeping information, and *retrieval* is getting information out of memory.

FIGURE 2.1

In one of the problems Piaget devised, a child is shown two clay balls of equal size and asked if they both contain the same amount of clay. Next, the researcher rolls one ball into a sausage shape and asks the child if the two shapes still contain the same amount of clay. A preoperational child will say that one now contains more clay than the other and will base his answer on their appearance: "The sausage has more because it's longer now." A concrete operational thinker will say that the two still contain the same amount of material because no clay was added or taken away from either. (Photo: Will Hart)

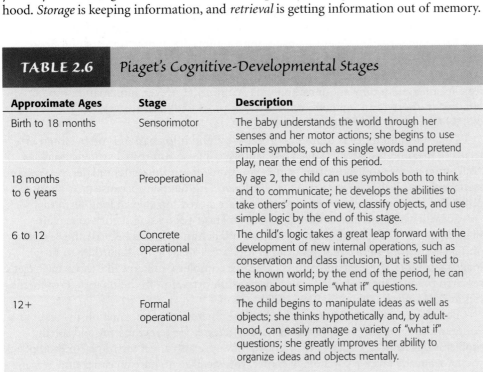

TABLE 2.6	Piaget's Cognitive-Developmental Stages	
Approximate Ages	**Stage**	**Description**
Birth to 18 months	Sensorimotor	The baby understands the world through her senses and her motor actions; she begins to use simple symbols, such as single words and pretend play, near the end of this period.
18 months to 6 years	Preoperational	By age 2, the child can use symbols both to think and to communicate; he develops the abilities to take others' points of view, classify objects, and use simple logic by the end of this stage.
6 to 12	Concrete operational	The child's logic takes a great leap forward with the development of new internal operations, such as conservation and class inclusion, but is still tied to the known world; by the end of the period, he can reason about simple "what if" questions.
12+	Formal operational	The child begins to manipulate ideas as well as objects; she thinks hypothetically and, by adulthood, can easily manage a variety of "what if" questions; she greatly improves her ability to organize ideas and objects mentally.

scheme in Piaget's theory, an internal cognitive structure that provides an individual with a procedure to use in a specific circumstance

assimilation the process of using a scheme to make sense of an event or experience

accommodation changing a scheme as a result of some new information

equilibration the process of balancing assimilation and accommodation to create schemes that fit the environment

information-processing theory a theoretical perspective that uses the computer as a model to explain how the mind manages information

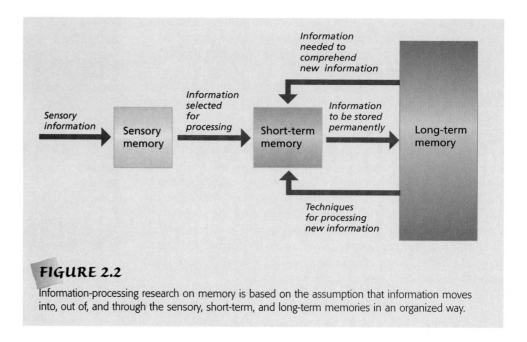

FIGURE 2.2

Information-processing research on memory is based on the assumption that information moves into, out of, and through the sensory, short-term, and long-term memories in an organized way.

Most memory research assumes that the human memory is made up of multiple components. The idea is that information moves through these components in an organized way (see Figure 2.2). The process of understanding a spoken word serves as a good example.

First, you hear the word when the sounds enter your *sensory memory*. Your experiences with language allow you to recognize the pattern of sounds as a word. Next, the word moves into your *short-term memory*, the component of the memory system where all information is processed. Thus, short-term memory is often called *working memory*. Knowledge of the word's meaning is then called up out of *long-term memory*, the component of the system where information is permanently stored, and placed in short-term memory, where it is linked to the word's sounds to enable you to understand it.

Each memory component manages information differently. Information flows through the sensory memory in a constant stream. Bits of information that are not attended to drop out quickly. The short-term memory is extremely limited in capacity—it can contain only about seven items at a time. However, information can be retained in short-term memory as long as it is processed in some way—as you do when you repeat your grocery list to yourself on the way to the store.

Long-term memory is unlimited in capacity, and information is often stored in terms of meaningful associations. For example, suppose you read a sentence such as "Bill wrote a letter to his brother." When you think about the sentence later, you might mistakenly recall that it contained the word *pen*. This happens because facts about the process of writing and the tools used to do it are stored together in long-term memory.

Some developmentalists have used information-processing theory to explain Piaget's stages. Their theories are called **neo-Piagetian theories** because they expand on Piaget's theory rather than contradict it (Case, 1985, 1997). According to neo-Piagetians, older children and adults can solve complex problems like those in Piaget's research because they can hold more pieces of information in their short-term memories at the same time than younger children can.

Besides age differences, there are individual differences in information-processing. For example, some people use more efficient strategies for remembering and solving problems than others. Differences in prior knowledge also affect memory. For example, if you have already taken a psychology course, you are likely to have an easier time remembering and understanding what you read in this book. In a sense, prior knowledge gives you a set of mental "hooks" on which to hang new information about psychology.

neo-Piagetian theory an approach that uses information-processing principles to explain the developmental stages identified by Piaget

EVALUATION OF COGNITIVE THEORIES

Research based on cognitive theories, especially the work of Piaget, has demonstrated that simplistic views, such as those of the conditioning theorists, cannot explain the development of the complex phenomenon that is logical thinking. Moreover, Piaget's research findings have been replicated in virtually every culture and in every cohort of children since his work was first published in the 1920s. Thus, not only did he formulate a theory that forced psychologists to think about child development in a new way, he also provided a set of findings that were impossible to ignore and difficult to explain. In addition, he developed innovative methods of studying children's thinking that continue to be important today (see the Research Report on page 38).

Nevertheless, Piaget turned out to be wrong about some of the ages at which children develop particular skills. As you will see in later chapters, researchers have found that children develop some intellectual skills at earlier ages than Piaget's findings suggested. Furthermore, Piaget was probably wrong about the generality of the stages themselves. Most 8-year-olds, for example, show concrete operational thinking on some tasks but not on others, and they are more likely to show complex thinking on familiar than on unfamiliar tasks. Thus, the whole process seems to be a great deal less stagelike than Piaget proposed.

Information-processing theory has helped to clarify some of the cognitive processes underlying Piaget's findings. Furthermore, it has greatly enhanced developmentalists' understanding of human memory. For example, information-processing research on the inaccuracies often found in eyewitness testimony is influencing the way police officers, prosecutors, and attorneys interview witnesses (Wells et al., 2000). Thus, information-processing theory is currently one of the most important psychological theories because of its adaptability to explaining and studying specific cognitive tasks such as how eyewitnesses remember what they have seen.

Critics of information-processing theory point out that human thinking is more complex than that of a computer. They also correctly point out that much information-processing research involves artificial memory tasks such as learning lists of words. Therefore, say critics, research based on the information-processing approach doesn't always accurately describe how memory works in the real world.

Piagetians claim that information-processing theory emphasizes explanations of single cognitive tasks at the expense of a comprehensive picture of development. Finally, critics of both cognitive theories say that they ignore the role of emotions in development. The cognitive theories are summarized in Table 2.7.

Before going on . . .

■ What did Piaget discover about the development of logical thinking in children, and how did he explain it?

■ What is the focus of information-processing theory?

■ List some contributions and criticisms of cognitive theories.

TABLE 2.7	*Cognitive Theories*		
		Evaluation	
Theory	**Main Idea**	**Strengths**	**Weaknesses**
Piaget's Theory of Cognitive Development	Reasoning develops in four universal stages from birth through adolescence; in each stage, the child builds a different kind of scheme.	Helps explain how children of different ages think about and act on the world	Stage concept may cause adults to underestimate children's reasoning abilities; there may be additional stages in adulthood.
Information-Processing Theory	The computer is used as a model for human cognitive functioning; encoding, storage, and retrieval processes change with age, causing changes in memory function; these changes happen because of both brain maturation and practice.	Helps explain how much information people of different ages can manage at one time and how they process it; provides a useful framework for studying individual differences in people of the same age	Human information processing is much more complex than that of a computer; the theory doesn't provide an overall picture of development.

Piaget's Clever Research

Piaget not only proposed a novel and provocative theory; he also devised creative strategies for testing children's understanding. Probably the most famous of all Piaget's clever techniques is his method for studying conservation, the understanding that matter does not change in quantity when its appearance changes. As shown in Figure 2.1, Piaget began with two balls of clay of equal size; he showed them to a child and let the child hold and manipulate them until she agreed that they had the same amount of clay. Then in full view of the child, Piaget rolled one of the balls into a sausage shape. Then he asked the child whether there was still the same amount of clay in the sausage and the ball or whether one had more. Children of 4 and 5 consistently said that the ball contained more clay; children of 6 and 7 consistently said that the shapes still had the same amount. Thus, the older children understood that the quantity of clay was conserved even though its appearance changed.

In another study, Piaget explored children's understanding that objects can belong to multiple categories. (For example, Fido is both a dog and an animal; a high chair is both a chair and furniture.) Piaget usually studied this by first having children create their own classes and subclasses and then asking them questions about these. One 5-year-old child, for example, played with a set of flowers and had made two heaps, one large group of primroses and a smaller group of

other mixed flowers. Piaget then had this conversation with the child (Piaget & Inhelder, 1959, p. 108):

PIAGET: If I make a bouquet of all the primroses and you make one of all the flowers, which will be bigger?

CHILD: Yours.

PIAGET: If I gather all the primroses in a meadow, will any flowers remain?

CHILD: Yes.

The child understood that there are flowers other than primroses but did not yet understand that all primroses are flowers—that the smaller, subordinate class is included in the larger class. Piaget's term for this concept was class inclusion.

In these conversations with children, Piaget was always trying to understand how the child thought, rather than trying to see whether the child could come up with the right answer. So he used an investigative method in which he followed the child's lead, asking probing questions or creating special exploratory tests to try to discover the child's logic. In the early days of Piaget's work, many American researchers were critical of this method, since Piaget did not ask precisely the same questions of each child. Still, the results were so striking, and so surprising, that they couldn't be ignored. And when stricter research techniques were devised, more often than not the investigators confirmed Piaget's observations.

Current Trends

A number of theories have generated interest among developmentalists in recent years because of their potential for explaining biological and cultural influences on development.

BIOLOGICAL THEORIES

Theories that propose links between physiological processes and development represent one of the most important current trends in developmental psychology (Parke, 2004). Some biological theories explain universal changes, while others address individual differences.

nativism the view that human beings possess unique genetic traits that will be manifested in all members of the species, regardless of differences in environments

Nativism, Ethology, and Sociobiology
Nativism is the view that humans possess unique genetic traits that will be manifested in all members of the species, regardless of differences in their environments. Nativist theory is supported when developmentalists identify behaviors that appear early in life, develop in almost all individuals in every cul-

ture, and do not exist in other species. For example, all healthy children learn language early in life without any specific instruction from adults, and, to date, scientists have found no evidence of grammatical language in nonhuman species.

Ethology emphasizes genetically determined survival behaviors that are assumed to have evolved through natural selection. For example, nests are necessary for the survival of young birds. Therefore, ethologists say, evolution has equipped birds with nest-building genes.

Similarly, ethologists believe that emotional relationships are necessary to the survival of human infants (Bowlby, 1969, 1980). They claim that evolution has produced genes that cause humans to form these relationships. For example, most people feel irritated when they hear a newborn crying. Ethologists say the baby is genetically programmed to cry in a certain way, and adults are genetically programmed to get irritated when they hear it. The caretaker responds to a crying baby's needs in order to remove the irritating stimulus of the noise. As the caretaker and infant interact, an emotional bond is created between them. Thus, genes for crying in an irritating manner increase infants' chances of survival.

Sociobiology is the study of society using the methods and concepts of biological science. When applied to human development, sociobiology emphasizes genes that aid group survival. Sociobiologists claim individual humans have the best chance for survival when they live in groups. Therefore, they claim, evolution has provided humans with genetic programming that helps us cooperate.

(Photo: © Tom Brown/Getty Images/Stone)

Ethologists assert that the first 2 years of life are a critical period for the establishment of relationships between infants and caregivers.

To support their views, sociobiologists look for social rules and behaviors that exist in all cultures. For example, every society has laws against murder. Sociobiologists believe that humans are genetically programmed to create rules based on respect for other people's lives. Evolution has selected these genes, they claim, because people need to respect each other's lives and to be able to cooperate.

Critics of nativism, ethology, and sociobiology claim that these theories underestimate the impact of the environment. For example, while the nativists' observation that all children learn languages in the same way is true, environmental factors affect the rate at which they learn them. Moreover, these theories are difficult to test. How can researchers test ethological theorists' claim that infant-caregiver attachment is universal because it has survival value, for example? Finally, critics say that these theories ignore the fact that societies invent ways of enhancing whatever behaviors might be influenced by universal genetic programming. For instance, as sociobiologists hypothesize, genes may be involved in the universal prohibition of murder, but societies invent strategies for preventing it. Moreover, these strategies differ across societies and in their effectiveness.

Behavior Genetics **Behavior genetics** focuses on the effect of heredity on individual differences. Traits or behaviors are believed to be influenced by genes when those of related people, such as children and their parents, are more similar than those of unrelated people. Behavior geneticists have shown that heredity affects a broad range of traits and behaviors, including intelligence, shyness, and aggressiveness.

Furthermore, the contributions of heredity to individual differences are evident throughout the lifespan. For example, researchers in the Netherlands have been studying a number of variables in identical and fraternal twins for several decades. As you'll learn in Chapter 3, identical twins are particularly important in genetic research because they have exactly the same genes. Moreover, it's useful to compare them to twins who are nonidentical because these individuals share the same environment but do not have the same genes. As you can see in Figure 2.3 (page 40), the Dutch

ethology a perspective on development that emphasizes genetically determined survival behaviors presumed to have evolved through natural selection

sociobiology the study of society using the methods and concepts of biology; when used by developmentalists, an approach that emphasizes genes that aid group survival

behavior genetics the study of the role of heredity in individual differences

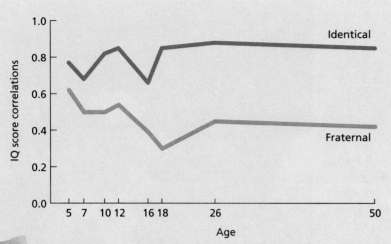

FIGURE 2.3

This figure illustrates the combined findings of several longitudinal and cross-sectional studies of Dutch twins (Posthuma, de Geus, & Boomsma, 2003). You will notice that in childhood, when fraternal twins share the same environment, their IQ scores are more strongly correlated than in adulthood, when they presumably no longer live together. By contrast, the IQ scores of identical twins are even more strongly correlated in adulthood than during the childhood years. This pattern suggests conclusions about both heredity and environment. Specifically, at least with regard to IQ scores, the influence of heredity appears to increase with age, while that of the environment declines.

researchers have found that IQ scores of identical twins are more strongly correlated than those of fraternal (nonidentical) twins from early childhood until middle age. Interestingly, too, such findings show that the environment affects IQ scores as well, but that its effects may be transient. This conclusion is suggested by the fact that the IQ scores of fraternal twins are more strongly correlated in childhood, when they are living together, than in adulthood, when they do not share the same environment.

VYGOTSKY'S SOCIOCULTURAL THEORY

Following the Bolshevik revolution of 1917, the new Soviet government hired Russian psychologist Lev Vygotsky, among others, to create a school system that would serve the ends of the new communist regime (Vygotsky, 1978). Although influenced by Freud, Pavlov, and Piaget, Vygotsky devised a theory of child development that was unique. His death in 1938 and the historical events that followed—World War II and the Cold War—resulted in his work's remaining largely unknown outside the Soviet Union for decades. Recently, however, developmentalists have become interested in his views on the influence of cultural forces on individual development (Thomas, 2000).

Vygotsky's **sociocultural theory** asserts that complex forms of thinking have their origins in social interactions rather than in the child's private explorations, as Piaget thought. According to Vygotsky, children's learning of new cognitive skills is guided by an adult (or a more skilled child, such as an older sibling), who structures the child's learning experience, a process Vygotsky called *scaffolding*. To create an appropriate scaffold, the adult must gain and keep the child's attention, model the best strategy, and adapt the whole process to the child's developmental level, or *zone of proximal development* (Landry, Garner, Swank, & Baldwin, 1996; Rogoff, 1990). Vygotsky used this term to signify tasks that are too hard for the child to do alone but that he can manage with guidance. For example, parents of a beginning reader provide a scaffold when they help him sound out new words.

Vygotsky's ideas have important educational applications. Like Piaget's, Vygotsky's theory suggests the importance of opportunities for active exploration. But assisted discovery would play a greater role in a Vygotskian than in a Piagetian classroom; the teacher would provide the scaffolding for children's discovery, through questions, demonstrations, and explanations (Tharp & Gallimore, 1988). To be effective, the assisted discovery processes would have to be within the zone of proximal development of each child.

CRITICAL THINKING ?

How is scaffolding involved when a parent helps a child with homework?

sociocultural theory Vygotsky's view that complex forms of thinking have their origins in social interactions rather than in an individual's private explorations

Developmental psychologist Lev Vygotsky hypothesized that social interactions among children are critical to both cognitive and social development.

BRONFENBRENNER'S ECOLOGICAL THEORY

Another approach gaining interest in developmental psychology is Urie Bronfenbrenner's **ecological theory,** which explains development in terms of relationships between people and their environments, or *contexts,* as Bronfenbrenner calls them (Bronfenbrenner, 1979, 1993). Bronfenbrenner attempts to classify all the individual and contextual variables that affect development and to specify how they interact.

According to Bronfenbrenner, the contexts of development are like circles within circles (see Figure 2.4). The outermost circle, the *macrosystem* (the cultural context), contains the values and beliefs of the culture in which a child is growing up. For example, a society's beliefs about the importance of education exist in the cultural context.

The next level, the *exosystem* (the socioeconomic context), includes the institutions of the culture that affect children's development indirectly. For example, funding for education exists in the socioeconomic context. The citizens of a specific nation may strongly believe that all children should be educated (cultural context), but their ability to provide universal education may be limited by the country's wealth (socioeconomic context).

The *microsystem* (the immediate context) includes those variables to which people are exposed directly, such as their families, schools, religious institutions, and neighborhoods. The *mesosystem* is made up of the interconnections between these components. For example, the specific school a child attends and her own family are part of the microsystem. Her parents' involvement in her school and the response of the school to their involvement are part of the mesosystem. Thus, the culture a child is born into may strongly value quality education. Moreover, her nation's economy may provide ample funds for schooling. However, her own education will be more strongly affected

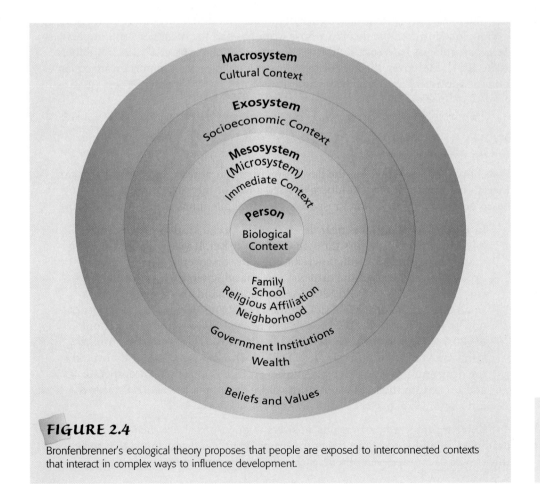

FIGURE 2.4

Bronfenbrenner's ecological theory proposes that people are exposed to interconnected contexts that interact in complex ways to influence development.

ecological theory Bronfenbrenner's theory that explains development in terms of relationships between individuals and their environments, or interconnected contexts

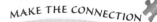

MAKE THE CONNECTION

Like the learning theories you read about earlier in the chapter, Bronfenbrenner's ecological theory emphasizes environmental factors. But what are some of the important differences between learning theories and Bronfenbrenner's perspective?

by the particular school she attends and the connections—or lack thereof—between her school and her family. Thus, the child's immediate context may be either consistent with the cultural and socioeconomic contexts or at odds with them.

Finally, the child's genetic makeup and developmental stage—her *biological context*—also influence her development. For example, a student who hasn't mastered the skill of reading isn't likely to benefit from an enriched literature program. Thus, her culture, the socioeconomic situation, the school she attends, and her own family may all be geared toward providing a quality education. However, her ability to benefit from it will be determined by the degree to which her education fits her individual needs.

Ecological theory provides a way of thinking about development that captures the complexity of individual and contextual variables. To date, its greatest contribution to developmental psychology has been its emphasis on the need for research examining interactions among these variables (Thomas, 2000). For example, ecological theory has helped developmentalists understand that studies of infant day care can't just compare infants in day care to infants in home care. Such studies must also consider family variables, such as parents' educational level, and day-care variables, such as the ratio of caretakers to infants. Since the 1980s, an increasing number of such studies have appeared.

 # Moral Development

Theorists representing various orientations think differently about moral development. However, the theorist whose work has had the most powerful impact has been psychologist Lawrence Kohlberg (Bergman, 2002; Colby et al., 1983; Kohlberg, 1976, 1981). Moreover, theories of moral reasoning have been important in explanations of adolescent antisocial behavior.

KOHLBERG'S THEORY OF MORAL REASONING

Piaget proposed two stages in the development of moral reasoning. Working from Piaget's basic assumptions, Kohlberg devised a way of measuring moral reasoning based on research participants' responses to moral dilemmas such as the following:

> In Europe, a woman was near death from a special kind of cancer. There was one drug that the doctors thought might save her. It was a form of radium that a druggist in the same town had recently discovered. The drug was expensive to make, but the druggist was charging ten times what the drug cost him to make. He paid $200 for the radium and charged $2000 for a small dose of the drug. The sick woman's husband, Heinz, went to everyone he knew to borrow the money, but he could only get together about $1000. . . . He told the druggist that his wife was dying, and asked him to sell it cheaper or let him pay later. But the druggist said, "No, I discovered the drug and I'm going to make money from it." So Heinz got desperate and broke into the man's store to steal the drug for his wife. (Kohlberg & Elfenbein, 1975, p. 621)

Kohlberg analyzed participants' answers to questions about such dilemmas (for example, "Should Heinz have stolen the drug? Why?") and concluded that there were three levels of moral development, each made up of two substages, as summarized in

CRITICAL THINKING 9

How would you respond to the Heinz dilemma? What does your response suggest about your level of moral reasoning?

TABLE 2.1A	Kohlberg's Stages of Moral Development	
Level	**Stages**	**Description**
Level I: Preconventional	Stage 1: Punishment and Obedience Orientation	The child or teenager decides what is wrong on the basis of what is punished. Obedience is valued for its own sake, but the child obeys because the adults have superior power.
	Stage 2: Individualism, Instrumental Purpose, and Exchange	Children and teens follow rules when it is in their immediate interest. What is good is what brings pleasant results.
Level II: Conventional	Stage 3: Mutual Interpersonal Expectations, Relationships, and Interpersonal Conformity	Moral actions are those that live up to the expectations of the family or other significant group. "Being good" becomes important for its own sake.
	Stage 4: Social System and Conscience (Law and Order)	Moral actions are those so defined by larger social groups or the society as a whole. One should fulfill duties one has agreed to and uphold laws, except in extreme cases.
Level III: Postconventional	Stage 5: Social Contract or Utility and Individual Rights	This stage involves acting so as to achieve the "greatest good for the greatest number." The teenager or adult is aware that most values are relative and laws are changeable, although rules should be upheld in order to preserve the social order. Still, there are some basic absolute values, such as the importance of each person's life and liberty.
	Stage 6: Universal Ethical Principles	The small number of adults who reason at stage 6 develop and follow self-chosen ethical principles in determining what is right. These ethical principles are part of an articulated, integrated, carefully thought-out, and consistently followed system of values and principles.

(Sources: Kohlberg, 1976; Lickona, 1978.)

Table 2.1a. It is important to understand that what determines the stage or level of a person's moral judgment is not any specific moral choice but the form of reasoning used to justify that choice. For example, either response to Kohlberg's dilemma—that Heinz should steal the drug or that he should not—could be justified with logic at any given stage.

Age and Moral Reasoning The stages are correlated somewhat loosely with age. Very few children reason beyond stage 1 or 2, and stage 2 and stage 3 reasoning are the types most commonly found among adolescents (Walker, de Vries, & Trevethan, 1987). Among adults, stages 3 and 4 are the most common (Gibson, 1990). Two research examples illustrate these overall age trends. The first, shown in Figure 2.1a, comes from Kohlberg's own longitudinal study of 58 boys, first interviewed when they were 10 and then followed for more than 20 years (Colby et al., 1983). Table 2.2a shows cross-sectional data from a study by Lawrence Walker and his colleagues (1987). They studied 10 boys and 10 girls at each of four ages, interviewing the parents of each child as well. The results of these two studies, although not identical, point to remarkably similar conclusions about the order of emergence of the various stages and about the approximate ages at which they predominate. In both studies, stage 2 reasoning dominates at around age 10, and stage 3 reasoning is most common at about age 16.

Preconventional Reasoning At level I, **preconventional morality,** the child's judgments are based on sources of authority who are close by and physically superior—usually the parents. Just as descriptions of others are largely external at this level, so the standards the child uses to judge rightness or wrongness are external rather than internal. In particular, it is the outcome or consequence of an action that determines the rightness or wrongness of the action.

preconventional morality in Kohlberg's theory, the level of moral reasoning in which judgments are based on authorities outside the self

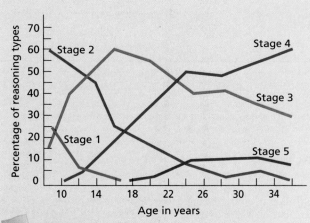

FIGURE 2.1A

These findings are from Colby and Kohlberg's long-term longitudinal study of a group of boys who were asked about Kohlberg's moral dilemmas every few years from age 10 through early adulthood. As they got older, the stage or level of their answers changed, with conventional reasoning appearing fairly widely at high school age. Postconventional, or principled, reasoning was not very common at any age. (Source: Colby et al., 1983, Figure 1, p. 46. © The Society for Research in Child Development.)

In stage 1 of this level—*punishment and obedience orientation*—the child relies on the physical consequences of some action to decide whether it is right or wrong. If he is punished, the behavior was wrong; if he is not punished, it was right. He is obedient to adults because they are bigger and stronger.

In stage 2—*individualism, instrumental purpose, and exchange*—the child or adolescent operates on the principle that you should do things that are rewarded and avoid things that are punished. For this reason, the stage is sometimes called *naive hedonism.* If it feels good or brings pleasant results, it is good. Some beginning of concern for other people is apparent during this stage, but only if that concern can be expressed as something that benefits the child or teenager himself as well. So he can enter into agreements such as "If you help me, I'll help you."

To illustrate, here are some responses to variations of the Heinz dilemma, drawn from studies of children and teenagers in a number of different cultures, all of whom were at stage 2:

He should steal the [drug] for his wife because if she dies he'll have to pay for the funeral, and that costs a lot. [Taiwan]

[He should steal the drug because] he should protect the life of his wife so he doesn't have to stay alone in life. [Puerto Rico] (Snarey, 1985, p. 221)

conventional morality in Kohlberg's theory, the level of moral reasoning in which judgments are based on rules or norms of a group to which the person belongs

Conventional Reasoning   At the next major level, the level of **conventional morality,** rules or norms of a group to which the individual belongs become the basis of moral judgments, whether that group is the family, the peer group, a church, or the nation. What the chosen reference group defines as right or good is right or good in the individual's view. Again, very few children exhibit conventional thinking, but many adolescents are capable of this kind of moral reasoning.

Stage 3 (the first stage of level II) is the stage of *mutual interpersonal expectations, relationships, and interpersonal conformity* (sometimes also called the *good boy/nice girl stage*). Regardless of age, individuals who reason at this stage believe that good behavior is what pleases other people. They value trust, loyalty, respect, gratitude, and maintenance of mutual relationships. Andy, a boy Kohlberg interviewed who was at stage 3, said:

I try to do things for my parents, they've always done things for you. I try to do everything my mother says, I try to please her. Like she wants me to be a doctor and I want to, too, and she's helping me get up there. (Kohlberg, 1964, p. 401)

TABLE 2.2A	Percentages of Children and Parents Who Show Moral Reasoning at Each of Kohlberg's Stages								
	Stage								
Age	1	1–2	2	2–3	3	3–4	4	4–5	5
6 (grade 1)	10%	70%	15%	5%	—	—	—	—	—
9 (grade 4)	—	25%	40%	35%	—	—	—	—	—
12 (grade 7)	—	—	15%	60%	25%	—	—	—	—
15 (grade 10)	—	—	—	40%	55%	5%	—	—	—
Parents	—	—	—	1%	15%	70%	11%	3%	—

(Source: Walker et al., from Table 1, p. 849, "Moral stages and moral orientations in real-life and hypothetical dilemmas," Child Development, 60 [1987], 842–858. By permission of the Society for Research in Child Development.)

Another mark of this third stage is that the individual makes judgments based on intentions as well as on outward behavior. If someone "didn't mean to do it," the wrongdoing is seen as less serious than if the person did it "on purpose."

Stage 4, the second stage of the conventional morality level, incorporates the norms of a larger reference group into moral judgments. Kohlberg labeled this the stage of social system and conscience. It is also sometimes called the *law-and-order orientation*. People reasoning at this stage focus on doing their duty, respecting authority, following rules and laws. The emphasis is less on what is pleasing to particular people (as in stage 3) and more on adhering to a complex set of regulations. However, the regulations themselves are not questioned, and morality and legality are assumed to be equivalent. Therefore, for a person at stage 4, something that is legal is right, whereas something that is illegal is wrong. Consequently, changes in law can effect changes in the moral views of individuals who reason at stage 4.

(Photo: © Bettmann/CORBIS)

Civil disobedience involves intentionally breaking laws one believes to be immoral. For example, in the early years of the U.S. civil rights movement, African Americans broke laws that excluded them from certain sections of restaurants by "sitting in" at whites-only lunch counters. Practitioners of civil disobedience do not try to evade the consequences of their actions, because they believe in upholding the law as a general principle even though they may view some specific laws as immoral. Thus, the thinking that underlies acts of civil disobedience represents Kohlberg's postconventional level of moral reasoning.

Postconventional Reasoning
The transition to level III, **postconventional morality,** is marked by several changes, the most important of which is a shift in the source of authority. Individuals who reason at level I see authority as totally outside of themselves; at level II, the judgments or rules of external authorities are internalized, but they are not questioned or analyzed; at level III, a new kind of personal authority emerges, in which an individual makes choices and judgments based on self-chosen principles or on principles that are assumed to transcend the needs and concerns of any individual or group. Postconventional thinkers represent only a minority of adults and an even smaller minority of adolescents.

In stage 5 at this level, which Kohlberg called the *social contract orientation,* such self-chosen principles begin to be evident. Rules, laws, and regulations are not seen as irrelevant; they are important ways of ensuring fairness. But people operating at this level also acknowledge that there are times when the rules, laws, and regulations need to be ignored or changed.

The American civil rights movement of the 1950s and 1960s is a good example of stage 5 reasoning in action. *Civil disobedience*—deliberately breaking laws that were believed to be immoral—arose as a way of protesting racial segregation. For example, in restaurants, African Americans intentionally took seats that were reserved for whites. It is important to note that the practice of civil disobedience does not usually involve avoiding the penalties that accompany criminal behavior. Indeed, some of the most effective and poignant images from that period of U.S. history are photographs of individuals who surrendered and were jailed for breaking segregation laws. This behavior illustrates the stage 5 view that, as a general principle, upholding the law is important, even though a specific law that is deemed to be immoral can—or even should—be broken when breaking it will serve to promote the common good.

In his original writing about moral development, Kohlberg also included a sixth stage, *the universal ethical principles orientation.* For example, in arguing against capital punishment, some people say that an individual's right to life is more important than society's right to exact justice from those who are convicted of heinous crimes. Such a claim might or might not be an example of stage 6 reasoning. The same could be said of the assertion that a fetus's right to life should supercede a woman's right to choose whether to bear a child. Remember, the key to assessing an individual's stage of moral development is to fully probe the reasoning behind his or her answer to a question about a moral dilemma. Sometimes this kind of probing reveals that arguments that, on first glance, appear to represent stage 6 thinking are actually based on the authority

postconventional morality in Kohlberg's theory, the level of moral reasoning in which judgments are based on an integration of individual rights and the needs of society

of a religious tradition or a highly respected individual, in which case the reasoning is conventional rather than postconventional. Occasionally, though, the individual making such an argument is able to explain it in terms of a universal ethical principle that must always be adhered to regardless of any other considerations. In the case of these two arguments, the universal ethical principle would be the idea that the maintenance of human life is the highest of all moral principles. Note, however, that a person reasoning at stage 6 would not argue that society has no right to punish criminals or that women have no right to decide whether to bear children. Instead, he or she would say that, in situations where upholding such rights involves termination of a human life, the right to life of the person whose life would be ended takes precedence. Moreover, a person reasoning at stage 6 might decide that the right to life is more important than other considerations with regard to the capital punishment question but less important with regard to the abortion question. He or she might also come to an entirely different conclusion when thinking about whether terminally ill people have the right to take their own lives. Thus, stage 6 reasoning involves balancing equally valid, but conflicting, moral principles against one another in order to determine which should be given precedence with respect to a specific moral issue.

Kohlberg argued that this sequence of reasoning is both universal and hierarchically organized. That is, each stage grows out of the preceding one. Kohlberg did not suggest that all individuals eventually progress through all six stages—or even that each stage is tied to specific ages. But he insisted that the order is invariant and universal. He also believed that the social environment determines how slowly or rapidly individuals move through the stages.

The evidence seems fairly strong that the stages follow one another in the sequence Kohlberg proposed. Long-term longitudinal studies of teenagers and young adults in the United States, Israel, and Turkey show that changes in participants' reasoning nearly always occur in the hypothesized order (Colby et al., 1983; Nisan & Kohlberg, 1982; Snarey et al., 1985; Walker, 1989). People do not skip stages, and movement down the sequence rather than up occurs only about 5–7% of the time.

Variations of Kohlberg's dilemmas have been used with children in a wide range of countries, including both Western and non-Western, industrialized and non-industrialized (Snarey, 1985). In every culture, researchers find higher stages of reasoning among older children, but cultures differ in the highest level of reasoning observed. In urban cultures (both Western and non-Western), stage 5 is typically the highest stage observed; in agricultural societies and those in which there is little opportunity for formal education, stage 4 is typically the highest. Collectively, this evidence seems to provide quite strong support for the universality of Kohlberg's stage sequence.

CAUSES AND CONSEQUENCES OF MORAL DEVELOPMENT

The most obvious reason for the general correlations between Kohlberg's stages and chronological age is cognitive development. Specifically, it appears that children must have a firm grasp of concrete operational thinking before they can develop or use conventional moral reasoning. Likewise, formal operational thinking appears to be necessary for advancement to the postconventional level.

To be more specific, Kohlberg and many other theorists suggest that the decline of egocentrism that occurs as an individual moves through Piaget's concrete and formal operational stages is the cognitive-developmental variable that matters most in moral reasoning. The idea is that the greater a child's or adolescent's ability to look at a situation from another person's perspective, the more advanced she is likely to be in moral reasoning. Psychologists use the term **role-taking** to refer to this ability (Selman, 1980). Research has provided strong support for the hypothesized link between role-taking and moral development (Kuhn, Kohlberg, Languer, & Haan, 1977; Walker, 1980).

Nevertheless, cognitive development isn't enough. Kohlberg thought that the development of moral reasoning also required support from the social environment.

role-taking the ability to look at a situation from another person's perspective

Specifically, he claimed that in order to foster mature moral reasoning, a child's or teenager's social environment must provide him with opportunities for meaningful, reciprocal dialogue about moral issues.

Longitudinal research relating parenting styles and family climate to levels of moral reasoning suggests that Kohlberg was right (Pratt, Arnold, & Pratt, 1999). Parents' ability to identify, understand, and respond to children's and adolescents' less mature forms of moral reasoning seems to be particularly important to the development of moral reasoning. This ability on the part of parents is important because people of all ages have difficulty understanding and remembering moral arguments that are more advanced than their own level (Narvaez, 1998). Thus, a parent who can express her own moral views in words that reflect her child's level of understanding is more likely to be able to influence the child's moral development.

As an individual's capacity for moral reasoning grows, so does her ability to think logically about issues in other domains. For example, the complexity of an individual's political reasoning is very similar to the complexity of her moral reasoning (Raaijmakers, Verbogt, & Vollebergh, 1998). Further, attitudes toward the acceptability of violence also vary with levels of moral reasoning. Individuals at lower levels are more tolerant of violence (Sotelo & Sangrador, 1999).

Perhaps most importantly, teenagers' level of moral reasoning appears to be positively correlated with prosocial behavior and negatively related to antisocial behavior (Schonert-Reichl, 1999). In other words, the highest levels of prosocial behavior are found among teens at the highest levels of moral reasoning (compared to their peers). Alternatively, the highest levels of antisocial behavior are found among adolescents at the lowest levels of moral reasoning.

CRITICISMS OF KOHLBERG'S THEORY

Criticisms of Kohlberg's theory have come from theorists representing different perspectives.

Culture and Moral Reasoning Cross-cultural research provides strong support for the universality of Kohlberg's stage sequence (Snarey, 1985, 1995). Nevertheless, cross-cultural researchers have argued that his approach is too narrow to be considered truly universal. These critics point out that there are many aspects of moral reasoning found in non-Western cultures that do not fit in well with Kohlberg's approach (Eckensberger & Zimba, 1997). The root of the problem, they say, is that Kohlberg's theory is strongly tied to the idea that justice is an overriding moral principle. To be sure, say critics, justice is an important moral concept throughout the world, and thus it isn't surprising that Kohlberg's stage sequence has been so strongly supported in cross-cultural research. However, these critics argue that the notion that justice supercedes all other moral considerations is what distinguishes Western from non-Western cultures. As these criticisms would predict, research has shown that the responses of individuals in non-Western cultures to Kohlberg's classic dilemmas often include ideas that are not found in his scoring system (Baek, 2002).

For example, in many cultures, respect for one's elders is an important moral principle that often overrides other concerns (Eckensberger & Zimba, 1997). Thus, if researchers alter the Heinz dilemma such that the sick woman is Heinz's mother rather than his wife, Western and non-Western research participants are likely to respond quite differently. Such differences are difficult to explain from the justice-based, stage-oriented perspective of Kohlberg's theory. Advocates for the theory have argued that respect for elders as the basis of moral reasoning represents Kohlberg's conventional level. Critics, by contrast, say that this classification underestimates the true moral reasoning level of individuals from non-Western cultures.

Moral Reasoning and Emotions   Researchers studying the link between moral emotions and moral reasoning have also criticized the narrowness of Kohlberg's justice-based approach. Psychologist Nancy Eisenberg, for example, suggests that *empathy,* the ability to identify with others' emotions, is both a cause and a consequence of moral development (Eisenberg, 2000). Similarly, Eisenberg suggests that a complete explanation of moral development should include age-related and individual variations in the ability to regulate emotions (such as anger) that can motivate antisocial behavior.

Likewise, Carol Gilligan claims that an ethic based on caring for others and on maintaining social relationships may be as important to moral reasoning as are ideas about justice. Gilligan's theory argues that there are at least two distinct "moral orientations": justice and care (Gilligan, 1982; Gilligan & Wiggins, 1987). Each has its own central injunction—not to treat others unfairly (justice) and not to turn away from someone in need (caring). Research suggests that adolescents do exhibit a moral orientation based on care and that care-based reasoning about hypothetical moral dilemmas is related to reasoning about real-life dilemmas (Skoe et al., 1999). In response, Kohlberg acknowledged in his later writings that his theory deals specifically with development of reasoning about justice and does not claim to be a comprehensive account of moral development (Kohlberg, Levine, & Hewer, 1983).

Possible sex differences in moral reasoning are another focus of Gilligan's theory. According to Gilligan, boys and girls learn both justice and care orientations, but girls are more likely to operate from the care orientation whereas boys are more likely to operate from a justice orientation. Because of these differences, girls and boys tend to perceive moral dilemmas quite differently.

Given the emerging evidence on sex differences in styles of interaction and in friendship patterns, Gilligan's hypothesis makes some sense. Perhaps girls, focused more on intimacy in their relationships, judge moral dilemmas by different criteria. But, in fact, research on moral dilemmas has not consistently shown that boys are more likely to use justice reasoning or that girls more often use care reasoning. Several studies of adults do show such a pattern (e.g., Lyons, 1983; Wark & Krebs, 1996). However, studies of children and teenagers generally have not (Jadack, Hyde, Moore, & Keller, 1995; Smetana, Killen, & Turiel, 1991; Walker et al., 1987). Further, recent evidence suggests that such sex differences, if they exist, may be restricted to North American culture (Skoe et al., 1999).

Moral Reasoning and Behavior   Finally, critics have questioned the degree to which moral reasoning predicts moral behavior. Researchers have found that moral reasoning and moral behavior are correlated, but the relationship is far from perfect. To explain inconsistencies between reasoning and behavior, learning theorists suggest that moral reasoning is situational rather than developmental. They point to a variety of studies to support this assertion.

First, neither adolescents nor adults reason at the same level in response to every hypothetical dilemma (Rique & Camino, 1997). An individual research participant might reason at the conventional level in response to one dilemma and at the postconventional level with respect to another. Second, the types of characters in moral dilemmas strongly influence research participants' responses to them, especially when the participants are adolescents. For example, hypothetical dilemmas involving celebrities as characters elicit much lower levels of moral reasoning from teenagers than those involving fictional characters such as Heinz (Einerson, 1998).

In addition, research participants show disparities in levels of moral reasoning invoked in response to hypothetical dilemmas and real-life moral issues. For example, Israeli Jewish, Israeli Bedouin, and Palestinian youths living in Israel demonstrate different levels of moral reasoning when responding to hypothetical stories such as the Heinz dilemma than they exhibit in discussing the moral dimensions of the long-standing conflicts among their ethnic groups (Elbedour, Baker, & Charlesworth, 1997). Thus, as learning theorists predict, it appears that situational factors may be more important variables for decisions about actual moral behavior than the level of moral reasoning exhibited in response to hypothetical dilemmas.

MORAL DEVELOPMENT AND ANTISOCIAL BEHAVIOR

The consistent finding of low levels of moral reasoning among adolescents who engage in serious forms of antisocial behavior has been of particular interest to developmentalists (Aleixo & Norris, 2000; Cheung, Chan, Lee, Liu, & Leung, 2001; Gregg, Gibbs, & Basinger, 1994; Ma, 2003; Smetana, 1990). Delinquency is distinguished from other forms of antisocial behavior, such as bullying, on the basis of actual law-breaking. Thus, the term **delinquency** applies specifically to adolescent behavior that violates the law. Serious forms of delinquency, such as rape and murder, have increased dramatically in the United States in recent years. Attempts to explain this phenomenon have resulted in research that has led to a more comprehensive understanding of youth violence.

Incidents such as the Columbine High School shooting in April 1999 capture a great deal of public attention and often lead to increased security measures in schools. However, statistically speaking, schools are actually quite safe. Only 1% of all violent deaths among youths in the United States occur in schools (NCIPC, 2000).

Delinquents appear to be behind their peers in moral reasoning because of deficits in role-taking skills. For example, researchers have found that teenagers who can look at actions they are contemplating from their parents' perspective are less likely to engage in delinquent behavior than adolescents who cannot do so (Wyatt & Carlo, 2002). Most delinquent teens also seem to be unable to look at their crimes from their victims' perspectives or to assess hypothetical crimes from the victims' perspectives. Thus, programs aimed at helping delinquents develop more mature levels of moral reasoning usually focus on heightening their awareness of the victim's point of view. However, few such programs have been successful (Armstrong, 2003; Moody, 1997; Putnins, 1997). Consequently, psychologists believe that there is far more to delinquency than just a lack of role-taking and moral reasoning skills.

First, it appears that there are at least two important subvarieties of delinquents, distinguished by the age at which the delinquent behavior begins. Childhood-onset problems are more serious and are more likely to persist into adulthood. Adolescent-onset problems are typically milder and more transitory, apparently more a reflection of peer-group processes or a testing of the limits of authority than a deeply ingrained behavior problem.

The developmental pathway for early-onset delinquency seems to be directed by factors inside the child, such as temperament and personality. In early life, these children throw tantrums and defy parents; they may also develop insecure attachments (Greenberg, Speltz, & DeKlyen, 1993). Once the defiance appears, if the parents are not up to the task of controlling the child, the child's behavior worsens. He may begin to display overt aggression toward others, who then reject him, which aggravates the problem. The seriously aggressive child is pushed in the direction of other children with similar problems, who then become the child's only supportive peer group (Shaw, Kennan, & Vondra, 1994).

By adolescence, these youngsters may exhibit serious disturbances in thinking (Aleixo & Norris, 2000). Most have friends drawn almost exclusively from among other delinquent teens (Tremblay, Masse, Vitaro, & Dobkin, 1995). Of course, this situation is reinforced by frequent rejection by nondelinquent peers (Brendgen, Vitaro, & Bukowski, 1998). Many of these adolescents have parents with histories of antisocial behavior as well (Gainey, Catalano, Haggerty, & Hoppe, 1997). Early-onset delinquents are also highly likely to display a whole cluster of other problem behaviors, including drug and alcohol use, truancy or dropping out of school, and early and risky sexual behavior, including having multiple sexual partners (Dishion, French, & Patterson, 1995) (see No Easy Answers).

delinquency antisocial behavior that includes law-breaking

Preventing Youth Violence

For most delinquent teens, law-breaking is limited to acts of malicious mischief, such as spray-painting obscenities on a wall. Some adolescents, however, engage in antisocial behavior that is far more serious and difficult to understand. Surveys showing that 20% of all violent crimes in the United States are committed by individuals under age 18 have increased public awareness of the growing problem of youth violence (National Center for Injury Prevention and Control [NCIPC], 2000).

One important key to preventing youth violence is to understand what distinguishes violent from nonviolent teenagers. Researchers have learned that many teens who progress from nonviolent to violent forms of delinquency have themselves been victims of such crimes (Van Dorn & Williams, 2003). As a result, they believe that establishing a reputation for engaging in violent behavior will protect them from further victimization. Others come from homes in which violence is often used to resolve conflicts. Moreover, most violent teenagers have poor social reasoning skills (Gleason, Jensen-Campbell, & Richardson, 2004).

Few programs designed to change aggressive and violent behavior in adolescents have been successful (Armstrong, 2003). However, as you've read, research suggests that many children who are violent in adolescence began to exhibit this pattern of behavior in the early elementary grades (Moffitt, 1993). Thus, it might seem possible to identify potentially violent children at an early age and place them in programs that would reshape their thinking and behavior so as to prevent them from becoming violent. Recent efforts along these lines suggest that this kind of strategy can be successful. However, as you might imagine, it isn't as easy as it might seem.

A number of psychologists have contributed to the development and evaluation of a program called the Fast Track Project, which involves several hundred aggressive elementary school children in four different U.S. cities (Coie, 1997; Dodge, 1997; McMahon, 1997). The children are divided into experimental and control groups. In special class sessions, children in the experimental group learn how to recognize others' emotions. They also learn strategies for controlling their own feelings, managing aggressive impulses, and resolving conflicts with peers.

The teachers of children in the experimental group are trained to use a series of signals to help children maintain control. For example, a red card or a picture of a red traffic light might be used to indicate unacceptable behavior. A yellow card would mean something like "Calm down. You're about to lose control." Parenting classes and support groups help parents learn effective ways of teaching children acceptable behavior, rather than just punishing unacceptable behavior. In addition, parents are encouraged to maintain communication with their children's teachers.

After several years of implementation, the program appears to have produced the following effects among children in the experimental group:

- Better recognition of emotions
- More competence in social relationships
- Lower ratings of aggressiveness by peers
- Lowered risk of being placed in special education classes

In addition, parents of control group children have learned how to use less physical punishment and how to have better control of their children's behavior.

Other programs of similar intensity have also been shown to be effective in preventing youth violence. Most such programs go beyond intervening with the teenagers and their families, with the aim of building a community that is committed to the prevention of youth violence (Sabol, Coulton, & Korbin, 2004). For instance, many school-based programs involve both violent and nonviolent students, as well as teachers and school officials (Sege, 2004). In one community intervention program, researchers worked with multifamily groups to build support networks (Smith et al., 2004).

Clearly, such interventions require a considerable commitment of time and resources. Furthermore, they aren't effective for every child. However, they represent the best options developmentalists have to offer at this point. When balanced against the suffering of the half million or so victims of youth violence each year in the United States or against the personal consequences of violent behavior for the young perpetrators of these crimes, the costs don't seem quite so extreme.

For young people whose delinquency appears first in adolescence, the pathway is different. They, too, have friends who are delinquents. However, associating with delinquent peers worsens their behavior, while the behavior of early-onset delinquents remains essentially the same, whether they have antisocial friends or are "loners" (Vitaro, Tremblay, Kerr, Pagani, & Bukowski, 1997). Moreover, the antisocial behavior patterns of adolescent-onset delinquents often change as their relationships change (Laird, Pettit, Dodge, & Bates, 1999). Consequently, peer influence seems to be the most important factor in the development of adolescent-onset delinquency.

Parenting style and other relationship variables seem to be additional factors in this type of antisocial behavior. Most of these teens have parents who do not monitor them sufficiently; their individual friendships are not very supportive or intimate; and they are drawn to a clique or crowd that includes some teens who are experimenting with drugs or mild law-breaking. After a period of months of hanging out with such a group of peers, previously nondelinquent adolescents show some increase in risky or antisocial behaviors, such as increased drug-taking (Berndt & Keefe, 1995a; Dishion et al., 1995; Steinberg, Fletcher, & Darling, 1994). However, when parents do provide good monitoring and emotional support, their adolescent child is unlikely to get involved in delinquent acts or drug use even if she hangs around with a tough crowd or has a close friend who engages in such behavior (Brown & Huang, 1995; Mounts & Steinberg, 1995).

Before going on . . .

■ What are the features of moral reasoning at each of Kohlberg's stages?

■ What are some important causes and effects in the development of moral reasoning?

■ How has Kohlberg's theory been criticized?

■ Describe the moral reasoning abilities and other characteristics of delinquents.

ECLECTICISM

Perhaps the most important current trend in the field is **eclecticism,** the use of multiple theoretical perspectives to explain and study human development (Parke, 2004). The interdisciplinary nature of the study of human development you read about in Chapter 1 is reflected in this new trend as well. Thus, today's developmental scientists try to avoid the kind of rigid adherence to a single theoretical perspective that was characteristic of theorists such as Freud, Piaget, and Skinner.

To better understand the eclectic approach, think about how ideas drawn from several sources might help us better understand a child's disruptive behavior in school. Observations of the child's behavior and her classmates' reactions may suggest that her behavior is being rewarded by the other children's responses (a behavioral explanation). Deeper probing of the child's family situation may indicate that her acting-out behavior may be an emotional reaction to a family event such as divorce (a psychoanalytic explanation).

The interdisciplinary nature of today's developmental science also contributes to eclecticism. For instance, an anthropologist might suggest that the rapid-fire communication media found in almost every home nowadays (e.g., television) require children to develop attention strategies that differ from those that are appropriate for classroom environments. As a result, children today exhibit more disruptive behavior in school than children in past generations because of the mismatch between the kinds of information delivery to which they are accustomed and those which are found in school.

By adopting an eclectic approach, developmentalists can devise more comprehensive theories from which to derive questions and hypotheses for further research. In other words, their theories and studies may more closely match the behavior of real people in real situations.

eclecticism the use of multiple theoretical perspectives to explain and study human development

Before going on . . .

■ What kinds of behaviors interest proponents of nativism, ethology, sociobiology, and behavior genetics?

■ How did Vygotsky use the concepts of scaffolding and the zone of proximal development to explain cognitive development?

■ What is the main idea of Bronfenbrenner's ecological theory?

■ What is eclecticism?

Comparing Theories

After learning about theories, students usually want to know which one is right. However, developmentalists don't think of theories in terms of right or wrong but, instead, compare theories on the basis of their assumptions and how useful they are in promoting understanding of development.

ASSUMPTIONS ABOUT DEVELOPMENT

When we say that a theory assumes something about development, we mean that it holds some general perspective to be true. We can think of a theory's assumptions in terms of its answers to three questions about development.

One question addresses the *active or passive* issue: *Is a person active in shaping his own development, or is he a passive recipient of environmental influences?* Theories that claim a person's actions on the environment are the most important determinants of development are on the active side. Cognitive theories, for example, typically view development this way. In contrast, theories on the passive side, such as those of Pavlov and Skinner, maintain that development results from the environment acting on the individual.

As you learned in Chapter 1, the *nature versus nurture* question—*How do nature and nurture interact to produce development?*—is one of the most important in developmental psychology. All developmental theories, while admitting that both nature and nurture are involved in development, make assumptions about their relative importance. Theories claiming that biology contributes more to development than does environment are on the nature side of the question. Those that view environmental influences as most important are on the nurture side. Other theories assume that nature and nurture are equally important, and that it is impossible to say which contributes more to development.

You may also recall from Chapter 1 that the *continuity versus discontinuity* issue is a source of debate among developmentalists. Here, the question is *Does development happen continuously or in stages?* Theories that do not refer to stages assert that development is a stable, continuous process. Stage theories, on the other hand, emphasize change more than stability. They claim that development happens in leaps from lower to higher steps.

For the three major families of theories you have read about in this chapter, Table 2.8 lists the assumptions each individual theory makes regarding these issues. Because each theory is based on different assumptions, each implies a different approach to studying

CRITICAL THINKING ?

How do the biological theories, Vygotsky's socio-cultural theory, and Bronfenbrenner's ecological theory answer the three questions about development?

TABLE 2.8	How Theories Answer Three Questions about Development		
Theories	**Active or Passive?**	**Nature or Nurture?**	**Stability or Change?**
Psychoanalytic Theories			
Psychosexual Theory	Passive	Nature	Change (stages)
Psychosocial Theory	Passive	Both	Change
Learning Theories			
Classical Conditioning	Passive	Nurture	Stability (no stages)
Operant Conditioning	Passive	Nurture	Stability
Social-Learning Theory	Active	Nurture	Stability
Cognitive Theories			
Cognitive-Developmental Theory	Active	Both	Change
Information-Processing Theory	Active	Both	Both

development. Consequently, research derived from each theory tells us something different about development. Moreover, a theory's assumptions shape the way it is applied in the real world.

For example, a teacher who approached instruction from the cognitive perspective would create a classroom in which children could experiment to some degree on their own. He would also recognize that children differ in ability, interests, developmental level, and other internal characteristics. He would believe that structuring the educational environment is important, but would assume that what each student ultimately learns will be determined by his own actions on the environment.

Alternatively, a teacher who adopted the learning perspective would guide and reinforce children's learning very carefully. Such a teacher would place little importance on ability differences among children. Instead, she would try to accomplish the same instructional goals for all children through proper manipulation of the environment.

USEFULNESS

Developmentalists also compare theories with respect to their usefulness. You should be aware that there is a fair amount of disagreement among psychologists on exactly how useful each theory is. Nevertheless, there are a few general criteria most psychologists use to evaluate the usefulness of a theory.

One way to evaluate usefulness is to assess a theory's ability to generate predictions that can be tested using scientific methods. For example, as you learned earlier in this chapter, one criticism of Freud's theory is that many of his claims are difficult to test. In contrast, when Piaget claimed that most children can solve concrete operational problems by age 7, he made an assertion that is easily tested. Thus, Piaget's theory is viewed by many developmentalists as more useful in this sense than Freud's. Vygotsky, learning theorists, and information-processing theorists also proposed many testable ideas. By contrast, according to some developmental psychologists, current biological and ecological theories are weak because they are difficult to test (Thomas, 2000).

Another criterion by which to judge the usefulness of a theory is its *heuristic* value, the degree to which it stimulates thinking and research. In terms of heuristic value, Freud's and Piaget's theories earn equally high marks. Both are responsible for an enormous amount of theorizing and research on human development, often by psychologists who strongly disagree with them. In fact, all of the theories in this chapter are important heuristically.

Yet another way of evaluating a theory's usefulness, though, is in terms of practical value. In other words, a theory may be deemed useful if it provides solutions to problems. Based on this criterion, the learning and information-processing theories seem to stand out because they provide tools that can be used to influence behavior. A person who suffers from anxiety attacks, for example, can learn to use biofeedback, a technique derived from conditioning theories, to manage anxiety. Similarly, a student who needs to learn to study more effectively can get help from study skills courses based on information-processing research.

Ultimately, of course, no matter how many testable hypotheses or practical techniques a theory produces, it has little or no usefulness to developmentalists if it doesn't explain the basic facts of development. Based on this criterion, learning theories, especially classical and operant conditioning, are regarded by many developmentalists as somewhat less useful than other perspectives (Thomas, 2000). Although they explain how specific behaviors may be learned, they cannot account for the complexity of human development, which can't be reduced to connections between stimuli and responses or between behaviors and reinforcers.

As you can see, the point of comparing theories is not to conclude which one is true. Instead, such comparisons help to reveal the unique contribution each can make to a comprehensive understanding of human development.

Before going on . . .

- What assumptions do the three families of theories make about development?

- On what criteria do developmentalists compare the usefulness of theories?

Summary

Psychoanalytic Theories

- Freud emphasized that behavior is governed by both conscious and unconscious motives and that the personality develops in steps: The id is present at birth; the ego and the superego develop in childhood. Freud also proposed psychosexual stages: the oral, anal, phallic, latency, and genital stages.
- Erikson emphasized social forces more than unconscious drives as motives for development. He proposed that personality develops in eight psychosocial stages over the course of the lifespan: trust versus mistrust; autonomy versus shame and doubt; initiative versus guilt; industry versus inferiority; identity versus role confusion; intimacy versus isolation; generativity versus stagnation; and integrity versus despair.
- Psychoanalytic concepts, such as the unconscious and identity, have contributed to psychologists' understanding of development. However, these theories propose many ideas that are difficult to test.

Learning Theories

- Classical conditioning—learning through association of stimuli—helps explain the acquisition of emotional responses.
- Operant conditioning involves learning to repeat or stop behaviors because of their consequences. However, consequences often affect behavior in complex ways in the real world.
- Bandura's social-learning theory places more emphasis on mental elements than other learning theories do and assumes a more active role for the individual.
- Learning theories provide useful explanations of how behaviors are acquired but fall short of a truly comprehensive picture of human development.

Cognitive Theories

- Piaget focused on the development of logical thinking. He discovered that such thinking develops across four childhood and adolescent stages: the sensorimotor, preoperational, concrete operational, and formal operational stages. He proposed that movement from one stage to another is the result of changes in mental frameworks called *schemes*.
- Information-processing theory uses the computer as a model to explain intellectual processes such as memory and problem-solving. It suggests that there are both age differences and individual differences in the efficiency with which humans use their information-processing systems.
- Research has confirmed the sequence of skill development Piaget proposed but suggests that young children are more capable of logical thinking than he believed. Information-processing theory has been important in explaining Piaget's findings and memory processes.

Current Trends

- Biological theories such as nativism, ethology, sociobiology, and behavior genetics have gained popularity as developmentalists have sought to better understand the role of physiological processes in development.
- Vygotsky's socio-cultural theory has become important to developmentalists' attempts to explain how culture affects development.
- Bronfenbrenner's ecological theory has helped developmental psychologists categorize environmental factors and think about the ways in which they influence individuals.
- Developmentalists who take an eclectic approach use theories derived from all the major families, as well as those of many disciplines, to explain and study human development.

Comparing Theories

- Theories vary in how they answer three basic questions about development: Are individuals active or passive in their own development? How do nature and nurture interact to produce development? Does development happen continuously or in stages?
- Useful theories allow psychologists to devise hypotheses to test their validity, are heuristically valuable, provide practical solutions to problems, and explain the facts of development.

Moral Development

- Kohlberg proposed six stages of moral reasoning, organized into three levels. Preconventional moral reasoning includes reliance on external authority: What is punished is bad, and what feels good is good. Conventional morality is based on rules and norms provided by outside groups, such as the family, church, or society. Postconventional morality is based on self-chosen principles. Research evidence suggests that these levels and stages are loosely correlated with age, develop in a specified order, and appear in this same sequence in all cultures studied so far.
- The acquisition of cognitive role-taking skills is important to moral development, but the social environment is important as well. Specifically, to foster moral reasoning, adults must provide children with opportunities for discussion of moral issues. Moral reasoning and moral behavior are correlated, though the relationship is far from perfect.
- Kohlberg's theory has been criticized by theorists who place more emphasis on learning moral behavior and others who believe that moral reasoning may be based more on emotional factors than on ideas about justice and fairness.
- Delinquent teens are usually found to be far behind their peers in both role-taking and moral reasoning. However, other factors, such as parenting style, may be equally important in delinquency.

Key Terms

accommodation (p. 34)

assimilation (p. 34)

behavior genetics (p. 39)

behaviorism (p. 29)

classical conditioning (p. 29)

cognitive theories (p. 33)

conventional morality (p. 44)

defense mechanisms (p. 24)

delinquency (p. 49)

eclecticism (p. 42)

ecological theory (p. 41)

ego (p. 24)

equilibration (p. 34)

ethology (p. 39)

extinction (p. 30)

id (p. 24)

information-processing theory
(p. 35)

learning theories (p. 29)

libido (p. 24)

nativism (p. 38)

neo-Piagetian theory (p. 36)

observational learning,
or modeling (p. 31)

operant conditioning (p. 30)

postconventional morality (p. 45)

preconventional morality (p. 43)

psychoanalytic theories (p. 24)

psychosexual stages (p. 24)

psychosocial stages (p. 26)

punishment (p. 30)

reinforcement (p. 30)

role-taking (p. 46)

scheme (p. 34)

shaping (p. 31)

sociobiology (p. 39)

socio-cultural theory (p. 40)

superego (p. 24)

Physical and Cognitive Development in Early Adulthood

You probably know someone like one of the people in the following list. What do all of them have in common?

© Davis Barber/PhotoEdit

Cassie, a 22-year-old single mother of a 4-year-old, lives with her parents, works full-time, and attends college classes at night.

Joe, a 25-year-old married machinist, is attending a trade school after 4 years of military service.

Marta, a 27-year-old divorced mother of a preschooler, works as a flight attendant.

Devon, a 20-year-old sophomore at a large university, is trying to choose between psychology and music as her major.

Renée, a married 30-year-old mother of two school-aged children, has just started college.

Marshall, a 33-year-old single man, has been a public school teacher for 10 years.

Each member of this diverse group is a young adult. If you think about the people you know who are between the ages of 20 and 40, they probably make up just as varied a group.

Clearly, young adulthood is the period of life when individuals' developmental pathways begin to diverge significantly. For example, in contrast to those of younger individuals, the educational experiences of young adults are highly diverse. Some go on to college as soon as they graduate from high school. Others work and attend college part-time. Still others work for a while or serve in the military and then further their educations.

Despite these variations, most social science researchers believe that it is still useful to divide the adult years into three roughly equal parts: early adulthood, from 20 to 40; middle adulthood, from 40 to about 65; and late adulthood, from 65 until death. This way of dividing adulthood reflects the fact that optimum physical and cognitive functioning, achieved in the 20s and 30s, begins to wane in some noticeable and measurable ways in the 40s and 50s. Moreover, several important role changes often occur in the early 40s: Children begin to leave home, careers near their peak, and so on.

We will follow the common usage and define "young," or "early," adulthood as the period from age 20 to age 40. In this chapter, you will read about the changes that occur in early adulthood, along with a number of variables that are associated with variation from the "typical" pathway. As you read this chapter, keep the following questions in mind:

- How does physical functioning change in the years from 20 to 40?

- What are the major health issues during early adulthood?

- How do thinking and problem-solving improve in early adulthood?

- How does post-secondary education help shape young adults' development?

CRITICAL THINKING

Before you read the rest of the chapter, think about how you might answer the following questions for yourself: In what ways have your body and mind changed since you were younger? How do you expect them to change as you get older? How has attending college affected your life, and what difference will it make in your future?

Physical Functioning

When developmentalists study children's development, they are looking at increases or improvements. When developmentalists study adults, especially adults' physical functioning, they begin to ask questions about loss of function, or decline.

PRIMARY AND SECONDARY AGING

Researchers distinguish between two types of aging. The basic, underlying, inevitable aging process is called **primary aging** by most developmentalists. To learn about its effects, they study adults who are disease-free and who have good health practices (Birren & Schroots, 1996).

Secondary aging, in contrast, is the product of environmental influences, health habits, or disease, and it is neither inevitable nor experienced by all adults. Research on age differences in health and death rates reveals the expected pattern. For example, 18- to 24-year-olds rarely die from disease (National Center for Health Statistics [NCHS], 1997). However, researchers have found that age interacts with other variables to influence health, a pattern suggesting the influence of secondary aging.

For example, age interacts with social class in a way that is revealed especially clearly in a set of survey data based on questions posed to more than 3,000 adults and analyzed by James House and his colleagues (House, Kessler, & Herzog, 1990; House et al., 1992). Figure 3.1 illustrates the study's results. As you can see, differences among young adults across social class groups are fairly small. However, with increasing age, the differences become much larger.

Similar social class differences in adult health have been found in other industrialized countries, such as Sweden, Ireland, and England, and they occur within ethnic groups in the United States as well as in the overall population (Eames, Ben-Schlomo, & Marmot, 1993; Kelleher, Friel, Gabhainn, & Tay, 2003; Thorslund & Lundberg, 1994). That is, among African Americans, Hispanic Americans, and Asian Americans, better-educated adults or those with higher incomes have longer life expectancies and better health than do those with less education or lower incomes (Guralnik, Land, Blazer, Fillenbaum, & Branch, 1993).

Social class differences in health may be due to group variations in patterns of primary aging. However, most developmentalists believe they represent secondary aging. In other words, the health differences result from income-related variations in both social environments and individual behavior. Consider the findings that people who live in low-income neighborhoods have higher rates of cardiovascular disease than those who live in more affluent areas and that social class differences in rates of such diseases are the most likely cause of income-related differences in mortality rates (Roux et al., 2001; Wong, Shapiro, Boscardin, & Ettner, 2002). One reason for these findings may be that doctors who practice in low-income neighborhoods tend to have less training than those who serve higher-income areas (Bach, Pham, Schrag, Tate, & Hargraves, 2004). These doctors are also less likely than their peers in higher-income neighborhoods to have access to hospitals equipped with advanced diagnostic and treatment facilities. Such findings suggest that even if residents in low-income areas have adequate health insurance, the care they receive— if they obtain that care in neighborhood clinics and physicians' offices—may be inferior to that available to people who live in other areas.

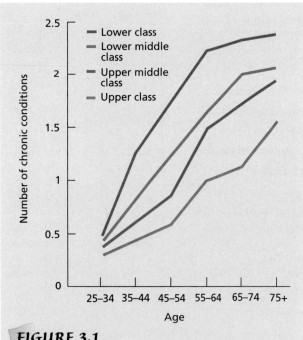

FIGURE 3.1

As people get older, they are more likely to experience some kind of chronic illness, but this change is earlier and more pronounced among poor and working-class adults. (Source: House et al., 1990, Figure 1, p. 396.)

primary aging age-related physical changes that have a biological basis and are universally shared and inevitable

secondary aging age-related changes that are due to environmental influences, poor health habits, or disease

Nevertheless, quality of health care is only part of the explanation for social class differences in secondary aging. Perhaps equally important is the finding that many of the same factors that contribute to economic differences are also related to health habits. Longitudinal studies show that, among individuals who drop out of high school, physical activity rates decline significantly during the late teens and remain low in adulthood (Kimm et al., 2002). Physical activity is a predictor of cardiovascular health, and educational level is associated with income. Moreover, the emotions underlying individuals' perceptions of their social class may be more important than their actual economic status. Some researchers have found that people who are unhappy with their economic situation are more likely to be sick than those who are relatively satisfied, regardless of income level (Operario, Adler, & Williams, 2004). Thus, as you can see, the link between social class and secondary aging is fairly complex.

Research also suggests that, regardless of income level, changes in behavior may prevent or even reverse the effects of aging. Such findings further strengthen the hypothesis that some changes that were formerly thought to be caused by primary aging may turn out to be the result of secondary aging (see No Easy Answers, page 60).

THE BRAIN AND NERVOUS SYSTEM

No matter what age an individual is, new synapses are forming, myelinization is occurring, and old connections are dying off. Further, there is recent evidence that, contrary to what neurologists have believed for a long time, some parts of the brain produce new neurons to replace those that die, even in the brains of older adults (Gould, Reeves, Graziano, & Gross, 1999). Interestingly, too, animal research suggests that production of these new neurons is stimulated by an enriched environment, as well as by physical exercise (Cao et al., 2004; Rhodes et al., 2003). Thus, just as is true in childhood and adolescence, a challenging environment probably supports brain development. At some point in development, though, usually in the late teens, developmental processes reach a balance and the brain attains a stable size and weight. Similarly, by early adulthood, most functions have become localized in specific areas of the brain (Gaillard et al., 2000).

Growth Spurts Neurologists have found that the pattern of peaks and valleys in the development of brain functions continues into adulthood. In fact, there may be two spurts in brain growth in early adulthood, like those you have read about in earlier chapters. A major spurt in the growth of the frontal lobes—the area of the brain devoted to logic, planning, and emotional control—begins around age 17. This spurt continues until age 21 or 22 (Spreen et al., 1995). Many neuropsychologists believe that this spurt is strongly connected to the increases in the capacity for formal operational thinking and other kinds of abstract reasoning that occur in late adolescence.

In addition to this brain growth spurt between 17 and 21, some neuropsychologists hypothesize that another peak in brain development happens in the mid- to late 20s (Fischer & Rose, 1994). They claim that the cognitive skills that emerge in the middle of the early adulthood period seem to depend on changes in the brain. For example, when you take a multiple-choice test, you need to be able to keep yourself from responding too quickly to the options in order to carefully weigh them all. Neuropsychologists suggest that this kind of *response inhibition* may depend on the ability of the frontal lobes of the brain to regulate the **limbic system,** or the emotional part of the brain. Many scientists believe that the capacity to integrate various brain functions in this way does not become fully developed until early adulthood (Spreen et al., 1995).

Still, the gradual loss of speed in virtually every aspect of bodily function appears to be the result of very gradual changes at the neuronal level, particularly the loss of dendrites and a slowing of the "firing rate" of nerves (Birren & Fisher, 1995; Earles & Salthouse, 1995; Salthouse, 1993). As you get older, it takes longer to warm up after you have been very cold or to cool off after you have been hot. Your reaction time to sudden events slows; you don't respond quite as quickly to a swerving car, for example.

limbic system the part of the brain that regulates emotional responses

There Is No Fountain of Youth

Spend a few hours watching television or leafing through magazines, and the advertisements will tell you something very significant about the adult population: Many of us appear to be looking for a quick and easy way to escape the ravages of age. A pill promises to cure a man's baldness. A cream is said to dissolve fat on women's thighs. As appealing as the idea of a fountain of youth is, the truth is that the best way to moderate the effects of primary aging on the body is to follow the hard road of behavioral change. The most significant barriers to remaining youthful are the result of secondary aging and are often preventable. Further, if you develop good habits while you are young, not only will it be easier to maintain those habits, but you will reap benefits over many years.

These are the most important changes you can make:

- Stop smoking. If you smoke now, stop. If you don't smoke, don't start.
- Exercise, exercise, exercise. Take the stairs instead of the elevator; walk to the grocery store or on other errands; ride a bike to work; get at least 20–30 minutes of vigorous exercise at least three times a week (more than that is even better).

- Eat a lower-fat diet. High fat in the diet has been linked to increased risks of both cancer and heart disease, as well as to obesity. The American Heart Association currently recommends that 30% of daily calories come from fat—well below the percentage in the average American diet. But there is good evidence that a level of 15–20% of calories from fat would be even better. Achieving this level means eating much less meat and dairy products and a lot more vegetables, fruits, grains, and beans. (Goodbye, fast foods!)

- Get enough calcium. This is especially important for women, who lose more calcium from their bones than do men, especially after menopause. And once the calcium is lost, it is very hard—perhaps impossible—to regain it. So here is one place where prevention is critical. Weight-bearing exercise helps to retain calcium, but taking calcium supplements from early adulthood is also a good idea.

All these functions are tied to particular parts of the nervous system. For example, the hypothalamus regulates body temperature. Declines in reaction times are probably linked to slower communication between the cerebral cortex and the reticular formation. In early adulthood, the nervous system is so redundant—with so many alternative pathways for every signal—that functional changes such as the slowing of neuronal responses have relatively little practical effect on behavior. But over the full sweep of the adult years, the loss of speed becomes very noticeable.

Sex Differences There is considerable controversy about the meaning of sex differences in the adult brain. As you should remember from earlier chapters, the brains of males and females differ to some extent at every age. However, sex differences are even more striking in the adult brain.

For example, the brain contains two types of tissue: *gray matter* and *white matter*. Gray matter is made up of cell bodies and axon terminals; white matter contains myelinated axons that connect one neuron to another. Men have a higher proportion of white matter than women do (Gur et al., 1999). In addition, the distributions of gray and white matter differ in the brains of men and women. Men have a lower proportion of white matter in the left brain than in the right brain. In contrast, the proportions of gray matter and white matter in the two hemispheres are equal in women's brains. Such findings have led some neuropsychologists to speculate that men's overall superior spatial perception is associated with sex differences in the distribution of gray and white matter.

Researchers also speculate that gender differences in emotional behavior may be explained by the finding that women have more gray matter in the area of the brain that controls emotions (Gur, Gunning-Dixon, Bilker, & Gur, 2002). However, studies have also shown differences between males and females in the role played by the ratio of gray matter to white matter. In one study, researchers found that the ratio was associated with individual differences in performance on verbal learning tasks among male participants but was not associated with differences in such performance among female participants (Yurgelun-Todd, Killgore, & Young, 2002).

There are other sex differences in adult brains. Some listening tasks activate the left hemisphere in men, whereas women respond to them with the right hemisphere (Spreen et al., 1995). Similarly, men and women appear to use different areas of the brain when determining the location of a sound (Lewald, 2004). However, there isn't yet enough consistency across studies to allow neuroscientists to draw definitive conclusions about sex differences in brain function. Moreover, these scientists are still a long way from finding direct links between neurological and behavioral sex differences.

OTHER BODY SYSTEMS

It's hard to draw a clear line between "early adulthood" and "middle adulthood" because the physical and mental changes are so gradual; even at 30, adults may find that it takes a bit more work to get into or stay in shape than it did at 20.

Young adults perform better than do the middle-aged or old on virtually every physical measure. Compared to older adults, adults in their 20s and 30s have more muscle tissue; maximum bone calcium; more brain mass; better eyesight, hearing, and sense of smell; greater oxygen capacity; and a more efficient immune system. The young adult is stronger, faster, and better able to recover from exercise or to adapt to changing conditions, such as alterations in temperature or light levels.

Declines in Physical Functioning   There is a gradual decline on almost every measure of physical functioning through the years of adulthood. Table 3.1 (page 62) summarizes these changes. Most of the summary statements in the table are based on both longitudinal and cross-sectional data; many are based on studies in which both experimental and control groups consisted of participants in good health. So developmentalists can be reasonably confident that most of the age changes listed reflect primary aging and not secondary aging.

The center column of the table lists the approximate age at which the loss or decline reaches the point where it becomes fairly readily apparent. Virtually all these changes begin in early adulthood. But the early losses or declines are not typically noticeable in everyday physical functioning during these years, except when a person is attempting to operate at the absolute edge of physical ability. Among top athletes, for example, the very small losses of speed and strength that occur in the late 20s and 30s are highly significant, often dropping 25-year-olds or 30-year-olds out of the group of elite athletes (see the Real World feature, page 64). Nonathletes, though, typically notice little or no drop in everyday physical functioning until middle age.

Research on peak performance in various sports suggests that elite athletes reach peak performance levels in their early twenties. Thirty-something cancer survivor Lance Armstrong's continued domination of the Tour de France has surprised many.

Another way to think of this change is in terms of a balance between physical demand and physical capacity (Welford, 1993). In early adulthood, almost all of us have ample physical capacity to meet the physical demands we encounter in everyday life. We can read the fine print in the telephone book without bifocals; we can carry heavy boxes or furniture when we move; our immune systems are strong enough to fight off most illnesses, and we recover quickly from sickness. As we move into middle adulthood, the balance sheet changes: We find more and more arenas in which our physical capacities no longer quite meet the demands.

Heart and Lungs   The most common measure of overall aerobic fitness is **maximum oxygen uptake (VO$_2$ max),** which reflects the ability of the body to take in and transport oxygen to various body organs. When VO$_2$ max is measured in a person at rest, scientists find only minimal decrements associated with age. But when they measure VO$_2$ max during exercise (such as during a treadmill test), it shows a systematic decline with age of about 1% per year, beginning between ages 35 and 40 (Goldberg,

maximum oxygen uptake (VO$_2$ max) a measure of the body's ability to take in and transport oxygen to various body organs

TABLE 3.1	A Summary of Age Changes in Physical Functioning

Body Function	Age at Which Change Begins to Be Clear or Measurable	Nature of Change
Vision	Mid-40s	Lens of eye thickens and loses accommodative power, resulting in poorer near vision and more sensitivity to glare
Hearing	50 or 60	Loss of ability to hear very high and very low tones
Smell	About 40	Decline in ability to detect and discriminate among different smells
Taste	None	No apparent loss in taste discrimination ability
Muscles	About 50	Loss of muscle tissue, particularly in "fast twitch" fibers used for bursts of strength or speed
Bones	Mid-30s (women)	Loss of calcium in the bones, called osteoporosis; also wear and tear on bone in joints, called osteoarthritis, more marked after about 60
Heart and lungs	35 or 40	Most functions (such as aerobic capacity or cardiac output) do not show age changes at rest, but do show age changes during work or exercise
Nervous system	Probably gradual throughout adulthood	Some loss (but not clear how much) of neurons in the brain; gradual reduction in density of dendrites; gradual decline in total brain volume and weight
Immune system	Adolescence	Loss in size of thymus; reduction in number and maturity of T cells; not clear how much of this change is due to stress and how much is primary aging
Reproductive system	Mid-30s (women)	Increased reproductive risk and lowered fertility
	Early 40s (men)	Gradual decline in viable sperm beginning at about age 40; very gradual decline in testosterone from early adulthood
Cellular elasticity	Gradual	Gradual loss of elasticity in most cells, including skin, muscle, tendon, and blood vessel cells; faster deterioration in cells exposed to sunlight
Height	40	Compression of disks in the spine, with resulting loss of height of 1 to 2 inches by age 80
Weight	Nonlinear	In U.S. studies, weight reaches a maximum in middle adulthood and then gradually declines in old age
Skin	40	Increase in wrinkles, as a result of loss of elasticity; oil-secreting glands become less efficient.
Hair	Variable	Hair becomes thinner and may gray

(Sources: Bartoshuk & Weiffenbach, 1990; Blatter et al., 1995; Braveman, 1987; Briggs, 1990; Brock, Guralnik, & Brody, 1990; Doty et al., 1984; Fiatarone & Evans, 1993; Fozard, 1990; Fozard, Metter, & Brant, 1990; Gray, Berlin, McKinlay, & Longcope, 1991; Hallfrisch, Muller, Drinkwater, Tobin, & Adres, 1990; Hayflick, 1994; Ivy, MacLeod, Petit, & Marcus, 1992; Kallman, Plato, & Tobin, 1990; Kline & Scialfa, 1996; Kozma, Stones, & Hannah, 1991; Lakatta, 1990; Lim, Zipursky, Watts, & Pfefferbaum, 1992; McFalls, 1990; Miller, 1990; Mundy, 1994; Scheibel, 1992, 1996; Shock et al., 1984; Weisse, 1992.)

Dengel, & Hagberg, 1996). Figure 3.2 graphs some typical results from both cross-sectional and longitudinal studies of women. Similar results are found with men (Kozma et al., 1991; Lakatta, 1990). Notice the slight decline in the years of early adulthood, followed by a somewhat more rapid drop in the middle years, a pattern that is highly typical of data on physical changes over adulthood. Similarly, under resting conditions, the quantity of blood flow from the heart (called *cardiac output*) does not decline with age; under exercise or work conditions, however, it declines significantly, dropping 30–40% between age 25 and age 65 (Lakatta, 1990; Rossman, 1980).

VO_2 max during exercise declines more with age than does VO_2 max at rest for a variety of reasons. Primary aging effects have been demonstrated in studies showing that, even in healthy individuals who exercise regularly, age is associated with a loss of arterial elasticity and with calcification of the valves that regulate the flow of blood to and from the heart (Cheitlin, 2003). As a result, the older adult's heart responds less efficiently to the demands of exercise than the younger adult's. Research has also revealed, however, that aerobic exercise can improve VO_2 max in both younger and older adults (Wilmore et al., 2001). Thus, age-related declines in this variable may reflect the cumulative effects of a sedentary lifestyle.

Strength and Speed The collective effect of changes in muscles and cardiovascular fitness is a general loss of strength and speed with age—not just in top athletes, but in all of us. Figure 3.3 shows both cross-sectional and 9-year longitudinal changes in grip strength in a group of men who participated in the Baltimore Longitudinal Studies of Aging (Kallman et al., 1990). Clearly, strength was at its peak in the men's 20s and early 30s and then declined steadily. Once again, though, such a difference might be the result of the fact that younger adults are more physically active or more likely to be engaged in activities or jobs that demand strength. Arguing against this conclusion, however, are studies of physically active older adults, who also show loss of muscle strength (e.g., Phillips, Bruce, Newton, & Woledge, 1992).

Reproductive Capacity The risk of miscarriage and other complications of pregnancy is higher in a woman's 30s than in her 20s. An equivalent change occurs in fertility— the ability to conceive—which is at its highest in the late teens and early 20s and drops steadily thereafter (McFalls, 1990; Mosher, 1987; Mosher & Pratt, 1987). Men's reproductive capacity declines as well, but far more slowly than is common among women. Moreover, older men have a diminished sperm count, but, as long as their reproductive organs remain disease free, men retain the ability to father children throughout their lives. Why does this pattern of reproductive aging exist?

Genetic studies in mice suggest that a single protein is responsible for the regulation of reproductive aging in both sexes (Baker et al., 2004). However, the end point of the reproductive aging process is different for men and women. Men's capacity diminishes, as stated earlier, but remains intact. By contrast, the end point of reproductive aging for women involves a total loss of the capacity for reproduction. Because of this difference, fertility problems in men (e.g., low sperm count) are almost always the result of some kind of disease or abnormal developmental process. By contrast, fertility problems in women are more often a by-product of the normal aging process.

As you will learn in Chapter 5, in preparation for menopause, ovulation becomes sporadic and unpredictable in many women, sometimes as soon as the early 30s. Consequently, the natural process of reproductive aging leads many women to experience periods of time during which conception is impossible. However, because menstrual cycles continue to occur, many women who are ovulating intermittently are unaware of the problem. Thus, to achieve conception, many women in their 30s turn to specialists in reproductive medicine who can help them identify the times when they are fertile or can prescribe drugs that stimulate the ovaries to produce more eggs, as discussed in the Research Report (page 65).

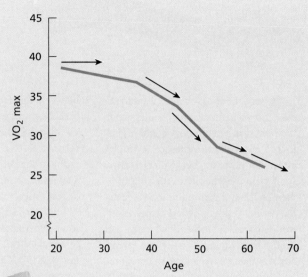

FIGURE 3.2

The continuous line shows VO₂ max averages for cross-sectional comparisons; the arrows show changes on the same measure for groups of women studied longitudinally. The two sets of findings match remarkably. Note that the largest drop was between ages 40 and 50. (Source: Plowman, Drinkwater, & Horvath, 1979, Figure 1, p. 514.)

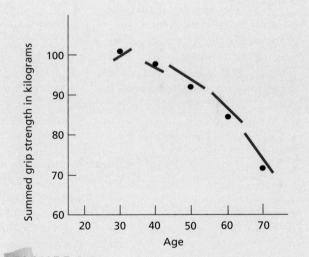

FIGURE 3.3

These data, from the Baltimore Longitudinal Study of Aging, show both cross-sectional data (the dots) and longitudinal data (the lines) for grip strength among men. Once again, there is striking agreement between the two sets of information. (Source: Kallman et al., 1990, Figure 2, p. M84.)

Immune System Functioning The two key organs in the immune system are the thymus gland and the bone marrow. Between them, they create two types of cells, B cells and T cells, each of which plays a distinct role. B cells fight against external

Age and Peak Sports Performance

One of the most obvious ways to confirm whether human bodies are at their physical peak in early adulthood is to look at sports performance. Olympic athletes or other top performers in any sport push their bodies to the limit of their abilities. If early adulthood is really the period of peak physical ability, most world-record-holders and top performers should be in their 20s or perhaps early 30s. Another way to approach the same question is to look at the average performance of top athletes in each of several age groups, including those in "master" categories (athletes who are 35 or older). Both types of analysis lead inescapably to the same conclusion: Athletic performance peaks early in life, although the exact timing of the peak varies somewhat from one sport to another.

Swimmers, for example, reach their peak very early—at about age 17 for women and about 19 for men. Golfers peak the latest, at about age 31 (Ericsson, 1990; Schulz & Curnow, 1988; Stones & Kozma, 1996). Runners fall in between, with top performances in their early or middle 20s, although the longer the distance, the later the peak. You can see that pattern in the figure, which represents the average age at which each of a series of top male runners ran his fastest time.

Cross-sectional comparisons of the top performances of competitors of different ages lead to the same conclusion. For example, Germany holds national

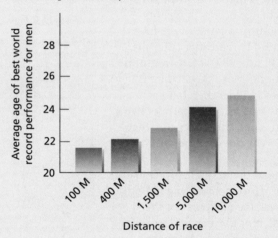

swimming championships each year, giving awards to the top performers in each 5-year age range from 25 through 70. The best times drop steadily with age (Ericsson, 1990).

At the same time, it is also true that older athletes can perform far better than has been commonly thought. World records for master athletes have been repeatedly broken over the past several decades; in many sports, present-day 50-year-olds are performing at higher levels than did Olympic athletes of 100 years ago. The human body, at any age, is more responsive to training than researchers even a decade ago had presumed. But it is still true that for those who achieve and maintain a high level of fitness throughout adult life, peak performance will come in early adulthood (Stones & Kozma, 1996).

threats by producing antibodies against such disease organisms as viruses or bacteria; T cells defend against essentially internal threats, such as transplanted tissue, cancer cells, and viruses that live within the body's cells (Kiecolt-Glaser & Glaser, 1995). It is T cells that decline most in number and efficiency with age (Garcia & Miller, 2001).

Changes in the thymus gland appear to be central to the aging process. This gland is largest in adolescence and declines dramatically thereafter in both size and mass. By age 45 or 50, the thymus has only about 5–10% of the cellular mass it had at puberty (Braveman, 1987; Hausman & Weksler, 1985). This smaller, less functional thymus is less able to turn the immature T cells produced by the bone marrow into fully "adult" cells. As a result, both of the basic protective mechanisms work less efficiently. Adults produce fewer antibodies than do children or teenagers. And T cells partially lose the ability to "recognize" a foreign cell, so that the body may fail to fight off some disease cells (cancer cells, for example). Thus, one of the key physical changes over the years of adulthood is an increasing susceptibility to disease.

But it is not entirely clear whether this susceptibility is due to primary or secondary aging. These changes in the immune system are found in healthy adults, which makes them look like part of primary aging. But there also is growing evidence that the functioning of the immune system is highly responsive to psychological stress and depression (Maier, Watkins, & Fleshner, 1994; Weisse, 1992). College students, for example, show lower levels of one variety of T cells ("natural killer" T cells) during

Assisted Reproductive Technology

Physicians define *infertility* as the failure to conceive after 12 consecutive months of unprotected intercourse (Mitchell, 2002). To help them conceive and deliver healthy babies, many infertile couples turn to physicians who are specialists in the use of *assisted reproductive techniques (ART)*. The use of *fertility drugs* to stimulate the ovaries to produce eggs is the most common approach to treating infertility. Increasing the number of eggs a woman produces increases the chances of a natural conception. Moreover, fertility drugs play an important role in other assisted reproductive techniques. They are often used along with *artificial insemination,* the process of injecting sperm into a woman's uterus at times when eggs are known to be present.

Fertility drugs are also employed in a more complex assisted reproductive technique known as *in vitro fertilization* (IVF; *in vitro* is Latin for *glass*), popularly known as the "test-tube baby" method. The first step in IVF involves using fertility drugs to stimulate the woman's ovaries to produce multiple eggs. The eggs are then extracted from the ovaries and combined with sperm in a laboratory dish. If conception takes place, one or more embryos—ideally at the six-to-eight-cell stage of development—are transferred to the woman's uterus in the hope that a normal pregnancy will develop. The eggs used in IVF can come from the woman who will carry the child or from a donor. Likewise, the sperm can be from the woman's partner or a donor. Extra embryos that result from an IVF cycle but are not used in that particular cycle can be frozen, or *cryopreserved.* These frozen embryos can be transferred at a later date, through a process known as *frozen embryo transfer (FET).*

An eight-celled embryo is ideal for an IVF transfer. Pictured here is an embryo on the day of transfer into a woman's uterus.

However, whether zygotes are cryopreserved or not, IVF is not a highly successful procedure. For one thing, the older a woman is, the lower the probability that she will be able to have a successful IVF pregnancy. Roughly 35% of 20- to 29-year-old IVF patients achieve a live birth, but only 13% or so of IVF procedures involving women over age 40 are successful (Schieve et al., 1999). It's important to note here, though, that these are aggregate statistics; each reproductive clinic keeps track of its own success rate, and these can vary considerably from one facility to another (Society for Assisted Reproductive Technology, 2004). Still, in even the most successful clinics, failure rates are high. Considering that most couples resort to IVF after months or years of frustration, it isn't surprising that failed IVF can result in depression among some of them (Weaver, Clifford, Hay, & Robinson, 1997). Moreover, IVF is expensive and is typically not covered by health insurance (Jain, Harlow, & Hornstein, 2002).

Successful IVF carries a different set of risks. Babies who are born as a result of IVF conception are more likely to be low-birth-weight and have birth defects than infants who are conceived naturally (Hansen, Kurinczuk, Bowev, & Webb, 2002: Schieve et al., 2002). The most important factor explaining these outcomes is the link between IVF and multiple gestation. Multiple birth is more frequent among IVF patients, primarily because doctors typically transfer several zygotes at once in order to increase the likelihood of at least one live birth (Society for Assisted Reproductive Technology, 2004). Consequently, 20–25% of IVF patients deliver twins, and another 2–5% give birth to triplets (Schieve et al., 1999). As you learned in Chapter 3, multiple pregnancies are associated with premature birth, low birth weight, and birth defects. Thus, reducing the frequency of multiple births among women undergoing treatment for infertility has become an important goal of reproductive medicine (Jain, Missmer, & Horn-

stein, 2004). To this end, the Society for Assisted Reproductive Technology (2004) has issued guidelines that strongly discourage physicians from transferring more than two embryos to a woman's uterus.

Nevertheless, researchers have found that, even when only one embryo is transferred, IVF is still associated with a higher rate of multiple births than is natural conception. For reasons that are not yet understood, implanted zygotes conceived through IVF are more likely to spontaneously divide into two embryos than are naturally conceived zygotes (Blickstine, Jones, & Keith, 2003). This finding suggests that multiple pregnancy must always be considered as a possible outcome when infertile couples are advised of the risks associated with IVF.

In addition, infants born as a result of IVF conception are twice as likely as naturally conceived infants to be low-birth-weight, even when they are singletons and are born at term. Likewise, birth defects are twice as common among IVF babies of normal birth weight and gestational age as among those who are conceived naturally (Hansen et al., 2002). The causes for these findings are not yet known, but identifying them so as to prevent the occurrence of these problems is one of the major goals of current research on assisted reproductive technology.

Despite the risks associated with IVF, most women who achieve successful pregnancies as a result of this technique deliver babies who are healthy and normal. Further, both comparative (IVF infants and children versus non-IVF ones) and longitudinal studies have shown that children conceived through IVF who are of normal birth weight and who do not have any birth defects develop identically to peers who were conceived naturally (Levy-Shiff et al., 1998; van Balen, 1998). Such findings should give encouragement and hope to those couples who must turn to assisted reproductive technology to fulfill their desire to have children.

exam periods than at other times (Glaser et al., 1992). And adults who have recently been widowed show a sharp drop in immune system functioning (Irwin & Pike, 1993). Chronic stress, too, has an effect on the immune system, stimulating an initial increase in immune efficiency, followed by a drop (Kiecolt-Glaser et al., 1987).

Collectively, this research points to the possibility that life experiences that demand high levels of change or adaptation will affect immune system functioning. Over a period of years and many stresses, the immune system may become less and less efficient. It may well be that the immune system changes with age in basic ways regardless of the level of stress. But it is also possible that what is thought of as normal aging of the immune system is a response to cumulative stress.

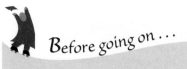

Before going on . . .

■ Define primary and secondary aging.

■ Why do neuroscientists think there may be a spurt in brain development in the mid-20s?

■ Describe the various changes in other body systems that happen in early adulthood.

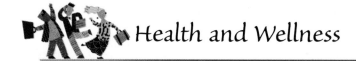

Health and Wellness

E arly adulthood is a relatively healthy period of life, but risky behaviors—having multiple sex partners or engaging in substance use, for example—along with generally poor health habits can be problematic.

SEXUALLY TRANSMITTED DISEASES

In contrast to other types of disease, most sexually transmitted diseases (STD)—including gonorrhea, syphilis, genital herpes, and HIV—are more common among young adults than any other age group (CDC, 1999a, 1999b, 2000a, 2000b).

Bacterial STDs Bacterial STDs are STDs caused by microorganisms that can be eradicated through the use of antibiotic medications. The most prevalent of the bacterial STDs is *chlamydia,* a bacterial infection that can be transmitted through many kinds of physical contact involving the genitals, as well as actual intercourse (CDC, 2003). Women are about three times as likely as men to suffer from chlamydia. Community studies show that as many as one-third of young women who are screened at family planning clinics are infected with chlamydia. Many of these women are symptom-free because the disease can remain hidden for several years. Unfortunately, undiagnosed chlamydia can lead to **pelvic inflammatory disease,** an infection of the female reproductive tract that can cause infertility.

Another bacterial STD is *gonorrhea.* Because of educational programs about the disease and increased use of condoms, the prevalence of gonorrhea has declined considerably in recent years (CDC, 2003b). However, the strains that infect today's gonorrhea sufferers are far more resistant to antibiotics than those that existed decades ago (CDC, 2003b). As a result, in some cases the disease is extremely difficult to cure and causes long-term damage to the reproductive systems of those who suffer from it. Men and women experience roughly equivalent rates of gonorrhea, but women's bodies are more susceptible to long-term damage from this infection.

Another bacterial STD is *syphilis,* a disease that can lead to serious mental disorders and death if not treated in the early stages of infection. Fortunately, widespread screening for the disease has led to significant declines in its prevalence. Only about 7,000 cases were reported to the Centers for Disease Control in 2002 (CDC, 2003b).

pelvic inflammatory disease an infection of the female reproductive tract that may result from a sexually transmitted disease and can lead to infertility

However, syphilis continues to be a much more extensive health problem in some groups. For example, during the late 1990s, the infection rate among African Americans was 34 times that of whites (CDC, 2003b). Thanks to intensive educational campaigns geared toward African Americans, the cross-racial difference in syphilis rates decreased substantially in the first years of the 21st century. However, public health officials note that the decrease in the disparity across races is due both to declining numbers among African Americans and to increasing numbers among whites. The increase in syphilis infection in the white population is confined to men, largely because the number of cases among homosexual males who live in highly populated urban areas continues to rise each year at an alarming rate (CDC, 2003b).

Viral STDs Unlike STDs caused by bacteria, STDs caused by viruses cannot be treated with antibiotics. In fact, these diseases are considered to be incurable. One such disease is *genital herpes.* This disease can be acquired through either intercourse or oral sex. The Centers for Disease Control report that 20% of the adult population in the United States is infected with herpes (CDC, 2001). Attacks of the disease, which include the development of painful blisters on the genitals, occur periodically in most people who carry the virus.

A more serious viral STD is *genital warts* caused by the *human papillomavirus (HPV)*. The primary symptom of the disease, the presence of growths on the genitals, is not its most serious effect. The virus is strongly associated with cervical cancer, accounting for more than 80% of all cases (Ochs, 1994). Studies indicate that, in the United States, 25% of women in their 20s, and 10% of women over 30 are infected with HPV (Stone et al., 2002).

HIV/AIDS The most feared STD is the *human immunodeficiency virus (HIV)*, the virus that causes *acquired immune deficiency syndrome (AIDS)*. Since HIV was discovered in the early 1980s, more than 900,000 cases have been documented and just over 500,000 people have died from the disease in the United States (National Institutes of Health, 2003). HIV is transmitted through an exchange of bodily fluids. Such exchanges can happen during sexual intercourse, when intravenous drug users share needles, or as a result of a blood transfusion or other kinds of invasive medical treatment. Male homosexuals have higher rates of HIV than other groups primarily because of the tendency to engage in anal intercourse, during which bodily fluids are more likely to be exchanged than in other kinds of sexual encounters.

Prevention Behavioral change is the key to STD prevention. Young adults have higher rates of these diseases than older people primarily because they engage in more sexually risky behavior. In particular, many young adults engage in casual, unprotected sex with multiple partners. To compound the problem, young adults seldom discuss STD prevention with potential sex partners. Further, most do not insist that their partners use condoms, and they delay seeking treatment for STD symptoms (Lewis, Malow, & Ireland, 1997; Schuster, 1997). Thus, reducing the rates of such risky behaviors could reduce the rates of STDs and prevent many young adults from experiencing the adverse health consequences associated with them.

HEALTH HABITS AND PERSONAL FACTORS

As you might expect, individual health habits, such as exercise, influence health in the early adult years and beyond. Social support networks and attitudes also affect health.

Health Habits The best evidence for the long-term effects of various health habits comes from the Alameda County Study, a major longitudinal epidemiological study

Sexually transmitted diseases are one of the most significant health risks of young adulthood. Casual sexual encounters with multiple partners carry with them a higher risk of contracting such diseases than do more careful relationship choices.

conducted in one county in California (Berkman & Breslow, 1983; Breslow & Breslow, 1993; Kaplan, 1992; Stallworth & Lennon, 2003). The study began in 1965, when a random sample of all residents of the county, a total of 6,928 people, completed an extensive questionnaire about many aspects of their lives, including their health habits and their health and disability. These participants were contacted again in 1974 and in 1983, when they again described their health and disability. The researchers also monitored death records and were able to specify the date of death of each of the participants who died between 1965 and 1983. They could then link health practices reported in 1965 to later death, disease, or disability. The researchers initially identified seven good health habits that they thought might be critical: getting physical exercise; not smoking, drinking, over- or undereating, or snacking; eating breakfast; and getting regular sleep.

Data from the first 9 years of the Alameda study show that five of these seven practices were independently related to the risk of death. Only snacking and eating breakfast were unrelated to mortality. When the five strong predictors were combined in the 1974 data, researchers found that, in every age group, those with poorer health habits had a higher risk of mortality. Not surprisingly, poor health habits were also related to disease and disability rates over the 18 years of the study. Those who described poorer health habits in 1965 were more likely to report disability or disease symptoms in 1974 and in 1983 (Breslow & Breslow, 1993; Guralnik & Kaplan, 1989; Strawbridge, Camacho, Cohen, & Kaplan, 1993). Moreover, the study showed that a sendentary lifestyle in early adulthood predisposes people to develop life-threatening illnesses such as diabetes in later years (Hu, Li, Colditz, Willet, & Manson, 2003).

The Alameda study is not the only one to show these connections between health habits and mortality. For example, a 20-year longitudinal study in Sweden confirms the link between physical exercise and lower risk of death (Lissner, Bengtsson, Bjorkelund, & Wedel, 1996). In addition, the Nurses' Health Study, a longitudinal investigation that examined the health behaviors of more than 115,000 nurses in the United States for almost 2 decades, found that the lower a woman's initial body-mass index (a measure of weight relative to height), the lower her likelihood of death (Manson et al., 1995).

These longitudinal studies suggest that the lifestyle choices of early adulthood have cumulative effects. For example, the effect of a high-cholesterol diet appears to add up over time. However, a radical lowering of fat levels in the diet may reverse the process of cholesterol build-up in the blood vessels (Ornish, 1990). Thus, the long-term effects of lifestyle choices made in early adulthood may be either negative or positive. So there is likely to be a payoff for changing your health habits.

CRITICAL THINKING ?

Think about your own less-than-ideal health habits. What rationalizations do you use to justify them to yourself?

Social Support Abundant research shows that adults with adequate *social support* have lower risk of disease, death, and depression than do adults with weaker social networks or less supportive relationships (e.g., Berkman, 1985; Berkman & Breslow, 1983; Cohen, 1991). However, a person's perception of the adequacy of her social contacts and emotional support is more strongly related to physical and emotional health than is the actual number of such contacts (Feld & George, 1994; Sarason, Sarason, & Pierce, 1990). Thus, it is not the objective amount of contact with others that is important, but how that contact is understood or interpreted.

The link between social support and health was revealed in some of the findings from the Alameda study. In this study, the *social network index* reflected an objective measurement: number of contacts with friends and relatives, marital status, church and group membership. Even using this less-than-perfect measure of support, the relationship is vividly clear: Among both men and women in three different age groups

(30–49, 50–59, and 60–69), those with the fewest social connections had higher death rates than those with more social connections. Since similar patterns have been found in other countries, including Sweden and Japan, this link between social contact and physical hardiness is not restricted to the United States or to Western cultures (Orth-Gomer, Rosengren, & Wilhelmsen, 1993; Sugisawa, Liang, & Liu, 1994).

The beneficial effect of social support is particularly clear when an individual is under high stress. An excellent example comes from research on depression among women in England (Brown, 1989, 1993; Brown & Harris, 1978). Researchers initially studied 419 women who ranged in age from 18 to 65, gathering information about the number of severely stressful events each woman had experienced in the year prior to the research (such as the death of someone close, a divorce or failed relationship, or the equivalent), about whether they were currently depressed, and about who—if anyone—served as an intimate confidant. The study found that, although stress was more strongly linked to depression than to social support, highly stressed women who had a close confidant, especially if that confidant was a husband or boyfriend, were much less likely to become depressed. That is, the social support of their partner or other confidant buffered them against the negative effects of the stress.

Research shows that social support, as exhibited between these two women, lowers the risk of disease, death, and depression in adults.

A Sense of Control Another personal characteristic that affects health is an individual's level of what Rodin has called *perceived control* (Rodin, 1990). Psychologist Albert Bandura talks about this same characteristic but refers to it as **self-efficacy,** the belief in one's ability to perform some action or to control one's behavior or environment, to reach some goal or to make something happen (Bandura, 1977b, 1982b, 1986). Such a belief is one aspect of the internal model of the self and is affected by one's experiences with mastering tasks and overcoming obstacles.

A similar idea comes from the work of Martin Seligman, who differentiates between positions of *optimism and helplessness* (Seligman, 1991). The pessimist, who feels helpless, believes that misfortune will last a long time, will undermine everything, and is his own fault. The optimist believes that setbacks are temporary and usually caused by circumstances. He is convinced that there is always some solution and that he will be able to work things out. Confronted by defeat, the optimist sees it as a challenge and tries harder, whereas the pessimist gives up. Both Bandura and Seligman propose that self-efficacy or optimism arises in childhood and adolescence, as a result of early experiences of effectiveness, success or failure, and frustration.

Research on the links between a sense of control and health shows that those with a more helpless attitude or with a low sense of self-efficacy are more likely to become depressed or physically ill ("Optimism can mean life," 1994a; Seligman, 1991; Syme, 1990). The most striking demonstration of this connection is from a 35-year study of a group of Harvard men who were first interviewed in their freshman years, in 1938–1940. Researchers were able to use material from interviews with these men when they were 25 to assess their degree of pessimism. Their physical health from ages 30 to 60 was then rated by physicians who examined the men every 5 years.

Pessimism was not related to health at 30, 35, or 40, but at every assessment from age 45 to age 60, those who had had a more pessimistic approach at age 25 had significantly poorer health, and this was true even after controlling statistically for physical and mental health at 25 (Peterson, Seligman, & Vaillant, 1988).

It is also possible to show that experimentally increasing the sense of control improves an adult's health, even immune function. On this point, there is cross-sectional, longitudinal, and experimental evidence (Welch & West, 1995). In the earliest and best-known study of this kind, researchers found that mortality rates of nursing home residents were lower among those who had been given control over even quite

self-efficacy the belief in one's capacity to cause an intended event to occur or to perform a task

simple aspects of their daily lives, such as whether to have scrambled eggs or omelettes for breakfast or whether to sign up to attend a movie (Rodin & Langer, 1977).

INTIMATE PARTNER ABUSE

Researchers define **intimate partner abuse** as physical acts or other behavior intended to intimidate or harm an intimate partner. Intimate partners are couples who are dating, cohabiting, engaged, or married or who were formerly partners. The more common term, *domestic abuse,* refers only to incidents involving individuals who live in the same household.

Prevalence Throughout the world, women are more likely than men to be victimized by intimate partners. In the United States, surveys suggest that about 25% of women have been physically abused by a partner, compared to only 8% of men (NCIPC, 2000). However, rates of abuse among women vary significantly around the world, as Figure 3.4 reveals (World Health Organization [WHO], 2000).

Rates vary across ethnic and sexual orientation groups within the United States as well. As many as half of all African American women in the United States have been physically abused by an intimate partner at some time in their adult lives (Wyatt, Axelrod, Chin, Carmona, & Loeb, 2000). Similarly, some studies suggest that Hispanic American women experience partner abuse more frequently than their white counterparts (Duncan, Stayton, & Hall, 1999). However, careful analyses of these findings show that the critical factor is socioeconomic status rather than race (Rennison & Planty, 2003). In other words, low-income women are more likely to be abused than those with higher incomes, and African American and Hispanic American households have lower average income levels than those of other ethnic groups.

The prevalence of abuse also differs across heterosexual and homosexual partnerships. Gay men are about as likely to be abused by a partner as are women in heterosexual relationships; rates are 22% and 25%, respectively (Waldner-Haugrud, Gratch, & Magruder, 1997). However, almost half of lesbians surveyed report that they have been physically assaulted by a partner (Waldner-Haugrud et al., 1997).

Causes of Partner Abuse Anthropologists believe that cultural attitudes contribute to rates of abuse (Hicks & Gwynne, 1996). Specifically, in many societies, women are regarded as property, and a man's "right" to beat his partner may be protected by law. In fact, there was a time when, based on English common law traditions, this was true in the United States.

Gender-role prescriptions may also contribute to abuse. For example, rates of abuse are particularly high among Japanese women, over 50% of whom claim to have been victimized (Kozu, 1999). Researchers attribute the prevalence of abuse to the cultural belief that Japanese husbands are absolute authorities over their wives and children. Further, to avoid bringing dishonor on her husband, the Japanese wife is obligated to conceal abusive incidents from those outside the family.

In addition to cultural beliefs, a number of characteristics of abusers and their victims are associated with intimate partner abuse. For example, the same cluster of personality traits in abusers contributes to abuse in both heterosexual and homosexual couples (Burke & Follingstad, 1999). The cluster includes a tendency toward irrational jealousy, a need for the partner's dependency and for control in a relationship, sudden mood swings, and a quick temper (Landolt &

(Photo: © Jonathan Nourok/PhotoEdit)

Criminologists point out that intimate partner abuse happens most often in the context of arguments over long-standing disagreements that take place when partners are home from work in the evening, on holidays, or on weekends, and/or have been drinking or using drugs.

intimate partner abuse physical acts or other behavior intended to intimidate or harm an intimate partner

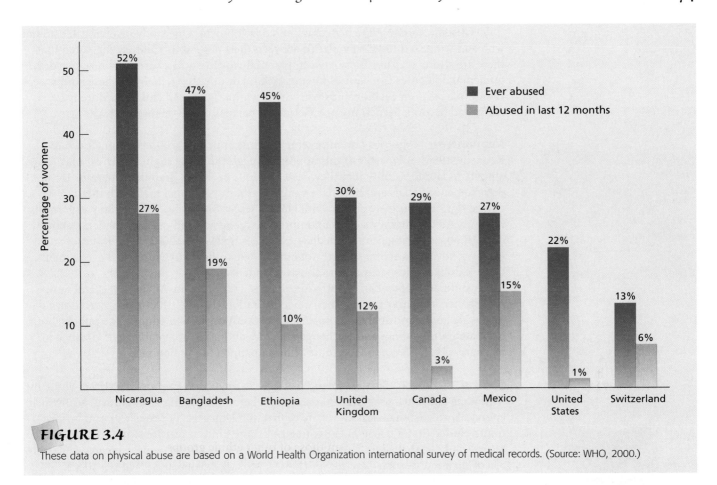

FIGURE 3.4

These data on physical abuse are based on a World Health Organization international survey of medical records. (Source: WHO, 2000.)

Dutton, 1997). Men who are generally aggressive are also more likely than less aggressive men to abuse their partners (Kane, Staiger, & Ricciardelli, 2000). In addition, men who are high school dropouts or who are frequently unemployed abuse their partners more often than other men (Kyriacou et al., 1999).

Abuse victims are more likely to have been abused as children than are their peers who are not involved in abusive relationships (Smith, White, & Holland, 2003; Wyatt et al., 2000). Age is also a factor. Young women between the ages of 16 and 24 are more likely to be abused than those who are older (Buss, 1999; Duncan et al., 1999). This pattern of age differences may result from younger women's lesser ability to function independently from abusive partners. They may lack the education and/or work experience necessary to gain employment. Finally, younger women are more likely to be caring for infants and young children for whom they cannot obtain day care. As a result, many such women remain in abusive relationships, believing they have no other choice (Kaplan & Sadock, 1991).

Alcohol and drug problems are more common among both abusers and victims than among nonabusive partners (Kyriacou et al., 1999; Schafer, Caetana, & Cunradi, 2004; Van Hightower & Gorton, 1998). One extensive study of more than 8,000 intra-family killings found that, in about half of spousal homicides, the perpetrator had been drinking alcohol or using drugs (Dawson & Langan, 1994). Similarly, in 50% of cases, the victim had been using alcohol or drugs.

Effects of Abuse on Individuals Women who are abused may develop feelings of anxiety, depression, shame, and low self-esteem (Buchbinder & Eisikovits, 2003; Kaplan & Sadock, 1991). Such feelings are intensified when victims believe they cannot escape from the abusive relationship. Some become so despondent that they consider or attempt suicide as an escape (NCIPC, 2000).

Witnessing abuse influences children's development. One study involving 420 adults who had witnessed physical violence between their parents as children suggested that there are strong relationships between parental violence and a variety of negative developmental outcomes (McNeal & Amato, 1998). For one thing, many of these adults were found to have poor relationships with their own partners and children. Moreover, many had become perpetrators or victims of partner abuse themselves.

Prevention   Vigorous law enforcement is one approach to prevention (Sacco & Kennedy, 1996). Advocates of this approach suggest that the stigma of arrest may force abusers to face the reality that they have a serious problem. Training programs for law enforcement officials and hospital emergency room personnel that teach them to recognize signs of abuse are also essential (Hamberger & Minsky, 2000). Many experts also recommend training physicians and nurses to recognize and question patients about signs of abuse during routine medical exams (Scholle et al., 2003). As a result of such training, advocates claim, perpetrators may be identified and prosecuted even when victims do not voluntarily report abusive incidents.

A different approach is to provide victims with problem-solving skills and temporary shelters that may prevent their revictimization (NCIPC, 2000). Further, community-wide and school-based approaches to prevention seek to educate the public about intimate partner abuse and to change attitudes about the acceptability of violence in intimate relationships, so that abuse will not happen in the first place.

Sexual Violence   **Sexual violence** is the term applied to episodes of partner abuse in which one individual uses force to coerce the other into engaging in sexual acts. Many such episodes involve strangers; however, more than three-quarters of sexually violent incidents in the United States occur in the context of some kind of relationship (NCIPC, 2000). Surveys indicate that about 20% of women have been victims of sexual violence, while only 3% of men report such experiences (Elliott, Mok, & Briere, 2004; NCIPC, 2000).

The psychological effects of being a victim of sexual violence include the development of sexual dysfunctions and posttraumatic stress disorder, as well as the possibility of physical trauma and pregnancy (Elliott et al., 2004). Men who are raped by other men also sometimes experience doubts about their sexual orientation (Kaplan & Sadock, 1991). Moreover, the psychological effects of sexual violence have been found to persist more than a decade in many victims (Elliott et al., 2004). Thus, being victimized by sexual violence can, overall, be one of the most traumatic episodes in a young adult's life.

One particularly troubling type of sexual violence among young adults is *date rape,* or rape that occurs in the context of a date. Men's belief that women say no when they mean yes is believed to contribute to such incidents. However, many cases of date rape are premeditated and involve the use of alcohol and drugs to loosen the inhibitions of the victim. Research indicates that such episodes may be more traumatic than rapes perpetrated by strangers because victims of date rape believe they should have been able to prevent the assault. Victims who were coerced with drugs and/or alcohol also frequently have incomplete memories of the event, a factor that increases their vulnerability to long-term negative emotional consequences (Gauntlett-Gilbert, Keegan, & Petrak, 2004).

Prevention of sexual violence often involves training potential victims to avoid situations in which such episodes are likely to occur (Kalmuss, 2004). Training in self-defense techniques, both verbal and physical, can also help women learn how to deal effectively with the initial phases of a threatened sexual assault (Hollander, 2004).

MENTAL HEALTH PROBLEMS

sexual violence the use of physical coercion to force a person to engage in a sexual act against his or her will

Studies in a number of developed countries show that the risk of virtually every kind of emotional disturbance is higher in early adulthood than in middle age (Kessler, Foster, Webster, & House, 1992; Regier et al., 1988). In fact, survey research suggests that as many as 10% of younger adults, those aged 18 to 24, have seriously considered committing suicide (Brener, Hassan, & Barrios, 1999).

Causes of Mental Disorders The most plausible explanation for the differing rates of mental illness between young adults and middle-aged adults is that early adulthood is the period in which adults have both the highest expectations and the highest levels of role conflict and role strain. These are the years when each of us must learn a series of major new roles (spouse, parent, worker). If we fall short of our expectations, emotional difficulties such as anxiety and depression become more likely.

Some people respond very effectively to the challenges of young adulthood, while others do not. For example, the personal factors you read about in an earlier section are important to mental health as well as physical health. However, with respect to mental illness, researchers' attention is becoming more focused on biological causes.

First, mental illnesses tend to run in families, suggesting a genetic factor. In fact, the number of close relatives a person has who suffer from depression or other mood disorders is the best predictor of the likelihood that the individual will develop a mood disorder (Kendler et al., 1995). In addition, an increasing number of studies demonstrate links between mental illnesses and disturbances in specific brain functions (Drevets et al., 1997; Monarch, Saykin, & Flashman, 2004). Consequently, the current view of most psychologists is that mental disorders result from an interaction of biological and environmental factors.

Anxiety, Mood, and Substance Use Disorders The most common mental disorders are those that are associated with fear and anxiety (Kessler et al., 1994). For example, *phobias* are fairly common. A **phobia** is an irrational fear of an object, a person, a place, or a situation. Most phobias are learned through association of the experience of being in a state of fear with a specific stimulus. For example, a college student who was injured in a car crash may avoid the intersection where the crash occurred, even though doing so adds time and distance to his daily trip from home to campus.

Since phobias are usually learned, therapeutic interventions usually involve some process of *un*learning the association. In fact, many people "cure" their own phobias simply by exposing themselves to the fear-producing stimulus until it no longer induces anxiety. Thus, the student who is phobic about a particular intersection may tell himself that he is being silly and force himself to drive through it repeatedly until the phobic reaction no longer occurs.

After anxiety disorders, problems associated with moods are the most common type of mental difficulty. Depression is the most frequent of these disorders. Rates of depression are higher in early adulthood than in either adolescence or middle age. Thus, paradoxically, the time of life in which people experience their peak of physical and intellectual functioning is also the time when they may be most prone to feelings of sadness. Depression rates may be higher in early adulthood because these are the years when people must create new attachment relationships while at the same time separating from parents (Erikson's task of *intimacy*). Consequently, brief periods during which a person is alone may result in feelings of loneliness and social failure that may lead to depression.

Alcoholism and significant drug addiction also peak between ages 18 and 40, after which they decline gradually. The rates of addiction are higher for men than for women, but the age pattern is very similar in both genders (Anthony & Aboraya, 1992). One large study in the United States found a rate of alcohol abuse or dependence of about 6% among young adults, compared with 4% among the middle aged and 1.8% for those over 65 (Regier et al., 1988).

Binge drinking (usually defined as consuming five or more drinks on one occasion) is also particularly common among college students in the United States. Although most binge drinkers do not think of themselves as having a problem with alcohol, they clearly display a variety of problem behaviors, including substantially higher rates of unprotected sex, physical injury, driving while intoxicated, and trouble with the police (Wechsler, Davenport, Dowdall, Moeykens, & Castillo, 1994; Wechsler, Dowdall, Maenner, Gledhill-Hoyt, & Lee, 1998). Thus, alarmed by surveys showing that as many as 50% of college students engage in binge drinking, a growing number of colleges and universities are strictly enforcing rules against on-campus substance

phobia an irrational fear of an object, a person, a place, or a situation

use (Wechsler et al., 1998). Many also provide students with treatment for alcohol and substance abuse problems.

Personality Disorders In a few cases, the stresses of young adulthood, presumably in combination with some biological factor, lead to serious disturbances in cognitive, emotional, and social functioning that are not easily treated. For example, a **personality disorder** is an inflexible pattern of behavior that leads to difficulties in social, educational, and occupational functioning. In many cases, the problems associated with these disorders appear early in life. However, the behavior pattern is usually not diagnosed as a mental disorder until late adolescence or early adulthood (APA, 2000). The five most common types of personality disorders are listed in Table 3.2.

Some young adults may exhibit behavior that suggests a personality disorder because of stressors such as the break-up of a long-term relationship. For this reason, mental health professionals have to assess an individual's long-term and current levels of functioning in order to diagnose personality disorders. Ethnic and cultural standards of behavior also have to be taken into account, and physical illnesses that can cause abnormal behavior, such as disturbances in the endocrine system, have to be ruled out. Clinicians also have to keep in mind that some of these disorders are closely related, such as the narcissistic and histrionic disorders, and that some individuals suffer from more than one.

Generally, to be diagnosed with any of the disorders in Table 3.2, a young adult has to have been exhibiting the associated behavior since mid- or late adolescence. In addition, the person should demonstrate the behavior consistently, across all kinds of situations. For example, a person who steals from an employer but generally respects the property rights of others outside the work environment would probably not be diagnosed with antisocial personality disorder. The individual's functioning at work, at school, or in social relationships also must be impaired to some degree. Psychological tests can be helpful in distinguishing whether an individual simply has a troublesome personality trait, such as suspiciousness, or a genuine mental illness, such as paranoid personality disorder.

Some personality disorders, such as antisocial and borderline disorders, get better on their own as adults gain maturity (APA, 2000). However, most of these disorders remain problematic throughout adult life. In addition, they are not easily treated. In most cases, they do not respond to psychotherapy, because those who suffer from them seem to believe their problems result from others' behavior rather than their own.

Schizophrenia Another type of serious mental illness that is often first diagnosed in early adulthood is **schizophrenia,** a mental disorder characterized by false beliefs known

personality disorder an inflexible pattern of behavior that leads to difficulty in social, educational, and occupational functioning

schizophrenia a serious mental disorder characterized by disturbances of thought such as delusions and hallucinations

TABLE 3.1	A Summary of Age Changes in Physical Functioning
Type	**Characteristics**
Antisocial	Difficulty forming emotional attachments; lack of empathy; little regard for the rights of others; self-centered; willing to violate the law or social rules to achieve a desired objective
Paranoid	Suspicious of others' behavior and motives; emotionally guarded and highly sensitive to minor violations of personal space or perceived rights
Histrionic	Irrational, attention-seeking behavior; inappropriate emotional responses; sexually seductive behavior and clothing
Narcissistic	Exaggerated sense of self-importance; craves attention and approval; exploits others; lack of empathy
Borderline	Unstable moods, relationships; fear of abandonment; tendency to self-injury; highly dependent on others; impulsive and reckless behavior

(Source: APA, 2000.)

as delusions and false sensory experiences called *hallucinations*. For example, a first-year biology student who breaks into a laboratory on his college campus to work on a cure for cancer he has just thought of may suffer from a *delusion of grandeur*. Likewise, a young woman who hears voices that guide her behavior is likely to be experiencing hallucinations.

For most people with schizophrenia, these disturbances of thought become so severe that they can no longer function at work, at school, or in social relationships. In fact, many engage in behavior that endangers themselves or others. For example, a person with schizophrenia may believe that he can fly and jump out of an upper-story window. Consequently, people with schizophrenia are frequently hospitalized. Fortunately, powerful antipsychotic medications can help most people with schizophrenia regain some degree of normal functioning. Yet many continue to experience recurring episodes of disturbed thinking even when medication helps them to gain control over their behavior.

Before going on . . .

- How are age, health habits, and stress related to illness?

- What habits are associated with good health?

- How do social support and a sense of control contribute to good health?

- What are the prevalence rates, causes, and effects of intimate partner abuse?

- What are the characteristics of people who suffer from anxiety or mood disorders, substance abuse, personality disorders, or schizophrenia?

Cognitive Changes

Like most aspects of physical functioning, intellectual processes are at their peak in early adulthood. Indeed, it now seems clear that the intellectual peak lasts longer than many early researchers had thought and that the rate of decline is quite slow. Current research also makes clear that the rate and pattern of cognitive decline vary widely—differences that appear to be caused by a variety of environmental and lifestyle factors, as well as by heredity.

FORMAL OPERATIONS AND BEYOND

Piaget's formal operational stage emerges in mid- to late adolescence but is not nearly so well developed then as his theory proposed. In fact, it appears that formal operational thinking is more characteristic of adults than of adolescents and is strongly tied to educational experiences. But some theorists dispute Piaget's hypothesis that the formal operations stage is the last stage of cognitive development.

A number of theorists argue that Piaget's concept of formal operations simply doesn't capture many of the kinds of thinking that adults are called on to do. They propose, instead, that new structures, or new stages, of thinking occur in adulthood. One such theorist is Gisela Labouvie-Vief, who argues that formal operational thinking is useful in early adulthood, when the young person has some need to explore or examine many life options (Labouvie-Vief, 1980, 1990). But once an adult has made his initial choices, he no longer has much need for formal operations; instead, he needs thinking skills that are specialized and pragmatic. Adults learn how to solve the problems associated with the particular social roles they occupy or the particular jobs they hold. In the process, they trade the deductive thoroughness of formal operations for what Labouvie-Vief calls *contextual validity*. In her view, this trade-off does not reflect a regression or a loss, but rather a necessary structural change.

(Photo: © Diana White/PhotoEdit)

What kind of thinking might this young couple be using to make a budget decision? Pragmatic? Concrete or formal operational?

Labouvie-Vief also makes the point that many young adults begin to turn away from a purely logical, analytic approach, toward a more open, perhaps deeper, mode of understanding that incorporates myth and metaphor and recognizes and accepts paradox and uncertainty. Michael Basseches calls this new adult type of thinking **dialectical thought** (Basseches, 1984, 1989). He suggests that whereas formal operational thought "involves the effort to find fundamental fixed realities—basic elements and immutable laws—[dialectical thought] attempts to describe fundamental processes of change and the dynamic relationships through which this change occurs" (1984, p. 24). According to this view, adults do not give up their ability to use formal reasoning. Instead, they acquire a new ability to deal with the fuzzier problems that make up the majority of the problems of adulthood—problems that do not have a single solution or in which some critical pieces of information may be missing. Choosing what type of refrigerator to buy might be a decision aided by formal operational thought. But such forms of logical thought may not be helpful in making a decision about whether to adopt a child or whether to place an aging parent in a nursing home. Basseches argues that such problems demand a different kind of thinking—not a "higher" kind of thinking, but a different one.

Still a third model of "postformal" thinking comes from Patricia Arlin, who argues that Piaget's stage of formal operations is a stage of problem solving (Arlin, 1975, 1989, 1990). Some adults, Arlin proposes, develop a further stage characterized by problem *finding*. This new mode, which includes much of what is normally called *creativity*, is optimal for dealing with problems that have no clear solution or that have multiple solutions. A person operating at this stage is able to generate many possible solutions to ill-defined problems and to see old problems in new ways. Arlin argues that problem finding is a clear stage following formal operations, but that it is achieved by only a small number of adults, such as those involved in advanced science or the arts.

Many of these new theories of adult cognition are intriguing, but they remain highly speculative, with little empirical evidence to back them up. More generally, psychologists do not yet agree on whether these new types of thinking represent "higher" forms of thought, built on the stages Piaget described, or whether it is more appropriate simply to describe them as different forms of thinking that may or may not emerge in adulthood. What may be most important about such theories is the emphasis on the fact that the normal problems of adult life, with their inconsistencies and complexities, cannot always be addressed fruitfully using formal operational logic. It seems entirely plausible that adults are pushed toward more pragmatic, relativistic forms of thinking and use formal operational thinking only occasionally, if at all. Postformal theorists agree that this change should not be thought of as a loss or a deterioration, but rather as a reasonable adaptation to a different set of cognitive tasks.

INTELLIGENCE AND MEMORY

Examination of intelligence and memory in early adulthood suggests that both continuity and change characterize these components of cognitive functioning (Schroeder & Salthouse, 2004). Verbal abilities, such as the number of words in one's vocabulary, grow during early adulthood. By contrast, spatial skills decline a bit. Thus, you may be wondering, Does an individual become more intelligent or less so over the years from 20 to 40? The answer to this question depends on how intellectual functioning is measured.

IQ Scores IQ scores remain quite stable across middle childhood, adolescence, and early adulthood. For example, a study of Canadian army veterans, tested first when they were in their early 20s and then again in their early 60s, yielded similar results; there was a correlation of .78 between verbal IQ scores achieved at the two ages (Gold et al., 1995). Over shorter intervals, the correlations were even higher.

CRITICAL THINKING 9

List two personal problems you have had to solve in the past 6 months. What kind of logic or thought process did you use to solve each one? Did your mode of thinking change in response to the nature of the problem?

dialectical thought a form of thought involving recognition and acceptance of paradox and uncertainty

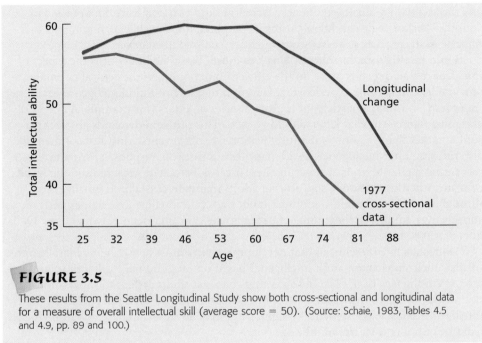

FIGURE 3.5

These results from the Seattle Longitudinal Study show both cross-sectional and longitudinal data for a measure of overall intellectual skill (average score = 50). (Source: Schaie, 1983, Tables 4.5 and 4.9, pp. 89 and 100.)

The best single source of evidence on the stability of IQ in adulthood is a remarkable 35-year study by Werner Schaie, referred to as the Seattle Longitudinal Study (1983, 1989, 1993, 1994, 1996; Schaie & Hertzog, 1983). Schaie began in 1956 with a set of cross-sectional samples; the participants in different samples were 7 years apart in age and ranged in age from 25 to 67. All participants took an IQ test at the outset of the study; a subset of the participants in each age group was then followed over 35 years and retested every 7 years. In 1963, another set of cross-sectional samples, covering the same age ranges, was tested, and a subset of these was retested 7, 14, 21, and 28 years later. Further samples were added in 1970, 1977, 1984, and 1991. This remarkable data-collection process enabled Schaie to look at IQ changes over 7-, 14-, 21-, and 28-year intervals for several sets of participants, each from a slightly different cohort. Figure 3.5 graphs one set of cross-sectional comparisons made in 1977, as well as 14-year longitudinal results smoothed over the whole age range. The test involved in this case is a measure of global intelligence on which the average score is set at 50 points (equivalent to an IQ of 100 on most other tests).

You can see that the cross-sectional comparisons show a steady drop in IQ. But the longitudinal evidence suggests that overall intelligence test scores actually rise in early adulthood and then remain quite constant until perhaps age 60, when they begin to decline. Since this pattern has also been found by other researchers (e.g., Sands, Terry, & Meredith, 1989; Siegler, 1983), there is good support for the temptingly optimistic view that intellectual ability remains essentially stable through most of adulthood.

Crystallized and Fluid Intelligence Looking at different components of intellectual ability gives a clearer picture of change and stability across the adult years. Theorists have suggested several ways to subdivide intellectual tasks. However, the most influential of these theories has been Raymond Cattell and John Horn's distinction between crystallized intelligence and fluid intelligence (Cattell, 1963; Horn, 1982; Horn & Donaldson, 1980).

Crystallized intelligence depends heavily on education and experience. It consists of the set of skills and bits of knowledge that every adult learns as part of growing up in any given culture, such as vocabulary, the ability to read and understand the newspaper,

crystallized intelligence knowledge and judgment acquired through education and experience and the ability to evaluate experience. Technical skills you may learn for your job or your life—balancing a checkbook, using a computer, making change, finding the mayonnaise in the grocery store—also represent crystallized intelligence.

Fluid intelligence, in contrast, involves more "basic" abilities—it is the aspect of intelligence that depends more on the efficient functioning of the central nervous system and less on specific experience. A common measure of fluid intelligence is a "letter series test," in which a participant is given a series of letters (for example, A C F J O) and must figure out what letter should go next. This problem demands abstract reasoning rather than reasoning about known or everyday events. Most tests of memory also measure fluid intelligence, as do many tests measuring response speed and those measuring higher-level or abstract mathematical skills. Schaie's results, and the results of many other investigators, suggest that adults maintain crystallized intelligence throughout early and middle adulthood, but that fluid intelligence declines fairly steadily over adulthood, beginning at perhaps age 35 or 40 (Horn & Donaldson, 1980; Li et al., 2004; Schaie, 1994).

Do results like these mean that developmentalists must revise their generally optimistic conclusions about adult intelligence based on longitudinal studies of total IQ scores? On the face of it, yes: On some kinds of tests, adults appear to show some decline beginning as early as their 40s. But Schaie notes that even the decline in fluid intelligence skills, while statistically significant, may not result in psychologically significant loss until at least late middle age.

Some theorists suggest that psychologically or functionally relevant declines may show up even in early adulthood, when adults are faced with highly complex or difficult tasks—tasks that stretch the individual's skills to the limit—just as significant declines in physical skill show up in early adulthood among top athletes (Baltes, Dittmann-Kohli, & Dixon, 1984, 1986). One of the ironies, then, is that adults whose occupations require them to function regularly at intellectually more taxing levels are likely to become aware of some subtle decline in intellectual skills earlier in adulthood than adults whose life circumstances make less stringent intellectual demands—even though the former individuals may continue to function at very high absolute levels of skill throughout their early and middle years.

So where does this leave us in answering the question about intellectual maintenance or decline over adulthood? It seems safe to conclude, at least tentatively, that intellectual abilities show essentially no decline in early adulthood except at the very top levels of intellectual demand. In middle adulthood, though, declines on fluid intelligence abilities—those tasks that are thought to represent the efficiency of the basic physiological process—become evident (Salthouse, 1991). Indeed, the rate of decline on measures of fluid intelligence closely matches the rate of decline in total brain size, suggesting a possible direct link (Bigler, Johnson, Jackson, & Blatter, 1995).

fluid intelligence the aspect of intelligence that reflects fundamental biological processes and does not depend on specific experiences

Memory   The pattern of results from studies of memory ability generally follows the pattern found in studies of fluid intelligence. Memory skills remain stable during early adulthood, decline somewhat during middle adulthood, and decline more noticeably in late adulthood. For example, measures of short-term memory—recalling something after only a short time, such as a phone number you've just looked up in the phone book—generally show a drop with age.

Age differences become more pronounced for measures of long-term memory—memory for items stored for longer periods or permanently. Both the process of getting memories into this long-term storage (a process called *encoding* by memory theorists) and the process of retrieving them again seem to be impaired among older adults, as compared to young adults (Salthouse, 1991). Some studies suggest that declines in metamemory and metacognitive skills are responsible for these impairments (Salthouse, Atkinson, & Berish, 2003).

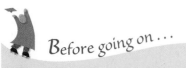

Before going on …

■ What are some theoretical proposals regarding a stage of cognitive development beyond Piaget's formal operational stage?

■ How do the concepts of crystallized and fluid intelligence help explain age-related changes in IQ scores?

Post-Secondary Education

In today's high-tech, global economy, **post-secondary education**—any kind of formal educational experience that follows high school—has become a necessity for virtually everyone (see Development in the Information Age). For some, post-secondary education may be a 1-year course of study that culminates in a certificate attesting to a marketable set of job skills, such as training in medical office management, For others, post-secondary education takes the form of enrollment in a 2- or 4-year college. At some point in their academic careers, most college students wonder whether all the hassles they experience are really worth the effort, as perhaps you may have. It should be somewhat heartening, then, to learn that college attendance is associated with a number of positive developmental outcomes.

DEVELOPMENTAL IMPACT

There is no longer any doubt about the economic value of post-secondary education, as Figure 3.6 suggests. Further, although some post-secondary education is better than none, people who succeed in completing a degree have a clear income advantage. Interestingly, although there are sex differences in the earnings of men and women at all educational levels, the advantage of post-secondary education seems to be as great for women as for men. (We will return to the issue of sex differences in compensation in Chapter 4.)

College graduates earn more than nongraduates for a variety of reasons (Pascarella & Terenzi, 1991). First, graduates get more promotions and are far less likely than nongraduates to be unemployed for prolonged periods of time. In fact, for minorities, a college education seems to outweigh the potential effects of racial prejudice in hiring decisions. Supervisors prefer minority college graduates to white nongraduates. In addition, college graduates have higher real and perceived status. This means that they are more likely than nongraduates to get high-status managerial, technical, and professional positions, and they are viewed by those who make hiring decisions as more

post-secondary education any kind of formal educational experience that follows high school

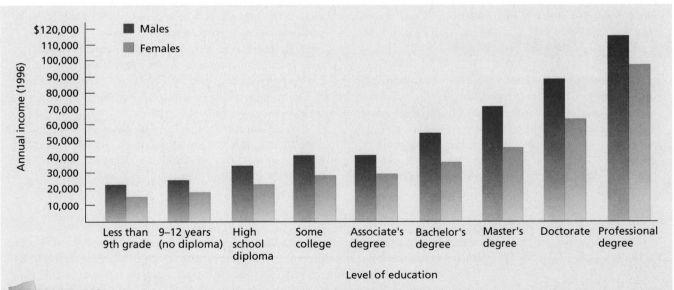

FIGURE 3.6

The association between education and income is clear. The longer a person stays in school, the more she earns. Degree attainment is strongly linked to income as well. The effect of education is similar for men and women, though men earn more at every level. (Source: U.S. Bureau of the Census, 1998.)

Development in the Information Age

Distance Learning

One of the most promising technological innovations in recent years has been the remarkable increase in the availability of opportunities for distance learning. Distance learning is any mode of instruction in which teacher and student are at a distance from each other. Information technologies—television, computers, and so on—serve as mediators between the two.

Of course, distance learning in the form of correspondence courses has been around for a long time. Likewise, colleges have offered classes via television for several decades. However, widespread access to the Internet has opened the door to a new era in distance learning. Thanks to the World Wide Web, students can enroll in institutions very far removed from their place of residence. They can also create a flexible schedule for themselves. For example, a student can download a professor's lecture at 4:00 a.m. if that is the hour that suits his particular needs. Thus, it isn't surprising that distance learning college students, especially nontraditional ones, report high levels of satisfaction with Web-based courses (Wernet, Olliges, & Delicath, 2000).

Most distance learning courses and programs are offered by traditional post-secondary institutions. In fact, as of the 2000–2001 academic year, more than 90% of colleges in the United States offered such courses (NCES, 2002). One of the nation's largest community college systems, Dallas Community College (DCC), enrolls more than 10,000 students in distance learning classes each semester (Carr, 2000). Many are Dallas residents, but some live very far from Dallas, even in foreign countries, and have discovered DCC's offerings via the Internet. They enroll, pay their tuition and fees, and buy their books via the Net as well.

The potential of the Internet to attract distance learning students and to allow them to register and pay for courses from a distance has led to the creation of new virtual colleges, or colleges that offer courses only on the Internet. Some are owned by nonprofit or governmental entities, but many are for-profit businesses. The stimulus for these new institutions is simple: North Americans currently spend more than $200 billion each

year on distance learning (Bulkeley, 1998). Thus, traditional colleges and universities see distance learning as an avenue to much-needed additional funds, and entrepreneurs see a potentially profitable market.

However, distance learning students drop out at much higher rates than do on-campus students (Carr, 2000). Most likely, the higher drop-out rate reflects the fact that nontraditional students enroll in distance courses at a higher rate than do traditional students. All the factors that make nontraditional students more likely to withdraw from on-campus courses probably affect their persistence in distance learning courses. In addition, weaker students may need the periodic contact with the instructor and other class members that on-campus courses can provide.

There are other concerns as well. Professors who teach online courses own the copyrights to all original materials they create and upload to their course Web sites. A copyright warning can be included, and professors can protect materials by requiring students to use passwords. Yet, once these documents are on the Net, they become widely accessible. Consequently, many professors shy away from putting time and effort into distance learning courses only to have their work illegally downloaded by others. This leads more institutions to increased use of prepackaged Internet courseware, which, in turn, leads to concerns about course quality and academic freedom.

Distance learning also raises new questions about fraud and cheating (Kennedy, Nowak, Raghuraman, Thomas, & Davis, 2000). When a professor requires distance students to participate in online chats, how does she know if a student has someone substitute for him? Moreover, concerns about fraud make it almost impossible to use conventional tests in online courses unless students can physically come to a testing center. Again, this raises questions about course quality and the equivalence of on-campus and online courses.

Predictions about the potential for distance learning to revolutionize post-secondary education are probably valid. However, as with other information-age innovations, there are costs as well as benefits.

desirable employees than are nongraduates. This finding raises the question of whether college graduates are really different from nongraduates or are simply perceived to be. However, longitudinal evidence suggests that the longer a person remains in college, the better her performance on Piaget's formal operational tasks and other measures of abstract reasoning (Lehman & Nisbett, 1990; Pascarella, 1999).

There is also evidence that, during their years of college enrollment, students' academic and vocational aspirations rise (Pascarella & Terenzi, 1991). For example, a young woman may enter college with the goal of becoming a biology teacher but graduate with the intention of going on to medical school. What seems critical to such decisions is that college-level classes allow students to make realistic assessments—for better or worse—of their academic abilities. Thus, another student may intend to be a doctor when he is a freshman but soon conclude that becoming a biology teacher is a more realistic, attainable goal, given his performance in college-level classes. Further, college attendance enhances students' internal locus of control and, as a result, helps them to understand how the daily behavioral choices they make shape their future lives (Wolfle & List, 2004).

In addition to cognitive and motivational benefits, going to college provides students with new socialization opportunities. Many students encounter people from racial or ethnic groups other than their own for the first time in college. Advances in moral and social reasoning, as well as increases in the capacity to empathize with others' feelings, are also linked to college attendance (Chickering & Reisser, 1993; Pascarella & Terenzi, 1991). However, the relationships among authoritative parenting, academic performance, and social adjustment you have read about so often in earlier chapters hold true for college students as well (Wintre & Yaffe, 2000). Thus, students' social experiences prior to entering post-secondary education seem to be critical to their ability to benefit fully from the college experience.

TRADITIONAL AND NONTRADITIONAL STUDENTS

Despite the advantages of a college degree, only about one-third of U.S. high school graduates become **traditional post-secondary students** by enrolling in college full-time directly after graduation (Horn & Premo, 1995). Certainly, economic factors are important to this decision; those who can afford to go to college full-time are more likely to do so. However, parental influence seems to be equally important. In one survey, researchers asked traditional post-secondary students who were in their first year of college why they had enrolled in college straight out of high school. Almost 40% responded that they enrolled out of a desire to conform to parental expectations (*Chronicle of Higher Education,* 1997).

Many traditional post-secondary students (14–16%) leave college at one time or another during their academic careers. But when they do, most are only temporarily college drop-outs. Thus, traditional post-secondary students have a very high graduation rate: Almost two-thirds obtain a college degree within 5 years (NCES, 1997).

More than 60% of college students are **nontraditional post-secondary students** (NCES, 2003). Researchers classify students as nontraditional if they (1) delay entering college more than 1 year after high school graduation, (2) are independent from parents, (3) are employed full-time while enrolled, (4) are enrolled part-time, (5) have one or more children, (6) possess a GED rather than a high school diploma, or (7) are single parents.

Clearly, many of these variables apply to traditional students as well. To clarify traditional and nontraditional status, researchers classify students as *minimally, moderately,* or *highly* nontraditional, based on the number of these factors present in their lives. As you can see from Figure 3.7 (page 82), there is a clear association between traditional or nontraditional status and college graduation. The more nontraditional factors a student possesses, the less likely he is to graduate from college.

A majority of traditional post-secondary students are likely to attain their educational objective, whether they are pursuing a bachelor's degree, an associate's degree, or a vocational certificate. However, nontraditional post-secondary students are almost twice as likely to complete their program of study when pursuing a vocational certificate as when working toward either an associate's or a bachelor's degree (NCES, 1997). About 54% succeed in getting a certificate, but only 26% and 31%, respectively, reach their goals of obtaining associate's and bachelor's degrees. Perhaps this is because nontraditional vocational students set more realistic goals for themselves. Alternatively, vocational programs may do a better job of supporting nontraditional students than academically oriented associate's and bachelor's degree programs.

Surveys of nontraditional students suggest that the supportiveness of an educational institution can be critical to helping then manage the conflicting demands of school, family, and work (Kirby, Biever, Martinez, & Gomez, 2004). These findings point

(Photo: © Royalty Free/CORBIS)

College attendance is associated with developmental advances in both the cognitive and social domains.

traditional post-secondary student a student who attends college full-time immediately after graduating from high school

nontraditional post-secondary student a student who either attends college part-time or delays enrollment after high school graduation

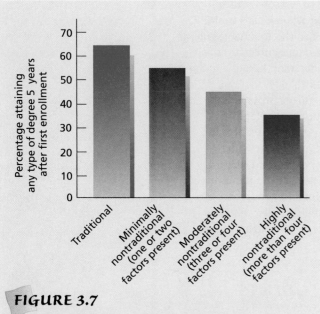

FIGURE 3.7

The greater the number of nontraditional factors present in a student's life, the less likely she is to complete a vocational certificate or college degree. Nontraditional factors include delayed entry into school, being independent from one's family; working full-time and/or attending school part-time; having one or more children, being a single parent, and having a GED rather than a high school diploma. (Source: NCES, 1997.)

to another important difference between traditional and nontraditional post-secondary students. Those who go directly from high school to college are concentrated in 4-year institutions, while the majority of nontraditional students attend 2-year colleges (NCES, 1997). Thus, graduation rates may vary across the two groups not only because of variables on which the students themselves differ but also because there are important differences between 2- and 4-year colleges. For example, 4-year institutions are more likely to have counseling centers where students can obtain career guidance and help with personal problems. Likewise, students at 4-year schools, especially those who live on campus, spend more time socializing with one another. Thus, they have a greater opportunity to establish social networks on which they can rely for support in times of difficulty. In contrast, students at 2-year colleges typically do not socialize with or even see one another outside of class. Thus, students in 4-year college settings may be better supported both formally and informally by the institutions they attend.

Fortunately, officials at 2-year colleges have begun to recognize the need for greater student support. Many are therefore developing innovative programs—such as on-campus child care—based on students' needs. Likewise, officials are attempting to provide greater financial and facility support for student organizations so that students will have more opportunities for social interaction.

STUDENTS WITH DISABILITIES

CRITICAL THINKING ?

Suppose a 30-year-old blue-collar worker who is married with two children and who has never been past high school decides to go to college. What obstacles will she have to overcome to succeed in earning a degree? How comfortable would she feel at the institution you are attending?

Thanks to a federal law passed by the U.S. Congress in 1990, the Americans with Disabilities Act, many students with disabilities have access to post-secondary education. Colleges are now required to provide them with the same kinds of modifications provided by special education services in the public school system. Thus, blind students are provided with readers and Braille textbooks, hearing-impaired students are accompanied by sign language interpreters when they attend class, and wheelchair-bound students are guaranteed that classroom doors will be wide enough to allow them to enter. Moreover, many high schools have created partnerships with community colleges to provide transitional programs for students with disabilities that help them acquire the study techniques and life management skills essential for success in college (Hart, Mele-McCarthy, Pasternack, Zimbrick, & Parker, 2004; Pearman, Elliot, & Aborn, 2004). Consequently, students with disabilities now make up about 9% of the college population in the United States (NCES, 2003).

Although it is still too early to draw firm conclusions from research on college students with disabilities, recent studies contain some hints about how such students fare. For example, one reason for recent increases in college enrollment among students with disabilities is their belief that the required instructional modifications make it possible for them to compete academically with other students. The most common modification for such students is extended time for taking tests (Ofiesh, Hughes, & Scott, 2004). Research suggests that, with extended time, students with disabilities are able to approach or meet the same standards of academic performance required of other students in college classes (Alster, 1997). Still, students with disabilities usually receive lower course grades than their non-disabled peers (Cosden & McNamara, 1997).

Research also suggests that students with disabilities perceive the college environment to be somewhat inhospitable to them. Although they perceive their peers to be accepting and supportive, many students with disabilities believe that college faculty do not fully accept them (Beilke & Yssel, 1999; Cosden & McNamara, 1997). They say that most professors are willing to comply with classroom modifications but have negative attitudes toward the required modifications and the students themselves.

GENDER AND THE COLLEGE EXPERIENCE

A slight majority of college students are female, and women have higher graduation rates than men at all degree levels and in both traditional and nontraditional post-secondary groups (NCES, 1997). Further, females maintain their graduation advantage over males even when they must overcome many obstacles associated with nontraditional status, such as single parenthood (Benshoff & Lewis, 1993).

Paradoxically, women's college entrance examination scores, especially in math, tend to be lower than men's. As a result, more males are admitted to selective universities. In addition, more men are accepted into honors programs. Thus, the different graduation rates of males and females are unlikely to be attributable to sex differences in intellectual ability. Rather, college men and women differ in attitudes and behavior in ways that significantly affect the likelihood of graduation (Noldon & Sedlacek, 1998).

In contrast to studies of sex bias at lower educational levels, studies in college classrooms have produced mixed results (Brady & Eisler, 1999). Some studies suggest that professors take male students more seriously than female students. Others seem to indicate that women feel less confident and more inhibited in their interactions with college faculty. Yet the most consistent finding is that there appear to be few, if any, overt indicators of sex bias in college classrooms (Brady & Eisler, 1999). Thus, one reason for the tendency of females to be more successful in college may be that they perceive the post-secondary environment as more intellectually supportive than the institutions they attended when they were younger.

However, intellectually talented women continue to be somewhat reluctant to pursue difficult majors (Jacobs et al., 1998). For the most part, this finding seems to be restricted to women whose talents are in science and mathematics. It seems that many young women, even those who are very capable, have doubts about their ability to succeed in such fields. However, when a wider array of interests and talents is taken into account, there seem to be few consistent sex differences in educational aspirations or academic self-concept among intellectually gifted college students (Achter, Lubinski, Benbow, & Eftekhari-Sanjani, 1999).

When research reveals sex differences in study strategies, they usually favor the females. For example, college women in both the United States and Europe use a greater number of study techniques than do men (Braten & Olaussen, 1998). By contrast, college men are more likely to cheat (Thorpe, Pittenger, & Reed, 1999). Moreover, the kinds of study strategies women use are those that are most likely to lead to long-term retention of information (Pearsall, Skipper, & Mintzes, 1997). Consequently, it isn't surprising that a recent study of gender differences in comprehensive final examination performance among Irish medical school students revealed that women significantly outscored men in several areas (McDonough, Horgan, Codd, & Casey, 2000). In areas in which women did not outscore men, they achieved equally high scores.

Women also appear to adapt easily to the demands of new educational experiences. For example, women outperform men in distance learning classes. They also usually begin with lower levels of computer skills than men. However, when they enroll in classes that require such skills, they learn them very quickly and exhibit levels of performance equal to those of men whose initial skill levels were higher (Clawson & Choate, 1999).

Behaviors outside the classroom may matter as well. For example, binge drinking is more prevalent among college men than women. Similarly, men seem to be more influenced by peer behavior than women do. If a man is with a group of men who are drinking, he is likely to do so as well. Women are more likely to make individual decisions about behaviors such as alcohol use (Senchak, Leonard, & Greene, 1998).

RACE AND THE COLLEGE EXPERIENCE

One longitudinal study involving several thousand college students found that most minority groups have lower drop-out rates than whites, even though minority college students typically possess a greater number of nontraditional factors (NCES, 1997). Researchers at the National Center for Educational Statistics found that 17% of Native Americans, 24% of Asian Americans, and 28% of Hispanic Americans, compared to 35% of whites, dropped out and did not return to college during the study's 5-year span. The study also found the drop-out rate of African American students to be 44%.

One approach to explaining the African American students' higher drop-out rates is to determine how they are similar to and different from the students in other groups. For example, African American high school students and beginning college students have educational and career aspirations that are similar to those of students in other groups (Brown, 1997). In addition, their goals seem to be as carefully and realistically formulated as those of students of other races. However, African American students are more likely than students of other races or ethnicities to perceive themselves as not fitting in, not really being a part of the college community (Gossett, Cuyjet, & Cockriel, 1998). In addition, for many African American students, the college campus is the first environment in which they personally experience overt expressions of racism. For example, an African American student may be assumed to be a janitorial employee by a faculty member or fellow student. Thus, African American students often perceive the college environment as hostile and cite personal experiences with overt racism among their reasons for dropping out (Schwitzer, Griffin, Ancie, & Thomas, 1999; Zea, Reisen, Bell, & Caplan, 1997).

A different approach is to find out how African American college students who obtain degrees differ from those who drop out. For example, a strong sense of racial identity is associated with persistence and academic performance in college for African American students (Rowley, 2000; Sellers, Chavous, & Cooke, 1998). Research also suggests that students who participate in programs aimed at helping minority students stay in college are more likely to graduate and to gain admission to professional and graduate schools than those who do not participate (Gary, Kling, & Dodds, 2004; Hesser, Cregler, & Lewis, 1998).

Researchers have also examined differences between African American students who attend predominantly white colleges and those who enroll in historically black institutions. One advantage of the latter institutions for students may be that most have a larger proportion of black faculty members with whom students can identify and to whom they feel comfortable expressing themselves. In fact, students who attend historically black schools view African American professors very positively and value their relationships with them (Chism & Satcher, 1998).

Interestingly, though, African American females at predominantly white schools appear to have higher levels of self-esteem than peers at historically black institutions (Poindexter-Cameron & Robinson, 1997). Still, cognitive development across the college years is strongly associated with the racial composition of the college for both male and female African American students. Those who attend historically black colleges show more improvement across a variety of cognitive measures, such as tests of reading comprehension, than do those who attend predominantly white schools (Flowers & Pascarella, 1999).

Before going on . . .

■ List some of the ways in which college attendance affects individual development.

■ How do traditional and nontraditional post-secondary students differ?

■ What does research suggest about the experiences of college students with disabilities?

■ How is the college experience different for men and women?

■ How does race affect the college experiences of African Americans?

Summary

Physical Functioning

- It is important to distinguish between the unavoidable effects of primary aging and the preventable consequences of secondary aging.
- The brain reaches a stable size and weight in early adulthood. There is strong evidence that at least one spurt in brain development occurs between ages 17 and 21. Neuropsychologists hypothesize that a second spurt occurs in the mid- to late 20s. Sex differences are apparent in the adult brain, although their significance has yet to be established.
- It is clear that adults are at their peak both physically and cognitively between ages 20 and 40. In these years, a person has more muscle tissue, more calcium in the bones, better sensory acuity, greater aerobic capacity, and a more efficient immune system.

Health and Wellness

- In contrast to other diseases, sexually transmitted diseases are more common among young adults than among older adults.
- The rate of loss of physical and cognitive abilities varies widely across individuals. Some of this difference seems to be explained by varying health habits. Adults with good health habits have lower risk of death and disease at any age.
- Social support and a sense of personal control also affect rates of disease and death, especially in the face of stress.
- Intimate partner abuse is a significant global health problem. Causal factors include cultural beliefs about gender roles, as well as personal variables such as alcohol and drug use.
- Rates of mental illness are higher in early adulthood than in middle adulthood; young adults are more likely to be depressed, anxious, or lonely than are the middle-aged. Early adulthood is the period during which personality disorders and schizophrenia are usually diagnosed.

Cognitive Changes

- There may be a change in cognitive structure in adult life, and theorists have suggested that cognitive development goes beyond Piaget's formal operational stage.
- Some studies of measures of intelligence show a decline with age, but the decline occurs quite late for well-exercised abilities (crystallized abilities) such as recall of vocabulary, everyday memory use, and normal problem solving. A measurable decline occurs earlier for so-called fluid abilities. Memory differences between younger and older adults are usually restricted to tasks involving speed of processing.

Post-Secondary Education

- Post-secondary education has beneficial effects on both cognitive and social development in addition to being associated with higher income.
- Nontraditional post-secondary students are more likely to obtain vocational certificates than bachelor's or associate's degrees.
- There is not yet enough research on students with disabilities to draw firm conclusions about their college experiences, but studies suggest that, with certain accommodations, they can be just as successful in college as students who do not have disabilities.
- Female students seem to have a number of important advantages over male students, including a higher graduation rate. However, many women lack confidence in their academic abilities and are reluctant to enter traditionally male occupations.
- African American students are less likely to complete post-secondary programs than other groups, perhaps because they perceive white-dominated educational environments as hostile.

Key Terms

crystallized intelligence (p. 77)
dialectical thought (p. 76)
fluid intelligence (p. 78)
intimate partner abuse (p. 70)
limbic system (p. 59)
maximum oxygen uptake (VO_2 max) (p. 61)

nontraditional post-secondary student (p. 81)
pelvic inflammatory disease (p. 66)
personality disorder (p. 74)
phobia (p. 73)
post-secondary education (p. 79)
primary aging (p. 58)

schizophrenia (p. 74)
secondary aging (p. 58)
self-efficacy (p. 69)
sexual violence (p. 72)
traditional post-secondary student (p. 81)

Social and Personality Development in Early Adulthood

In early adulthood, individuals turn away from the preoccupation with self-definition that is characteristic of adolescence and take on a series of roles that involve new relationships with other people.

© Richard T. Nowitz/CORBIS

For example, from their wedding day forward, newlyweds are known both as individuals and as spouses. The bride is also now a daughter-in-law as well as a daughter; the groom has become a son-in-law in addition to continuing to be his parents' son. It is also likely that the two young adults have already taken on occupational roles, and they may become parents within a few years.

The timing and content of the various adult roles obviously differ from one culture to another, from one cohort to another, and even from one individual to another. For example, the median age for first marriage among women in the United States rose from 21 in 1970 to 25 in 2000—a very large change in a fairly short span of years (U.S. Bureau of the Census, 2000). Marriage remains an important milestone of the young adult years, as evidenced by the fact that the percentage of women who have never married drops from 70% among 20-year-old females to 14% among 35- to 39-year-old females; the percentage of men who have never married drops from 85% to 21% for the same ages (U.S. Bureau of the Census, 2000). In addition, most people become parents for the first time in early adulthood. Thus, regardless of variations in timing, adults' social connections become far more complex between the ages of 20 and 40—through marriage, divorce, parenthood, and career development.

In this chapter you will learn about how these role transitions affect young adults' development. As you read, keep the following questions in mind:

- How do theorists view social and personality development in early adulthood?
- How do young adults go about establishing intimate relationships?
- How do intimate relationships shape young adults' lives?
- What factors contribute to career choice, job satisfaction, and sex differences in work patterns?

Theories of Social and Personality Development

Social scientists have not done very well at devising theories to explain lovely romantic moments like these.

intimacy versus isolation
Erikson's early adulthood stage, in which an individual must find a life partner or supportive friends in order to avoid social isolation

intimacy the capacity to engage in a supportive, affectionate relationship without losing one's own sense of self

life structure in Levinson's theory, the underlying pattern or design of a person's life at a given time, which includes roles, relationships, and behavior patterns

(Photo: © Timothy Shonnard/Getty Images/Stone)

(Photo: © David Young-Wolff/PhotoEdit)

Psychoanalytic theories view adult development, like development at younger ages, as a result of a struggle between a person's inner thoughts, feelings, and motives and society's demands. Other perspectives provide different views of this period. Integrating ideas from all of them allows us to better understand early adult development.

ERIKSON'S STAGE OF INTIMACY VERSUS ISOLATION

For Erikson, the central crisis of early adulthood is **intimacy versus isolation.** The young adult must find a life partner, someone outside her own family with whom she can share her life, or face the prospect of being isolated from society. More specifically, **intimacy** is the capacity to engage in a supportive, affectionate relationship without losing one's own sense of self. Intimate partners can share their views and feelings with each other without fearing that the relationship will end. They can also allow each other some degree of independence without feeling threatened.

As you might suspect, successful resolution of the intimacy versus isolation stage depends on a good resolution of the identity versus role confusion crisis. Erikson predicted that individuals who reached early adulthood without having established a sense of identity would be incapable of intimacy. That is, such young adults would be, in a sense, predestined to social isolation.

Still, a poor sense of identity is only one barrier to intimacy. Misunderstandings stemming from sex differences in styles of interaction can also get in the way. To women, intimacy is bound up with self-disclosure. Thus, women who are involved with a partner who does not reveal much that is personal perceive the relationship as lacking in intimacy. However, most men don't see self-disclosure as essential to intimacy. Consequently, many men are satisfied with relationships that their female partners see as inadequate.

Though many people involved in intimate relationships wish their relationships were better, most adults succeed in establishing some kind of close relationship. Not everyone marries, of course, but many adults develop affectionate, long-lasting friendships that are significant sources of support for them and may, in some cases, serve the same functions as having an intimate life partner.

LEVINSON'S LIFE STRUCTURES

Levinson's concept of *life structure* represents a different approach to adult development (Levinson, 1978, 1990). A **life structure** includes all the roles an individual occupies, all of his or her relationships, and the conflicts and balance that exist among them. Figure 4.1 illustrates how life structures change over the course of adulthood.

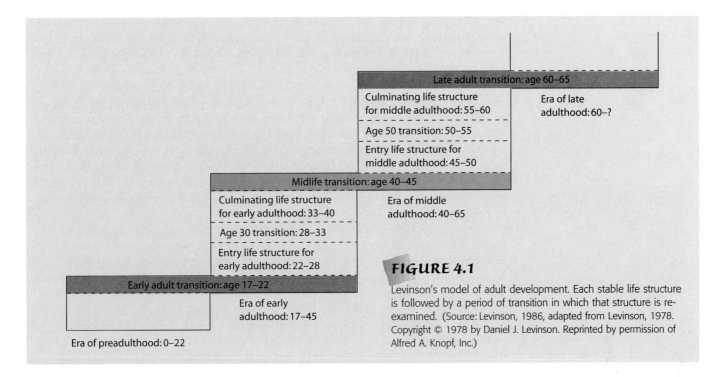

FIGURE 4.1

Levinson's model of adult development. Each stable life structure is followed by a period of transition in which that structure is re-examined. (Source: Levinson, 1986, adapted from Levinson, 1978. Copyright © 1978 by Daniel J. Levinson. Reprinted by permission of Alfred A. Knopf, Inc.)

Like Erikson, Levinson theorized that each of these periods presents adults with new developmental tasks and conflicts. He believed that individuals respond psychologically to these tasks and conflicts by creating new life structures. Consequently, adults cycle through periods of stability and instability.

As adults enter a period in which a new life structure is required, there is a period of adjustment, which Levinson called the *novice* phase. In the *mid-era* phase, adults become more competent at meeting the new challenges through reassessment and reorganization of the life structure they created during the novice phase. Stability returns in the *culmination* phase, when adults have succeeded in creating a life structure that allows them to manage the demands of the new developmental challenges with more confidence and less distress.

For example, marriage requires a new life structure. Even if the newlyweds have known each other for a very long time or have been living together, they have not known each other in the roles of husband and wife. Moreover, they have never had in-laws. So, young adults who marry acquire a whole new set of relationships. At the same time, they face many new day-to-day, practical issues such as how finances will be managed, how housekeeping chores will be done, and whose family they will visit on which holidays. As Levinson's theory predicts, newlyweds usually go through a period of adjustment, during which they experience more conflict than before the wedding, and after which things are much calmer. The calm comes, as Levinson would put it, when each spouse has achieved a new life structure that is adapted to the demands of marriage.

Both Erikson and Levinson regard formation of an intimate relationship with another adult as a central developmental task of early adulthood. However, neither addresses the process of just how an adult goes about finding a suitable partner. However, other theorists focus specifically on the mating process.

CRITICAL THINKING

Have you experienced periods of loneliness? If so, how do you think the state of your love life at the time contributed to your feelings?

EVOLUTIONARY THEORY AND MATE SELECTION

As you should remember from Chapter 2, evolutionary explanations of behavior focus on survival value. Heterosexual relationships ensure the survival of the species, of course, because they are the context in which conception takes place. However, when choosing a mate, heterosexuals don't simply look for someone of the opposite sex.

Instead, mating is a selective process, and evolutionary theorists often cite research on sex differences in mate preferences and mating behavior in support of their views.

Cross-cultural studies conducted over a period of several decades suggest that men prefer physically attractive, younger women, while women look for men whose socio-economic status is higher than their own, who offer earning potential and stability (Buss, 1999; Schmidt, Shackelford, & Buss, 2001). Moreover, in the short run, men appear to be willing to lower their standards when forced to choose between a partner who meets their standards and no partner at all. Thus, availability strongly influences men's selection of short-term mates. In contrast, women seem to have little interest in short-term mating unless it will lead to a beneficial long-term relationship. For example, evolutionary theorists hypothesize that *mate-switching*—using an affair to lead to a long-term relationship with a higher-status man—is an important motive in women's extramarital affairs.

The reasons behind men's and women's divergent mating goals are explained by **parental investment theory** (Trivers, 1972). This theory proposes that men value health and availability in their mates and are less selective because their minimum investment in parenting offspring—a single act of sexual intercourse—requires only a few minutes. In contrast, women's minimum investment in childbearing involves nurturing an unborn child in their own body for 9 months as well as enduring the potentially physically traumatic experience of giving birth. Given their minimum investments, men seek to maximize the likelihood of survival of the species by maximizing the number of their offspring; women seek to minimize the number of their offspring because their investment is so much greater.

Further, evolutionary theorists argue that both men and women realize that a truly adaptive approach to child-rearing requires much more than a minimum investment (Buss, 1999). Human offspring cannot raise themselves. Therefore, men value health and youth in their mates not only because these traits suggest fertility but also because a young, healthy woman is likely to live long enough to raise the children. Moreover, men are willing to abandon their focus on short-term mating in order to gain continuing and exclusive sexual access to a desirable mate through committed, long-term relationships such as marriage. Making such a commitment ensures that any offspring the woman produces will be the man's own and that the children will have a mother to raise them.

Similarly, women realize that to be able to nurture children to adulthood, they must have an economic provider so that they will be able to invest the time needed to raise offspring. Consequently, they look for men who seem to be capable of fulfilling these requirements. Further, women's mating behavior is affected by the higher costs they bear if a selected mate fails to fulfill expectations. Faced with the prospect of having to provide children with both economic support and physical nurturing if a mate fails to "bring home the bacon," women choose mates more carefully and more slowly than men; they prefer not to engage in sexual intercourse until they have tested a man's trustworthiness and reliability (Buss & Schmitt, 1993).

As mentioned above, consistent sex differences in mate preferences and mating behavior have been found across many cultures, and evolutionary theorists suggest that this cross-cultural consistency is strong evidence for a genetic basis for the behavior. However, these claims take us back to the basic nature-versus-nurture arguments we have examined so many times before. Certainly, these sex differences are consistent, but they could be the result of variations in gender roles that are passed on within cultures.

SOCIAL ROLE THEORY AND MATE SELECTION

Social role theory provides a different perspective on sex differences in mating (Eagly & Wood, 1999). According to this view, such sex differences are adaptations to gender roles that result from present-day social realities rather than from natural selection pressures that arose in a bygone evolutionary era. Social role theorists point out that

parental investment theory the theory that sex differences in mate preferences and mating behavior are based on the different amounts of time and effort men and women must invest in child-rearing

social role theory the idea that sex differences in mate preferences and mating behavior are adaptations to gender roles

gender-based divisions of labor in child-rearing are just as consistent across cultures as sex differences in mating. Men look for women who can perform domestic duties (healthy and young), and women look for men who will be good economic providers (higher socioeconomic status and good earning potential).

For example, one team of researchers found that college-educated women with high earning potential prefer to date and marry men whose income potential is higher than their own (Wiederman & Allgeier, 1992). In fact, the more a woman expects to earn herself, the higher are her income requirements in a prospective mate. This study was widely cited by evolutionary theorists as supporting their view that such preferences are genetic and are not influenced by cultural conditions.

However, a different perspective on the same study, proposed by social role theorists, led to a different conclusion (Eagly & Wood, 1999). These theorists suggest that today's high-income women desire to have and raise children almost as much as earlier generations of women. What is different about them, compared to their mothers and grandmothers, is that they want to be able to both pursue a career and raise a family. To meet both goals, most women plan to take time out from their careers to have and raise children (a pattern you will read more about later in this chapter). To be able to do so without lowering their standard of living substantially, these women require a mate who can earn a lot of money. Thus, social role theorists say, such research findings can be explained by social role theory just as well as by evolutionary theory.

In addition, social role theorists point out that high-income women desire high-income husbands because members of both sexes prefer mates who are like themselves. People are drawn to those who are similar in age, education, social class, ethnic group membership, religion, attitudes, interests, and temperament. Sociologists refer to this tendency as **assortative mating,** or **homogamy.** Further, partnerships based on homogamy are much more likely to endure than are those in which the partners differ markedly (Murstein, 1986).

In addition to assortative mating, choosing a partner appears to involve some kind of exchange process. Each individual has certain assets to offer to a potential mate. Exchange theorists argue that people try for the best bargain, or the best exchange, they can manage (Edwards, 1969). According to this model, women frequently exchange their sexual and domestic services for the economic support offered by a man (Schoen & Wooldredge, 1989). However, social role theorists suggest that, over the past few decades, women have improved their income-producing prospects considerably. As a result, if social role theory is correct, women today should be less concerned about a potential mate's earning potential than women were in the past.

To test this hypothesis, social role theorists reanalyzed a very large set of cross-cultural data, a data set produced and interpreted by evolutionary psychologist David Buss in support of parental investment theory (Buss et al., 1990). In their reanalysis, advocates of social role theory found that both men's and women's mate preferences changed as women gained economic power (Eagly & Wood, 1999): Women's emphasis on potential mates' earning power declined, and men's focus on potential mates' domestics skills decreased.

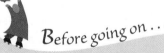

Before going on . . .

■ What did Erikson mean when he described early adulthood as a crisis of intimacy versus isolation?

■ What is a life structure? Why and how does it change?

■ What types of research findings do evolutionary theorists cite to support their views on mate selection?

■ How can social role theory contribute to an understanding of partner selection?

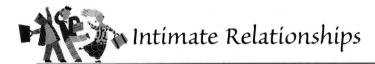

Intimate Relationships

Theories notwithstanding, everyday observations of adults reveal that an intimate relationship forms the secure base from which most young adults move out into the adult world. Census reports show that approximately 60% of adults in the United States share their homes with an intimate partner (U.S. Bureau of the Census, 2003b). In 91% of such households, the couple are married. In households headed by unmarried

assortative mating (homogamy) sociologists' term for the tendency to mate with someone who has traits similar to one's own

couples, 89% are opposite-sex partners and 11% are of the same sex. In addition, single-hood is a growing trend. In 1970, only 5.4% of females and 7.2% of males 35 to 39 years old in the United States had never been married. By 1998, these figures had risen to 14% of females and 22% of males in this age group (U.S. Bureau of the Census, 2003a). Thus, behavioral scientists have had to expand research on intimacy to include all of these variations.

MARRIAGE

Are you surprised to learn that, in the United States, nearly 300,000 couples get married every month and there are 2.4 million formal weddings every year (Hallmark Corporation, 2004; Sutton & Munson, 2004)? Clearly, the institution of marriage is alive and well (see No Easy Answers). Moreover, most marriages endure. The often-quoted statistic of a 50% divorce rate is derived from dividing the number of marriages each year by the number of divorces. For instance, in 2002, 8 in every 1,000 adults in the United States married, while 4 in every 1,000 divorced (U.S. Bureau of the Census, 2003a). Like cross-sectional studies, though, such statistics often reflect cohort differences. Longitudinal studies of marital duration suggest that only about 20% of marriages end in divorce (U.S. Bureau of the Census, 1997). Moreover, after a couple have been married for 8 years, the probability that they will divorce declines to nearly zero.

Not only is marriage an enduring institution—it is associated with a number of important health benefits. Married adults are happier and healthier, live longer, and have lower rates of a variety of psychiatric problems than do adults without committed partners, findings that are discussed further in the Research Report (page 95) (Coombs, 1991; Glenn & Weaver, 1988; Lee, Seccombe, & Shehan, 1991; Ross, 1995; Sorlie, Backlund, & Keller, 1995). Clearly, though, not all marriages are happy ones. What are the factors that contribute to marital satisfaction?

Relationship Quality   Many powerful influences on marital success are in place long before a marriage even begins. Each partner brings to the relationship certain skills, resources, and traits that affect the emerging partnership system. The personality characteristics of the partners seem to be especially important (Arrindell & Luteijn, 2000; Haring, Hewitt, & Flett, 2003). For example, a high degree of neuroticism in one or both partners usually leads to dissatisfaction and instability in the relationship (Robins, Caspi, & Moffitt, 2000). Likewise, attitudes toward divorce affect marital stability. Couples who have favorable attitudes are less likely to be satisfied with their marriages than those who view divorce as highly undesirable (Amato & Rogers, 1999).

Another important factor appears to be the security of each partner's attachment to his or her family of origin. Theorists speculate that the parental attachment relationship contributes to the construction of an internal model of intimate relationships that children bring with them into adulthood and into their marriages (e.g., Crowell & Waters, 1995; Feeney, 1994; Fuller & Fincham, 1995; Hazan & Shaver, 1987; Owens et al., 1995; Rothbard & Shaver, 1994). Research supports this hypothesis. For example, one study found that nearly two-thirds of a sample of about-to-be-married young people showed the same attachment category (secure, dismissing, or preoccupied) when they described their love relationship as when they described their relationship with their parents (Owens et al., 1995). However, once the marriage takes place, spouses must know when and how to let go of their families of origin in favor of the new family they are in the process of establishing. Research shows that, among newly-weds, the frequency of arguments about in-laws is exceeded only by the frequency of disagreements about financial matters (Oggins, 2003).

Emotional affection contributes to relationship quality as well. The most compelling theory of romantic love comes from Robert Sternberg, who argues that love has three key components: (1) *intimacy,* which includes feelings that promote closeness

Avoiding Bridal Stress Disorder

Imagine that you just got engaged to be married and shared the news with your best friend. What kinds of questions do you think your friend would ask about your future plans? The answer may depend on whether you are male or female. If you are female (and so is your best friend), the questions are likely to focus on the characteristics of your wedding ceremony. The most recent studies show that weddings continue to be a feminine domain, with future brides far more concerned about the particulars of the event than future grooms are (Knox, Zusman, McGinty, & Abowitz, 2003).

(Photo: © Allan Hall Photography. Used with permission.)

Marriage rituals, of course, have been an integral part of societies all over the world for thousands of years. The difference between the modern-day version and those that were common in earlier days is one of degree. Until fairly recently, elaborate weddings were reserved for the wealthy. However, according to the largest manufacturer of wedding stationery in the United States, the Hallmark Corporation (2004), the *average* formal wedding now costs about $20,000 and takes place after 7–12 months planning.

With so much money at stake and with the potential for hurt feelings on the part of acquaintances who aren't invited to the reception or cousins who aren't asked to be bridesmaids, not to mention concerns about how she will look in a wedding gown, wedding planning can be a stressful experience for the bride-to-be. Consequently, there are now dozens of books and several Internet sites devoted to advice on how to reduce wedding-related stress. One such site even purports to address prevention of "bridal stress disorder" (see http://www.uniquethemeweddings.com).

It's doubtful that the stresses associated with wedding planning constitute an actual psychological disorder, but these stresses, like many others in life, can significantly diminish an individual's quality of life. Psychological research

says that the best approach to managing wedding-related stress is one that balances *problem-focused coping* and *emotion-focused coping* (Folkman & Lazarus, 1980). Problem-focused coping involves managing the actual source of stress. When brides-to-be set firm budget guidelines for themselves and research ways to limit spending in order to conform to them, they are engaging in this kind of coping. Emotion-focused coping has to do with managing emotional responses to current or potential stressors. A bride-to-be who treats herself to a massage in the midst of the wedding-planning frenzy is using emotion-focused coping. Emotion-focused coping also comes into play as brides-to-be remember that stress-inducing events such as bridal showers are a part of their own deliberate choice to have a formal wedding (Montemurro, 2002). Similarly, brides who temper their emotional responses to a groom's apathy about wedding details by acknowledging that such issues are more important to them than to their fiancé are likely to experience less stress (Knox, Zusman, McGinty, & Abowitz, 2003).

Brides-to-be who want to reduce their stress levels should also keep in mind that merchants whose businesses focus exclusively on weddings, such as bridal gown boutiques, train their salespeople to present themselves as professionals who are willing to take control of every aspect of wedding planning (Corrado, 2002). Researchers have found that many brides-to-be succumb to this sales strategy and allow the standards of such wedding-planning "experts" to supercede their own values and goals. While it might seem that letting someone else take over would reduce stress, it may actually increase stress. Research on stress management suggests that maintaining a sense of personal control is one of the most important principles of stress reduction (Rodin & Salovey, 1989). Thus, future brides would be well advised to look upon wedding professionals as important sources of information but to be certain that their own standards remain the driving force behind their wedding plans.

Finally, most engaged couples nowadays enroll in wedding gift registries so that those who want to give them gifts will know what kinds of dishes, sheets, and other household items they want. However, the best gift for a couple to request might be a new service, offered by many marital therapists, called *marriage insurance*—a series of post-wedding counseling sessions that help couples cope with the transition to marriage (Thomas, 2003). Including on their list such a gift may help future brides remember that a beautiful wedding doesn't ensure a happy marriage. This kind of long-term perspective may help the bride-to-be focus less on the details of the wedding day and more on building a relationship with her partner that will last a lifetime.

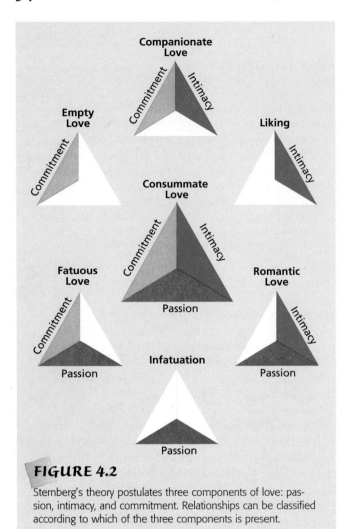

FIGURE 4.2

Sternberg's theory postulates three components of love: passion, intimacy, and commitment. Relationships can be classified according to which of the three components is present.

and connectedness; (2) *passion,* which includes a feeling of intense longing for union with the other person, including sexual union; and (3) *commitment to a particular other,* often over a long period of time (Sternberg, 1987). When these three components are combined in all possible ways, you end up with the seven subvarieties of love listed in Figure 4.2. Sternberg's theory suggests that the characteristics of the emotional bond that holds a couple together influence the unique pattern of interaction that develops in each intimate relationship.

How a couple manage conflict is also an important predictor of relationship quality. Drawing on a large body of research, psychologists have identified three quite different types of stable, or enduring, marriages (Gottman, 1994b). **Validating couples** have disagreements, but the disagreements rarely escalate. Partners express mutual respect, even when they disagree, and listen well to each other. **Volatile couples** squabble a lot, disagree, and don't listen to each other very well when they argue. But they still have more positive than negative encounters, showing high levels of laughter and affection. **Avoidant couples,** called "conflict minimizers," don't try to persuade each other; they simply agree to disagree, without apparent rancor, a pattern sometimes described as "devitalized."

Similarly, psychologists find two types of unsuccessful marriages. Like volatile couples, **hostile/engaged couples,** have frequent hot arguments, but they lack the balancing effect of humor and affection. **Hostile/detached couples** fight regularly (although the arguments tend to be brief), rarely look at each other, and lack affection and support. In both unsuccessful types, the ratio of negative to positive encounters gets out of balance, and the marriage spirals downward toward dissolution.

validating couples partners who express mutual respect, even in disagreements, and are good listeners

volatile couples partners who argue a lot and don't listen well, but still have more positive than negative interactions

avoidant couples partners who agree to disagree and who minimize conflict by avoiding each other

hostile/engaged couples partners who have frequent arguments and lack the balancing effect of humor and affection

hostile/detached couples partners who fight regularly, rarely look at each other and lack affection and support

Divorce For couples whose marriages end in divorce, the experience is often one of the most stressful of their entire lives. Not surprisingly, divorce is associated with increases in both physical and emotional illness. Recently separated or divorced adults have more automobile accidents, are more likely to commit suicide, lose more days at work because of illness, and are more likely to become depressed (Bloom, White, & Asher, 1979; Menaghan & Lieberman, 1986; Stack, 1992a, 1992b; Stack & Wasserman, 1993). They also report strong feelings of failure and a loss of self-esteem, as well as loneliness (Chase-Lansdale & Hetherington, 1990). These negative effects are strongest in the first months after the separation or divorce, much as we see the most substantial effects for children during the first 12 to 24 months (Chase-Lansdale & Hetherington, 1990; Kitson, 1992).

The psychological effects of divorce are often significantly exacerbated by serious economic effects, particularly for women. Because most men have had continuous work histories, they commonly leave a marriage with far greater earning power than do women. Not only do women typically lack high earning capacity; they also usually retain custody of any children, with attendant costs. Several longitudinal studies in both the United States and European countries show that divorced men generally improve their economic position, while divorced women are strongly adversely affected, with an average decline of 40–50% of household income (e.g., Morgan, 1991; Smock, 1993). Long-term economic loss from divorce is especially likely for working-class women or those with relatively low levels of education. Women who were earning above-average incomes before their divorce are more likely to recover financially, even if they do not remarry (Holden & Smock, 1991).

Sex Differences in the Impact of Marriage

As you have learned, married adults appear to be healthier and happier than their single counterparts. Why? One possible explanation of this pattern is that some sort of self-selection is occurring: People who are healthy and happy are simply more likely to marry. Logical as it may sound, researchers have found little support for this explanation (Coombs, 1991; Waite, 1995). A second alternative is that married adults follow better health practices. For example, Dutch researchers find that married adults are less likely to smoke or drink to excess and more likely to exercise than are unmarried adults (Joung, Stronks, van de Mheen, & Mackenbach, 1995).

However, an important finding in this body of research is that, at least in the United States, men generally benefit more from marriage than do women on measures of physical and mental health. That is, married men are generally the healthiest and live the longest, while unmarried men are collectively the worst off. The two groups of women fall in between, with married women at a slight advantage over unmarried women. But unmarried women are considerably healthier and happier than are unmarried men. Why should this difference exist?

An interesting two-phase study of marital quality and health looked for a possible correlation between levels of a stress-related hormone called *cortisol* and marriage quality (Kiecolt-Glaser, 2000). Researchers focused on cortisol because it is known to increase when individuals experience negative emotions, and it is one of many stress hormones that are thought to impair immune system functioning. Thus, it may be an important mechanism through which relationship quality affects health.

Investigators measured newlyweds' cortisol levels after they had discussed issues involving conflict, such as in-law relationships and finances. As expected, both husbands' and wives' cortisol levels were somewhat elevated after these discussions. Next, researchers asked couples to tell the story of how they met. As expected, in the majority of both husbands and wives, cortisol levels dropped as they discussed the emotionally neutral topic of relationship history. However, cortisol levels dropped least in those participants who were the most emotionally negative (as measured by number of negative words used) in describing their relationships. This component of the study demonstrated a direct link between stress hormones and marital negativity.

In addition, an important sex difference emerged. When couples described negative events in their relationships, wives' cortisol levels increased while husbands' levels remained constant. This finding suggests that women may be more physiologically sensitive to relationship negativity than men. These results may help explain why marriage is a more consistent protective factor for men than for women.

Sex differences were also apparent in the study's second phase, during which researchers surveyed participants 8 to 12 years later to find out whether they were still married. Remarkably, they found that the higher the wife's cortisol response to emotional negativity in the first phase, the more likely the couple were to be divorced. Consequently, researchers hypothesized that women's physiological responses to marital quality are an important determinant of relationship stability.

For many adults, divorce also affects the sequence and timing of family roles. Even though divorced women with children are less likely to remarry than those who are childless, remarriage expands the number of years of childbearing for many divorced women (Lampard & Peggs, 1999; Norton, 1983). The total number of years of child-rearing may also be significantly larger for divorced men, especially those who remarry younger women with young children. One effect of this is to reduce the number of years a man (or woman) may have between the departure of the last child and the time when elder parents need economic or physical assistance.

COHABITING HETEROSEXUAL COUPLES

As noted, a significant proportion of unmarried couples in the United States live together. Most such couples plan to marry. However, research has shown that those who cohabit before marriage are less satisfied with their marriages and more likely to divorce than are those who marry without cohabiting (DeMaris & Rao, 1992; Hall & Zhao, 1995; Thomson & Colella, 1992). Research has also shown that this relationship exists across historical cohorts. That is, couples who cohabited prior to marriage during the 1980s and 1990s display the same rates of marital dissatisfaction and divorce as those who cohabited in the 1960s and 1970s (Dush, Cohan, & Amato, 2003).

Several theories have been proposed to explain the relationship between premarital cohabitation and divorce. First, couples who cohabit are less *homogamous* (similar) than those who do not (Blackwell & Lichter, 2000). For instance, in about 12% of cohabiting couples in the United States partners are of different races, compared to only 6% of marriages (U.S. Bureau of the Census, 2003b). Cohabiting couples also differ more often in religious beliefs, educational levels, and socioeconomic status (Blackwell & Lichter, 2000). Homogamy contributes to relationship stability. Thus, the difference in marital stability between premarital cohabitants and noncohabitants may be a matter of self-selection, not the result of some causal process attributable to cohabitation itself.

Other developmentalists believe that these findings result from the tendency of researchers to lump all kinds of cohabiting couples into a single category. This kind of aggregation, they say, may distort a study's findings because it ignores that there are two rather distinct types of heterosexual cohabitation (Kline, Stanley, Markman, & Olmos-Gallo, 2004). One type involves couples who are fully committed to a future marriage. In most cases, these couples have firm wedding plans and choose to live together for convenience or for economic reasons. In the second type of cohabitation, the relationship between the two partners is more ambiguous. Many such couples regard future marriage as a possibility but also believe that the relationship may be temporary.

Sociologist Jay Teachman points out that one important difference between these two types of couples is previous cohabitation and premarital sexual experience (Teachman, 2003). His findings are derived from the National Survey of Family Growth, a longitudinal study that focuses on women's family transitions. Teachman's analyses of these data show that married women whose premarital cohabitation and sexual experience was limited to their future husband are no more likely to divorce than women who did not cohabit prior to marriage. Thus, says Teachman, the critical variable at work in the cohabitation-divorce relationship is the fact that a large proportion of cohabitants have been in prior cohabiting or sexual relationships.

Researchers have also identified interaction differences between cohabitants with firm intentions to marry and those whose future plans are less clear. For instance, cohabiting men who intend to marry their partner do more housework than men who are not so committed (Ciabittari, 2004). This difference may be the result of communication patterns that distinguish cohabiting women of the two types. In other words, cohabiting women who intend to marry their partner may do a better job of communicating their expectations about a fair division of labor. Another important finding is that cohabiting couples who are clear about their intentions to marry are happier during the period of cohabitation than couples whose future plans are more ambiguous (Brown, 2003). Thus, looking at the kinds of interaction patterns that exist among cohabitants who intend to marry helps us understand why, after marriage, they differ little in satisfaction and stability from those who do not cohabit until after marriage (Brown, 2003; Brown & Booth, 1996; Kline et al., 2004; Teachman, 2003).

GAY AND LESBIAN COUPLES

As noted earlier, about 11% of unmarried cohabiting couples in the United States are partners of the same sex. Further, there is a growing international movement to legalize same-sex marriage. As a result, in recent years, developmentalists have become interested in whether the same factors that predict satisfaction and stability in heterosexual partnerships also relate to these variables in same-sex partnerships (Kurdek, 1998).

One factor that appears to be just as important to same-sex unions as it is to opposite-sex relationships is attachment security (Elizur & Mintzer, 2003). Moreover, as is true for heterosexual couples, neuroticism in one or both partners is related to relationship quality and length (Kurdek, 1997, 2000). Homosexual couples argue about the same things as heterosexual couples, and, like marriages, gay and lesbian relationships are of higher quality if the two partners share similar backgrounds and are equally committed to the relationship (Krueger-Lebus & Rauchfleisch, 1999; Kurdek, 1997; Peplau, 1991; Solomon, Rothblum, & Balsam, 2004).

Despite these similarities, there are important differences between the two kinds of relationships. For one, gay and lesbian partners are often more dependent on each other for social support than men and women in heterosexual partnerships are. This happens because many homosexuals are isolated from their families, primarily because of their families' disapproval of their sexual orientation (Hill, 1999). Thus, many gays and lesbians build *families of choice* for themselves. These social networks typically consist of a stable partner and a circle of close friends. They provide for gay and lesbian couples the kind of social support that most heterosexual adults receive from their families of origin (Kurdek, 2003; Weeks, 2004).

Another difference is in the nature of the power relation between the partners. Homosexual couples seem to be more egalitarian than heterosexual couples, with less specific role prescriptions. It is quite uncommon in homosexual couples for one partner to occupy a "male" role and the other a "female" role. Instead, power and tasks are more equally divided. However, some research indicates that this is more true of lesbian couples, among whom equality of roles is frequently a strong philosophical ideal, than of gay couples (Kurdek, 1995a).

Finally, homosexual and heterosexual partners appear to differ with regard to expectations for monogamy. Both men and women in heterosexual relationships overwhelmingly state that they expect their partners to be sexually faithful to them. Similarly, lesbian partners often insist on sexual exclusivity. However, gay men, even those in long-term partnerships, do not necessarily regard sexual fidelity as essential to their relationships. Couples therapists report that monogamy is important to gay men, but it is an issue that is considered to be negotiable by most (LaSala, 2001).

SINGLEHOOD

Many adults are single by preference. The impact of singlehood on an adult's life often depends on the reason for his or her relationship status. For instance, continuous singlehood is associated with greater individual autonomy and capacity for personal growth than is a life path that has included divorce or loss of a spouse (Marks & Lamberg, 1998). Another important point to keep in mind is that many single adults participate in intimate relationships that do not involve either cohabitation or marriage. These people show up in surveys and census reports as "single" but might be better described as "partnered." Even among singles who have an intimate partner, though, close relationships with their families of origin are more likely to be an important source of psychological and emotional intimacy than they are for individuals who are married or cohabiting (Allen & Pickett, 1987; Campbell, Connidis, & Davies, 1999). Further, close friends are likely to play a more

Close friends play an important role in the social networks of singles.

(Photo: © Brian Bailey/Getty Images/Stone)

Before going on . . .

■ How do marriage and divorce affect the lives of young adults?

■ What factors contribute to the relationship between premarital cohabitation and divorce?

■ In what ways are gay and lesbian couples similar to and different from heterosexual couples?

■ How do singles accomplish Erikson's psychosocial developmental task of intimacy?

prominent role in the social networks of singles than among marrieds or cohabitants.

The number of years an individual has been single appears to be an important factor in the influence of singlehood on his or her development. Developmentalists have found that there is a transition during which long-term singles move from thinking of themselves as people who will be married or partnered in the future to viewing themselves as single by choice (Davies, 2003). Afterward, singlehood becomes an important, positive component of the individual's identity. This kind of self-affirmation may protect singles from some of the negative health consequences associated with singlehood that you read about earlier.

Parenthood and Other Relationships

The second major new role typically acquired in early adulthood is that of parent. The transition into this new role brings with it unique stresses, and, to make matters more complicated, it usually happens at a time when most other social relationships are in transition as well.

PARENTHOOD

Most parents would agree that parenthood is a remarkably mixed emotional experience. On one hand, the desire to become a parent is, for many adults, extremely strong. Thus, fulfilling that desire is an emotional high point for most. On the other hand, parenthood results in a number of stressful changes.

The Desire to Become a Parent In the United States, nine out of every ten women aged 18 to 34 have had or expect to have a child (U.S. Bureau of the Census, 1997). Despite the opportunistic attitude toward mating that evolutionary theory ascribes to men, the percentage of men who feel strongly that they want to become parents and who view parenting as a life-enriching experience is actually greater than the percentage of women who feel this way (Horowitz, McLaughlin, & White, 1998; Muzi, 2000). Furthermore, most expectant fathers become emotionally attached to their unborn children during the third trimester of pregnancy and eagerly anticipate the birth (White, Wilson, Elander, & Persson, 1999).

Postpartum Depression Between 10% and 25% of new mothers experience a severe mood disturbance called *postpartum depression (PPD)*—a disorder found among mothers in Australia, China, Sweden, and Scotland as well as in the United States (Campbell, Cohn, Flanagan, Popper, & Meyers, 1992; Guo, 1993; Lundh & Gyllang, 1993; Oates et al., 2004; Webster, Thompson, Mitchell, & Werry, 1994). Women who develop PPD suffer from feelings of sadness for several weeks after the baby's birth. Most cases of PPD persist only a few weeks, but 1–2% of women suffer for a year or more. Moreover, more than 80% of women who suffer from PPD after their first pregnancy experience the disorder again following subsequent deliveries (Garfield, Kent, Paykel, Creighton, & Jacobson, 2004).

Women whose bodies produce unusually high levels of steroid hormones toward the end of pregnancy are more likely to develop

For most couples in long-term relationships, especially those who are married, having a child is an important goal.

postpartum depression (Harris et al., 1994). The disorder is also more common in women whose pregnancies were unplanned, who were anxious about the pregnancy, or whose partner was unsupportive (Campbell et al., 1992; O'Hara, Schlechte, Lewis, & Varner, 1992). The presence of major life stressors during pregnancy or immediately after the baby's birth—such as a move to a new home, the death of someone close, or job loss—increases the risk of PPD (Swendsen & Mazure, 2000). Fatigue and difficult temperament in the infant can also contribute to PPD (Fisher, Feekery, & Rowe-Murray, 2002).

However, the best predictor of postpartum depression is depression during pregnancy (Da Costa, Larouche, Dritsa, & Brender, 2000; Martinez-Schallmoser, Telleen, & MacMullen, 2003). Thus, many cases of PPD can probably be prevented by training health professionals to recognize depression in pregnant women. Similarly, family members of women with absent or unsupportive partners can help them locate agencies that provide material and social support.

The Transition Experience Even when new mothers are emotionally healthy, the transition to parenthood can be very stressful. New parents may argue about child-rearing philosophy, as well as how, when, where, and by whom child-care chores should be done (Reichle & Gefke, 1998). Both parents are usually also physically exhausted, perhaps even seriously sleep-deprived, because their newborn keeps them up for much of the night. Predictably, new parents report that they have much less time for each other—less time for conversation, for sex, for simple affection, or even for doing routine chores together (Belsky, Lang, & Rovine, 1985).

Some cultures have developed ritualized rites of passage for this important transition, which can help new parents manage stress. For example, in Hispanic cultures, *la cuarenta* is a period of 40 days following the birth of a child, during which fathers are expected to take on typically feminine tasks such as housework. Extended family members are also expected to help out. Researchers have found that Hispanic couples who observe *la cuarenta* adjust to parenthood more easily than those who do not (Niska, Snyder, & Lia-Hoagberg, 1998).

Developmental Impact of Parenthood Despite its inherent stressfulness, the transition to parenthood is associated with positive behavior change: Sensation-seeking and risky behaviors decline considerably when young adults become parents (Arnett, 1998). However, marital satisfaction tends to decline after the birth of a child. The general pattern is that such satisfaction is at its peak before the birth of the first child, after which it drops and remains at a lower level until the last child leaves home.

In a review of all the research on this point, one psychologist concluded that this curvilinear pattern "is about as close to being certain as anything ever is in the social sciences" (Glenn, 1990, p. 853). Figure 4.3 (page 100) illustrates the pattern, based on results from an early and widely quoted study (Rollins & Feldman, 1970). The best-documented portion of this curvilinear pattern is the drop in marital satisfaction after the birth of the first child, for which there is both longitudinal and cross-sectional evidence. More recent studies suggest that the decline in marital satisfaction is characteristic of contemporary cohorts of new parents as well, and researchers have found a pattern of marital satisfaction similar to that reported by Rollins and Feldman across a variety of cultures (Ahmad & Najam, 1998; Gloger-Tippelt & Huerkamp, 1998; Twenge, Campbell, & Foster, 2003).

A number of variables contribute to just how dissatisfied a couple becomes. One important factor is the division of labor. The more a partner feels that he or she is carrying an unfair proportion of the economic, household, or child-care workload, the greater his or her loss of satisfaction (Wicki, 1999). Support from extended family members is another variable that predicts maintenance or loss of satisfaction (Lee & Keith, 1999).

Some developmentalists suggest that the relative effectiveness of the coping strategies couples use to adjust to their new roles determines how their relationship satisfaction will

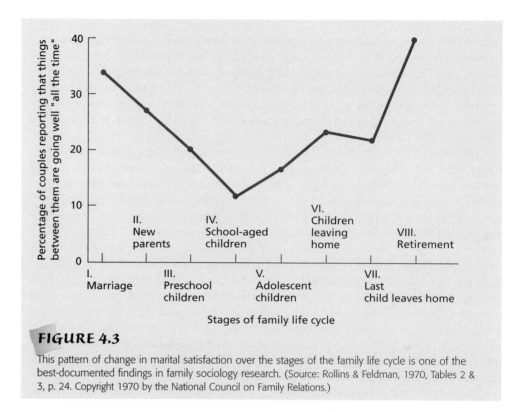

FIGURE 4.3

This pattern of change in marital satisfaction over the stages of the family life cycle is one of the best-documented findings in family sociology research. (Source: Rollins & Feldman, 1970, Tables 2 & 3, p. 24. Copyright 1970 by the National Council on Family Relations.)

be affected by the birth of a child (Belsky & Hsieh, 1998). For example, couples who have established effective conflict-resolution strategies before the birth of a child experience less loss of satisfaction (Cox, Paley, Burchinal, & Payne, 1999; Lindahl, Clements, & Markman, 1997). The quality of new parents' attachment to their own parents also predicts how much their relationship satisfaction declines after the birth of a child (Gloger-Tippelt & Huerkamp, 1998). In fact, young adults with anxious or avoidant attachments to their own parents expect the transition to parenthood to be a negative experience more often than do those whose attachments are secure (Rholes, Simpson, Blakely, Lanigan, & Allen, 1997).

It's important to keep in mind, though, that new parents who are married or cohabiting experience a much smaller decline in overall life satisfaction than new single parents, whose lives are far more complicated and stressful (Lee, Law, & Tam, 1999). Likewise, single parents are more likely to suffer from health problems and are less likely to advance to management positions at work (Khlat, Sermet, & Le Pape, 2000; Tharenou, 1999). Instead of focusing on declines in relationship satisfaction, some developmentalists suggest that more attention be paid to the consistent finding that having a parenting partner—especially one to whom one is married—is a significant protective factor in managing the stressful transition to parenthood.

Childlessness   Like parenthood, childlessness affects the shape of an adult's life, both within marriages and in work patterns. Without the presence of children, marital satisfaction fluctuates less over time. Like all couples, those who do not have children are likely to experience some drop in satisfaction in the first months and years of marriage. But over the range of adult life, their curve of marital satisfaction is much flatter than the one shown in Figure 4.3 (Houseknecht, 1987; Somers, 1993). Childless couples in their 20s and 30s consistently report higher cohesion in their marriages than do couples with children.

Childlessness also affects the role of worker, especially for women. Childless married women, like unmarried women, are much more likely to have full-time continuous careers. However, a survey involving more than 2,000 participants found that single, childless women had no higher rates of managerial advancement than mothers

(Tharenou, 1999). Thus, one of the disadvantages associated with childlessness may be that it is always socially a bit risky to be seen as "different" from others in any important way (Mueller & Yoder, 1999). Tharenou's survey's finding that married fathers whose wives were not employed were more likely to advance than workers of any other marital or parental status supports this conclusion.

SOCIAL NETWORKS

Creating a partnership may be the most central task of the process of achieving intimacy, but it is certainly not the only reflection of that basic process. In early adult life, each of us creates a social network made up of family and friends as well as our life partner.

Family If you ask children and adults "Who is the person you don't like to be away from?" or "Who is the person you know will always be there for you?" children and teenagers most often list their parents, while adults most often name their spouse or partner and almost never mention their parents (Hazan, Hutt, Sturgeon, & Bricker, 1991). However, most adults feel emotionally close to their parents and see or talk to them regularly (Belsky, Jaffee, Caspi, Moffitt, & Silva, 2003; Campbell et al., 1999; Lawton, Silverstein, & Bengtson, 1994).

A good illustration comes from a relatively old study (Leigh, 1982). Researchers interviewed about 1,300 adults who varied with respect to their stage in the traditional family life cycle. Each adult reported how frequently he or she saw, spoke with, or wrote to parents, brothers and sisters, cousins, and other family members. Figure 4.4 shows the percentage of the young adult respondents who said they had at least monthly contact with their parents, the percentage who had weekly contact with parents, and the percentage who had weekly contact with siblings. Clearly, some contact is the norm, and frequent contact is common.

Not surprisingly, the amount and kind of contact an adult has with kin are strongly influenced by proximity. Adults who live within 2 hours of their parents and siblings see them far more often than those who live farther away. But distance does not prevent a parent or sibling from being part of an individual adult's social network. These relationships can provide support in times of need, even if physical contact is infrequent.

CRITICAL THINKING **9**

List all the people in your current social network. What is the relative importance of family and friends for you?

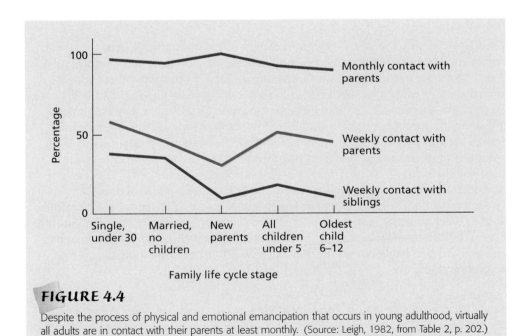

FIGURE 4.4

Despite the process of physical and emotional emancipation that occurs in young adulthood, virtually all adults are in contact with their parents at least monthly. (Source: Leigh, 1982, from Table 2, p. 202.)

There are also important cultural differences in young adults' involvement with their families. For example, one study compared the development of social independence among Australian, Canadian, and Japanese children and adults (Takata, 1999). In all three cultures, the sense of being independent from parents and family increased with age. However, Australian and Canadian participants appeared to develop self-perceptions of independence earlier in life. Consequently, Japanese young adults reported a greater sense of connectedness to their families of origin than either Australian or Canadian young adults.

Although patterns of interaction with family members are similar across U.S. racial groups, Hispanic Americans perceive family ties to be more important than young adults of other races or ethnicities (Schweizer, Schnegg, & Berzborn, 1998). Given a choice, many non-Hispanics de-emphasize kin networks in early adulthood, whereas Hispanic Americans embrace them enthusiastically (Vega, 1990). In the Hispanic American culture, extensive kin networks are the rule rather than the exception, with frequent visiting and exchanges not only between parents, children, and siblings, but with grandparents, cousins, aunts, and uncles (Keefe, 1984). These frequent contacts are not only perceived as enjoyable, but also seen as vital signs of the closeness of kin relationships.

African American young adults also tend to value family connections highly, although the reasons are somewhat different. For one thing, African American young adults are less likely to marry than are young adults in other groups, a pattern resulting in part from the high level of unemployment among young African American men (Burgess, 1995). Consequently, more African American young adults live in multigenerational households with their parents, grandparents, or other relatives than do their peers in other groups; many African American households consist of two generations of adult women and one or more children (Hatchett, Cochran, & Jackson, 1991). African American young adults tend to report higher levels of intimacy and warmth in relationships with parents than do whites, Asian Americans, or Hispanic Americans, so it's not surprising that they feel more comfortable living with family than other young adults do (Kane, 1998). Frequent kin contact is also a significant part of the daily life of most African American adults who do not live in extended family households (Hatchett & Jackson, 1993). African Americans also are more likely to form what have been called "pseudo-kin networks," or "fictive" kin relationships—close family-like relationships between neighbors or peers, who provide each other with a wide variety of aid (Taylor, Chatters, Tucker, & Lewis, 1990).

Friends   Friends, too, are important members of a social network, even those with whom young adults interact exclusively online (see Development in the Information Age). We choose our friends as we choose our partners, from among those who are similar to us in education, social class, interests, family background, or family life cycle stage. Cross-sex friendships are more common among adults than they are among 10-year-olds, but they are still outnumbered by same-sex friendships. Young adults' friends are also overwhelmingly drawn from their own age group. Beyond this basic requirement of similarity, close friendship seems to rest on mutual openness and personal disclosure.

Because of the centrality of the task of intimacy in early adulthood, most researchers and theorists assume that young adults have more friends than do middle-aged or older adults. Research has offered some hints of support for this idea, but it has been a difficult assumption to test properly. Developmentalists lack longitudinal data and do not agree on definitions of friendship, which makes combining data across studies very difficult.

Sex Differences in Relationship Styles   As in childhood, there are very striking sex differences in both the number and the quality of friendships in the social network of

Development in the Information Age

Internet Relationships

Do you have friends you associate with exclusively online? If so, you have something in common with millions of Americans, especially those in younger age groups, 70–90% of whom have online friends (Parks & Roberts, 1998; Wolak, Mitchell, & Finkelhor, 2002). Many of these friendships blossom into face-to-face dating relationships.

The appeal of Internet dating for many seems to be its capacity to allow individuals to bypass conventional relationship "filters"—physical attractiveness, socioeconomic status, and age. Through e-mail, bulletin boards, and chat rooms, cyber-daters can get to know one another psychologically, without the distraction of characteristics that are easily discernible in face-to-face relationships. Cross-cultural research also suggests that interpersonal communication on the Net is viewed as more pleasurable than in-person communication (Chou, Chou, & Tyang, 1998).

However, some psychologists speculate that, in contrast to conventional dating, Internet relationships may retard development of social skills in young people, because online relationships don't allow for the kind of immediate behavioral feedback, such as facial expressions, that face-to-face relationships typically provide (Schnarch, 1997). Further, the more time people spend on the Internet, the less time they spend in other kinds of social interactions where such feedback is available (Kraut et al., 1998).

Another major drawback to Internet dating is the possibility of being deceived. Thus, Internet relationships may be preferable in situations where deception is desirable. For example, adults who want to entice children or teenagers into sexual relationships often use deception. Likewise, married people who want to present themselves to potential partners as single can do so more easily online.

Not surprisingly, extramarital affairs that begin or are carried out exclusively on the Internet are a growing phenomenon. In fact, their prevalence has led marital counselors to redefine the word "affair." Historically, an affair has involved sexual contact. But online affairs often lack any face-to-face contact, sexual or otherwise. Still, sexual tension and stimulation are typically a large part of online affairs. Partners trade pictures, sometimes sexually provocative ones, and engage in flirtatious sexual banter while online. Researchers have found that most men and women believe that these kinds of interactions represent sexual infidelity (Whitty, 2003). Consequently, marital counselors now define an affair as a relationship that involves psychological intimacy, secrecy, and sexual chemistry, in order to help clients understand that marital fidelity involves something more than just sexual monogamy (Glass, 1998).

No doubt the phenomenon of Internet dating will continue to grow. Thus, there is a need for research that will lead to a better understanding of how online relationships develop and dissolve, as well as how they affect individual development.

---

young adults. Women have more close friends, and their friendships are more intimate, with more self-disclosure and more exchange of emotional support. Young men's friendships, like those of boys and older men, are more competitive. Male friends are less likely to agree with each other or to ask for or provide emotional support to one another (Dindia & Allen, 1992; Maccoby, 1990). Adult women friends talk to one another; adult men friends do things together.

Whether one sees the female pattern or the male pattern as "better" or "worse" obviously depends on one's gender and point of view. Theorists continue to argue the point (Antonucci, 1994). Most research shows men to be less satisfied with their friendships than women are (although the sexes are equally satisfied with their family relationships), and women clearly gain in quite specific ways from the buffering effect of their social network. But men also gain from their style of relationship. Women's style, for example, sometimes has the effect of burdening them too much with emotional obligations, whereas men are more able to focus on their work (Antonucci, 1994b). Value judgments aside, the important point remains: Men and women appear to create different kinds of relationships, and this difference permeates U.S. culture.

Another facet of this difference is that women most often fill the role of **kin-keeper** (Moen, 1996). They write the letters, make the phone calls, arrange the gatherings of

kin-keeper a family role, usually occupied by a woman, which includes responsibility for maintaining family and friendship relationships

Before going on . . .

■ Describe the transition to parenthood and the developmental effects of becoming a parent and remaining childless.

■ How are family and friends important to young adults?

family and friends. (In later stages of adult life, it is also the women who are likely to take on the role of caring for aging parents—a pattern you'll learn more about in Chapter 6.)

Taken together, all this means that women have a much larger "relationship role" than men do. In virtually all cultures, it is part of the female role to be responsible for maintaining the emotional aspects of relationships—with a spouse, with friends, with family, and, of course, with children.

The Role of Worker

In addition to the roles of spouse or partner and parent, a large percentage of young adults are simultaneously filling yet another major and relatively new role: that of worker. Most young people need to take on this role to support themselves economically. But that is not the only reason for the centrality of this role. Satisfying work also seems to be an important ingredient in mental health and life satisfaction, for both men and women (Meeus, Dekovic & Iedema, 1997; Tait, Padgett, & Baldwin, 1989). However, before looking at what developmentalists know about career steps and sequences in early adulthood, let's examine how young people choose an occupation.

CHOOSING AN OCCUPATION

As you might imagine, a multitude of factors influence a young person's choice of job or career: family background and values; intelligence and education; gender; and personality (in addition to other factors such as ethnic group, self-concept, and school performance).

Family Influences   Typically, young people choose occupations at the same general social class level as those of their parents—although this is less true today than it was a decade or two ago (Biblarz, Bengtson, & Bucur, 1996). In part, this effect operates through the medium of education. For example, researchers have found that young adults whose parents are college graduates are less likely to enlist in the military than those whose parents have less education (Bachman, Segal, Freedman-Doan, & O'Malley, 2000). Such findings suggest that parents who have higher-than-average levels of education themselves are more likely to encourage their children to go on to post-secondary education. Such added education, in turn, makes it more likely that the young person will qualify for middle-class jobs, for which a college education is frequently a required credential.

Families also influence job choices through their value systems. In particular, parents who value academic and professional achievement are far more likely to have children who attend college and choose professional-level jobs. This effect is not just social-class difference in disguise. Among working-class families, it is the children of those who place the strongest emphasis on achievement who are most likely to move up into middle-class jobs (Gustafson & Magnusson, 1991). Further, families whose career aspirations for their children are high tend to produce young adults who are more intrinsically motivated as employees (Cotton, Bynum, & Madhere, 1997).

(Photo: © Scott Olson/Getty Images)

Young adults who enter military service differ from peers who go to college or into civilian careers. Their parents are less likely to have gone to college and more likely to be poor than parents of young adults who do not go into military service. However, some families encourage their young adult children to join the military in order to have access to educational opportunities that they cannot afford to provide for them but that often accompany military service.

Similarly, parental moral beliefs influence young adults' willingness to enter various occupations (Bregman & Killen, 1999). For example, young adults whose families believe that drinking alcohol is morally wrong are unlikely to choose alcohol-related occupations such as bartending, waiting tables in a restaurant where liquor is served, or working at a liquor store.

Education and Intelligence   Education and intelligence also interact very strongly to influence not just the specific job a young person chooses but also career success over the long haul. The higher your intelligence, the more years of education you are likely to complete; the more education you have, the higher the level at which you enter the job market; the higher the level of entry, the further you are likely to go over your lifetime (Brody, 1992; Kamo, Ries, Farmer, Nickinovich, & Borgatta, 1991).

Intelligence has direct effects on job choice and job success as well. Brighter students are more likely to choose technical or professional careers. And highly intelligent workers are more likely to advance, even if they enter the job market at a lower level than those who are less intelligent (Dreher & Bretz, 1991).

Gender   Specific job choice is also strongly affected by gender. Despite the women's movement and despite the vast increase in the proportion of women working, it is still true that sex-role definitions designate some jobs as "women's jobs" and some as "men's jobs" (Reskin, 1993; Zhou, Dawson, Herr, & Stukas, 2004). Stereotypically male jobs are more varied, more technical, and higher in both status and income (e.g., business executive, carpenter). Stereotypically female jobs are concentrated in service occupations and are typically lower in status and lower paid (e.g., teacher, nurse, secretary). One-third of all working women hold clerical jobs; another quarter are in health care, teaching, or domestic service.

Children learn these cultural definitions of "appropriate" jobs for men and women in their early years, just as they learn all the other aspects of sex roles. So it is not surprising that most young women and men choose jobs that fit these sex-role designations. Nonstereotypical job choices are much more common among young people who see themselves as androgynous or whose parents have unconventional occupations. For instance, young women who choose traditionally masculine careers are more likely to have a mother who has had a long-term career and are more likely to define themselves either as androgynous or as masculine (Betz & Fitzgerald, 1987; Fitzpatrick & Silverman, 1989).

Personality   A fourth important influence on job choice is the young adult's personality. John Holland, whose work has been the most influential in this area, proposes six basic personality types, summarized in Table 4.1 (page 106) (Holland, 1973, 1992). Holland's basic hypothesis is that each of us tends to choose, and be most successful at, an occupation that matches our personality.

Research in non-Western as well as Western cultures, and with African Americans, Hispanic Americans, and Native Americans as well as whites in the United States, has generally supported Holland's proposal (e.g., Kahn, Alvi, Shaukat, Hussain, & Baig, 1990; Leong, Austin, Sekaran, & Komarraju, 1998; Tokar, Fischer, & Subich, 1998; Tracey & Rounds, 1993; Upperman & Church, 1995). Ministers, for example, generally score highest on Holland's social scale, engineers highest on the investigative scale, car salespeople on the enterprising scale, and career army officers on the realistic scale.

People whose personalities match their jobs are also more likely to be satisfied with their work. Moreover, obtaining a personality assessment prior to making an occupational choice is associated with greater feelings of confidence about the decision (Francis-Smythe & Smith, 1997).

TABLE 4.1	Holland's Personality Types and Work Preferences

Type	Personality and Work Preferences
Realistic	Aggressive, masculine, physically strong, often with low verbal or interpersonal skills; prefer mechanical activities and tool use, choosing jobs such as mechanic, electrician, or surveyor
Investigative	Oriented toward thinking (particularly abstract thinking), organizing, and planning; prefer ambiguous, challenging tasks, but are low in social skills; are often scientists or engineers
Artistic	Asocial; prefer unstructured, highly individual activity; are often artists
Social	Extraverts; people-oriented and sociable and need attention; avoid intellectual activity and dislike highly ordered activity; prefer to work with people and choose service jobs like nursing and education
Enterprising	Highly verbal and dominating; enjoy organizing and directing others; are persuasive and strong leaders, often choosing careers in sales
Conventional	Prefer structured activities and subordinate roles; like clear guidelines and see themselves as accurate and precise; may choose occupations such as bookkeeping or filing

(Source: Holland, 1973, 1992.)

JOBS OVER TIME

Once the job or career has been chosen, what kinds of experiences do young adults have in their work life? Do they become more or less satisfied with their work over time? Are there clear career steps that might be considered stages?

Job Satisfaction   Many studies show that job satisfaction is at its lowest in early adulthood and rises steadily until retirement, a pattern that has been found in repeated surveys of both male and female respondents (Glenn & Weaver, 1985). Researchers know that this is not just a cohort effect, because similar findings have been reported over many years of research, and that it is not entirely culture-specific, since it has been found in many industrialized countries.

But what might cause the pattern? Some research points to the possibility that this pattern is the effect of time on the job rather than age (e.g., Bedeian, Ferris, & Kacmar, 1992). Older workers are likely to have had their jobs longer, which may contribute to several sources of satisfaction, including better pay, more job security, and more authority. But there may be some genuine age effects at work, too. The jobs young people hold are likely to be dirtier, physically harder, and less complex and interesting (Spenner, 1988).

However, research also suggests that there are a number of important variables that contribute to job satisfaction in young adults. As with almost every life situation, individual personality traits such as neuroticism affect job satisfaction (Blustein, Phillips, Jobin-Davis, & Finkelberg, 1997; Judge, Bono, & Locke, 2000). In addition, young adults engaged in careers for which they prepared in high school or college have higher levels of satisfaction (Blustein et al., 1997). Race is also related to job satisfaction, with white workers reporting higher levels of satisfaction than minority workers (Weaver & Hinson, 2000).

In addition to personal factors, a number of workplace variables influence job satisfaction. For example, the degree to which a work setting encourages or discourages young employees makes a difference (Blustein et al., 1997). Encouragement may be part of a set of workplace variables that contribute to positive affect, or feelings of emotional contentment, among workers, which, in turn, leads to higher levels of job satisfaction. Research suggests that workers are most satisfied when they experience more pleasant than unpleasant emotions while working (Fisher, 2000).

Career Ladders   In most careers, workers tend to move from step to step through a series of milestones that make up a **career ladder.** In academic jobs, the sequence is

career ladder the milestones associated with a particular occupation

from instructor to assistant professor, associate professor, and then full professor. In an automobile plant, the ladder may go from assembly-line worker to foreman, general foreman, superintendent and on up. In the corporate world, there may be many rungs in a management career ladder.

What kind of progress up the career ladder do young adults typically make? To answer such a question properly, of course, researchers need to conduct longitudinal studies. There have not been many of these, but fortunately there are a few, including a 20-year study of AT&T managers (Bray & Howard, 1983) and a 15-year study of workers in a large manufacturing company (Rosenbaum, 1984). This research suggests several generalizations about the developmental progression of work careers in early adulthood. First, college education makes a very large difference, as you should remember from Chapter 3. Even when the effects of differing intellectual ability are accounted for, research shows that those with college educations advance further and faster.

Second, early promotion is associated with greater advancement over the long haul. In the manufacturing company that Rosenbaum studied, 83% of those who were promoted within the first year eventually got as far as lower management, while only 33% of those who were first promoted after 3 years of employment got that far.

Third, and perhaps most important, most work advancement occurs early in a career path, after which a plateau is reached. The policy in the manufacturing company that Rosenbaum studied was for all workers—whether they had a college degree or not—to enter at the submanagement level. The first possible promotional step was to the job of foreman; promotion to lower management was the second possible step. The majority of promotions to either position occurred when workers were between the ages of 29 and 34; by age 40, virtually all the promotions that a person was going to receive had already happened. The same pattern is evident in other career paths as well, such as those of accountants and academics, so it is not unique to business career ladders (Spenner, 1988).

Such a pattern may be unique, however, to adults who enter a profession in their 20s and stay in it through most of their adult lives. There are at least a few hints from research with women—whose work histories are frequently much less continuous than men's—that time-in-career rather than age may be the critical variable for the timing of promotions. There may be a window of 10–15 years between the time you enter a profession and the time you reach a plateau. If you begin in your 20s, you are likely to have peaked by your mid-30s. But if you begin when you are 40, you may still have 15 years in which to advance.

Another View of Work Sequences Another way to describe the work experience of young adults is in terms of a series of stages, a model proposed originally by Donald Super (Super, 1971, 1986). First comes the *trial stage,* roughly between the ages of 18 and 25, more or less equivalent to the first phase of the young adult period proposed by Levinson (refer back to Figure 4.1). In this stage, the young person must decide on a job or career, and he searches for a fit between his interests and personality and the jobs available. The whole process involves a good deal of trial and error as well as luck or chance. Perhaps because many of the jobs available to those in this age range are not terribly challenging and because many young adults have not yet found the right fit, job changes are at their peak during this period.

Next comes the *establishment stage* (also called the *stabilization stage*), roughly from age 25 to age 45. Having chosen an occupation, the young person must learn the ropes and begin to move through the early steps in some career ladder as he masters the needed skills, perhaps with a mentor's help. In this period, the worker also focuses on fulfilling whatever aspirations or goals he may have set for himself. In Levinson's terms, he tries to fulfill his dream. The young scientist pushes himself to make an important discovery; the young attorney strives to become a partner; the young business executive tries to move as far up the ladder as he can; the young blue-collar worker may aim for job stability or promotion to foreman. It is in these years that most promotions do in fact occur, although it is also the time when the job plateau is reached.

(Photo: © Rolf Bruderer/CORBIS)

(Photo: © Rob Crandal/The Image Works)

Women are working in larger and larger numbers, but fewer than a third work continuously during the early adult years.

SEX DIFFERENCES IN WORK PATTERNS

Some of what you have read so far about work patterns is as true for women as it is for men. For example, women's work satisfaction goes up with age (and with job tenure), just as men's does. But women's work experience in early adulthood differs from men's in one strikingly important respect: The great majority of women move in and out of the work force at least once, often many times (Drobnic, Blossfeld, & Rohwer, 1999).

This pattern has numerous repercussions for women's work roles. For example, women who work continuously have higher salaries and achieve higher levels in their jobs than do those who have moved in and out of employment (Betz, 1984; Van Velsor & O'Rand, 1984). Many researchers use the term *mommy track* to refer to this in-and-out pattern of work. One important factor that helps explain why women who choose the mommy track typically earn less and are less likely to be promoted than women who work continuously is that these women tend to choose careers—such as teaching and nursing—that are more amenable to this kind of work pattern (Blanchard & Lichtenberg, 2003). Such professions usually pay less than other professions that require an equal amount of training.

Women's work patterns are obviously changing rapidly. For example, researchers found that a large group of female college seniors majoring in business who were interviewed in 1988 expected to work an average of 29.1 years, whereas their male peers expected to work for 37.7 years (Blau & Ferber, 1991). Only a few years later, a Canadian study found that most of the high school girls the researchers interviewed in the early 1990s expected both to be continuously employed and to have a family in adulthood (Davey, 1998). However, when they were reinterviewed 4 years later, these young women had begun to think about potential conflicts between career and family goals. Most still expected to be continuously employed, but many indicated that they would prefer to take time out from their careers to achieve family goals such as raising children. So, although the cultural climate has changed drastically with regard to women's work patterns, the essential conflict women feel with regard to work and family, which is the driving force behind discontinuous patterns of employment, continues to be evident in current cohorts.

The evidence on women's patterns of discontinuous employment raises the more general question of how individuals and couples balance the roles of worker and parent

MAKE THE CONNECTION

In Chapter 8, you learned about gender schema theory. How would this theory explain women's responses to conflicts between work and family roles?

and those of worker and spouse. It is an interesting testimony to the strength of cultural gender roles that people have no trouble thinking of a man as simultaneously a worker, a parent, and a spouse, but they think it is problematic for a woman to be all three at once. Women do, in fact, feel more role conflict among these three roles than men do, for several clear reasons (Higgins, Duxbury, & Lee, 1994).

The most obvious reason is that if the hours spent in family work (child care, cleaning, cooking, shopping, etc.) and in paid employment are added together, employed women are working more hours a week than are their husbands or partners, as suggested by Figure 4.5—despite the fact that men whose wives are employed are doing more child care than men in previous generations did (Higgins et al., 1994). Further, unmarried men are as likely as their female counterparts to anticipate the need to balance work and family roles after marriage (Kerpelman & Schvaneveldt, 1999).

However, wives still do roughly twice as much housework (child care, cooking, cleaning, running errands, and so forth) as husbands, even when both work full-time (Blair & Johnson, 1992). African American and Hispanic American men appear to spend slightly more time in household labor than do white men, but the range of variation is not large (Shelton & John, 1993). Thus, although the gap is decreasing, women still devote much more time to family roles than do men.

Women also feel more conflict between family and work roles because of the way sex roles are defined in most cultures. The woman's role is to be relationship-oriented, to care for others, to nurture. To the extent that a woman has internalized that role expectation—and most have—she will define herself, and judge herself, more by how well she performs such caring roles than by how well she performs her job role. Joseph Pleck argues that this means that the boundaries between work and family roles are therefore "asymmetrically

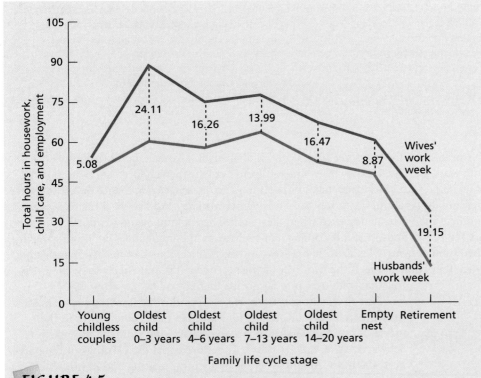

FIGURE 4.5

When both partners work full time, women still do more housework and child care, so their total work week is many hours longer—contributing significantly to women's greater sense of conflict between work and family roles. Note that the gap is greatest right after the birth of the first child—perhaps a time when the man is most likely to be intensely committed to his career. (Source: Rexroat & Shehan, 1987, Fig. 1, p. 746.)

The Real World

Strategies for Coping with Conflict between Work and Family Life

If you are like many of today's college students, especially women, you view your future as including marriage, parenthood, and a successful career (Hoffnung, 2004). But can a person really balance the demands of all three of these roles? While there is no magic formula for creating such a balance and eliminating conflict and distress, there are some strategies that can help. These suggestions are phrased as advice to women, because it is women who experience the greatest role conflict. But men can certainly profit from the same information.

The most helpful strategy overall is something psychologists call *cognitive restructuring*—recasting or reframing the situation for yourself in a way that identifies the positive elements. Cognitive restructuring might include reminding yourself that you had good reasons for choosing to have both a job and a family and recalling other times when you have coped successfully with similar problems (Paden & Buehler, 1995).

A related kind of restructuring involves redefining family roles. In several older studies, psychologists found that women who found ways to redistribute basic household tasks to other family members (husband and children) or who simply gave up doing some tasks experienced less stress and conflict (Hall, 1972, 1975). You might make a list of all the household chores you and your partner do and go over the list together, eliminating whatever items you can and reassigning the others. Men can clean toilets; clutter can be dealt with less frequently (or not at all!); meals can perhaps be simpler. If economic resources are sufficient, help can also be hired.

You can also redefine the sex roles themselves. Where is it written that only women can stay home with a sick child? It is probably written in your internal model of yourself or in your gender schema. Many women find it difficult to give up such responsibilities, even when they cause severe role conflict, because such nurturing is part of their image of themselves. As one woman whose husband was very involved in the care of their infant said,

> I love seeing the closeness between him and the baby, especially since I didn't have that with my father, but if he does well at his work and his relationship with the baby, what's my special contribution? (Cowan & Cowan, 1987, p. 168)

It may be helpful to try to discover whether the current division of labor in your own household exists because others in the household don't do their share or because of your own inner resistance to changing your view of yourself and your basic contribution to the family unit.

Finally, you may find it helpful to take a class in time management. Research reveals that good planning can, in fact, reduce the sense of strain you feel (Paden & Buehler, 1995). You have probably already heard lots of advice about how to organize things better. Easier said than done! But there are techniques that can help, and many of these are taught in workshops and classes in most cities.

What does not help is simply trying harder to do it all yourself. Women who continue to try to fulfill several roles perfectly report maximum strain and stress. Something has to give, whether it is your standards for housework or your sense of your female role. Combining a number of roles is inherently full of opportunities for conflict. At best, you may manage a delicate balance. At worst, you will find yourself overwhelmed.

CRITICAL THINKING ?

What plans do you have to combine work and family? Might your planning, or your thinking, change as a result of what you have read so far?

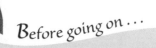

Before going on . . .

■ What factors influence a person's choice of occupation?

■ How do the concepts of job satisfaction and the career ladder contribute to an understanding of how jobs change over time?

■ Describe women's patterns of work and how they relate to on-the-job achievement and income. What are the potential conflicts among work and family roles, and how do they differ for men and women?

permeable" for the two sexes (Pleck, 1977). That is, for a woman, family roles spill over into work life. She not only takes time off from her job when children are born, but also stays home with a sick child, takes time off to go to a teacher's conference or a PTA meeting, and thinks about her family tasks during her workday. Women view themselves as mothers and wives all day, even when they work. These simultaneous, competing demands are the very definition of role conflict. For men, work and family roles are more sequential than simultaneous. Men view themselves as workers during the day, husbands and fathers when they come home. If the two roles conflict for men, it is more likely to be the work role that spills over into family life than the other way around.

Not all the intersections of family and work roles are problematic for women. For example, working women have more power in their marriages or partnerships than do nonworking women (Blumstein & Schwartz, 1983; Spitze, 1988). The more equal the earnings of the partners, the more equality there is in decision making and in household work. But it remains true that the most striking single fact about work and family roles in this age of high women's employment is that women struggle more than men do to resolve the conflict between the two. It is also clear that this conflict is vastly greater during early adulthood, when children are young and need constant care, than it is in middle or later adult life. In many respects, it is this complex intersection of spousal, parental, and work roles that is the defining feature of early adult life in industrialized societies (see the Real World feature).

Summary

Theories of Social and Personality Development

- Erikson proposed that young adults face the crisis of intimacy versus isolation. Those who fail to establish a stable relationship with an intimate partner or a network of friends become socially isolated.
- Levinson hypothesized that adult development involves alternating periods of stability and instability, through which adults construct and refine life structures.
- Evolutionary theories of mate selection suggest that sex differences in mate preferences and mating behavior are the result of natural selection.
- Social role theory emphasizes factors such as gender roles, similarity, and economic exchange in explaining sex differences in mating.

Intimate Relationships

- Personality characteristics, as well as attachment and love, contribute to marital success. Marriage is associated with a number of health benefits, while divorce tends to increase young adults' risk of depression.
- People who cohabit prior to marriage are more likely to divorce. However, research has shown that among cohabiting couples in which the intention to marry is firm and the woman has had no prior cohabitation experience, divorce or dissatisfaction with the relationship is no more likely than among couples who do not live together before marriage.
- The factors that contribute to relationship satisfaction are similar across homosexual and heterosexual couples. However, the two types of couples often differ in the power relation within the partnership. Further, monogamy is not as important to gay male couples as it is to lesbian or heterosexual partners.
- Singles who do not have intimate partners rely on family and friends for intimacy. After many years of singlehood, unpartnered adults tend to incorporate "singleness" into their sense of personal identity.

Parenthood and Other Relationships

- Most men and women want to become parents, because they view raising children as a life-enriching experience.
- The transition to parenthood is stressful and leads to a decline in relationship satisfaction. Factors such as the division of labor between mother and father, individual personality traits, and the availability of help from extended family members contribute to relationship satisfaction.
- Young adults' relationships with their parents tend to be steady and supportive, even if less central than they were at earlier ages. The quality of attachment to parents continues to predict a number of important variables in early adulthood.
- Each young adult creates a network of relationships with friends as well as with a partner and family members.

The Role of Worker

- The specific job or career a young adult chooses is affected by his or her education, intelligence, family background and resources, family values, personality, and gender. The majority of adults choose jobs that fit the cultural norms for their social class and gender. More intelligent young people, and those with more education, are more upwardly mobile.
- Job satisfaction rises steadily throughout early adulthood, in part because the jobs typically available to young adults are less well paid, more repetitive, and less creative and allow the worker very little power or influence. The work role has two stages in early adulthood: a trial stage, in which alternative pathways are explored, and an establishment stage, in which the career path is established.
- For most women, the work role includes an additional in-and-out stage, in which periods of focusing on family responsibilities alternate with periods of employment. The more continuous a woman's work history, the more successful she is likely to be at her job.
- When both partners work, the family responsibilities are not equally divided: Women continue to perform more work in the home and feel more role conflict.

Key Terms

assortative mating (homogamy) (p. 91)
avoidant couples (p. 94)
career ladder (p. 106)
hostile/detached couples (p. 94)
hostile/engaged couples (p. 94)

intimacy (p. 88)
intimacy versus isolation (p. 88)
kin-keeper (p. 103)
life structure (p. 88)

parental investment theory (p. 90)
social role theory (p. 90)
validating couples (p. 94)
volatile couples (p. 94)

Physical and Cognitive Development in Middle Adulthood

CHAPTER 5

The great baseball player Satchel Paige, who was still pitching in the major leagues at age 62, once said, "Age is mind over matter. If you don't mind, it doesn't matter."

© Kathy Ferguson-Johnson/PhotoEdit

It's a nice summary of the physical changes of the middle years. Yes, there are changes. Memory does get less efficient in some situations in mid-life; vision and hearing get worse; people slow down slightly and become somewhat weaker. But among adults who are otherwise healthy, the amount of loss is far less than folklore would have us believe. Further, along with obvious losses come important gains. Indeed, although early adulthood may be the physical high point of adulthood, there is a great deal of evidence that middle adulthood is the intellectual and creative peak.

In this chapter you will learn that, with advancing age, the story of human development seems to become more an account of differences than a description of universals. This happens because there are so many factors—behavioral choices, poor health, and so on—that determine the specific developmental pathway an adult follows. Most middle-aged adults are healthy, energetic, and intellectually productive, but others are in decline. Moreover, because developmental psychology has focused more on younger individuals, there simply isn't as much knowledge about universal changes in adulthood. As you read this chapter, keep the following questions in mind:

- How do the nervous system, reproductive system, and other body systems change between age 40 and age 60?

- What are the major issues of physical and mental health in middle adulthood?

- In what ways does cognitive function improve and/or decline?

Physical Changes

For a quick overview of the common physical changes of middle age, take another look at Table 3.1 (page 62), which summarizes most of the evidence. Changes or declines in many physical functions occur very gradually through the 40s and 50s. For a few physical functions, however, change or decline is already substantial in the middle adult years.

THE BRAIN AND NERVOUS SYSTEM

Relatively little is known about the normal, undamaged brains of middle-aged adults. This is because research has focused on changes associated with trauma and disease rather than changes due to primary aging. However, it is possible to make a few general statements.

After a period of stability across adolescence and the first decade of early adulthood, synaptic density begins to decline around age 30 (Huttenlocher, 1994). The decline continues throughout middle adulthood and the later years and is accompanied by decreases in brain weight. However, it's important to note that new synapses are continuing to form in middle age. Earlier in life, though, new synapses form more rapidly or at the same rate as old connections are lost. In middle age, it appears, more synapses are lost than are formed. The effect of the loss of synaptic density on brain function has yet to be determined.

In addition, developmentalists know that behavioral choices and mental health affect the adult brain. For example, alcoholics and nonalcoholics differ in the distribution of electrical activity in the brain (Duffy, 1994). The brains of depressed and nondepressed adults differ as well. Further, a number of serious mental illnesses, such as schizophrenia, are associated with structural variations in the brain. What researchers don't know yet is whether the brains of alcoholics, depressed persons, or schizophrenics were different from the brains of others before the onset of their difficulties. The longitudinal research necessary to answer such questions hasn't yet been done.

Besides studying the effects of trauma and disease, neuropsychologists are also involved in investigating a very important issue in the study of aging—whether declines in cognitive functions are caused by a loss of neurological processing resources. To find out, researchers examine how the brains of young and middle-aged people respond to cognitive tasks. Such studies have produced a rather complex set of findings.

One fairly consistent finding is that cognitive tasks activate a larger area of brain tissue in middle-aged adults than they do in younger adults (Gunter, Jackson, & Mulder, 1998). Of course, neuropsychologists don't know why, but they speculate that cognitive processing is less selective in middle-aged adults than it is in younger adults. It's as if the middle-aged brain has a more difficult time finding just the right neurological tool to carry out a particular function, and so it activates more tools than are necessary. This lack of selectivity could account for differences between age groups in the speed at which cognitive tasks are carried out.

One way of examining this hypothesis is to see if it explains individual differences as well as age variation. Typically, when middle-aged and young adults are compared, the range of individual differences within each age group is far greater than the average difference between the two age groups. Researchers find that in participants in both age groups who perform poorly on tasks such as remembering lists of associated words (*table-chair*) or nonassociated words (*knife-car*), larger areas of the brain are activated than in those who perform well.

In addition, the brains of high performers are more sensitive to different kinds of tasks. For example, recalling nonassociated words requires a larger area of activation (more neurological tools) than recalling associated words, because nonassociated words are more difficult to memorize. The more difficult task activates more of the brain than the easy one does in all adults. But in both young and middle-aged high performers, the difference in brain activation on difficult and easy tasks is much greater.

The brains of middle-aged and younger adults also respond differently to sensory stimuli. For example, when participants are presented with a simple auditory stimulus such as a musical tone, patterns of brain waves in different areas vary across age groups (Yordanova, Kolev, & Basar, 1998). Research along this line has suggested that middle-aged adults may have less ability to control attention processes by inhibiting brain responses to irrelevant stimuli (Amenedo & Diaz, 1998, 1999). Their difficulty with attentional control could be another reason for the average difference in processing speed between young and middle-aged adults.

Such findings might lead you to conclude that, in everyday situations requiring intense concentration and rapid judgments, middle-aged adults would perform more poorly than their younger counterparts. Interestingly, though, recent research on lapses of concentration and poor decision-making among drivers shows just the opposite (Dobson, Brown, Ball, Powers, & McFadden, 1999). Younger drivers exhibit more lapses in attention and driving errors than middle-aged drivers. These lapses and errors, combined with younger drivers' greater likelihood of driving after drinking alcohol, help account for the different accident rates of young and middle-aged adults. Such findings, when considered with those on age differences in brain function, illustrate the difficulty researchers face in finding direct relationships between age-related brain differences and cross-age variations in behavior.

THE REPRODUCTIVE SYSTEM

If you were asked to name a single significant physical change occurring in the years of middle adulthood, chances are you'd say *menopause*—especially if you're a woman. The more general term is the **climacteric,** which refers to the years of middle or late adulthood in both men and women during which reproductive capacity declines or is lost.

Male Climacteric In men, the climacteric is extremely gradual, with a slow loss of reproductive capacity, although the rate of change varies widely from one man to the next, and there are documented cases of men in their 90s fathering children. On average, the quantity of viable sperm produced declines slightly, beginning perhaps at about age 40. The testes also shrink very gradually, and the volume of seminal fluid declines after about age 60.

The causal factor is most likely a very slow drop in testosterone levels, beginning in early adulthood and continuing well into old age. This decline in testosterone is implicated in the gradual loss of muscle tissue (and hence strength) that becomes evident in the middle and later years, as well as in the increased risk of heart disease in middle and old age. It also appears to affect sexual function. In particular, in the middle years, the incidence of erectile dysfunction begins to increase—although many things other than the slight decline in testosterone contribute to this change, including an increased incidence of poor health (especially heart disease), obesity, use of blood pressure medication (and other medications), alcohol abuse, and smoking. *Erectile dysfunction,* sometimes called *impotence,* is the inability to achieve or maintain an erection.

Lifestyle changes can sometimes restore sexual function. In one study, researchers enrolled 35- to 55-year-old obese men with erectile dysfunction in a 2-year weight loss program that required participants to make changes in their diets and exercise habits (Esposito et al., 2004). About one-third of the men experienced improvements in erectile dysfunction along with reductions in body fat.

Among healthy middle-aged men, performance anxiety is a frequent cause of erectile dysfunction. The drug *sildenafil* (Viagra) has been found to be effective in treating this problem (Rosen, 1996). However, physicians warn that men with erectile dysfunction should avoid so-called natural treatments such as food supplements because most of them have not been studied in placebo-controlled experiments (Rowland & Tai, 2003).

climacteric the term used to describe the adult period during which reproductive capacity declines or is lost

During middle age, supportive partners help each other cope with the changes in sexual function that are brought about by the natural aging of the reproductive system.

Moreover, men who turn to supplements for symptom relief may delay seeking medical attention and, as a result, may continue to suffer from a serious underlying condition without realizing it.

Menopause Declines in key sex hormones are also clearly implicated in the set of changes in women called **menopause,** which means literally the cessation of the menses. Secretion of several forms of estrogen by the ovaries increases rapidly during puberty, triggering the onset of menstruation as well as stimulating the development of breasts and secondary sex characteristics. In the adult woman, estrogen levels are high during the first 14 days of the menstrual cycle, stimulating the release of an ovum and the preparation of the uterus for possible implantation. *Progesterone*, which is secreted by the ruptured ovarian follicle from which the ovum emerges, rises during the second half of the menstrual cycle and stimulates the sloughing off of accumulated material in the uterus each month if conception has not occurred.

The average age of menopause for both African American and white American women, and for women in other countries for which data are available, is roughly age 50; anything between ages 40 and 60 is considered within the normal range (Bellantoni & Blackman, 1996). About 1 woman in 12 experiences menopause before the age of 40, referred to by physicians as *premature menopause* (Wich & Carnes, 1995).

Menopausal Phases Menopause, like puberty, is often thought of as a single event. However, it actually occurs over several years, and researchers generally agree that it consists of three phases. First, during the **premenopausal phase,** estrogen levels begin to fluctuate and decline, typically in the late 30s or early 40s, producing irregular menstrual periods in many women. The ovaries are less sensitive to cyclical hormonal signals, and many women experience *anovulatory cycles,* or cycles in which no ovum is released. Even though no ovum is produced, estrogen levels are high enough in premenopausal women to produce periodic bleeding. However, the lack of ovulation results in a dramatic drop in progesterone. Thus, many experts believe that the menstrual irregularity associated with the premenopausal period is due to progesterone loss rather than estrogen loss (Lee, 1996).

During the **perimenopausal phase,** estrogen levels decrease and women experience more extreme variations in the timing of their menstrual cycles. In addition, about 75% of perimenopausal women experience *hot flashes,* sudden sensations of feeling hot. Of those who have hot flashes, 85% will have them for more than a year; a third or more will have them for 5 years or more (Kletzky & Borenstein, 1987). It is hypothesized that fluctuating levels of estrogen and other hormones cause a woman's blood vessels to expand and contract erratically, thus producing hot flashes (see No Easy Answers, pages 118–119).

During a hot flash, the temperature of the skin can rise as much as 1–7 degrees in some parts of the body, although the core body temperature actually drops (Kronenberg, 1994). Hot flashes last, on average, about 3 minutes and may recur as seldom as daily or as often as three times per hour (Bellantoni & Blackman, 1996). Most women learn to manage these brief periods of discomfort if they occur during the day. However, hot flashes frequently disrupt women's sleep. When this happens, it sets in motion a series of changes that are actually due to sleep deprivation rather than menopause. For example, lack of sleep can lead to mental confusion, difficulty with everyday memory tasks, and emotional instability. Thus, perimenopausal women may have the subjective feeling that they are "going crazy" when the real problem is that hot flashes are preventing them from getting enough sleep. The general light-headedness and shakiness that accompany some women's hot flashes can add to this sensation.

Eventually, estrogen and progesterone drop to consistently low levels and menstruation ceases altogether. Once a women has ceased to menstruate for a year, she is in the **postmenopausal phase.** In postmenopausal women, estradiol and estrone, both types

menopause the cessation of monthly menstrual cycles in middle-aged women

premenopausal phase the stage of menopause during which estrogen levels fall somewhat, menstrual periods are less regular, and anovulatory cycles begin to occur

perimenopausal phase the stage of menopause during which estrogen and progesterone levels are erratic, menstrual cycles may be very irregular, and women begin to experience symptoms such as hot flashes

postmenopausal phase the last stage of menopause beginning when a woman has had no menstrual periods for a year or more

of estrogen, drop to about a quarter or less of their premenopausal levels. Progesterone decreases even more, as a result of the cessation of ovulation, although the adrenal glands continue to provide postmenopausal women with some progesterone.

The reduction in estrogen during the perimenopausal and postmenopausal phases also has effects on genital and other tissue. The breasts become less firm, the genitals and the uterus shrink somewhat, and the vagina becomes both shorter and smaller in diameter. The walls of the vagina also become somewhat thinner and less elastic and produce less lubrication during intercourse (McCoy, 1998; Wich & Carnes, 1995).

Psychological Effects of Menopause
One other aspect of the climacteric in women deserves some mention. It has been part of folklore for a very long time that menopause involves major emotional upheaval as well as clear physical changes. Women were presumed to be emotionally volatile, angry, depressed, even shrewish during these mid-life years. Studies have shown that, in accordance with this myth, women are likely to view menopausal moods and behavior as being beyond their control (Lawlor & Choi, 1998; Poole, 1998). However, research findings are mixed.

Several relevant, well-designed longitudinal studies have examined this aspect of menopause. In the largest of these studies, researchers followed a group of 3,049 women aged 40 to 60 over a 10-year period (Busch, Zonderman, & Costa, 1994). Four of the studies reported no connection between menopausal status and a rise in depression or other psychological symptoms (Busch et al., 1994; Hallstrom & Samuelsson, 1985; Matthews et al., 1990; McKinlay, McKinlay, & Brambilla, 1987). By contrast, a more recent longitudinal study found that depressive symptoms increase during menopause (Freeman et al., 2004). Nevertheless, experts note that serious depression, as defined by the DSM-IV-TR criteria for major depressive disorder, is no more frequent among menopausal women than among those who are nonmenopausal.

What does seem to be associated with moods and social functioning during menopause is, among other things, a woman's overall negativity and number of life stressors before entering menopause (Dennerstein, Lehert, Burger, & Dudley, 1999; Dennerstein, Lehert, & Guthrie, 2002; Woods & Mitchell, 1997). In other words, a woman's negativity may be attributed to menopause when, in reality, it may be a long-standing component of her personality. Alternatively, she may have a particularly stressful life, and menopausal symptoms are just one more source of difficulty.

In addition, the actual level of symptoms women experience makes a difference. It isn't surprising that women who are most uncomfortable because of hot flashes and other physical changes, and whose symptoms last the longest, experience the most depression and negative mood. At any rate, research suggests that once they reach the postmenopausal phase, these women's dispositions change.

Researchers have also found that menopausal women who suffer from sleep deprivation due to hot flashes at night, or night sweats, may be misdiagnosed with generalized anxiety disorder. Not only are the symptoms of the two conditions similar, but electroencephalographic studies reveal that the patterns of brain activity across the two conditions are quite similar, too (Terashima et al., 2004).

Sexual Activity
Despite changes in the reproductive system, the great majority of middle-aged adults remain sexually active, although the frequency of sex declines somewhat during these years (Association of Reproductive Health Professionals, 2000; Laumann, Gagnon, Michael, & Michaels, 1994; Michael, Gagnon, Laumann, & Kolata, 1994). It is unlikely that this decline during mid-life is due wholly or even largely to drops in sex hormone levels; women do not experience major estrogen declines until their late 40s, but the decline in sexual activity begins much sooner. And the drop in testosterone among men is so gradual and slight during these years that it cannot be the full explanation. An alternative explanation is that the demands of other roles are simply so pressing that middle-aged adults find it hard to find time for sex. Increasing rates of chronic diseases such as diabetes and arthritis may also explain the declines in the frequency of sexual activity among people in their 50s (Association of Reproductive Health Professionals, 2000).

CRITICAL THINKING 9

What is your own view of menopause? How much has your view been influenced by negative stereotypes of menopausal women in the media?

The Pros and Cons of Hormone Replacement Therapy

Most of the physical symptoms and effects of menopause—including hot flashes, thinning of the vaginal wall, and loss of vaginal lubrication—can be dramatically reduced by taking estrogen and progesterone. Moreover, hormone replacement is associated with a reduction in mood swings in menopausal women (Klaiber, Broverman, Vogel, Peterson, & Snyder, 1997). However, researchers have found that women are very poorly informed about both menopause itself and the potential risks and benefits of hormone replacement therapy. Apparently, unlike women in nonindustrialized societies, who rely on older women for information, women in the industrialized world rely on drug manufacturers' advertisements on television and in women's magazines for information about menopause (Berg & Lipson, 1999; Clinkingbeard, Minton, Davis, & McDermott, 1999; Whittaker, 1998). Analyses of these sources of information have shown that they contain more misleading than helpful information (Gannon & Stevens, 1998). Thus, a woman who wants to make an informed decision about alternatives for dealing with the effects of menopause has to look beyond these information sources.

Hormone replacement therapy has had a somewhat checkered history. In the 1950s and 1960s, estrogen therapy became extremely common. In some surveys, as many as half of all postmenopausal women in the United States reported using replacement estrogen, many of them over periods of 10 years or more (Stadel & Weiss, 1975). In the 1970s, however, new evidence showed that the risk of endometrial cancer (cancer of the lining of the uterus) increased threefold to tenfold in women taking replacement estrogen (Nathanson & Lorenz, 1982). Not surprisingly, when this information became public, the use of estrogen therapy dropped dramatically.

The next phase of the debate emerged when a flurry of studies published in the 1980s and early 1990s showed that a combination of estrogen and progesterone, at quite low dosages, had the same benefits as estrogen alone and eliminated the increased risk of endometrial cancer. Studies also suggested that the use of replacement estrogen might reduce the risk of coronary heart disease by about half and significantly retard the development of osteoporosis (Barrett-Connor & Bush, 1991; Cauley et al., 1995; Ross, Paganini-Hill, Mack, & Henderson, 1987; Stampfer et al., 1991; Working Group for the PEPI Trial, 1995). Further, estrogen was being investigated as a possible preventive measure against Alzheimer's disease. Thus, in the 1990s, doctors often recommended hormone replacement therapy even to menopausal women who had few or no symptoms.

Everything changed again in 2002 with the publication of the results of the Women's Health Initiative (WHI), a longitudinal placebo-controlled study of hormone replacement therapy (Writing Group for the Women's Health Initiative Investigators, 2002). These results included alarming evidence showing that long-term use of either estrogen alone or combined estrogen-progesterone hormone replacement therapy significantly increased the risk of both breast and ovarian cancers (Chlebowski et al., 2003; Lacey et al., 2002). Data from the Heart and Estrogen Replacement Study (HERS) also showed that estrogen-progesterone therapy provided women with no protection against cardiovascular disease and may even have increased the severity of the disease among study participants who already had it (Grady et al., 2002; Hulley et al., 2002). The evidence suggesting that hormone replacement therapy might seriously harm women's health was so strong that the WHI was immediately terminated; all of the study's participants who had been given hormone replacement med-

THE SKELETAL SYSTEM

osteoporosis loss of bone mass with age, resulting in more brittle and porous bones

Another change that begins to be quite significant in middle adulthood is a loss of calcium from the bones, resulting in reduced bone mass and more brittle and porous bones. This process is called **osteoporosis.** Bone loss begins at about age 30 for both men and women, but in women the process is accelerated by menopause. The major consequence of this loss of bone density is a significantly increased risk of fractures, beginning as early as age 50 for women, much later for men. In the United States, it is estimated that almost one in four women will experience a hip fracture before the age of 80 (Lindsay, 1985). Among older women (and men), such fractures can be a major cause of disability and reduced activity, so osteoporosis is not a trivial change.

ications were advised to stop taking them (Writing Group for the Women's Health Initiative Investigators, 2002). Further, research failed to support the hypothesized link between estrogen and Alzheimer's disease, and some studies showed that estrogen treatment might actually increase the incidence of the disorder (Nelson, Humphrey, Nygren, Teutsch, & Allan, 2002; Shumaker et al., 2003).

To date, the accumulated evidence indicates that the only consistent benefits associated with hormone replacement therapy are the reduction of hot flashes and protection against osteoporosis (Nelson, 2004; Nelson et al., 2002; Torgerson & Bell-Syer, 2001). However, there may be ways of achieving these results without the risks associated with hormone replacement therapy. For instance, *selective serotonin reuptake inhibitors* (SSRIs), such as Prozac, have shown promise as a possible treatment for hot flashes (Stearns, Beebe, Iyengar, & Dube, 2003). In addition, the drug *alendronate* (Fosamax) is now being studied as a possible preventive measure against the development of osteoporosis (Greenspan, Resnick, & Parker, 2003).

Furthermore, researchers are taking a closer look at the claims made by many advocates of a "natural" approach to menopause (e.g., Lee, 1996). One area of research focuses on *bioidentical* hormones, or those that mimic the chemical structure and dosage levels of the body's own hormones. Advocates claim that bioidentical hormones are associated with little or no risk of cancer or other harmful effects. However, so far there have been very few controlled studies of these hormones, and no longitudinal research whatsoever (Jensen, 2003). The studies that have been done suggest that bioidentical hormones may be helpful in reducing the symptoms of menopause, but there is no evidence that they are less risky than conventional hormone replacement therapy

(Jensen, 2003). Moreover, research examining menopause-related claims made by the manufacturers of nutritional supplements such as clover extract and isoflavone-rich soy protein have shown that these substances offer little in the way of symptom relief and may interfere with other medications (Kreijkamp-Kaspers et al., 2004; Tice et al., 2003).

Researchers have also begun to compare various forms of hormones to determine which are least harmful. One form of estrogen, *17β-estradiol*, appears to be associated with fewer harmful effects than other forms of the hormone, for example, (Nelson, 2004). Some modes of hormone delivery may be less harmful than others as well. Studies have shown that hormones can be readily absorbed from creams applied either to the skin or directly to the vagina and from patches worn on any area of the body (Nelson, 2004). Doctors believe that creams and patches may be less risky than pills that must be metabolized through the digestive system (American College of Obstetricians and Gynecologists [ACOG], 2004b).

As a result of the most recent findings, the American College of Obstetricians and Gynecologists recommends that women be extremely cautious about entering into any regimen involving hormone replacement (ACOG, 2004b). First, they say that women should aim for the lowest dosage that provides symptom relief and avoid taking hormones for more than a year or two. Second, they suggest that hormone treatment be symptom-specific. For example, if a woman's main complaint is vaginal dryness, then the best treatment for her is a vaginal cream. They also suggest that women consider alternative treatments such as SSRIs. Finally, ACOG recommends that women undergoing any kind of treatment for menopausal symptoms see their doctors regularly and follow their instructions with regard to cancer screenings (e.g., mammograms).

In women, it is clear that bone loss is linked quite directly to estrogen and progesterone levels. Researchers know that these hormones fall dramatically after menopause, and it is the timing of menopause rather than age that signals the increase in rate of bone loss. Researchers also know that the rate of bone loss drops to premenopausal levels among women who take replacement hormones, all of which makes the link quite clear (Duursma, Raymakers, Boereboom, & Scheven, 1991). While the overall pattern of bone loss seems to be a part of primary aging, the amount of such loss nonetheless varies quite a lot from one individual to another. Table 5.1 (page 120) lists the known risk factors for osteoporosis.

Aside from taking replacement hormones, women can help prevent osteoporosis with one or both of the following strategies. First, they can get enough calcium during early

(Photo: © David Madison/Getty Images/Stone)

Any weight-bearing exercise—even walking—will help prevent osteoporosis.

TABLE 5.1	Risk Factors for Osteoporosis
Risk Factor	**Explanation**
Race	Whites are at higher risk than other races.
Gender	Women have considerably higher risk than men.
Weight	Those who are underweight are at higher risk.
Timing of climacteric	Women who experience early menopause and those who have had their ovaries removed are at higher risk, presumably because their estrogen levels decline at earlier ages.
Family history	Those with a family history of osteoporosis are at higher risk.
Diet	A diet low in calcium during adolescence and early adulthood results in lower peak levels of bone mass, and hence greater risk of falling below critical levels later. Whether there is any benefit in increasing intake of calcium postmenopausally remains in debate. Diets high in either caffeine (especially black coffee) or alcohol are also linked to higher risk.
Exercise	Those with a sedentary lifestyle are at higher risk. Prolonged immobility, such as bed rest, also increases the rate of bone loss. Exercise reduces the rate of bone loss.

(Sources: Duursma et al., 1991; Gambert, Schultz, & Hamdy, 1995; Goldberg & Hagberg, 1990; Gordon & Vaughan, 1986; Lindsay, 1985; Morrison et al., 1994; Smith, 1982.)

adulthood so that peak levels of bone mass are as robust as possible. Second, throughout adult life women can get regular exercise, particularly weight-bearing exercise such as walking or strength training. In one study, a group of middle-aged or older women were randomly assigned to a strength-training program consisting of twice-weekly sessions for a year. They showed a gain in bone density over the year, whereas women in a control group without such weight training showed a loss (Nelson et al., 1994).

VISION AND HEARING

One of the most noticeable physical changes occurring in the middle years is a loss of visual acuity. Most people find that they need reading glasses or bifocals by the time they are 45 or 50. Two changes in the eyes, collectively called **presbyopia,** are involved. First, the lens of the eye thickens. In a process that begins in childhood but produces noticeable effects only in middle adulthood, layer after layer of slightly pigmented material accumulates on the lens. Because light coming into the eye must pass through this thickened, slightly yellowed material, the total amount of light reaching the retina decreases, which reduces a person's overall sensitivity to light waves, particularly short wavelengths that are perceived as blue, blue-green, and violet (Fozard, 1990).

Because of this thickening of the lens, it is also harder and harder for the muscles surrounding the eye to change the shape of the lens to adjust the focus. In a young eye, the shape of the lens readily adjusts for distance, so no matter how near or far away some object may be, the light rays passing through the eye converge where they should, on the retina in the back of the eye, giving a sharp image. But as the thickening increases, the elasticity of the lens declines and it can no longer make these fine adjustments. Many images become blurry. In particular, the ability to focus clearly on near objects deteriorates rapidly in the 40s and early 50s. As a result, middle-aged adults often hold books and other items farther and farther away, because only in that way can they get a clear image. Finally, of course, they cannot read print at the distance at which they can focus, and they are forced to wear reading glasses or bifocals. These same changes also affect the ability to adapt quickly to variations in levels of light or glare, such as from passing headlights when driving at night or in the rain. So driving may become more stressful. All in all, these changes in the eyes, which appear to be a genuine part of primary aging, require both physical and psychological adjustment.

(Photo: © Myrleen Ferguson Cate/PhotoEdit)

By age 45 or 50, nearly everyone needs glasses, especially for reading.

presbyopia normal loss of visual acuity with aging, especially the ability to focus the eyes on near objects

The equivalent process in hearing is called **presbycusis.** The auditory nerves and the structures of the inner ear gradually degenerate as a result of basic wear and tear, resulting primarily in losses in the ability to hear sounds of high and very low frequencies. But these changes do not accumulate to the level of significant hearing loss until somewhat later in life than is typical for presbyopia. Hearing loss is quite slow until about age 50, and only a small percentage of middle-aged adults require hearing aids (Fozard, 1990). After age 50 or 55, however, the rate of hearing loss accelerates. Such a pattern of loss also appears to be an aspect of primary aging. But some secondary aging processes are involved as well. In particular, the amount of hearing loss is considerably greater in adults who work or live in very noisy environments—or who listen regularly to very loud music (Baltes, Reese, & Nesselroade, 1977).

Before going on . . .

- What do researchers know about brain function in middle age?

- How does reproductive function change in men and women in middle age?

- What is osteoporosis, and what factors are associated with it?

- How do vision and hearing change in middle age?

Health and Wellness

N o single variable affects the quality of life in middle and late adulthood as much as health. A middle-aged person in good health often functions as well and has as much energy as much younger adults. However, mid-life is the era during which the poor health habits and risky behaviors of earlier years begin to catch up with us.

HEALTH TRENDS AT MID-LIFE

In general, middle-aged adults report that they experience annoying aches and pains with greater frequency than when they were younger (Helme, 1998). Moreover, many middle-aged adults, especially women, are unhappy with their bodies; most would prefer to be thinner (Allaz, Bernstein, Rouget, Archinard, & Morabia, 1998). In addition, the number of truly healthy adults declines in mid-life. Perhaps half of adults between 40 and 65 have either some diagnosed disease or disability or a significant but undiagnosed problem, such as the early stages of heart disease. Still, 40-year-olds' life expectancy is remarkably high, as you can see from Figure 5.1 (page 112), and has been rising over the past few decades (Centers for Disease Control [CDC], 1998c; U.S. Bureau of the Census, 1990, 1995a). However, middle-aged adults have more chronic diseases and disabilities, such as diabetes and arthritis, than those who are younger (CDC, 1998a; U.S. Bureau of the Census, 1992). Similarly, disease-related death rates increase significantly in middle adulthood, as you can see from Figure 5.2 (page 112). The two leading causes of death in middle age are heart disease and cancer.

CARDIOVASCULAR DISEASE

The term **cardiovascular disease (CVD)** covers a variety of physical problems, but the key problem is in the arteries. In individuals suffering from CVD, the arteries become clogged with *plaque* (a fibrous or fatty substance), in a process called **atherosclerosis.** Eventually, vital arteries may become completely blocked, producing what laypeople call a heart attack (if the blockage is in the coronary arteries) or a stroke (if the blockage is in the brain). Atherosclerosis is not a normal part of aging. It is a disease, increasingly common with age, but not inevitable.

presbycusis normal loss of hearing with aging, especially of high-frequency tones

cardiovascular disease (CVD) a set of disease processes in the heart and circulatory system

atherosclerosis narrowing of the arteries caused by deposits of a fatty substance called plaque

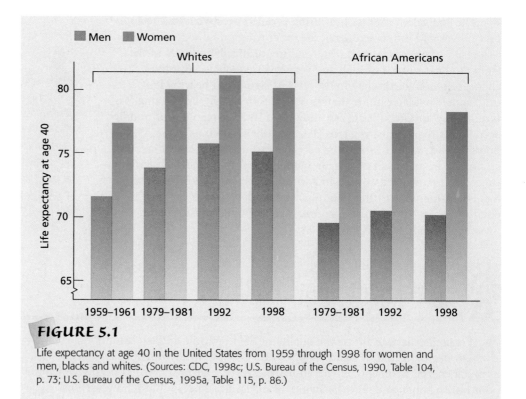

FIGURE 5.1

Life expectancy at age 40 in the United States from 1959 through 1998 for women and men, blacks and whites. (Sources: CDC, 1998c; U.S. Bureau of the Census, 1990, Table 104, p. 73; U.S. Bureau of the Census, 1995a, Table 115, p. 86.)

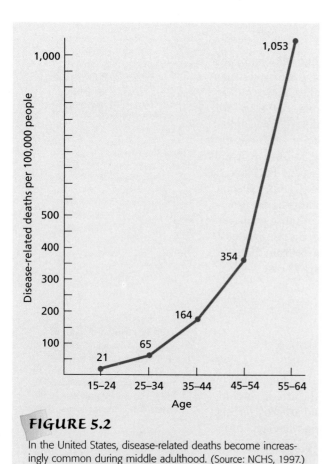

FIGURE 5.2

In the United States, disease-related deaths become increasingly common during middle adulthood. (Source: NCHS, 1997.)

The rate of CVD has been dropping rapidly in the United States and in most other industrialized countries in recent years. Between 1973 and 1987, for example, it decreased 42% among those under age 55 and dropped by a third for those aged 55 to 84—fairly startling declines that have contributed greatly to the increased life expectancy among today's adults (Davis, Dinse, & Hoel, 1994). During the 1990s, CVD declined another 20% among adults of all ages (U.S. Department of Health and Human Services, 1998b). Yet CVD remains the leading cause of death among adults in the United States and throughout the developed world. In fact, in the United States, heart disease causes more deaths than all other diseases combined (NCHS, 2000).

General Risk Factors   The best information about who is at risk for CVD comes from a number of long-term epidemiological studies, such as the Framingham study and the Nurses' Health Study, in which the health and habits of large numbers of individuals have been tracked over time. In the Framingham study, 5,209 adults were first studied in 1948, when they were aged 30 to 59. Their health (and mortality) has since been assessed repeatedly, which makes it possible to identify characteristics that predict CVD (Anderson, Castelli, & Levy, 1987; Dawber, Kannel, & Lyell, 1963; Garrison, Gold, Wilson, & Kannel, 1993; Kannel & Gordon, 1980). More recent studies continue to suggest the same risk factors (Dwyer et al., 2004; U.S. Department of Health and Human Services, 1998b). The left side of Table 5.2 lists the well-established risk factors that emerged from the

Framingham study and similar studies, along with a few other risk factors that are more speculative.

Because lists like the one in Table 5.2 have appeared in numerous popular magazines and newspapers, there's not likely to be much that is news here, but there are still a few important points to be made. First, the great majority of Americans have at least one of these risk factors. The Centers for Disease Control found that out of more than 91,000 adults interviewed in 1992, only 12.6% of men and 17.9% of women between 35 and 49 had none of the controllable risk factors for CVD (smoking, overweight, inactivity, high blood pressure, high cholesterol, and diabetes) (CDC, 1994). In the 50- to 64-year-old group, even fewer people (9.4% of men and 11.6% of women) showed no risk factors. So, although rates of both smoking and high cholesterol have declined since the significance of these two risk factors became widely publicized, most Americans could still do a much better job of reducing their heart disease risks.

Second, it is important to understand that these risks are cumulative in the same way that the health habits investigated in the Alameda County study seem to be

CRITICAL THINKING **9**

How many of the risk factors in Table 15.2 apply to you?

TABLE 5.2	Risk Factors for Heart Disease and Cancer	
Risk	**Heart Disease**	**Cancer**
Smoking	Major risk; the more you smoke, the greater the risk. Quitting smoking reduces risk.	Substantially increases the risk of lung cancer; also implicated in other cancers.
Blood pressure	Systolic pressure above 140 or diastolic pressure above 90 linked to higher risk.	No known risk.
Weight	Some increased risk with any weight above the normal range; risk is greater for those with weight 20% or more above recommended amount.	Being overweight is linked to increased risk of several cancers, including breast cancer, but the risk is smaller than for heart disease.
Cholesterol	Clear risk with elevated levels of low-density lipoproteins.	No known risk.
Inactivity	Inactive adults have about twice the risk of those who exercise.	Inactivity is associated in some studies with higher rates of colon cancer.
Diet	High-fat, low-fiber diet increases risk; antioxidants such as Vitamin E, Vitamin C, or beta-carotene may decrease risk.	Results are still unclear; a high-fat diet is linked to risk of some cancers; high-fiber diets appear to be protective for some cancers.
Alcohol	Moderate intake of alcohol, especially wine, linked to decreased CVD risk. Heavy drinking can weaken the heart muscle.	Heavy drinking is associated with cancers of the digestive system.
Heredity	Those with first-degree relatives with CVD have seven to ten times the risk; those who inherit a gene for a particular protein are up to twice as likely to have CVD.	Some genetic component with nearly every cancer.

(Sources: Centers for Disease Control, 1994; Dwyer et al., 2004; Gaziano & Hennekens, 1995; Hunter et al., 1996; Lee, Manson, Hennekens, & Paffenbarger, 1993; Manson et al., 1995; Manson et al., 2002; Morris, Kritchevsky, & Davis, 1994; Rich-Edwards, Manson, Hennekens, & Buring, 1995; Risch, Jain, Marrett, & Howe, 1994; Rose, 1993; Stampfer et al., 1993; Trichopoulou, Costacou, Bamia, & Trichopoulou, 2003; Willett et al., 1992, 1995; Woodward & Tunstall-Pedoe, 1995.)

cumulative: The more high-risk behaviors or characteristics you have, the higher your risk of heart disease; the effect is not just additive. For example, high cholesterol is three times more serious in a heavy smoker than in a nonsmoker (Tunstall-Pedoe & Smith, 1990).

Personality and Health Personality may also contribute to heart disease. The **type A personality pattern** was first described by two cardiologists, Meyer Friedman and Ray Rosenman (1974; Rosenman & Friedman, 1983). They were struck by the apparently consistent presence among patients who suffered from heart disease of several other characteristics, including competitive striving for achievement, a sense of time urgency, and hostility or aggressiveness. These people, whom Friedman and Rosenman named type A personalities, were perpetually comparing themselves to others, always wanting to win. They scheduled their lives tightly, timed themselves in routine activities, and often tried to do such tasks faster each time. They had frequent conflicts with their co-workers and family. Type B people, in contrast, were thought to be less hurried, more laid back, less competitive, and less hostile.

Early research by Friedman and Rosenman suggested that type A behavior was linked to higher levels of cholesterol, and hence to increased risk of CVD, even among people who did not suffer from observable heart disease. Contradictory results from more extensive studies since then, however, have forced some modifications in the original hypothesis (e.g., Miller, Turner, Tindale, Posavac, & Dugoni, 1991; O'Connor, Manson, O'Connor, & Buring, 1995).

For one thing, not all facets of the type A personality, as originally described, seem to be equally significant for CVD. The most consistent link has been found between CVD and hostility; hard-driving competitiveness is less consistently linked to CVD. Time pressure is not consistently related to CVD at all (Friedman, Hawley, & Tucker, 1994; Miller, Smith, Turner, Guijarro, & Hallet, 1996).

What is more, for individuals who are already at high risk of CVD—because of smoking, high blood pressure, or the like—information about levels of hostility does not add to the accuracy of heart disease predictions. That is, if two adults each have high blood pressure and high cholesterol, they are both equally at risk of heart disease, even if one of them also displays high levels of hostility and the other does not. It is only among people who do not show other risk factors that measures of hostility add helpful information to the prediction. The effect is fairly small, but in large samples of otherwise low-risk adults, those who are hostile and competitive are slightly more likely to develop CVD than those who are more easygoing.

Most people who have analyzed this research would now agree that there is some kind of connection between personality and CVD. What is less clear is just which aspects of personality are most strongly predictive. Some research suggests that measures of neuroticism or depression may be even better risk predictors than measures of hostility (e.g., Cramer, 1991).

CANCER

The second leading cause of death in middle and old age (in industrialized countries, at least) is cancer. In middle-aged men, the likelihood of dying of heart disease or cancer is about equal. Among middle-aged women, though, cancer is considerably more likely than heart disease to cause death.

Like heart disease, cancer does not strike in a totally random fashion. Indeed, as you can see in the right-hand column of Table 5.2, some of the same risk factors are implicated in both diseases. Most of these risk factors are at least partially under your own control. It helps to have established good health habits in early adulthood, but it is also clear from the research that improving your health habits in middle age can reduce your risks of both cancer and heart disease.

The most controversial item listed in Table 5.2 is diet; in particular, scientists debate the role of dietary fat as a potential risk factor. Some of the strongest evidence for a link

type A personality pattern a personality type associated with greater risk of coronary heart disease; it includes competitive achievement striving, a sense of time urgency, and, sometimes, hostility or aggressiveness

between diet and cancer comes from cross-national comparisons. For example, the typical Japanese diet contains only about 15% fat whereas the typical U.S. diet is closer to 40% fat, and cancer is much less common in Japan. The possibility of a causal link between dietary fat and cancer is further strengthened by the observation that in those areas in Japan where Western dietary habits have been most extensively adopted, cancer rates have risen to nearer Western levels (Weisburger & Wynder, 1991).

Comparisons of diet and cancer rates in many nations show similar patterns. This is especially clear in results from a study of U.N. data (Kesteloot, Lesaffre, & Joossens, 1991). Researchers obtained two kinds of information for each of 36 countries: (1) the death rate from each of several types of cancer and (2) the estimated per-person intake of fat from dairy products or lard. (Only dairy fat and lard are included because these are the major sources of saturated fats, thought to be more strongly implicated in disease.) Figure 5.3 shows the relationship between deaths from rectal cancer and fat consumption, one of the clearest connections, by country; the average correlation between the two was .64. The average correlations for other types of cancer were .60 for breast cancer in women, .70 for prostate cancer in men, .47 for colon cancer in women, and .43 for colon cancer in men. For all cancers combined, the correlations were .58 in men and .65 in women.

The Japanese, whose diet is very low in fat, have lower rates of some kinds of cancer than North Americans and Europeans.

While the debate over the role of diet continues, there is now little doubt that several types of cancers are caused by infectious agents (Ewald, 2000). For example, in Chapter 3 you learned about the link between the human papilloma virus (HPV) and cervical cancer (Castellsagué et al., 2002). This sexually transmitted disease is apparently also responsible for many cancers of the mouth, nose, and throat, presumably because of oral sex, and for some cases of anal cancer in gay men (Frisch et al., 1997; Mork et al., 2001).

Studies have shown that Epstein-Barr virus is also associated with cancers of the nose and throat, as well as one type of non-Hodgkin's lymphoma (Chien et al., 2001).

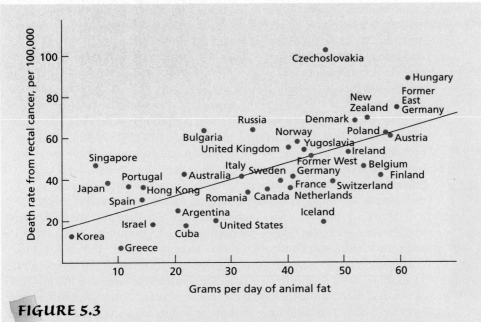

FIGURE 5.3

This figure shows the relationship between deaths from rectal cancer and fat consumption, one of the strongest correlations found in a large set of data relating diet to cancer rates compiled by the United Nations. (Source: Kesteloot, Lesaffre, & Joossens, 1991.)

Another virus, hepatitis B, is linked to liver cancer (Yang et al., 2002). Thus, screening people who do not yet have symptoms of these viral infections may help to identify cancers at very early stages of development, when they are most curable.

Correlations between bacterial infections and cancer have also been identified. For example, *Helicobacter pylori* has been implicated in many studies of stomach cancer and one type of non-Hodgkin's lymphoma (Uemura et al., 2001). This microorganism also causes stomach ulcers. Typically, antibiotic treatment clears up both the infection and the ulcers and, coincidentally, reduces the risk of stomach cancer. However, most people who carry *H. pylori* do not have ulcers or any other symptoms. Moreover, a fairly high proportion of people, especially those in developing nations with poor water purification systems, carry the infection (Brown, 2000). Consequently, researchers are currently trying to determine whether treating carriers who are asymptomatic will reduce rates of stomach cancer. Others are examining whether improvements in sanitary conditions in developing nations will lead to lower rates of *H. pylori* infection and stomach cancer.

Studies of the role of infection in the development of cancer provide yet another example of the importance of health-related choices. Specifically, safe sex practices can limit an individual's risk of contracting sexually transmitted diseases and the cancers in which they have been implicated. Moreover, vaccines against many viruses, including hepatitis B, are widely available. Drinking bottled water in locations or in situations in which the safety of the water supply is in question may also protect people from cancer-related bacterial infections such as *H. pylori*.

GENDER AND HEALTH

Figure 5.1 makes clear that women's life expectancy is greater than men's. But what is not evident is an interesting paradox: Women live longer, but they have more diseases and disabilities. Women are more likely to describe their health as poor, to have chronic conditions such as arthritis, and to be limited in their daily activities. Such differences have been found in every country in which the pattern has been studied, including nonindustrialized countries (Rahman, Strauss, Gertler, Ashley, & Fox, 1994).

This difference is already present in early adulthood and grows larger with age. By old age, women are substantially more likely than men to be chronically ill (Guralnik et al., 1993; Kunkel & Applebaum, 1992). In early adulthood, this gender difference in disease rate can be largely attributed to health problems associated with childbearing. At later ages, the difference cannot be explained in this same way.

How is it possible that men die younger but are healthier while they are alive? Researchers suggest that the apparent paradox can be resolved by considering sex differences in potentially fatal conditions such as cardiovascular disease (Verbrugge, 1989). In the United States, 143 of every 100,000 men between the ages of 45 and 54 die of heart disease annually, compared with only 50 of every 100,000 women (U.S. Bureau of the Census, 2003a). This difference in rates of heart disease diminishes once women are past menopause, although it does not disappear totally even in late old age.

It isn't just that men have higher rates of CVD; they also are more likely to die from the disease once it has been acquired. One reason may be that the heart muscles of women who have CVD seem to be better able to adapt to stresses such as physical exertion (van Doornen, Snieder, & Boomsma, 1998). In addition, once they suffer a heart attack, women recover to a higher level of physical functioning than men do (Bosworth et al., 2000). Sex differences in health habits also seem to contribute to women's greater ability to recover from CVD. For example, women are more likely to get regular checkups and to seek help early in an illness than men are (Addis & Mahalik, 2003; Verbrugge & Wingard, 1987).

Chances are this man will die before his wife does, but she will be more troubled by chronic illnesses in her middle and later years.

By contrast, women are more likely than men to suffer from nonfatal chronic ailments such as arthritis. Because chronic pain is characteristic of arthritis, the activities of women who suffer from it are often limited. Understandably, too, living with chronic pain affects their general sense of well-being.

SOCIOECONOMIC CLASS, RACE, AND HEALTH

While emphasizing preventive actions such as exercise, developmentalists cannot ignore the importance for health and mental ability in middle adulthood of those familiar demographic variables social class and race. If you look again at Figure 3.1 (page 58), you'll see that social class is a more significant predictor of variations in health in middle age than at any other time of adult life. In middle adulthood, occupational level and education (both of which correlate strongly with socioeconomic class) are most predictive of health. Figure 3.1 does not break this pattern down by race, but research suggests that the same link between social class and health is found among Hispanic Americans and African Americans (Chatters, 1991; James, Keenan, & Browning, 1992; Markides & Lee, 1991).

Race is also linked to overall health. For example, African Americans have shorter life expectancies than white Americans, as Figure 5.1 shows. There are also racial differences in incidence of specific diseases (CDC, 2003a). In recent years, public health officials in the United States have begun to study and address these disparities. These efforts have focused on three diseases: cardiovascular disease, diabetes, and cancer.

Cardiovascular Disease Although cardiovascular disease (heart attack and stroke) is the leading cause of death in all racial groups, it disables and/or kills a higher proportion of African Americans, Mexican Americans, and Native Americans than of either white or Asian Americans (U.S. Department of Health and Human Services, 1998b; Wong et al., 2002). Rates of disease are higher in these groups because they are more likely to possess every risk factor listed in Table 5.2.

Among minority women, the major factor seems to be obesity. More than half of African American and Mexican American women are overweight, compared to 34% of white women (U.S. Department of Health and Human Services, 1998b). Among men, the key risk factor is high blood pressure, or **hypertension** (U.S. Department of Health and Human Services, 1998b). About 25% of white men have elevated blood pressure, compared to 35% of African American men. Mexican American men are more likely than white American men to have hypertension, although precise incidence rates have yet to be determined (U.S. Department of Health and Human Services, 1998b).

Diabetes The proportion of adults in the United States who suffer from diabetes is growing in all racial groups but minorities have significantly higher rates of the condition than whites (CDC, 2003a; Wong, Shapiro, Boscardin, & Ettner, 2002; U.S. Department of Health and Human Services, 1998c). Men and women have equal rates of this disease. In particular, 10.8% of African Americans, 10.6% of Mexican Americans, and 9% of Native Americans have diabetes, compared to 7.8% of whites. Public health officials estimate that there is at least one undiagnosed case of diabetes for every two individuals who have been diagnosed. Thus, public education about diabetes has become a major health goal in the United States, because the disease can lead to severe complications such as cardiovascular disease, kidney failure, and blindness (CDC, 1998a). Just as they are more likely than whites to have the disease in the first place, minority adults who have been diagnosed with diabetes are more likely than their white counterparts to develop complications (U.S. Department of Health and Human Services, 1998c). Although diabetes itself kills few people, it is the underlying cause of so many other potentially deadly diseases and conditions that death rates

hypertension elevated blood pressure

You can inherit it.
You can be
born with it.
You can get it
during pregnancy.
You can develop it from
the way you live.
So is there anyway
— to be safe from
diabetes?

I am one of the 18 million Americans managing life with diabetes.
Join me, Novo Nordisk and the Entertainment Industry Foundation
in the fight to change the way this disease is treated, one
person at a time.

To learn more, or to take an easy test for diabetes,
ask your doctor. For more information, visit
www.DiabetesAware.com

novo nordisk   EIF
                ENTERTAINMENT
                INDUSTRY FOUNDATION

Public health officials in the United States believe that public awareness of the risks associated with diabetes will encourage people to seek treatment for the disease earlier, thereby avoiding some of its more serious complications.

among adults who have diabetes are about twice as high at every age as those among individuals who do not have this disease (CDC, 1998a).

Public health officials don't yet have an explanation for racial differences in diabetes rates. However, they hypothesize that complication rates vary because minorities tend to develop the disease earlier in life than whites do (U.S. Department of Health and Human Services, 1998c). Therefore, it affects all of their body systems for a longer period of time. Once diagnosed, minority adults often have less access to regular medical care than whites. However, researchers have found that, even among diabetic whites and African Americans who have the same health insurance benefits and equal access to diabetes care services, African Americans are less likely to seek care for complications at a point when medical intervention can be most effective (U.S. Department of Health and Human Services, 1998c).

For example, because of the disease's effects on the kidneys, some diabetics develop circulation problems in their lower extremities that can cause complications that result in amputation. These problems are evidenced by sores on the feet and legs that do not heal. If diabetics obtain medical intervention when such wounds first appear, the likelihood of amputation can be significantly reduced. Unfortunately, because they delay seeking care, African Americans with diabetes are more likely than their white counterparts to have a lower limb amputated (U.S. Department of Health and Human Services, 1998c). Public health officials do not yet have an explanation for this behavioral difference. However, they agree that educating minority adults who have diabetes about the necessity of obtaining immediate care for any kind of problem is critical to reducing complication rates among them.

Cancer African Americans also have higher incidences of most types of cancer and have poorer survival rates once cancer is diagnosed, perhaps because they receive medical care later in the illness (Blakeslee, 1994; Chatters, 1991). For example, African American men have the highest rate of prostate cancer in the world (CDC, 2000a). In the United States, 55.5% of white cancer patients survive at least 5 years; among African Americans, the comparable figure is 40.4% (U.S. Bureau of the Census, 1995b). Other groups also have higher rates of specific cancers than do white Americans (U.S. Department of Health and Human Services, 1998a). For example, Native American men are more likely than white American men to develop lung cancer or colorectal cancer. In addition, Vietnamese American and Hispanic American women have higher rates of cervical cancer than white women.

The main cause for cross-racial variations in cancer incidence and death rates, according to public health officials, is failure to receive routine cancer screenings. Minority men and women are less likely than whites to obtain mammograms, Pap smears, and colorectal examinations. Thus, improving minorities' access to and knowledge about cancer screening services is critical to reducing cancer deaths in these groups (U.S. Department of Health and Human Services, 1998a). Likewise, ensuring that screened adults have access to follow-up care is another public health goal. Moreover, public health officials are concerned that minority cancer rates are likely to increase in the future because the prevalence of tobacco use is higher among minority teens than among white youth and is increasing (CDC, 1998c).

Development in the Information Age

Is the Internet Addictive?

Although new technologies are usually associated with the young, surveys suggest that middle-aged and even older adults spend more time "surfing the Net" than those who are younger (Hinden, 2000; T. Miller, 1996). Recently, some mental health professionals have raised concerns about the amount of time some individuals spend online. Some claim to have discovered a new disorder they call *Internet addictive disorder,* or IAD (Griffiths, 1999). The criteria for the disorder are the same as for other addictions. Specifically, to be diagnosed with IAD, a person must demonstrate a pattern of Internet use that interferes with normal educational, occupational, and social functioning.

To be sure, there are individuals who spend a great deal of time online and who admit that Internet use often interferes with other activities (Brenner, 1997). However, to justify the use of the term *addiction* in relation to a specific activity, the activity itself must have some addictive power. For example, alcohol induces an altered state of consciousness that users find desirable. The altered state reinforces the behavior of consuming alcohol. Thus, those who propose that IAD exists are, by implication, saying that the experience of being online has the capacity to induce some kind of reinforcing state in users.

Some Internet users report that online communication is more pleasurable than face-to-face social encounters (Chou et al., 1999). But is this sense of pleasure enough to bring about an addiction, or is socializing on the Internet nothing more than an easy way to escape the usual pressures of social interaction? Similarly, use of online pornography for sexual gratification is clearly a problem for some people (Cooper, Putnam, Planchon, & Boies, 1999). However, is it any different from use of conventional sources of pornography such as adult magazines and videos?

In fact, research has suggested that excessive Internet use may be part of a behavior pattern that is consistent across several media (Greenberg, Lewis, & Dodd, 1999). Those who are "addicted" to the Internet also spend inordinate amounts of time watching television and playing video games. They are also more likely to be addicted to alcohol and other substances.

Thus, rather than being a distinct addictive disorder, what seems more likely is that excessive Internet use is a new means by which people can escape from everyday problems. In this way, the Net is no different from books, television, movies, or even drugs. The Net may simply provide people who have some kind of tendency toward a specific addictive problem—such as an obsession with pornography or gambling—with an additional avenue through which to express this tendency (Fabi, 2004; Griffiths, 2003). Thus, mental health professionals who oppose the idea of Internet addiction suggest that excessive time online either is a symptom of another disorder—such as an obsession with pornography or gambling—or simply reflects fascination with a new medium (Griffiths, 1999; Grohol, 1999).

MENTAL HEALTH

As you learned in Chapter 3, most types of mental health problems are considerably more common in early adulthood than in the middle years of adult life. However, about two-thirds of adults diagnosed with serious mental disorders in early adulthood continue to have difficulties in middle age (Meeks, 1997). Further, though most addictive disorders begin in adolescence or early adulthood, they frequently go undiagnosed until the middle adulthood years, when they begin to have dramatic effects on health and other areas of functioning that sufferers or their families can no longer deny (see Development in the Information Age).

Alcoholism, defined as physical and psychological dependence on alcohol, takes a particularly heavy toll during middle age. For example, some parts of the brains of middle-aged alcoholics are smaller and less responsive to stimuli than the brains of nonalcoholics (Laakso et al., 2000; Polo, Escera, Gual, & Grau, 1999). Functional deficits among alcoholics include problems with memory and language. Cardiovascular disease is more prevalent among alcoholics as well, because long-term exposure to alcohol weakens the muscles of the heart along with the valves and walls of the body's

alcoholism physical and psychological dependence on alcohol

Before going on . . .

■ What are the major trends in health during middle adulthood?

■ How does coronary heart disease develop?

■ What factors contribute to cancer?

■ What are some important differences in the health of middle-aged men and women?

■ How are socioeconomic status and race related to health in middle adulthood?

■ What are some of the consequences of alcoholism for middle-aged adults?

blood vessels. Further, long-term heavy drinking damages the digestive system, impairs the immune system, and contributes to losses in muscle strength (Laso et al., 1999; Tarter et al., 1997). In women, alcoholism is associated with a delay in the course of the phases of menopause (Torgerson, Thomas, Campbell, & Reid, 1997).

The result of this interaction between aging and alcohol abuse is that alcoholics face an increased risk of health problems and death (Dawson, 2000). A longitudinal study involving more than 40,000 males in Norway found that the rate of death prior to age 60 was significantly higher among alcoholics than among nonalcoholics (Rossow & Amundsen, 1997). Not surprising, perhaps, is the finding that alcoholics were three times as likely to die in automobile accidents as their nonalcoholic peers. However, alcoholics were also almost three times as likely to die of heart disease and had twice the rate of deaths from cancer.

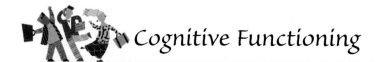

Cognitive Functioning

In the middle adult years, some cognitive abilities improve, while others slow down a bit. Still, many adults have acquired large bodies of knowledge and skill that help them compensate for losses and solve problems within their areas of expertise more efficiently than younger adults do.

A MODEL OF PHYSICAL AND COGNITIVE AGING

Many of the various bits and pieces of information you've encountered so far about physical and cognitive changes in adulthood can be combined in a single model, suggested by Nancy Denney and illustrated in Figure 5.4 (Denney 1982, 1984). Denney proposed that on nearly any measure of physical or cognitive functioning, age-related changes follow a typical curve, like those shown in the figure. But she also argued that

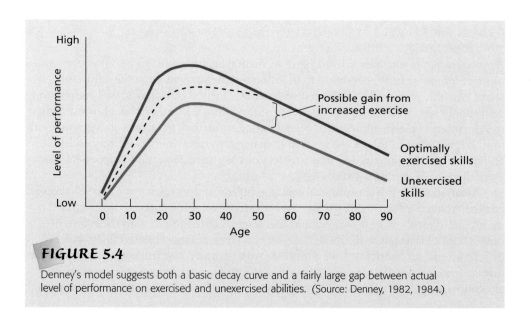

FIGURE 5.4

Denney's model suggests both a basic decay curve and a fairly large gap between actual level of performance on exercised and unexercised abilities. (Source: Denney, 1982, 1984.)

the height of this curve varies, depending on the amount an individual exercises some ability or skill. Denney used the word *exercise* very broadly, to refer not only to physical exercise but also to mental exercise and to the extent to which some specific task has been performed before. Unexercised abilities generally have a lower peak level of performance; exercised abilities generally have a higher peak.

Many laboratory tests of memory, for example, such as memorizing lists of names, tap unexercised abilities. Everyday memory tasks, such as recalling details from a newspaper column, tap much more exercised abilities. The distinction is somewhat similar to the distinction between crystallized and fluid abilities (see Chapter 3). Most crystallized abilities are at least moderately exercised, whereas many fluid abilities are relatively unexercised. But Denney was making a more general point: Whether abilities are crystallized or fluid, those that are more fully exercised will have a higher peak.

The gap between the curve for unexercised abilities and the curve for maximally exercised abilities represents the degree of improvement that would be possible for any given skill. Any skill that is not fully exercised can be improved if the individual begins to exercise that ability. There is clear evidence, for example, that aerobic capacity (VO_2 max) can be increased at any age if a person begins a program of physical exercise (e.g., Blumenthal et al., 1991; Buchner, Beresford, Larson, LaCroix, & Wagner, 1992; Cheitlin, 2003). Nonetheless, in Denney's model, the maximum level an adult will be able to achieve, even with optimum exercise, will decline with age, just as performance of top athletes declines, even with optimum training regimens. One implication of this is that young adults are more likely to be able to get away with laziness or poor study habits and still perform well; as they age, this becomes less and less true, because they are fighting against the basic decay curve of aging.

The dashed line in Figure 5.4 represents a hypothetical curve for a skill that is not optimally exercised but is still used fairly regularly. Many verbal skills fall into this category, as do problem-solving skills. Because skills like these are demanded in a great many jobs, they are well exercised in most adults in their 20s, 30s, 40s, and 50s and are therefore well maintained, creating a flat-topped curve. But if Denney is correct, then at some point even optimum exercise will no longer maintain these abilities at that same level, and some decline will occur.

This model does not take into account all the facts. In particular, Denney's model does not easily handle the wide degree of variation from one individual to the next in the pattern of skill maintenance or decline over age (Schaie, 1990). But what Denney's model does do is emphasize that there is an underlying decay curve. Those in middle adulthood may perform as well as or better than the average young adult in arenas in which they regularly exercise their skills. However, with increasing age, this high level of function requires more and more effort, until eventually every adult reaches a point at which even maximum effort will no longer maintain peak function.

HEALTH AND COGNITIVE FUNCTIONING

You should remember from Chapter 3 that it is often difficult to separate the effects of primary and secondary aging, because they happen at the same time. Denney's model helps illuminate the links between primary aging and cognitive functioning in middle age. Research examining correlations between health and cognition helps developmentalists understand the effects of secondary aging. Specifically, many of the same characteristics that are linked to increased or decreased risk of heart disease and cancer are also linked to the rate of change or the maintenance of intellectual skill in the middle years.

One illustration of this relationship comes from Warner Schaie's analysis of data from the Seattle Longitudinal Study (1983). He found that those research participants who had some kind of cardiovascular disease (either coronary heart disease or high blood pressure) showed earlier and larger declines on intellectual tests than did those who were disease-free. Other researchers have found similar linkages. Even adults

(Photo: © Tom Stewart/CORBIS)

Research shows that middle-aged adults who are physically active have lower mortality rates over the next 20–30 years than their peers who are less active. Physical exercise during middle age is also positively correlated with scores on tests of intellectual functioning.

whose blood pressure is controlled by medication seem to show earlier declines (Sands & Meredith, 1992; Schultz, Elias, Robbins, Streeten, & Blakeman, 1986). Schaie cautions against taking these findings too far. The size of the effect is quite small, and it may operate indirectly rather than directly. For example, adults with cardiovascular disease may become physically less active as a response to their disease. The lower level of activity, in turn, may affect the rate of intellectual decline. This raises the possibility that exercise may be one of the critical factors in determining an individual person's overall physical health and cognitive performance during middle adulthood. A growing amount of information confirms such an effect.

One particularly large and well-designed study of the effects of exercise on physical health involved 17,321 Harvard alumni who had been students between 1916 and 1950. In 1962 or 1966, when the men were in their 30s, 40s, or 50s, each man provided detailed information about his daily levels of physical activity (Lee, Hsieh, & Paffenbarger, 1995). (The measures of physical activity were quite detailed. Each man reported how many blocks he normally walked each day, how often he climbed stairs, the amount of time per week he normally engaged in various sports, and so on. All the answers were then converted into estimates of calories expended per week. For example, walking 1 mile on level ground uses roughly 100 calories; climbing one flight of stairs uses about 17.) The researchers tracked all these men until 1988 to identify who had died and of what cause. The link between the level of physical activity and death rates over the succeeding 25 years is shown clearly in Figure 5.5: The more exercise a man reported, the lower his mortality risk.

Researchers were careful to exclude from the study any man who was known to suffer from heart disease or other disease at the onset of the study, in the 1960s. Furthermore, the groups differed *only* in level of energy expenditure; they did not differ in age or whether they smoked, had high blood pressure, were overweight, or had a family history of early death—which makes the effect of exercise even clearer. To be sure, because the level of exercise was each man's own choice, there may have been other differences separating the various exercise groups that could account for the dif-

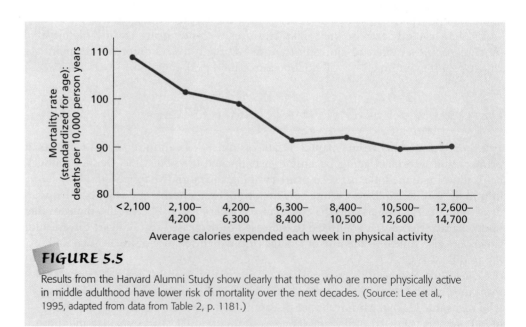

FIGURE 5.5

Results from the Harvard Alumni Study show clearly that those who are more physically active in middle adulthood have lower risk of mortality over the next decades. (Source: Lee et al., 1995, adapted from data from Table 2, p. 1181.)

ferent death rates. But the pattern, which has been replicated in other groups of both men and women, is so substantial and striking that alternative explanations are hard to come by (e.g., Blair et al., 1995; Lissner et al., 1996). By far the most likely explanation is that there is a causal connection between longevity and level of physical activity.

Physical exercise also seems to help maintain cognitive abilities in the middle adult years, very likely because it helps to maintain cardiovascular fitness (Rogers, Meyer, & Mortel, 1990). Among physically healthy middle-aged and older adults, those who are more physically active—doing gardening, heavy housework, or aerobic exercise such as walking, running, or swimming—score higher on tests of reasoning, reaction time, and short-term memory (Van Boxtel et al., 1997).

A different approach to studying exercise and cognitive functioning would involve randomly assigning some people to an exercise program and some to a nonexercise control group, and then seeing whether the two groups differed in their cognitive functioning after a period of exercise. The results of the small number of studies of this type have been quite mixed. Every study finds that exercise increases measures of physical functioning, such as VO_2 max, even in very elderly adults. Some—but not all—such studies also show that exercise improves thinking (Hawkins, Kramer, & Capaldi, 1992; Hill, Storandt, & Malley, 1993). Other studies do not come to that conclusion (e.g., Buchner et al., 1992; Emery & Gatz, 1990). In most cases, the experimental exercise program lasts only a few months, and that may not be sufficient to make any difference in mental functioning. Still, because researchers already know that exercise is linked to lower levels of disease and greater longevity, prudence alone would argue for including it in your life.

CHANGES IN MEMORY AND COGNITION

When developmentalists study changes in cognitive functioning in middle age, they find almost precisely what Denney's model and Schaie's longitudinal study suggest. That is, lack of mental exercise tends to be correlated with declines in memory and cognitive skills, but major deficits are not found until after age 60 to 65.

Memory Function   Drawing conclusions about memory function in middle age is difficult because studies of age differences in adult memory rarely include middle-aged people. Typically, researchers compare very young adults, such as college students, to adults in their 60s and 70s. When the two groups are found to differ, psychologists often infer that middle-aged adults' performance falls somewhere between the two. In other words, they assume that memory function declines steadily, in linear fashion, across the adult years—an assumption that may not be true.

One thing developmentalists do know about memory is that the subjective experience of forgetfulness clearly increases with age. The older we get, the more forgetful we think we are (Commissaris, Ponds, & Jolles, 1998). However, it may be that the memory demands of middle-aged adults' everyday lives are greater than those of young adults'. Remember, working memory is limited, and the more you try to remember at one time, the more you will forget.

Middle-aged adults are very proficient at overcoming perceived memory limitations by using reminders, or *cues*, to help themselves remember information. Thus, the middle-aged person who knows that she may forget where her car is parked makes a point of noting nearby landmarks that will help her remember its location. This may be because middle-aged adults, in contrast to those who are older, continue to have a high sense of self-efficacy with respect to memory (Lineweaver & Hertzog, 1998). In other words, they believe their efforts will make a difference, so they actively work to improve their memories.

Nevertheless, there seem to be some real differences in the memory performance of young and middle-aged adults. For example, visual memory, the ability to remember

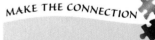

MAKE THE CONNECTION

Look back at the information on cross-sectional and longitudinal research designs in Chapter 1. How might cohort differences affect the results of studies comparing cognitive functioning of middle-aged adults to that of both younger and older adults? What kind of design would minimize such cohort effects? If such a study were begun today, how long would it be before researchers could derive useful conclusions from the data?

Some declines in cognitive performance, such as increased reaction times, are evident even when middle-aged individuals are engaged in activities with which they have had many years of relevant experience. However, expertise is associated with the development of cognitive strategies that help to buffer the effects of aging (Morrow et al., 2003). Consequently, middle-aged adults are able to maintain high levels of performance on cognitively demanding tasks, such as flying a commercial airliner.

an object you have seen for just a few seconds, declines in middle age (Fahle & Daum, 1997; Giambra, Arenberg, Zonderman, Kawas, & Costa, 1995). Further, the more complex the visual stimulus and the longer the interval between presentation and recall, the greater the difference. By contrast, memory for auditory stimuli seems to remain stable throughout adulthood.

Performance on more complex memory tasks, such as remembering lists of words and passages of text, also declines with age, but usually not until after about age 55. In contrast, recognition of words and texts appears to remain stable throughout adulthood (Zelinski & Burnight, 1997). Such findings suggest that there are age differences in working memory. Research examining short-term memory capacity at various ages shows that it remains very stable throughout early, middle, and late adulthood. What changes, apparently, is the ability to make efficient use of available capacity (Lincourt, Rybash, & Hoyer, 1998).

Semantic and Episodic Memories

Researchers can gain additional insight into age-related memory changes by studying how well young and middle-aged adults encode different kinds of memories. **Episodic memories** are recollections of personal events or episodes. **Semantic memories** represent general knowledge. For example, a person's memories of a vacation in Hawaii are episodic, and her knowledge that Hawaii was the 50th state is semantic.

Researchers find that young and middle-aged adults differ more with respect to new episodic memories than they do with respect to semantic memories (Maylor, 1998; Nilsson, Baeckman, Erngrund, & Nyberg, 1997). For example, a middle-aged person attending a baseball game may forget where he parked his car (episodic memory). However, he is unlikely to forget the basic rules of the game (semantic memory).

Yet it is too simplistic to say that episodic encoding is better in younger than in older adults. The difference is a bit more complex than that. Research examining the memories of adults for highly memorable episodes, often called *flashbulb memories,* has demonstrated that age has no effect on our ability to recall such events. For example, in one study, researchers asked young, middle-aged, and older adults to recount where they were and what they were doing when they heard about the verdict in the O. J. Simpson trial (Bluck, Levine, & Laulhere, 1999). Respondents of all ages remembered the event with equal clarity. Younger respondents were somewhat more likely to report details. However, other research on such memories suggests that memory for details surrounding such episodes is subject to suggestion and overconfidence (Neisser & Harsch, 1992; Niedzwienska, 2003). Moreover, longitudinal studies of individuals' flashbulb memories of the terrorist attacks of September 11, 2001, have shown that memory for details of such events declines over time (Smith, Bibi, & Sheard, 2003). So the younger participants may have thought they remembered details when, in reality, their minds were simply filling in gaps in their memories with assumed details.

Practiced and Unpracticed Skills

In general, adults maintain or even gain in skill on any task that they practice often or that is based on specific learning. For example, verbal abilities increase in middle age (Giambra et al., 1995; Salthouse, 2004). It appears that vocabulary—or, more precisely, performance on vocabulary tests—doesn't begin to decline until about age 65. And the "use it or lose it" dictum seems to hold true for cognitive abilities. That is, adults who engage in intellectually challenging activities show fewer losses in cognitive skills than those who do not (Salthouse, 2004; Schaie, Nguyen, Willis, Dutta, & Yue, 2001).

Similarly, expertise in a particular field helps to compensate for age-related deficits in cognitive functioning (Colonia-Willner, 1999; Morrow et al., 2003; Tsang, 1998). For

episodic memories recollections of personal events

semantic memories general knowledge

example, in one study, researchers examined 17- to 79-year-old participants' ability to recognize melodies performed at varying tempos (Andrews, Dowling, Bartlett, & Halpern, 1998). Some tunes were played very rapidly and then slowed until participants could recognize them. Both age and years of musical training predicted participants' ability to recognize melodies presented in this way, but the relationship between age and recognition was much weaker than the relationship between recognition and musical training. Other melodies were played too slowly to be recognized at the beginning and then speeded up. Interestingly, only musical training correlated with recognition of tunes played this way; there was no association with age whatsoever.

When researchers examine middle-aged adults' performance on unfamiliar or unpracticed skills, such as a timed arithmetic test or a three-dimensional spatial task, the effects of aging are apparent. In particular, mental processes get steadily slower with age (Salthouse, 1991). Still, longitudinal research suggests that, even in these unfamiliar domains, the actual losses for most adults in this age range are small (Giambra et al., 1995). Major declines seem to happen after about age 60. Such results support conclusions such as that expressed by psychologist Warner Schaie:

> It is my general conclusion that reliably replicable age changes in psychometric abilities of more than trivial magnitude cannot be demonstrated prior to age 60, but that reliable decrements can be shown to have occurred for all abilities by age 74. (Schaie, 1983a, p. 127)

New Learning When it comes to acquiring new knowledge, middle-aged adults seem to be just as capable as younger adults of learning and remembering new information. In fact, middle-aged college students tend to be more academically successful than their younger peers (Burley, Turner, & Vitulli, 1999). Psychologists hypothesize that this difference is due to both motivational differences and the greater amount of background knowledge and experience possessed by older students.

Interestingly, surveys suggest that employers believe young adults to be more capable of learning new job skills than are those who are older. However, research seems to show that there are few, if any, differences in the rates at which young and middle-aged adults learn new job skills (Forte & Hansvick, 1999). Particularly with regard to computer skills, once the skills have been acquired, there are no age-related differences in performance.

Schematic Processing The literature on memory change with age also offers support for Labouvie-Vief's view that what happens to cognition in adulthood involves not only decline but also changes in emphasis, or structure. Labouvie-Vief, as you may recall from Chapter 3, suggests that middle adults tend to shift away from the logical or formal operational approach, which dominates thinking in adolescence and young adulthood, to a more pragmatic approach aimed at solving everyday problems—a process some developmentalists call *schematic processing* (Labouvie-Vief, 1990). In other words, the schemas used by a middle-aged adult to process information are qualitatively different from those used earlier in life. Such a schematic difference might lead middle-aged adults to pay more attention to overarching themes than to details. In memory, this difference in schematic processing might be reflected in a decline in memory for surface detail, accompanied by an increase in memory for themes and meanings.

A study in which researchers asked adults of various ages to read a story and then to recall it immediately afterward, in writing, yielded support for this hypothesis (Adams, 1991). Younger adults were more likely to report specific events or actions in the story, while middle-aged adults recalled more of the psychological motivations of the characters and offered more interpretations of the story in their recall. What this may mean is that, along with a shift in schematic processing, the encoding process changes as we get older. We may not attempt to encode as much detail, but may store more summarizing information.

CREATIVITY

A somewhat different question about cognitive functioning in the middle years of adulthood—one that may have more direct relevance for one's work life—has to do with creativity and productivity (see the Real World feature). Some widely quoted early research suggested that peak creativity, like peak physical functioning, occurs in early adulthood (Lehman, 1953). The technique used in this study involved identifying a series of major scientific discoveries of the past several hundred years and finding out how old each scientist was at the time of that discovery. Most were quite young, especially those who worked in more theoretical sciences and in mathematics. The classic example is Einstein, who was 26 when he developed the theory of relativity. These are interesting patterns, but this approach may be going at the question backwards. The alternative is to study scientists or other problem-solvers throughout their working lives and see whether the average person (someone who *isn't* an Einstein) is more productive and creative in early or middle adult life.

More recently, one psychologist has moved a step in this direction by looking at the lifetime creativity and productivity of thousands of notable scientists from the 19th century and earlier (Simonton, 1991, 2000). Simonton identified the age at which these individuals (nearly all men) published their first significant work, their best work, and their last work. In every scientific discipline represented, the thinkers produced their best work at about age 40, on average. But most of them were publishing significant, even outstanding, research through their 40s and into their 50s. In fact, researchers propose that the reason people tend to do their best work at about 40 is not that the mind works better at that age, but that productivity is at its highest at that time. Chance alone suggests that the best work will come during the time when the most work is being done.

Lifetime creative output of modern-day scientists follows a similar pattern. Mathematicians, psychologists, physicists, and other scientists born in the 20th century have consistently shown their maximum productivity (usually measured by the number of papers published in a single year) when they were about 40. But research quality (as measured by the number of times each research paper is cited by peers) remains high through age 50 or even 60 (Horner, Rushton, & Vernon, 1986; Simonton, 1988).

Among musicians or other artists, peak creativity may occur later or be maintained far longer. For example, in one study, researchers asked judges to rate the aesthetic qualities of musical compositions by the 172 composers whose works are most often performed (Simonton, 1988). Works created late in life ("swan songs") were most likely to be evaluated as masterpieces by the judges.

It is also possible to approach the question of how age is related to creativity or professional effectiveness experimentally. One such study broadened examination of adult creativity beyond the realm of scientific research by focusing on business executives (Streufert, Pogash, Piasecki, & Post, 1990). The researchers created four-person decision-making teams, made up of mid-level managers from state and federal government and private industry. On 15 of the teams, the participants were all between ages 28 and 35. Members of another 15 teams were middle-aged (aged 45 to 55), and another 15 teams included only older adults (aged 65 to 75). Each team was given a wonderfully complex simulated task: They were asked to manage an imaginary developing country called Shamba. They were given packets of information about Shamba ahead of time and could request additional information during their group work, done via a computer—which was of course programmed to make the experience of the different groups as much alike as possible, although the participants did not know that. Every team faced a crisis in Shamba at about the same time in their work.

Researchers recorded all the questions, suggestions, and plans generated by each team, from which they created a series of measures of activity rate, speed of response, depth of analysis, diversity of suggestions, and strategic excellence of each group's performance. The teams of young and middle-aged participants differed significantly on

CRITICAL THINKING

Why do you think that some people associate creativity with youth, when there are so many highly creative middle-aged and older adults?

Maintaining the Creative "Edge" at Mid-Life and Beyond

In a fascinating set of interviews, a number of highly successful and creative people described how they viewed creativity ("The creators," 2000). Interviewees ranged in age from 50 (musician Bobby McFerrin) to 93 (architect Phillip Johnson). Interestingly, all reported that they viewed themselves as more creative than they had been when they were younger. Their comments suggested that the creative process is a highly individualized intellectual activity. However, what was remarkable was that, by middle age, all had arrived at firm conclusions about what did and did not work for them. So, some part of the maintenance of creativity included acceptance of their own creative idiosyncrasies. Some, for example, expressed the need for external motivation, such as a deadline. Guitarist B. B. King, 74, said, "If you want me to be creative, give me the line to cross and when I have to cross it" (p. 44). Others were more motivated by self-imposed standards than by externals. For example, writer Isabel Allende, 57, reported that she always begins a new work on January 8, because the date is a personally meaningful anniversary for her. Advertising writer Stan Freberg, 73, claimed that when he

needs an idea, he takes a shower, because he often gets inspiration while in the shower.

A second theme pervaded these reports. Each creative person, in one way or another, recognized the value of accumulated knowledge and experience. They also tended to acknowledge important sources of this knowledge, such as parents, spouses, and friends. Consequently, these people saw their creative work not only as the product of their own abilities but also as the result of a complex network of influential individuals, life experiences, and their own capacity to reflect on their lives.

From these extraordinary individuals we can learn two important things about maintaining creativity and productivity in the middle and late adult years: First, being consciously aware of one's own creative process—and accepting its boundaries—seems to be critical. Second, some degree of humility, a sense of indebtedness to those who have contributed to and supported one's creative development, appears to be associated with continuing productivity in the middle and late adult years.

only 3 of the 16 measures: The younger teams did more things (made more decisions and took more actions), asked for more additional information (often excessively, to the point of creating information overload), and suggested a greater diversity of actions. Middle-aged teams asked for just about the right amount of information—not too much to overload the system, but enough to make good decisions—and used the information effectively. On most of the measures the researchers devised, there were no differences between the young and middle-aged. In contrast, the oldest teams performed less well on virtually every measure. These findings suggest that the ability to apply creative thinking efficiently to complex problems may, indeed, be at its peak in the middle adult years.

Before going on . . .

■ How does Denney's model explain the relationships among exercise, physical health, and cognitive functioning in middle adulthood?

■ What does research reveal about the link between health and cognitive functioning?

■ Describe differences between young and middle-aged adults in cognition and memory function.

■ What does research evidence suggest about age-related changes in creativity?

Summary

Physical Changes

● Brain size diminishes a bit in the middle adult years. Some changes in brain function suggest that middle-aged adults are more subject to distraction. However, middle-aged adults often outperform younger adults on everyday tasks that require concentration and rapid judgments, such as driving.

● The loss of reproductive capacity, called the climacteric in both men and women, occurs very gradually in men, but more rapidly in women. Menopause is a three-phase process that results from a series of hormonal changes.

● Bone mass declines significantly beginning at about age 30; accelerated declines in women at menopause are linked to decreased levels of estrogen and progesterone. Faster bone loss occurs in women who experience early menopause, who are underweight, who exercise little, or who have low-calcium diets.

- Thickening of the lens of the eye, with accompanying loss of elasticity, reduces visual acuity noticeably in the 40s or 50s. Hearing loss is more gradual.

Health and Wellness

- The rate of illness and death rises noticeably in middle adulthood. Young adults have more acute illnesses; middle-aged adults have more chronic illnesses. The two major causes of death in middle adulthood are cancer and heart disease.
- Cardiovascular disease is not a normal part of aging; it is a disease for which there are known risk factors, including smoking, high blood pressure, high blood cholesterol, obesity, and a high-fat diet.
- Cancer, too, has known risk factors, including smoking, obesity, and an inactive lifestyle. The role of a high-fat diet has been debated, but most evidence supports the hypothesis that such a diet contributes to the risk. Recent research shows that several cancers are caused by infectious agents (viral and bacterial).
- Women tend to live longer than men but are more likely to suffer from chronic illnesses.
- Low-income adults have more chronic illnesses and a higher rate of death than those who are better off economically. African Americans, Hispanic Americans, and Native Americans are more likely to suffer from cardiovascular disease, cancer, and diabetes than whites.
- Middle-aged adults have lower rates of mental health problems of virtually every kind than young adults. Alcoholism usually starts at younger ages but often remains undiagnosed until middle age.

Cognitive Functioning

- Denney's model of aging suggests that exercising either physical or cognitive abilities can improve performance at any age, but the upper limit on improvement declines with increasing age.
- Some studies suggest that differences in health contribute to variations in cognitive functioning among middle-aged adults. Exercise clearly affects the physical health of middle-aged adults, but research is less conclusive with regard to its effects on cognitive functioning.
- Verbal abilities continue to grow in middle age. Some loss of memory speed and skill occurs, but by most measures the loss is quite small until fairly late in the middle adult years. Expertise helps middle-aged adults compensate for losses in processing speed.
- Creative productivity also appears to remain high during middle adulthood, at least for adults in challenging jobs (the category of adults on whom most of this research has focused).

Key Terms

alcoholism (p. 129)
atherosclerosis (p. 121)
cardiovascular disease (CVD) (p. 121)
climacteric (p. 115)
episodic memories (p. 134)

hypertension (p. 127)
menopause (p. 116)
osteoporosis (p. 118)
perimenopausal phase (p. 116)
postmenopausal phase (p. 116)

premenopausal phase (p. 116)
presbycusis (p. 121)
presbyopia (p. 120)
semantic memories (p. 134)
type A personality pattern (p. 124)

Social and Personality Development in Middle Adulthood

CHAPTER 6

When 43-year-old John F. Kennedy was elected to the U.S. presidency in 1960, many of his critics expressed the view that he was too young to be president.

© Ariel Skelley/CORBIS

139

Similarly, in 1980, when Ronald Reagan was elected president at age 68, some thought he was too old to perform effectively. Both views reflect cultural beliefs about the social clock. Middle adulthood is seen as the time when people are best able, developmentally, to manage the weighty demands associated with positions of authority. Thus, those just entering middle adulthood, as Kennedy was in 1960, are thought to be insufficiently mature for such positions, while those who are beyond the middle years, like 68-year-old Reagan, may be seen as no longer sufficiently competent.

Such beliefs and expectations are not entirely unfounded. When middle-aged adults get together with acquaintances, friends, or relatives at events such as high school or family reunions, they find most of their agemates to be in the most powerful positions of their lives. Most have higher incomes than they ever had before or ever will again, and a greater proportion of them hold positions of authority in business, education, and government than was true when they were younger.

The social clock is evident in family relationships as well. The middle-aged cohort of any family tends to have the most responsibility, "sandwiched" between adolescent or young adult children and aging parents. When a younger or older family member requires help, the middle-aged members are expected to respond.

What seems most striking about everyday life in middle age is how much less constricting social roles feel. Most middle-aged adults are spouses, parents, and workers, but by age 40 or 50, these roles have changed in important ways. Children have begun to leave home, which dramatically alters and reduces the intensity of the parental role; job promotions have usually reached their limit, so workers have less need to learn new work skills. And when both parenting and work are less demanding, partners can find more time for themselves and for each other. As you read this chapter, keep the following questions in mind:

- How does Erikson view social and personality development in middle adulthood, and what evidence exists to support the "crisis" view of mid-life?

- How do family roles and relationships change in middle adulthood, and how do individual personalities and life pathways influence development?

- What are the major career issues facing middle-aged adults?

Theories of Social and Personality Development

You should remember from Chapter 2 that Erik Erikson viewed middle age as a period when attention turns to creation of a legacy. Adults do this by influencing the lives of those in younger generations. Yet many have characterized middle age less positively, suggesting that it is a period of intense crisis.

ERIKSON'S GENERATIVITY VERSUS STAGNATION STAGE

Middle-aged adults are in Erikson's **generativity versus stagnation stage.** Their developmental task is to acquire a sense of **generativity,** which involves an interest in establishing and guiding the next generation. Generativity is expressed not only in bearing or rearing one's own children, but through teaching, serving as mentor, or taking on leadership roles in various civic, religious, or charitable organizations. Merely having children is not enough for developing generativity in Erikson's terms. The optimum expression of generativity requires turning outward from a preoccupation with self, a kind of psychological expansion toward caring for others. Those who fail to develop generativity often suffer from a "pervading sense of stagnation and personal impoverishment [and indulge themselves] as if they were their own one and only child" (Erikson, 1963, p. 267).

Research has produced hints of such a developmental stage, but the findings are much less clear than data on changes in earlier years. One cross-sectional study of young, mid-life, and older women found that generativity increased in middle age, as Erikson's theory suggests (Zucker, Ostrove, & Stewart, 2002). Contrary to what his theory would predict, however, the oldest group of participants, whose average age was 66, cited generative concerns as being important to them just as frequently as the middle-aged group did. These findings support Erikson's claim that generativity is more common in middle than in early adulthood, but they also indicate that generativity continues to be important in old age. Other research suggests that generativity is a more prominent theme in the lives of middle-aged women than in the lives of middle-aged men (Morfei, Hooker, Carpenter, Mix, & Blakeley, 2004).

Despite these inconsistencies, studies support Erikson's belief that generativity is related to mental health among middle-aged adults. For instance, researchers have found that generativity is positively related to satisfaction in life and work and to emotional well-being (Ackerman, Zuroff, & Moskowitz, 2000). Further, in a study that measured middle-aged women's sense of being burdened by caring for elderly parents, those who exhibited the highest levels of generativity felt the least burdened by elder care (Peterson, 2002).

Erikson's theory also raises questions about the impact of childlessness on adult development. One very interesting analysis comes from a 40-year longitudinal study of a group of inner-city, nondelinquent boys who had originally served as a comparison group in a study of delinquent boys (Snarey, Son, Kuehne, Hauser, & Vaillant, 1987). Of the 343 married men who were still part of this sample in their late 40s, 29 had fathered no children. Researchers found that the way a man had responded earlier to his childlessness was predictive of his psychological health at age 47. At that age, each man was rated on his degree of generativity. A man was considered to be "generative" if he had participated in some kind of mentoring or other teaching or supervising of children or younger adults. Among those with no children, those who were rated as most generative were likely to have responded to their childlessness by finding another child to nurture. They adopted a child, became Big Brothers, or helped with the rearing of someone else's child, such as a niece or nephew. Those childless men rated as nongenerative were more likely to have chosen a pet as a child substitute.

CRITICAL THINKING

Make a list of ways to express generativity other than by bringing up your own children and helping them get a start in life.

generativity versus stagnation stage the seventh of Erikson's stages, in which middle-aged adults find meaning in contributing to the development of younger individuals

generativity a sense that one is making a valuable contribution to society by bringing up children or mentoring younger people in some way

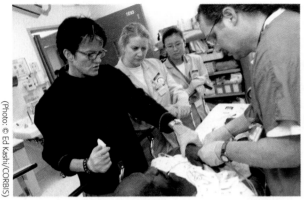

(Photo: © Ed Kashi/CORBIS)

At work, these health care professionals must fulfill highly demanding, emotionally intense roles. Long work days filled with life-and-death decisions may leave them too emotionally and physically drained to cope with the expectations associated with family roles. Moreover, many of them must be on call 24 hours a day. As a result, family interactions may frequently be interrupted by the demands of their jobs. Thus, they may experience both role strain and role conflict.

Such findings raise the possibility that some aspects of psychological growth in early adulthood may depend on bearing and rearing one's own children or another child who calls forth one's nurturing and caring qualities—just as Erikson proposed. However, critics have suggested that studies of generativity have focused on well-educated, white, middle-aged adults. Researchers who have examined the issue of generativity in other groups have found that generativity is somewhat related to education (McAdams, Hart, & Maruna, 1998). Still, researchers have found consistent patterns of generativity-related behaviors and attitudes among poor as well as middle-class adults and across a variety of ethnic groups (McAdams et al., 1998; Schulz, 1998). Thus, expressions of generativity appear to be normal middle-aged experiences that are relatively independent of ethnicity and economic factors.

MID-LIFE CRISIS: FACT OR FICTION?

You may recall that the crisis concept is central to Erikson's theory, and a specific mid-life crisis has been part of several other theories as well, including Levinson's. Levinson argued that each person must confront a constellation of difficult tasks at mid-life: accepting one's own mortality, recognizing new physical limitations and health risks, and adapting to major changes in most roles. Dealing with all these tasks, according to Levinson, is highly likely to exceed an adult's ability to cope, thus creating a crisis.

When developmentalists look at the relevant research evidence, however, they often question Erikson's conclusions. Psychologist David Chiriboga argues that "there is mounting evidence from research studies that serious mid-life problems are actually experienced by only 2% to 5% of middle agers" (Chiriboga, 1989, p. 117). There is evidence that the rate of depression peaks among women in their late 30s and early 40s (Anthony & Aboraya, 1992). But even at the peak, the rate is only about 4.5%—hardly evidence of a universal crisis. Other researchers used a mid-life crisis scale, including items about inner turmoil, marital or job dissatisfaction, and a sense of declining power (Costa & McCrae, 1980b; McCrae & Costa, 1984). They compared the responses of over 500 participants in a cross-sectional study of men ranging in age from 35 to 70. They could find no age at which scores on the mid-life crisis scale were significantly high. Others who have devised mid-life crisis scales have arrived at the same conclusion, as have those who have studied responses to stress (e.g., Farrell & Rosenberg, 1981; Pearlin, 1975). Epidemiological studies also do not show any clear rise in mid-life of such likely signs of crisis as divorce, alcoholism, or depression in men (Hunter & Sundel, 1989). And, finally, longitudinal studies do not lend much comfort to mid-life crisis advocates. For example, researchers found no indication that any kind of crisis was common at mid-life among the participants in the Berkeley/Oakland longitudinal study (Haan, 1981).

There are clearly stresses and tasks that are unique to this period of life. But there is little sign that these stresses and tasks are more likely to overwhelm an adult's coping resources at this age than at any other (Gallagher, 1993).

ROLE TRANSITIONS

The concept of roles provides a different perspective on adjustment to the various transitions of adulthood. This important idea, which developmentalists borrowed from sociology, has been discussed in several previous chapters. Any social system can be thought of as being made up of interlocking positions (also called *statuses*) such as "employer," "worker," "teacher," "student," "retired person," and "widow." A *role* is the content of a social position—the behaviors and characteristics expected of a person filling that position (Marshall, 1996). Thus, a role is a kind of job description.

Several aspects of the concept of roles are important for an understanding of development. First, roles are at least partially culture- and cohort-specific. "Teacher," for example, may be a different role (a different set of expected behaviors) in one culture than in another or in the same culture from one time to another.

Second, each of us must occupy multiple roles at the same time, and this inevitably produces frictions of various kinds. For example, a woman can be a member of a profession (say, a psychologist) while simultaneously occupying the roles of wife, mother, stepmother, grandmother, daughter, sister, sister-in-law, aunt, niece, friend, author, board member, singer, and volunteer. There will certainly be times when all these roles don't fit together tidily.

Sociologists use the term **role conflict** to describe any situation in which two or more roles are at least partially incompatible, either because they call for different behaviors or because their separate demands add up to more hours than there are in the day. Role conflict happens, for example, when a middle-aged father must choose between helping his aging parents with financial or health problems and attending his teenaged son's football games. A person experiences **role strain** when her own qualities or skills do not measure up to the demands of some role. For example, a 40-year-old worker who is forced to return to college to acquire new skills after a job layoff and who feels anxious about her ability to succeed is experiencing role strain.

The concept of roles can also help explain changes in adult life, because certain roles shift predictably with age. Each age level has accompanying roles. Even more conspicuously, family roles change in predictable ways, and one could argue that adult life marches to the rhythm of these shifts in family roles.

Evelyn Duvall described a sequence of eight family life stages, listed in Table 6.1. Each stage involves either adding or deleting some role or changing the content of a central role (Duvall, 1962). Duvall's idea has served as an organizing model for a great deal of sociological research on adulthood. Instead of comparing adults of different ages, researchers have compared adults in different life-cycle stages, creating a variant of the cross-sectional design. The basic idea, obviously, is that an individual's behavior and attitudes are shaped by the roles he occupies. And since these roles change with age in systematic and predictable ways, adults will also change systematically and predictably. Knowing that a person has a new infant tells you something about his life. If you knew that another person's youngest child had just gone off to college, you would quite correctly infer very different things about her daily existence.

But the idea of family life stages, helpful as it has been, has two major flaws. First, the model totally omits a number of important roles, such as the role of grandparent

TABLE 6.1	Duvall's Stages of the Family Life Cycle
Stage	**Description**
1	Adult is newly married, with no children; the person assumes the spousal role.
2	First child is born; role of parent is added.
3	Oldest child is between 2 and 6; role of parent changes.
4	Oldest child is in school; parental role changes again.
5	Oldest child is an adolescent; parental role changes again.
6	Oldest child leaves home; parental role involves helping child become independent.
7	All children have left home—sometimes called the postparental stage.
8	One or both spouses have retired; worker role ends.

(Source: Duvall, 1962.)

role conflict any situation in which two or more roles are at least partially incompatible, either because they call for different behaviors or because their separate demands add up to more hours than there are in the day

role strain the strain experienced by an individual whose own qualities or skills do not measure up to the demands of some role

and that of caregiver to one's own aging parents. The model also does not reflect the years beyond age 65; it is as if the model assumes that no further changes in roles or life patterns occur after retirement. Yet it is increasingly clear that substantial variations in life patterns and roles exist among those over 60. Indeed, gerontologists today customarily divide the later adult years into three periods: the young old (60 to about 75), the old old (from 75 to about 85), and the oldest old (those over 85).

An even more telling problem with Duvall's simple model of family life stages is that in modern industrialized societies, a great many people simply don't move through this sequence of roles in the listed order. Increasing numbers of today's adults do not marry or do not have children; many divorce and move through complex cycles or combinations of family roles.

Yet the concept of the family life cycle has important elements that both sociologists and psychologists would like to retain. Although the sequence and timing may vary, the particular family life cycle an individual experiences clearly has an important effect on his or her life pattern (Aldous, 1996). And in any given culture or cohort, some role shifts are likely to be shared, such as retirement in one's 60s in most industrialized countries. One sociologist suggests that the life course should be thought of as containing a number of transitions, defined as "changes in status that are discrete and bounded in duration," such as shifting from being single to being married or from working to being retired (George, 1993, p. 358). Transitions that are highly predictable and widely shared in any given culture or cohort are called *life course markers.* In recent cohorts in industrialized countries, many of the family life transitions that used to be concentrated in early adulthood—such as marriage and first parenthood—have become less predictable, with highly variable timing and sequence. At the same time, some transitions in middle and late adulthood—such as the death of a parent while one is in middle age or voluntary retirement in one's 60s—have become more prevalent and predictable. Sociologists believe that some aspects of Duvall's basic theoretical perspective remain useful, despite the fact that family life stages are not precisely the same for all adults (e.g., Caspi & Elder, 1988). The specific sequence of roles or the timing of those roles may change from one cohort to the next, from one culture to the next, or even between different subgroups within a given culture, but dealing with some sequence of roles is the very stuff of adult life.

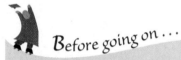

Before going on . . .

■ Briefly describe Erikson's generativity versus stagnation stage and the evidence that supports his theory.

■ What does research suggest about the existence of a universal mid-life crisis?

■ What do the concepts of role conflict and role strain add to an understanding of middle adulthood?

Changes in Relationships and Personality

As suggested previously, family roles are still an important part of life in middle age. However, these roles change significantly during this period of life.

PARTNERSHIPS

Several lines of evidence suggest that, on average, marital stability and satisfaction increase in mid-life as conflicts over child-rearing and other matters decline (Swensen, Eskew, & Kohlhepp, 1981; Veroff, Douvan, & Kulka, 1981; Wu & Penning, 1997). In addition, as couples get older, the number of shared friends they have increases and the number of non-shared friends decreases (Kalmijn, 2003). As a result, the social network tends to get a bit tighter—and probably more supportive—in middle age. This may be one reason for age-related improvements in relationship satisfaction. So, despite considerable diversity among mid-life marriages and partnerships, overall they are less conflicted than those of young adults.

Improvements in marital satisfaction may also derive from middle-aged adults' increased sense of control—a kind of marital self-efficacy (Lachman & Weaver, 1998). It is likely that middle-aged partners' identification of successful problem-solving strategies contributes to the sense that they have control over their relationship. Research has provided useful illustrations of this point. For example, researchers typically find that marital problem themes among middle-aged couples are remarkably similar to those of younger adults. Wives complain of an unjust division of labor; husbands express dissatisfaction with limits on their freedom. Yet relationship stability among middle-aged couples is maintained through the practice of what one researcher called "skilled diplomacy," an approach to solving problems that involves confrontation of the spouse about an issue, followed by a period during which the confronting spouse works to restore harmony (Perho & Korhonen, 1999). Skilled diplomacy is practiced more often by wives than by husbands, but it appears to be an effective technique for marital problem-solving no matter which spouse uses it.

As age-related increases in marital satisfaction would predict, middle-aged couples are far less likely to divorce than those who are younger (Uhlenberg, Cooney, & Boyd, 1990). Moreover, research suggests that middle-aged women are better able to cope with divorce then younger women (Marks & Lambert, 1998). Perhaps a "mellowing" of personality (which you will read about later in this chapter) renders the middle-aged woman more resilient in the face of such traumatic events.

Once the children are grown and gone, many couples find it easier to spend time together—perhaps one of the reasons that marital satisfaction generally rises in middle age.

CHILDREN AND PARENTS

The discussion of the relationship between young adults and their families in Chapter 4 focused almost entirely on connections *up* the chain of family generations—that is, relationships between the young adults and their own middle-aged parents. When looking at family rela-

Research suggests that middle-aged women are more resilient than younger women in managing transitions such as divorce.

tionships from the perspective of middle age, we have to look in both directions: down the generational chain to relationships with grown children and up the chain to relationships with aging parents.

Each of the positions in a family's generational chain has certain role prescriptions (Hagestad, 1986, 1990). In middle adulthood, the family role involves not only giving assistance in both directions in the generational chain but also shouldering the primary responsibility for maintaining affectional bonds. These responsibilities produce what is sometimes called the mid-life "squeeze," and those being squeezed form the "sandwich generation."

Such a squeeze was illustrated in the results of interviews with over 13,000 adults in one frequently cited national survey. Among many other things, respondents were asked about the amount of help of various kinds—financial, child care, household assistance, and so forth—they gave to and received from both adult children and aging parents (Bumpass & Aquilino, 1995). The results, graphed in Figure 6.1, make clear that those between ages 40 and 65 give more help than they receive in both directions within the family—to adult children and to aging parents—a pattern confirmed in a variety of other studies, in Canada as well as the United States (e.g., Gallagher, 1994; Hirdes & Strain, 1995).

(Photo: © Jeff Greenberg/PhotoEdit)

(Photo: © David Young-Wolff/PhotoEdit)

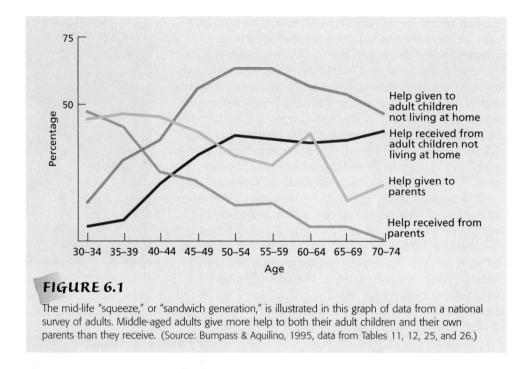

FIGURE 6.1

The mid-life "squeeze," or "sandwich generation," is illustrated in this graph of data from a national survey of adults. Middle-aged adults give more help to both their adult children and their own parents than they receive. (Source: Bumpass & Aquilino, 1995, data from Tables 11, 12, 25, and 26.)

Whether most middle-aged adults experience this combination of responsibilities as a burden is not clear from the available information (Bengtson, Rosenthal, & Burton, 1996). Doubtless some do and some do not, depending on the degree of infirmity of the aging parents, the nature of the relationship the middle-aged adult has with those aging parents, and the degree of help required by the young adult children. A 50-year-old whose divorced daughter has returned with young grandchildren to live at home or one who has a parent living nearby and suffering from the early stages of Alzheimer's is far more likely to experience major role strain than is someone of the same age who babysits the grandchildren from time to time and helps her aging parents by doing occasional shopping, snow shoveling, or house-cleaning. But, on average, it is clear that middle adulthood is likely to be a time when more help is given than is received.

A quite different look at patterns of family interaction among middle-aged adults is taken in sociologist Gunhild Hagestad's classic three-generation family study (Hagestad, 1984). Hagestad was interested not so much in patterns of aid as in attempts to influence other generations in the family. Middle-aged adults in this sample of 148 families typically spent more effort trying to influence their children than their parents, but both kinds of effort occurred fairly regularly. Their most successful efforts to influence their aging parents came in the form of practical advice about where to live or how to manage the household and money. Attempts to change their parents' views about social issues or family dynamics largely fell on deaf ears. Influence attempts directed at their young adult children were aimed mostly at shaping the children's transition into key adult roles. So, for example, the older adults talked about educational choices, work, money, and personal lifestyle.

Influence attempts did not radiate exclusively from the middle-aged generation. Both the young adult children and the aging parents in this study tried to influence the middle-aged generation, with varying degrees of success. Hagestad found that parents, whatever their age, kept trying to influence their children, and that children, whatever their age, continued to resist such influence and advice. Advice from child to parent was much more likely to be successful. Only about a third of the influence attempts from parents to children were effective, whereas about 70% of the influence attempts in the other direction were received positively.

Hagestad also found that each family seemed to have a particular agenda, or set of themes, that cropped up again and again in descriptions of interactions across the generations. Some families spent a lot of time talking about money; others never mentioned this subject. Some focused on family dynamics or on health issues. Themes like this were particularly clear in the all-male or all-female lineage. In more than half of the families Hagestad studied, the three generations of women regularly talked about some aspect of interpersonal relationships, particularly family dynamics, while such themes never surfaced in the male lineage. Grandfathers, fathers, and grown sons were more likely to talk with one another about work, education, or money.

Other studies of multigenerational families, both in the United States and in Germany, confirm these patterns. When women family members have conflicts, they are most likely to be over how members of the family ought to relate to one another. When fathers, sons, and grandsons have conflicts, they are likely to be about nonfamily issues, such as politics or social issues (e.g., Hagestad, 1985; Lehr, 1982).

Hagestad's research gives a glimpse into the complex workings of family relationships across several generations. But further understanding of family relationships for middle-aged adults can be gained by considering specific aspects of their situation. Research on the "empty nest" and "revolving door," on grandparenthood, and on the care of aging parents creates a more complete picture of this sandwich generation.

CRITICAL THINKING **9**

What do men and women talk about at multigenerational gatherings of your own family?

EMPTYING THE NEST

Folklore in Western cultures predicts that some or even most women become depressed or upset once the "nest" is empty, because they are losing the central role of mother. Of course, it is possible that such a pattern exists in some cultures, but it seems not to be true of U.S. culture, at least not for the great majority of middle-aged women. Suicide rates do go up for women in mid-life, but the rise begins between the ages of 31 and 40, when children are still at home, and then drops for women over 50, which is when the empty nest typically occurs. Similarly, the highest rates of depression among mid-life women appear in the late 30s and early 40s, also before the children have left home.

More to the point, when women are asked specifically about positive and negative transitions in their lives, those who list the departure of the last child are more likely to describe this event as positive than negative. In one study of 60 women between the ages of 45 and 60, researchers found that only a third of the participants described any significant transition point when the last child left home (Harris, Ellicott, & Holmes, 1986). Of these, 25% reported that the transition involved a distinct "mellowing," increased marital satisfaction, or increased inner stability; 17% reported that the transition involved an adjustment to the departure of the children. More recent studies, in both the United States and other countries, have produced similar findings (Segatto & Di Filippo, 2003). The few women who do experience some distress in this role transition appear to be those whose sense of self-identity has been heavily focused on the role of mother. In contrast, women in this age range who are in the labor force are much more likely to experience the empty nest as positive.

THE REVOLVING DOOR

Because research findings regarding the positive aspects of emptying the nest are so strong, researchers have recently turned their attention to the *revolving door,* the pattern in which adult children return to their parents' home (Dennerstein, Dudley, & Guthrie, 2002). Studies show that conflicts between parents and resident adult children are common (Muzi, 2000). Both parents and children feel that they have inadequate privacy. Middle-aged parents' sense of obligation to their children may cause them to feel that they can't pursue their own goals until they have helped

(Photo: Courtesy of Drs. Booker and Madeline Wright. Used with permission.)

Contrary to popular belief, when this woman's daughter leaves the nest in a few years, it will be a joyful experience.

their late-blooming children to become self-sufficient. As a child's departure is further and further delayed, frustrations can accumulate.

The percentage of adult children living with their middle-aged parents seems to be increasing. In 1970, only 8% of 25-year-olds lived with their parents. By the 1990s, estimates of the proportion of young adults residing with parents ranged from 12% to 20% (Muzi, 2000; U.S. Bureau of the Census, 1995b). Delayed marriage and a rise in the divorce rate probably explain this increase.

Research suggests that, even though conflict occurs, more than half of parents with adult resident children manage to work out good systems for handling the potential stresses and say that they are satisfied with their arrangement (Aquilino & Supple, 1991). In fact, some parents enjoy greater social support from their resident children than from their children who live away from home (Umberson, 1992). But there is little doubt that such an arrangement brings a new set of tasks and roles, and that it is linked to somewhat higher stress levels in many families.

GRANDPARENTING

Middle-aged adults typically move into several new roles—for example, becoming in-laws as their children marry (see the Real World feature). In addition, in the United States, about a third of adults become grandparents by their late 40s, and half of women become grandmothers by their early 50s (Bumpass & Aquilino, 1995). As the average age of childbearing has risen in recent cohorts, the timing of grandparenthood may shift to a slightly later age, but such a shift would not change the basic fact that this role is normally acquired in middle adulthood.

Most grandparents—92% in one study—express high levels of satisfaction with this role (Kaufman & Elder, 2003; Peterson, 1999; Segatto & Di Filippo, 2003). A majority see or talk to their grandchildren regularly. They may write, call, or visit as often as every couple of weeks, and most describe their relationships as warm and loving. Likewise, many studies have demonstrated the positive impact of warm relationships with grandparents on children's development (Adkins, 1999).

Grandparents seem to be an especially important source of stability in the lives of children of divorced parents. However, court rulings in the United States make clear that the rights of grandparents are limited by the rights of parents (Jacoby, 2000). In extreme cases, such as when a grandparent is dying or has never been allowed to visit a grandchild, grandparents may sue parents, whether divorced or married, for the right to see their grandchildren. However, courts have ruled that, under most circumstances, denying visitation to a grandparent is within a parent's constitutionally protected right to make decisions about a child's upbringing.

(Photo: © Jack Monnier/Getty Images/Stone)

This girl seems delighted with her grandmother, with whom she seems to have what Cherlin and Furstenberg would call a "companionate" relationship.

Fortunately, most parents welcome the involvement of their own parents in their children's lives, and surveys suggest that grandparents and grandchildren engage in many of the same activities—watching television, shopping, attending religious services—that parents and children share (Waggoner, 2000). However, while parenthood clearly involves full-time responsibility, there are many degrees of being a grandparent.

remote relationships relationships in which grandparents do not see their grandchildren often

companionate relationships relationships in which grandparents have frequent contact and warm interactions with grandchildren

Most behavioral scientists place grandparents in one of several categories derived from a study in which researchers interviewed a nationally representative sample of over 500 grandparents (Cherlin & Furstenberg, 1986). Twenty-nine percent of grandparents in the study had **remote relationships;** they saw their grandchildren relatively infrequently and had little direct influence over their grandchildren's lives. The most common reason for this remoteness was physical distance.

By contrast, this statement by one of the grandmothers in the study illustrates a different kind of relationship, for which researchers used the term **companionate relationship:**

Me, a Mother-in-Law?

Most middle-aged adults are happy to see their adult children marry and form their own families. However, somewhere in the midst of the excitement a middle-aged woman experiences when an adult child gets married comes the realization that she is going to acquire one of the most maligned social roles there is: that of mother-in-law. Mother-in-law jokes abound in films and TV shows, and relationships between mothers-in-law and their children's spouses are regularly characterized as full of tension and conflict. Typically, it is the relationship between the mother-in-law and the daughter-in-law that is depicted most negatively. Thus, it isn't surprising that most middle-aged women don't look forward to becoming mothers-in-law. But is the negative stereotyping of mothers-in-law justified?

Research in some societies (e.g., rural communities in Latin America, India, and Korea) suggests that the stereotype is somewhat accurate. In these societies, the mother-in-law has a well-defined social role. Newlyweds usually reside with the husband's parents, and the mother-in-law is the supervisor of the young wife and is responsible for socializing her into the family. The mother-in-law is also typically responsible for teaching new mothers cultural procedures associated with caring for newborns (Hyun et al., 2002). In such cultures, wives remain under the authority of their mothers-in-law for many years, usually until the older woman is no longer physically able to fulfill her role's requirements.

Despite the cultural reinforcement of the relationship between mother-in-law and daughter-in-law in traditional societies, these relationships are often high in conflict (Chiapin, DeAraujo, & Wagner, 1998). Most such conflicts involve the husband: The daughter-in-law thinks her husband is too loyal to his mother, or the mother-in-law thinks her son's wife is trying to undermine her relationship with him. Some mothers-in-law go so far as to physically abuse daughters-in-law, and abusive husbands sometimes receive praise from their mothers for keeping young wives in line (Fernandez, 1997).

However, some mothers-in-law may be treated poorly by daughters-in-law. For example, in rural China, a daughter-in-law is expected to care for her elderly mother-in-law. Research suggests that many daughters-in-law fail to live up to this cultural obligation (Yang & Chandler, 1992). This is especially devastating for the mother-in-law, because, in China, the elderly are completely dependent on their adult children for economic support.

Parallels to these situations exist in more industrialized societies like the United States. Mothers-in-law are perceived as interfering in the marital relationship; daughters-in-law are accused of trying to turn their husbands against their mothers. Consequently, family therapists have devised recommendations to help middle-aged women adjust to the mother-in-law role and to forestall conflict (Greider, 2000). Here are a few such recommendations:

(Photo: © HBO/WORLDWIDE PANTS INC./ THE KOBAL COLLECTION)

- Don't give unsolicited advice or make unannounced visits.
- When asked for your advice, share your experience in a nonjudgmental way.
- Don't criticize your daughters- or sons-in-law behind their backs.
- Don't insist on being visited every weekend or holiday.
- Respect your children's wishes regarding how grandchildren are to be cared for.

When you have grandchildren, you have more love to spare. Because the discipline goes to the parents and whoever's in charge. But you just have extra love and you will tend to spoil them a little bit. And you know, you give. (Cherlin & Furstenberg, 1986, p. 55)

Just over half of the survey's participants exhibited such attitudes toward their grandchildren and responded that they had very warm, pleasurable relationships with them. Yet these grandparents also said that they were glad they no longer had the day-to-day responsibility. They could love the grandchildren and then send them home.

The third and least common (16%) type of relationship was exhibited by grandparents who had **involved relationships** with their grandchildren. These grandparents were everyday participants in the rearing of their grandchildren. Some of them lived in three-generation households with one or more children and grandchildren; some had nearly full-time care of the grandchildren. But involved relationships also occurred in some cases in which the grandparent had no daily responsibility for the grandchildren's care but created an unusually close link.

involved relationships relationships in which grandparents are directly involved in the everyday care of grandchildren or have close emotional ties with them

Within American society, involved grandparent care is more common among African Americans than among whites, and more common among poor than among middle-class grandparents. Surveys suggest that the prevalence of custodial grandparenting may be three times as high among African Americans (Tolson & Wilson, 1990). Moreover, about 20% of low-income grandparents have full-time responsibility for a grandchild (Pearson, Hunter, & Cook, 1997). Several studies suggest that, even when they do not have full-time responsibility for grandchildren, African American and Hispanic American grandparents have closer and more frequent contact with their grandchildren than white American grandparents do (Bengtson, 1985; Kivett, 1991). However, the incidence of custodial grandparenting has increased in all ethnic and socioeconomic groups in recent years (Goodman & Silverstein, 2002). Across groups, about 10% of grandparents have had full-time responsibility for a grandchild for 6 months or longer.

No matter what the family's ethnicity and socioeconomic status, full-time grandparent care is especially likely when the grandchild's mother is unmarried. In such cases, the grandmother frequently takes on child-care responsibilities so that her daughter can continue in school or hold down a job. That such assistance is indeed helpful is indicated by the fact that teenaged mothers who have such help from their own mothers complete more years of education and have more successful work careers in adulthood (Taylor et al., 1990).

Gender is related to grandparenting as well. Among all ethnic groups, the role of grandmother is likely to be both broader and more intimate than that of grandfather (Hagestad, 1985). In addition, young grandparents, those in their 40s, have less day-to-day contact with grandchildren than those who are older, perhaps because they often are still working (Watson, 1997). As a result, they know less about and are less involved in their grandchildren's everyday lives than older grandparents are.

The role of grandparent obviously brings many middle-aged and older adults a good deal of pleasure and satisfaction. However, grandparents who see their grandchildren more often do not describe themselves as happier than those who see theirs less often (Palmore, 1981). Thus, for most adults in middle age, grandparenthood is not central to their lives, to their sense of self, or to their overall morale.

CARING FOR AGING PARENTS

Another role that may be added at mid-life, and that *does* have a powerful effect on overall life satisfaction, is the role of major caregiver for aging parents (see No Easy Answers). The great majority of adults, in virtually every culture, feel a strong sense of filial responsibility. When their parents need assistance, they endeavor to provide it (Ogawa & Retherford, 1993; Wolfson, Handfield-Jones, Glass, McClaran, & Keyserlingk, 1993). Interestingly, young adults seem to feel a stronger sense of obligation than those who are middle-aged (Stein et al., 1998). This may be because their parents are still healthy and fairly young and they have not yet had to face the prospect of caring for them. In contrast, for middle-aged people, the day-to-day problem of how to care for aging parents is more of a present reality. However, just how many adults actually take on this role is surprisingly unclear.

Much of the information that developmentalists have comes from studies of elderly adults who are asked about the kind and amount of care they receive from their children. But this information does not reveal much about the typical experience of the middle-aged adult. For example, researchers know that 18% of the elderly people in the United States who have adult children live with one of those children (Crimmins & Ingegneri, 1990; Hoyert, 1991). But because most elders have more than one child, it is not true that 18% of middle-aged children have a parent

(Photo: © Michael Newman/PhotoEdit)

Daughters, far more than sons, are likely to take on the role of significant caregiver for a disabled parent or a parent with dementia, as this daughter has done now that her mother is suffering from Alzheimer's disease.

Who Cares for Aging Parents?

One of the most difficult dilemmas of mid-life arises when elderly parents become incapable of caring for themselves. Inevitably, the issue of who will care for them creates conflicts. The financial burden involved in admitting aging parents to nursing homes renders that option impossible for many. Others avoid the nursing home option because they feel a sense of moral obligation to care for their parents directly. Ultimately, even if elders move to long-term care facilities, someone has to take primary responsibility for overseeing their care.

Families typically negotiate the caregiving task along a number of dimensions, including each family member's competing demands and availability of resources (Ingersoll-Dayton, Neal, Ha, & Hammer, 2003). Within a group of siblings, the one most likely to take on the task of caregiving is the one who has no children still at home, is not working, is not married, and lives closest to the aging parent (Brody, Litvin, Albert, & Hoffman, 1994; Stoller, Forster, & Duniho, 1992). The child with the strongest attachment to the parent is also most likely to provide help, although distance and time factors often override this effect (Whitbeck, Simons, & Conger, 1991).

Most of these factors combine to make a daughter or daughter-in-law the most likely candidate for the role of caregiver. Some studies have found that as many as 90% of the primary caregivers for elders with Alzheimer's are either daughters or daughters-in-law (Daire, 2004). But it makes a difference whether the frail elder is a mother or a father. Daughters are four times as likely as sons to help an older mother, but only 40% more likely than sons are to help a frail

father (Lee, Dwyer, & Coward, 1993). Because women (mothers) live longer than men and are thus more likely to require help, this tendency for children to provide relatively more help to the same-sex parent means that women have a much higher probability of providing such care.

Another factor that increases daughters' involvement in parental care is simple proximity. Perhaps because of greater emotional closeness to their parents or their socialization for the role of kin-keeping, daughters are more likely to live near their parents. And parents, when they approach their later years, are more likely to move to be close to a daughter than to a son.

Yet sons are quite often involved in the care of an elder. If a son is unmarried, he is more likely to take on the caregiving role than is a married sister (Stoller et al., 1992). And if both a son and a daughter are involved, the two often divide the responsibilities, with sons providing more financial assistance or instrumental support (mowing the lawn, home repairs, perhaps shopping) and daughters more often providing help with physical activities of daily living, such as dressing, cleaning, and cooking (Campbell & Martin-Matthews, 2003).

But despite these complexities, the inescapable conclusion is that women are far more likely than men to take on the role of caregiver of an aging parent, just as women are more likely to take on the role of caregiver with children. Whether this will change in the next few decades, as many more middle-aged women enter or remain in the labor force, remains to be seen.

---

living with them. Nor is it true that all those home-sharing elders are disabled or in need of regular care. So this kind of study does not show how many of the middle-aged are providing regular or extensive care to an elder parent.

Better information comes from a small number of cross-sectional studies in which representative samples of middle-aged adults have been asked how much and what kind of assistance they provide to their parents (e.g., Rosenthal, Matthews, & Marshall, 1989; Spitze & Logan, 1990). In one such study, researchers interviewed 1,200 middle-aged adults in upstate New York. Figure 6.2 (page 152) shows that in this sample, on average, only about 11% of adults between 40 and 65 were providing as much as 3 hours per week of assistance to an older parent—a relatively low level of care. Combining this information with evidence from other similar research gives an estimate that between 10% and 15% of middle-aged adults are providing some kind of regular care for an older parent at any given time (Scharlach & Fredricksen, 1994). But let's be careful about what this number means.

First, studies like these give only information about one point in time, not longitudinal information. So they do not reveal what percentage of adults will take on such a caregiving role at some time in their lives. Several researchers have tried to make such an estimate, but they have used widely varying definitions of "providing care." Research using broad definitions (for example, counting anyone providing any kind of care for a nonresident, seriously ill or disabled relative in the past year) suggests that roughly 40% of middle-aged women will be involved in at least some minimal caregiving in their lifetimes (Himes, 1994).

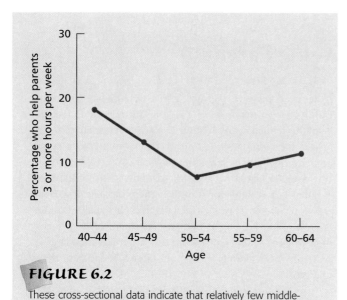

FIGURE 6.2

These cross-sectional data indicate that relatively few middle-aged adults are involved in extensive caregiving for one or both parents at any one time. But such evidence does not indicate what percentage of adults will fulfill such a role at some time in their lives. (Source: Spitze & Logan, 1990, from Table 2, p. 189.)

Using longitudinal data and a much stricter definition of care, other researchers find that about a quarter of women provide significant levels of care to their own parents or parents-in-law at some time in their middle adult years (Robison, Moen, & Dempster-McClain, 1995). Furthermore, the likelihood of such a role rose steadily from one cohort to the next in the 20th century. Only 17% of women born between 1905 and 1917 were ever major caregivers for a parent, whereas a third of those in the cohort born from 1927 to 1934 took on such a role. As life expectancy continues to rise, the likelihood of caring for an aging parent will rise still further. But even with such increases, it seems clear that while the role of caregiver for an aging parent is a common one in mid-life, it is not a standard experience, even for those in current cohorts. Moreover, future cohorts of elderly are likely to be healthier and more financially secure than today's older adults. Consequently, the experience of caring for an elder may actually become rarer.

Just what impact does caregiving have on the middle-aged adult? In the past decade, there have been hundreds of studies exploring the impact on the caregiver of tending to the daily needs of a parent (or spouse) who is disabled or frail or has dementia. In the large majority of studies, the recipient of care has been diagnosed with Alzheimer's disease or some other dementia. Such individuals gradually lose their ability to perform ordinary daily tasks, may ultimately be unable to dress or feed themselves, and may not recognize their caregivers. Providing care for such an individual, especially if the caregiver is also trying to meet the needs of her (or his) own job and family, may drain both energy and finances.

Not surprisingly, such a demanding role takes its toll. The cumulative evidence indicates that such caregivers are more depressed and have lower marital satisfaction than those in comparison groups of similar age and social class (Hoyert & Seltzer, 1992; Jutras & Lavoie, 1995; Li & Seltzer, 2003; Schulz, Visintainer, & Williamson, 1990). However, one study comparing African American and white American caregivers found heightened depression only among the white caregivers, an interesting finding that should be investigated further (Haley et al., 1995). Some research also suggests that those who care for frail elders are more often ill themselves or have some reduced efficiency of immune system function (Dura & Kiecolt-Glaser, 1991; Hoyert & Seltzer, 1992; Kiecolt-Glaser et al., 1987). Collectively, these effects are often termed **caregiver burden.**

However, remember that many of these studies involve participants who were recruited from among support groups of families with Alzheimer's patients. It is reasonable to suppose that those who join such support groups may be those for whom caregiving is especially burdensome. Second, although scores on standard scales of depression do indeed rise among those taking on the caregiving role, few of these adults show all the symptoms of full-scale clinical depression. Third, much less is known about the level of caregiver burden experienced by those who provide relatively low levels of assistance, such as 3 hours per week or less. It seems reasonable to assume that there is a significant difference between daily care for an elder with dementia and occasional lawn-mowing or shopping assistance. Finally, it is clear that certain factors can significantly lessen the burden, even for those with major caregiving responsibilities. Those who have good support networks (including a supportive spouse), as well as help from other caregivers, experience fewer negative consequences (Brody, Litvin, Hoffman, & Kleban, 1992; Pearlin, Aneshensel, Mullan, & Whitlatch, 1996; Schulz & Williamson, 1991).

For the majority of mid-life adults, the relationship with aging parents is far more positive. Most give more assistance to their parents than they did before, but they also continue to see them regularly for ceremonial and celebratory occasions and to feel

caregiver burden a term for the cumulative negative effects of caring for an elderly or disabled person

affection as well as filial responsibility (Stein et al., 1998). Parents are also symbolically important to middle-aged adults, because as long as they are alive, they occupy the role of elder in the family lineage. When they are gone, each generation moves up a notch in the sequence: Those in the middle generation must come to terms with the fact that they have now become the elders and are confronted directly with their own mortality.

FRIENDS

The scant research on friendships in middle adulthood suggests that the total number of friendships is lower in these years than in young adulthood (Kalmijn, 2003). For example, in one small study, researchers interviewed three generations of women in each of 53 families, some white American and some Hispanic American (Levitt, Weber, & Guacci, 1993). Each woman was asked to describe her close relationships. Among both groups, the young adult women had more friends in their social networks than did their middle-aged mothers.

At the same time, there are other bits of research suggesting that mid-life friendships are as intimate and close as those at earlier ages. For example, researchers have analyzed information from the files of 50 participants in the now-familiar Berkeley/Oakland longitudinal study, who had been interviewed or tested repeatedly from adolescence through age 50 (Carstensen, 1992). These analyses revealed that the frequency of interaction with best friends dropped between age 17 and age 50, but that the best-friend relationships remained very close.

These studies suggest that the social network of middle-aged adults is relatively small, although relationships are just as intimate as they were at earlier ages. It may be that the social network shrinks as adults age because there is less need for it. Role conflict and role strain decline significantly in middle age, and the need for emotional support from a social network outside the family seems to decrease accordingly (Due, Holstein, Lund, Modvig, & Avlund, 1999). Yet, because the relationships that do endure are close, the social network is available when needed. Friendship depends less on frequent contact than on a sense that friends are there to provide support as needed. Thus, the nature of friendship itself may be different in middle age.

CONTINUITY AND CHANGE IN PERSONALITY

Can developmentalists tell what kind of person someone will be in middle adulthood, based on what is known about his childhood, adolescence, or early adult life? Looking at poorly adjusted people as they grow older provides a view of continuity different from that of correlation studies of personality traits. For example, as you know, neuroticism is fairly consistent across ages. In fact, a recent longitudinal study revealed that emotional negativity in adolescence is linked to poor mental health in middle adulthood (Offer et al., 1998). In this study, male participants were tested at ages 14, 19, and 48. Researchers found that negative emotional traits in adolescence strongly predicted less-than-optimal mental health status in both early adulthood and middle age.

Despite the evidence for continuity, most people believe that personality changes with age, and most expect themselves to change. In one study, researchers examined 26- to 67-year-olds' current perceptions of their own personalities in terms of the Big Five (Fleeson & Heckhausen, 1997). They also asked participants to describe themselves when they were 20 to 25 years old and to speculate about how their personalities might change by the time they reached age 70. Further, participants were asked to describe an ideal personality they would like to have. All respondents believed that their personalities had changed since they were younger and that they would change in the future. Their ideas about the kinds of changes that would take place included both gaining and losing some traits. The researchers pointed out that these respondents perceived much

CRITICAL THINKING ❓

Has your personality changed since you were younger? In what ways? How do you expect it to change as you get older?

more change in personality than is shown by longitudinal studies of the Big Five traits. Apparently, we believe we change much more than we actually do.

However, there is some evidence of real change in personality in adulthood. For example, most observers agree that during the years from 40 to 65, most adults decline in achievement striving, independence, assertiveness, and individualism, which tend to peak at about mid-life. In fact, several studies suggest that people become more prosocial and less individualistic in middle and late adulthood (e.g., Van Lange et al., 1997). Interestingly, though, this change seems to be linked to secure attachment in infancy and childhood, so it has elements of both continuity and change.

Studies of negative and positive emotionality suggest a similar pattern. Even though negative emotionality in early adulthood is moderately to strongly correlated with negative emotionality in middle adulthood, longitudinal studies show that many individuals, particulary women, become *less* negative over time (Helson & Klohnen, 1998; Srivastava, John, Gosling, & Potter, 2003). Similarly, agreeableness appears to increase with age (Srivastava, John, Gosling, & Potter, 2003). At the same time, tolerance for risk-taking and impulsivity decline with age (Deakin, Aitken, Robbins, & Sahakian, 2004). Apparently, then, when researchers consider large groups—which they must do to correlate variables such as personality factors—they find that personality is fairly stable over time. However, the correlations can mask a number of individual cases in which there is a great deal of change. Consequently, the best conclusion to draw is that stability is the general pattern, but the increased individual variability in personality that is typically found among middle-aged and older adults suggests that change is clearly possible and may even be common (Nelson & Dannefer, 1992).

Cohort differences must also be kept in mind when interpreting research results. For example, one recent study found that middle-aged women from the Baby Boom generation, most of whom have worked outside the home for a large proportion of their adult lives, may possess characteristics that have not been found in research on earlier cohorts (Stewart & Ostrove, 1998). Historically, researchers consistently found that menopause and the empty nest were the primary landmarks middle-aged women used to characterize their lives. Baby Boom women, however, seem to be more likely to engage in the sort of comprehensive life review that previously was more characteristic of middle-aged men. Physical and family changes appear to continue to be important for these women at mid-life, but career issues and the potential for reshaping their lives as they age seem also to be crucial.

tenacious goal pursuit a behavior pattern in which individuals remain committed to goals that are difficult, and may be impossible, for them to achieve

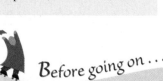

Before going on . . .

■ What contributes to the "mellowing" of marital relationships in middle age?

■ What is the family role of middle-aged adults with respect to older and younger generations?

■ What is the evidence regarding the existence of an "empty nest syndrome"?

■ What is the "revolving door," and how does it affect middle-aged adults?

■ How does the grandparent role affect middle-aged adults?

■ How might caregiver burden affect a middle-aged adult's life?

■ How do social networks change during middle adulthood?

■ What is the evidence for continuity and change in personality throughout adulthood?

Cross-sectional studies suggest that the mechanism behind personality change in middle adulthood may be an increasing ability to maintain control of one's emotions in a variety of situations (Gross et al., 1997). Supporting this hypothesis is the finding from several cross-sectional studies that introversion, or self-examination, increases slightly over the adult years (e.g., Costa et al., 1986). However, research on introversion is inconsistent. Several studies have found no indication of an increase in introversion in late middle age or among older adults, either in participants' current descriptions of themselves or in their recollections of themselves at earlier ages (Ryff, 1984; Ryff & Heincke, 1983).

Another possible cause of change is growth in personal flexibility. Researchers have examined the tendency of adults to either remain committed to difficult goals or adjust their goals when an objective seems to be impossible to achieve (Brandtstädter & Baltes-Götz, 1990; Brandtstädter & Greve, 1994). An individual high in **tenacious goal pursuit** would agree with statements like these (Brandtstädter & Baltes-Götz, 1990, p. 216):

The harder a goal is to achieve, the more desirable it often appears to me.
Even if everything seems hopeless, I still look for a way to master the situation.

Someone high in **flexible goal adjustment** would agree with the following (pp. 215–216):

I can adapt quite easily to changes in a situation.
In general, I'm not upset very long about an opportunity passed up.
I usually recognize quite easily my own limitations.

Tenacious goal pursuit tends to decrease in middle adulthood, while flexible goal adjustment rises, suggesting a kind of "mellowing" of personality in the middle years.

Mid-Life Career Issues

Work in mid-life is characterized by two paradoxes: First, work satisfaction is at its peak in these years, despite the fact that most adults receive few work promotions in middle age. Second, the quality of work performance remains high, despite declines in some cognitive and physical skills.

WORK SATISFACTION

Despite the plateau in promotions that occurs for most adults in the middle years, job satisfaction is typically at its peak, as is a sense of power, or job clout. One reason for these increases may be that careers become more stable in middle age, with fewer interruptions caused by either voluntary or involuntary job changes (Boxall, Macky, & Rasmussen, 2003). Still, patterns of work and work satisfaction do vary between men and women in middle adulthood.

A cross-sectional study of a nationally representative sample of men suggested that, for them, work satisfaction increases in middle age because the issue of work is less central to their lives (Tamir, 1982). Among young adult men (aged 25–39) in this study, job satisfaction was strongly correlated with various measures of personal satisfaction; for the middle-aged men (aged 40–65), it was not. Middle-aged men, in other words, have begun to disengage from their work as a primary source of personal fulfillment or satisfaction, even though they are likely to be more pleased with the work itself.

Whether the same is true of women workers at mid-life is not so clear. For women who begin to work steadily only in their 30s or 40s, the middle adult years may be the time of most rapid work advancement rather than simple maintenance of previous gains. For such women, work satisfaction might have as strong a correlation with overall life satisfaction as it does for young adult men.

Interestingly, though, a shift to full-time employment once the nest is empty is not a very common pattern for women, at least in current cohorts. Longitudinal data from the 10-year Michigan Panel Study of Income Dynamics suggest that most middle-aged women began paid employment while their children were still at home (Moen, 1991). Few began work for the first time after their last child left home. When women did return to full-time work in middle adulthood, the most likely reasons were divorce and widowhood, not the final departure of children.

Moreover, patterns of work satisfaction among middle-aged women may be more complex than those of men (Auster, 2001). For example, men's satisfaction is generally linked to objective measures of achievement such as promotions and salary history (Allen, Poteet, & Russell, 1998). In contrast, even among very successful women, work satisfaction often depends on how they view the career decisions they made in early adulthood. Many in one study believed that they had given family concerns too high a priority in deciding

(Photo: © Photodisc/Getty Images)

Studies show that men are more likely than women to use problem-focused strategies to cope with job stress. By contrast, women use emotion-focused coping more often than men. These differences help explain why middle-aged men and women differ in work satisfaction.

flexible goal adjustment a behavior pattern in which individuals adjust goals in order to enhance the likelihood of success

what kind of career to pursue and claimed that they should have given less primacy to marital and family responsibilities and chosen a different career field (Stewart & Ostrove, 1998). For such women, work satisfaction tends to be low. However, many respond by making mid-life career changes or pursuing additional education.

Cross-gender variations in patterns of work and job satisfaction are accompanied by sex differences in coping styles at work (Perho & Korhonen, 1999). Men and women cite the same sources of work dissatisfaction in middle age: time pressure, difficult co-workers, boring tasks, and fear of losing one's job. However, they cope with these challenges differently. Men are more likely to negotiate with supervisors and co-workers directly to effect change. In contrast, women tend to withdraw and to engage in collective complaining with female co-workers. Still, women are better able than men to balance their dissatisfactions with areas of contentment. Consequently, a statement such as "I don't like the boss, but the hours fit my needs" is more likely to come from a woman than a man. Because of their different coping styles, men are more likely to improve their level of satisfaction in situations where change is possible. By contrast, women are probably better able to cope with work settings where they must adjust to dissatisfaction because the situation can't be changed.

Despite their differences, both men and women in mid-life have a greater sense of control over their work lives than younger adults do (Lachman & Weaver, 1998). One reason for the increased feeling of control may be that social-cognitive skills improve from early to middle adulthood (Blanchard-Fields, Chen, Schocke, & Hertzog, 1998; Hess, Bolstad, Woodburn, & Auman, 1999). Middle-aged adults are better than they were when younger at "sizing up" people, relationships, and situations. At the same time, by middle age, they have become proficient at directing their own behavior in ways that allow them to maintain levels of personal satisfaction even in unpleasant circumstances.

JOB PERFORMANCE

In the great majority of occupations, job performance remains high throughout middle adulthood (McEvoy & Cascio, 1989). The few exceptions are those occupations in which physical strength or speedy reaction time is a critical element; some examples are longshoreman, air traffic controller, truck driver, professional athlete, and the like. In these jobs, performance begins to decline at mid-life or earlier, just as you would expect (Sparrow & Davies, 1988). In fact, many adults in such occupations change jobs at mid-life in anticipation of—or because of—such declines. But in most occupations that demand high levels of cognitive skill, performance remains at essentially the same level throughout middle adulthood (Salthouse & Maurer, 1996).

Researchers Paul Baltes and the late Margaret Baltes argue that maintaining high job productivity or performance is possible because adults, faced with small but noticeable erosions of cognitive or physical skill, engage in a process the Balteses call "selective optimization with compensation" (Baltes & Baltes, 1990). Three subprocesses are involved:

■ *Selection.* Workers narrow their range of activities—for example, by focusing on only the most central tasks, delegating more responsibilities to others, or giving up or reducing peripheral job activities.

■ *Optimization.* Workers deliberately "exercise" crucial abilities—such as by taking added training or polishing rusty skills—so as to remain as close to maximum skill levels as possible.

■ *Compensation.* Workers adopt pragmatic strategies for overcoming specific obstacles—for example, getting stronger glasses or hearing aids, making lists to reduce memory loads, or even carefully emphasizing strengths and minimizing weaknesses when talking to co-workers or bosses.

A growing body of evidence supports the Balteses' view (Baltes & Heydens-Gahir, 2003). Researchers have tested this model in a study of 224 working adults aged 40 to 69 (Abraham & Hansson, 1995). Measuring each of the three aspects of the proposed compensatory process as well as job competence, they found that the link between the use of selection, optimization, and compensation on the one hand and the quality of work performance on the other got stronger with increasing age. That is, the older the worker, the more it mattered whether she used helpful compensatory practices. In the older groups (primarily those in their 50s and early 60s), those who used the most selection, optimization, and compensation had the highest work performance. But among the younger workers in this sample (those in their early 40s), the same relationship did not hold. This is obviously only one study, but the results provide some support for the idea that job performance remains high during middle age at least in part because adults take deliberate compensatory actions.

UNEMPLOYMENT AND CAREER TRANSITIONS

In today's rapidly changing job market, it is not unusual for men and women to change occupations. However, career transitions can be more difficult in middle age than earlier in adulthood. For one thing, as you learned in Chapter 5, potential employers tend to believe that young adults are more capable of learning a new job than are middle-aged applicants, even though research suggests that this generalization is untrue (Forte & Hansvick, 1999). Employers give middle-aged applicants higher ratings on variables such as dependability, but they tend to think that younger applicants will be able to acquire new skills (especially computer skills) more rapidly. Thus, mid-life career changers must often overcome ageism in obtaining new employment.

Career counselors also point out that to understand mid-life career changes, it is useful to categorize workers on the basis of their reasons for changing occupations (Zunker, 1994). They suggest that people change careers for either external or internal reasons and can thus be classified as either *involuntary* or *voluntary* career changers.

Involuntary Career Changers Involuntary career changers are people who are in transition for external reasons: Their skills have become obsolete, their jobs have been eliminated through organizational restructuring, or they have been laid off because of shifting economic conditions. They experience heightened levels of anxiety and depression and higher risk of physical illness in the months after the job loss (Crowley, Hayslip, & Hobdy, 2003; He, Colantonio, & Marshall, 2003; Isaksson, Johansson, Bellaagh, & Sjöberg, 2004; Kessler, Turner, & House, 1988; Liem & Liem, 1988; Price, 1992). Such effects are not unique to workers in the United States. Similar results have been found in studies in England, Denmark, and other Western developed countries (e.g., Iversen & Sabroe, 1988; Warr, Jackson, & Banks, 1988). You can see an example of this effect in Figure 6.3, which shows results from a study comparing 146 unemployed and 184 employed men and women (Kessler et al., 1988). Interestingly, just as remarriage alleviates many of the stresses associated with divorce, re-employment seems to restore health, emotional stability, and a sense of well-being quite rapidly.

The causal link between job loss and emotional or physical distress is both direct and indirect. The financial strain of job loss is itself a major contributor to heightened levels of anxiety and depression. When job loss does not create significant financial strain—such as when a spouse continues to work at a well-paying job or the family has other resources—the negative effect of job loss is only about half as great (Kessler et al., 1988).

The indirect effects of job loss include changes in family relationships and loss of self-esteem. Most strikingly, marital relationships deteriorate rapidly after one or the other spouse has been laid off. The number of hostile or negative interactions increases, and the number of warm and supportive interactions declines—which means that the crucial ratio of positive to negative interactions spirals downward.

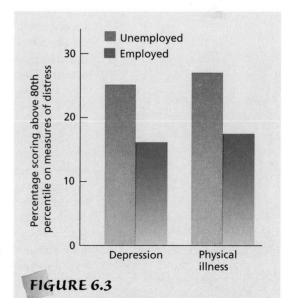

FIGURE 6.3

Adults who are involuntarily unemployed report more distress on nearly every measure, including both depression and physical illness, as shown by the results of a study in Michigan. (Source: Kessler et al., 1988, from Table 2, p. 74.)

Involuntary career changers must confront a series of stressful situations, such as applying for unemployment benefits.

Separation and divorce become much more common as a result (Conger, Patterson, & Ge, 1995; Crouter & McHale, 1993; Elder & Caspi, 1988; McLoyd, Jayaratne, Ceballo, & Borquez, 1994).

These negative effects of unemployment are seen in both young and middle-aged adults, but those aged 30 to 60 seem to show the largest effects—the greatest increases in physical illness and the biggest declines in mental health (Warr et al., 1988). This pattern makes some sense in terms of the stages of work lives you read about in Chapter 4. During the trial stage, young adults between 18 and 29 may interpret periods of unemployment as a normal part of the trial-and-error process of finding the right job. But workers in the stabilization stage may interpret job loss quite differently—either as a sign of personal failure or as an unrecoverable loss of security. Younger workers are also more likely to be unmarried, with fewer economic responsibilities, and they may be able to return to live with their parents during a period of unemployment. For them, the stress is therefore less pronounced.

The dynamics of job loss appear to be much the same for workers of every racial group. For example, unemployed African American adults, like other unemployed groups, show higher rates of distress and illness and lower levels of life satisfaction (Bowman, 1991). But in the United States and in most European countries, unemployment is considerably more common among African Americans than among whites. As Vonnie McLoyd, who has studied the effects of unemployment on African Americans, observes,

> Even in the best of times, the official unemployment rate of black workers typically is twice that of white workers. Blacks' increased vulnerability to unemployment is attributable to several factors, including lesser education, lesser skill training, less job seniority, [and] fewer transportable job skills. (1990, p. 316)

What is more, recent changes in the U.S. job market have made this problem worse. There have been heavy job losses in manufacturing and other blue-collar job sectors in which African American men are most likely to be employed. African American women, more often employed in the service sector, have been less severely affected by these changes.

The magnitude of the effect of unemployment may also be larger for African Americans than for white Americans because being unemployed is so often accompanied by a lack of any sense of personal control over the situation. When jobs become increasingly scarce, even hard work and diligence will not necessarily pay off in terms of employment. A sense of victimization is a common result, as are increased ill health and depression. Because many African Americans, confronted with widespread racism or chronic urban poverty, already experience very high levels of stress, unemployment increases the risks proportionately more.

Predictably, the Big Five personality dimensions, especially neuroticism and openness to experience, contribute to mental health during involuntary career transitions across all racial and ethnic groups (Heppner, Fuller, & Multon, 1998). Nevertheless, mental health professionals suggest that the impact of an involuntary career change on an individual's life may be more directly affected by his or her coping skills (Zunker, 1994). For example, the person must be able to assess the situation realistically. If new work skills are needed, then the person must be able to formulate and carry out a plan for obtaining such skills. Researchers have found that mid-life career changers who have good coping skills and use them to manage involuntary transitions are less likely to become depressed (Cook & Heppner, 1997).

As with all types of stress, the effects of unemployment can be partially buffered by having adequate social support (Vinokur & van Ryn, 1993). Further, involuntary career changers benefit from career counseling that addresses both their occupational needs and their psychosocial development (Schadt, 1997). Counselors can help people who are forced to change jobs learn to think of the transition as an opportunity to re-examine goals and priorities—to treat the crisis as an opportunity (Zunker, 1994).

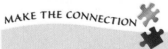

MAKE THE CONNECTION

How might a middle-aged adult use the postformal thinking you learned about in Chapter 13 to cope with an involuntary career transition?

Counselors also urge involuntary career changers to avoid acting impulsively. They suggest viewing the transition as a process that begins with a review of the individual's work history, interests, skills, and values. Based on the information gathered, the career changer should formulate an occupational goal and a plan for obtaining training, if needed. Finally, the person should develop a strategy to reduce the likelihood of another involuntary transition in the future, such as an educational plan for keeping work skills up to date.

Voluntary Career Changers Voluntary career changers leave one career to pursue another for a variety of internal reasons (Allen, Dreves, & Ruhe, 1999). For example, they may believe that the new job will be more fulfilling. One pattern occurs when workers look at the next step on the career ladder and decide they don't want to pursue further advancement in their current occupation. For example, both male and female certified public accountants are more likely to leave their profession for this reason than for any other (Greenhaus, Collins, Singh, & Parasuraman, 1997). Others change careers in order be able to express aspects of their personalities that they believe aren't utilized in their present jobs (Young & Rodgers, 1997).

Twin studies suggest that the tendency to change careers voluntarily in adulthood may have a genetic basis (McCall, Cavanaugh, Arvey, & Taubman, 1997). These findings further suggest that such transitions are a by-product of personality. Specifically, voluntary job changers appear to have a higher tolerance for risk-taking than do people who generally do not actively seek to change jobs (Roth, 2003). Most also appear to be people who do not regard either working or job-seeking as particularly stressful (Mao, 2003). Although voluntary career changers have a better sense of control over their situation than do people whose job changes are forced on them, the transition may still be stressful. Spouses and family members may not understand why the person wants to change careers. Moreover, changing careers can involve periods of unemployment and, often, a reduction in income. Thus, voluntary career changers manifest many of the same symptoms of anxiety and depression seen in involuntary career changers. Consequently, they, too, benefit from social support and career counseling.

PREPARING FOR RETIREMENT

Many middle-aged adults begin to prepare for retirement as early as 15 years before their anticipated retirement date. One aspect of such preparation is a gradual reduction in workload. For example, Figure 6.4 shows the hours worked per year for men and women

CRITICAL THINKING 9

Think about the middle-aged people you know. Do any of them seem to be winding down their involvement in work?

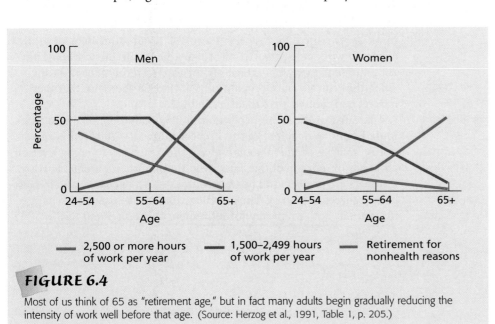

2,500 or more hours of work per year — 1,500–2,499 hours of work per year — Retirement for nonhealth reasons

FIGURE 6.4

Most of us think of 65 as "retirement age," but in fact many adults begin gradually reducing the intensity of work well before that age. (Source: Herzog et al., 1991, Table 1, p. 205.)

One difference between Baby Boomers and earlier cohorts is that among Baby Boomers, more women are involved in retirement planning.

in a random national sample of 1,339 U.S. adults (Herzog, House, & Morgan, 1991). You can see that the percentage of men and women working very long hours (2,500 hours per year or more, which averages out to 48 hours a week) drops among those aged 55 to 64.

However, it may be too early to form conclusions about how people prepare for retirement. After all, the notion of retirement is relatively new and tends to be exclusive to industrialized cultures. Even among the most prosperous nations, the idea of a period of leisure following many years of work did not exist prior to the mid-20th century. Thus, all our notions about preparation for retirement are based on a small number of cohorts, all of whose members were born in the first half of the 20th century. Comparisons of their behavior to that of the current generation of middle-aged adults suggest that ideas about preparing for retirement have changed.

The retirement preparations of the Baby Boom cohort, who are all now middle-aged, are quite different from those of their parents (Monroy, 2000). For one thing, among their parents, retirement planning was primarily a male responsibility. In contrast, Baby Boom women are also doing retirement planning, sometimes together with their husbands, but sometimes independently (Dietz, Carrozza, & Ritchey, 2003; Glass & Kilpatrick, 1998). Further, retirement-minded Boomers are largely responsible for the growth of electronic financial services because of their enthusiastic response to the availability of such services on the Internet.

Most Baby Boomers expect to die in their mid-80s or later but expect to retire fairly early, in their early 60s (Monroy, 2000). This means that their expected length of retirement is 20 years or more, far longer than that of earlier generations. Moreover, Baby Boomers believe that they need higher retirement incomes than their parents. Most have enjoyed a more comfortable standard of living than earlier generations, in part because of the proliferation of the two-income family. They expect some decline in income after their retirement, but generally much less change in their standard of living. Further, most do not expect that Social Security payments will be adequate to meet their needs.

Because of their expected length of retirement and income requirements, traditional ideas about preparation for retirement don't seem to fit the Baby Boomers. For example, earlier cohorts tended to put funds they expected to use for retirement into very safe investments (certificates of deposit, government bonds, and the like). However, many Baby Boomers have put their retirement nest eggs into the stock market. Further, they have borrowed rather than saved to achieve their investment objectives. Consequently, financial analysts claim that many individual Boomers may be in precarious situations when they reach retirement age because they are not saving enough money and have substantial debt (Glass & Kilpatrick, 1998; Monroy, 2000). In addition, while their parents' generation tended to think of retirement exclusively in terms of leisure time, most Boomers expect to work at least part-time during their retirement years (Lim, 2003). In fact, many Boomers look forward to retirement as a time when they can try out occupations that interest them but that they haven't had time to pursue earlier in life.

Because of the retirement wealth many Baby Boomers have accumulated and their intentions to keep working after they retire, economic analysts predict that as a group they are likely to enjoy levels of affluence in retirement that far exceed those of their parents. Further, Boomers are projected to be the healthiest, best-educated, and longest-living retirees in history. Thus, they are likely to substantially change ideas about both preparing for retirement and retirement itself.

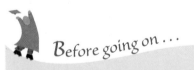

Before going on . . .

■ Why are levels of job satisfaction higher among middle-aged workers than among younger workers?

■ Describe the job performance strategies used by middle-aged workers.

■ What are the factors that contribute to career transitions in mid-life?

■ How do Baby Boomers differ from previous cohorts with respect to preparation for retirement?

Summary

Theories of Social and Personality Development

- Erikson proposed that the primary developmental task of middle adulthood is to acquire a sense of generativity through mentoring younger individuals.
- Many different models of the "mid-life crisis" in middle adulthood have been proposed, but none has been strongly supported by research.
- Sociologists explain adult development in terms of role transitions. Duvall's stage theory of role transitions has provided a framework for research, but it is not comprehensive enough to explain adult development.

Changes in Relationships and Personality

- Marital satisfaction is typically higher at mid-life than it is earlier. This higher level of satisfaction appears to be due primarily to a decline in problems and conflicts.
- Middle-aged adults have significant family interactions both up and down the generational chain. The two-way responsibilities can create a mid-life "squeeze," or a "sandwich generation." Middle adults provide more assistance in both directions and attempt to influence both preceding and succeeding generations.
- There is little sign that middle-aged parents experience negative reactions to the "empty nest," when the last child leaves home. On the contrary, the reduction in role demands may contribute to the rise in life satisfaction at this age.
- The "revolving door" is the pattern in which adult children who have been living independently return to live in their parents' home. Generally, this pattern is associated with declines in life satisfaction among middle-aged adults. However, some enjoy the companionship provided by adult children.
- Most adults become grandparents in middle age. The majority have warm, affectionate relationships with their grandchildren, although there are also many remote relationships. A minority of grandparents are involved in day-to-day care of grandchildren.
- Only a minority of middle-aged adults seem to take on the role of significant caregiver for an aging parent. Those who do report feeling a considerable burden and experience increased depression, particularly if the parent being cared for suffers from some form of dementia. Women are two to four times as likely as men to fulfill the role of caregiver to a frail elder.
- Friendships appear to be somewhat less numerous in middle adulthood, although they appear to be as intimate and central to the individual.
- The Big Five personality traits and other aspects of personality are correlated across early and middle adulthood. There is evidence for personality change in middle age as well. There are some signs of "mellowing," a lowering of intensity and striving, but middle-aged adults vary more in personality traits than do younger adults.

Mid-Life Career Issues

- Job satisfaction is at its peak in middle adulthood, and productivity remains high. But the centrality of the work role appears to wane somewhat, and job satisfaction is less clearly linked to overall life satisfaction than at earlier ages. Research suggests that patterns of work and satisfaction are different for men and women in middle age.
- Levels of job performance in middle adulthood are consistent with those at earlier ages, with the exception of work that involves physical strength or reaction time.
- Involuntary career changes are associated with anxiety and depression. Even many middle-aged adults who make voluntary career transitions experience negative emotions.
- Middle-aged adults prepare for retirement in several ways, not only by specific planning but also by reducing the number of hours they work.

Key Terms

Policy Question

What Types of Couples Should Be Sanctioned by Society?

During the sexual revolution of the 1960s and early 1970s, young adults often referred to marriage as "just a piece of paper." The real bond between intimate partners was psychological, many asserted, and need not be validated by a government license. This view became the driving force behind a movement away from marriage and toward cohabitation. At the same time, gay rights advocates began to suggest that, if being a couple is essentially a psychological union, then sexual orientation should be irrelevant. That is, they argued, homosexuals are capable of establishing the same kinds of interpersonal relationships as heterosexuals. Therefore, heterosexual unions should not be seen as superior in any way simply because they are legally sanctioned by society.

However, changing ideas about relationships, instead of causing marriage to disappear, have led to an increase in the number of legal options available to intimate partners. Thus, it seems that both heterosexual and homosexual couples, rather than regarding a license as "just a piece of paper," continue to want to have their relationships recognized by society in some official way. Currently, the notion that same-sex couples should have the same marital rights as opposite-sex couples is at the center of a heated public debate.

Domestic Partnerships and Civil Unions

For quite some time, homosexual rights activists have argued that same-sex couples need a legal means by which to make health insurance and other employee benefits available to their partners. In the absence of a legal relationship, they have pointed out, homosexuals have no right to authorize or terminate medical treatment for an ailing or injured partner. On a more personal level, many gay and lesbian couples, especially those in long-term relationships, want access to a public, socially recognized way to declare their affection for and commitment to each other (Solomon, Rothblum, & Balsam, 2004).

In the first wave of official responses to these concerns, numerous jurisdictions enacted laws that allow both opposite-sex and same-sex couples to enter into *registered domestic partnerships*. Some jurisdictions, including a number of states and cities in the United States, require employers to provide to domestic partners the same benefits that are available to married employees' spouses. In most cases, however, domestic partners have fewer rights, privileges, and legal obligations to each other (such as joint responsibility for debts) than do spouses.

The *civil union* is a newer type of relationship, created specifically to answer homosexual couples' demands for rights equivalent to those of married heterosexuals. In 2000, the first civil union legislation was passed in the state of Vermont. The only legal difference between a civil union and a marriage is that the latter is restricted to male-female cou-

(Photo: © Jonathan Nourok/Getty Images/Stone)

Legislators in the United States have responded to the demands of gay rights advocates to expand marriage to include homosexual couples by creating registered domestic partnerships and civil unions.

ples. Civil unions differ from domestic partnerships in that couples in civil unions have the same rights and obligations as those who are married. Further, those who decide to end their relationships must do so in family court, adhering to the same set of rules that apply to divorce, although the term *dissolution* is used rather than divorce.

The Right-to-Marry Movement

Despite the increasing availability of domestic partnerships and civil unions, many homosexual rights activists say that homosexual couples will never have the same status as heterosexual couples until they are allowed to marry (Patterson, 2004). Advocates of same-sex marriage argue that, unlike domestic partnerships and civil unions, marriage is a legal relationship that is universally recognized. They point out, for instance, that the U.S. Constitution guarantees that marriages performed in one state must be recognized in all others. No such protections exist for domestic partnerships and civil unions. Moreover, many argue that marriage is a civil right and that laws restricting marriage to opposite-sex couples are discriminatory.

Same-sex marriage advocates also claim that allowing homosexual couples to marry may be beneficial to the larger society (Green, 2004). They point to studies showing that married heterosexuals enjoy better mental health than those who are not married. Advocates say that marriage may similarly enhance the mental health of gays and lesbians by providing them with protection against the stresses associated with exposure to homophobia.

The efforts of activists who support same-sex marriage have led to a number of policy changes. In Denmark, the Netherlands, and some Canadian provinces, marital rights have been extended to same-sex couples (Associated Press, 2000). In the United States, judges in several states have ruled that laws

restricting marriage to opposite-sex couples are unconstitutional (Peterson, 2004). Lawsuits challenging the constitutionality of restrictive marriage laws are pending in many other states (Peterson, 2004).

Nevertheless, a clear majority of people in the United States oppose same-sex marriage (Morris & Langer, 2004; Public Agenda, 2004a). Moreover, proposals to legalize same-sex marriage through public referenda have been soundly defeated in several states; likewise, referenda in favor of limiting marriage to opposite-sex couples have passed by substantial majorities (Peterson, 2004). Many religious groups, such as the Roman Catholic church, oppose any kind of legal status for homosexual couples because they believe that homosexuality is immoral (United States Conference of Catholic Bishops, 2003).

Other opponents of same-sex marriage have challenged the assumptions underlying the right-to-marry movement. The movement, they claim, inappropriately defines marriage as a public declaration of love between romantic partners. By contrast, these critics say, marriage is a cultural invention that was designed to provide children with a stable environment in which to grow up (Sprigg, 2004; Young & Nathanson, 2003). Therefore, marriage carries the same kinds of legal and familial obligations in societies where parents arrange marriages for their infant children as it does in cultures in which men and women marry because they fall in love. Consequently, these critics say, relationships between individuals who cannot naturally procreate, while they may be intensely loving and may even be legally recognized in some way, will never be true marriages. This argument also asserts that society has an obligation to promote heterosexual relationships by providing spouses with legal protections that are unavailable to others because marriage is the primary structure through which cultural knowledge is transmitted to children (Young & Nathanson, 2003). In other words, they say, marriage is essential to the survival of the culture; thus, experimentation with this critically important institution ought to be avoided.

The activities of groups and individuals who believe that the heterosexual nature of marriage should be preserved have resulted in a number of legislative actions aimed at countering the right-to-marry movement. In 1998, President Bill Clinton signed into law the *Defense of Marriage Act (DOMA)*, a law defining marriage as limited to one man and one woman. At about the same time, more than 30 states adopted their own version of DOMA (Public Agenda Inc., 1999). However, a number of lawsuits have claimed that DOMA violates the equal protection clauses of most state constitutions and of the U.S. Constitution. To address this issue, legislators in most states are trying to enact constitutional amendments that restrict marriage to opposite-sex couples (Peterson, 2004). In the future, advocates for maintaining traditional marriage hope to amend the U.S. Constitution so that policies regarding who can and cannot marry are uniform throughout the United States.

The prevalence of legal relationships among homosexuals may increase in the future, as societal views of homosexuality and the meaning of marriage continue to change.

Your Turn

The influence of the right-to-marry movement has been felt throughout the industrialized world. What is the situation in your area? Use your research skills to find answers to these questions:

● How have policymakers in your area responded to the same-sex marriage movement? (Go to http://www. stateline.org and http://www.gay-civil-unions.com to find out.) How much support does the movement have in your state's legislature and among the citizens of your state?

● What do your classmates and friends think about the idea of same-sex marriage?

● Find out whether your city and/or state has a domestic partnership law. If so, does the law guarantee employer benefits such as health insurance coverage to domestic partners?

● Interview a marriage therapist. What does this professional think about the effects of legal status on partners' commitment to each other, the quality of their relationship, and their development as individuals?

Physical and Cognitive Development in Late Adulthood

C H A P T E R

7

In an earlier edition of this book, Helen Bee wrote about her 81-year-old father's tendency to use the term "my brains" to refer to a notebook in which he kept information such as frequently used phone numbers, appointments, birthdays, and the like.

© R. W. Jones/CORBIS

He developed this behavior in response to his self-observed increasing forgetfulness, and the substitute "brains" enabled him to get through each day without having to rely on his own brain. As this anecdote illustrates, for many older adults, the experience of aging is a process of learning to offset weaknesses, such as increasing forgetfulness, with strengths, such as practicality and inventiveness.

As the example of Helen Bee's father illustrates, older adults often find ingenious ways of managing age-related changes. Thus, one of the most striking characteristics of old age is the degree to which the experience of growing old varies from one individual to another. In this chapter, we will examine this variability along with changes that appear to affect almost everyone. As you read, keep the following questions in mind:

- How variable is the aging process?

- What physical changes are associated with late adulthood, how do theorists explain them, and how do they affect the lives of older adults?

- What are the major mental health concerns of late adulthood?

- How does aging affect memory, and what theories have psychologists formed regarding the development of wisdom and creativity in old age?

Variability in Late Adulthood

The scientific study of aging is known as **gerontology.** For many years, gerontologists thought about old age almost exclusively in terms of decline and loss. However, perspectives on the later years are rapidly changing, and late adulthood is now thought of as a period of tremendous individual variability rather than one of universal decline (Weaver, 1999).

CHARACTERISTICS OF THE ELDERLY POPULATION

Stereotypes of the elderly abound—they are the stuff of jokes and fairy tales, and today they are reinforced in the media. But real people often belie the stereotypes.

Life Expectancy   You might be surprised to learn that life expectancy increases as adults get older. For example, in the United States, the average 65-year-old man lives to about age 80, but once a man reaches 80, he is likely to live to be 90 (Federal Interagency Forum on Aging-Related Statistics [FIFARS], 2000). Life expectancy among women is even longer. The average 65-year-old woman lives to the age of 85, and the average 85-year-old woman can expect to live to over 90. Because of this sex difference in life expectancy, there are more elderly women than men. Life expectancy varies by racial group as well. In general, 65- to 74-year-old white Americans have longer life expectancies than African Americans in this age group, perhaps because of different rates of cancer and the other diseases you learned about in Chapter 5. However, by age 75, the life expectancies of white American and African American elders are essentially equivalent (FIFARS, 2000).

Subgroups   Gerontologists point out that there are important differences among the *young old* (aged 60–75), the *old old* (aged 75–85), and the *oldest old* (aged 85 and over). The oldest old are the fastest-growing segment of the population in the United States, which means that terms such as *octogenarian* (a person in his or her 80s) and *centenarian* (a person over 100 years of age) will be used far more often than in the past. From 1960 to 1994, the over-65 population in the United States doubled, while the over-85 population tripled (FIFARS, 2000). By contrast, the overall U.S. population grew only 45% during the same period. Moreover, demographers project that the over-85 population in the United States will exceed 19 million by 2050. Furthermore, every industrialized country in the world is experiencing this same kind of growth in the elderly population (Century Foundation, 1998).

The oldest old are more likely to suffer from significant physical and mental impairments than are the young old or the old old. Consequently, the increase in their numbers means that the population of **frail elderly,** older adults who cannot care for themselves, is also likely to grow significantly. Demographers and economists have become concerned about the ability of young and middle-aged adults to support the growing number of elderly (see No Easy Answers).

Even with the best health habits, relatively few individuals reach the age of 100, or centenarian status. Nevertheless, the proportion of centenarians in the population is growing more rapidly than any other age group (Perls, Silver, & Lauerman, 1998). At the beginning of the 20th century, there was only 1 centenarian for every 100,000 people in the United States. By the end of the century, the rate was 1 centenarian per 10,000 people, or a total of about 50,000 individuals over the age of 100. Demographers project that by 2010 the centenarian population will quadruple, reaching more than 200,000. Similar increases are projected to happen every decade, which will result in a centenarian population of over 1,000,000 persons by the middle of the 21st century—more than 90% of whom will be female.

At Boston University School of Medicine, a team of researchers headed by Dr. Thomas Perls has been studying centenarians for more than a decade. Their project is known as the

gerontology the scientific study of aging

frail elderly older adults whose physical and/or mental impairments are so extensive that they cannot care for themselves

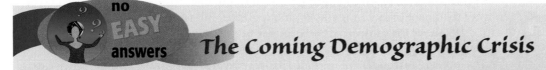

The Coming Demographic Crisis

Every industrialized nation in the world will face a demographic crisis in the near future. The reason for this crisis is that an extraordinarily large number of people were born in the years from 1946 until the early 1960s. (In the United States, this cohort is known as the Baby Boomers.) When the people born in this period reached maturity, however, they had many fewer children than their parents did. As a result, when the first wave reaches 65 in 2011, there will be fewer young and middle-aged adult workers for each of them than there are for each of the current cohort of elderly adults (Century Foundation, 1998). Consequently, governments may lack sufficient tax revenues to pay for the many benefits they have guaranteed to senior citizens.

With respect to pension plans, such as the Social Security system in the United States, there are really only two options: decreasing benefits to recipients or increasing taxes on workers. Moreover, economic analysts report that neither option alone will solve the problem. Any workable solution must include both reducing the financial burden of elderly entitlements and generating additional revenues.

Unfortunately, polls suggest that the public is opposed to both options (Public Agenda, Inc., 1999). Voters in the United States overwhelmingly oppose reducing benefits for the current cohort of retired people and are only slightly less opposed to reducing benefits for future retirees. At the same time, most workers believe that their Social Security taxes are already too high but do not want the government to use other funds, such as those generated by income taxes, to pay for Social Security benefits. Moreover, U.S. workers blame the problem on government mismanagement rather than on the mathematical inevitabilities of the demographic crisis. Consequently, lawmakers face a dilemma: A solution must be found, or governments may go bankrupt trying to fulfill their obligations to future elderly citizens. However, any solution politicians impose on voters is likely to be unpopular.

(Photo: © Mark Richards/PhotoEdit)

For these reasons, policy makers are looking for ways to make elderly entitlement reform more palatable to voters. For example, one proposal involves workers' taking responsibility for their own retirement income by directing how their Social Security taxes are to be invested. The appeal of this option is that it offers workers more autonomy. However, unlike the current system, it would not include a guaranteed retirement income. Those who invest wisely will enjoy a comfortable retirement; those who are less astute may be left with little or nothing.

Surveys suggest that the public wants both autonomy over retirement investments and a guaranteed income (Public Agenda, Inc., 1999). People would like to be able to invest their own Social Security taxes and retain the present system. Clearly, U.S. voters are reluctant to acknowledge that it is impossible to create a system that offers benefits without costs. As a result, workers in the United States are likely to end up with a solution that is imposed on them by legislators rather than one that represents a public consensus.

New England Centenarian Study (NECS). Predictably, these researchers have found that attainment of centenarian status runs in families: Individuals who are more than 100 years old tend to have parents and siblings who also lived to the age of 100. Moreover, most centenarians come from large families. One comparison study showed that people who died in their 60s or 70s had an average of 3.2 siblings, while participants in the NECS averaged more than four. Scientists associated with the NECS hypothesize that the greater number of siblings may reflect a genetic predisposition to better general health.

Superior health is also proposed as an explanation for the somewhat surprising finding that female centenarians are four times as likely to have given birth to a child during their 40s than women who die in their 60s or 70s. However, the general health hypothesis has not yet been supported by research. What does seem clear, however, is that centenarians are individuals who have lived extraordinarily healthy lives (Perls, Levenson, Regan, & Puca, 2002). Most have little or no evidence of cardiovascular disease, and a surprisingly large proportion (more than 30%) have experienced no or very minimal declines in cognitive abilities (Silver, Jilinskaia, & Perls, 2001).

Whatever the cause of extreme longevity, the increasing number of centenarians is likely to change developmentalists' understanding of old age. Perhaps future lifespan development textbooks will include chapters devoted specifically to these super-elders.

Health As Figure 7.1 indicates, a majority of older adults across all three age subgroups regard their health as good (FIFARS, 2000). These data contradict stereotypes of old age as a period of illness. However, the proportions of elderly with good health are a great deal lower than the equivalent proportions for young and middle-aged adults. Thus, as you might suspect, health is the single largest factor determining the trajectory of an adult's physical or mental status over the years beyond age 65. As you read more about the prevalence of disability and disease among older adults, keep Figure 7.1 in mind. You will see that these data are a testimony to the emotional resilience of older adults, a majority of whom are able to maintain an optimistic view of themselves and their lives in the face of growing physical challenges.

Further, their optimistic view seems to help protect older adults against the long-term effects of serious health threats such as strokes. Researchers have found that elders who rate their health as good, regardless of how an objective observer might rate it, recover more physical and cognitive functions after a stroke than their peers who rate their health more poorly (Hillen, Davies, Rudd, Kieselbach, & Wolfe, 2003). Older adults who are already suffering from one or more chronic diseases at 65 show far more rapid declines than do those who begin late adulthood with no disease symptoms. In part, of course, this is an effect of the disease processes themselves. Cardiovascular disease results, among other things, in restricted blood flow to many organs, including the brain, with predictable effects on an adult's ability to learn or remember. Longitudinal studies show that adults with this disease show earlier declines in all mental abilities (Schaie, 1996). And, of course, those suffering from the early stages of Alzheimer's disease or another disease that causes dementia will experience far more rapid declines in mental abilities than will those who do not have such diseases.

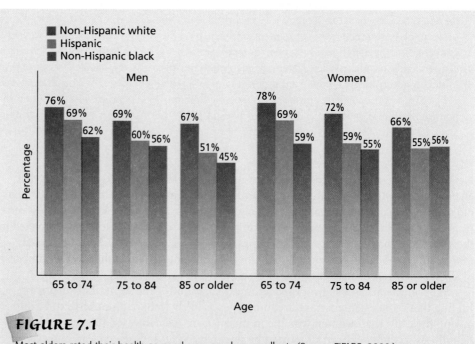

FIGURE 7.1

Most elders rated their health as good, very good, or excellent. (Source: FIFARS, 2000.)

Cognitive Functioning Researchers found a great deal of variability in a 7-year longitudinal study of the cognitive abilities of 102 older adults, first tested when they were between ages 62 and 86 (Willis, Jay, Diehl, & Marsiske, 1992). Over the ensuing 7 years, when most of the participants shifted from being young old to being old old, 62% of the group either remained at their original level of competence or showed improvement in competence on everyday intellectual tasks, while the remaining 38% showed decline (Willis et al., 1992). These results are supported by the graph in Figure 7.2, which illustrates that a majority of elderly adults, even among those who are over 85, do not suffer from cognitive impairments.

Gerontologists have also learned that variations in sex hormones are related to variations in cognitive performance. In one study, researchers examined cognitive functioning in men who were receiving sex-hormone-blocking drugs in connection with treatment for prostate cancer (Almeida, Waterreus, Spry, Flicker, & Martins, 2004). When these men discontinued treatment, their levels of sex hormones returned to normal, and their cognitive functioning improved dramatically.

Similarly, studies show that estrogen levels and cognitive functioning are correlated in women. Some early studies indicated that postmenopausal women who received hormone replacement therapy showed improved memory function (Costa, Reus, Wolkowitz, Manfredi, & Lieberman, 1999; Duka, Tasker, & McGowan, 2000). However, the collective findings of numerous studies examining the effects of hormone replacement therapy on cognitive functioning suggest that giving women hormone supplements does *not* improve their cognitive functioning. In fact, as you learned in Chapter 5, hormone replacement therapy may actually increase women's chances of developing serious cognitive dysfunctions (Shumaker et al., 2003). So, the nature of the relationship between sex hormones and cognitive functioning is not yet understood.

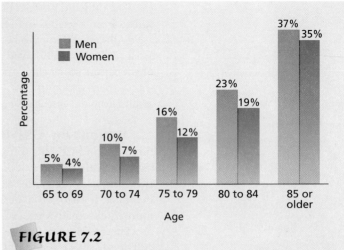

FIGURE 7.2

The graph represents the percentages of young old, old old, and oldest old adults in the United States who have cognitive impairments. (Source: FIFARS, 2000.)

Mental Exercise Can mental exercise improve mental functioning, just as physical exercise improves physical functioning? Studies with rats show that older rats placed in very rich, interesting environments experience growth in brain tissue, whereas rats placed in neutral or boring environments experience a decrease in brain mass (Cotman & Neeper, 1996). Neurophysiologists involved in this animal research are convinced that something analogous occurs among humans—that older adults who continue to challenge themselves with complex mental activities can delay or even reverse the normal decline in brain mass that is part of primary aging.

Correlational evidence supports this argument (Salthouse, 2004). For example, in one study, researchers found that older adults who played bridge regularly had higher scores on tests of both memory and reasoning than did non–bridge players. The two groups did not differ in education, health, exercise levels, or life satisfaction or on measures of physical and cognitive functioning that have little relationship to bridge playing, such as reaction time and vocabulary size (Clarkson-Smith & Hartley, 1990).

Use it or lose it? These men keep their minds sharp by playing games that require complex memory and strategy skills.

The difficulties inherent in this research are obvious: Most strikingly, such research suffers from a serious self-selection problem. People who strive to remain mentally active are doubtless different to begin with from those who make less effort (Hultsch, Hertzog, Small, & Dixon, 1999). And teasing out the unique effect of mental activity from the roles of education, social class, and health is clearly very difficult. But it seems reasonable that some—perhaps significant—enhancement or better maintenance of intellectual skills results from an "engaged" and intellectually active lifestyle (Gold et al., 1995).

Limitations on Activities Gerontologists generally define a *disability* as a limitation in an individual's ability to perform certain roles and tasks, particularly self-help tasks and other chores of daily living (Jette, 1996). Daily living tasks are grouped into two categories: **Activities of daily living,** or **ADLs,** include bathing, dressing, and using the toilet. **Instrumental activities of daily living,** or **IADLs,** include activities that are more intellectually demanding, such as managing money.

Figure 7.3 gives a sense of how many elderly adults in the United States have difficulty performing such tasks (FIFARS, 2000). As you can see, a significant proportion of elders have at least some degree of disability. However, the proportions have declined in recent years, and the majority of elderly adults have no difficulty performing ADLs or IADLs.

As you might expect, proportions of older adults with disabilities rise with age. Roughly half of those over 85 report at least some level of difficulty performing some basic daily life activities (Jette, 1996). But this means that half of these oldest old do *not* have such problems. To be sure, surveys generally exclude adults who are living in institutions, the vast majority of whom are severely disabled, according to the usual definition. And, of course, many of those with significant disability die before age 85, leaving only the healthiest still surviving among the oldest old. Still, it is important to understand that among the oldest old who live outside of nursing homes, the proportion who have some disability is nowhere near 100%. Even more encouraging is the finding that the rate of disability among the old old and the oldest old has been declining slowly but steadily in the past few decades in the United States, perhaps because of better health care or better health habits (Kolata, 1996).

As you can see from Figure 7.4, the physical problems or diseases that are most likely to contribute to some functional disability in late adulthood are arthritis and

activities of daily living (ADLs) self-help tasks such as bathing, dressing, and using the toilet

instrumental activities of daily living (IADLs) more intellectually demanding daily living tasks such as doing housework, cooking, and managing money

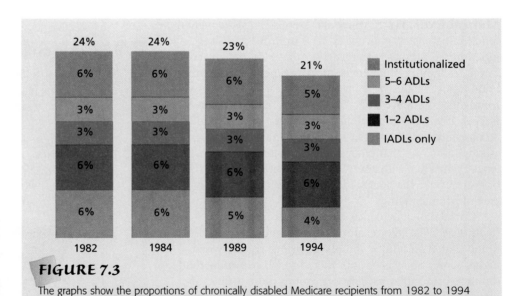

FIGURE 7.3

The graphs show the proportions of chronically disabled Medicare recipients from 1982 to 1994 who had limitations on one or more activities of daily living (ADLs, which are self-care tasks such as bathing) and on instrumental activities of daily living (IADLs, which are more complex tasks such as cooking and money management). (Source: FIFARS, 2000.)

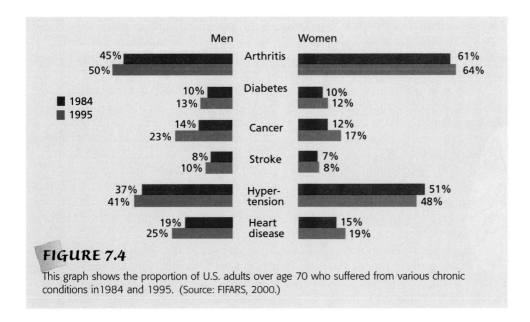

FIGURE 7.4

This graph shows the proportion of U.S. adults over age 70 who suffered from various chronic conditions in 1984 and 1995. (Source: FIFARS, 2000.)

hypertension. Not everyone with these problems is disabled. But the risk of some kind of functional disability is two to three times higher among elders who suffer from these diseases than among those who do not (Verbrugge, Lepkowski, & Konkol, 1991). As the figure also indicates, except for hypertension among women, the prevalence of these conditions and diseases increased from 1984 to 1995. These increases are most likely the result of population growth among the oldest old, who are more likely than the young old and the old old to be in ill health.

You can also see from Figure 7.4 that women are considerably more likely than men to suffer from arthritis, so they are also more often limited in their ability to carry out the various movements and tasks necessary for independent life (Brock et al.,1990). Since women are more likely to be widowed and thus to lack a partner who can assist with these daily living tasks, it is not surprising that more women than men live with their children or in nursing homes.

Racial and Ethnic Differences Among ethnic minorities, as among white Americans, individual variability in old age is the rule rather than the exception. Certainly, averages for life expectancy and disabling conditions such as heart disease differ across groups. For example, the prevalence of arthritis among elderly white Americans is about 58%, whereas 50% of Hispanic Americans and 67% of African Americans have this potentially disabling condition (FIFARS, 2000). Nevertheless, as Figure 7.1 showed, a majority of elders across these three ethnic groups rate their health as good to excellent. (The one exception is African American men over age 85.)

Moreover, everything you have learned so far about the correlations between health habits and health status in adulthood is just as applicable to minorities as to whites. Thus, improved diet, increased physical activity, and participation in treatment programs for debilitating chronic ailments can potentially benefit elders of any race or ethnic group.

LONGEVITY

The shift in thinking about old age is evident in the fact that gerontologists have begun to devote a great deal of attention to studying why some people live to the age of 100 and beyond. By this time, you've learned enough about development to predict that, like most other developmental variables, longevity will appear to result from interactions among heredity, environment, and behavioral choices.

The Maximum Lifespan

For humans, the maximum lifespan seems to be about 110 or 120 years. For turtles, the lifespan is far longer, and for chickens, far shorter. Such differences among species have persuaded some biologists that there may be some universal genetic process that limits lifespan (e.g., Hayflick, 1977, 1987).

Advocates of this view support their argument with research demonstrating that cells taken from the embryos of different species and placed in nutrient solution double only a fixed number of times, after which the cell colony degenerates. Human embryo cells double about 50 times; those from the Galapagos tortoise double roughly 100 times; chicken cells double only about 25 times. Furthermore, cells taken from human adults double only about 20 times, as if they had already "used up" some of their genetic capacity. The theoretical proposal that emerges from such observations is that each species is subject to a time limit, known as the **Hayflick limit** (because it was proposed by biologist Leonard Hayflick), beyond which cells simply lose their capacity to replicate themselves (Norwood, Smith, & Stein, 1990).

The genetic limits argument has been strengthened by the recent discovery that each chromosome in the human body (and presumably in other species, too) has, at its tip, a string of repetitive DNA called a **telomere** (Angier, 1992; Campisi, Dimri, & Hara, 1996). Among other functions, telomeres appear to serve as a kind of timekeeping mechanism for the organism. Researchers have found that the number of telomeres is reduced slightly each time a cell divides, so the number remaining in a 70-year-old is much lower than what is found in a child. This raises the possibility that there may be a crucial minimum number of telomeres; when the total falls below that number, disease or death comes fairly quickly.

Individual Heredity

Whatever the maximum possible human lifespan, it is clear that there is a large range of individual differences in how long people live. Some general tendency to "live long and prosper" (to quote Mr. Spock from *Star Trek*) is clearly inherited (Heun & Bonsignore, 2004). Identical twins are more similar in length of life than are fraternal twins, and adults whose parents and grandparents were long-lived are also likely to live longer (Plomin & McClearn, 1990).

Twin studies in Sweden showed that identical twins have more similar illness rates than do fraternal twins (Pedersen & Harris, 1990). Similarly, for the Harvard men in the Grant study sample discussed in Chapter 1, there was a small but significant correlation between health and the longevity of each man's parents and grandparents. Only about a quarter of those whose oldest grandparent had lived past 90 had any kind of chronic illness at age 65, compared with nearly 70% of those whose oldest grandparent had died at 78 or younger (Vaillant, 1991).

Hayflick limit the genetically programmed time limit to which each species is theoretically proposed to be subject, after which cells no longer have any capacity to replicate themselves accurately

telomere a string of repetitive DNA at the tip of each chromosome in the body that appears to serve as a kind of timekeeping mechanism

(Photo: © A. Ramey/Stock Boston, LLC)

There are many ways to maintain physical fitness in old age. In China, elderly people often can be found practicing Tai Chi in the early morning.

Health Habits

The same health habits that are important predictors of longevity and health in early adulthood continue to be significant predictors in late adulthood. For example, a 17-year follow-up of participants in the Alameda County epidemiological study who were 60 or over at the start of the study showed that smoking, low levels of physical activity, and being significantly underweight or overweight were linked to increased risk of death over the succeeding 17 years (Kaplan, 1992). Many other large epidemiological studies confirm such connections (e.g., Brody, 1996; Paffenbarger, Hyde, Wing, & Hsieh, 1987).

Perhaps the most crucial variable is physical exercise, which has been clearly linked not only to greater longevity but also to lower rates of diseases such as heart disease, cancer, osteoporosis, diabetes, gastrointestinal problems, and arthritis (Brody, 1995; Deeg, Kardaun, & Fozard, 1996). Good evidence on this point comes from a longitudinal study of nearly 7,000 participants who were all 70 or older when they were first tested in 1984 (Wolinsky, Stump, & Clark, 1995). They were then retested every 2 years until 1990. Those who reported in 1984 that they had a regular exercise routine or walked a mile or more at least once a week maintained better physical functioning over the succeeding years, were less likely to die, and were less likely to be in a nursing home by 1990. These outcomes remained likely even when the variations in health in 1984 were factored out—that is, it isn't that healthy adults were more likely to exercise, but that exercise kept people healthier.

CRITICAL THINKING

How many people in your family have lived past the age of 80? Did those who died younger do so because of a controllable lifestyle factor, such as smoking?

This point is reinforced by studies in which older adults were assigned randomly to exercise and nonexercise groups (e.g., Blumenthal et al., 1991; Tsang & Hui-Chan, 2003). In these studies, too, those who exercised had better scores on various measures of physical functioning. One such experiment, with a group of adults who were all over age 80, found that muscular strength increased and motor skills improved after only 12 weeks of exercise (Carmeli, Reznick, Coleman, & Carmeli, 2000).

Physical exercise also seems to help maintain higher levels of cognitive performance among the elderly (Albert et al., 1995; Lytle, 2004). Studies with rats, for example, show that older rats who exercise regularly on treadmills have higher levels of a nerve growth factor that keeps neurons healthy (Cotman & Neeper, 1996). Studies of humans, naturally enough, provide less direct evidence, but nonetheless point in the same direction. Some particularly clear evidence comes from a study in which researchers followed a group of 85 men from age 65 through age 69. All the men were well educated and were in good health at the start of the study, with no symptoms of heart disease or dementia (Rogers et al., 1990). In the succeeding 4 years, a third of the men chose to continue working, mostly at fairly high-level jobs. Another third retired but remained physically active, while the remaining third retired and became physically (and mentally) inactive. The inactive participants showed progressive declines on a measure of blood flow to the brain and performed significantly less well than either the active retired men or the still-working men on a battery of cognitive tests.

If anything, physical exercise seems to be even more important in the later years than at earlier ages. For example, one investigation used medical records and self-reports of exercise to examine the degree to which physical activity influenced height loss in the elderly (Sagiv, Vogelaere, Soudry, & Shrsam, 2000). Investigators found that study participants who had exercised regularly lost significantly less height over a 30-year period than those who had not exercised. Further, exercise after age 40 seemed to be especially important in preventing height loss.

Some authors have suggested that as much as half of the decline in various aspects of physical (and perhaps cognitive) functioning in late adulthood could be prevented through improved lifestyle, particularly exercise. Yet less than a fifth of older adults in the United States exercise regularly (McAuley, 1993; Wolinsky et al., 1995). People give many reasons for not exercising, including poor health, arthritic pain, time demands of caring for an ailing spouse, culturally based assumptions about appropriate behavior for older persons, embarrassment about exposing an aging body to others in an exercise program, lack of fitness facilities or lack of transportation to such facilities, fears of various kinds, and plain lethargy.

Before going on . . .

■ In what ways do older adults vary across age groups and individually?

■ What are the factors that contribute to longevity?

Physical Changes

Despite variability in health and functioning among the elderly, there are several changes in physical functioning that characterize the late adult years for almost everyone.

THE BRAIN AND NERVOUS SYSTEM

If you look back at Table 3.1 (p. 62), you'll see four main changes in the brain during the adult years: a reduction of brain weight, a loss of gray matter, a decline in the density of dendrites, and slower synaptic speed. The most central of these changes is the loss of dendritic density. Dendrites are "pruned" during the first few years after birth so that redundant or unused pathways are eliminated. The loss of dendrites in middle and late adulthood does not seem to be the same type of pruning. Rather, it appears to be a decrease in useful dendritic connections.

However, research suggests that experience as well as aging is involved in the loss of dendritic density. Neurologists have found that, across the years from 60 to 90, adults with higher levels of education show significantly less atrophy of the cerebral cortex than those who have fewer years of schooling (Coffey, Saxton, Ratcliff, Bryan, & Lucke, 1999). Moreover, the brains of well and poorly educated elderly adults do not differ in areas that are less involved in academic learning than the cerebral cortex is. This finding suggests that education itself is the cause of the reduced atrophying of the cerebral cortex rather than some general factor, such as socioeconomic status, that is coincidentally related to education.

Dendritic loss also results in a gradual slowing of synaptic speed, with a consequent increase in reaction time for many everyday tasks. Neural pathways are redundant enough that it is nearly always possible for a nerve impulse to move from neuron A to neuron B or from neuron A to some muscle cell. Neurologists usually refer to this redundancy as **synaptic plasticity.** But with the increasing loss of dendrites, the shortest route may be lost, so plasticity decreases and reaction time increases.

One final change in the nervous system, about which physiologists disagree, is the loss of neurons themselves. For many years, it was believed that an adult lost 100,000 neurons every day. It now appears that this conclusion, like many such conclusions about primary aging, was based on cross-sectional comparisons that included many older adults who had diseases known to affect brain composition and functioning. Researchers have not yet reached a consensus on just how much loss occurs among healthy aging adults, but most agree that 100,000 neurons per day is a considerable overestimation (e.g., Ivy et al., 1992; Scheibel, 1996).

Current estimates are that the brain has perhaps 1 trillion neurons (Morgan, 1992). A loss of 100,000 per day, even if it began at birth and lasted for a lifespan of 100 years, would be only about 4 billion neurons, leaving the vast majority (over 99%) still intact. It is only when the brain loses a significant amount of interconnectivity, which occurs as dendrites decrease in number, that "computational power" declines and symptoms of old age appear (Scheibel, 1992, p. 168). In addition, as you learned in Chapter 3, scientists have only recently discovered that new neurons are produced in some parts of the brain even in adulthood, although the effect of this neuron regeneration is not yet known (Gould et al., 1999).

THE SENSES AND OTHER BODY SYSTEMS

In Chapter 5, you read about declines in sensory and other physical functions that occur in middle age. Such deficits become larger in late adulthood, and several more serious threats to the health of these systems arise.

Vision   In addition to presbyopia (farsightedness), late adulthood can bring other vision defects due to body changes. For example, blood flow to the eye decreases (perhaps as a side effect of atherosclerosis), which results in an enlarged "blind spot" on the retina and thus a reduced field of vision. The pupil does not widen or narrow as much or as quickly as it previously did, which means that the older adult has more difficulty seeing at night and responding to rapid changes in brightness (Kline & Scialfa, 1996).

synaptic plasticity the redundancy in the nervous system that ensures that it is nearly always possible for a nerve impulse to move from one neuron to another or from a neuron to another type of cell (e.g., a muscle cell)

In addition, a significant minority of older adults suffer from diseases of the eye that further diminish visual acuity and adaptability. Only about 2% of U.S. adults under age 65 suffer from *cataracts*, a condition in which the lens inside the eye becomes clouded and obscures vision. For those over 75, the rate is roughly ten times that figure (U.S. Bureau of the Census, 1995a). Thus, many older adults must adapt to significant impairments of vision, and the process of adaptation doesn't always go smoothly. Researchers have found that middle-aged adults adjust more easily to the difficulties associated with living with a serious vision impairment (Lindo & Nordholm, 1999). Moreover, vision loss has a greater negative effect on an elderly adult's sense of well-being. Fortunately, many age-related diseases of the eye can be effectively treated with medications and/or surgery.

(Photo: © Wally McNamee/CORBIS)

Hearing aids improve many older adults' quality of life.

Hearing You'll recall from Chapter 5 that wear and tear on the auditory system results in some hearing loss (*presbycusis*) beginning in middle adulthood, but these gradual losses don't typically add up to functionally significant loss until late adulthood. Auditory problems, unlike many other disabilities of old age, are more likely to be experienced by men than by women. This sex difference is normally attributed to differential exposure to noise: More men have worked in environments with high levels of noise (at least in current cohorts of older adults in developed countries).

Hearing difficulties in late adulthood have several components: First, there is the loss of ability to hear high-frequency sounds. Both cross-sectional and longitudinal studies suggest that, for the range of sounds used in normal human speech, the loss after age 60 is such that a given sound has to be about 1–2 decibels louder each year for the individual to report that he hears it (Fozard, 1990; Kline & Scialfa, 1996).

Second, most older adults develop difficulties with word discrimination. Even when the sound is loud enough, older adults have more difficulty identifying individual words they have just heard (Schieber, 1992). In addition, many adults over the age of 60 have problems hearing under noisy conditions. The loss of ability to discriminate individual words is even greater in such situations, so large gatherings become increasingly difficult for older adults.

Tinnitus, a persistent ringing in the ears, also increases in incidence with age, although this problem appears to be independent of the other changes just described. Roughly 10% of adults over 65 experience this problem (U.S. Bureau of the Census, 1995a), which may be caused by exposure to noise, although that is not well established.

Even mild hearing loss can pose communication problems in some situations. Those with such problems may be perceived by others as disoriented or suffering from poor memory, especially if the person with the hearing loss is unwilling to admit the problem and ask for a comment or instruction to be repeated. Nonetheless, the older adult with a hearing impairment is *not* necessarily socially isolated or unhappy. Mild and moderate hearing losses, even if uncorrected with a hearing aid, are simply not correlated with measures of general social, emotional, or psychological health among elderly adults. It is only severe hearing loss that is associated with an increase in social or psychological problems, including heightened rates of depression (Corso, 1987; Schieber, 1992).

Presbycusis and the other changes in hearing seem to result from gradual degeneration of virtually every part of the auditory system. Older adults secrete more ear wax, which may block the ear canal; the bones of the middle ear become calcified and less elastic; the cochlear membranes of the inner ear become less flexible and less responsive; and the nerve pathways to the brain show some degeneration (Schieber, 1992).

Taste, Smell, and Touch The ability to taste the four basic flavors (salty, bitter, sweet, and sour) does not seem to decline over the years of adulthood. Taste receptor cells (taste buds) have short lives and are continually replaced (Bornstein, 1992). But other changes in the taste system affect older adults, such as the secretion of somewhat less saliva, producing a sensation of "wooly mouth" for some. Many elders also report

CRITICAL THINKING ❓

How do you think a hearing impairment is likely to affect the life of an older adult? Aside from wearing a hearing aid, how could a person with a moderate hearing impairment adapt his life so as to reduce the impact of the disability?

tinnitus persistent ringing in the ears

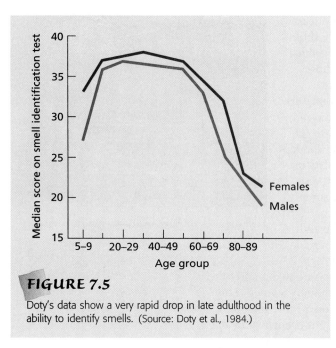

FIGURE 7.5

Doty's data show a very rapid drop in late adulthood in the ability to identify smells. (Source: Doty et al., 1984.)

that flavors seem blander than in earlier years, leading them to prefer more intense concentrations of flavors, particularly sweetness (de Graaf, Polet, & van Staveren, 1994). But it may well be that this perception of flavor blandness is due largely to a loss of the sense of smell.

The sense of smell clearly deteriorates in old age. The best information comes from a cross-sectional study in which researchers tested nearly 2,000 children and adults on their ability to identify 40 different smells—everything from pizza to gasoline (Doty et al., 1984). As Figure 7.5 reveals, young and middle-aged adults had equally good scores on this smell identification test, but scores declined rapidly after age 60. However, the loss of sensitivity to odors is far greater among elderly men than elderly women (Morgan, Covington, Geisler, Polich, & Murphy, 1997).

Interestingly, like hearing loss, the loss of the sense of smell seems to have an environmental component. Specifically, both men and women who worked in factories (where, presumably, they were exposed to more pollutants) show much greater losses of sense of smell in old age than do those who worked in offices (Corwin, Loury, & Gilbert, 1995).

These changes in taste and smell can reduce many pleasures in life. But they can also have practical health consequences. Smells enhance the pleasure of food, so as the sense of smell becomes less acute, elders are less motivated to prepare tasty food. In some cases, this can result in inadequate nutrition or significant dietary imbalances.

Similarly, loss of sensitivity to touch can lead to significant declines in the quality of life. For example, the skin of elderly adults is less responsive to cold and heat (Stevens & Choo, 1998). Research suggests that the loss of sensitivity occurs in a pattern that is a reversal of the proximodistal principle of growth. In other words, the extremities, usually the feet, are the first body parts to decline in sensitivity. Consequently, elderly people are less able to benefit from the potential comforts associated with physical stimuli. For example, for an elderly person to be able to feel a warm bath, the water temperature may have to be so high that it will burn the skin.

THEORIES OF BIOLOGICAL AGING

What are the causes of physical aging? Current theorists agree that the most likely explanation lies in basic cellular processes, which appear to change with age in specific ways that reduce the efficiency of cellular functioning. A number of theoretical variations on this theme have been proposed.

Genetically Programmed Senescence   Senescence is the gradual deterioration of body systems that happens as organisms age. **Programmed senescence theory** suggests that age-related physical declines result from species-specific genes for aging. Evolutionary theorists argue that programmed senescence prevents older, presumably less fit, individuals from becoming parents at an age when they are unlikely to be able to raise offspring to maturity (Buss, 1999). The idea is that these aging genes are equipped with some kind of built-in clock that prevents the genes from having an effect when humans are in their reproductive years but switches them on once the reproductive peak has passed.

senescence physical changes and declines associated with aging

programmed senescence theory the view that age-related declines are the result of species-specific genes for aging

Repair of Genetic Material and Cross-Linking   Another theory of aging focuses on the cells' ability to repair breaks in DNA. Breaks in DNA strands are common events, resulting from unknown metabolic processes. Because the organism is apparently unable to repair all the damage, the theory proposes, the accumulation of unrepaired breaks results over time in a loss of cellular function, and the organism ages (Tice & Setlow, 1985).

A related theory focuses on another cellular process called cross-linking, which occurs more often in cell proteins of older adults than in those of younger adults. **Cross-linking** occurs when undesirable chemical bonds form between proteins or fats. In skin and connective tissue, for example, two proteins called *collagen* and *elastin* form cross-linkages, either between their molecules or within a given molecule. The resulting molecules cannot assume the correct shape for proper function, leading to effects such as wrinkling of the skin and arterial rigidity. (An equivalent process, by the way, occurs in old rubber, which explains why windshield wipers become stiffer over time.)

Free Radicals A third type of cellular process that may contribute to aging relates to the body's ability to deal with free radicals. **Free radicals,** which are molecules or atoms that possess an unpaired electron, are a normal by-product of body metabolism and also arise as a result of exposure to certain substances in foods, sunlight, X-rays, or air pollution. These radicals, especially the subgroup called *oxygen free radicals,* enter into many potentially harmful chemical reactions, resulting in irreparable cellular damage that accumulates with age. For example, oxidation reactions caused by free radicals can damage cell membranes, thereby reducing the cell's protection against toxins and carcinogens. Oxygen free radicals are also implicated in the body's reaction to cholesterol: Oxidation helps to transform some types of cholesterol into a form that adheres to artery walls, narrowing them and increasing the risk of heart attack and stroke (Brody, 1994).

A different line of evidence for this theory comes from research in which scientists genetically engineered a group of fruit flies to enhance the flies' built-in capacity to defend against free radicals (Orr & Sohal, 1994). These altered flies lived roughly one-third longer than normal fruit flies did—a result that raises the possibility that scientists might eventually be able to alter the limit of the human lifespan via genetic engineering.

Research on diet variations also points to the possibility that some foods, especially those high in fat and/or food additives such as preservatives, promote the formation of oxygen free radicals, whereas others, referred to as *antioxidants,* inhibit the formation of these radicals or promote chemical processes that help the body defend against them. Foods high in vitamins C and E and beta carotene (vitamin A) all belong in the latter group (Ornish, 1993). Several large epidemiological studies show that people who eat diets high in antioxidants or who take regular supplements of vitamin E or beta carotene live somewhat longer and have lower rates of heart disease (Blumberg, 1996).

Furthermore, recent research on dietary supplementation suggests that some kinds of vision loss in old age may be reversed when elders increase their intake of antioxidants. Researchers at Johns Hopkins University gave patients who suffered from various kinds of retinal degeneration large doses of an antioxidant called *lutein,* a yellow pigment found in egg yolks and in some vegetables (Dgnelie, Zorge, & McDonald, 2000). They found that participants' visual acuity began to improve within just 2 weeks and continued to get better for several months.

Such findings do not mean that age-related problems such as heart disease and vision loss are *caused* by antioxidant deficiencies. Moreover, not all studies of antioxidant supplemention show positive effects (e.g., Alpha-Tocopherol Beta Carotene Cancer Prevention Study Group, 1994). However, studies that do demonstrate such benefits add support to the general notion that many of the effects of aging are modifiable and perhaps even preventable.

Terminal Drop Some theorists claim that physical and mental declines in old age are actually part of the dying process. For example, the **terminal drop hypothesis** asserts that all adults retain excellent physical and mental function until just a few years before death, at which time there are significant declines in all functions (Kleemeier, 1962). However, longitudinal research suggests that declines in most functions are

cross-linking the formation of undesirable bonds between proteins or fats

free radicals molecules or atoms that possess an unpaired electron

terminal drop hypothesis the hypothesis that mental and physical functioning decline drastically only in the few years immediately preceding death

gradual across late adulthood (Berg, 1996; Birren & Schroots, 1996). Only changes in cognitive functions seem to fit the terminal drop pattern (Johansson et al., 2004).

BEHAVIORAL EFFECTS OF PHYSICAL CHANGES

The great majority of older adults cope effectively with most everyday tasks—buying groceries, managing their finances, reading bus schedules, planning their lives, and so on—despite changes in vision, hearing, and other physical functions (Willis, 1996). Thus, in addition to knowing what these changes are and how they might be explained, it's important to know just how they affect older adults' daily lives.

General Slowing The biggest single behavioral effect of age-related physical changes is a general slowing down. Dendritic loss at the neuronal level clearly contributes substantially to this general slowing, but other factors are also involved, including arthritic changes in the joints and loss of elasticity in the muscles. Everything takes longer—writing things down, tying one's shoes, and adapting to changes in temperature or changes in light conditions (Schaie & Willis, 1991). Even tasks that involve word skills, which tend to decline very little in accuracy with age, nonetheless are done more slowly (Lima, Hale, & Myerson, 1991; Madden, 1992).

Further, many developmentalists believe that the decline in the speed of nerve impulses is responsible for age-related difficulties in translating thoughts into action. For example, neurologists sometimes assess nervous system functioning by having patients demonstrate a physical action involving a tool, such as hammering. Demonstrating an appropriate hand posture and moving the arm in an appropriate way are taken as indicators of neurological health. Developmentalists have found that healthy individuals in late adulthood make more initial errors than younger adults in trying to carry out such activities (Peigneux & van der Linden, 1999). However, they correct their errors just as quickly as those who are younger. Consequently, neuropsychologists think that general slowing of brain activity interferes with older adults' retrieval of the knowledge they need to accomplish the task and that they use behavioral feedback to compensate for mistakes.

Age-related physical changes add up to really significant differences in functioning in a complex motor activity such as driving. Young adults have more auto accidents than any other age group, primarily because they drive too fast. But older adults have more accidents per miles driven (Bianchi, 1993). Of course, other physical changes beyond general slowing contribute to driving problems in old age. Changes in the eyes mean that older adults have more trouble reading signs at night and adjusting to the glare of oncoming headlights. In addition, reduced range of motion in the neck, which often accompanies arthritis, may contribute to automobile accidents involving elderly drivers. Older adults also say that they have more trouble judging their own speed and that the instrument panel is too dim to be seen (Kline et al., 1992). Similarly, they seem to be less able to judge the speed of oncoming traffic when trying to execute turns and carry out other driving maneuvers (Keskinen, Ota, & Katila, 1998). And the general increase in reaction time affects elders' ability

(Photo: © Tom Prettyman/PhotoEdit)

This older man has bought himself a very sporty car and doubtless thinks of himself as still a skillful driver. But it is nonetheless true that many of the physical changes associated with aging will make it harder for him to respond quickly, to see clearly in glare, and to adapt rapidly to changing driving conditions.

to switch attention from one thing to the next or to react quickly and appropriately when a vehicle or obstacle appears unexpectedly.

Changes in temperature sensitivity, together with general slowing, lead to increases in accidental burns. For example, the elderly are more likely to burn themselves when they mistakenly pick up a hot pan while cooking. The neurological message "Put down this pan because it's going to burn your skin" moves from the hand to the brain almost instantaneously in a young or middle-aged adult. In older adults, however, a greater amount of heat is required to initiate the message, the message itself travels to the brain more slowly, and the response from the brain that signals the hand to let go of the pan travels more slowly as well. Consequently, burns are far more common in late adulthood than earlier.

Sleeping and Eating Patterns   Another common effect of physical change is a shift in sleep patterns in old age, which occurs among both healthy and less healthy elders. Adults older than 65 typically wake up more frequently in the night and show decreases in rapid eye movement (REM) sleep, the lighter sleep state in which dreaming occurs. Older adults are also more likely to wake early in the morning and go to bed early at night. They become "morning people" instead of "night people" (Hoch, Buysse, Monk, & Reynolds, 1992; Richardson, 1990). And because their night sleep is more often interrupted, older adults also nap more during the day in order to accumulate the needed amount of sleep. These changes in sleep and activity patterns are presumed to be related to changes in nervous system functioning.

The ability of the brain to regulate appetite also changes with advancing age. When you eat, your blood sugar rises, resulting in a chemical message to the brain that creates a sensation called **satiety,** the sense of being full. The feeling of satiety continues until your blood sugar drops, at which time another chemical message is sent to the brain that causes you to feel hunger. In older adults, the satiety part of the pattern seems to be impaired (Keene, Hope, Rogers, & Elliman, 1998). As a result, older adults may feel hungry all the time and may overeat. To compensate, they come to rely more on habits such as taking their meals at certain times and eating the same foods every day. Thus, they may seem to be unnecessarily rigid to those who are younger when, in reality, their adherence to a particular eating regime is simply a (perhaps unconscious) way of coping with a physiological change.

Motor Functions   The various physical changes associated with aging also combine to produce a reduction in stamina, dexterity, and balance. The loss of stamina clearly arises in large part from changes in the cardiovascular system, as well as from changes in muscles. Dexterity is lost primarily as a result of arthritic changes in the joints.

Another significant change, one with particularly clear practical ramifications, is a gradual loss of the sense of balance (Guralnik et al., 1994; Simoneau & Liebowitz, 1996; Slobounov, Moss, Slobounova, & Newell, 1998). Older adults, who may be quite mobile in their home environments, are likely to have greater difficulty handling an uneven sidewalk or adapting their bodies to a swaying bus. Such situations require the ability to adjust rapidly to changing body cues and the muscular strength to maintain body position, both of which decline in old age. So older adults fall more often. About one-quarter of the young old and more than a third of the old old interviewed for one study reported having fallen in the previous year (Hornbrook, Stevens, & Wingfield, 1994). Because of osteoporosis, such falls in old age more often result in a fracture, which can be a very serious health complication for an older adult.

Older adults also have more problems with fine-motor movements (Smith et al., 1999). Such losses are small and gradual with respect to well-practiced skills such as handwriting. However, research suggests that some fine-motor activities, especially those that require learning a new pattern of movement, may be extremely difficult for elderly people. For example, older adults take far longer than young and middle-aged adults do to learn complex computer mouse skills such as clicking and dragging objects across the screen (Smith, Sharit, & Czaja, 1999).

CRITICAL THINKING 🅀

How might age-related changes in facial muscles contribute to stereotypes about "grumpiness" in the elderly?

satiety the feeling of fullness that follows a meal

Sexual Activity Another behavior that is affected by the cumulative physical changes of aging is sexual behavior. You read in Chapter 5 that the frequency of sexual activity declines gradually in middle adulthood. Both cross-sectional and longitudinal data suggest that this trend continues in late adulthood (Marsiglio & Donnelly, 1991; Palmore, 1981).

The decline in the frequency of sexual activity in late adulthood doubtless has many causes (National Institute on Aging [NIA], 2000b). The continuing decline in testosterone levels among men clearly plays some role. The state of one's overall health plays an increasingly larger role with advancing age. For example, blood pressure medication sometimes produces impotence as a side effect; chronic pain may also affect sexual desire. Stereotypes that portray old age as an essentially asexual period of life may also have some effect.

Despite declining frequency, though, more than 70% of adults continue to be sexually active in old age (Bartlik & Goldstein, 2000). Moreover, the physiological capacity to respond to sexual stimulation, unlike other aspects of functioning, appears not to diminish with age. Indeed, some studies suggest that older adults, especially women, are more sexually adventurous; that is, they appear to be more willing to engage in sexual experimentation than young and middle-aged adults (Purnine & Carey, 1998).

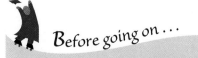

Before going on · · ·

- How does the brain change in late adulthood?
- What changes happen in other body systems of older adults?
- How do theories explain biological aging?
- What are the behavioral effects of changes in the various body systems of older adults?

Mental Health

The best-known mental health problems of old age are the **dementias,** a group of neurological disorders involving problems with memory and thinking that affect an individual's emotional, social, and physical functioning. Dementia is the leading cause of institutionalization of the elderly in the United States (FIFARS, 2000) (see the Real World feature). However, depression is also a concern in the late adult years.

ALZHEIMER'S DISEASE AND OTHER DEMENTIAS

Alzheimer's disease (technically known as *dementia of the Alzheimer's type*) is a very severe form of dementia. The early stages of Alzheimer's disease usually become evident very slowly, beginning with subtle memory difficulties, repetitive conversation, and disorientation in unfamiliar settings. Then, memory for recent events begins to go. Memory for long-ago events or for well-rehearsed cognitive procedures, such as simple calculations, is often retained until late in the illness, presumably because these memories can be accessed through many alternative neural pathways (Martin et al., 2003).

Eventually, however, an individual with Alzheimer's disease may fail to recognize family members and may be unable to remember the names of common objects or how to perform such routine activities as brushing her teeth or dressing. Those afflicted with Alzheimer's suffer declines in the ability to communicate, as well as the ability to carry out daily self-care routines. The changes in appetite regulation you read about earlier in this chapter are particularly problematic for those with Alzheimer's, because they can't rely on habit to regulate their eating behavior, as healthy older people do. Left to their own devices, Alzheimer's victims may consume as many as three or four complete meals at one sitting without realizing how much they have eaten. Consequently, their eating behavior must be closely supervised.

Alzheimer's patients also have difficulty processing information about others' emotions, such as facial expressions (Burnham & Hogervorst, 2004). Some have problems controlling their own emotions and display sudden bursts of anger or even rage. Others exhibit an increased level of dependency and clinginess toward family or friends

dementia a neurological disorder involving problems with memory and thinking that affect an individual's emotional, social, and physical functioning

Alzheimer's disease a very severe form of dementia, the cause of which is unknown

The Real World

Institutionalization among the Elderly

Research results such as those graphed in Figures 7.3 and 7.4 suggest that the average older adult will spend at least a few years with some kind of disability or chronic disease. How often do such problems require nursing home care? There are several answers to that question, depending on what statistics you look at.

One frequently quoted statistic is that only 4% of all adults over 65 in the United States are in any kind of institutional care (FIFARS, 2000). More older women than men are in nursing homes, simply because women's average lifespan is longer than men's. A second important piece of information is the estimate that the average 65-year-old man in the United States can expect to spend about 5 months in such an institution before he dies. The average woman can expect to spend 16 to 17 months (Manton, Stallard, & Liu, 1993). But neither of these statistics answers what is perhaps the most important question: What is the probability that any given 65-year-old will spend time in a nursing home or other institution? In the United States, that probability is about 40% (Belgrave, Wykle, & Choi, 1993; Kane & Kane, 1990). That is, roughly 40% of current older adults can expect to spend at least some time in a nursing home before death. Considered together, these several pieces of data suggest that some kind of institutional care during late adulthood is common but by no means universal, and that such care is most often fairly brief. Only a quarter of those over 65 can expect to spend as long as a year in a nursing home.

The actual experiences of those in nursing homes paint both rosy and gloomy pictures. It is true that placement in a nursing home is often followed by death within a relatively short time. But it is not true that nursing home care necessarily shortens a person's life. Only when an older adult has been placed in an institution (or any other living situation) involuntarily is there evidence that the move itself is a causal factor in rapid decline and death. Involuntarily institutionalized elders show much higher death rates in the ensuing months and years than do equivalently disabled elders who remain at home, although even this effect is not inevitable (Lawton, 1985, 1990). When the institution offers residents high levels of warmth, individuation, and opportunity for choice and control, even an involuntary move need not accelerate the process of physical or mental decline (Fields, 1992).

Nursing homes have a bad reputation—and, unfortunately, in the past some of that reputation was deserved. Only as research has revealed more about the needs and abilities of the elderly has institutional care for this group improved. Given that the number of elderly in the United States is increasing, it's important that those currently caring for the elderly and those who are getting older themselves have a realistic view of the likelihood of entering an institution and how being in an institution affects the elderly. The public must demand that institutional care for the elderly meet high standards and take more varied forms, so that, should some kind of institutional care become necessary (as well it might), the elders involved have the best possible experience.

(Raskind & Peskind, 1992). Research suggests that the incidence of depression among elders with Alzheimer's disease may be as high as 40% (Harwood et al., 2000).

Diagnosing and Treating Alzheimer's Disease   Alzheimer's disease can be definitively diagnosed only after a person has died. At autopsy, the brains of Alzheimer's victims are far more likely to contain extensive *neurofibrillary tangles* than are the brains of individuals with other kinds of dementia (Silver, Newell, Brady, Hedley-White, & Perls, 2002). Neurofibrillary tangles are stringy masses of tissue that appear to "clog" connections between neurons. They are typically surrounded by deposits of proteins and other substances called *plaques.*

The difficulty involved in diagnosing Alzheimer's disease is magnified by the fact that nearly 80% of elderly individuals complain of memory problems (Hanninen et al., 1996). As a result, researchers are currently looking for a set of predictors that may distinguish individuals who are in the process of developing Alzheimer's from those who are suffering from the effects of normal aging. A few indicators, such as the syndrome known as *mild cognitive impairment,* show promise (see the Research Report). At present, though, a diagnosis of Alzheimer's disease represents a health professional's best educated guess about the source of an individual's cognitive difficulties.

Mild Cognitive Impairment and Alzheimer's Disease

When an elder seeks help for memory problems or difficulties with logical thinking but is clearly not suffering from any kind of dementia, health care professionals usually try to determine whether he should be diagnosed with *mild cognitive impairment (MCI)* or with *age-associated cognitive decline (AACD)*. Criteria for both diagnoses include a gradual decline in cognitive function along with low scores on standardized tests (compared to scores of others of the same age). Physicians must also rule out the possibility that the individual is suffering from a specific disorder that might account for his symptoms (e.g., brain tumor, stroke, depression). Of the two disorders, AACD is the more common, afflicting just under one-third of older adults (Hanninen et al., 1996). By contrast, MCI is found in about 9% of elders (Tervo et al., 2004).

The procedures involved in determining which diagnosis is appropriate can take several weeks to complete and must usually be repeated a few months later. Although this process can be frustrating for elderly adults and their caregivers, getting the correct diagnosis is important because MCI is believed to be a precursor to Alzheimer's disease, while AACD is not. Thus, the prognosis for individuals with MCI is quite different from that for elders with AACD. Moreover, many researchers think that the progression to dementia in patients with MCI can be slowed or even prevented through the use of drugs that have shown to be effective against fully developed Alzheimer's (Amieva et al., 2004; Maruyama et al., 2003).

However, the idea that MCI is an early stage in the development of Alzheimer's disease is somewhat controversial. Some of the strongest evidence in favor of the stage hypothesis has involved brain-imaging and DNA studies. Generally, imaging studies show similar patterns of brain degeneration in individuals with MCI and Alzheimer's disease (Johnson, Vogt, Kim, Cotmam, & Head, 2004), and these patterns appear to be distinguishable from those associated with both normal aging and other kinds of dementia. Similarly, defects in the *apolipoprotein E* gene are strongly associated with both Alzheimer's disease and MCI (Tervo et al., 2004).

Additional support for the stage view comes from other kinds of physiological research. For example, individuals with either MCI or Alzheimer's disease differ from normal older adults in the degree to which free-radical-fighting substances such as vitamin C are present in their bloodstreams (Rinaldi et al., 2003). Further, studies examining substances in the cerebrospinal fluid of normal elderly adults, elders with MCI, and Alzheimer's sufferers indicate that both MCI and Alzheimer's are associated with rapid neuronal death (Maruyama et al., 2003).

Despite these compelling lines of evidence, it is abundantly clear that MCI does not inevitably lead to Alzheimer's disease. Longitudinal studies show that only one-third of adults aged 70 and over exhibit full-blown dementia within 2 years of receiving the diagnosis of MCI (Amieva et al., 2004). In addition, the cognitive functioning of many MCI sufferers remains entirely stable for many years.

Scientists on both sides of the debate about the nature of the MCI–Alzheimer's link agree that continued research into the correlation between the two is important to discovering the disease process that underlies the symptoms of Alzheimer's disease. Such research could lead to preventive measures that spare many MCI sufferers from this devastating disease.

A few drugs—such as *galantamine,* a drug that increases the amounts of some neurotransmitters in the brain—appear to slow down progress of Alzheimer's disease (Kurz, Erkinjuntti, Small, Lilienfeld, & Damaraju, 2003). Researchers are also studying the potential uses of anti-inflammatory drugs (e.g., aspirin) and antioxidant supplements (e.g., vitamin E) in the treatment and prevention of the disease (Sano et al., 1997). Experimental studies have shown that training Alzheimer's sufferers to use specific strategies (e.g., making notes in a journal) can to some degree improve their performance of everyday memory tasks such as associating names with faces and remembering to take medication (Lowenstein, Acevedo, Czaja, & Duara, 2004).

Heredity and Alzheimer's Disease Genetic factors seem to be important in some, but not all, cases of Alzheimer's (Heun & Bonsitnore, 2004). Researchers have now found three separate genes that appear to be implicated. The most common of these is a gene on chromosome 19 that controls production of a particular protein

(Rose, 1995). When errors in the production of this protein occur, the dendrites and axons of neurons in the brain become tangled and, as a result, do not function as efficiently. Heavy drinking during middle age may be an important factor in "turning on" this potentially harmful gene (Anttila et al., 2004).

Even in families with very high prevalences of Alzheimer's disease, ages of onset are highly variable. In one family study, age of onset ranged from 44 to 67 years (Axelman, Basun, & Lannfelt, 1998). Morever, there were wide variations in the severity of the disease's behavioral effects and in the length of time the victims lived once they developed Alzheimer's.

Other Types of Dementia Strictly speaking, dementia is a symptom and not a disease, and neurological research indicates that Alzheimer's and non-Alzheimer's dementias involve very different disease processes (Fokin, Ponomareva, Androsova, & Gavrilova, 1997). For example, signs of dementia frequently appear after a person suffers multiple small strokes; in this case, the condition is called **multi-infarct dementia.** The brain damage caused by such strokes is irreversible. However, in contrast to the situation with most cases of Alzheimer's disease, various forms of therapy—occupational, recreational, and physical—can improve victims' functioning (see Development in the Information Age, page 184).

In addition, dementia can be caused by depression, cardiovascular disease, metabolic disturbances, drug intoxication, Parkinson's disease, hypothyroidism, multiple blows to the head (frequent among boxers), a single head trauma, some kinds of tumors, vitamin B_{12} deficiency, anemia, or alcohol abuse (Anthony & Aboraya, 1992; Butters et al., 2004; Suryadevara, Storey, Aronow, & Ahn, 2003). Clearly, many of these causes are treatable; indeed, roughly 10% of all patients who are evaluated for dementia turn out to have some reversible problem. So, when an older person shows signs of dementia, it is critical to arrange for a careful diagnosis.

Incidence of Alzheimer's and Other Dementias Evidence from research in China, Sweden, France, Great Britain, Italy, the United States, Canada, and Japan, as well as studies involving several U.S. ethnic groups, shows that somewhere between 2% and 8% of all adults over age 65 exhibit significant symptoms of some kind of dementia, and about half of them have Alzheimer's disease (Corrada, Brookmeyer, & Kawas, 1995; Gurland et al., 1999; Rockwood & Stadnyk, 1994). Experts also agree that the rates of all kinds of dementias, including Alzheimer's disease, rise rapidly among people in their 70s and 80s. For example, a large, careful study in Canada showed that 11.1% of adults over 75 and 26.0% of those over 85 suffered from moderate to severe symptoms of dementia (Rockwood & Stadnyk, 1994). Similarly, about 64% of participants in the New England Centenarian Study displayed some signs of dementia (Silver et al., 2001).

DEPRESSION

The earliest studies of age differences in depression suggested that older adults were at higher risk for this disorder than any other age group, which contributed to a widespread cultural stereotype of the inevitably depressed elder. Certainly, suicide statistics suggest that depression increases in old age (see Figure 7.6, page 184). However, the full story on depression in late adulthood is complex.

Diagnosis, Definitions, and Prevalence Ageism can influence the diagnosis of depression in the elderly. Signs of depression in older adults may be dismissed as old-age "grumpiness" by family members (NIA, 2000a). And, when health care professionals recognize the signs of depression in elderly adults, they often fail to offer them effective treatments (Fischer, Wei, Solberg, Rush, & Heinrich, 2003). Alternatively, depression may be mistaken for dementia because it can cause confusion and memory loss.

multi-infarct dementia a form of dementia caused by one or more strokes

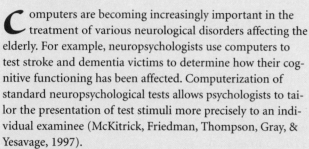

Development in the Information Age

Computers and Dementia

Computers are becoming increasingly important in the treatment of various neurological disorders affecting the elderly. For example, neuropsychologists use computers to test stroke and dementia victims to determine how their cognitive functioning has been affected. Computerization of standard neuropsychological tests allows psychologists to tailor the presentation of test stimuli more precisely to an individual examinee (McKitrick, Friedman, Thompson, Gray, & Yesavage, 1997).

For example, a common assessment task involves presenting test-takers with a series of digits and asking them to add the numbers two at a time. A computer can present a sample problem to determine how long an individual examinee takes to respond. After making that determination, the computer can then present problems at a rate that will allow the examinee sufficient time to respond. Certainly, human examiners can do the same thing, but they are less precise.

Neuropsychologists also use computers in rehabilitation programs. For example, many stroke victims have problems with comprehending speech and/or speaking themselves. Researchers have found that computerized speech rehabilitation programs are highly effective at improving the language skills of such people (Katz & Wertz, 1997; Waller, Dennis, Brodie, & Cairns, 1998).

(Photo: © Bob Daemmrich/Stock Boston, LLC)

Dementia sufferers benefit from computerized rehabilitation as well. For example, one program trains those with Alzheimer's and other types of dementia to remember routes from one place to another by guiding them through a virtual apartment. Neuropsychologists report that practicing route-learning in the virtual environment improves these patients' ability to remember such routes in their own living environments (Schreiber, Lutz, Schweizer, Kalveram, & Jaencke, 1998; Schreiber, Schweizer, Lutz, Kalveram, & Jaencke, 1999).

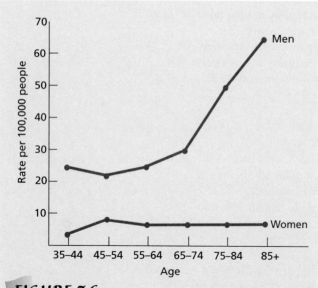

FIGURE 7.6

The data on which this figure is based indicate that suicide rates increase substantially in old age among men but remain fairly stable among women. (Sources: NCHS, 1999a; U.S. Bureau of the Census, 1997.)

Furthermore, standard questionnaires used to assess depression usually include questions about physical symptoms that commonly accompany that disorder, such as loss of appetite, sleep disturbances, and lack of energy. Older adults are more likely to report such symptoms no matter what their emotional state, and so are more likely to wind up with high scores on these standardized depression scales. As a result, elders may be diagnosed with depression when they are not actually depressed.

It is also important to distinguish between depressed mood and full-fledged clinical depression. The latter involves problems (e.g., feelings of hopelessness, insomnia, lack of appetite, loss of interest in social activities) that are of long duration and are severe enough to interfere with a person's ability to carry out normal activities (APA, 1994). By contrast, chronic depressed mood among the elderly, known as **geriatric dysthymia,** typically does not progress to clinical depression and has been found to be related to life stresses (Kocsis, 1998).

Estimates of the prevalence of depression depend on how it is defined. Studies by researchers who define depression as the presence of any kind of depressive symptom suggest that as many as a quarter of the old old and the oldest old suffer from depression, a higher proportion than in any other adult group (FIFARS, 2000). However, researchers using stricter definitions often find that the reporting of depressive symptoms by elderly adults declines slightly after age 75 and that only 4% of those older than that are depressed (Forsell & Winblad, 1999). Moreover, evidence suggests that true clinical depression is, if anything, less common among older adults than among younger adults, while dysthymia increases somewhat in frequency in late old age (Beekman, Copeland, & Prince, 1999; Gatz, Kasl-Godley, & Karel, 1996).

Risk Factors The risk factors for depression and dysthymia among the elderly are not difficult to identify: inadequate social support, inadequate income, emotional loss (such as following the death of spouse, family, or friends) and nagging health problems. However, the strongest predictor appears to be health status. Across all ethnic and socioeconomic groups, the more disabling conditions older adults have, the more depressive symptoms they have (Black, Markides, & Miller, 1998; Curyto, Chapleski, & Lichtenberg, 1999; FIFARS, 2000; Lam, Pacala, & Smith, 1997; Okwumabua, Baker, Wong, & Pilgram, 1997). Determining the direction of causation in the association between health status and depression is difficult because depression impairs an older adult's ability to respond to therapeutic interventions that might be helpful (Mast, Azar, MacNeil, & Lichtenberg, 2004). To put it differently, elders who have chronic health conditions such as arthritis are more likely to be depressed than their peers who do not, but depression is a risk factor for a poor response to therapy. Thus, for many elderly adults, the link between health and depression becomes circular.

Gender is also a risk factor; depressed women outnumber depressed men two to one among the elderly, just as they do at younger ages (FIFARS, 2000; Forsell & Winblad, 1999). It's not easy, however, to sort out the causes of this difference. For one thing, women appear to be more resilient in response to many life stressors. The death of a spouse, for example, is more likely to lead to depression in a man than in a woman (Byrne & Raphael, 1999; Chen et al., 1999). Such findings suggest that depression in women may more often be the result of an accumulation of everyday stresses, whereas traumatic events are more likely to bring on feelings of depression in men. Another possible explanation is that women are more willing to seek help for depression and, as a result, are more often diagnosed.

There is a fair amount of consistency in findings that elders living in poverty are at higher risk for depression than others (Beekman et al., 1999). Education is also independently related to depression; that is, poorly educated older adults are more likely to be depressed (Gallagher-Thompson, Tazeau, & Basilio, 1997; Miech & Shanahan, 2000). The association between education and depression exists among elderly adults at all levels of income and in all racial and ethnic groups.

Ethnic and Cultural Differences Poverty and education account for only some of the ethnic differences in depression among older adults. Other differences are explained by health status. That is, on average, minorities have poorer health than whites in the United States; so, on average, most minority groups have higher rates of depression.

For example, the prevalence of depressive symptoms in elderly Native Americans may be as high as 20% (Curyto et al., 1999). You may remember from Chapter 15 that Native Americans suffer from chronic illnesses at higher rates than white Americans. Moreover, among depressed Native Americans, those with the greatest number of physical limitations are the most depressed (Curyto et al., 1999).

The rate of depression among Chinese American and Mexican American elders may also be near 20% (Black et al., 1998; Lam et al., 1997). There is an association between health and depression in these groups, just as there is in others (Schneider, 2004). However, researchers point out that, in addition, many older Chinese Americans and Mexican Americans are recent immigrants to the United States and have poor English skills. These factors may help explain their higher incidence of depression, because length of time in the United States and knowledge of English are negatively associated with depression in these groups (Black et al., 1999; Lam et al., 1997). This means that the longer older Chinese Americans and Mexican Americans have been in

geriatric dysthymia chronic depressed mood in older adults

African American elders may be less likely to be depressed than their peers in other ethnic groups because they may treat sad feelings as a spiritual issue rather than a mental health problem.

the United States, and the better integrated they are into the society, the less likely they are to be depressed.

Isolated symptoms of depression, such as insomnia and poor appetite, have sometimes been found to occur more often in elderly African Americans than in elderly members of other minority groups or in elderly white Americans (Blazer, Landerman, Hays, Simonsick, & Saunders, 1998; Foley, Monjan, Izmirlian, Hays, & Blazer, 1999). But the entire cluster of depressive symptoms appears to occur much less often in African Americans, even those who are the least healthy (Leo et al., 1997). For example, a study of several thousand men admitted to veterans' hospitals revealed that African Americans were half as likely as whites to be depressed (Kales, Blow, Bingham, Copeland, & Mellow, 2000). Furthermore, a study in which researchers reviewed the medical records of several hundred African American and white American patients produced similar findings (Leo et al., 1997). However, in both studies, researchers found that elderly African Americans were more likely than elderly white Americans to suffer from schizophrenia. In addition, among those older African Americans who are depressed, the tendency toward suicidal thoughts may be greater than it is among depressed older white Americans (Leo et al, 1997).

Researchers often attribute low rates of depression in African Americans to underdiagnosis. They hypothesize that African Americans' lack of access to mental health services, reluctance to seek help, and unwillingness to take antidepressant medications contribute to underdiagnosis (Blazer, Hybels, Simonsick, & Hanlon, 2000; Steffens, Artigues, Ornstein, & Krishnan, 1997). However, some developmentalists take issue with this view. These critics point to cultural differences between African Americans and other groups. Specifically, African Americans are more likely to view feelings of sadness as a spiritual issue rather than a mental health problem. Research examining the association between depression and religious beliefs and activities has shown that the tendency to turn to faith and the church for support in times of emotional difficulty is much more prevalent among African Americans than among white Americans (Husaini, Blasi, & Miller, 1999; Steffens et al., 1997). In fact, research demonstrates that religious faith and practice are associated with lower incidences of long-term depression in most ethnic groups, no matter what religion is considered (Braam, Beekman, Deeg, Smit, & van Tilburg, 1997; Idler & Kasl, 1997a; Meisenhelder & Chandler, 2000; Musick, Koenig, Hays, & Cohen, 1998; Tapanya, Nicki, & Jarusawad, 1997). And, as you will learn in Chapter 8, these effects are a result of the way elders think about their lives in religious terms, rather than being due to self-selection or the social support provided to elders by religious institutions.

Suicide As is true for individuals in younger age groups, there is a strong relationship between depression and suicide among the elderly. An analysis of suicide notes showed that the reasons given by individuals who commit suicide are consistent across age groups as well (Foster, 2003). People who end their own lives most often speak of a sense of hopelessness and despair in the messages they leave behind. However, the suicide notes of elders often contain a theme that is seldom present in those of younger individuals—the idea that one is a burden to others.

Despite higher rates of depression among women and some minority groups in the United States, elderly white men are more likely to commit suicide than any other group (National Center for Health Statistics, 1999a). Thus, white males are largely responsible for the dramatic increase with age in male suicide illustrated in Figure 7.6. However, the overall age-related pattern of sex differences indicated by the figure exists among minority groups as well (U.S. Bureau of the Census, 1994).

The reasons for this dramatic sex difference are not entirely clear. It's important to note, though, that suicide at all ages is predicted by the same factors: a sense of hopelessness, unemployment, psychological disorders, alcoholism, social isolation, and poor physical health (Beck, Brown, Berchick, Stewart, & Steer, 1990; Kaplan & Sadock, 1991). Some theorists believe that elderly men are at higher risk for suicide, even though elderly women are more often depressed, because men are more likely than women to have several of these risk factors in combination (Kaplan & Sadock, 1991).

In addition, loss of economic status through retirement may be more troubling for men than for women in present cohorts of the elderly, because traditional socialization patterns may have led men to equate earnings with self-worth (Mooney, Knox, & Schacht, 2000). Similarly, declining health may cause an elderly man to view himself as a burden on others. The death of a spouse may also be a factor in many male suicides because, as you will learn in Chapter 9, men do not adjust as well as women do to the death of a spouse (Stroebe & Stroebe, 1993). Finally, as is true of younger people, older women attempt suicide more often than older men do, but the men complete the act more often, mostly because they are more likely than women to choose violent methods such as firearms.

Interacting with children may help prevent depression in late adulthood.

Therapy and Medication   Therapies for depression are the same for older adults as for those who are younger. Psychotherapy is often recommended, especially interventions that help sufferers develop optimistic thought patterns (NIA, 2000a). However, as with younger adults, therapy appears to be most effective when combined with antidepressant medications ("Depressed elderly," 1999).

Longitudinal studies suggest that the use of antidepressant medications increases rather dramatically with age. One study involving more than 4,000 elderly white and African Americans tracked their medication use for 10 years, beginning in the mid-1980s. At the beginning of the study, approximately 5% of white Americans and 2% of African Americans were taking antidepressant medicines. Remarkably, by 1996, 14% of the white participants and 5% of the African Americans were taking such medications (Blazer et al., 2000).

Experts point out that appropriate use of antidepressant medications among the elderly is critical. For one thing, antidepressants may reduce the effectiveness of the life-sustaining drugs some older adults take (NIA, 2000a). In addition, antidepressants are linked to an increased incidence of falls among the institutionalized elderly. One study found a remarkable 80% increase in falls in a group of more than 2,000 nursing home residents who began taking antidepressants (Bender, 1999).

Prevention   Given that poor overall health status predicts depression in the elderly, one important aspect of preventing depression is to help older adults improve their health. For example, arthritis limits the activities of more elders than any other chronic condition (FIFARS, 2000). There are many new and effective treatments for arthritis, of which older adults may be unaware. So one indirect way of preventing depression is to educate older adults and their health care providers about such treatments and to encourage the elders to get help.

Social involvement may also be important in preventing depression in the elderly. For example, in one study, researchers in Mexico examined how participation in activities with children, such as attending children's plays or helping plan children's parties, might affect nursing home residents' emotions (Saavedra, Ramirez, & Contreras, 1997). Researchers found that such activities significantly improved participants' emotional states. So periodic involvement with children might be an effective way to prevent depression in institutionalized elders.

In addition, research on the connection between religion and depression suggests that caretakers can help elders avoid depression by supporting their spiritual needs. Many older adults need help getting to religious services; those who live in institutions may need to have services brought to them. Declines in vision may mean that an elderly person can no longer read religious books and may deeply appreciate having someone read to him or provide him with recordings. Helping elders maintain religious faith and practice in these ways may be an important key to reducing depression rates.

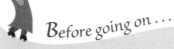

Before going on . . .

■ What is Alzheimer's disease, and how does it differ from other dementias?

■ What does research suggest about depression among older adults?

(Photo: © Ellen Senisi/The Image Works)

Cognitive Changes

Among the young old (aged 65–75), cognitive changes are still fairly small, and these older adults show little or no average decline on a few measures, such as vocabulary knowledge. But the old old and the oldest old show average declines on virtually all measures of intellectual skill, with the largest declines evident on any measures that involve speed or unexercised abilities (Cunningham & Haman, 1992; Giambra et al., 1995). Recall Schaie's comment, quoted in Chapter 5, that "reliable decrement can be shown to have occurred for all abilities by age 74" (Schaie, 1983, p. 127). By the 80s, the declines are substantial on most abilities (Schaie, 1993).

MEMORY

As you learned in Chapter 5, forgetfulness becomes more frequent with age (Ponds, Commissaris, & Jolles, 1997). However, it's important to remember that the same basic rules seem to apply to memory processes among both older and younger adults. For both groups, for example, recognition is easier than recall, tasks that require speed are more difficult, and metamemory skills are important to memory function (Olin & Zelinski, 1997). Further, in many studies, older adults achieve scores very similar to those of younger adults on tests of memory accuracy, although they typically take longer to complete memory tasks and make more errors (Babiloni et al., 2004).

Short-Term Memory Function   One area in which researchers see significant changes in late adulthood is in short-term, or working, memory capacity (Hester, Kinsella, & Ong, 2004; Jenkins, Myerson, Hale, & Fry, 1999). You should remember from earlier chapters that there is a limitation on the number of items a person can retain in her memory at once. The more pieces of information she has to handle, the more she forgets, and the poorer her performance on memory and other kinds of cognitive tasks. Thus, the more any given cognitive task makes demands on working memory, the larger the decline with age.

A good illustration comes from a study involving a familiar, everyday task—remembering telephone numbers (West & Crook, 1990). Participants were shown a series of seven-digit or ten-digit telephone numbers on a computer screen, one at a time. The participant said each number as it appeared; then the number disappeared from the screen and the participant had to dial the number she had just seen on a push-button phone attached to the computer. On some trials, the participants got a busy signal when they first dialed and then had to dial the number over again. Figure 7.7 shows the relationship between age and the correct recall of the phone numbers under these four conditions.

Notice that there is essentially no decline with age in immediate recall of a normal seven-digit telephone number (the equivalent of what you do when you look a number up in the phone book, say it to yourself as you read it, and then dial it immediately). When the length of the number increases to the ten digits used for long-distance numbers, however, a decline with age becomes evident, beginning at about age 60. And with even a brief delay between saying the number and dialing it, the decline occurs earlier.

However, patterns of age differences are not identical for all memory tasks. For example, older adults typically perform more poorly than younger adults on tasks involving *retrospective memory*, or recalling something in the past (Henry,

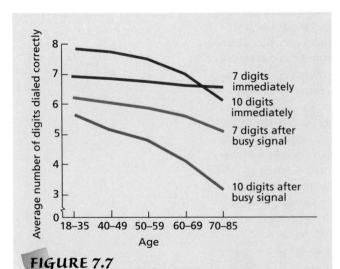

FIGURE 7.7

The graph shows the results from West and Crook's study of memory for telephone numbers. Notice that there is no loss of memory in middle adulthood for the most common condition: a seven-digit number dialed immediately. But if the number of digits increases or if you have to remember the number a bit longer, some decline in memory begins around age 50 or 60. (Source: West & Crook, 1990, from Table 3, page 524.)

MacLeod, Phillips, & Crawford, 2004). By contrast, older adults' performance on *prospective memory tasks* (which require individuals to remember to do something in the future) depends on the type of task involved. On laboratory prospective memory tasks that have little relevance to everyday life, young adults do somewhat better than elders. However, several naturalistic studies have shown that older adults out-perform those who are younger on everyday memory tasks of this kind (Henry et al., 2004; Rendell & Thomson, 1999).

Strategy Learning A study of older adults in Germany provides a good example of research findings on strategy learning and memory in older adults (Baltes & Kliegl, 1992; Kliegl, Smith, & Baltes, 1990). Researchers tested 18 college students and 19 old, but physically healthy, adults who ranged in age from 65 to 80, with an average age of 71.7 years. Participants were shown sets of pictures of 30 familiar buildings in Berlin and asked to use the pictures to create associations that would help them remember a list of 30 words. For example, a castle might be paired with the word "bicycle." A typical association would be to imagine someone riding a bicycle in front of a castle. The pictures in each set were displayed for different amounts of time, ranging from 20 seconds each to 1 second each. After participants attempted to learn each list of words, the experimenters asked what images they had used and suggested possible improvements. Training sessions were interspersed with test sessions to check on the participants' progress.

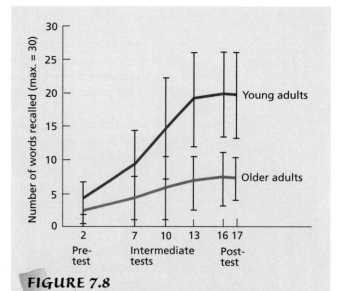

FIGURE 7.8

These results from Kliegl's study show that older adults can learn complex information-processing skills and improve their performance after training, but they don't gain as much as younger adults do. However, this study also suggests that, given enough time, older adults can learn new strategies. (Source: Kliegl et al., 1990, adapted from Figure 2, p. 899.)

Figure 7.8 shows the results for pictures and words presented at 5-second intervals. You can see that the older adults showed improvement after training, but their performance was poorer than that of younger adults. These findings suggest that the learning process simply takes longer for older adults—more time is needed to create the mental image and to link that image up with the word in the list. However, when older adults were allowed more time to associate each picture and word, their performance was more similar to that of younger participants.

Studies comparing younger and older adults' performance on arithmetic tasks involving the "five rule" show a somewhat different pattern, however. The "five rule" is researchers' term for the common finding that arithmetic problems involving multiples of five are easier to work with than problems that do not involve these multiples. For instance, people more quickly say that $5 \times 12 = 50$ is false than that $4 \times 12 = 50$ is false. Researchers have found that the five rule is used far less often by elderly than by younger research participants (Lemaire & Lecacheur, 2004). Such findings suggest that the tendency to apply some cognitive strategies automatically—that is, without giving them much thought—may decline with age.

Everyday Memory One common argument from those who take an optimistic view of the effects of aging on cognitive functioning is that older adults may be able to remember just as well as younger adults but may simply be less motivated to memorize lists of unrelated words given to them by researchers in a laboratory. However, on virtually all everyday tasks—remembering the main points of a story or a newspaper article; recalling movies, conversations, grocery lists, or recipes; recalling the information from a medicine label; remembering whether they did something ("Did I turn off the stove before I left the house?"); or remembering where they heard something (called *source memory*)—older adults perform less well than younger adults (Brown, Jones, & Davis, 1995; Light, 1991; Mäntylä, 1994; Maylor, 1993; Salthouse, 1991; Verhaeghen & Marcoen, 1993; Verhaeghen, Marcoen, & Goossens, 1993). These results have been found in longitudinal as well as cross-sectional studies, particularly after age 70 (Arenberg, 1983; Hultsch, Hertzog, Small, McDonald-Miszczak, & Dixon, 1992; Zelinski, Gilewski, & Schaie, 1993).

Still, task-specific knowledge seems to make a difference among the elderly. For example, older adults who have larger vocabularies outperform peers who know fewer words on tasks involving rapid recognition of words (Kitzan, Ferraro, Petros, & Ludorf, 1999). Researchers know that prior knowledge is the critical factor in such findings, because elders with large vocabularies perform just as poorly as their less knowledgeable peers on tasks involving nonsense words.

Preliminary Explanations   How do researchers account for these changes in memory? Extensive statistical analyses of memory function suggest that only a few variables may account for all of the age differences in memory so far identified (Salthouse, 1998; Salthouse & Czaja, 2000; Verhaeghen & Salthouse, 1997). However, exactly what those variables are remains unclear.

One likely candidate appears to be the speed of the whole memory process (Hertzog, Dixon, Hultsch, & MacDonald, 2003; MacDonald, Hultsch, Strauss, & Dixon, 2003). Older adults take longer to register some new piece of information, encode it, and retrieve it. Some of the clearest evidence of the important role of speed in memory decline in old age comes from an extensive series of studies by Timothy Salthouse (e.g., Salthouse, 1991, 1993, 1996, 2004).

He has tested both basic reaction speed and memory or other cognitive skills in adults of various ages. According to Salthouse, a very large portion of the age decline in memory can be accounted for simply by slower reaction times in older adults. He is convinced that the loss of speed occurs at the level of the central nervous system and not in the peripheral nerves. So physiological changes in neurons and the accompanying loss of nerve conductance speed may be the root causes of these changes in memory.

Virtually all experts now agree with Salthouse that loss of speed is a key aspect of the process of memory decline, and studies have shown that quantitative losses in speed of information-processing very strongly predict qualitative changes in memory function (Byrne, 1998; Maylor, Vousden, & Brown, 1999). But most also believe that speed is not the entire explanation. There appear to be other factors as well, such as changes in attention strategies that lead to less effective processing of information (Gottlob & Madden, 1999).

WISDOM AND CREATIVITY

Theorists who study cognition in older adults have recently begun to ask whether elders might have some advantages over the young because of their accumulation of knowledge and skills. In other words, older adults might be more wise. Researchers have not yet agreed on a common definition of wisdom, but most authors emphasize that it goes beyond mere accumulations of facts. **Wisdom** reflects understanding of "universal truths" or basic laws or patterns; it is knowledge that is blended with values and meaning systems; it is knowledge based on the understanding that clarity is not always possible, that unpredictability and uncertainty are part of life (Baltes & Smith, 1990; Baltes, Smith, & Staudinger, 1992; Baltes, Staudinger, Maercker, & Smith, 1995; Csikszentmihalyi & Rathunde, 1990; Sternberg, 1990).

You may be wondering how researchers measure wisdom. The leading researcher in this field, Paul Baltes, has devised one useful technique (Baltes & Staudinger, 2000). Baltes presents research participants with stories about fictional characters who are trying to make some major life decision. For example, one dilemma Baltes has used involves a 15-year-old girl who wants to get married. Participants' responses to the stories are judged according to five criteria Baltes hypothesizes to be central to wisdom as it relates to solving practical life problems:

- Factual knowledge
- Procedural knowledge
- Understanding relevance of context
- Understanding relevance of values
- Recognition that it is impossible to know in advance how any decision will ultimately affect one's life

CRITICAL THINKING

Make a list of the people you think of as wise. How old are they? Is old age necessary for wisdom? If not, how do you think wisdom is acquired?

wisdom a cognitive characteristic that includes accumulated knowledge and the ability to apply that knowledge to practical problems of living, popularly thought to be more commonly found in older adults

A person would be judged to be low in wisdom if her response to the 15-year-old's desire to marry were something like "A 15-year-old getting married? That's stupid. I would tell the girl to forget about it until she's older." The answer of a person judged to be high in wisdom would be more complex. A wise person might point out, "There are circumstances when marriage at such a young age might be a good decision. Is she motivated by a desire to make a home for a child she is expecting? Also, the girl might come from a culture where marriage at 15 is quite common. You have to consider people's motivations and their backgrounds to understand their decisions. You also have to know how the person involved views the situation to be able to give advice."

Virtually all theorists who have written about wisdom assume that it is more likely to be found in the middle-aged and the elderly. However, Baltes has found that younger adults perform as well as older adults in response to the fictional dilemma task. In fact, Baltes has found that, rather than age, intelligence and professional experience are correlated with responses to the dilemma task. So, Baltes's research seems to suggest that the popular notion that age and wisdom are associated is probably not true. Wisdom does not appear to be a characteristic of the elderly that distinguishes them from other subgroups of adults.

Critics have suggested that Baltes is simply measuring general cognitive ability rather than what is usually thought of as wisdom. Nevertheless, Baltes's research has produced an important finding about wisdom and old age: In contrast to performance on information-processing tasks such as memorizing nonsense words, performance on wisdom tasks does not decline with age (Baltes & Staudinger, 2000). Moreover, the speed of accessing wisdom-related knowledge remains constant across adulthood, unlike speed of information processing in other domains. In addition, other researchers (e.g., Orwoll & Perlmutter, 1990) have found that those older adults singled out by their peers as wise are more likely to rank high in what Erikson called ego integrity and are more likely to show concern for humanity as a whole.

Enhanced creativity may also be an element of cognition in older adults. As you learned in Chapter 5, some highly creative individuals, especially composers and artists, reach their peak in late adulthood. To describe the potential for creative work in the later years, a leading gerontologist, Gene Cohen, has developed a four-stage theory of mid- to late-life creativity (G. Cohen, 2000). Cohen believes that these phases apply to ordinary people who are more creative than others in their everyday lives as well as to "professional creators" such as composers and artists.

Cohen proposes that at around age 50, creative individuals enter a *reevaluation phase,* during which they reflect on past accomplishments and formulate new goals. The reevaluation process, along with an increasing sense of time limitations, leads to an intensification of the desire to create and produce. During the next stage, the *liberation phase,* individuals in their 60s become freer to create, because most have retired from everyday work. Most are also more tolerant of their own failures, and thus are willing to take risks that they would not have taken at earlier ages. In the *summing-up phase,* creative people in their 70s have a desire to knit their accomplishments together into a cohesive, meaningful story. They begin to view their early accomplishments in terms of how those accomplishments prefigured later achievements. Finally, in the *encore phase,* during the 80s and beyond, there is a desire to complete unfinished works or to fulfill desires that have been put aside in the past.

(Photo: © Vincent DeWitt/Stock Boston, LLC.)

Seeking advice from an elder who is presumed to be wise is one way young adults act on the belief that those who are older have accumulated knowledge and information that can benefit them.

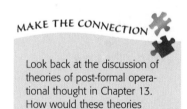

MAKE THE CONNECTION

Look back at the discussion of theories of post-formal operational thought in Chapter 13. How would these theories explain abrupt opinion change in the elderly?

Before going on . . .

■ Describe memory differences that distinguish older and younger adults, and suggest some possible explanations for these age differences.

■ What do theory and research on wisdom and creativity reveal about cognitive functioning in late adulthood?

Summary

Variability in Late Adulthood

- Developmentalists group the elderly into three subgroups: the young old (60–75), the old old (75–85), and the oldest old (85 and older). The oldest old are the fastest-growing group of the elderly in the United States. There are vast individual differences in the timing and pace of all the physical and mental changes associated with aging.
- Heredity, overall health, current and prior health habits (particularly exercise), and availability of adequate social support all influence functioning and longevity. Skills that are not used regularly show more rapid decline.

Physical Changes

- Changes in the brain associated with aging include, most centrally, a loss of dendritic density of neurons, which has the effect of slowing reaction time for almost all tasks.
- Older adults have more difficulty adapting to darkness and light. Loss of hearing is more common and more noticeable after 65 than at earlier ages; many older adults experience loss of hearing for high sounds, some loss of ability to discriminate words, and greater difficulty hearing under noisy conditions. Taste discrimination remains largely unchanged with age, but ability to discriminate smells declines substantially in late adulthood.
- Theories of biological aging emphasize the possible existence of genetic limiting mechanisms and/or the cumulative effects of malfunctions within cells.

- General slowing alters behavior in old age and makes tasks such as driving more dangerous. Older adults also change their sleeping and eating patterns. Motor abilities decline, causing more accidents due to falls. Sexual activity also decreases in frequency, although most older adults continue to be sexually active.

Mental Health

- Dementia is rare before late adulthood, becoming steadily more common with advancing age. The most common cause of dementia is Alzheimer's disease. It's difficult to diagnose definitively, and its causes are not fully understood.
- Mild or moderate depression appears to rise in frequency after age 70 or 75. Serious clinical depression, however, appears not to become more common in old age. Ethnic groups vary in rates of depression, with older African Americans being the least likely to be depressed.

Cognitive Changes

- The elderly experience difficulties in a variety of mental processes, which appear to reflect a general slowing of the nervous system and perhaps a loss of working-memory capacity.
- Wisdom and creativity may be important aspects of cognitive functioning in old age.

Key Terms

activities of daily living (ADLs) (p. 170)
Alzheimer's disease (p. 180)
cross-linking (p. 177)
dementia (p. 180)
frail elderly (p. 166)
free radicals (p. 177)
geriatric dysthymia (p. 185)

gerontology (p. 166)
Hayflick limit (p. 172)
instrumental activities of daily living (IADLs) (p. 170)
multi-infarct dementia (p. 183)
programmed senescence theory (p. 176)

satiety (p. 179)
senescence (p. 176)
synaptic plasticity (p. 174)
telomere (p. 172)
terminal drop hypothesis (p. 177)
tinnitus (p. 175)
wisdom (p. 190)

Social and Personality Development in Late Adulthood

In an autobiography written when he was in his late 60s, comedian Groucho Marx, who died at 87, said, "Age is not a particularly interesting subject. Anyone can get old.

© Frank Siteman/Getty Images/Stone

All you have to do is live long enough" (Marx, 1987). Marx's observation implies that there is little value in regarding the attainment of old age as the only thing about oneself that is interesting or remarkable. Indeed, an important part of maintaining a sense of self in late adulthood is recognizing whatever it is about one's life that could not have been done by anyone else. But maintaining a sense of personal uniqueness can be especially challenging for older adults, who are often stereotyped by others as sick, disabled, or incompetent.

As you learned in Chapter 17, the biological clock ticks loudly in late adulthood. But the experiences of these years, as in every period of life, extend far beyond the physical domain. Indeed, as you will learn in this chapter, changes in roles and relationships are perhaps just as significant as physical ones. And for many older adults, these changes are perceived not as losses but as opportunities to create new roles and to make old age a time of personal and social gains. As you read this chapter, keep the following questions in mind:

- How do theorists describe the important aspects of social and personality development in late life?

- What factors predict successful aging, and how does religious coping affect older adults' physical and mental health?

- In what ways do social relationships change in late adulthood?

- How do retirement and continued work affect the lives of older adults?

Theories of Social and Personality Development

If the social and personality changes of young adulthood can be described as "individuation" and those of middle adulthood can be described (more tentatively) as "mellowing," how might the changes of late adulthood be described? Several theorists have hypothesized specific forms of change, but there is little agreement among them and very little information supporting any of their theories.

ERIKSON'S STAGE OF EGO INTEGRITY VERSUS DESPAIR

Erikson termed the last of his eight life crises the **ego integrity versus despair stage.** He thought that the task of achieving **ego integrity,** the sense that one has lived a useful life, began in middle adulthood but was most central in late adulthood. To achieve ego integrity, the older adult must come to terms with who she is and has been, how her life has been lived, the choices that she has made, the opportunities gained and lost. The process also involves coming to terms with death and accepting its imminence. Erikson hypothesized that failure to achieve ego integrity in late adulthood would result in feelings of hopelessness and despair because there would be too little time to make changes before death.

Developmentalists have essentially no longitudinal or even cross-sectional data to suggest whether older adults are more likely than younger or middle-aged adults to achieve such self-acceptance. What they have instead are a few bits of information suggesting that adults become more reflective and somewhat more philosophical in orientation as they move through the late adulthood years (Prager, 1998). Moreover, those who use their growing capacity for philosophical reflection to achieve a degree of self-satisfaction are less fearful of death. There is also some evidence that older adults are more likely than young and middle-aged adults to respond to thwarted personal goals with feelings of sadness—a hint that the kind of despair Erikson talked about may be more common in old age than earlier in life (Levine & Bluck, 1997).

One aspect of Erikson's theory that has received a great deal of attention from researchers is the notion that the process of **reminiscence,** thinking about the past, is a necessary and healthy part of achieving ego integrity, and thus an important aspect of old age and preparation for death. However, few developmentalists today would say that the only—or even the most important—purpose of these processes is to help an individual prepare for death. Instead, recent research has examined the link between reminiscence and health.

First, it's important to note that adults of all ages engage in reminiscence. In fact, young adults reminisce more often than middle-aged or older adults (Parker, 1999). Moreover, the emotional effects of reminiscence are correlated with age. For younger adults, reminiscence often evokes negative emotions, whereas it is generally a positive activity for elders.

Developmentalists hypothesize that young and older adults feel differently about reminiscence because they use it for different purposes (Webster & McCall, 1999). Young adults often use reminiscence to search for tried and true methods of solving problems ("How did I handle this the last time it happened?"). For older adults, reminiscence is more often seen as a way of communicating their experiences to younger individuals. In fact, elders who do not have this intergenerational view of reminiscence do not engage in reminiscence as much as peers who do (Muthesius, 1997).

OTHER THEORIES OF LATE-LIFE PSYCHOSOCIAL FUNCTIONING

As you learned in Chapter 6, the ideas of Paul Baltes and the late Margaret Baltes about selection, optimization, and compensation have been important in the study of mid-

ego integrity versus despair stage the last of Erikson's psychosocial stages, in which older adults must achieve a sense of satisfaction with their lives

ego integrity the feeling that one's life has been worthwhile

reminiscence reflecting on past experience

Some older adults are quite content with solitary lives, but disengagement from social contacts is neither a typical nor an optimal choice for most elders.

CRITICAL THINKING ?

Think about the oldest person in your family. Which do you think describes him or her better—activity theory or disengagement theory?

activity theory the idea that it is normal and healthy for older adults to try to remain as active as possible for as long as possible

disengagement theory the theory that it is normal and healthy for older adults to scale down their social lives and to separate themselves from others to a certain degree

Before going on . . .

■ Does research support the existence of Erikson's stage of ego integrity versus despair?

■ What are the main ideas of activity theory and disengagement theory?

dle-aged adults' psychosocial functioning. They are often applied to the study of older adults as well. Recall that the Balteses proposed that, as adults get older, they maintain high levels of performance by focusing on their strengths. In this way, they compensate for weaknesses. You may remember the example of pianist Arthur Rubenstein given in Chapter 1. In his later years, Rubenstein performed only pieces that he knew very well. Thanks to his use of selective optimization and compensation, he was able to delight concert-goers well into his 80s.

Another theoretical perspective on old age focuses on the question of whether it is normal, necessary, or healthy for older adults to remain active as long as possible, or whether the more typical and healthy pattern is some kind of gradual turning inward. The perspective typically referred to as **activity theory** argues that the psychologically and physically healthiest response to old age is to maintain the greatest possible level of activity and involvement in the greatest possible number of roles.

Activity theorists often cite research demonstrating that the most active older adults report slightly greater satisfaction with themselves or their lives, are healthiest, and have the highest morale (Adelmann, 1994; Bryant & Rakowski, 1992; McIntosh & Danigelis, 1995). The effect is not large, but its direction is consistently positive: More social involvement is linked to better outcomes, even among elders who suffer from disabilities such as arthritis, for whom active social participation may be physically painful (Zimmer, Hickey, & Searle, 1995). Yet it is also true that every in-depth study of lifestyles of older adults identifies at least a few who lead socially isolated lives but remain contented, sometimes because they are engaged in an all-consuming hobby (e.g., Maas & Kuypers, 1974; Rubinstein, 1986).

An alternative theory on social and personality development in old age is disengagement theory, first proposed as a formulation of the central psychological process for older adults (Cumming, 1975; Cumming & Henry, 1961). In its current form, **disengagement theory** proposes that aging has three aspects:

Shrinkage of life space. As people age, they interact with fewer and fewer others and fill fewer and fewer roles.

Increased individuality. In the roles and relationships that remain, the older individual is much less governed by strict rules or expectations.

Acceptance of these changes. The healthy older adult actively disengages from roles and relationships, turning increasingly inward and away from interactions with others.

The first two of these aspects seem largely beyond dispute. What has been controversial about disengagement theory is the third aspect. Advocates argue that the normal and healthy response to the shrinkage of roles and relationships is for the older adult to step back still further, to stop seeking new roles, to spend more time alone, to turn inward. In essence, they propose a kind of personality change, not just a decline in involvement.

Clearly, it is possible to choose a highly disengaged lifestyle in late adulthood and to find satisfaction in it. But such disengagement is neither normal for the majority of older adults nor necessary for overall mental health in the later years. For most elders, some level of social involvement is a sign—and probably a cause—of higher morale and lower levels of depression and other psychiatric symptoms (Zunzunegui, Alvarado, Del Ser, & Otero, 2003). Roles and relationships may rule our lives less in late adulthood than at earlier ages, but they still seem to be essential ingredients for emotional balance, at least for most of us.

Individual Differences

Individual differences continue to make substantial contributions to the experiences of older men and women. In fact, research suggests that differences in a variety of behaviors are related to overall quality of life as well as to longevity. Similarly, individual differences in reliance on religious beliefs and institutions as sources of support are also correlated with well-being in late adulthood.

THE SUCCESSFUL AGING PARADIGM

In recent years, one of the dominant themes in gerontology literature has been the concept of successful aging. As defined by authors John Rowe and Robert Kahn, **successful aging** has three components: good physical health, retention of cognitive abilities, and continuing engagement in social and productive activities (Rowe & Kahn, 1997, 1998). An additional aspect of successful aging is an individual's subjective sense of life satisfaction. (Table 8.1 describes these components.) The idea of successful aging is part of the overall trend in gerontology (which you read about in Chapter 7) toward viewing old age in terms of variability rather than universal decline. In addition, the concept attempts to integrate physical, social, and personality development in order to create a comprehensive picture of what it means to age successfully.

The three dimensions of successful aging described by Rowe and Kahn are, of course, not entirely independent. For example, good health makes it more likely that an older adult will retain her mental abilities, and better mental functioning enables her to remain socially active. The concept of successful aging is referred to as a *paradigm* because it presents patterns for or examples of such aging. Rather than stating a theory of development, the paradigm of successful aging offers a way of thinking about late adulthood and about how earlier decisions and patterns of behavior contribute to quality of life at later ages.

Staying Healthy and Able By now, you should be familiar with the factors that predict health and physical functioning across the lifespan: diet, exercise, avoidance of tobacco, and so on. In a sense, older people reap the consequences of the behavioral choices they made when younger. However, there are also aspects to staying healthy and able that most of us never face until old age.

For example, when an older adult suffers a stroke or fractures a bone, his willingness to engage in the sometimes painful process of rehabilitation significantly affects his degree of recovery. Researchers have found that older adults vary considerably in their willingness to comply with physicians and therapists who supervise their rehabilitation

TABLE 8.1	The Components of Successful Aging
Health	Good health must be maintained through middle and late adulthood.
Mental Activity	Engaging in cognitively stimulating activities and hobbies helps older adults retain mental abilities.
Social Engagement	Remaining socially active is critical; social contacts that involve helping others are especially important.
Productivity	Volunteer activities can help by engaging retired adults in productive pursuits.
Life Satisfaction	Older adults must learn how to adjust expectations such that life satisfaction remains high.

successful aging the term gerontologists use to describe maintaining one's physical health, mental abilities, social competence, and overall satisfaction with one's life as one ages after such events. In both the United States and Japan, an individual's willingness to adopt recovery goals suggested by rehabilitation professionals is related to recovery prospects (Ushikubo, 1998). Those who believe they can reach the suggested goals appear to be the most willing to do the work required for optimal recovery of functioning. Not surprisingly, these individuals gain the most from rehabilitation. So life-long health habits contribute to successful aging, but individuals' responses to the health crises of old age also matter.

Retaining Cognitive Abilities   The degree to which elders maintain cognitive functioning seems to be linked to education. As you learned in Chapter 7, those who are the best educated show the least cognitive decline. Moreover, researchers who have examined correlations between cognitive functioning and the other two dimensions of successful aging—physical health and social engagement—have found that verbal intelligence and education are related to both (Jorm et al., 1998). Cross-cultural research has found relationships among cognitive functioning, health, and social involvement in Taiwanese and North American elders, as well as in both Mexican Americans and white Americans (Hazuda, Wood, Lichtenstein, & Espino, 1998; Ofstedal, Zimmer, & Lin, 1999).

In addition to education, the complexity of the cognitive challenges older adults are willing to take on influences their cognitive functioning. For example, older adults are sometimes reluctant to use new technologies such as automatic teller machines (Echt, Morrell, & Park, 1998). Psychologists suggest that self-stereotyping contributes to this reluctance; older people may believe that they can't learn as well as younger people can, and so they stick to established routines. However, neuropsychologists suggest that such avoidance of learning may actually contribute to cognitive decline (Volz, 2000). New learning, these scientists hypothesize, helps to establish new connections between neurons, connections that may protect the aging brain against deterioration. Thus, what might be called *cognitive adventurousness,* a willingness to learn new things, appears to be a key component of successful aging.

Social Engagement   Social connectedness and participation in productive activities are clearly important to successful aging. For example, nursing home residents report greater satisfaction with their lives when they have frequent contact with family and friends (Guse & Masesar, 1999). Similarly, among elders with disabilities, frequency of contact with family and friends is associated with reduced feelings of loneliness (Bondevik & Skogstad, 1998).

However, social support does not mean dependence on others. In fact, rehabilitation professionals have found that elderly adults who expect to have someone help them with daily living activities are less likely to recover fully from strokes or other potentially debilitating medical conditions than peers who have no one to help them (Ushikubo, 1998). Moreover, one study of recovering cardiac patients found that social support contributed to mental well-being but was negatively correlated with physical recovery, especially among women (Bosworth et al., 2000).

Research on dependency suggests that the past thinking of behavioral scientists about the role of social support may have been too simplistic. It seems that social support contributes to successful aging because it provides opportunities for older adults to give support as well as to receive it. For example, research involving elderly Mexican immigrants to the United States suggests that those who have better functional integration into a community—that is, those who are fulfilling some kind of purposeful role—exhibit higher levels of physical and emotional functioning than those who are socially isolated (Hazuda et al., 1998).

Similarly, researchers studying Japanese elders found that a majority of them say that helping others contributes to their own health and personal sense of well-being (Krause, Ingersoll-Dayton, Liang, & Sugisawa, 1999). In addition, researchers have found that elderly residents of Israeli *kibbutzim* (collective communities) display exceptionally high levels of functioning compared to Israeli elders who do not live in *kibbutzim* (Leviatan, 1999). The key to this successful aging, developmentalists believe, is that the social structure of the kibbutz offers older adults many opportunities to occupy meaningful roles, to remain socially connected to peers, and to contribute to the development of younger community members.

Of course, you might argue that elders who are the healthiest are naturally going to be the best able to make a social contribution. However, developmentalists have found correlations between feeling useful and having a sense of well-being even among older adults who are very unhealthy. For example, researchers who have asked U.S. nursing home residents to rate various quality-of-life factors have found that they often give high ratings to "opportunities to help others" (Guse & Masesar, 1999). Thus, even when elderly adults have significant disabilities, many are still oriented toward helping others and feel more satisfied with their lives when they can do so.

For some elders, remaining productive means venturing into new hobbies such as painting, sculpting, or other artistic pursuits.

Productivity Contributing to a social network may be one important way of remaining productive, especially for older adults who are retired. **Volunteerism,** or performing unpaid work for altruistic reasons, has been linked to successful aging. Remarkably, a California study involving nearly 2,000 older adults found that mortality rates were 60% lower among volunteers than among nonvolunteers (Oman, Thoresen, & McMahon, 1999). Studies have also shown that volunteerism improves older adults' overall life satisfaction (Glass & Jolly, 1997). Moreover, volunteers appear to be healthier than nonvolunteers (Krause et al., 1999). As noted earlier, however, selection effects may account for some of these observed effects—that is, the healthiest elders may volunteer the most.

Surveys suggest that 10–30% of older adults are involved in volunteer activities (Chou, Chouw, & Chi, 2003; Federal Interagency Forum on Aging-Related Statistics [FIFARS], 2000; Oman et al., 1999). Furthermore, surveys of school volunteer programs in the United States have shown that older adults contribute more to such programs than adults in any other age group (Strom & Strom, 1999). So it seems that the volunteer activities of older adults have the potential to benefit society as well as their own physical and mental health (Warburton, Le Brocque, & Rosenman, 1998).

Some older adults remain productive by venturing into new pursuits, such as taking music lessons, attending college classes, or learning to paint or sculpt. Researchers conducting a study of 36 artists over age 60 asked them to explain how artistic productivity contributed to their successful aging (Fisher & Specht, 1999). Their responses contained several themes: Producing art gave them a purpose in life, opportunities to interact with like-minded peers, and a sense of competence. These responses are perhaps not surprising, and they probably vary little from those that might be offered by younger artists. However, the older artists also claimed that creating art helped them stay healthy. Thus, creative productivity may help older adults maintain an optimistic outlook, which, as you have learned, contributes to physical health.

Life Satisfaction *Life satisfaction,* or a sense of personal well-being, is also an important component of successful aging. Many of the factors that predict life satisfaction are very similar to the variables that you have already learned are predictive of successful aging. For example, one characteristic linking successful aging to life satisfaction is a sense of control, which you read about in Chapter 3 (Rodin, 1986). Even life events that could be highly stressful, such as financial problems, may have little negative effect if the individual feels he has some choice (Krause, Jay, & Liang, 1991). Thus, involuntary retirement or involuntary institutionalization typically has negative effects, whereas planned and chosen retirement or a voluntary move to a nursing home does not.

What is critical to life satisfaction in almost all cases is an individual's perception of her own situation, which seems to be more important than objective measures

MAKE THE CONNECTION

Look back at the discussions of post-secondary education in Chapter 3 and career selection in Chapter 4. Formulate a model that explains how the experiences of early adulthood contribute to successful aging.

volunteerism performance of unpaid work for altruistic motives

(Gana, Alphilippe, & Bailly, 2004). Perceived adequacy of social support and perceived adequacy of income are critical. Moreover, self-ratings of health, rather than objective measures of health, may be the most significant predictors of life satisfaction and morale (Draper, Gething, Fethney, & Winfield, 1999).

Research also suggests that social comparisons—how well an older adult thinks he is doing compared to others his age—are just as important to these perceptions as the older adult's awareness of the changes he has undergone since his younger years (Robinson-Whelen & Kiecolt-Glaser, 1997). A majority of older adults, no matter what their personal circumstances, believe that most others their age are worse off than they are (Heckhausen & Brim, 1997). Developmentalists speculate that the tendency to see others as having more problems is an important self-protective psychological device employed by those who are aging successfully (Frieswijk, Buunk, Steverink, & Slaets, 2004).

Criticisms of the Successful Aging Paradigm

Critics of the successful aging paradigm suggest that the concept can be misleading. For one thing, they say, the paradigm has the potential to become a new kind of ageist stereotype, one that portrays older adults who suffer from disabilities as incompetent (Minkler & Fadem, 2002; Scheidt, Humpherys, & Yorgason, 1999). Such critics point out that, for many elderly adults, no amount of optimism, willingness to rehabilitate, social support, or involvement in intellectually demanding activities can moderate their physical limitations. For example, studies comparing the performance of university professors over age 70 and graduate students on reading comprehension tests show that some degree of age-based cognitive decline can be expected, even among very bright, highly experienced, and productive adults (Christensen, Henderson, Griffiths, & Levings, 1997). Thus, these critics claim, the danger of the successful aging paradigm is that it can give the erroneous impression that all the effects of aging are under one's control (Holstein & Minkler, 2003).

Another danger in shifting the focus of gerontology research from disease and decline to quality of life, some critics say, is that medical research still has enormous potential for discovering cures for many of the diseases of old age (Portnoi, 1999). Critics fear that emphasis on successful aging may cause public and institutional support for disease-related research to decline. These critics point out that there is good reason to believe that many conditions now thought to be part of "normal" aging are actually disease processes for which medical science can find effective treatments (Portnoi, 1999).

Nevertheless, critics concede that the successful aging paradigm has broadened gerontologists' approaches to studying old age. Thus, they agree that its influence has been largely positive. Still, keeping their criticisms in mind can help balance the optimism of the successful aging paradigm against the realities of life in late adulthood and the need to continue to encourage researchers to search for treatments for age-related diseases such as Alzheimer's.

RELIGIOUS COPING

Religion appears to be one factor contributing to individual differences in life satisfaction. Psychologists use the term **religious coping** to refer to the tendency to turn to religious beliefs and institutions in times of stress or trouble. People of all ages use religious coping. However, many developmentalists suggest that religious coping may be particularly important in the later years because of the high number of life stressors—including deaths of loved ones, chronic illnesses, and declining sensory abilities. And elders themselves often cite religious coping as their primary means of managing stress (Barusch, 1999).

religious coping the tendency to turn to religious beliefs and institutions for support in times of difficulty

Racial and Sex Differences   As you learned in Chapter 7, the tendency to turn to religion for comfort is stronger among African Americans than among other racial or ethnic groups. For example, research suggests that participation in church social activities is linked to high reported levels of well-being among older African Americans more than among older white Americans (Bryant & Rakowski, 1992; Husaini et al., 1999; Walls & Zarit, 1991). Further, the negative correlation between church involvement and depressive feelings is stronger for elderly African American cancer sufferers than for their white counterparts (Musick et al., 1998).

Strong religious beliefs appear to be positively associated with elders' health and well-being.

In addition, some studies suggest that women make more use of religious coping than men do (e.g., Coke, 1992). Most developmentalists attribute this finding to sex differences in social behavior that are observed across the lifespan. However, it's important to keep in mind that, even though the frequency with which religious coping is used may differ according to race and gender, its effects seem to be similar in all racial and ethnic groups and for both women and men. These effects can be best examined by separating the psychological and social components of religious coping.

Religious Beliefs   The psychological component of religious coping involves people's beliefs and attitudes. A number of investigators have examined links between religious beliefs and various measures of well-being among the elderly. For example, elders who place a great deal of emphasis on religious faith worry much less than those who do not (Tapanya et al., 1997). Moreover, associations between religious faith and physical and mental health have been found among older adults of diverse faiths— Christians, Buddhists, Muslims, Hindus, Taoists, and Sikhs—and from a variety of cultures and ethnic groups (Krause et al., 1999; Meisenhelder & Chandler, 2000; Tapanya et al., 1997; Zhou, Yao, & Xu, 2002).

The positive effects of religious coping seem to arise from its influence on how elders think about their lives. For example, older adults who rate their religious beliefs as highly important to them are more likely than others to think that their lives serve an important purpose (Gerwood, LeBlanc, & Piazza, 1998). In addition, religious faith seems to provide older adults with a theme that integrates the various periods of their lives. As a result, religious elders are more likely than their nonreligious peers to view old age as a chapter in an ongoing story rather than as primarily a period of loss of capacities. Further, among low-income elders, divine power is viewed as a resource on which those who have little social power in the material world can rely (Barusch, 1999).

CRITICAL THINKING **9**

How do you think your friends' and relatives' use of religious coping affects their attitudes and behavior?

Attendance at Religious Services   The social aspect of religious coping most often examined by researchers is attendance at religious services. Research suggests that adults who regularly attend such services are physically and emotionally healthier than their nonattending peers (Bosworth, Park, McQuoid, Hays, & Steffens, 2003; Idler & Kasl, 1997a). Once again, selection effects are possible. However, longitudinal studies suggest that patterns of attendance, as well as the association between attendance and health, change little when elders become ill or disabled (Idler & Kasl, 1997b).

In addition, attendance at religious services is linked to health habits. For example, African American elders with hypertension who attend church regularly are more likely than those who attend intermittently to comply with medical advice regarding blood pressure medication; also, the average blood pressure readings of the regular attendees are lower (Koenig et al., 1998). Researchers don't know why, but one explanation might be that church attendance provides opportunities for interaction with peers who suffer from the same disorder. In the context of such interactions, African American elders may receive encouragement to persevere in dealing with such chronic ailments as hypertension by complying with medical advice.

Elders themselves cite a number of reasons for the benefits of religious involvement. For example, many say that religious institutions provide them with opportunities to help others (Krause et al., 1999). Intergenerational involvement is another aspect of religious participation often mentioned by older adults. For many, religious institutions provide a structure within which they can pass on their knowledge and beliefs to younger individuals.

Alternative Explanations   Researchers must always consider selection effects when examining links between variables such as religious coping and health. There are other possible confounding factors as well. For example, religious and nonreligious elders may differ in personality traits. It seems likely that those with higher levels of extraversion would be the most comfortable in religious social environments—and scientists know that extraversion is correlated with successful aging. Thus, the connection between religious coping and health in old age may be a manifestation of personality rather than an independent effect of religion.

In addition, research on the association between religious faith and health focuses on the personal relevance of spirituality rather than on intellectual acceptance of a set of doctrines. So it may be the intensity and the personal nature of these beliefs, rather than the fact that they have a religious focus, that are responsible for the correlations.

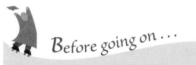

Before going on...

■ Describe the successful aging paradigm, noting the ways in which it is manifested in the lives of older adults.

■ How does religious coping influence physical and mental health in late adulthood?

In addition, in most research studies, the participants have had long-standing belief and attendance patterns. Thus, these elders may persist in religious faith and involvement, even when they are ill or disabled, because it helps them achieve a sense of continuity of identity. That is, religious involvement may allow an older adult to feel that, despite physical losses, she is still the same person. So it may be that the sense of personal integration that religion provides is responsible for the correlations. Whatever the reasons, the research evidence suggests that supporting the spiritual needs of the elderly may be just as important to maintaining their health and functioning as meeting their physical and material needs.

Social Relationships

The social roles older adults occupy are usually different from those they held at younger ages. In addition, both consistency and change characterize social relationships during this period.

SOCIAL ROLES

Clearly, role changes are inevitable in old age, and physical and cognitive changes are responsible for many of them. Some, however, are the result of ageism. Appearance cues—wrinkles and gray hair and the like—are often the basis for judgments about the competence of those who are older (Hummert, Garstka, & Shaner, 1997). The older people look, the more negatively others stereotype them, and negative stereotypes are more often applied to older women than to older men. Consequently, older adults may be unjustly forced out of roles by younger adults.

Surprisingly, though, elderly adults are just as likely as their younger peers to hold ageist stereotypes. In fact, some data suggest that older adults are actually *more* likely than younger adults to be prejudiced against their elderly peers (Hummert, Garstka, & Shaner, 1997). Thus, an older adult's beliefs about his own competence or attractiveness may be as important to his decisions about role transitions as the prejudices of others.

Moreover, sociologists point out that the roles that older adults do retain have far less content—that is, far fewer duties or expectations (Rosow, 1985). For example, most older adults continue to occupy the role of parent, but this role typically becomes far less demanding. Unless she had children very late in life or her children encountered unusual difficulties in getting established in their own lives, by the time an individual reaches age 65, her last child has long since become fully independent. Similarly, in other arenas, elders may occupy roles that have titles but few duties. A retired university professor, for instance, may have the title of Professor Emeritus, a position that carries a few benefits but essentially no obligations. In other organizations, an older individual may be given the title of Honorary Chairperson.

In a practical sense, the decline in role content means that the daily routines of many older adults are no longer structured by specific roles. But is this good or bad? Some developmentalists see this loss of role definition as carrying with it a significant risk of isolation or alienation. Further, in one survey, a majority of British elders cited meaningful social roles as essential to life satisfaction (Bowling et al., 2003).

Others see distinct advantages to this "roleless" time in late life. One such advantage is a greater "license for eccentricity" (Bond & Coleman, 1990, p. 78). Because they do not have to fit into the sometimes tight confines of role expectations, older adults feel far freer to express their own individuality—in dress, language, and personal preferences. This change may begin even earlier than late adulthood; the gradual assertion of individuality seems to be characteristic of middle adulthood for many. But certainly older adults benefit from a kind of institutionalized acceptance of eccentricity.

LIVING ARRANGEMENTS

Most older adults prefer to live in private homes. However, the physical changes associated with aging mean that some kind of change in living arrangements generally must be made at some point in an individual's later years.

Aging in Place   Elders' preference for living in a private home environment has led to a pattern known as **aging in place.** Aging in place involves making modifications to a private residence in response to the changing needs of older adults, such as making doorways wider to accommodate a wheelchair. It may also include hiring a *home health aide* to provide assistance with ADLs when necessary. At the core of the aging-in-place concept is the idea that, as much as possible, changing a normal living environment to meet an elder's needs is preferable to moving the elder to an institutional environment. Aging in place can involve the services of a wide range of health care professionals, including physical therapists and mental health counselors. Researchers have found that comprehensive home-based care of this kind has strong positive effects on elders' physical and mental health (Gill et al., 2002). Thus, compared to institutional care, aging in place is believed by many to be both more supportive of elders' psychosocial needs and less costly.

For more than 70% of the adults over the age of 65 in the United States, aging in place means living in their own homes either alone or with a spouse, although, as you can see in Figure 8.1 (page 204), the percentage who live alone varies across ethnic groups. Another variation on the aging-in-place theme arises when an older adult moves into the home of a relative, usually one of his own children. In many such cases, modifications must be made to the caretaker's home in order to meet the elder's needs, and a home health aide may be hired to help with ADLs. In the United States, just over 20% of older adults live in the homes of relatives, usually their adult children. Four factors influence an older adult's decision to live with an adult child:

aging in place living in a non-institutional environment, to which modifications have been made to accommodate an older adult's needs

■   *Health.* Elders who need help with ADLs because of health problems are more likely to live in the homes of family members than are those who can manage the physical demands of living independently (Choi, 2003).

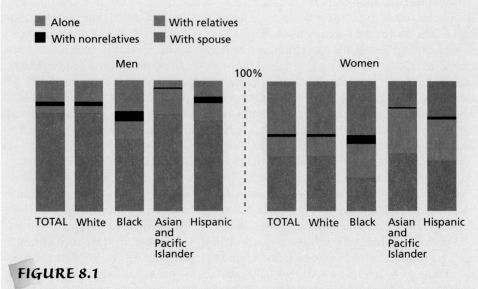

FIGURE 8.1

This graph shows the living arrangements of noninstitutionalized U.S. adults in 1998. You can see that for those elders who were not living with a spouse, living alone was the most common alternative, followed by living with relatives. Only a small percentage lived with nonrelatives. (Source: FIFARS, 2000.)

- *Income.* Those with lower incomes are more likely to live with family members (Choi, 1991).

- *Adult children's characteristics.* Elders with several daughters are more likely than those with few daughters to live with grown children (Soldo, Wolf, & Agree, 1990). Married adults are more likely than those who are single to take in their aging parents (Choi, 2003).

- *Ethnicity.* Hispanic American, African American, and Asian American elders are more likely to live with relatives than are those in other groups (Choi, 2003; FIFARS, 2000).

Residential Options for Older Adults   Older adults who are no longer able to live independently or who don't want to deal with the demands of caring for a home often turn to one of several residential options. An *independent living community* is an apartment complex or housing development in which all the residents are over a certain age, typically 55 or 60. In most such communities, residents join together for a variety of social activities and outings. Thus, independent living communities offer older adults the opportunity to remain socially active without having to travel far from home. However, these communities typically do not provide residents with any kind of health care assistance.

When older adults need more help than is available in an independent living community, an *assisted living facility* is another option. Just over 2% of older adults in the United States live in these facilities (Centers for Medicare and Medicaid Services [CMS], 2004). The average age of assisted living residents is 80, and most require help with one or two activities of daily living (toileting, bathing, etc.). In most assisted living facilities, residents live in small apartments and get help with housework and meal preparation along with ADL assistance. Nurses are on site around the clock and can be called upon in emergencies, but residents are generally responsible for routine health care such as taking medications. Still, elders who move from their own homes to an assisted living facility have less stress and an enhanced sense of well-being just knowing that help is close by if they need it (Cutchin, Owen, & Chang, 2003; Fonda, Clipp, & Maddox, 2002). Assisted living facilities also provide senior citizens with organized social activities. Researchers have found that participation in these activities is important to the overall life satisfaction and mental health of elders who live in assisted living facilities (Zimmerman et al., 2003).

When older adults need more help with ADLs than is available in an assisted living facility, many turn to nursing homes, or *skilled nursing facilities.* As you learned in Chapter 7, about 4% of the elderly adults in the United States live in nursing homes. The typical nursing home resident is a female in her late 70s or early 80s (CMS, 2004). Most require help with three to four ADLs. About half of nursing home residents have dementia. Of course, the decision to admit an elderly adult to a skilled nursing facility can be difficult (see No Easy Answers, page 498). However, for older adults who require 24-hour supervision, particularly those with dementia, nursing homes often represent the best residential option.

Finally, *continuing-care retirement communities (CCRCs)* offer a continuum of care ranging from independent living to skilled nursing care. Residents can move from one level of care to another on an as-needed basis while remaining within the same community. For example, an elder who lives in the independent living part of the facility can temporarily move to the skilled nursing sector for a few days or weeks while she recovers from surgery or an accident. Similarly, a resident who is in the process of developing dementia may start out in independent living and move to assisted living before finally being admitted to skilled nursing care.

Only a tiny fraction of older adults in the United States currently live in this new kind of community, but interest in CCRCs is growing. Like assisted living facilities, they are most popular with seniors who pay for their own care. The flexibility and social continuity provided by CCRCs are the keys to their appeal.

Cultural Differences in Living Arrangements Living arrangements for the elderly vary across nations, particularly when Western and non-Western countries are compared. A set of beliefs known as **filial piety** is a common feature of Asian cultures. Central to this set of beliefs is the notion that children have a duty to care for their elderly parents. As a result, few elders in such societies live on their own. In Japan, for example, only one-third of older adults live alone or with a spouse (Tsuya & Martin, 1992). Most of the remaining two-thirds live with their children. Asian elders who are dependent on their adult children are less likely to be depressed than those who live independently, and many Asian countries have no formal employer- or government-sponsored pension programs for the elderly (Chou, Chi, & Chow, 2004; McDonald, 2004; Min, 2004).

The concept of filial piety exists in Western cultures as well. However, among Westerners, filial piety is more often based on affection and attachment than on a sense of duty (Datta, Poortinga, & Marcoen, 2003). Spiritual and religious values also often motivate families to provide care for their elders (Pierce, 2001). Further, individualistic values motivate elderly adults in Western cultures to take into account their children's own financial and social resources, as well as their need for independence, when making judgments about whether their children have met their filial piety obligations (Iecovich & Lankri, 2002). Thus, unlike elders in Asian cultures, adults in Western societies who must depend on their children for financial help, especially men, often experience emotional distress (Nagumey, Reich, & Newsom, 2004).

Nevertheless, as you can see in Figure 8.2, the majority of the social contacts of elders in the United States involve interactions with family members. Thus, Western views of filial piety clearly do not lead to isolation of the elderly. Moreover, the Western idea that elders should remain financially independent as long as possible is the philosophical basis of government- and employee-sponsored pension programs, without which many senior citizens would be destitute.

(Photo: © Michael Newman/PhotoEdit)

In Asian countries, most elderly adults live with their adult children.

filial piety the idea that children have a duty to care for their aging parents

Deciding on Nursing Home Care

In Chapter 7 you read about the numbers of older adults living in nursing homes and other institutions. How do they and their families decide that a nursing home is the best form of care?

Because of the costs involved and the fact that nursing home placement decisions are often made in the midst of a crisis, many families choose a facility on the basis of cost alone (Castle, 2002). In the United States, nursing home costs vary widely from one region to another. In the South and West, the daily cost may be as little as $110, while in the Northeast, nursing home care can cost more than $300 per day in major metropolitan areas. The median cost is about $160 per day, or nearly $5000 per month (Mature Market Institute, 2003b). Specialized care for residents with Alzheimer's disease costs even more.

Unless an elder is recovering from a serious illness or injury, nursing home costs are not covered by Medicare. Moreover, when Medicare does provide coverage, it is usually for only the first 100 days of care. About two-thirds of nursing home residents receive additional support from Medicaid (CMS, 2004). Ironically, then, even though a nursing home is the most expensive kind of residence for the elderly, the residents of such facilities tend to have lower incomes than those who live in other kinds of facilities (CMS, 2004).

High-income elders can afford to pay for their care out of pocket. Yet many are concerned about the unpredictability of nursing home costs and worry that the assets they have accumulated during a lifetime of work will be completely depleted if they become disabled and require such care. In addition, many middle-class families are caught in the double bind of being too well off to qualify for Medicaid while at the same time lacking the financial resources to pay for nursing home care. These elders don't want to become a financial burden on their grown children, many of whom are still raising their own children. For these reasons, a growing number of healthy middle-class and upper-income elderly adults are purchasing long-term-care insurance (Mature Market Institute, 2003a). In addition, assisted living facilities are gaining popularity among families whose elderly members can get by with a lower level of care than is provided in nursing homes. In fact, the number of residents in assisted living facilities increased by 50% between 1998 and 2003 (Mature Market Institute, 2003a). Assisted living facilities cost about half as much as nursing homes, and many of them have developed innovative approaches to providing lower-cost care, even for elders with the most serious disabilities.

Whether families choose a nursing home or an assisted living facility for their elderly members, the larger problem for many is balancing the older adult's need for independence and control against the needs of younger family members who have lives of their own to lead. What often tips the balance, one way or the other, is whether any family member is able or willing to provide assistance and whether other community services are available. For some families, aging-in-place strategies may make it possible to continue to care for an elder who is frail or suffers from dementia at home.

Certainly, if average nursing home care were of much higher quality than it is now, with built-in opportunities for personal control, challenging activities, and first-rate medical care, and if such care were covered by Medicare or other national health insurance, choosing such an option might be less difficult. But until that better day arrives, the choice of nursing home care—for oneself or for an aging parent—is likely to continue to be difficult.

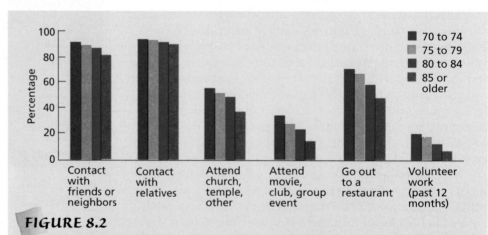

FIGURE 8.2

Survey participants were asked what social activities they had engaged in within the previous 2 weeks. As this figure suggests, older adults are very socially active. Activities such as dining out and going to movies decline with age, but contacts with family and friends remain fairly stable. (Source: FIFARS, 2000.)

The spread of Western ideas to non-Western societies via mass media and other means appears to be changing the concept of filial piety in Asian countries. Researchers have found that the concept of filial piety held by both middle-aged and elderly adults in highly Westernized areas, such as Hong Kong, is much more like that of North Americans and Europeans than that of traditional Asian culture (Ng, Ying, Phillips, & Lee, 2002). These changes have had a number of adverse consequences for elderly Asians. In some locales, older adults have been reduced to begging on the streets because their children aren't taking care of them and there are no government programs to help them. In response, many countries are enacting legislation that criminalizes a family's failure to provide for elders (Min, 2004). Others are recognizing that a shift toward Western values will necessitate adoption of Western-style government programs for the elderly (McDonald, 2004).

Affection between married partners and pleasure in each other's company clearly do not disappear in old age.

PARTNERSHIPS

Figure 18.3 shows the percentages of married, divorced, widowed, and never married individuals across elderly age groups in the United States. Because men typically marry younger women and because women live longer than men, a man can normally expect to have a spouse or intimate partner until he dies. The normal expectation for a woman is that she will eventually be without such a partner, often for many years. Clearly the percentages in Figure 8.3 support these expectations and help explain why there are more women than men in nursing homes and among the victims of elder abuse (see the Real World, page 208). But what are the marital relationships of older adults like?

Cross-sectional comparisons show that marital satisfaction is higher in the late adult years than when children are still at home. But this high marital satisfaction may have a somewhat different basis than that of the early years of marriage. In late adulthood, marriages tend to be based less on passion and mutual disclosure and more on loyalty, familiarity, mutual investment in the relationship, and companionship (Bengtson et al., 1990; Fouquereau & Baudoin, 2002). In Sternberg's terms (look back at Figure 4.2, page 94), late adult marriages are more likely to reflect companionate love than romantic or even consummate love.

Of course, this does not mean that the marriages of older adults are necessarily passionless. That may well be true of some marriages, but there is evidence to the contrary

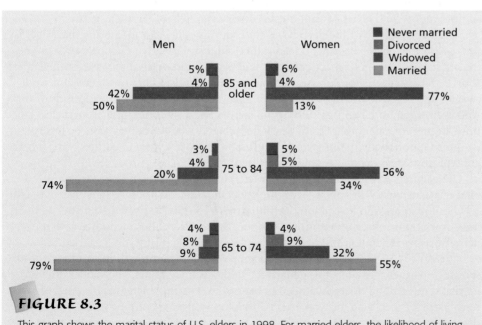

FIGURE 8.3

This graph shows the marital status of U.S. elders in 1998. For married elders, the likelihood of living with a spouse declines with age, especially among older women. (Source: FIFARS, 2000.)

The Real World

Elder Abuse

Elder abuse has received a great deal of media coverage in recent years, but it is not especially common; current estimates are that only about 3% of U.S. elders are physically abused (Bengtson, Rosenthal, & Burton, 1996). Physical abuse is most likely to be directed at elders who have some type of dementia, and abuse by spouses is twice as likely as abuse by children (Pillemer & Finkelhor, 1988). However, many experts believe that elder abuse is underreported because health care providers do not get enough training in recognizing its effects (Thobaben & Duncan, 2003).

Researchers have identified several risk factors for elder abuse, including mental illness or alcoholism in the abuser, financial dependency of the abuser on the victim, social isolation, and external stresses (Pillemer & Suitor, 1990, 1992). A likely victim of abuse is an elderly widow sharing her household with a dependent son who has a mental disorder or a drug or alcohol problem; the mother is typically too dependent on her son to kick him out and too ashamed of the abuse to tell others about it (Bengtson et al., 1996). Abuse is also more likely when the elder with dementia is physically violent and when a husband has physically abused his wife throughout their adult lives and simply continues to do so in old age.

Other forms of elder abuse may be far more subtle, including financial exploitation or failure to provide needed aid. The existence of such destructive forms of interaction is a clear reminder that older adults' relationships with their kin are not all sweetness and light. But it is also important to remember that these highly negative patterns are the exception rather than the rule. For most elders, relationships with children and other kin may be a mixture of positive and negative, but the scale most often tips toward the positive.

for many. You'll recall from Chapter 7 that the majority of older adult couples are still sexually active and may be somewhat more sexually adventurous than younger adults. Collectively, older couples report higher levels of pleasure and lower levels of conflict in their relationships than do middle-aged couples. When older couples do have conflicts, they resolve them in more affectionate and less negative ways (Carstensen, Gottman, & Levenson, 1995; Levenson, Carstensen, & Gottman, 1993). Older couples also spend more time with each other than with family or friends, and although much of this time is spent in passive or basic maintenance activities—watching TV, doing housework, running errands—it is also true that those married elders who spend more time with their spouses report high levels of happiness (Larson, Mannell, & Zuzanek, 1986).

Further evidence of the deep bond that continues to exist in late-life marriages is the remarkable degree of care and assistance older spouses give each other when one or the other is disabled. For married elders with some kind of disability, by far the largest source of assistance is the spouse, not children or friends. Many husbands and wives care for spouses who are ill or who suffer from dementia for very long periods of time. And even when both spouses suffer from significant disabilities, they nonetheless continue to care for each other "until death do us part." Marriages may thus be less romantic or less emotionally intense in late adulthood than they were in earlier years, but they are typically satisfying and highly committed.

Researchers have found similar characteristics and effects in long-term gay and lesbian relationships (Grossman, Daugelli, & Hershberger, 2000). Like heterosexuals, elderly homosexuals who have a long-term partner typically identify the partner as their most important source of emotional support. In addition, those who live with a partner report less loneliness and better physical and mental health.

It is the loss of the marriage or partnership relationship through the death of the spouse or partner that alters this pattern for so many older adults. The gender difference in marital status among elders illustrated in Figure 8.3 is further increased by a higher rate of remarriage for men than for women, a pattern found among both the widowed and the divorced at every age. Twenty percent of single men over 65 remarry, compared with only 2% of women. Older unmarried men are also more likely to date and more likely to live with someone (Bulcroft & Bulcroft, 1991). By contrast, research suggests that widows have little interest in dating or remarriage (Talbott, 1998). Despite older women's reluctance to remarry, studies of the emotional impact of remarriage in late adulthood suggest that both men and women benefit emotionally (Curran, McLanahan, & Knab, 2003; Winter, Lawton, Casten, & Sando, 2000). When researchers examine self-ratings of life satisfaction, elderly newlyweds rate their personal happiness higher than do either long-married or single peers.

Married older adults, like married adults of any age, have certain distinct advantages: They have higher life satisfaction, better health, and lower rates of institutionalization (Iwashyna & Christakis, 2003). Such differential advantages are generally greater for married older men than for married older women (again, this is also true among younger adults). This difference might be interpreted as indicating that marriage affords more benefits to men than to women or that men rely more on their marriage relationship for social support and are thus more affected by its loss. Whatever the explanation, it seems clear that, for older women, marital status is less strongly connected to health or life satisfaction, but still strongly connected to financial security.

Elderly newlyweds report higher levels of personal happiness than either long-married or single peers.

FAMILY RELATIONSHIPS

Folklore and descriptions of late adulthood in the popular press suggest that family, particularly children and grandchildren, forms the core of the social life of older adults, perhaps especially those who are widowed. Older adults do describe intergenerational bonds as strong and important; most report a significant sense of family solidarity and support (Bengtson et al., 1996). These bonds are reflected in, among other things, regular contact between elders and family members. Moreover, researchers have found that family relationships become more harmonious as adults get older (Akiyama, Antonucci, Takahashi, & Langfahl, 2003). Thus, they represent an important component of most elders' overall life satisfaction.

Contacts with Adult Children In one national sample of over 11,000 adults aged 65 and older, 63% reported that they saw at least one of their children once a week or more often, another 16% saw a child one to three times a month, and only 20% saw their children as rarely as once a month or less (Crimmins & Ingegneri, 1990). Regular contact is made easier by the fact that even in the highly mobile U.S. society, three-quarters of elders live within an hour's travel of at least one of their children. Very similar figures are reported by researchers in other developed countries such as England, so this pattern is not unique to the United States (Jerrome, 1990).

Part of the regular contact between elders and their adult children, of course, involves giving aid to or receiving it from the elder person—a pattern you learned about in Chapter 6. Most of the time, when older adults need help that cannot be provided by a spouse, it is provided by other family members, principally children. One representative set of data comes from the National Survey of Families and Households, which used a large national sample of more than 1,500 U.S. adults over 65 who had at least one living child. In this group, 52% were receiving some household help and 21% were receiving some financial help from at least one child (Hoyert, 1991).

However, relationships between older parents and their adult children cannot be reduced simply to the exchange of aid. A great deal of the interaction is social as well as functional, and the great majority of older adults describe their relationships with their adult children in positive terms. Most see their children not only out of a sense of obligation or duty but because they take pleasure in such contact, and a very large percentage describe at least one child as a confidant (Connidis & Davies, 1992).

Most elders enjoy maintaining relationships with younger family members. However, research suggests that such connections are not essential to life satisfaction in old age.

Effects of Relationships with Adult Children

Some studies indicate that when relationships between elders and adult children are warm and close, they are more important to elders' sense of well-being than any other kind of social relationship (Pinquart & Soerensen, 2000). By contrast, other researchers have found that elders who see their children more often or report more positive interactions with their children do not describe themselves as happier or healthier overall than do those who have less frequent contact or less positive relationships with their children (e.g., Mullins & Mushel, 1992). Moreover, such results have been obtained in very different cultural settings, such as in India and among Mexican Americans (Lawrence, Bennett, & Markides, 1992; Venkatraman, 1995). In all these studies, the older adults reported regular contact with their children and said that they enjoyed it, but these relationships did not seem to enhance happiness or health. Moreover, research has shown that childless elders are just as happy and well adjusted as those who have children (Connidis & McMullin, 1993). Many developmentalists have concluded that good relationships and regular contact with adult children can add to an elderly adult's quality of life, but are not necessary for it.

One possible explanation for this inconsistency in findings is that the relationship with one's children is still governed by role prescriptions, even in old age. It may be friendly, but it is not chosen in the same way that a relationship with a friend is. With your friend, you feel free to be yourself and feel accepted as who you are. With your children, you may feel the need to live up to their demands and expectations.

Grandchildren and Siblings As you learned in Chapter 6, interactions between grandchildren and middle-aged grandparents are beneficial to both. However, in late adulthood, contact between grandchildren and grandparents declines as the grandchildren become adults themselves (Barer, 2001; Silverstein & Long, 1998). Thus, grandchildren are rarely part of an elderly adult's close family network.

Interestingly, though, it appears that relationships with siblings may become more important in late adulthood, especially after both parents have died (Bedford, 1995; Gold, 1996). Siblings seldom provide much practical assistance to one another in old age, but they can and often do serve two other important functions. First, siblings can provide a unique kind of emotional support for one another, based on shared reminiscences and companionship. Once parents are gone, no one else knows all the old stories, all the family jokes, the names and history of former friends and neighbors. Second, many elders see their siblings as a kind of "insurance policy" in old age, a source of support of last resort (Connidis, 1994).

FRIENDSHIPS

CRITICAL THINKING

Why do you think most older adults' friends are long-standing ones? What social or psychological barriers might there be to creating new friendships in old age?

Because older adults' friends generally come from the same cohort and have been their friends for a number of years, they can provide the same sense of generational solidarity that siblings may provide. The small amount of research on late-life friendships supports the hypothesis that the number of friendships diminishes gradually from age 65 onward (e.g., Blieszner & Adams, 1992; Levitt, Weber, & Guacci, 1993). However, friendships gain importance in the lives of elders, even as they diminish in number.

Mounting evidence suggests that contact with friends has a significant impact on overall life satisfaction, on self-esteem, and on the amount of loneliness reported by older adults (Antonucci, Lansford, & Akiyama, 2001; Antonucci, 1990; Jerrome, 1990). Moreover, for those elders whose families are unavailable, friendships seem to provide an equally effective support network (Takahashi, Tamura, & Tokoro, 1997). This is particularly true of unmarried elders, but is at least somewhat true of married ones as well.

Friends meet different kinds of needs for older adults than do family members. For one thing, relationships with friends are likely to be more reciprocal or equitable, and developmentalists know that equitable relationships are more valued and less stressful. Friends provide companionship, opportunities for laughter, and shared activities. In one Canadian study, for example, friends were second only to spouses as sources of companionship among those over 65 (Connidis & Davies, 1992). Friends may also provide assistance with daily tasks, such as shopping or housework, although they typically provide less help of this kind than do family members.

Friends seem to play an important role in late adulthood, perhaps because they share the same background and memories—like favorite old tunes and dances.

GENDER AND RACIAL DIFFERENCES IN SOCIAL NETWORKS

As at earlier ages, women and men in late adulthood appear to form different kinds of social networks, with men's friendships involving less disclosure and less intimacy than women's. In addition, older women's networks tend to be larger and closer than those of older men. Developmentalists attribute these findings to a continuation of a pattern evident across most of the lifespan (Barker, Morrow, & Mitteness, 1998). If you think back on what you learned about sex differences in the chapters on childhood, adolescence, early adulthood, and middle adulthood, sex differences in late adulthood social networks should not be surprising.

However, it would be a mistake to assume that, because men have smaller social networks, their relationships are unimportant to them. Some developmentalists suggest that research on social networks may be biased in such a way that women will always be found to have stronger networks. This bias, critics say, originates in the fact that research emphasizes shared activities and frequency of contact more than the quality of the relationships. Indeed, when quality of relationships is considered, research shows that men's social networks are just as important to them and provide them with the same kinds of emotional support as women's networks, even though men's networks tend to be smaller (Riggs, 1997).

African Americans tend to have warmer relationships with their siblings and to live with their children more often than white Americans do. In addition, they show two other distinctive patterns in their social networks. They create strong relationships with "fictive kin," a type of relationship you first learned about in Chapter 4. In African American groups, friends often acquire the status of a close sibling, aunt, uncle, or grandparent. Such fictive kin may be important sources of both emotional and instrumental support among elders of all ethnic groups, but the pattern is particularly prevalent among African Americans (Johnson & Barer, 1990; MacRae, 1992).

Other ethnic groups, including Hispanic Americans and Asian Americans, are also often found to have more extensive social networks than white Americans. However, the correlations between social networks and various measures of well-being seem to be similar across these groups (Barker et al., 1998; Baxter et al., 1998; Takahashi et al., 1997). Moreover, most studies suggest that the quality of the social network, not just its size, is important. Thus, as the earlier discussion of successful aging suggested, the number of contacts with family and friends and the quality of interactions with them are important predictors of elders' well-being.

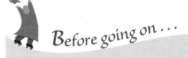

Before going on . . .

- How do social roles change in late adulthood?

- What are the living arrangements of most elderly people in the United States and other industrialized countries?

- How do intimate partnerships contribute to development in late adulthood?

- What is the significance for older adults of family relationships?

- How do friends affect elders' life satisfaction?

- What are some gender and ethnic differences in older adults' social networks?

Career Issues in Late Life

A remarkable capacity for adaptation marks the transition from work to retirement. Although this transition certainly brings the loss of a major role, virtually all the folklore about the negative effects of this particular role loss turns out to be wrong, at least for current older cohorts in developed countries. Developmentalists' knowledge about the process of retirement has been greatly enhanced by a series of excellent longitudinal studies, each following a group of men or women from before retirement into the years past retirement. In one particularly helpful analysis, Erdman Palmore and his colleagues combined the results of seven such studies, yielding a sample of over 7,000 adults, each interviewed at least twice and often many more times (Palmore, Burchett, Fillenbaum, George, & Wallman, 1985). Although these data are not completely current, they comprise by far the most comprehensive set of longitudinal data available.

TIMING OF RETIREMENT

One inaccurate bit of folklore is that 65 is the normal age of retirement. As recently as 1970, 65 was indeed the most common age of retirement for men in the United States. One reason for the uniformity was that many employers forced all workers to retire at 65. However, during the 1980s, age-discrimination legislation outlawed mandatory retirement in the United States (Mooney, Knox, & Schacht, 2000).

Knowing that there is a ban on mandatory retirement might lead you to believe that people are continuing to work to more advanced ages. However, the trend is quite the opposite. Although most older adults plan to continue working at least part-time during retirement (Lim, 2003; Mature Market Institute, 2004), the average age of retirement from full-time work has been declining in recent years throughout the industrialized world. One reason for this trend is that many government agencies and private businesses now offer older workers financial incentives ("golden handshakes") to retire. For example, in many countries, 60 is currently the pensionable age; in many others, such as the United States, 65 is the age at which a worker can begin to receive a full pension, although a reduced pension may be drawn earlier (Inkeles & Usui, 1989).

Some European countries are trying to reverse the trend toward younger retirement by gradually raising the age of eligibility for public pensions. A similar change has been proposed in the United States, and such public policy changes may affect individual retirement decisions in the future. But in the United States currently, the most common retirement age for men is 62; only about 40% of men between the ages of 62 and 64 and 25% of men between 65 and 69 are still in the full-time work force (Quadagno & Hardy, 1996). A similar shift toward leaving the labor force earlier has also occurred for women. Still, as you learned in Chapter 6, a majority of the current cohort of middle-aged adults (the Baby Boomers) expect to work at least part-time during retirement, so these figures are likely to change in the future.

REASONS FOR RETIREMENT

Research suggests that financial incentives are only one reason for retiring. Studies point to a collection of "pushes" and "pulls" that combine to influence each person's decision to retire (Kohli, 1994; Quadagno & Hardy, 1996).

Age Age itself is obviously an important ingredient in the retirement equation. Internal models play an important role here. If a person's "expected life history" includes retirement at age 62 or 65, he will be strongly inclined to retire at that age, regardless of other factors.

CRITICAL THINKING

Think about your own attitudes toward retirement. Do you expect this life change to be positive and enjoyable, or do you anticipate it with dread or some anxiety? What do you think has shaped your attitudes?

Health Poor health provides a particularly strong push toward early retirement (Schulz, 1995). Poor health lowers the average age of retirement by 1–3 years, an effect seen among Hispanic Americans and African Americans as well as among white Americans, and in countries other than the United States (Hayward, Friedman, & Chen, 1996; McDonald & Wanner, 1990; Sammartino, 1987; Stanford, Happersett, Morton, Molgaard, & Peddecord, 1991). However, among those who retire at 65 or later, health is a less powerful factor, presumably because most of these later retirees are in good health.

Family Considerations Family composition is important in the decision to retire. Those who are still supporting minor children retire later than do those in the postparental stage. Thus, men and women who bear their children very late, those who acquire a second and younger family in a second marriage, and those rearing grandchildren are likely to continue to work until these children have left home.

Financial Support Equally important in the timing of retirement is the availability of adequate financial support for retirement. Those who anticipate receiving pension support in addition to Social Security or who have personal savings to draw on retire earlier than do those who have no such financial backup.

Anticipated pension and health frequently work in opposite directions, because many working-class men and women who have worked in unskilled jobs can expect little supplementary retirement income and are in poor health. In general, working-class adults retire earlier than do middle-class and upper-class adults, often as a result of ill health and social norms, but many poor and working-class adults continue to work well past the normal retirement age in order to supplement their incomes.

On the other end of the social class scale, health and the adequacy of pensions work against each other in the opposite way. Adults in higher socioeconomic groups generally have both better health and better pensions; they also tend to have more interesting jobs. The three factors combine to produce somewhat later retirement for this group.

Work Characteristics Those who like their work and are highly committed to it, including many self-employed adults, retire later—often quite a lot later—than do those who are less gratified by their work. Those in challenging and interesting jobs are likely to postpone retirement until they are pushed by ill health or attracted by some extra financial inducement. For them, availability of a normal pension is less of an influence (Hayward & Hardy, 1985).

A quite different kind of work influence occurred in the 1990s in occupations or industries in which the work force suffered major "downsizing." A great many workers, blue collar and white collar alike, were pushed to accept early retirement, as their employers offered them special incentives (Hardy & Quadagno, 1995).

Sex Differences None of the reasons for retirement, except age, is as significant for women as for men (Palmore et al., 1985). Women retire at about the same age as men do, on average, but retirement benefits, health, or job characteristics do not predict just when they will retire. The most reliable predictor of retirement for a woman is whether her husband has retired (Weaver, 1994). An opposing force that tends to keep women in the labor force is the lure of higher earnings that will augment future Social Security benefits—a factor that may be especially important for current cohorts of women nearing retirement, many of whom entered the labor force only in middle adulthood.

By contrast, the factors that lead to positive views of retirement are very similar for men and women. For example, one study found that health was the most important predictor of quality of life in retirement for both sexes (Quick & Moen, 1998). However, extensive pre-retirement planning seemed to be more important for men. Almost all of the study's male participants had worked continuously until retirement. Although some of the retired women had worked continuously, others had spent a significant number of years in the home or in part-time employment. The researchers found that those who had worked continuously expressed more satisfaction with the quality of their retirement.

EFFECTS OF RETIREMENT

There are a number of shifts that take place at retirement, some positive and some negative. But, overall, retirement seems to have positive effects on the lives of older adults.

Income   One potentially significant change at retirement is a change in income. In the United States, retired adults have five potential sources of income: government pensions, such as Social Security; other pensions, such as those offered through an employer or the military; earnings from continued work; income from savings or other assets; and, for those living below the poverty line, public assistance, including food stamps and Supplemental Security Income. For most elderly in the United States, Social Security is the largest source of income (FIFARS, 2000).

Of course, statistics on income sources indicate nothing about changes in income level after retirement. Here again, Palmore's longitudinal data can be helpful. These data suggest that incomes decline roughly 25% after retirement. But this figure paints a misleadingly negative picture of the actual financial status of retired persons.

In the United States, as in many developed countries, many retired adults own their own homes and thus have no mortgage payments, and their children are self-reliant. Furthermore, retirees are eligible for Medicare as well as for many special senior citizen benefits. When these factors are taken into consideration, retired adults in the United States, Australia, and most European countries have, on average, incomes that are at 85–100% of pre-retirement levels (Smeeding, 1990).

Poverty   It used to be that post-retirement income losses resulted in high poverty rates among the elderly. However, over the past several decades, poverty rates among the elderly have declined substantially. In 1959, 35% of adults over 65 in the United States were living below the poverty line. In 1998, slightly more than 11% were at that low economic level (FIFARS, 2000).

A variety of factors are responsible for declining poverty rates among the elderly. For one thing, significant improvements in Social Security benefits in the United States (and equivalent improvements in many other countries), including regular cost-of-living increases, have meant that the relative financial position of the elderly has improved more than that of any other age group in the population. Moreover, more elderly adults than ever before are high school or college graduates. In 1950, only 18% of adults over 65 were high school graduates, compared to two-thirds of the over-65 population in 1998 (FIFARS, 2000). Thus, most elderly adults today had better jobs and earned a great deal more money before retirement than did members of previous cohorts. As a result, today's elders have more savings and better retirement benefits.

However, low rates of poverty in the total elderly population obscure much higher rates in various subgroups. Although Figure 18.4 shows declines in the elderly poverty rates of the various ethnic groups in the United States from 1979 to 1989, large disparities across groups remain (FIFARS, 2000).

Ethnic group differences in poverty are, no doubt, related to differences in educational attainment. Among older adults in the United States today, nearly three-quarters of whites and about two-thirds of Asian Americans are high school graduates. So it is perhaps not surprising that these two groups have the lowest poverty rates. By contrast, less than half of the elders in other ethnic and racial groups graduated from high school. Consequently, the employment histories of these groups are different, leading to income disparities in retirement. However, in future cohorts of retirees, these disparities are likely to diminish because of greatly increased rates of high school graduation and college attendance among younger minorities (U.S. Bureau of the Census, 1995a).

Similarly, single older adults continue to be more likely to be poor than their married peers, and among older singles, women are more likely to be poor than men (16% versus 9%, respectively) (FIFARS, 2000). Different poverty rates for single men and women in old age arise from a number of differences in adult life experiences.

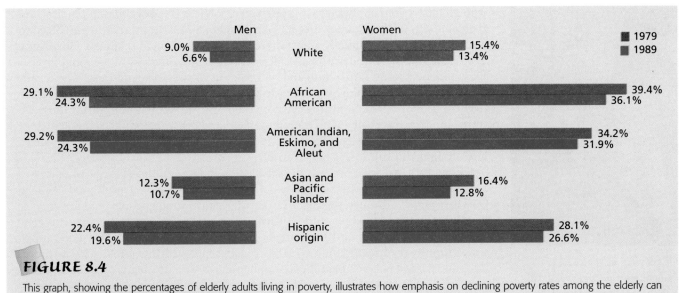

FIGURE 8.4

This graph, showing the percentages of elderly adults living in poverty, illustrates how emphasis on declining poverty rates among the elderly can obscure important variations across groups. (Source: U.S. Bureau of the Census, 1995a.)

Current cohorts of older women are much less likely than their male peers to have had paid employment, are less likely to have earned retirement benefits even if they did work, and generally worked for lower wages (Hardy & Hazelrigg, 1993). As a result, many older widows rely entirely on Social Security income. Women in younger cohorts are more likely to have been employed and to have participated in a retirement plan, but, as you learned in earlier chapters, gender differences in work patterns still exist. Thus, there are likely to be gender differences in poverty rates in future cohorts of retirees, though these will probably shrink a bit.

Health, Attitudes, and Emotions Longitudinal studies indicate quite clearly that health does not change, for better or worse, simply because of retirement. When ill health accompanies retirement, the causal sequence is nearly always that the individual retired because of poor health. Among those in good health at retirement age, retirement itself has little or no effect on health status over the succeeding years (Palmore et al., 1985). This clear set of research results is interesting because it suggests that retirement is not a highly stressful life change for the vast majority of adults.

Similarly, the bulk of the evidence suggests that retirement has essentially no impact on overall life satisfaction or subjective well-being. Longitudinal studies that have included measures of such attitudes show little difference in scores before and after retirement, and those recently retired show little sign of an increase in depression (Palmore et al., 1985). For most, retirement is not perceived as a stressor at all.

One set of data that makes this point particularly clearly comes from a study of a group of more than 1,500 men over a period of years (Bossé, Aldwin, Levenson, & Workman-Daniels, 1991). In the most recent interviews, participants were asked to indicate which of 31 possibly stressful life events they had experienced in the past year and to rate the overall stressfulness of each of these events. Retirement was ranked 30th out of 31 in overall stressfulness, below even such items as "move to a less desirable residence" and "decrease in responsibilities or hours at work or where you volunteer." Of those who had retired in the previous year, seven out of ten said that they found retirement either not stressful at all or only a little stressful. Among the 30% of retired men in this study who did list some problems with retirement, poor health and poor family finances were the most likely causes. Those with marital problems were also likely to report more daily hassles in their retired lives.

Other evidence suggests that those who respond least well to retirement are those who had the least control over the decision (Smith & Moen, 2004). For example, those

Elders who have moved to resort communities specifically designed for retired people have made what social scientists call an amenity move.

who go into retirement because of a late-career job loss show declines in physical and mental health (Gallo, Bradley, Siegel, & Kasl, 2000). Similarly, those who are forced to retire by poor health typically adjust more poorly to retirement (Hardy & Quadagno, 1995). Even workers who accept special early retirement offers from their employers are likely to report lower satisfaction and higher levels of stress than do those who feel they had more control over the retirement decision (Herzog et al., 1991). Retirement is also likely to be more stressful for those whose economic situation is poor or for those who must simultaneously cope with both retirement and other major life changes, such as widowhood (Stull & Hatch, 1984). But for those for whom retirement is anticipated and on time, this role loss is not stressful.

It appears that what predicts life satisfaction in late adulthood is not whether a person has retired but whether he was satisfied with life in earlier adulthood. We take ourselves with us through the years: Grumpy, negative young people tend to be grumpy, negative old people, and satisfied young adults find satisfaction in retirement as well. The consistency of this finding is quite striking and provides very good support for continuity theories of adulthood. Work does shape daily life for 40 years or more of adulthood, but a person's happiness or unhappiness with life, her growth or stagnation, seems less a function of the specifics of the work experience than a function of the attitudes and qualities she brings to the process.

Mobility   For many adults, retirement brings an increase in choices about where to live. When your job or your spouse's job no longer ties you to a specific place, you can choose to move to sunnier climes or to live nearer one of your children. Surprisingly, however, most retirees stay fairly close to the place they have called home for many years (Burkhauser, Butrica, & Wasylenko, 1995; De Jong, Wilmoth, Angel, & Cornwell, 1995).

Charles Longino, who has been one of the most diligent investigators of residential moves among the elderly, suggests that elderly adults make three types of moves (Jackson, Longino, Zimmerman, & Bradsher, 1991; Litwak & Longino, 1987; Longino, 1990; Longino, Jackson, Zimmerman, & Bradsher, 1991). The first type, which he calls an amenity move, is the one most of us probably think of when we think of older adults changing residences. If an older adult makes such a move, it is almost always right around the time of retirement. Most typically, an **amenity move** is in a direction away from the older person's children, frequently to a warmer climate. Florida, California, and Arizona are the most popular destinations for amenity moves in the United States. In Canada, amenity moves are most often westward, particularly to British Columbia; in Britain, the equivalent move is to the seaside.

Those who make amenity moves are likely to be still married and relatively healthy and to have adequate or good retirement income (De Jong et al., 1995; Hazelrigg & Hardy, 1995). Often the relocating couple has vacationed in the new location; many have planned the move carefully over a number of years (Cuba & Longino, 1991). Most report higher levels of life satisfaction or morale after such a move, although some move back to where they came from because they find themselves too isolated from family and friends.

Another pattern of amenity move is to move seasonally rather than making a permanent move to a new location. Some elders, often called "snowbirds," spend the winter months in sunnier areas and the summer months at home, nearer their families. One survey of older retired residents of Minnesota found that 9% followed such a pattern (Hogan & Steinnes, 1994).

The second type of move, which Longino calls **compensatory (kinship) migration,** occurs when the older adult—most often, a widow living alone—develops such a level of chronic disability that she has serious difficulty managing an independent household. When a move of this type occurs, it is nearly always a shift to be closer to a daughter, son, or some other relative who can provide regular assistance. In some cases, this means moving in with that daughter or son, but often the move is to an apartment or house nearby or into a retirement community in which the individual can live independently but has supportive services available. The final type of move in late adulthood is what Longino calls **institutional migration,** to nursing home care.

amenity move post-retirement move away from kin to a location that has some desirable feature, such as year-round warm weather

compensatory (kinship) migration a move to a location near family or friends that happens when an elder requires frequent help because of a disability or disease

institutional migration a move to an institution such as a nursing home that is necessitated by a disability

Of course, very few older adults actually move three times. Longino's point is that these are three very different kinds of moves, made by quite different subsets of the population of elderly and at different times in the late adult years. Amenity moves usually occur early, kinship or compensatory migration is likely to occur in middle to late old age, and institutional migration clearly occurs late in life. Only the first of these types of moves reflects the increase in options that may result from retirement.

One of the most recent developments in connection with post-retirement mobility is the trend among universities and colleges to make their on-campus housing facilities available to alumni and senior citizens who want to attend college (Kressley & Huebschmann, 2002). This trend is in response to the significant portion of elders who want to spend their increased leisure time on intellectual pursuits (Trentin, 2004). Moreover, increased enrollment by older adults has helped some institutions overcome the financial difficulties associated with declining college attendance among young adults.

About 47% of older men and 37% of older women in the United States are employed at least part-time (FIFARS, 2000). Further, a fairly high proportion of middle-aged people say they plan to work at least part-time after retirement. Consequently, employers are eager to learn how to best train older workers.

CHOOSING NOT TO RETIRE

A significant number of adults plan to continue working past the typical retirement age (Mature Market Institute, 2004). This subgroup includes two types of people: (1) those who will never retire from their long-time occupations and (2) those who will retire from their regular occupations and venture into new lines of work, often part-time.

Continuing in a Life-Long Occupation Developmentalists know almost nothing about women who choose not to retire, but they do know something about men who shun retirement. Some are men with very limited education, poor retirement benefits, and thus very low incomes. Many of these men continue working out of economic necessity.

A larger fraction of those who shun retirement are highly educated, healthy, highly work-committed professionals, whose wives often are also still working (Parnes & Sommers, 1994). Many of them have been highly work-committed all their adult lives. For example, men in the National Longitudinal Surveys sample, a group that has been studied over a period of 25 years, were asked in their 50s whether they would continue working if they suddenly found themselves with enough money to live comfortably. Those who said they would continue working are much more likely to shun retirement and to be still working in their 70s and 80s (Parnes & Sommers, 1994). For these men, work continues to provide more satisfaction than they expect retirement to offer.

Learning New Job Skills Perhaps the greatest obstacle to employment for older adults is that many potential employers express concerns about older adults' ability to learn new job skills (Forte & Hansvick, 1999). However, studies of age differences in learning demonstrate that the learning process itself does not change with age. The same factors—interest, anxiety, motivation, quality of instruction, self-efficacy, and so on—predict learning success in both older and younger adults (Chasseigne, Grau, Mullet, & Cama, 1999; Gardiner, Luszcz, & Bryan, 1997; Mead & Fisk, 1998; Plaud, Plaud, & von Duvillard, 1999; Truluck & Courtenay, 1999). Thus, it seems reasonable that many aspects of effective training programs designed for younger workers, such as financial incentives for accomplishment of training goals, should also apply to older employees.

Moreover, an extensive body of research shows that, with appropriately paced training, older adults can significantly improve their performance on many cognitive tasks that are relevant to the workplace (Baltes & Kliegl, 1992; Dittmann-Kohli,

Research suggests that older adults respond to computer training very much the way younger adults do. Most get over their anxiety about computers after receiving training, and they can become just as proficient as younger adults, although they may require slower-paced training.

Development in the Information Age

Older Adults in the Technological Workplace

Computer skills are now required for most jobs, including many held by older adults. As a result, computer and software makers are producing and funding training programs and research aimed at promoting computer use and computer skills among the elderly ("Microsoft senior initiative," 1998).

Older adults are somewhat more anxious about learning computer skills than those who are younger (Czaja & Sharit, 1998). However, knowledge and training reduce their anxiety, often to levels that are comparable to those of young and middle-aged adults (Dyck, Gee, & Smither, 1998; Ellis & Allaire, 1999). Moreover, among elders, anxiety does not appear to interfere with skill learning (Laguna & Babcock, 1997).

Productivity studies suggest that older workers can be just as productive as younger employees in jobs involving computer usage. In fact, at least one study found that workers over the age of 60 made fewer data-entry mistakes (Czaja, Sharit, Nair, & Rubert, 1998). The study's authors suggested that employers can expect an equal amount of work output from older and younger computer workers because older employees' lower error rate compensates for their slower speed.

Older adults seem to benefit most from training that is specially designed to take into account their motor difficulties and slower speed of cognitive processing. In some cases, training programs have been specifically tailored to the different needs of the young old and the old old (Mead & Fisk, 1998). For example, researchers used repetition strategies to train young old and old old adults to use automated teller machines (ATMs). They found that both groups benefited more from action training than from verbal explanations of how to use the machine. However, the old old group made more errors and required more repetitions of the various steps involved in ATM use. Studies involving other kinds of technology skills have also shown that the old old take longer to learn new skills than the young old (Echt et al., 1998). However, ultimately, the old old seem to be no less able to learn new skills than young old, middle-aged, and young adults.

Before going on . . .

■ At what age do most men and women retire in the United States?

■ What are the factors that influence the decision to retire?

■ How does retirement affect income, health, attitudes, emotions, and mobility?

■ What does research suggest about the decision not to retire?

Lachman, Kliegl, & Baltes, 1991; Kliegl, Smith, & Baltes, 1989, 1990; Verhaeghen, Marcoen, & Goossens, 1992). Pacing is important, because these studies do suggest that learning new skills sometimes takes longer for older adults. However, even training in the use of new technologies usually results in similar or identical skill levels among younger and older adults (see Development in the Information Age).

Workplace Functioning With respect to aspects of job functioning other than learning of new skills, supervisors typically give older adults higher ratings than younger adults (Forte & Hansvick, 1999). For example, they view older employees as more reliable. In addition, managers typically report that although younger workers produce a greater quantity of work, the quality of older employees' work is better (Rao & Rao, 1997). Consequently, many employers view older adults as desirable employees.

Summary

Theories of Social and Personality Development

- Erikson's concept of ego integrity has been influential, but research does not indicate that the development of ego integrity is necessary to adjustment in old age. The notion of reminiscence has been helpful in researchers' attempts to understand development in late adulthood. However, research does not provide strong support for the hypothesis that reminiscence is necessary to successful aging.
- Similarly, disengagement has been found not to be essential in old age; high life satisfaction and good mental health are found most often among elders who disengage the least.

Individual Differences

- Successful aging is defined as maintenance of health along with cognitive and social functioning. Productivity and life satisfaction are also elements of successful aging.
- Religious coping has psychological and social components. It is associated with a lower mortality rate as well as with better physical and mental health.

Social Relationships

- Late adulthood is a time when people discard some roles. Remaining roles have less content. Having fewer roles may offer greater license for individuality.
- Among unmarried elders in the United States, living alone is the most common living arrangement. However, a number of residential options are available for seniors who do not want to care for a home or who have become physically disabled. Cultural differences in living arrangements for the elderly are based on variations in beliefs about filial piety.

- Marriages in late adulthood are, on average, highly satisfying for both spouses, who exhibit strong loyalty and mutual affection. If one spouse is disabled, the healthier spouse is likely to provide care. Married elders, as a group, are somewhat healthier and more satisfied with their lives than are single elders; this difference is larger among men than women.
- The majority of elders have at least one living child, and most take pleasure in seeing their children regularly. There is some indication that relationships with siblings may become more significant in late adulthood than at earlier ages.
- Degree of contact with friends is correlated with overall life satisfaction among older adults.
- Women in this age group continue to have larger social networks than men do, and African Americans tend to have larger social networks than white Americans.

Career Issues in Late Life

- The typical age of retirement is closer to 62 than 65 in the United States and in most Western developed countries.
- Time of retirement is affected by health, family responsibilities, adequacy of anticipated pension income, and satisfaction with one's job.
- Income typically decreases with retirement, but income adequacy does not decline very much. Among elders, women and minorities are most likely to live in poverty.
- Retirement appears not to be a stressful life change for the great majority of people. It is not the cause of deterioration in physical or mental health. The minority of older adults who find retirement stressful are likely to be those who feel they have least control over the decision to retire.
- Those who choose not to retire do so for economic reasons or because of particularly strong commitments to work. Research indicates that older adults can learn new job skills but may do so at slower rates than younger workers.

Key Terms

activity theory (p. 196)
aging in place (p. 203)
amenity move (p. 216)
compensatory (kinship) migration
   (p. 216)

disengagement theory (p. 196)
ego integrity (p. 195)
ego integrity versus despair stage
   (p. 195)
filial piety (p. 205)

institutional migration (p. 216)
religious coping (p. 200)
reminiscence (p. 195)
successful aging (p. 197)
volunteerism (p. 199)

Policy Question

How Should Stem Cell Research Be Funded and Regulated?

Stem cells are partially developed, unspecialized cells. In response to biochemical signals that scientists don't yet understand, they develop into mature, specialized cells (Stewart, 2004). The potential of stem cells for curing many diseases associated with aging, such as Parkinson's disease and Alzheimer's disease, has received a great deal of media attention in recent years. There are experts who say that stem cell research may lead to treatments that reverse the effects of aging. For instance, stem cells may be used to stop the loss of muscle mass that normally accompanies aging, and stem cells in hair follicles have been touted as a potential cure for baldness (Blanpain, Lowry, Geoghegan, Polak, & Fuchs, 2004; Stewart, 2004). Such claims have resulted in widespread public interest in stem cell research. Policymakers are interested in age-related applications of stem cell research because of the anticipated health care costs associated with the demographic crisis you read about in Chapter 17 (the elderly are the fastest growing segment of the population).

Nevertheless, public policies related to stem cell research are so controversial that in 2004, for the first time, both major political parties in the United States included statements on stem cell research in their platforms (Foust, 2004). The Democratic Party platform supports increased funding for all kinds of stem cell research, while that of the Republic Party urges policymakers to withhold funds from research involving the destruction of human embryos. Before examining the arguments involved in the stem cell research debate, it is essential that you understand a bit about the different kinds of stem cells and the current state of scientific knowledge about how they might be used to treat diseases.

Types of Stem Cells

A zygote results from the union of a sperm and an egg. The zygote is a kind of stem cell scientists refer to as *totipotent* because it is capable of developing into an entire human being. As the zygote divides, each resulting cell retains the characteristic of totipotentiality until the eight-cell stage is reached. In other words, each of the cells in an eight-cell embryo can develop into an entire human body.

Once the number of cells exceeds eight, each cell can develop into one of the body's 216 different cell types, but none can become an entire human body. Stem cells of this kind are called *pluripotent*. As the embryo develops, cells become committed to specific tissues and lose their pluripotent characteristics. Understanding how pluripotent cells develop into specialized tissues and applying that knowledge to the treatment of disease and injury is the goal of embryonic stem cell research. Such research involves extracting undifferentiated stem cells from embryos and experimenting with them in the laboratory.

Some cells that are committed to a particular kind of tissue retain some degree of plasticity, even though they are not pluripotent. Such cells represent a third kind of stem cell called *multipotent* and are present in the body at all stages of development, including adulthood. For example, multipotent stem cells in bone marrow can become any kind of blood cell the body needs. Likewise, multipotent stem cells in muscle tissue can become muscle cells, fat cells, or connective tissue (Stewart, 2004). When tissues are damaged by injury, disease, or the natural aging process, the body initiates a developmental process through which these multipotent cells mature into precisely the kind of tissue the body needs to repair itself. In the stem cell research debate, when people talk about "adult" stem cells, they are referring to these multipotent cells.

Why Is Stem Cell Research Controversial?

Many people object to embryonic stem cell research because it requires the destruction of a human embryo (Shannon, 2004). These opponents equate destroying an embryo with killing a human being. They argue that destruction of human life is always wrong, regardless of its stage of development and no matter how noble the purpose of such killing is.

In response, advocates of embryonic stem cell research argue that the human embryo is not yet a person, so its destruction is not equivalent to taking the life of a fully developed human being (Shannon, 2004). Furthermore, because embryonic stem cell research involves excess embryos that are created for in vitro fertilization (IVF), many argue that they would be destroyed whether they were used for research or not. Thus, advocates ask, why not use them to benefit others?

However, the debate takes a different turn when the issue of creating embryos strictly for the purpose of research is raised. Many who would endorse using excess IVF embryos for research balk at the idea that human sperm and ova might be joined in a test tube for the sole purpose of experimentation. They argue that leftover embryos from IVF were conceived with the intention of allowing them to develop into fully grown human beings. For this reason, they say, using their tissue to help others is morally acceptable, much like transplanting the organs of an individual who dies into the bodies of others who need them to live.

By contrast, research involving multipotent cells extracted from the tissues of children and/or adults is unhampered by such ethical dilemmas (Stewart, 2004). What is controversial, however, is the degree to which funds ought to be differentially allocated to embryonic and multipotent stem cell research. Some say that most funding should go to embryonic stem cell studies because pluripotent cells hold the best hope for curing diseases. Others argue that money is better spent on furthering scientists' understanding of how the body uses multipotent cells in natural healing processes. Research can be cited in support of both positions.

(Photo: AP/Wide World Photos)

Can Stem Cells Cure Diseases?

Experts point out that scientists are still years away from knowing whether embryonic stem cells can be used to treat diseases (Stewart, 2004). Experiments have shown that it is possible to extract pluripotent cells from developing embryos and grow them in the laboratory. In fact, a few such cells can turn into millions in a matter of weeks (National Institutes of Health, 2004). Moreover, scientists have learned how to keep them from differentiating into specialized cells. In other words, they know how to maintain the cells' pluripotent characteristics. What isn't known, though, is exactly how to initiate and control specialization.

Recently, however, British scientists succeeded in developing neurons from embryonic stem cells (National Institutes of Health, 2004). These neurons were then implanted in the brains of mice with a condition similar to Parkinson's disease. Remarkably, most of the mice showed improvements in motor function after receiving the laboratory-grown neurons. These findings have been widely cited by advocates for embryonic stem cell research.

However, even the most ardent advocates of embryonic stem cell research warn that much remains to be learned before similar experiments can be carried out with human beings. For one thing, they caution that stem cell transplants, like organ transplants, can be rejected by the body that receives them. Moreover, studies suggest that laboratory-grown cells may be more likely than naturally developed cells to develop into malignant tumors (Stewart, 2004). Consequently, embryonic stem cells cannot be used to treat diseases in human beings until much more is known about how to control the tissue rejection and tumor development processes.

There is no doubt that multipotent, or adult, stem cells, can be used to treat diseases. In fact, bone marrow stem cells have been used in the treatment of blood diseases for decades (Stewart, 2004). And in recent years, scientists have identified many new adult stem cell "populations"—in muscle tissue, the liver, the brain, the skin, hair follicles, and many other tissues (National Institutes of Health, 2004). Thus, most experts agree that the potential for using multipotent stem cells to treat disease—or even to moderate the effects of aging—is

tremendous. Moreover, scientists have recently discovered that some adult stem cells are pluripotent (National Institutes of Health, 2004).

(Photo: AP/Wide World Photos)

Nevertheless, new tissues grown from multipotent stem cells are unlikely to become a panacea for disease or a fountain of youth. Rejection isn't an issue, of course, when an individual receives new tissue grown from his or her own stem cells. However, the tendency of these cells to develop into malignant tumors is just as great as that of embryonic stem cells. Another difficulty is that genes in the stem cells of individuals who suffer from genetic disorders carry the same defects as those in their fully developed organs. Thus, gene therapy would be required before their stem cells could be used to fight such diseases.

In addition, stem cells extracted from adults' bodies grow much more slowly than those from embryos, and the older adults are, the more slowly their stem cells grow (Stewart, 2004). The slow growth rate of adults' stem cells represents an important obstacle to using them for research. In clinical applications, it might mean that new tissue could not be grown in time to treat a life-threatening disease or injury.

Stem Cell Research Policies

On August 9, 2001, President George W. Bush issued a directive that, with few exceptions, banned the use of U.S. taxpayer dollars for embryonic stem cell research (Office of the White House Press Secretary, 2001). However, this policy left privately funded embryonic stem cell research almost completely unregulated, and the number of private facilities devoted to such research in the United States has increased dramatically since the policy was enacted (Vergano, 2004). Moreover, President Bush's policy encouraged the U.S. Congress to appropriate additional funding for multipotent stem cell research.

By contrast, most other nations in the industrialized world have established policies that favor publicly funded over privately funded embryonic stem cell research (Rosenthal, 2004). To ensure continued funding, researchers must abide by strict

ethical guidelines. Further, these nations' policies place a higher priority on embryonic than on multipotent stem cell research.

Your Turn

In summary, stem cell research policy in the United States might be characterized as follows: (1) emphasis on private rather than public funding for embryonic stem cell research, (2) little regulation of privately funded embryonic stem cell research, and (3) prioritization of multipotent over embryonic stem cell research. Other nations' policies could be summarized as follows: (1) emphasis on public rather than private funding for embryonic stem cell research, (2) strict regulation of embryonic stem cell research, and (3) prioritization of embryonic over multipotent stem cell research. Which approach do you think is better? Finding the answers to these questions may help you decide.

- How do organizations for (e.g., the American Medical Association) and against (e.g., U.S. Conference of Catholic Bishops) embryonic stem cell research explain and support their positions?

- What do the Democratic Party and Republican Party platforms say about the issue? (Go to http://www.democrats.org/pdfs/2004platform.pdf and http://www.gopconvention.com/platform/2004platform.pdf to find out.)

- How do scientists grow stem cells in the laboratory?

- What are the top five diseases that scientists currently believe are most likely to be helped through stem cell research?

- Other than the treatment of diseases, what applications might there be for stem cell research?

Death, Dying, and Bereavement

9

We began our study of the human lifespan with an examination of birth and went on to consider a multitude of changes in the physical, cognitive, and social domains from infancy to late adulthood.

© Robert Brenner/PhotoEdit

Now we turn to the end of life. A particularly eloquent expression of the inevitability of death came from Stewart Alsop, a writer who kept a diary of the last years of his life, as he was dying of leukemia. In one of the very late entries in this journal, he said, "A dying man needs to die as a sleepy man needs to sleep, and there comes a time when it is wrong, as well as useless, to resist" (Alsop, 1973, p. 299). Alsop's statement calls to mind one of the important individual variables you have read about often in earlier chapters—the timing of a universal developmental event in a particular individual's life.

Like Alsop, many people contract fatal diseases and consciously face the inevitability of impending death for a period of months or years. Sometimes an unexpected event—perhaps an accident or a crime—ends a child's or young adult's life prematurely. For most of us, though, death comes in late adulthood and results from the subtle interplay between primary and secondary aging. Consequently, a good deal of what you will learn about dying and death will concern older adults. But the story must begin earlier, with an examination of people's understanding of and attitudes toward dying and death.

In this chapter you will learn about the physical, psychological, and social aspects of death. You will also learn how children's and teens' understanding of death differs from that of adults. The chapter also discusses individuals' responses to their own impending deaths and to the deaths of loved ones. As you read, keep the following questions in mind:

- What are three definitions of death, and how does where a person dies affect the experience of dying?

- How does the meaning of death change over the lifespan?

- How did Elizabeth Kübler-Ross and her critics think about the process of dying?

- In what ways do people experience the psychological process of grieving?

- How do psychoanalytic and attachment theorists explain grieving, and what theories do their critics propose?

The Experience of Death

Most of us use the word *death* as if it described a simple phenomenon. You are either alive or dead. But, in fact, death is a process as well as a state, and physicians have different labels for different aspects of this process. Moreover, for both the deceased and the bereaved, the experience of death is shaped by the circumstances surrounding the end of life.

DEATH ITSELF

The term **clinical death** refers to the few minutes after the heart has stopped pumping, when breathing has stopped and there is no evident brain function, but during which resuscitation is still possible. Heart attack patients are sometimes brought back from clinical death; presumably those who report near-death experiences were in a state of clinical death.

Brain death describes a state in which the person no longer has reflexes or any response to vigorous external stimuli and no electrical activity in the brain. When the cortex, but not the brain stem, is affected, the person may still be able to breathe without assistance and may survive for long periods in a vegetative state or on life-support systems. When the brain stem is also dead, no body functioning can occur independently, and the individual is said to be legally dead (Detchant, 1995). Brain death most often occurs after a period of 8–10 minutes of clinical death, but there are cases in which brain death has occurred because of brain injury, as in an auto accident, and other body functions can still be maintained artificially. In such cases, other body organs, such as the heart and kidneys, can be used for organ donation, as long as they are removed without delay.

Social death occurs at the point when the deceased person is treated like a corpse by others; for instance, someone may close the eyes or sign a death certificate. Once social death has been acknowledged, family and friends must begin to deal with the loss.

WHERE DEATH OCCURS

In the United States and in other industrialized countries, the great majority of adults die in hospitals, rather than at home or even in nursing homes. Naturally, there is a great deal of variation, depending on such factors as age and type of disease or injury. Among the old old, for example, death in a nursing home is quite common. Among younger adults, in contrast, hospital death is the norm. Similarly, adults with progressive diseases, such as cancer or AIDS, are typically in and out of the hospital for months or years before death; at the other end of the continuum are many who are hospitalized with an acute problem, such as a heart attack or pneumonia, and who die soon thereafter, having had no prior hospitalization. In between fall those who have experienced several different types of care in their final weeks or months, including hospitalization, home health care, and nursing home care. Despite such diversity, it is still true that the majority of deaths, particularly among the elderly, are preceded by some weeks of hospitalization (Merrill & Mor, 1993; Shapiro, 1983).

In recent years, however, an alternative form of terminal care that has become common is **hospice care,** an approach to caring for the dying that emphasizes individual and family control of the process. The hospice movement was given a boost by the writings of the late Elisabeth Kübler-Ross, who emphasized the importance of a "good death," or a "death with dignity," in which the patient and the patient's family have more control over the entire process (Kübler-Ross, 1974). Many health care professionals, particularly in England and the United States, believe that such a good death is

clinical death a period during which vital signs are absent but resuscitation is still possible

brain death the point at which vital signs, including brain activity, are absent and resuscitation is no longer possible

social death the point at which family members and medical personnel treat the deceased person as a corpse

hospice care an approach to care for the terminally ill that emphasizes individual and family control of the process of dying

The Meaning of Death across the Lifespan

As an adult, you understand that death is irreversible, that it comes to everyone, and that it means a cessation of all function. But do children and teenagers understand these aspects of death? And what does death mean to adults of different ages?

CHILDREN'S AND ADOLESCENTS' UNDERSTANDING OF DEATH

Results from a variety of studies suggest that preschool-aged children typically understand none of these aspects of death. They believe that death can be reversed, for instance, through prayer, magic, or wishful thinking; they believe that dead persons can still feel or breathe. They also believe that at least some people—those who are clever or lucky, or members of their own families—can avoid death (Lansdown & Benjamin, 1985; Speece & Brent, 1984, 1992). Research shows that young children's ideas about death are rooted in their lack of understanding of life (Slaughter & Lyons, 2003). This link between understanding life and understanding death has been illustrated in a series of studies showing that teaching young children about the nature of biological life helps them understand what causes death and why it is irreversible.

By the time they start school, just about the time Piaget described as the beginning of concrete operations, most children seem to understand both the permanence and the universality of death. This understanding is clear from children's own comments. In one study, children were told a story about two children who used to go into a candy store kept by an old lady who had recently died (Lansdown & Benjamin, 1985). After they heard the story, the participants were asked some questions about the old lady and about what it meant that she was dead.

> A 5-year-old: "Someone came into the shop to kill her. She'll see them again and she'll die again. She can try to get up."
> A 7-year-old: "They never come alive again. You can't move because your heart has stopped. People wish you can come alive but you can't. Children can't die because they start at one and go to 100."
> A 9-year-old: "Their heart can't take it any longer and they die. Babies can die of cancer, kidney problems. Heaven is much nicer than down here."
> (Lansdown & Benjamin, 1985, p. 20)

The first of these children did not yet understand the permanence of death, and the second did not understand its universality, but the third seems to have grasped all three.

Some investigators have found that children who understand conservation are also more likely to understand the permanence and universality of death, but not everyone has found such a link (Speece & Brent, 1984). Instead, as is true of so many other milestones of this age range, the child's specific experience seems to make a good deal of difference. Four- and five-year-olds who have had direct experience with the death of a family member are more likely to understand the permanence of death than are those who have had no such personal experience (Stambrook & Parker, 1987).

Adolescents understand the finality of death better than children do. Moreover, in an abstract sense, they understand that death is inevitable. Unrealistic beliefs about personal death, however, appear to contribute to adolescent suicide. Typically, teens who attempt suicide claim to understand that death is final, but many tell researchers and counselors that the purpose of their suicidal behavior was to achieve a temporary escape from a stressful personal problem (Blau, 1996). Further, researchers have found that some teenagers who attempt suicide believe that death is a pleasurable experience for most people who die (Gothelf et al., 1998). Certainly, such distorted beliefs may be

These children being comforted by an adult at a loved one's grave are likely to have far more mature concepts of death than others their age who have not encountered death firsthand.

the result of the powerful emotions that lead teens to attempt suicide, rather than the product of adolescent thinking. However, suicidal adults typically think of death, even when it is desired, as painful and unpleasant. So there may be a developmental difference between suicidal adolescents' and suicidal adults' understanding of death.

Like those of children, adolescents' ideas about death are affected by their personal experiences. Experiencing the death of a family member or friend, especially someone who is near the teenager's own age, tends to shake an adolescent's confidence in her own immortality. In fact, research suggests that the loss of someone close, such as a sibling, may lead an adolescent to critically re-examine her ideas about death—both as a general concept and as something that is inevitable for herself (Batten & Oltjenbruns, 1999).

THE MEANING OF DEATH FOR ADULTS

Adults' ideas about death vary with age. Death seems remote to most young adults. The notion of personal mortality is a more common focus of thought in middle age, and by the later years, the idea of death becomes very personally relevant for most adults.

(Photo: © Richard Lord/PhotoEdit)

After the death of John F. Kennedy, Jr., members of the public left thousands of flowers and gifts in front of his Manhattan apartment building in a spontaneous gesture of grief. Based on analyses of such responses to the deaths of public figures, some developmentalists believe that young adults idealize celebrities who die in early adulthood in order to avoid confronting their own mortality.

Early Adulthood In recent years, research examining young adults' views on death has been guided by a theoretical concept similar to the personal fable. Psychologists point out that young adults have a sense of **unique invulnerability**—a belief that bad things, including death, happen to others but not to themselves. Although young adults are more realistic about personal mortality than adolescents are, researchers find that many believe they possess unique personal characteristics that somehow protect them against death. For example, researchers often ask participants of various ages to use life-expectancy statistics and risk-factor self-ratings to predict the age at which they will die. Such studies usually find that young adults overestimate their own life expectancy (Snyder, 1997). Moreover, young adults are more likely than those who are middle-aged or older to show increased fear of death following open discussions of the process of dying (Abengozar, Bueno, & Vega, 1999).

Here again, actual experience with death makes a difference. For example, nursing students display less fear of death than college students pursuing other careers, and their anxieties about death lessen with each additional year of training (Sharma, Monsen, & Gary, 1997). Moreover, the sudden loss of a loved one appears to shake a young adult's belief in unique invulnerability and, as a result, is often more traumatic for younger than for older adults. In fact, such losses frequently lead to suicidal thoughts in young adults. Young adults who have recently lost a loved one in an accident or to a homicide or suicide are about five times as likely to formulate a suicide plan as young adults who have not had such a loss, although most never follow through with their plans (Prigerson et al., 1999).

Analyses of public reactions to the deaths of relatively young celebrities, such as Princess Diana and John F. Kennedy, Jr., provide additional insight into young adults' ideas about death. As you may have noticed, perceptions of these public figures often change dramatically after their deaths, and they are given heroic status (Bourreille, 1999). Moreover, public interest in the events surrounding their deaths, as evidenced by the frequency of tabloid headline stories devoted to them, continues for many years afterward (Brown, Basil, & Bocarnea, 2003). Psychologists hypothesize that such early deaths challenge young people's beliefs in unique invulnerability and, therefore, provoke defensive reactions that cause them to place those who die young in a special category. In other words, to maintain belief in their own unique invulnerability, young

unique invulnerability the belief that bad things, including death, happen only to others people must come up with reasons why death came early to John F. Kennedy, Jr. but will not happen to them. As a result, they elevate such figures to near-sainthood.

Middle and Late Adulthood In middle and late adulthood, an understanding of death goes well beyond the simple acceptance of finality, inevitability, and universality. A death changes the roles and relationships of everyone else in a family. For example, when an elder dies, everyone else in that particular lineage "moves up" in the generational system. As you learned in Chapter 6, the death of a parent can be particularly unsettling for a middle-aged adult if the adult does not yet consider himself ready to assume the elder role.

An individual's death also affects the roles of people beyond the family, such as younger adults in a business organization, who then take on new and perhaps more significant roles. Retirement serves the same function, as an older adult steps aside for a younger one. But death brings many permanent changes in families and social systems.

At an individual level, the prospect of death may shape one's view of time (Kalish, 1985). In middle age, most people exhibit a shift in their thinking about time, thinking less about "time since birth" and being more aware of "time till death," a transition clearly reflected in the comment of this middle-aged adult:

> Before I was 35, the future just stretched forth. There would be time to do and see and carry out all the plans I had. . . . Now I keep thinking, will I have time enough to finish off some of the things I want to do? (Neugarten, 1970, p. 78)

Such an "awareness of finitude" is not a part of every middle-aged or older adult's view of death (Marshall, 1975). One study of a group of adults aged 72 and older found that only about half thought in terms of "time remaining" (Keith, 1981/1982). Interestingly, those who did think of death in these terms had less fear of death than did those who thought of their lives as "time lived." Other research confirms this: Middle-aged and older adults who continue to be preoccupied with the past are more likely to be fearful and anxious about death (Pollack, 1979/1980).

Death as Loss The most pervasive meaning of death for adults of all ages is loss. Which of the many potential losses is feared or dreaded the most seems to change with age. Young adults are more concerned about loss of opportunity to experience things and about the loss of family relationships; older adults worry more about the loss of time to complete inner work. Such differences are evident in the results of a classic study in which researchers interviewed roughly 400 adults, equally divided into four ethnic groups: African American, Japanese American, Mexican American, and white American (Kalish & Reynolds, 1976). Among many other questions, researchers asked, "If you were told that you had a terminal disease and 6 months to live, how would you want to spend your time until you died?" Think about this question for a moment yourself. Then look at Table 9.2 (page 230), which shows both the ethnic differences and the age differences in responses to this question.

You can see that the only sizable ethnic difference was that Mexican Americans were the most likely to say that they would increase the time they spent with family or other loved ones. Age differences were more substantial. Younger adults were more likely to say that they would seek out new experiences; older adults were considerably more likely to say that they would turn inward—an interesting piece of support for disengagement theory.

FEAR OF DEATH

Surveys show that more than 80% of adults in the United States say that they do not fear death (Public Agenda, 2004b). However, survey questions such as "Do you fear death?" are far too simplistic to capture how people really feel about an issue as momentous as their own death. Thus, psychologists who study people's death-related

CRITICAL THINKING 9

When you think of your own age, do you think of time since birth, time till death, or both? If you think in terms of time till death, can you remember when you switched to this view?

TABLE 9.2	*Responses to Hypothetical Impending Death (percentages)*						
	Ethnic Group				**Age Group**		
	African American	**Japanese American**	**Mexican American**	**White American**	**20–39**	**40–59**	**60+**
Make a marked change in lifestyle (e.g., travel, have new experiences)	16	24	11	17	24	15	9
Center on inner life (e.g., read, contemplate, pray)	26	20	24	12	14	14	37
Focus concern on others; be with loved ones	14	15	38	23	29	25	12
Attempt to complete projects, tie up loose ends	6	8	13	6	11	10	3
No change in lifestyle	31	25	12	36	17	29	31

(Source: Kalish & Reynolds, 1976, p. 205, Item 037.)

MAKE THE CONNECTION

Look back at the discussion of disengagement theory in Chapter 18. Based on this chapter's discussion of the meanings of death for adults, do you think that Cumming and Henry were correct about disengagement being a natural process toward the end of life? Or did they perhaps place it too early in late adulthood and apply it too sweepingly? Explain.

fears have tried a number of ways to elicit more thoughtful responses than are typically generated by surveys.

One such approach is to ask participants to indicate, on a 5-point scale, how disturbed or anxious they feel when thinking about various aspects of death or dying, such as "the shortness of life" or "never thinking or experiencing anything again" or "your lack of control over the process of dying" (Lester, 1990). Another approach asks participants to respond to statements such as "I fear dying a painful death" or "Coffins make me anxious" or "I am worried about what happens to us after we die" (Thorson & Powell, 1992).

Fear of Death across Adulthood   Although you might think that those closest to death would fear it the most, research suggests that middle-aged adults are most fearful of death. For young adults, the sense of unique invulnerability probably prevents intense fears of death. In middle-age, though, belief in one's own immortality begins to break down, resulting in increasing anxiety about the end of life. However, by late life, the inevitability of death has been accepted, and anxieties are focused on how death will actually come about.

The difference between the middle-aged and the aged is especially clear from a study in which researchers interviewed a sample of adults, aged 45 to 74, chosen to represent the population of Los Angeles (Bengtson, Cuellar, & Ragan, 1977). Figure 9.1 shows the percentage of people in each age group who said they were "very afraid" or "somewhat afraid" of death. The fact that the shape of the curve is so remarkably similar for all three ethnic groups makes the results even more persuasive. And although these are cross-sectional results, similar patterns have emerged from cross-sectional comparisons done in the 1960s and the 1980s, which makes the conclusion that much more credible (e.g., Gesser, Wong, & Reker, 1987/1988).

However, older adults do not become less preoccupied with death. On the contrary, the elderly think and talk more about death than do those at any other age. Predictably, these discussions lead to less fear and anxiety about death among older adults (Abengozar et al., 1999). Thus, to an older person, death is highly important, but it is apparently not as frightening as it was at mid-life. Older adults are more likely to fear the period of uncertainty before death than they are to fear death itself (Sullivan, Ormel, Kempen, & Tymstra, 1998). They are anxious about where they may die, who will care for them until they do, and whether they will be able to cope with the pain and loss of control and independence that may be part of the last months or years of life (Marshall & Levy, 1990).

Religious Beliefs Researchers typically find that adults who are religious are less afraid of death than are those who describe themselves as less religious (Ardelt, 2003; Kalish, 1985; Lin, 2003; Thorson & Powell, 1990). In some instances, however, researchers have found that both those who are deeply religious and those who are totally irreligious report less fear of death. Thus, the most fearful may be those who are uncertain about or uncommitted to any religious or philosophical tradition.

Religious beliefs may moderate fears of death because religious people tend to view death as a transition from one form of life to another, from physical life to some kind of immortality. In the United States, roughly 70% of the population believes in some kind of life after death (Klenow & Bolin, 1989/1990). Such a belief is more common among women than among men, and more common among Catholics and Protestants than among Jews, but there is no age difference. Twenty-year-olds are just as likely to report such a belief as are those over 60.

In addition to framing death as a transition rather than an end, religious beliefs provide adults with death stories that help them cope with both their own deaths and those of loved ones (Winter, 1999). For example, Jewish scriptures, the Christian Bible, and the Muslim Quran all contain many stories that convey the idea that death comes when one's purpose in life has been fulfilled. Many such stories also teach that each individual life is part of a larger, multi-generational story. In this larger context, death is portrayed as a necessary part of the transfer of responsibility from one generation to another. This kind of philosophical approach to death leads believers to focus on the contributions to family and community that they have made during their lives rather than on the losses they will experience at their deaths.

Personal Worth Feelings about death are also linked to one's sense of personal worth or competence. Adults who feel that they have achieved the goals they set out to achieve or who believe that they have become the person they wanted to be are less anxious about death than are those who are disappointed in themselves (Neimeyer & Chapman, 1980/1981). Adults who believe that their lives have had some purpose or meaning also appear to be less fearful of death, as do those who have some sense of personal competence (Durlak, 1972; Pollack, 1979/1980).

Such findings suggest the possibility that adults who have successfully completed the major tasks of adult life, who have adequately fulfilled the demands of the roles they occupied, and who have developed inwardly are able to face death with greater equanimity. Adults who have not been able to resolve the various tasks and dilemmas of adulthood face their late adult years more anxiously, even with what Erikson described as despair. Fear of death may be merely one facet of such despair.

PREPARATION FOR DEATH

Preparation for death occurs on a number of levels (see No Easy Answers). At a practical level, regardless of age, most adults agree that it is important to make preparations for death (Steinhauser et al., 2001). According to most people, in addition to purchasing life insurance and making a will, such preparations should include issuing directives regarding end-of-life care, often called a *living will*. Individuals can use living wills to

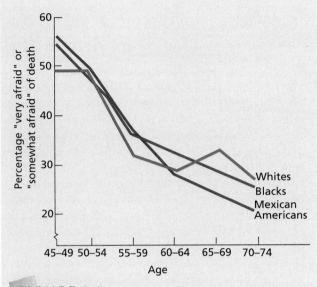

FIGURE 9.1

The remarkable similarity in the pattern of results for these three ethnic groups lends support to the generalization that older adults are less afraid of death than are the middle-aged. (Source: Bengtson et al., 1977, Figure 1, p. 80.)

Saying Goodbye

The Kaliai, a small Melanesian society in Papua New Guinea, believe that all deaths are caused by a person or spirit whom the dying person has offended in some way (Counts, 1976/1977). Any person who feels that he is near death moves from his house into a temporary shelter, where he attempts to appease whichever person or spirit he thinks he may have offended. He also attempts to thwart death through the use of various medicines and cures. When death becomes imminent, family members and friends return items borrowed from the dying person and pay debts they owe him. Likewise, the dying person returns borrowed items and repays debts owed to family and friends. The Kaliai believe that this process of bringing relationships into balance prepares the dying person for an afterlife in which he will become a powerful superhuman being.

But how do you say goodbye to a dying loved one, or how does a dying person say goodbye to loved ones, in a culture where discussions of death are largely taboo? Research suggests that in the United States, even physicians who routinely treat terminally ill patients are reluctant to state directly that a patient is going to die (Lutfey & Maynard, 1998). Moreover, the sufferer and her loved ones may avoid discussions of death because admitting that death is approaching may be seen as rejection of the possibility of recovery. Family members may believe that discussing death will undermine the terminally ill patient's optimism and ability to fight the disease. Likewise, those who are dying may not want to make their loved ones feel bad. Still, most people in these situations feel that they must balance the need for closure against fears of fostering pessimism. Consequently, many terminally ill adults and their families create indirect methods of saying farewell.

A study in Australia gives a glimpse of the variety of such goodbyes devised by the dying (Kellehear & Lewin, 1988/1989). Researchers interviewed 90 terminally ill cancer patients, all of whom expected to die within a year. Most had known of their cancer diagnosis for at least a year prior to the interview but had only recently been given a short-term prognosis. As part of the interview, these 90 people were asked if they had already said farewell to anyone, and to describe any plans they had for future farewells. To whom did they want to say goodbye, and how would they say it?

About a fifth of these people planned no farewells. Another three-fifths thought it was important to say goodbye, but wanted to put it off until very near the end so as to distress family and friends as little as possible. They hoped that there would then be time for a few final words with spouses, children, and close friends. The remaining fifth began their farewells much earlier and used many different avenues. In a particularly touching farewell gesture, one woman who had two grown daughters but no grandchildren knitted a set of baby clothes for each daughter, for the grandchildren she would never see.

Kellehear and Lewin make the important point that such farewells are a kind of gift. They signal that the dying person feels that someone is worthy of a last goodbye. Such farewells may also represent a balancing of the relationship slate just as important as the balancing of material possessions is among the Kaliai.

Farewells also may allow the dying person to disengage more readily when death comes closer, and to warn others that death is indeed approaching. Hearing someone say farewell may thus help the living to begin a kind of anticipatory grieving, and in this way prepare better for the loss.

make clear to health care professionals and to their families that they either do or do not wish to have their lives prolonged with feeding tubes and other devices. Moreover, most people agree that advance funeral planning can help bereaved family members deal with the many decisions they must make in the hours and days following the death of a loved one. However, researchers have found that older adults are far more likely than younger adults to have actually made such preparations (Bravo, Dubois, & Paquet, 2003).

At a somewhat deeper level, adults may prepare for death through some process of reminiscence. Deeper still, there may be unconscious changes that occur in the years just before death, which might be thought of as a type of preparation. You read about the physical and mental changes associated with terminal drop in Chapter 7. Research has pointed to the possibility that there may be terminal psychological changes as well.

For example, in a still influential study, researchers studied a group of older adults longitudinally, interviewing and testing each participant regularly over a period of 3 years (Lieberman, 1965; Lieberman & Coplan, 1970). After the testing, investigators kept track of the participants and noted when they died. They were able to identify one group of

40 participants who had all died within 1 year of the end of the interviewing and to compare them with another group of 40, matched to the first group by age, sex, and marital status, who had survived at least 3 years after the end of the testing. By comparing the psychological test scores obtained by those in these two groups during the course of the 3 years of testing, researchers could detect changes that occurred near death.

The study's results revealed that those nearer death not only showed terminal drop on tests of memory and learning, but also became less emotional, introspective, and aggressive or assertive and more conventional, docile, dependent, and warm. In those near death, all these characteristics increased over the 3 years of interviewing, a pattern that did not occur among those of the same age who were further from death. Thus, conventional, docile, dependent, and nonintrospective adults did not die sooner; rather, these qualities became accentuated in those who were close to death.

This is only a single study. As always in such cases, it's important to be careful about drawing sweeping conclusions from limited evidence. But the results are intriguing and suggestive. They paint a picture of a kind of psychological preparation for death—conscious or unconscious—in which an individual "gives up the fight," becoming less active physically and psychologically. Thus, near death, individuals do not necessarily become less involved with other people, but they do seem to show some kind of disengagement.

Before going on . . .

■ What are the characteristics of children's and adolescents' ideas about death?

■ How do young, middle-aged, and older adults think about death?

■ What factors are related to fear of death in adults?

■ How do adults prepare for death?

The Process of Dying

The late Elisabeth Kübler-Ross (1926–2004) was a Swiss-American psychiatrist who studied the experiences of the dying and their loved ones. In the 1960s, Kübler-Ross formulated a model that asserted that those who are dying go through a series of psychological stages. These stages of dying, which were formulated on the basis of interviews with approximately 200 adults who were dying of cancer, continue to be highly influential, although Kübler-Ross's model has many critics. In addition, research suggests that individual differences affect the process of dying in important ways.

KÜBLER-ROSS'S STAGES OF DYING

In Kübler-Ross's early writings, she proposed that those who know they are dying move through a series of steps, or stages, arriving finally at the stage she called *acceptance* (see Table 9.3, page 234). Kübler-Ross's ideas and her terminology are still widely used. In fact, surveys of death education programs suggest that Kübler-Ross's model is the only systematic approach to the dying process to which health professionals-in-training are exposed (Downe-Wamboldt & Tamlyn, 1997). Thus, you should at least be familiar with the stages she proposed.

Kübler-Ross's model predicts that most people who are confronted with a terminal diagnosis react with some variant of "Not me!" "It must be a mistake," "I'll get another opinion," or "I don't feel sick." All of these are forms of *denial*, a psychological defense that may be highly useful in the early hours and days after such a diagnosis. Denial of this kind may be helpful in insulating a person's emotions from the trauma of hearing such news. Keeping emotions in check in

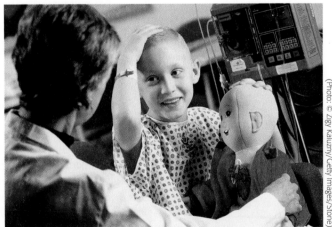

(Photo: © Zigy Kaluzny/Getty Images/Stone)

Children use some of the same defenses as adults to deal with impending death. Young cancer patients may deny or bargain—for instance, "If I take my medicine I'll be able to go back to school in the fall."

TABLE 9.3	*Stages of Dying Proposed by Kübler-Ross*
Denial	People's first reaction to news of a terminal diagnosis is disbelief.
Anger	Once the diagnosis is accepted as real, individuals become angry.
Bargaining	Anger and stress are managed by thinking of the situation in terms of exchanges (e.g., If I take my medicine, I will live longer; if I pray hard enough, God will heal me).
Depression	Feelings of despair follow when the disease advances despite the individual's compliance with medical and other advice.
Acceptance	Grieving for the losses associated with one's death results in acceptance.

this way may help an individual formulate a rational plan of action based on "what if it's true?" Having a plan of action may help moderate the effects of acknowledging the reality of the diagnosis. Kübler-Ross thought that these extreme forms of denial would fade within a few days, to be replaced by *anger.*

The model further suggests that anger among the dying expresses itself in thoughts like "It's not fair!" but a dying person may also express anger toward God, the doctor who made the diagnosis, nurses, or family members. The anger seems to be a response not only to the diagnosis itself but also to the sense of loss of control and helplessness that many patients feel in impersonal medical settings.

Bargaining follows anger in the Kübler-Ross model. This is a form of defense in which the patient tries to make "deals" with doctors, nurses, family, or God: "If I do everything you tell me, then I'll live till spring." Kübler-Ross gave a particularly compelling example of this defense reaction: A patient with terminal cancer wanted to live long enough to attend the wedding of her eldest son. The hospital staff, to help her try to reach this goal, taught her self-hypnosis to deal with her pain, and she was able to attend the wedding. Kübler-Ross reported, "I will never forget the moment when she returned to the hospital. She looked tired and somewhat exhausted and—before I could say hello—said, 'Now don't forget, I have another son!'" (1969, p. 83).

Bargaining may be successful as a defense for a while, but the model predicts that, eventually, bargaining breaks down in the face of signs of declining health. At this point, Kübler-Ross's theory predicts, the patient enters the stage of *depression.* According to Kübler-Ross, depression, or despair, is a necessary preparation for the final stage of *acceptance.* In order to reach acceptance, the dying person must grieve for all that will be lost with death.

CRITICISMS AND ALTERNATIVE VIEWS

Kübler-Ross's model has provided a common language for those who work with dying patients, and her highly compassionate descriptions have, without doubt, sensitized health care workers and families to the complexities of the process of dying. At some moments, what the patient needs is cheering up; at other moments, he simply needs someone to listen to him. There are times to hold his hand quietly and times to provide encouragement or hope. Many new programs for terminally ill patients are clearly outgrowths of this greater sensitivity to the dying process.

These are all worthwhile changes. But Kübler-Ross's basic thesis—that the dying process necessarily involves these specific five stages, in this specific order—has been widely criticized, for several good reasons.

Methodological Problems   Kübler-Ross's hypothesized sequence was initially based on clinical observation of 200 patients, and she did not provide information about how frequently she talked to them or over how long a period she continued to assess them. She also did not report the ages of the patients she studied, although it is clear that many were middle-aged or young adults, for whom a terminal illness was obviously "off time." Nearly all were apparently cancer patients. Would the same processes be evident in those dying of other diseases, for which it is much less common to have a specific diagnosis or a short-term prognosis? In other words, Kübler-Ross's observations might be correct, but only for a small subset of dying individuals.

Cultural Specificity A related question has to do with whether reactions to dying are culture-specific or universal. Kübler-Ross wrote as if the five stages of dying were universal human processes. However, cross-cultural studies suggest that cultures vary considerably in what they believe to be a "good death" (Westerhof, Katzko, Dittman-Kohli, & Hayslip, 2001). For individuals in Western societies, such as the United States, maintenance of individual autonomy over the dying process is of paramount importance. The idea that a dying person should have the right to take his or her own life is more widely accepted in individualistic than in collectivist cultures (Kemmelmeier, Wieczorkowska, Erb, & Burnstein, 2002). Thus, certain aspects of Kubler-Ross's theory, such as the concepts associated with the bargaining stage, may be less important to people in collectivist cultures than they were to the people who participated in her initial studies.

Similarly, in some Native American cultures, death is to be faced and accepted with composure. Because it is part of nature's cycle, it is not to be feared or fought (DeSpelder & Strickland, 1983). And, in Mexican culture, death is seen as a mirror of the person's life. Thus, your way of dying tells much about what kind of person you have been. Furthermore, in Mexican culture, death is discussed frequently, even celebrated in a national feast day, the Day of the Dead (DeSpelder & Strickland, 1983). Would it be reasonable to expect denial, anger, bargaining, and so on, in the context of such cultural expectations?

Finally, you have already read about the influence of religious beliefs on adults' ideas about death. The belief that death is a transition to immortality implies that one should face death with a sense of joy. Exhibitions of denial, anger, and bargaining may seem to indicate a lack of faith and, as a result, may be actively avoided by dying people who are religious. Thus, Kübler-Ross's model may fail to predict reactions to impending death by the religious.

The Stage Concept The most potent criticism of Kübler-Ross's model, however, centers on the issue of stages. Many clinicians and researchers who have attempted to study the process systematically have found that not all dying patients exhibit these five emotions, let alone in a specific order. Of the five, only depression seems to be common among Western patients. Further, neither Kübler-Ross's acceptance nor Cumming and Henry's disengagement (discussed in Chapter 8) appears to be a common end point of the dying process (Baugher, Burger, Smith, & Wallston, 1989/1990). Some patients display acceptance; others remain as active and engaged as possible right up to the end. Edwin Shneidman (1980, 1983), a major theorist and clinician in the field of **thanatology** (the scientific study of death and dying), puts it this way:

> I reject the notion that human beings, as they die, are somehow marched in lock step through a series of stages of the dying process. On the contrary, in working with dying persons, I see a wide [array] of human feelings and emotions, of various human needs, and a broad selection of psychological defenses and maneuvers—a few of these in some people, dozens in others—experienced in an impressive variety of ways. (1980, p. 110)

Instead of stages, Shneidman suggests that the dying process has many "themes" that can appear, disappear, and reappear in any one patient in the process of dealing with death. These themes include terror, pervasive uncertainty, fantasies of being rescued, incredulity, feelings of unfairness, a concern with reputation after death, and fear of pain.

Another alternative to Kübler-Ross's model is a "task-based" approach suggested by Charles Corr (1991/1992). In his view, coping with dying is like coping with any

thanatology the scientific study of death and dying

other problem or dilemma: You need to take care of certain specific tasks. He suggests four such tasks for the dying person:

■ Satisfying bodily needs and minimizing physical stress
■ Maximizing psychological security, autonomy, and richness of life
■ Sustaining and enhancing significant interpersonal attachments
■ Identifying, developing, or reaffirming sources of spiritual energy, and thereby fostering hope

Corr does not deny the importance of the various emotional themes described by Shneidman. Rather, he argues that for health professionals who deal with dying individuals, it is more helpful to think in terms of the patient's tasks, because the dying person may need help in performing some or all of them.

Whichever model one uses, what is clear is that there are no common patterns that typify most or all reactions to impending death. Common themes exist, but they are blended together in quite different patterns by each person who faces this last task.

RESPONSES TO IMPENDING DEATH

Individual variations in responding to imminent death have themselves been the subject of a good deal of research interest in the past few decades. In one study involving 26 terminally ill men, researchers found that many of the men believed that they could avoid entering into the process of actively dying by continuing to engage in their favorite hobbies (Vig & Pearlman, 2003). Such findings raise questions about whether attitudes and behavioral choices can influence the course of a terminal disease.

The most influential research along these lines has been the work of Steven Greer and his colleagues (Greer, 1991; Greer, Morris, & Pettingale, 1979; Pettingale, Morris, Greer, & Haybittle, 1985). They followed a group of 62 women diagnosed in the 1970s with early stages of breast cancer. Three months after the original diagnosis, each woman was interviewed at some length and her reaction to the diagnosis and to her treatment was classed in one of five groups:

■ *Denial (positive avoidance).* Person rejects evidence about diagnosis; insists that surgery was just precautionary.
■ *Fighting spirit.* Person maintains an optimistic attitude and searches for more information about the disease. These patients often see their disease as a challenge and plan to fight it with every method available.
■ *Stoic acceptance (fatalism).* Person acknowledges the diagnosis but makes no effort to seek any further information, or person ignores the diagnosis and carries on normal life as much as possible.
■ *Helplessness/hopelessness.* Person acts overwhelmed by diagnosis; sees herself as dying or gravely ill and as devoid of hope.
■ *Anxious preoccupation.* Women in this category had originally been included in the helplessness group, but they were separated out later. The category includes those whose response to the diagnosis is strong and persistent anxiety. If they seek information, they interpret it pessimistically; they monitor their body sensations carefully, interpreting each ache or pain as a possible recurrence.

Greer then checked on the survival rates of these five groups after 5, 10, and 15 years. Table 9.4 shows the 15-year survival rates. Only 35% of those whose initial reaction had been either denial or fighting spirit had died of cancer 15 years later, compared with 76% of those whose initial reaction had been stoic acceptance, anxious preoccupation, or helplessness/hopelessness. Because those in the five groups did not differ initially in the stage of their disease or in their treatment, these results support the hypothesis that psychological responses contribute to disease progress—just as coping strategies more generally affect the likelihood of disease in the first place.

TABLE 9.4	15-Year Outcomes among Women Cancer Patients			
	Outcome 15 Years Later			
Psychological Attitude 3 Months after Surgery	Alive and Well	Died from Cancer	Died from Other Causes	Total
Denial	5	5	0	10
Fighting spirit	4	2	4	10
Stoic acceptance	6	24	3	33
Anxious preoccupation	0	3	0	3
Helplessness/hopelessness	1	5	0	6
Total	16	39	7	62

(Source: Greer, 1991, from Table 1, p. 45.)

Similar results have emerged from studies of patients with melanoma (a form of skin cancer), as well as other cancers, and from several studies of AIDS patients (Juan et al., 2003; Reed, Kemeny, Taylor, Wang, & Visscher, 1994; Solano et al., 1993; Temoshok, 1987). And at least one study of coronary bypass patients showed that men who had a more optimistic attitude before the surgery recovered more quickly in the 6 months after surgery and returned more fully to their presurgery pattern of life (Scheier et al., 1989). In general, individuals who report less hostility, who express more stoic acceptance and more helplessness, and who fail to express negative feelings die sooner (O'Leary, 1990). Those who struggle the most, who fight the hardest, who express their anger and hostility openly, and who also find some sources of joy in their lives live longer. In some ways, the data suggest that "good patients"—those who are obedient and who do not question or fight with their doctors or make life difficult for those around them—are in fact likely to die sooner. Difficult patients, who question and challenge those around them, last longer.

Furthermore, a few studies have linked these psychological differences to immune system functioning. A particular subset of immune cells called NK cells, thought to form an important defense against cancer, have been found in lower numbers among patients who report less distress and who seem better adjusted to their illness (O'Leary, 1990). And one study of AIDS patients showed that T-cell counts declined more rapidly among those who responded to their disease with repression (similar to the stoic acceptance and helplessness groups in the Greer study), while those who showed a fighting spirit had slower loss of T cells (Solano et al., 1993).

Despite the consistency of these results, two important cautions are in order before you leap to the conclusion that a fighting spirit is the optimum response to any disease. First, some careful studies find no link between depression, stoic acceptance, or helplessness and more rapid death from cancer (e.g., Cassileth, Walsh, & Lusk, 1988; Richardson, Zarnegar, Bisno, & Levine, 1990). Second, it is not clear that the same psychological response is necessarily appropriate for every disease. Consider heart disease, for example. There is a certain irony in the fact that many of the responses to cancer that appear to be optimum could be considered as reflections of a type A personality. Because having a type A personality constitutes a risk factor for heart disease, a "fighting spirit" response to a diagnosis of advanced heart disease might not be the most desirable. The growing body of research on responses to diseases does confirm, though, that there are connections between psychological defenses or ways of coping and physical functioning, even in the last stages of life.

Another important ingredient in an individual's response to imminent death is the amount of social support he has. Those with positive and supportive relationships describe lower levels of pain and less depression during their final months of illness (Carey, 1974; Hinton, 1975). Such well-supported patients also live longer. For example, both African American and white American heart attack patients who live alone are more likely to have a second heart attack than are those who live with someone else. Similarly, those with significant levels of atherosclerosis live longer if they have a confidant than if they do not (Case, Moss, Case, McDermott, & Eberly, 1992; Williams, 1992).

This link between social support and length of survival has also been found in experimental studies in which patients with equivalent diagnoses and equivalent medical care have been randomly assigned either to an experimental group in which they participate in regular support group sessions or to a control group in which they have no such support system. In one study of a group of 86 women with metastatic breast cancer (that is, cancer that had spread beyond the original site), researchers found that the average length of survival was 36.6 months for those who had access to the support group compared with 18.9 months for those in the control group (Spiegel, Bloom, Kraemer, & Gottheil, 1989). Thus, just as social support helps to buffer children and adults from some of the negative effects of many kinds of nonlethal stress, so it seems to perform a similar function for those facing death.

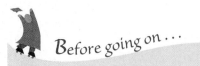

Before going on . . .

- Describe Kübler-Ross's stages of dying.

- What are some other views of the process of dying?

- How do people vary in the ways they adapt to impending death?

The Experience of Grieving

In virtually every culture, the immediate response to a death is some kind of funeral ritual. However, a death ritual is only the first step in the process of **grieving**—the emotional response to a death—which may take months or years to complete.

PSYCHOSOCIAL FUNCTIONS OF DEATH RITUALS

Funerals, wakes, and other death rituals help family members and friends manage their grief by giving them a specific set of roles to play. Like all roles, these include both expected behaviors and prohibited or discouraged behaviors. The content of these roles differs markedly from one culture to the next, but their clarity in most cases gives a shape to the days or weeks immediately following the death of a loved person. In American culture, the rituals prescribe what one should wear, who should be called, who should be fed, what demeanor one should show, and far more. Depending on one's ethnic or religious background, one may gather family and friends for a wake or to "sit shiva," a traditional Jewish 7-day period of mourning during which family members stay in the same home and formally mourn a deceased loved one. One may be expected to respond stoically or to wail and tear one's hair. Friends and acquaintances, too, have guiding rules, at least for those first few days. They may bring food, write letters of condolence, offer help, and attend wakes and funerals.

Death rituals also bring family members together as no other occasion does (with the possible exception of weddings). Frequently, cousins and other distant relatives see one another for the first time in many years at funerals. Such occasions typically inspire shared reminiscences and renew family relationships that have been inactive for a long time. In this way, death rituals can strengthen family ties, clarify the new lines of influence or authority within a family, and "pass the torch" in some way to the next generation. Likewise, funerals help establish deaths as shared milestones for family members—"that was before Grandpa died" or "the last time I saw her was at Grandpa's funeral." A death can become an important organizer of experience that separates the past from the present. Dividing time in this way seems to help survivors cope with grief (Katz & Bartone, 1998).

CRITICAL THINKING

Do the various funerals or death rituals you have participated in seem to have served the purposes described in the text?

grieving the emotional response to a death

Death rituals are also designed to help the survivors understand the meaning of death itself, in part by emphasizing the meaning of the life of the person who has died. It is not accidental that most death rituals include testimonials, biographies, and witnessing. By telling the story of a person's life and describing that life's value and meaning, others can more readily accept the person's death.

Finally, death rituals may give some transcendent meaning to death itself by placing it in a philosophical or religious context (Pangt & Lam, 2002). In this way, they provide comfort to the bereaved by offering answers to that inevitable question "Why?"

THE PROCESS OF GRIEVING

The ritual of a funeral, in whatever form it occurs, can provide structure and comfort in the days immediately following a death. But what happens when that structure is gone? How do people handle the sense of loss? Answering that question requires a look at a number of factors associated with grief.

Each culture has its own death rituals. The customarily quiet graveside service in the United States would seem strange to people in many other societies.

Age of the Bereaved Children express feelings of grief very much the same way teens and adults do. Like adults, children demonstrate grief through sad facial expressions, crying, loss of appetite, and age-appropriate displays of anger such as temper tantrums (Oatley & Jenkins, 1996). Funerals seem to serve the same adaptive function for children as for adults, and most children resolve their feelings of grief within the first year after the loss. In addition, knowing that a loved one or even a pet is ill and in danger of death helps children cope with the loss in advance, just as it does for those who are older (Jarolmen, 1998).

Although the behavioral aspects of adolescents' grief responses vary little from those of adults, teens may be more likely than children or adults to experience prolonged grief. One study found that more than 20% of a group of high school students who had a friend killed in an accident continued to experience intense feelings of grief 9 months after the death (Dyregrov, Gjestad, Bie Wikander, & Vigerust, 1999). Adolescents may also grieve longer than children or adults for lost siblings; in some cases, teens continue to have problems with grief-related behaviors, such as intrusive thoughts about the deceased, for as long as 2 years after the death of a sibling (Lohan & Murphy, 2001/2002). Other research suggests that adolescent girls whose mothers have died run a particularly high risk of developing long-term, grief-related problems (Lenhardt & McCourt, 2000). Teenagers may also be more likely than adults to experience grief responses to the deaths of celebrities or to idealize peers' suicides (see Development in the Information Age).

Adolescents' grief responses are probably related to their general cognitive characteristics. You should remember from Chapters 11 and 12 that adolescents often judge the real world by idealized images. Consequently, a teenager may become caught up in fantasizing about how the world would be different if a friend or loved one had not died. In addition, prolonged grieving among adolescents may be rooted in their tendency to engage in "what if" thinking. This kind of thinking may lead teens to believe that they could have prevented the death and, thus, cause them to develop irrational guilt feelings (Cunningham, 1996).

Mode of Death How an individual dies contributes to the grief process of those who are in mourning. For example, widows who have cared for spouses during a period

Development in the Information Age

"Copycat" Suicides

In Shakespeare's *Romeo and Juliet,* the teenaged hero takes his own life because he believes that his beloved has already done so. When Juliet revives and discovers Romeo's body, she commits suicide as well. Many believe that Shakespeare's characterization is a realistic portrayal of an emotionally distressed adolescent's typical reaction to suicide—imitation, or a "copycat" suicide. Based on this belief, many observers have raised concerns about the potential effects of emotion-provoking suicide stories in both fiction and the news media (Samaritans, 1998).

In general, research suggests that concerns about fictional suicides are unfounded. For example, a few years ago, the British public responded with outrage to a TV program that depicted a 15-year-old girl's attempted suicide with a drug overdose. These concerns were based on the fear that teenaged viewers who were experiencing emotional problems might be likely to imitate the character's behavior. Yet surveys that followed the airing of the program found no increase in frequency of suicide attempts among teenagers. Moreover, few of those who did attempt suicide had seen the program (Simkin, Hawton, Whitehead, Fagg, & Eagle, 1995). Follow-up studies of other suicide-related programs on television have produced similar findings.

News accounts of suicides are a different matter. However, news stories about suicides influence adults' behav-

ior more often than that of teens. Research suggests that, when the news media present sensational coverage of a particular mode of suicide, the number of people who attempt and complete suicides using that method increases. The number of individuals who attempted suicide by setting themselves ablaze, for instance, increased dramatically in Great Britain after several news programs carried reports, including graphic film footage, of a single self-immolation suicide (Ashton & Donnan, 1981). Likewise, suicide attempts involving throwing oneself in front of a subway train became so frequent in Vienna after sensational news reports of such incidents that members of the press agreed among themselves to no longer report them (Sonneck, Etzersdorfer, & Nagel-Kuess, 1992).

Despite inconsistencies in research examining the phenomenon of copycat suicide, mental health professionals believe that fictional or journalistic accounts of suicide may influence behavior in individual cases. They suggest that a 15-year-old girl who has already been thinking about taking a drug overdose may become more likely to do so after viewing a television program in which a character carries out a similar suicide plan. Similarly, an individual who wants to add drama to a planned suicide attempt may be inspired by news reports of an unusual method of suicide. Thus, mental health professionals warn that news and entertainment media should avoid romanticizing and sensationalizing suicide (Samaritans, 1998).

Some September 11 survivors have become involved in political activism geared toward preventing future terrorist attacks.

of illness prior to death are less likely to become depressed after the death than those whose spouses die suddenly (Carnelley, Wortman, & Kessler, 1999). Grief-related depression seems to emerge during the spouse's illness rather than after the death. The spouse's death is thought of as an escape from suffering for the one who dies and a release from grieving for the caregiver. Similarly, a death that has intrinsic meaning, such as that of a young soldier who dies defending his country, is not necessarily easier to cope with but does provide the bereaved with a sense that the death has not been without purpose (Malkinson & Bar-Tur, 1999). Consequently, mourners have a built-in cognitive coping device—a rational explanation for the death—that allows them to grieve but also protects them from long-term depression.

However, sudden and violent deaths evoke more intense grief responses (Murphy, Johnson, & Lohan, 2003). One study found that 36% of widows and widowers whose spouses had died in accidents or by suicide were suffering from post-traumatic stress symptoms (e.g., nightmares) 2 months after the death, compared to only 10% of widows and widowers whose spouses had died of natural causes (Zisook, Chentsova-Dutton, & Shuchter, 1998). Moreover, almost all of those whose spouses had died unnaturally and who had PTSD symptoms were also depressed.

Death in the context of a natural disaster is also associated with prolonged grieving and development of symptoms of PTSD (Kilic & Ulusoy, 2003). Such events bring to mind the inescapable reality of the fragility of human life. Public memorial services in which the common experiences of survivors are recognized and the differences between controllable and noncontrollable aspects of life are emphasized can help survivors cope with this kind of grief.

Public memorials can also be helpful to survivors whose loved ones have died as a result of what might be called "politically motivated" mass murders—such as the 1995 bombing of a federal government office building in Oklahoma City and the terrorist attacks of September 11, 2001 (Shapiro, 2002). Moreover, political activism on the part of survivors aimed at preventing future events of this kind may be helpful to policymakers and also may serve as a coping mechanism for those who engage in it (Shapiro, 2002).

Finally, suicide is associated with a unique pattern of responses among survivors (Bailley, Kral, & Dunham, 1999). In general, family and close friends of someone who commits suicide experience feelings of rejection and anger. Moreover, their grief over the loss of the loved one is complicated by the feeling that they could or should have done something to prevent the suicide. They are less likely to discuss the loss with other family members or with friends because of their sense that a suicide in the family is a source of shame. For these reasons, suicide survivors may be more likely than others who have lost loved ones to experience long-term negative effects.

WIDOWHOOD

The relationship between the deceased and those who are in mourning affects the grieving process. For example, bereaved parents often report that their health is poorer than before a child's death, and many continue to experience intense feelings of sadness for several years (Arbuckle & De Vries, 1995; Malkinson & Bar-Tur, 1999) (see The Real World, page 534). Similarly, children who lose a sibling sometimes worry that thoughts produced by sibling rivalry, such as wishing a brother or sister would die, caused the death (Crehan, 2004). As a general rule, though, the most difficult death to recover from is that of a spouse (Kaslow, 2004).

Widowhood and Physical Health The experience of widowhood appears to have both immediate and longer-term effects on the immune system (Beem et al., 1999; Gallagher-Thompson, Futterman, Farberow, Thompson, & Peterson, 1993; Irwin & Pike, 1993). (The term *widowhood* applies to both men and women; *widow* refers to women and *widower* to men.) In one Norwegian study, researchers measured immune functioning in widows twice, shortly after their husbands' deaths and 1 year later (Lindstrom, 1997). Investigators found that the widows' immune systems were suppressed somewhat immediately after the death but in most cases had returned to normal a year later.

Similarly, a study comparing widows to married women in the Netherlands found that widows' immune responses continued to differ from those of married participants 7 months after the spouses' deaths, even though psychological differences (such as feelings of sadness) between the two groups had disappeared (Beem et al., 1999). Thus, the bereaved may continue to suffer at a biochemical level even after obvious signs of grieving have subsided. Moreover, the association between death of a spouse and ensuing illness in the surviving partner may be the result of the effects of grief on the body's defenses against disease agents such as viruses and bacteria.

Widowhood and Mental Health In the year following bereavement, the incidence of depression among widows and widowers rises substantially, though rates of death and disease rise only slightly (Reich, Zautra, & Guarnaccia, 1989; Stroebe & Stroebe, 1993). In one important longitudinal study, researchers repeatedly interviewed

When an Infant Dies

Many parents grieving for a lost infant do not receive adequate support from either their social networks or health professionals (Vaeisaenen, 1998). It is important for those who are in a position to support grieving parents to understand that the grief that follows the death of an infant is no less intense than any other kind of bereavement. In fact, it may be more complex.

When an older child dies, parents have a relationship history and an intimate knowledge of the child's personality on which to build reminiscences. Such cognitive devices help them reorganize their attachment to the lost child so that they are able to release the child psychologically. But with an infant, there is little or no relationship history to draw on. The parents, of course, feel deep emotions of attachment, but the cognitive elements that help parents cope with the loss of a child are absent. For these reasons, bereaved parents of a dead infant often have a greater need for support from family, friends, and health professionals than even they themselves realize (Vaeisaenen, 1998).

Well-intentioned friends or family may pressure the couple to cope with their loss by simply replacing the infant with another one. However, research suggests that starting another pregnancy soon after the loss of an infant doesn't necessarily end either a mother's or a father's grief, although it does tend to protect both against long-term negative effects such as depression (Franche & Bulow, 1999). Moreover, parents may fear that a subsequent child will also die in infancy and may try to avoid becoming emotionally attached to a newborn (Wong, 1993). This could have adverse effects on the whole family.

Health professionals have compiled a few guidelines that can be useful to family members or friends in supporting parents who have lost an infant (Wong, 1993):

- Don't try to force bereaved parents to talk about their grief or the infant if they don't want to.
- Always refer to the deceased infant by name.
- Express your own feelings of loss for the infant, if they are sincere.
- Follow the parents' lead in engaging in reminiscences about the baby's looks or personality.
- Discourage the parents from resorting to drugs or alcohol to manage grief.
- Assure grieving parents that their responses are normal and that it will take time to resolve the emotions associated with losing an infant.
- Don't pressure the parents to "replace" the baby with another one.
- Don't offer rationalizations (e.g., "Your baby's an angel now") that may offend the parents.
- Do offer support for the parents' own rationalizations.
- Be aware that the infant's siblings, even those who are very young, are likely to experience some degree of grief.

a sample of 3,000 adults, all age 55 or older at the beginning of the study (Norris & Murrell, 1990). Forty-eight of these adults were widowed during the $2\frac{1}{2}$ years of the study, which allowed investigators to look at depression and health status before and immediately after bereavement. They found no differences in physical health between widowed and nonwidowed participants, but they did note a rise in depression among the widowed immediately following the loss and then a decline within a year after bereavement, a set of results illustrated in Figure 9.2.

However, other researchers have found that older adults whose spouses have died differ in mental health for several years following the death from peers whose spouses are still alive (Bennett, 1997). So it appears that declines in physical and mental health follow bereavement fairly consistently, but how long such effects last may be highly variable. Several factors contribute to this variability.

One such factor is mental health history. Older adults who enter widowhood with a history of depression are *more* likely to experience depression after the death of their spouse (Zisook, Paulus, Shuchter, & Judd 1997). Lack of social support, both actual and perceived, also contributes to variability in depression among widows and widowers (Reed, 1998; Tomita et al., 1997). Moreover, the quality of the relationship of the widow or widower with the deceased spouse is related to depressive symptoms. Perhaps surprisingly, relationships characterized by emotional distance and conflict are *more* likely to lead to depression than those that were warm (van Doorn, Kasl, Beery, Jacobs, & Prigerson, 1998).

Economic changes accompany the loss of a spouse and add to the overall stress involved in the transition to widowhood. Women typically suffer greater economic losses after the death of a spouse than men do, usually because they lose their husbands' income or pension (Zick & Holden, 2000). However, the household incomes of both widows and widowers are lower than those of married elders (Federal Interagency Forum on Aging-Related Statistics, [FIFARS], 2000). Thus, the degree to which an individual's economic status changes as a result of a spouse's death is probably another factor that contributes to individual differences in the long-term effects of bereavement.

Pathological Grief Some psychologists argue that **pathological grief,** depression-like symptoms following death of a loved one, should be thought of as a separate disorder from depression (Stroebe et al., 2000). They suggest that individuals who continue to experience grief symptoms such as loss of appetite more than 2 months following loss of a loved one may be developing pathological grief.

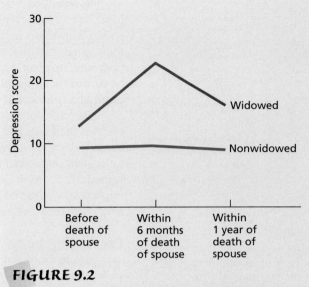

FIGURE 9.2

Those about to be widowed are more depressed than their age-mates who are not, and they also show a distinct increase in depression in the months immediately after the spouse's death. (Source: Norris & Murrell, 1990, from Table 1, p. 432.)

Diagnosis and treatment of pathological grief may be important for preventing problems in both mental and physical health among widows and widowers. Researchers have found that survivors whose grief symptoms continue for 6 months or longer are more likely to suffer long-term depression, as well as physical ailments such as cancer and heart disease (Prigerson et al., 1997). Moreover, they continue to show important differences in physical and mental functioning for up to 2 years after their spouse's death.

However, it's important to keep in mind that many aspects of grief are culturally determined. Beliefs about how long mourning should last and how the bereaved should behave vary widely from one culture to another (Braun & Nichols, 1997; Rubin & Schechter, 1997). For example, Orthodox Jewish men traditionally do not shave or trim their beards for 30 days after the death of a family member. Furthermore, mourning traditions among Orthodox Jews require abstaining from entertainment such as attending the theater or seeing movies for an entire year after the death of someone close (Bial, 1971).

Since inattention to grooming and lack of interest in social activities are also sometimes signs of depression, observers who are unfamiliar with Orthodox Jewish mourning practices might conclude that those who follow them are exhibiting pathological rather than normal grieving. Thus, mental health professionals are advised to learn about an individual's cultural beliefs before forming conclusions about grief-related behavior. Likewise, friends, neighbors, and co-workers of someone who is mourning the death of a spouse or other close family member should be careful to interpret any grief-related behaviors within the context of the person's cultural background.

Sex Differences The death of a spouse appears to be a more negative experience for men than for women, despite the fact that there seem to be no sex differences in the actual grieving process following such a loss (Quigley & Schatz, 1999). The risk of death from either natural causes or suicide in the months immediately after widowhood is significantly greater among men than among women (Stroebe & Stroebe, 1993). Depression and suicidal thoughts are also more common in widowers than in widows (Byrne & Raphael, 1999; Chen et al., 1999). Further, men seem to have a more difficult time than women do in returning to the levels of emotional functioning they exhibited before the spouse's death (van Grootheest, Beekman, van Groenou, & Deeg, 1999).

These differences are most often interpreted as yet another sign of the importance of social support. Social activities are very important in the lives of widows. In contrast, researchers have found that widowers withdraw from social activities to a far greater degree than widows do in the months immediately following bereavement (Bennett, 1998).

pathological grief symptoms of depression brought on by the death of a loved one

However, some developmentalists have suggested that activities-oriented studies have led to a stereotype that characterizes widowers as lonely and isolated. In fact, research involving in-depth examinations of widowers' friendships, rather than just their social activities, suggests that social relationships are very important in the lives of men who have lost a spouse (Riggs, 1997). Thus, differences in social involvement may be part of the explanation for sex differences in health and depression following the death of a spouse, but they do not appear to tell the whole story.

The results of a carefully designed longitudinal study of Australian widowers and married men over age 65 suggest that alcohol use may play a role in the greater prevalence of depression among widowers (Byrne, Raphael, & Arnold, 1999). Researchers found that more than twice as many widowers as married men (19% versus 8%) consumed five or more alcoholic drinks per day. Although alcohol may temporarily relieve unpleasant feelings of grief, it is a central nervous system depressant, and prolonged heavy drinking can lead to depression.

Preventing Long-Term Problems Some research suggests that the "talk it out" approach to managing grief can be helpful in preventing grief-related depression, especially when feelings are shared with others who have had similar experiences, in the context of a support group (Francis, 1997). Research also indicates that developing a coherent personal narrative of the events surrounding the spouse's death helps widows and widowers manage grief (Neimeyer, Prigerson, & Davies, 2002; van den Hoonaard, 1999). Participating in support groups—or even jointly recalling relevant events with close family members—can facilitate the formation of such stories.

Clearly, this kind of psychosocial management of grief requires time. Mental health professionals advise employers that providing bereaved employees (especially those whose spouses have died) with sufficient time off to grieve may be critical to their physical and mental health. In the long run, illness and depression among bereaved workers who return to their jobs too soon may be more costly to employers than providing additional time off (Eyetsemitan, 1998).

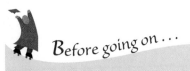

Before going on . . .

■ How do funerals and ceremonies help survivors cope with grief?

■ How do the age of the bereaved and the mode of death affect the grieving process?

■ How does grief affect the physical and mental health of widows and widowers?

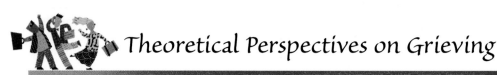

Theoretical Perspectives on Grieving

There are a number of ways of looking at the emotion of grief, but the two that have had the greatest influence on the way psychologists think about grief are Freud's psychoanalytic theory and Bowlby's attachment theory.

FREUD'S PSYCHOANALYTIC THEORY

From the psychoanalytic perspective, the death of a loved one is an emotional trauma. As with any trauma, the ego, or mind, tries to insulate itself from the unpleasant emotions such losses induce through the use of defense mechanisms, including denial and repression. However, Freud believed that defense mechanisms were only temporary devices for dealing with negative emotions. Eventually, he thought, the individual must examine the emotions and their source directly. Otherwise, such emotions lead to the development of physical symptoms and, perhaps, mental illnesses.

Freud's view has been very influential in grief counseling and in popular notions about the necessity of "working through" grief in order to avoid its long-term negative effects. It is generally accepted that bereaved individuals need to talk openly about their loss. Thus, grief counselors often recommend that friends of a bereaved person encourage the person to cry or express grief in other ways.

Psychoanalytically based grief therapy for children often emphasizes the use of defense mechanisms other than denial and repression to cope with grief. Following this approach, therapists sometimes encourage children to express their feelings through art. The idea is that this kind of defense mechanism, known as *sublimation,* will lead to better health outcomes than avoidance of emotions through more negative defense mechanisms (Glazer, 1998). Similarly, some therapists advocate encouraging children to use another defense mechanism, *identification,* to manage their grief. This goal can be accomplished by having the child watch popular films depicting children's grief, such *as The Lion King;* discuss the young characters' feelings; and compare the characters' emotions to their own (Sedney, 1999).

In addition, the psychoanalytic perspective has shaped grief research by characterizing the loss of a loved one as a trauma. An important concept in such research is that the more traumatic the death, the more likely it is to be followed by physical or mental problems. In fact, researchers have found that people who lose loved ones in sudden, tragic ways, such as to a drunk-driving accident or a murder, are more likely to display symptoms of post-traumatic stress disorder (Murphy et al., 1999; Sprang & McNeil, 1998).

BOWLBY'S ATTACHMENT THEORY

John Bowlby and other attachment theorists argue that intense grief reactions are likely to occur at the loss of any person to whom one is attached, whether a partner, a parent, or a child (Bowlby, 1980; Sanders, 1989; Stroebe, 2002). Moreover, their theories predict that the quality of attachment to the loved one should be related in some way to the experience of grief. Research seems to confirm this aspect of their view. The stronger the attachment between a mourner and a lost loved one, the deeper and more prolonged the grief response (van Doorn et al., 1998; Waskowic & Chartier, 2003). By contrast, the death of someone who is part of one's social network but not an intimate confidant or an attachment figure is less likely to trigger an intense emotional reaction (Murrell & Himmelfarb, 1989).

Bowlby proposed four stages of grief, and Catherine Sanders, another attachment theorist, proposed five stages, but as you can see in Table 9.5 (page 246), the two systems overlap a great deal. In the first period, that of shock or numbness, people say things that reveal their state of mind:

"I feel so vague. I can't keep my mind on anything for very long." (Bowlby, 1980, p. 47)

"I'm afraid I'm losing my mind. I can't seem to think clearly." (Bowlby, 1980, p. 48)

"It was so strange. I was putting on my makeup, combing my hair, and all the time it was as if I were standing by the door watching myself go through these motions." (Sanders, 1989, p. 56).

In the stage of awareness of loss, or yearning, when anger is a common ingredient, people say things such as "His boss should have known better than to ask him to work so hard." Bowlby suggested that this is equivalent to the behavior observed in young children when temporarily separated from their closest attachment figures; they go from room to room in search of this favored person. Adults who are widowed do some of the same searching—sometimes physically, sometimes mentally.

In the stage of disorganization and despair, the restlessness of the previous period disappears and is replaced by a great lethargy. One 45-year-old whose child had just died described her feelings:

I can't understand the way I feel. Up to now, I had been feeling restless. I couldn't sleep. I paced and ranted. Now, I have an opposite reaction. I sleep a lot. I feel fatigued and worn out. I don't even want to see the friends who have kept me going. I sit and stare, too exhausted to move. . . . Just when I thought I should be feeling better, I am feeling worse. (Sanders, 1989, p. 73)

TABLE 9.5		Stages of Grief	
Stage	**Bowlby's Label**	**Sanders's Label**	**General Description**
1	Numbness	Shock	Characteristic of the first few days after the death of the loved one and occasionally longer; mourner experiences disbelief, confusion, restlessness, feelings of unreality, a sense of helplessness.
2	Yearning	Awareness	The bereaved person tries to recover the lost person; may actively search or wander as if searching; may report that he sees the dead person; mourner feels full of anger, anxiety, guilt, fear, frustration; may sleep poorly and weep often.
3	Disorganization and despair	Conservation/ withdrawal	Searching ceases and the loss is accepted, but acceptance of loss brings depression and despair or a sense of helplessness; this stage is often accompanied by great fatigue and a desire to sleep all the time.
4	Reorganization	Healing and renewal	Sanders views this as two periods, Bowlby as only one. Both see this as the period when the individual takes control again. Some forgetting occurs and some sense of hope emerges, along with increased energy, better health, better sleep patterns, and reduced depression.

(Sources: Bowlby, 1980; Sanders, 1989.)

Finally, the resolution of the grieving process comes in Bowlby's stage of reorganization. Sanders hypothesized that this stage comprises two separate periods: healing and renewal. The outcome, from both Bowlby's and Sanders's perspectives, is that the grieving person begins to be able to maintain control. Sleep patterns return to normal, and a more optimistic outlook is typical.

These descriptions of the grieving process are highly evocative and can be useful in counseling grieving individuals. Discussion of the stages helps those who are grieving communicate with therapists about how they are feeling and describe the kinds of symptoms they are experiencing. Stage approaches also help survivors realize that their emotions and physical symptoms are normal and that the grieving process is complex.

However, as with the concept of stages of dying, there are two important questions about these proposed stages of grieving:
(1) Do they really occur in fixed stages?
(2) Does everyone feel all these feelings, in whatever sequence?
The answer to both questions, as you'll see, seems to be no.

CRITICAL THINKING

Think about a loss in your own life. (Even losing a pet causes grief.) Do Bowlby's and Sanders's stages seem to fit your experience?

ALTERNATIVE PERSPECTIVES

A growing set of "revisionist" views of grieving gives a rather different picture from that of either Freud or the attachment theorists. First, research suggests that, contrary to psychoanalytic hypotheses, avoiding expressions of grief neither prolongs the experience of grief nor leads inevitably to physical or mental health problems. In fact, at least one study suggests that bereaved individuals who avoid talking about the deceased or their feelings of loss actually experience milder grief and are less likely to suffer long-term effects (Bonanno, Znoj, Siddique, & Horowitz, 1999).

Second, many researchers and theorists find that grieving simply does not occur in fixed stages, with everyone following the same pattern (Wortman & Silver, 1990). There may be common themes, such as anger, guilt, depression, and restlessness, but these do not seem to appear in a fixed order.

One compromise model suggests that each of the key themes in the grieving process has a likely trajectory, as suggested in Figure 9.3 (Jacobs et al., 1987/1988). For example, numbness may be most prominent in the days immediately following the loved one's death. After a few months, the grieving person may feel numb at times, but depression may be a more dominant theme. The basic idea, obviously, is that many themes are present at the same time, but that one or another may dominate, in an approximate sequence. Thus, it may well be that disbelief is highest immediately after the death, and that depression peaks some months later—which makes the process look stagelike, although in fact both elements are present throughout. Some bereaved people might move more quickly and others more slowly through these various emotions.

In contrast, other revisionist theorists and researchers contend that for some adults, grieving simply does not include all these elements. Psychologists Camille Wortman and Roxane Silver have amassed an impressive amount of evidence to support such a view (Wortman & Silver, 1989, 1990, 1992; Wortman, Silver, & Kessler, 1993). They dispute the traditional view of grieving expressed in both Freud's and Bowlby's theories. First, Wortman and Silver do not agree that distress is an inevitable response to loss. Second, their research challenges the notion that failure to experience distress is a sign that the individual has not grieved "properly."

Based on their findings, Wortman and Silver conclude that there are at least four distinct patterns of grieving (Wortman & Silver, 1990):

- *Normal.* The person feels great distress immediately following the loss, with relatively rapid recovery.
- *Chronic.* The person's distress continues at a high level over several years.
- *Delayed.* The grieving person feels little distress in the first few months but high levels of distress some months or years later.
- *Absent.* The person feels no notable level of distress either immediately or at any later time.

Contrary to the predictions of stage theories of grief, it turns out that the pattern of absent grief is remarkably common. In Wortman and Silver's own first study, 26% of bereaved participants showed essentially no distress, either immediately after the death or several years later, a pattern confirmed in other research (Levy, Martinkowski, & Derby, 1994; Wortman & Silver, 1990). The least common pattern is delayed grief. Only

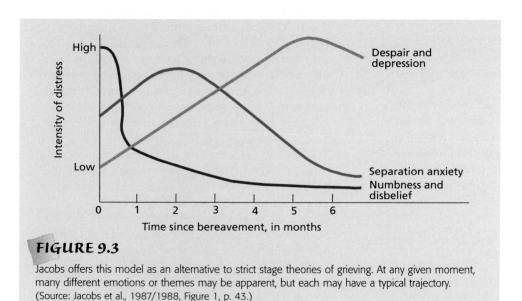

FIGURE 9.3

Jacobs offers this model as an alternative to strict stage theories of grieving. At any given moment, many different emotions or themes may be apparent, but each may have a typical trajectory. (Source: Jacobs et al., 1987/1988, Figure 1, p. 43.)

1–5% of adults appear to show such a response to loss, while as many as a third show chronic grief. Thus, Wortman and Silver find little support for either aspect of the traditional view: High levels of distress are neither an inevitable nor a necessary aspect of the grieving process. Many adults seem to handle the death of a spouse, a child, or a parent without significant psychological dislocation—although it remains true that, on average, bereaved persons have more depression, less life satisfaction, and a greater risk of illness than the nonbereaved.

As yet, developmentalists know relatively little about the characteristics of individuals who react to bereavement in the very different ways outlined by Wortman and Silver, although their research gives a few hints (Wortman et al., 1993). In their studies, widows who had had the best marriages showed the most persistent grief reactions. More surprisingly, Wortman and Silver found that those widows who had had the strongest sense of personal control, self-esteem, or mastery prior to the spouse's death had the most difficulty after his death, as if the loss of the spouse had undermined this very sense of control. Research in Germany suggests that neuroticism may be another important factor; researchers there found that widows who were high in neuroticism before bereavement showed stronger and more persistent negative effects after the deaths of their spouses (Stroebe & Stroebe, 1993).

Finally, it's important not to lose sight of the fact that loss can lead to growth. Indeed, the majority of widows say not only that they changed as a result of their husbands' deaths, but that the change was toward greater independence and greater skill (Wortman & Silver, 1990). Like all crises and all major life changes, bereavement can be an opportunity as well as—or instead of—a disabling experience. Which way a person responds is likely to depend very heavily on the patterns established from early childhood: in temperament or personality, in internal working models of attachment and self, in intellectual skills, and in social networks. Ultimately, we respond to death—our own or someone else's—as we have responded to life.

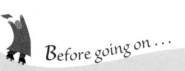

Before going on . . .

- How does Freud's psychoanalytic theory view grief?

- What do Bowlby and Sanders suggest about the connection between attachment and grief, and what stages of grieving have they proposed?

- How have other theorists criticized the psychoanalytic and attachment theories of the grief process, and what alternative perspectives do they propose?

Summary

The Experience of Death

- Death is a somewhat nonspecific term. Medical personnel refer to *clinical death* and *brain death; social death* occurs when the deceased person is treated like a corpse by those around him.

- The great majority of adults in industrialized countries die in hospitals. Hospice care emphasizes patient and family control of the dying process and palliative care rather than curative treatment. Some studies suggest that patients and families are slightly more satisfied with hospice care than hospital care, but hospice care is also highly burdensome for the caregiver.

The Meaning of Death across the Lifespan

- Until about age 6 or 7, children do not understand that death is permanent and inevitable and involves loss of function. Teens understand the physical aspects of death much better than children do, but they sometimes have distorted ideas about it, especially their own mortality.

- Many young adults believe they possess unique characteristics that protect them from death. For middle-aged and older adults, death has many possible meanings: a signal of changes in family roles, a transition to another state (such as a life after death), and a loss of opportunity and relationships. Awareness of death may help a person organize her remaining time.

- Fear of death appears to peak in mid-life, after which it drops rather sharply. Older adults talk more about death but are less afraid of it. Deeply religious adults are typically less afraid of death.

- Many adults prepare for death in practical ways, such as by buying life insurance, writing a will, and making a living will. Reminiscence may also serve as preparation. There are some signs of deeper personality changes immediately before death, including more dependence and docility and less emotionality and assertiveness.

The Process of Dying

- Kübler-Ross suggested five stages of dying: denial, anger, bargaining, depression, and acceptance. Research fails to support the hypothesis that all dying adults go through all five stages or that the stages necessarily occur in this order. The emotion most commonly observed is depression.
- Critics of Kübler-Ross suggest that her findings may be culture-specific. They also argue that the process of dying is less stagelike than her theory claims.
- Research with cancer and AIDS patients suggests that those who are most pessimistic and docile in response to diagnosis and treatment have shorter life expectancies. Those who fight hardest, and even display anger, live longer. Dying adults who have better social support, either from family and friends or through specially created support groups, live longer than those who lack such support.

The Experience of Grieving

- Funerals and other rituals after death serve important functions, including defining roles for the bereaved, bringing family together, and giving meaning to the deceased's life and death.

- Grief responses depend on a number of variables. The age of the bereaved and the mode of death shape the grief process.
- In general, the death of a spouse evokes the most intense and long-lasting grief. Widows and widowers show high levels of illness and death in the months immediately after the death of a spouse, perhaps as a result of the effects of grief on the immune system. Widowers appear to have a more difficult time than widows managing grief.

Theoretical Perspectives on Grieving

- Freud's psychoanalytic theory emphasizes loss as an emotional trauma, the effects of defense mechanisms, and the need to work through feelings of grief.
- Bowlby's attachment theory views grief as a natural response to the loss of an attachment figure. Attachment theorists suggest that the grief process involves several stages.
- Alternative views suggest that neither Freud's nor Bowlby's theory accurately characterizes the grief experience. Responses are more individual than either theory might suggest.

Key Terms

brain death (p. 224)	hospice care (p. 224)	social death (p. 224)
clinical death (p. 224)	palliative care (p. 225)	thanatology (p. 235)
grieving (p. 238)	pathological grief (p. 243)	unique invulnerability (p. 228)

Policy Question

Do People Have a Right to Die?

One element of having greater control over the process of dying might be the ability to choose the timing of death—a highly controversial topic. Today, most medical ethicists distinguish between two forms of euthanasia (also known as "mercy killing"). Passive euthanasia occurs when a person (typically, a physician) hastens a death by not using life support systems or medication that would prolong the life or by withdrawing life support or other treatment that may be keeping a patient alive. Active euthanasia (also called assisted suicide) occurs when a physician or other individual (at a patient's request) hastens the patient's death by active means, such as by administering a fatal dose of a drug.

Living Wills

There is little controversy about passive euthanasia. Most people agree that individuals should be able to determine the degree to which life-support technology will be used to delay their own deaths. Thus, an increasing number of adults have made living wills specifying that life-support systems or resuscitation should not be used in case of their clinical death or near death. Such living wills essentially ask physicians to participate in passive euthanasia.

However, it turns out that living wills are often not followed, both because health care professionals who treat a patient in an emergency do not know of the living will and because many physicians find it extremely difficult to "give up"—not to use the full array of treatments available to them to prolong a life. Many other physicians, particularly those who have treated a patient over many years, are entirely comfortable urging patients or family members to discontinue some life-prolonging treatment, thus hastening the patient's death.

Consequently, several states have passed legislation designed to ensure compliance with living wills. Some laws require hospitals to ask all those who are admitted whether they have made such a document. In other states, laws specifically limit the applicability of living wills (which are often vague about which specific technologies can and can't be used) to practices such as tube feeding.

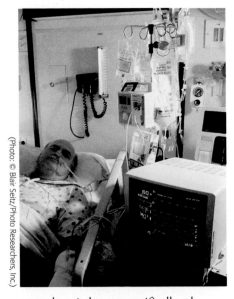

(Photo: © Blair Seitz/Photo Researchers, Inc.)

Many hospitals now specifically ask terminal patients during the admission process how they want to be treated in the event that they become mentally incapacitated.

The Assisted Suicide Debate

By contrast, assisted suicide (or any other form of active euthanasia) is far less common and much more controversial. The debate over physician-assisted suicide was brought to public attention in the United States by the actions of Dr. Jack Kevorkian, a physician who helped several terminally ill and severely handicapped individuals end their own lives. In the United States at present, the legal status of active euthanasia is tangled. Explicit attempts to legalize assisted suicide through voters' initiatives have been defeated in several states; one such referendum passed in Oregon in 1994, but its implementation was delayed by court action until 1997. Many other state legislatures have explicitly banned assisted suicide, and, in a unanimous ruling in 1997, the U.S. Supreme Court upheld such laws.

The only place in the world where assisted suicide is fully and explicitly legal is in the Netherlands. A law passed in 2001 legalized the long-standing Dutch custom of providing terminally ill patients with lethal doses of pain-killing drugs ("Dutch senate OKs doctor-assisted suicide," 2001). Individuals who wish to die must be terminally ill and have no hope of recovery, and must obtain the approval of two physicians. Children under 12 are prohibited from requesting to die, and those between 12 and 15 must have parental consent. The parents of a 16- or 17-year-old must be notified of the child's request but do not have the right to prevent the assisted suicide from being carried out.

Many of those who oppose active euthanasia believe that each individual life is sacred. Therefore, they believe, decisions about when to end life should be subject only to divine authority. These critics also view assisted suicide as just another form of suicide—a practice they consider to be immoral.

Other opponents argue against active euthanasia on the grounds that it might be extremely difficult to set limits on the process, even with strict guidelines—a position often labeled "the slippery slope argument" (Twycross, 1996). Advocates for the disabled have been particularly vocal in putting forward this point of view (Smith, 2004). They claim that once assisted suicide becomes widely viewed as morally acceptable, society may come to the point where those who are infirm or severely disabled will be subtly (or not so subtly) encouraged to end their own lives in order

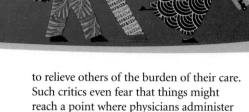

to relieve others of the burden of their care. Such critics even fear that things might reach a point where physicians administer fatal drugs without the patient's consent.

A third argument against any form of active euthanasia is that modern pain management techniques allow even those with extremely painful terminal illnesses to be comfortable in the last days or weeks of their lives. Thus, it is not necessary to hasten death in order to prevent pain. Some physicians also believe that the availability of assisted suicide may cause insurance companies and hospitals to fail to make patients aware of the wide array of pain management techniques because the deaths of these patients will save them money. Similarly, some social workers have pointed out that when patients who have considered assisted suicide learn about social and medical resources that are available to help them cope, they often change their minds (Hornik, 1998).

For these reasons, as well as the personal religious beliefs of some, about three-quarters of a sample of 3,000 oncologists (physicians who specialize in treating cancer) in a survey carried out by the National Institutes of Health were found to oppose active euthanasia of any kind (Emanuel et al., 2000). Instead, they advocate palliative-care education for all physicians to make them aware of the benefits of hospice care, as well as the most effective ways of relieving patients' pain. They also suggest that physicians treating terminal patients engage their patients in frank discussions about pain relief as early in the course of their illness as possible. Through such discussions, doctors and patients can decide together what pain relief measures will be taken.

Studies involving patients who refuse treatments such as chemotherapy suggest that such individuals often want to live as long as possible. However, they do not want to go through the difficulties associated with the treatments (Abrams, 1998). Such findings suggest that observers should be cautious about jumping to the conclusion that a person who doesn't want medical treatment is interested in hastening death.

Opponents of assisted suicide also question terminally ill patients' psychological fitness for making the decision to end their lives. Some fear that such patients may be depressed and that a request to hasten death is really no different from any other kind of suicide attempt. In other words, it is an act born of emotional despair, not rationality. The distinction is important, they say, because the philosophical rationale of assisted suicide laws is that choosing to die involves a rational decision-making process.

To address this concern, assisted suicide legislation, including the Oregon law, typically includes a mandatory

(Photo: © AFP/Getty Images)

In 1999, Dr. Jack Kevorkian, who lost his license to practice medicine several years earlier, was convicted of murder by a Michigan jury. He is currently in prison.

waiting period between a request for death and the fulfillment of the request. During the waiting period, a psychiatrist or psychologist is supposed to assess the mental state of the patient to determine whether he or she is competent to make the life-ending decision.

However, mental health professionals generally lack confidence in their ability to make such judgments (Fenn & Ganzini, 1999). Many believe that such an assessment is possible only when a practitioner has known the patient for a long period of time. Moreover, there is a possibility that a professional's own opinion about the moral acceptability of assisted suicide will influence the assessment of mental competency in such cases. To address these issues, the American Psychological Association and other interested organizations are attempting to develop guidelines and standards to be used in such assessments (Werth, 2000).

Those who favor assisted suicide legislation note that modern medical technology has increasingly made it possible to prolong life well past the point at which death, in earlier decades, would naturally have occurred. Further, proponents of assisted suicide argue that many terminal patients are unable to carry out their own suicides, and therefore require the help of a physician. However, opponents counter that asking another person to help with a suicide is a far cry from giving a person "death with dignity." As one German physician who opposes assisted suicide expressed it, "Everyone has the right to a dignified death, but nobody has the right to be killed" (Cohen, 2000).

Your Turn

- Find out from a local medical society whether hospitals and physicians in your area generally honor living wills. Does your state require medical personnel to ask all hospitalized people whether they have a living will?

- The medical society should also be able to tell you whether your state allows family members to authorize health professionals to terminate aspects of care such as tube feeding in cases where a terminally ill or seriously injured individual can't speak for himself.

- Has anyone in your state ever been prosecuted for helping a dying person hasten death? If so, what were the circumstances and outcome of the case(s)?

- Are there efforts under way in your state to legalize assisted suicide? If so, what do opinion polls suggest about voter support for such laws?

References

ABC News. (2000, August 22). *Poll: Americans like public school.* Retrieved August 23, 2000, from http://www.abcnews.com.

Abdelrahman, A., Rodriguez, G., Ryan, J., French, J., & Weinbaum, D. (1998). The epidemiology of substance use among middle school students: The impact of school, familial, community and individual risk factors. *Journal of Child & Adolescent Substance Abuse, 8,* 55–75.

Abengozar, C., Bueno, B., & Vega, J. (1999). Intervention on attitudes toward death along the life span. *Educational Gerontology, 25,* 435–447.

Abraham, J. D., & Hansson, R. O. (1995). Successful aging at work: An applied study of selection, optimization, and compensation through impression management. *Journals of Gerontology: Psychological Sciences, 50B,* P94–P103.

Abrams, E. J., Matheson, P. B., Thomas, P. A., Thea, D. M., Krasinski, K., Lambert, G., Shaffer, N., Bamji, M., Hutson, D., Grimm, K., Kaul, A., Bateman, D., Rogers, M., & New York City Perinatal HIV Transmission Collaborative Study Group (1995). Neonatal predictors of infection status and early death among 332 infants at risk of HIV-1 infection monitored prospectively from birth. *Pediatrics, 96,* 451–458.

Abrams, R. (1998). Physician-assisted suicide and euthanasia's impact on the frail elderly: Something to think about. *Journal of Long Term Home Health Care: The Pride Institute Journal, 17,* 19–27.

Accardo, P., Tomazic, T., Fete, T., Heaney, M., Lindsay, R., & Whitman, B. (1997). Maternally reported fetal activity levels and developmental diagnoses. *Clinical Pediatrics, 36,* 279–283.

Achter, J., Lubinski, D., Benbow, C., & Eftekhari-Sanjani, H. (1999). Assessing vocational preferences among gifted adolescents adds incremental validity to abilities: A discriminant analysis of educational outcomes over a 10-year interval. *Journal of Educational Psychology, 91,* 777–786.

Ackerman, B., Brown, E., & Izard, C. (2004). The relations between contextual risk, earned income, and the school adjustment of children from economically disadvantaged families. *Developmental Psychology, 40,* 204–216.

Ackerman, S., Zuroff, D., & Moskowitz, D. (2000). Generativity in midlife and young adults: Links to agency, communion and subjective well-being. *Aging and Human Development, 50,* 17–41.

Adams, C. (1991). Qualitative age differences in memory for text: A life-span developmental perspective. *Psychology & Aging, 6,* 323–336.

Adams, M., & Henry, M. (1997). Myths and realities about words and literacy. *School Psychology Review, 26,* 425–436.

Adams, M. J. (1990). *Beginning to read: Thinking and learning about print.* Cambridge, MA: The MIT Press.

Addis, M., & Mahalik, J. (2003). Men, masculinity, and the contexts of help seeking. *American Psychologist, 58,* 5–14.

Adelman, W., & Ellen, J. (2002). Adolescence. In A. Rudolph, R. Kamei, & K. Overby (Eds.), *Rudolph's fundamental of pediatrics* (3rd ed., pp. 70–109). New York: McGraw-Hill.

Adelmann, P. K. (1994). Multiple roles and physical health among older adults: Gender and ethnic comparisons. *Research on Aging, 16,* 142–166.

Adesman, A. R. (1996). Fragile X syndrome. In A. J. Capute & P. J. Accardo (Eds.), *Developmental disabilities in infancy and childhood, Vol. II: The spectrum of developmental disabilities* (pp. 255–269). Baltimore: Paul H. Brookes.

Adkins, V. (1999). Grandparents as a national asset: A brief note. *Activities, Adaptation, & Aging, 24,* 13–18.

Agnew, J., Dorn, C., & Eden, G. (2004). Effect of intensive training on auditory processing and reading skills. *Brain & Language, 88,* 21–25.

Ahadi, S. A., & Rothbart, M. K. (1994). Temperament, development, and the big five. In C. F. Halverson, Jr., G. A. Kohnstamm, & R. P. Martin (Eds.), *The developing structure of temperament and personality from infancy to adulthood* (pp. 189–207). Hillsdale, NJ: Erlbaum.

Ahmad, G., & Najam, N. (1998). A study of marital adjustment during first transition to parenthood. *Journal of Behavioural Sciences, 9,* 67–86.

Ahmed, E., & Braithwaite, V. (2004). Bullying and victimization: Cause for concern for both families and schools. *Social Psychology of Education, 7,* 35–54.

Aiken, L. (1997). *Psychological testing and assessment* (9th ed.). Boston: Allyn & Bacon.

Ainsworth, M. D. S. (1989). Attachments beyond infancy. *American Psychologist, 44,* 709–716.

Ainsworth, M. D. S., Blehar, M., Waters, E., & Wall, S. (1978). *Patterns of attachment.* Hillsdale, NJ: Erlbaum.

Ainsworth, M. D. S., & Marvin, R. S. (1995). On the shaping of attachment theory and research: An interview with Mary D. S. Ainsworth (Fall 1994). *Monographs of the Society for Research in Child Development, 60* (244, Nos. 2–3), 3–21.

Akers, J., Jones, R., & Coyl, D. (1998). Adolescent friendship pairs: Similarities in identity status development, behaviors, attitudes, and interests. *Journal of Adolescent Research, 13,* 178–201.

Akiba, D. (1998). Cultural variations in body esteem: How young adults in Iran and the United States view their own appearances. *The Journal of Social Psychology, 138,* 539–540.

Akiyama, H., Antonucci, T., Takahashi, K., & Langfahl, E. (2003). Negative interactions in close relationships across the life span. *Journals of Gerontology, Series B: Psychological Sciences & Social Sciences, 58B,* P70–P79.

Aksu-Koc, A. A., & Slobin, D. I. (1985). The acquisition of Turkish. In D. I. Slobin (Ed.), *The crosslinguistic study of language acquisition: Vol. 1: The data* (pp. 839–878). Hillsdale, NJ: Erlbaum.

Alan Guttmacher Institute. (2004). *U.S. teenage pregnancy statistics with comparative statistics for women aged 20–24.* Retrieved July 9, 2004, from http://www.guttmacher.org/pubs/teen_stats.html.

Albert, M. S., Jones, K., Savage, C. R., Berkman, L., Seeman, T., Blazer, D., & Rowe, J. W. (1995). Predictors of cognitive change in older persons: MacArthur studies of successful aging. *Psychology and Aging, 10,* 578–589.

Aldous, J. (1996). *Family careers: Rethinking the developmental perspective.* Thousand Oaks, CA: Sage.

Aleixo, P., & Norris, C. (2000). Personality and moral reasoning in young offenders. *Personality & Individual Differences, 28,* 609–623.

Alexander, G., & Hines, M. (1994). Gender labels and play styles: Their relative contribution to children's selection of playmates: *Child Development, 65,* 869–879.

Allaz, A., Bernstein, M., Rouget, P., Archinard, M., & Morabia, A. (1998). Body weight preoccupation in middle-aged and ageing women: A general population survey. *International Journal of Eating Disorders, 23,* 287–294.

Allen, C., & Kisilevsky, B. (1999). Fetal behavior in diabetic and nondiabetic pregnant women: An exploratory study. *Developmental Psychobiology, 35,* 69–80.

Allen, K., & Rainie, L. (2002). *Parents online.* Retrieved March 16, 2004, from http://www.pewinternet.org.

Allen, K. R., & Pickett, R. S. (1987). Forgotten streams in the family life course: Utilization of qualitative retrospective interviews in the analysis of lifelong single women's family careers. *Journal of Marriage & the Family, 49,* 517–526.

Allen, T., Poteet, M., & Russell, J. (1998). Attitudes of managers who are more or less career plateaued. *Career Development Quarterly, 47,* 159–172.

Allen, W., Dreves, R., & Ruhe, J. (1999). Reasons why college-educated women change employment. *Journal of Business & Psychology, 14,* 77–93.

Almeida, O., Waterreus, A., Spry, N., Flicker, L., & Martins, R. (2004). One year follow-up study of the association between chemical castration, sex hormones, beta-amyloid, memory and depression in men. *Psychoneuroendocrinology, 29,* 1071–1081.

Alpha-Tocopherol Beta Carotene Cancer Prevention Study Group (1994). The effect of vitamin E and beta carotene on the incidence of lung cancer and other cancers in male smokers. *New England Journal of Medicine, 330,* 1029–1035.

Alsaker, F. D. (1995). Timing of puberty and reactions to pubertal change. In M. Rutter (Ed.), *Psychosocial disturbances in young people: Challenges for prevention* (pp. 37–82). Cambridge, England: Cambridge University Press.

Alsaker, F. D., & Olweus, D. (1992). Stability of global self-evaluations in early adolescence: A cohort longitudinal study. *Journal of Research on Adolescence, 2,* 123–145.

Alsop, S. (1973). *Stay of execution.* New York: Lippincott.

Alspaugh, J. (1998). Achievement loss associated with the transition to middle school and high school. *Journal of Educational Research, 92,* 20–25.

Alster, E. (1997). The effects of extended time on algebra test scores for college students with and without learning disabilities. *Journal of Learning Disabilities, 30,* 222–227.

Alvidrez, J., & Weinstein, R. (1999). Early teacher perceptions and later student academic achievement. *Journal of Educational Psychology, 91,* 731–746.

Amato, P., & Rogers, S. (1999). Do attitudes toward divorce affect marital quality? *Journal of Family Issues, 20,* 69–86.

Amato, P. R. (1993). Children's adjustment to divorce: Theories, hypotheses, and empirical support. *Journal of Marriage & the Family, 55,* 23–38.

Amato, S. (1998). Human genetics and dysmorphy. In R. Behrman & R. Kliegman (Eds.), *Nelson essentials of pediatrics* (3rd ed., pp. 129–146). Philadelphia: W. B. Saunders.

Ambert, A. (2001). *Families in the new millennium.* Boston: Allyn & Bacon.

Ambuel, B. (1995). Adolescents, unintended pregnancy, and abortion: The struggle for a compassionate social policy. *Current Directions in Psychological Science, 4,* 1–5.

Amenedo, E., & Diaz, F. (1998). Aging-related changes in processing of non-target and target stimuli during an auditory oddball task. *Biological Psychology, 48,* 235–267.

Amenedo, E., & Diaz, F. (1999). Aging-related changes in the processing of attended and unattended standard stimuli. *Neuroreport: For Rapid Communication of Neuroscience Research, 10,* 2383–2388.

American Academy of Pediatrics (AAP). (1999). Committee on public education. *Pediatrics, 104,* 341–343.

American Academy of Pediatrics (AAP). (2002). *Television: How it affects children.* Retrieved July 2, 2004, from http://www.aap.org/family/tv1.htm.

American Academy of Pediatrics Committee on Psychosocial Aspects of child and Family Health. (1998). Guidance for effective discipline. *Pediatrics, 101,* 723–728.

American Association of Family Physicians. (1998). *Epilepsy and pregnancy: What you should know.* Retrieved March 6, 2001, http://www.aafp.org/afp/971015ap/971015c.html.

American College of Obstetrics and Gynecology (ACOG). (2001, December 12). *ACOG addresses latest controversies in obstetrics.* Retrieved April 1, 2004, from http://www.acog.org.

American College of Obstetrics and Gynecology. (2002, November 29). *Rubella vaccination recommendation changes for pregnant women.* Retrieved April 2, 2004, from http://www.acog.org.

American College of Obstetrics and Gynecology. (2004a). *Ethics in obstetrics and gynecology.* Washington, DC: Author.

American College of Obstetrics and Gynecology. (2004b). *Hormone therapy after the WHI: Time to strike a balance.* Retrieved August 26, 2004, from http://www.acog.org.

American Demographics. (2001). *It's all homework.* Retrieved June 23, 2004, from http://articles.findarticles.com/p/articles/mi_m4021/is_2001_Nov_1/ai_79501196.

American Medical Association. (1990). Legal interventions during pregnancy: Court-ordered medical treatments and legal penalties for potentially harmful behavior by pregnant women. *Journal of the American Medical Association, 264,* 2663–2667.

American Psychiatric Association. (2000). *Diagnostic and statistical manual of mental disorders* (4th ed., Text Revision). Washington, DC: Author.

Amieva, H., Lentenneur, L., Dartigues, J., Rouch-Leroyer, I., Sourgen, C., D'Alchée-Birée, F., Dib, M., Barberger-Gateau, P., Orgogozo, J., & Fabrigoule, C. (2004). Annual rate and predictors of conversion to dementia in subjects presenting mild cognitive impairment criteria defined according to a population-based study. *Dementia & Geriatric Cognitive Disorders, 18,* 87–93.

Anan, R., & Barnett, D. (1999). Perceived social support mediates between prior attachment and subsequent adjustment: A study of urban African American children. *Developmental Psychology, 35,* 1210–1222.

Anderman, E. (1998). The middle school experience: Effects on the math and science achievement of adolescents with LD. *Journal of Learning Disabilities, 31,* 128–138.

Anderman, E., Maehr, M., & Midgley, C. (1999). Declining motivation after the transition to middle school: Schools can make a difference. *Journal of Research & Development in Education, 32,* 131–147.

Anderman, E., & Midgley, C. (1997). Changes in achievement goal orientations, perceived academic competence, and grades across the transition to middle-level schools. *Contemporary Educational Psychology, 22,* 269–298.

Anderman, L. (1999). Classroom goal orientation, school belonging and social goals as predictors of students' positive and negative affect following the transition to middle school. *Journal of Research & Development in Education, 32,* 89–103.

Anderman, L., & Anderman, E. (1999). Social predictors of changes in students' achievement goal orientations. *Contemporary Educational Psychology, 24,* 21–37.

Anderson, C., & Dill, K. (2000). Video games and aggressive thoughts, feelings, and behavior in the laboratory and in life. *Journal of Personality & Social Psychology, 78,* 772–790.

Anderson, K. M., Castelli, W. P., & Levy, D. (1987). Cholesterol and mortality: 30 years of follow-up from the Framingham study. *Journal of the American Medical Association, 257,* 2176–2180.

Anderson, R. (1998). Examining language loss in bilingual children. *Electronic Multicultural Journal of Communication Disorders, 1.*

Andersson, H. (1996). The Fagan Test of Infant Intelligence: Predictive validity in a random sample. *Psychological Reports, 78,* 1015–1026.

Andreou, E., & Metallidou, P. (2004). The relationship of academic and social cognition to behaviour in bullying situations among Greek primary school children. *Educational Psychology, 24,* 27–41.

Andrews, M., Dowling, W., Bartlett, J., & Halpern, A. (1998). Identification of speeded and slowed familiar melodies by younger, middle-aged, and older musicians and nonmusicians. *Psychology & Aging, 13,* 462–471.

Angier, N. (June 9, 1992). Clue to longevity found at chromosome tip. *New York Times,* pp. B5, B9.

Anglin, J. M. (1993). Vocabulary development: A morphological analysis. *Monographs of the Society for Research in Child Development, 58* (Serial No. 238).

Anglin, J. M. (1995, March). *Word learning and the growth of potentially knowable vocabulary.* Paper presented at the biennial meetings of the Society for Research in Child Development, Indianapolis, IN.

Anisfeld, M. (1991). Neonatal imitation. *Developmental Review, 11,* 60–97.

Annett, M. (2003). Do the French and the English differ for hand skill asymmetry? Handedness subgroups in the sample of Doyen and Carlier (2002) and in English schools and universities. *Laterality: Asymmetries of Body, Brain & Cognition, 8,* 233–245.

Annunziato, P. W., & Frenkel, L. M. (1993). The epidemiology of pediatric HIV-1 infection. *Pediatric Annals, 22,* 401–405.

Anthony, J., & Lonigan, C. (2004). The nature of phonological awareness: Converging evidence from four studies of preschool and early grade school children. *Journal of Educational Psychology, 96,* 43–55.

Anthony, J. C., & Aboraya, A. (1992). The epidemiology of selected mental disorders in later life. In J. E. Birren, R. B. Sloane, & G. D. Cohen (Eds.), *Handbook of mental health and aging* (2nd ed., pp. 28–73). San Diego, CA: Academic Press.

Antonucci, T. C. (1990). Social supports and social relationships. In R. H. Binstock & L. K. George (Eds.), *Handbook of aging and the social sciences* (3rd ed., pp. 205–226). San Diego, CA: Academic Press.

Antonucci, T. C. (1994). A life-span view of women's social relations. In B. F. Turner & L. E. Troll (Eds.), *Women growing older: Psychological perspectives* (pp. 239–269). Thousand Oaks, CA: Sage.

Antonucci, T., Lansford, J., & Akiyama, H. (2001). Impact of positive and negative aspects of marital relationships and friendships on well-being of older adults. *Applied Developmental Science, 5,* 68–75.

Antrop, I., Roeyers, H., Van Oost, P., & Buysse, A. (2000). Stimulation seeking and hyperactivity in children with ADHD. *Journal of Child Psychology, Psychiatry & Allied Disciplines, 41,* 225–231.

Anttila, T., Helkala, E., Vitanen, M., Kareholt, I., Fratiglioni, L., Winblad, B., Soininen, H., Tuomilehto, J., Nissinen, A., & Kivipelto, M. (2004). Alcohol drinking in middle age and subsequent risk of mild cognitive impairment and dementia in old age: A prospective population based study. *British Medical Journal, 329,* 539.

Apgar, V. A. (1953). A proposal for a new method of evaluation of the newborn infant. *Current Research in Anesthesia and Analgesia, 32,* 260–267.

Aquilino, W. S., & Supple, K. R. (1991). Parent-child relations and parent's satisfaction with living arrangements when adult children live at home. *Journal of Marriage & the Family, 53,* 13–27.

Aranha, M. (1997). Creativity in students and its relation to intelligence and peer perception. *Revista Interamericana de Psicologia, 31,* 309–313.

Arbuckle, N. W., & De Vries, B. (1995). The long-term effects of later life spousal and parental bereavement on personal functioning. *The Gerontologist, 35,* 637–647.

Archer, S. (1999, April 12). *Crackdown on delinquent parents.* Retrieved December 6, 1999, from www.WorldNetDaily.com.

Ardelt, M. (2003). Effects of religion and purpose in life on elders' subjective well-being and attitudes toward death. *Journal of Religious Gerontology, 14,* 55–77.

Arditti, J. (1991). Child support noncompliance and divorced fathers: Rethinking the role of paternal involvement. *Journal of Divorce & Remarriage, 14,* 107–120.

Arenberg, D. (1983). Memory and learning do decline late in life. In J. E. Birren, J. M. A. Munnichs, H. Thomae, & M. Marios (Eds.), *Aging: A challenge to science and society, Vol. 3: Behavioral sciences and conclusions* (pp. 312–322). New York: Oxford University Press.

Arlin, P. K. (1975). Cognitive development in adulthood: A fifth stage? *Developmental Psychology, 11,* 602–606.

Arlin, P. K. (1989). Problem solving and problem finding in young artists and young scientists. In M. L. Commons, J. D. Sinnott, F. A. Richards, & C. Armon (Eds.), *Adult development, Vol. 1: Comparisons and applications of developmental models* (pp. 197–216). New York: Praeger.

Arlin, P. K. (1990). Wisdom: The art of problem finding. In R. J. Sternberg (Ed.), *Wisdom. Its nature, origins, and development* (pp. 230–243). New York: Cambridge University Press.

Arluk, S., Swain, D., & Dowling, E. (2003). Childhood obesity's relationship to time spent in sedentary behavior. *Military Medicine, 168,* 583–586.

Armstrong, T. (2003). Effect of moral reconation therapy on the recidivism of youthful offenders: A randomized experiment. *Criminal Justice & Behavior, 30,* 668–687.

Arnett, J. (1998). Risk behavior and family role transitions during the twenties. *Journal of Youth & Adolescence, 27,* 301–320.

Arrindell, W., & Luteijn, F. (2000). Similarity between intimate partners for personality traits as related to individual levels of satisfaction with life. *Personality & Individual Differences, 28,* 629–637.

Asendorpf, J. B., Warkentin, V., & Baudonnière, P. (1996). Self-awareness and other-awareness. II: Mirror self-recognition, social contingency awareness, and synchronic imitation. *Developmental Psychology, 32,* 313–321.

Ashton, J., & Donnan, S. (1981). Suicide by burning as an epidemic phenomenon: An analysis of 82 deaths and inquests in England and Wales in 1978–1979. *Psychological Medicine, 11,* 735–739.

Aslin, R. (1987). Motor aspects of visual development in infancy. In N. P. Salapatek & L. Cohen (Eds.), *Handbook of infant perception, Vol. 1: From sensation to perception* (pp. 43–113). Orlando, FL: Academic Press.

Aslin, R., Saffran, J., & Newport, E. (1998). Computation of conditional probability statistics by 8-month-old infants. *Psychological Science, 9,* 321–324.

Assibey-Mensah, G. (1997). Role models and youth development: Evidence and lessons from the perceptions of African-American male youth. *Western Journal of Black Studies, 21,* 242–252.

Associated Press. (1996, July 17). Carolina ruling favors unborn; court describes fetus as a person. *Washington Times,* p. A1.

Associated Press. (1998a, October 27). More subpoenas issued in TAAS inquiry.

Associated Press. (1998b, October 12). TAAS preparation is big business.

Associated Press. (2000, September 18). Netherlands' homosexuals get right to "marry" legally. *Washington Times/National Edition,* p. 24.

Association of Reproductive Health Professionals (ARHP). (2000). *Mature sex.* Retrieved August 26, 2004, from http://www.ahrp.org/maturesex.

Astington, J., & Jenkins, J. (1999). A longitudinal study of the relation between language and theory-of-mind development. *Developmental Psychology, 35,* 1311–1320.

Astington, J. W., & Gopnik, A. (1991). Theoretical explanations of children's understanding of the mind. In G. E. Butterworth, P. L. Harris, A. M. Leslie, & H. M. Wellman (Eds.), *Perspectives on the child's theory of mind* (pp. 7–31). New York: Oxford University Press.

Astington, J. W., & Jenkins, J. M. (1995, March). *Language and theory of mind: A theoretical review and a longitudinal study.* Paper presented at the biennial meetings of the Society for Research in Child Development, Indianapolis, IN.

Astor, R. (1994). Children's moral reasoning about family and peer violence: The role of provocation and retribution. *Child Development, 65,* 1054–1067.

Attie, I., Brooks-Gunn, J., & Petersen, A. (1990). A developmental perspective on eating disorders and eating problems. In M. Lewis & S. M. Miller (Eds.), *Handbook of developmental psychopathology* (pp. 409–420). New York: Plenum.

Auster, E. (2001). Professional women's midcareer satisfaction: Toward an explanatory framework. *Sex Roles, 44,* 719–750.

Avis, J., & Harris, P. L. (1991). Belief-desire reasoning among Baka children: Evidence for a universal conception of mind. *Child Development, 62,* 460–467.

Axelman, K., Basun, H., & Lannfelt, L. (1998). Wide range of disease onset in a family with Alzheimer disease and a His163Tyr mutation in the presenilin-l gene. *Archives of Neurology, 55,* 698–702.

Aylward, G. (2002). Cognitive and neuropsychological outcomes: More than IQ scores. *Mental Retardation & Developmental Disabilities Research Reviews, 8,* 234–240.

Babiloni, C., Babiloni, F., Carducci, F., Cappa, S., Cincotti, F., Del Percio, C., Miniussi, C., Moretti, D., Rossi, S., Sosta, K., & Rossini, P. (2004). Human cortical rhythms during visual delayed choice reaction time tasks: A high-resolution EEG study on normal aging. *Behavioural Brain Research, 153,* 261–271.

Bach, P., Pham, H., Schrag, D., Tate, R., & Hargraves, L. (2004). Primary care physicians who treat blacks and whites. *New England Journal of Medicine, 351,* 575–584.

Bachman, J., Safron, D., Sy, S., & Schulenberg, J. (2003). Wishing to work: New perspectives on how adolescents' part-time work intensity is linked to educational disengagement, substance use, and other problem behaviours. *International Journal of Behavioral Development, 27,* 301–315.

Bachman, J., Segal, D., Freedman-Doan, P., & O'Malley, P. (2000). Who chooses military service? Correlates of propensity and enlistment in the U. S. Armed Forces. *Military Psychology, 12,* 1–30.

Bachman, J. G., & Schulenberg, J. (1993). How part-time work intensity relates to drug use, problem behavior, time use, and satisfaction among high school seniors: Are these consequences or merely correlates? *Developmental Psychology, 29,* 220–235.

Baddeley, A. (1998). *Human memory: Theory and practice* (Rev. ed.) Boston: Allyn & Bacon.

Baek, H. (2002). A comparative study of moral development of Korean and British children. *Journal of Moral Education, 31,* 373–391.

Bahrick, L., & Lickliter, R. (2000). Intersensory redundancy guides attentional selectivity and perceptual learning in infancy. *Developmental Psychology, 36,* 190–201.

Bailey, J., Brobow, D., Wolfe, M., & Mikach, S. (1995). Sexual orientation of adult sons of gay fathers. *Developmental Psychology, 31,* 124–129.

Bailey, J., Pillard, R., Dawood, K., Miller, M., Farrer, L., Trivedi, S., & Murphy, R. (1999). A family history study of male sexual orientation using three independent samples. *Behavior Genetics, 29,* 7986.

Bailey, J. M., & Pillard, R. C. (1991). A genetic study of male sexual orientation. *Archives of General Psychiatry, 48,* 1089–1096.

Bailey, J. M., Pillard, R. C., Neale, M. C., & Agyei, Y. (1993). Heritable factors influence sexual orientation in women. *Archives of General Psychiatry, 50,* 217–223.

Bailey, J. M., & Zucker, K. J. (1995). Childhood sex-typed behavior and sexual orientation: A conceptual analysis and quantitative review. *Developmental Psychology, 31,* 43–55.

Bailey, S., & Zvonkovic, A. (2003). Parenting after divorce: Nonresidential parents' perceptions of social and institutional support. *Journal of Divorce & Remarriage, 39,* 59–80.

Baillargeon, R. (1987). Object permanence in very young infants. *Developmental Psychology, 23,* 655–664.

Baillargeon, R. (1994). How do infants learn about the physical world? *Current Directions in Psychological Science, 3,* 133–140.

Baillargeon, R., & DeVos, J. (1991). Object permanence in young infants: Further evidence. *Child Development, 62,* 1227–1246.

Baillargeon, R., Spelke, E. S., & Wasserman, S. (1985). Object permanence in five-month-old infants. *Cognition, 20,* 191–208.

Bailley, S., Kral, M., & Dunham, K. (1999). Survivors of suicide do grieve differently: Empirical support for a common sense proposition. *Suicide & Life-Threatening Behavior, 29,* 256–271.

Baird, P. A., Sadovnick, A. D., & Yee, I. M. L. (1991). Maternal age and birth defects: A population study. *Lancet, 337,* 527–530.

Baker, D., Jeganathan, K., Cameron, D., Thompson, M., Juneja, S., Kopecka, A., Kumar, R., Jenkins, R., de Groen, P., Roche, P., & van Deursen, J. (2004). BubR1 insufficiency causes early onset of aging-associated phenotypes and infertility in mice. *Nature Genetics, 36,* 744–749.

Balaban, M. T. (1995). Affective influences on startle in five-month-old infants: Reactions to facial expressions of emotion. *Child Development, 66,* 28–36.

Baldwin, D. A. (1995, March). *Understanding relations between constraints and a socio-pragmatic account of meaning acquisition.* Paper presented at the biennial meetings of the Society for Research in Child Development, Indianapolis, IN.

Ball, E. (1997). Phonological awareness: Implications for whole language and emergent literacy programs. *Topics in Language Disorders, 17,* 14–26.

Baltes, B., & Heydens-Gahir, H. (2003). Reduction of work-family conflict through the use of selection, optimization, and compensation behaviors. *Journal of Applied Psychology, 88,* 1005–1018.

Baltes, P., & Staudinger, U. (2000). Wisdom: A metaheuristic (pragmatic) to orchestrate mind and virtue toward excellence. *American Psychologist, 55,* 122–136.

Baltes, P., Staudinger, U., & Lindenberger, U. (1999). Lifespan psychology: Theory and application to intellectual functioning. *Annual Review of Psychology, 50,* 471–507.

Baltes, P. B., & Baltes, M. M. (1990). Psychological perspectives on successful aging: The model of selective optimization with compensation. In P. B. Baltes & M. M. Baltes (Eds.), *Successful aging* (pp. 1–34). Cambridge, England: Cambridge University Press.

Baltes, P. B., Dittmann-Kohli, F., & Dixon, R. A. (1984). New perspectives on the development of intelligence in adulthood: Toward a dual-process conception and a model of selective optimization with compensation. In P. B. Baltes & O. G. Brim, Jr. (Eds.), *Life-span development and behavior* (pp. 34–77). New York: Academic Press.

Baltes, P. B., Dittmann-Kohli, F., & Dixon, R. A. (1986). Multidisciplinary propositions on the development of intelligence during adulthood and old age. In A. B. Sørensen, F. E. Weinert, & L. R. Sherrod (Eds.), *Human development and the life course: Multidisciplinary perspectives* (pp. 467–508). Hillsdale, NJ: Erlbaum.

Baltes, P. B., & Kliegl, R. (1992). Further testing of limits of cognitive plasticity: Negative age differences in a mnemonic skill are robust. *Developmental Psychology, 28,* 121–125.

Baltes, P. B., Reese, H. W., & Lipsitt, L. P. (1980). Life-span developmental psychology. *Annual Review of Psychology, 31,* 65–110.

Baltes, P. B., Reese, H. W., & Nesselroade, J. R. (1977). *Life-span developmental psychology: Introduction to research methods.* Monterey, CA: Books/Cole.

Baltes, P. B., & Smith, J. (1990). Toward a psychology of wisdom and its ontogenesis. In R. J. Sternberg (Ed.), *Wisdom. Its nature, origins, and development* (pp. 87–120). Cambridge, England: Cambridge University Press.

Baltes, P. B., Smith, J., & Staudinger, U. M. (1992). Wisdom and successful aging. In T. B. Sonderegger (Ed.), *Nebraska Symposium on Motivation, 1991* (pp. 123–168). Lincoln: University of Nebraska Press.

Baltes, P. B., Staudinger, U. M., Maercker, A., & Smith, J. (1995). People nominated as wise: A comparative study of wisdom-related knowledge. *Psychology & Aging, 10,* 155–166.

Bamford, F. N., Bannister, R. P., Benjamin, C. M., Hillier, V. F., Ward, B. S., & Moore, W. M. O. (1990). Sleep in the first year of life. *Developmental Medicine & Child Neurology, 32,* 718–724.

Bandura, A. (1977a). *Social learning theory.* Englewood Cliffs, NJ: Prentice-Hall.

Bandura, A. (1977b). Self-efficacy: Toward a unifying theory of behavioral change. *Psychological Review, 84,* 91–125.

Bandura, A. (1982). The psychology of chance encounters and life paths. *American Psychologist, 37,* 747–755.

Bandura, A. (1986). *Social foundations of thought and action: A social cognitive theory.* Englewood Cliffs, NJ: Prentice-Hall.

Bandura, A. (1989). Social cognitive theory. *Annals of Child Development, 6,* 1–60.

Bandura, A. (1997). *Self-efficacy: The exercise of control.* New York: Freeman.

Bandura, A., Ross, D., & Ross, S. A. (1961). Transmission of aggression through imitation of aggressive models. *Journal of Abnormal & Social Psychology, 63,* 575–582.

Bandura, A., Ross, D., & Ross, S. A. (1963). Imitation of film-mediated aggressive models. *Journal of Abnormal & Social Psychology, 66,* 3–11.

Baranchik, A. (2002). Identifying gaps in mathematics preparation that contribute to ethnic, gender, and American/foreign differences in precalculus performance. *Journal of Negro Education, 71,* 253–268.

Barbarin, O. (1999). Social risks and psychological adjustment: A comparison of African American and South African children. *Child Development, 70,* 1348–1359.

Barber, B., & Olsen, J. (2004). Assessing the transitions to middle and high school. *Journal of Adolescent Research, 19,* 3–30.

Barenboim, C. (1981). The development of person perception in childhood and adolescence: From behavioral comparisons to psychological constructs to psychological comparisons. *Child Development, 52,* 129–144.

Barer, B. (2001). The "grands and greats" of very old black grandmothers. *Journal of Aging Studies, 15,* 1–11.

Barker, J., Morrow, J., & Mitteness, L. (1998). Gender, informal social support networks, and elderly urban African Americans. *Journal of Aging Studies, 12,* 199–222.

Barkley, R. (1990). *Attention-deficit hyperactivity disorder.* New York: Guilford Press.

Barlow, J., & Lewandowski, L. (2000, August). *Ten-year longitudinal study of preterm infants: Outcomes and predictors.* Paper presented at the annual meeting of the American Psychological Association, Washington, DC.

Barnard, K. E., Hammond, M. A., Booth, C. L., Bee, H. L., Mitchell, S. K., & Spieker, S. J. (1989). Measurement and meaning of parent-child interaction. In J. J. Morrison, C. Lord, & D. P. Keating (Eds.), *Applied developmental psychology, Vol. 3* (pp. 40–81). San Diego, CA: Academic Press.

Barness, L., & Curran, J. (1996). Nutrition. In R. E. Behrman, R. M. Kliegman, & A. M. Arvin (Eds.), *Nelson's textbook of pediatrics* (15th ed., pp. 141–184). Philadelphia: Saunders.

Barnett, W. S. (1993). Benefit-cost analysis of preschool education: Findings from a 25-year follow-up. *American Journal of Orthopsychiatry, 63,* 500–508.

Barnett, W. S. (1995). Long-term effects of early childhood programs on cognitive and school outcomes. *The Future of Children, 5* (3), 25–50.

Barr, R., Marrott, H., & Rovee-Collier, C. (2003). The role of sensory preconditioning in memory retrieval by preverbal infants. *Learning & Behavior, 31,* 111–123.

Barrett-Connor, E., & Bush, T. L. (1991). Estrogen and coronary heart disease in women. *Journal of the American Medical Association, 265,* 1861–1867.

Barron, V., & Menken, K. (2002). *What are the characteristics of the bilingual education and ESL teacher shortage?* National Clearinghouse for English Language Acquisition & Language Instruction Educational Programs Factsheet. Retrieved June 23, 2004, from http://www.ncela.gwu.edu/expert/faq/14shortage.htm.

Bartlik, B., & Goldstein, M. (2000, June). Maintaining sexual health after menopause. *Psychiatric Services Journal, 51,* 751–753.

Bartoshuk, L. M., & Weiffenbach, J. M. (1990). Chemical senses and aging. In E. L. Schneider & J. W. Rowe (Eds.), *Handbook of the biology of aging* (3rd ed., pp. 429–444). San Diego, CA: Academic Press.

Barusch, A. (1999). Religion, adversity and age: Religious experiences of low-income elderly women. *Journal of Sociology & Social Welfare, 26,* 125–142.

Basham, P. (2001). Home schooling: From the extreme to the mainstream. *Public Policy Sources/The Fraser Institute, 51.* Retrieved June 23, 2004, from http://www.fraserinstitute.ca/admin/books/files/homeschool.pdf.

Bass, D. M. (1985). The hospice ideology and success of hospice care. *Research on Aging, 7,* 307–328.

Basseches, M. (1984). *Dialectical thinking and adult development.* Norwood, NJ: Ablex.

Basseches, M. (1989). Dialectical thinking as an organized whole: Comments on Irwin and Kramer. In M. L. Commons, J. D. Sinnott, F. A. Richards, & C. Armon (Eds.), *Adult development: Vol. 1. Comparisons and applications of developmental models* (pp. 161–178). New York: Praeger.

Bates, E. (1993). Commentary: Comprehension and production in early language development. *Monographs of the Society for Research in Child Development, 58* (3–4, Serial No. 233), 222–242.

Bates, E., Bretherton, I., & Snyder, L. (1988). *From first words to grammar: Individual differences and dissociable mechanisms.* Cambridge, England: Cambridge University Press.

Bates, E., Marchman, V., Thal, D., Fenson, L., Dale, P., Reznick, J. S., Reilly, J., & Hartung, J. (1994). Developmental and stylistic variation in the composition of early vocabulary. *Journal of Child Language, 21,* 85–123.

Bates, E., O'Connell, B., & Shore, C. (1987). Language and communication in infancy. In J. D. Osofsky (Ed.), *Handbook of infant development* (2nd ed., pp. 149–203). New York: Wiley.

Bates, J. E. (1989). Applications of temperament concepts. In G. A. Kohnstamm, J. E. Bates, & M. K. Rothbart (Eds.), *Temperament in childhood* (pp. 321–356). Chichester, England: Wiley.

Batten, M., & Oltjenbruns, K. (1999). Adolescent sibling bereavement as a catalyst for spiritual development: A model for understanding. *Death Studies, 23,* 529–546.

Bauer, P., Schwade, J., Wewerka, S., & Delaney, K. (1999). Planning ahead: Goal-directed problem solving by 2-year-olds. *Developmental Psychology, 35,* 1321–1337.

Baugher, R. J., Burger, C., Smith, R., & Wallston, K. (1989/1990). A comparison of terminally ill persons at various time periods to death. *Omega, 20,* 103–115.

Bauminger, N., & Kasari, C. (1999). Brief report: Theory of mind in high-functioning children with autism. *Journal of Autism & Developmental Disorders, 29,* 81–86.

Baumrind, D. (1967). Child care practices anteceding three patterns of preschool behavior. *Genetic Psychology Monographs, 75,* 43–88.

Baumrind, D. (1971). Current patterns of parental authority. *Developmental Psychology Monograph, 4* (1, Part 2).

Baumrind, D. (1972). Socialization and instrumental competence in young children. In W. W. Hartup (Ed.), *The young child: Reviews of research, Vol. 2* (pp. 202–224). Washington, DC: National Association for the Education of Young Children.

Baumrind, D. (1980). New directions in socialization research. *American Psychologist, 35,* 639–652.

Baumrind, D. (1991). Effective parenting during the early adolescent transition. In P. A. Cowan & M. Hetherington (Eds.), *Family transitions* (pp. 111–163). Hillsdale, NJ: Erlbaum.

Baxter, J., Shetterly, S., Eby, C., Mason, L., Cortese, C., & Hamman, R. (1998). Social network factors associated with perceived quality of life: The San Luis Valley Health and Aging Study. *Journal of Aging & Health, 10,* 287–310.

Baydar, N., & Brooks-Gunn, J. (1991). Effects of maternal employment and child-care arrangements on preschoolers' cognitive and behavioral outcomes: Evidence from the children of the National Longitudinal Survey of Youth. *Developmental Psychology, 27,* 932–945.

Baydar, N., Brooks-Gunn, J., & Furstenberg, F. F. (1993). Early warning signs of functional illiteracy: Predictors in childhood and adolescence. *Child Development, 64,* 815–829.

Bayley, N. (1969). *Bayley scales of infant development.* New York: Psychological Corporation.

Bayley, N. (1993). *Bayley scales of infant development: Birth to two years.* San Antonio, TX: Psychological Corporation.

Beaty, L. (1999). Identity development of homosexual youth and parental and familial influences on the coming out process. *Adolescence, 34,* 597–601.

Beaudry, M., Dufour, R., & Marcoux, S. (1995). Relation between infant feeding and infections during the first six months of life. *Journal of Pediatrics, 126,* 191–197.

Beautrais, A., Joyce, P., & Mulder, R. (1999). Personality traits and cognitive styles as risk factors for serious suicide attempts among young people. *Suicide & Life-Threatening Behavior, 29,* 37–47.

Beck, A., Brown, G., Berchick, R., Stewart, B., & Steer, R. (1990). Relationship between hopelessness and ultimate suicide: A replication with psychiatric outpatients. *American Journal of Psychiatry, 147,* 190–195.

Bedeian, A. G., Ferris, G. R., & Kacmar, K. M. (1992). Age, tenure, and job satisfaction: A tale of two perspectives. *Journal of Vocational Behavior, 40,* 33–48.

Bedford, V. (1995). Sibling relationships in middle and old age. In R. Blieszner & V. H. Bedford (Eds.), *Handbook of aging and the family.* Westport, CT: Greenwood Press.

Bee, H. L., Barnard, K. E., Eyres, S. J., Gray, C. A., Hammond, M. A., Spietz, A. L., Snyder, C., & Clark, B. (1982). Prediction of IQ and language skill from perinatal status, child performance, family characteristics, and mother-infant interaction. *Child Development, 53,* 1135–1156.

Beekman, A., Copeland, J., & Prince, M. (1999). Review of community prevalence of depression in later life. *British Journal of Psychiatry, 174,* 307–311.

Beem, E., Hooijkaas, H., Cleriren, M., Schut, H., Garssen, B., Croon, M., Jabaaij, L., Goodkin, K., Wind, H., & de Vries, M. (1999). The immunological and psychological effects of bereavement: Does grief counseling really make a difference? A pilot study. *Psychiatry Research, 85,* 81–93.

Behrend, D., Scofield, J., & Kleinknecht, E. (2001) Beyond fast mapping: Young children's extensions of novel words and novel facts. *Developmental Psychology, 37,* 690–705.

Beilke, J., & Yssel, N. (1999). The chilly climate for students with disabilities in higher education. *College Student Journal, 33,* 364–371.

Belgrave, L. L., Wykle, M. L., & Choi, J. M. (1993). Health, double jeopardy, and culture: The use of institutionalization by African-Americans. *The Gerontologist, 33,* 379–385.

Bell, J., & Bromnick, R. (2003). The social reality of the imaginary audience: A ground theory approach. *Adolescence, 38,* 205–219.

Bell, L. G., & Bell, D. C. (1982). Family climate and the role of the female adolescent: Determinants of adolescent functioning. *Family Relations, 31,* 519–527.

Bellantoni, M. F., & Blackman, M. R. (1996). Menopause and its consequences. In E. L. Schneider & J. W. Rowe (Eds.), *Handbook of the biology of aging* (4th ed., pp. 415–430). San Diego, CA: Academic Press.

Belsky, J. (1985). Prepared statement on the effects of day care. In Select Committee on Children, Youth, and Families, House of Representatives, 98th Congress, Second Session, *Improving child care services: What can be done?* Washington, DC: U.S. Government Printing Office.

Belsky, J. (1992). Consequences of child care for children's development: A deconstructionist view. In A. Booth (Ed.), *Child care in the 1990s: Trends and consequences* (pp. 83–94). Hillsdale, NJ: Erlbaum.

Belsky, J. (2001). Developmental risks (still) associated with early child care. *Journal of Child Psychology & Psychiatry & Allied Disciplines, 42,* 845–859.

Belsky, J. (2002). Quantity counts: Amount of child care and children's socioemotional development. *Journal of Developmental & Behavioral Pediatrics, 23,* 167–170.

Belsky, J., & Hsieh, K. (1998). Patterns of marital change during the early childhood years: Parent personality, coparenting, and division-of-labor correlates. *Journal of Family Psychology, 12,* 511–528.

Belsky, J., Hsieh, K., & Crnic, K. (1996). Infant positive and negative emotionality: One dimension or two? *Developmental Psychology, 32,* 289–298.

Belsky, J., Jaffee, S., Caspi, A., Moffitt, T., & Silva, P. (2003). Intergenerational relationships in young adulthood and their life course, mental health, and personality correlates. *Journal of Family Psychology, 17,* 460–471.

Belsky, J., Lang, M. E., & Rovine, M. (1985). Stability and change in marriage across the transition to parenthood: A second study. *Journal of Marriage & the Family, 47,* 855–865.

Belsky, J., & Rovine, M. (1988). Nonmaternal care in the first year of life and the security of infant-parent attachment. *Child Development, 59,* 157–167.

Bem, S. L. (1974). The measurement of psychological androgyny. *Journal of Consulting & Clinical Psychology, 42,* 155–162.

Benbow, C. P. (1988). Sex differences in mathematical reasoning ability in intellectually talented preadolescents: Their nature, effects, and possible causes. *Behavioral & Brain Sciences, 11,* 169–232.

Bender, B. G., Harmon, R. J., Linden, M. G., & Robinson, A. (1995). Psychosocial adaptation of 39 adolescents with sex chromosome abnormalities. *Pediatrics, 96,* 302–308.

Bender, K. (1999). Assessing antidepressant safety in the elderly. *Psychiatric Times, 16.* Retrieved February 7, 2001, from http://www.mhsource.com/pt/p990151.html.

Bendersky, M., & Lewis, M. (1994). Environmental risk, biological risk, and developmental outcome. *Developmental Psychology, 30,* 484–494.

Benenson, J., & Benarroch, D. (1998). Gender differences in responses to friends' hypothetical greater success. *Journal of Early Adolescence, 18,* 192–208.

Benenson, J. F. (1994). Ages four to six years: Changes in the structures of play networks of girls and boys. *Merrill-Palmer Quarterly, 40,* 478–487.

Bengtson, V., Rosenthal, C., & Burton, L. (1990). Families and aging: Diversity and heterogeneity. In R. H. Binstock & L. K. George (Eds.), *Handbook of aging and the social sciences* (3rd ed., pp. 263–287). San Diego, CA: Academic Press.

Bengtson, V., Rosenthal, C., & Burton, L. (1996). Paradoxes of families and aging. In R. H. Binstock & L. K. George (Eds.), *Handbook of aging and the social sciences* (4th ed., pp. 253–282). San Diego, CA: Academic Press.

Bengtson, V. L. (1985). Diversity and symbolism in grandparent roles. In V. L. Bengtson & J. F. Robertson (Eds.), *Grandparenthood* (pp. 11–26). Beverly Hills, CA: Sage.

Bengtson, V. L., Cuellar, J. B., & Ragan, P. K. (1977). Stratum contrasts and similarities in attitudes toward death. *Journal of Gerontology, 32,* 76–88.

Bennett, M. (1997). A longitudinal study of wellbeing in widowed women. *International Journal of Geriatric Psychiatry, 12,* 61–66.

Bennett, M. (1998). Longitudinal changes in mental and physical health among elderly, recently widowed men. *Mortality, 3,* 265–273.

Benshoff, J., & Lewis, H. (1993). *Nontraditional college students.* ERIC No. ED 34 7483 92.

Berg, J., & Lipson, J. (1999). Information sources, menopause beliefs, and health complaints of midlife Filipinas. *Health, 20,* 81–92.

Berg, S. (1996). Aging, behavior, and terminal decline. In J. E. Birren & K. W. Schaie (Eds.), *Handbook of the psychology of aging* (4th ed., pp. 323–337). San Diego, CA: Academic Press.

Bergeman, C. S., Chipuer, H. M., Plomin, R., Pedersen, N. L., McClearn, G. E., Nesselroade, J. R., Costa, P. T., & McCrae, R. R. (1993). Genetic and environmental effects on openness to experience, agreeableness, and conscientiousness: An adoption/twin study. *Journal of Personality, 61,* 159–179.

Bergeson, T., & Trehub, S. (1999). Mothers' singing to infants and preschool children. *Infant Behavior & Development, 22,* 53–64.

Bergman, R. (2002). Why be moral? A conceptual model from developmental psychology. *Human Development, 45,* 104–124.

Berkman, L. F. (1985). The relationship of social networks and social support to morbidity and mortality. In S. Coen & S. L. Syme (Eds.), *Social support and health* (pp. 241–262). Orlando, FL: Academic Press.

Berkman, L. F., & Breslow, L. (1983). *Health and ways of living: The Alameda County Study.* New York: Oxford University Press.

Berkowitz, G. S., Skovron, M. L., Lapinski, R. H., & Berkowitz, R. L. (1990). Delayed childbearing and the outcome of pregnancy. *New England Journal of Medicine, 322,* 659–664.

Berliner, D., & Biddle, B. (1997). *The manufactured crisis: Myths, fraud, and the attack on America's public schools.* New York: Addison-Wesley.

Berndt, T. J. (1992). Friendship and friends' influence in adolescence. *Current Directions in Psychological Science, 1,* 156–159.

Berndt, T. J., & Keefe, K. (1995a). Friends' influence on adolescents' adjustment to school. *Child Development, 66,* 1312–1329.

Berndt, T. J., & Keefe, K. (1995b, March). *Friends' influence on school adjustment: A motivational analysis.* Paper presented at the biennial meetings of the Society for Research in Child Development, Indianapolis, IN.

Berne, L., & Huberman, B. (1996, February). Sexuality education works: Here's proof. *Education Digest,* 25–29.

Bernhard, J., Lefebvre, M., Kilbride, K., Chud, G., & Lange, R. (1998). Troubled relationships in early childhood education: Parent-teacher interactions in ethnoculturally diverse child care settings. *Early Education & Development, 9,* 5–28.

Berninger, V., Abbott, R., Zook, D., Ogier, S., et al. (1999). Early intervention for reading disabilities: Teaching the alphabet principle in a connectionist framework. *Journal of Learning Disabilities, 32,* 491–503.

Berthier, N., DeBlois, S., Poirier, C., Novak, M., & Clifton, R. (2000). Where's the ball? Two- and three-year-olds reason about unseen events. *Developmental Psychology, 36,* 394–401.

Berzonsky, M. (2003). The structure of identity: Commentary on Jane Kroger's view of identity status transition. *Identity, 3,* 231–245.

Betancourt, H., & Lopez, S. R. (1993). The study of culture, ethnicity, and race in American psychology. *American Psychologist, 48,* 629–637.

Betancourt, L., Fischer, R., Gianetta, J., Malmud, E., Brodsky, N. & Hurt, H. (1999). Problem-solving ability of inner-city children with and without in utero cocaine exposure. *Journal of Developmental Disabilities, 20,* 418–424.

Betz, E. L. (1984). A study of career patterns of women college graduates. *Journal of Vocational Behavior, 24,* 249–263.

Betz, N. E., & Fitzgerald, L. F. (1987). *The career psychology of women.* Orlando, FL: Academic Press.

Bhatt, R., Wilk, A., Hill, D., & Rovee-Collier, C. (2004). Correlated attributes and categorization in the first half-year of life. *Developmental Psychobiology, 44,* 103–115.

Bial, M. (1971). *Liberal Judaism at home.* New York: Union of American Hebrew Congregations.

Bialystok, E. (1997). Effects of bilingualism and biliteracy on children's emerging concepts of print. *Developmental Psychology, 33.*

Bialystok, E., & Majumder, S. (1998). The relationship between bilingualism and the development of cognitive processes in problem solving. *Applied Psycholinguistics, 19,* 69–85.

Bialystok, E., Majumder, S., & Martin, M. (2003). Developing phonological awareness: Is there a bilingual advantage? *Applied Linguistics, 24,* 27–44.

Bialystok, E., Shenfield, T., & Codd, J. (2000). Languages, scripts, and the environment: Factors in developing concepts of print. *Developmental Psychology, 36,* 66–76.

Bianchi, A. (1993, January-February). Older drivers: The good, the bad, and the iffy. *Harvard Magazine,* pp. 12–13.

Biblarz, T. J., Bengtson, V. L., & Bucur, A. (1996). Social mobility across three generations. *Journal of Marriage & the Family, 58,* 188–200.

Bigler, E. D., Johnson, S. C., Jackson, C., & Blatter, D. D. (1995). Aging, brain size, and IQ. *Intelligence, 21,* 109–119.

Bigler, R., & Liben, S. (1993). The role of attitudes and interventions in gender-schematic processing. *Child Development, 61,* 1440–1452.

Billy, J. O. G., Brewster, K. L., & Grady, W. R. (1994). Contextual effects on the sexual behavior of adolescent women. *Journal of Marriage & the Family, 56,* 387–404.

Binet, A., & Simon, T. (1905). Méthodes nouvelles pour le diagnostic du niveau intellectuel des anormaux [New methods for diagnosing the intellectual level of the abnormal]. *L'Anée Psychologique, 11,* 191–244.

Bingham, C. R., Miller, B. C., & Adams, G. R. (1990). Correlates of age at first sexual intercourse in a national sample of young women. *Journal of Adolescent Research, 5,* 18–33.

Birch, D. (1998). The adolescent parent: A fifteen-year longitudinal study of school-age mothers and their children. *International Journal of Adolescent Medicine & Health, 19,* 141–153.

Biringen, Z. (2000). Emotional availability: Conceptualization and research findings. *American Journal of Orthopsychiatry, 70,* 104–114.

Biro, F. M., Lucky, A. W., Huster, G. A., & Morrison, J. A. (1995). Pubertal staging in boys. *Journal of Pediatrics, 127,* 100–102.

Birren, J. E., & Fisher, L. M. (1995). Aging and speed of behavior: Possible consequences for psychological functioning. *Annual Review of Psychology, 56,* 329–353.

Birren, J. E., & Schroots, J. J. F. (1996). History, concepts, and theory in the psychology of aging. In J. R. Birren & K. W. Schaie (Eds.), *Handbook of the psychology of aging* (4th ed., pp. 3–23). San Diego, CA: Academic Press.

Biswas, M. K., & Craigo, S. D. (1994). The course and conduct of normal labor and delivery. In A. H. DeCherney & M. L. Pernoll (Eds.), *Current obstetric and gynecologic diagnosis and treatment* (pp. 202–227). Norwalk, CT: Appleton & Lange.

Bittner, S., & Newberger, E. (1981). Pediatric understanding of child abuse and neglect. *Pediatric Review, 2,* 198.

Black, K., & McCartney, K. (1997). Adolescent females' security with parents predicts the quality of peer interactions. *Social Development, 6,* 91–110.

Black, K. A., & McCartney, K. (1995, March). *Associations between adolescent attachment to parents and peer interactions.* Paper presented at the biennial meetings of the Society for Research in Child Development, Indianapolis, IN.

Black, S., Markides, K., & Miller, T. (1998). Correlates of depressive symptomatology among older community-dwelling Mexican Americans: The hispanic EPESE. *Journals of Gerontology, Series B: Psychological Sciences & Social Sciences, 53B,* S198–S208.

Blackman, J. A. (1990). Update on AIDS, CMV, and herpes in young children: Health, developmental, and educational issues. In M. Wolraich & D. K. Routh (Eds.), *Advances in developmental and behavioral pediatrics Vol. 9* (pp. 33–58). London: Jessica Kingsley Publishers.

Blackwell, D., & Lichter, D. (2000). Mate selection among married and cohabiting couples. *Journal of Family Issues, 21,* 275–302.

Blair, S. L., & Johnson, M. P. (1992). Wives' perceptions of the fairness of the division of household labor: The intersection of housework and ideology. *Journal of Marriage & the Family, 54,* 570–581.

Blair, S. N., Kohl, H. W., III, Barlow, C. E., Paffenbarger, R. S., Gibbons, L. W., & Macera, C. A. (1995). Changes in physical fitness and all-cause mortality. *Journal of the American Medical Association, 273,* 1093–1098.

Blake, I. K. (1994). Language development and socialization in young African-American children. In P. M. Greenfield & R. R. Cocking (Eds.), *Cross-cultural roots of minority child development* (pp. 167–195). Hillsdale, NJ: Erlbaum.

Blakemore, J., LaRue, A., Olejnik, A. (1979). Sex-appropriate toy preference and the ability to conceptualize toys as sex-role related. *Developmental Psychology, 15,* 339–340.

Blakeslee, S. (April 13, 1994). A genetic factor may help to explain variations in lung cancer rates. *New York Times,* p. B10.

Blanchard, C., & Lichtenberg, J. (2003). Compromise in career decision making: A test of Gottfredson's theory. *Journal of Vocational Behavior, 62,* 250–271.

Blanchard-Fields, F., Chen, Y., Schocke, M., & Hertzog, C. (1998). Evidence for content-specificity of causal attributions across the adult life span. *Aging, Neuropsychology, & Cognition, 5,* 241–263.

Blanpain, C., Lowry, W., Geoghegan, A., Polak, L., & Fuchs, E. (2004). Self-renewal, multipotency, and the existence of two cell populations within an epithelial stem cell niche. *Cell, 118,* 635–648.

Blatter, D. D., Bigler, E. D., Gale, S. D., Johnson, S. C., Anderson, C. V., Burnett, B. M., Parker, N., Kurth, S., & Horn, S. (1995). Quantitative volumetric analysis of brain MR: Normative database spanning five decades (16–65). *American Journal of Neuroradiology, 16,* 241–251.

Blau, F. D., & Ferber, M. A. (1991). Career plans and expectations of young women and men: The earnings gap and labor force participation. *The Journal of Human Resources, 26,* 581–607.

Blau, G. (1996). Adolescent depression and suicide. In G. Blau & T. Gullotta (Eds.), *Adolescent dysfunctional behavior: Causes, interventions, and prevention* (pp. 187–205). Newbury Park, CA: Sage.

Blazer, D., Hybels, C., Simonsick, E., & Hanlon, J. (2000). Marked differences in antidepressant use by race in an elderly community sample: 1986–1996. *American Journal of Psychiatry, 157,* 1089–1094.

Blazer, D., Landerman, L., Hays, J., Simonsick, E., & Saunders, W. (1998). Symptoms of depression among community-dwelling elderly African American and White older adults. *Psychological Medicine, 28,* 1311–1320.

Blickstine, I., Jones, C., & Keith, L. (2003). Zygotic-splitting rates after single-embryo transfers in in vitro fertilization. *New England Journal of Medicine, 348,* 2366–2367.

Blieszner, R., & Adams, R. G. (1992). *Adult friendship.* Newbury Park, CA: Sage.

Block, J. (1971). *Lives through time.* Berkeley, CA: Bancroft.

Block, J., & Robins, R. W. (1993). A longitudinal study of consistency and change in self-esteem from early adolescence to early adulthood. *Child Development, 64,* 909–923.

Bloom, B. L., White, S. W., & Asher, S. J. (1979). Marital disruption as a stressful life event. In C. Levinger & O. C. Moles (Eds.), *Divorce and separation: Context, causes, and consequences* (pp. 184–200). New York: Basic Books.

Bloom, L. (1973). *One word at a time.* The Hague: Mouton.

Bloom, L. (1991). *Language development from two to three.* Cambridge, England: Cambridge University Press.

Bloom, L. (1993). *The transition from infancy to language: Acquiring the power of expression.* Cambridge, England: Cambridge University Press.

Bloom, L. (1997, April). *The child's action drives the interaction.* Paper presented at the biennial meetings of the Society for Research in Child Development, Washington, DC.

Bluck, S., Levine, L., & Laulhere, T. (1999). Autobiographical remembering and hypermnesia: A comparison of older and younger adults. *Psychology & Aging, 14,* 671–682.

Blumberg, F., & Sokol, L. (2004). Boys' and girls' use of cognitive strategies when learning to play video games. *Journal of General Psychology, 131,* 151–158.

Blumberg, J. B. (1996). Status and functional impact of nutrition in older adults. In E. L. Schneider & J. W. Rowe (Eds.), *Handbook of the biology of aging* (4th ed., pp. 393–414). San Diego, CA: Academic Press.

Blumenthal, J. A., Emery, C. F., Madden, D. J., Schniebolk, S., Walsh-Riddle, M., George, L. K., McKee, D. C., Higginbotham, M. B., Cobb, R. R., & Coleman, R. E. (1991). Long-term effects of exercise on physiological functioning in older men and women. *Journals of Gerontology: Psychological Sciences, 46,* P352–361.

Blumstein, P., & Schwartz, P. (1983). *American couples.* New York: Morrow.

Blustein, D., Phillips, S., Jobin-Davis, K., & Finkelberg, S. (1997). A theory-building investigation of the school-to-work transition. *Counseling Psychology, 25,* 364–402.

Bogenschneider, K., Wu, M., Raffaelli, M., & Tsay, J. (1998). "Other teens drink, but not my kid": Does parental awareness of adolescent alcohol use protect adolescents from risky consequences? *Journal of Marriage & the Family, 60,* 356–373.

Bohman, M., & Sigvardsson, S. (1990). Outcome in adoption: Lessons from longitudinal studies. In D. M. Brodzinsky (Ed.), *The psychology of adoption* (pp. 93–106). New York: Oxford University Press.

Boldizar, J. (1991). Assessing sex-typing and androgyny in children. *Developmental Psychology, 27,* 506–535.

Bonanno, G., Znoj, H., Siddique, H., & Horowitz, M. (1999). Verbal-autonomic dissociation and adaptation to midlife conjugal loss: A follow-up at 25 months. *Cognitive Therapy & Research, 23,* 605–624.

Bond, J., & Coleman, P. (Eds.). (1990). *Aging in society.* London: Sage.

Bond, L., Braskamp, D., & Roeber, E. (1996). *The status report of the assessment programs in the United States.* Oakbrook, IL: North Central Regional Educational Laboratory. ERIC No. ED 401 333.

Bond, M. H., Nakazato, H., & Shiraishi, D. (1975). Universality and distinctiveness in dimensions of Japanese person perception. *Journal of Cross-Cultural Psychology, 6,* 346–357.

Bonde, E., Obel, C., Nedergard, N., & Thomsen, P. (2004). Social risk factors as predictors for parental report of deviant behaviour in 3-year-old children. *Nordic Journal of Psychiatry, 58,* 17–23.

Bondevik, M., & Skogstad, A. (1998). The oldest old, ADL, social network, and loneliness. *Western Journal of Nursing Research, 20,* 325–343.

Bong, M. (1998). Tests of the internal/external frames of reference model with subject-specific academic self-efficacy and frame-specific academic self-concepts. *Journal of Educational Psychology, 90,* 102–110.

Boone, R., Higgins, K., Notari, A., & Stump, C. (1996). Hypermedia pre-reading lessons: Learner-centered software for kindergarten. *Journal of Computing in Childhood Education, 7,* 39–70.

Borkenau, P., & Ostendorf, F. (1990). Comparing exploratory and confirmatory factor analysis: A study on the five-factor model of personality. *Personality & Individual Differences, 11,* 515–524.

Borkowski, M., Hunter, K., & Johnson, C. (2001). White noise and scheduled bedtime routines to reduce infant and childhood sleep disturbances. *Behavior Therapist, 24,* 29–37.

Bornholt, L., & Goodnow, J. (1999). Cross-generation perceptions of academic competence: Parental expectations and adolescent self-disclosure. *Journal of Adolescent Research, 14,* 427–447.

Bornstein, M., Tamis-LeMonda, D., Tal, J., Ludemann, P., Toda, S., Rahn, C., Pecheux, M., Azuma, H., & Vardi, D. (1992). Maternal responsiveness to infants in three societies: The United States, France, and Japan. *Child Development, 63,* 808–821.

Bornstein, M. H. (1992). Perception across the life span. In M. H. Bornstein & M. E. Lamb (Eds.), *Developmental psychology: An advanced textbook* (3rd ed., pp. 155–210). Hillsdale, NJ: Erlbaum.

Bosch, L., & Sebastian-Galles, N. (1997). Native-language recognition abilities in 4-month-old infants from monolingual and bilingual environments. *Cognition, 65,* 33–69.

Bossé, R., Aldwin, C. M., Levenson, M. R., & Workman-Daniels, K. (1991). How stressful is retirement? Findings from the normative aging study. *Journals of Gerontology: Psychological Sciences, 46,* P9–14.

Bosworth, H., Park, K., McQuoid, D., Hays, J., & Steffens, D. (2003). The impact of religious practice and religious coping on geriatric depression. *International Journal of Geriatric Psychiatry, 18,* 905–914.

Bosworth, H., Siegler, I., Brummett, B., Barefoot, J., Williams, R., Clapp-Channing, N., & Mark, D. (2000, August). *Health-related quality of life in a coronary artery sample.* Paper presented at the annual meeting of the American Psychological Association. Washington, DC.

Botwinick, J., & Storandt, M. (1974). *Memory, related functions and age.* Springfield, IL: Charles C Thomas.

Bouchard, T. J., Jr., & McGue, M. (1981). Familial studies of intelligence: A review. *Science, 212,* 1055–1059.

Bourreille, C. (1999). Diana/Diana. *Cahiers Jungiens de Psychanalyse, 96,* 75–76.

Bowen, J., Gibson, F., & Hand, P. (2002). Educational outcome at 8 years for children who were born extremely prematurely: A controlled study. *Journal of Pediatrics & Child Health, 38,* 438–444.

Bowerman, M. (1985). Beyond communicative adequacy: From piecemeal knowledge to an integrated system in the child's acquisition of language. In K. E. Nelson (Ed.), *Children's language, Vol. 5* (pp. 369–398). Hillsdale, NJ: Erlbaum.

Bowker, A. (2004). Predicting friendship stability during early adolescence. *Journal of Early Adolescence, 24,* 85–112.

Bowlby, J. (1969). *Attachment and loss, Vol. 1: Attachment.* New York: Basic Books.

Bowlby, J. (1973). *Attachment and loss, Vol. 2: Separation, anxiety, and anger.* New York: Basic Books.

Bowlby, J. (1980). *Attachment and loss, Vol. 3: Loss, sadness, and depression.* New York: Basic Books.

Bowlby, J. (1988a). Developmental psychiatry comes of age. *American Journal of Psychiatry, 145,* 1–10.

Bowlby, J. (1988b). *A secure base.* New York: Basic Books.

Bowler, D., Briskman, J., & Grice, S. (1999). Experimenter effects on children's understanding of false drawings and false beliefs. *Journal of Genetic Psychology, 160,* 443–460.

Bowling, A., Fleissig, A., Gabriel, Z., Banister, D., Dyjes, J., Dowding, L., Sutton, S., & Evans, O. (2003). Let's ask them: A national survey of definitions of quality of life and its enhancement among people aged 65 and over. *International Journal of Aging & Human Development, 56,* 269–306.

Bowman, P. J. (1991). Joblessness. In J. J. Jackson (Ed.), *Life in black America* (pp. 156–178). Newbury Park, CA: Sage.

Boxall, P., Macky, K., & Rasmussen, E. (2003). Labour turnover and retention in New Zealand: The causes and consequences of leaving and staying with employers. *Asia Pacific Journal of Human Resources, 41,* 195–214.

Boyatzis, C. J., Matillo, G., Nesbitt, K., & Cathey, G. (1995, March). *Effects of "The Mighty Morphin Power Rangers" on children's aggression and pro-*

social behavior. Paper presented at the biennial meetings of the Society for Research in Child Development, Indianapolis, IN.

Braam, A., Beekman, A., Deeg, D., Smit, J., & van Tilburg, W. (1997). Religiosity as a protective or prognostic factor of depression in later life: Results from a community survey in the Netherlands. *Longitudinal Aging Study, 96,* 199–205.

Bradbury, K., & Katz, J. (2002). Women's labor market involvement and family income mobility when marriages end. *New England Economic Review, Q4,* 41–74.

Bradley, R. H., Caldwell, B. M., Rock, S. L., Barnard, K. E., Gray, C., Hammond, M. A., Mitchell, S., Siegel, L., Ramey, C. D., Gottfried, A. W., & Johnson, D. L. (1989). Home environment and cognitive development in the first 3 years of life: A collaborative study involving six sites and three ethnic groups in North America. *Developmental Psychology, 25,* 217–235.

Bradmetz, J. (1999). Precursors of formal thought: A longitudinal study. *British Journal of Developmental Psychology, 17,* 61–81.

Brady, K., & Eisler, R. (1999). Sex and gender in the college classroom: A quantitative analysis of faculty-student interactions and perceptions. *Journal of Educational Psychology, 91,* 124–145.

Brand, A., & Brinich, P. (1999). Behavior problems and mental health contacts in adopted, foster, and nonadopted children. *Journal of Child Psychology & Psychiatry & Allied Disciplines, 40,* 1221–1229.

Brandon, P. (1999). Determinants of self-care arrangements among school-age children. *Children & Youth Services Review, 21,* 497–520.

Brandon, P., & Hofferth, S. (2003). Determinants of out-of-school childcare arrangements among children in single-mother and two-parent families. *Social Science Research, 32,* 129–147.

Brandtstädter, J., & Baltes-Götz, B. (1990). Personal control over development and quality of life perspectives in adulthood. In P. Baltes & M. M. Baltes (Eds.), *Successful aging* (pp. 197–224). Cambridge, England: Cambridge University Press.

Brandtstädter, J., & Greve, W. (1994). The aging self: Stabilizing and protective processes. *Developmental Review, 14,* 52–80.

Braten, I., & Olaussen, B. (1998). The learning and study strategies of Norwegian first-year college students. *Learning & Individual Differences, 10,* 309–327.

Braun, K., & Nichols, R. (1997). Death and dying in four Asian American cultures: A descriptive study. *Death Studies, 21,* 327–359.

Braveman, N. S. (1987). Immunity and aging immunologic and behavioral perspectives. In M. W. Riley, J. D. Matarazzo, & A. Baum (Eds.), *Perspectives in behavioral medicine: The aging dimension* (pp. 94–124). Hillsdale, NJ: Erlbaum.

Bravo, G., Dubois, M., & Pâquet, M. (2003). Advance directives for health care and research prevalence and correlates. *Alzheimer Disease & Associate Disorders, 17,* 215–222.

Bray, D. W., & Howard, A. (1983). The AT&T longitudinal studies of managers. In K. W. Schaie (Ed.), *Longitudinal studies of adult psychological development* (pp. 266–312). New York: Guilford Press.

Brazelton, T. B. (1984). *Neonatal Behavioral Assessment Scale.* Philadelphia: Lippincott.

Bregman, G., & Killen, M. (1999). Adolescents' and young adults' reasoning about career choice and the role of parental influence. *Journal of Research on Adolescence, 9,* 253–275.

Bremner, J. (2002). The nature of imitation by infants. *Infant Behavior & Development, 25,* 65–67.

Brendgen, M., Vitaro, F., & Bukowski, W. (1998). Affiliation with delinquent friends: Contributions of parents, self-esteem, delinquent behavior, and rejection by peers. *Journal of Early Adolescence, 18,* 244–265.

Brener, N., Hassan, S., & Barrios, L. (1999). Suicidal ideation among college students in the United States. *Journal of Consulting & Clinical Psychology, 67,* 1004–1008.

Brennan, F., & Ireson, J. (1997). Training phonological awareness: A study to evaluate the effects of a program of metalinguistic games in kindergarten. *Reading & Writing, 9,* 241–263.

Brenner, V. (1997). Psychology of computer use: XLVII. Parameters of Internet use. *Psychological Reports, 80,* 879–882.

Breslau, N., & Chilcoat, H. (2000). Psychiatric sequelae of low birth weight at 11 years of age. *Biological Psychiatry, 47,* 1005–1011.

Breslau, N., DelDotto, J. E., Brown, G. G., Kumar, S., Ezhuthachan, S., Hufnagle, K. G., & Peterson, E. L. (1994). A gradient relationship between low birth weight and IQ at age 6 years. *Archives of Pediatric & Adolescent Medicine, 2148,* 377–383.

Breslau, N., Johnson, E., & Lucia, V. (2001). Academic achievement of low birthweight children at age 11: The role of cognitive abilities at school entry. *Journal of Abnormal Child Psychology, 29,* 273–279.

Breslow, L., & Breslow, N. (1993). Health practices and disability: Some evidence from Alameda County. *Preventive Medicine, 22,* 86–95.

Bretscher, M., Rummans, T., Sloan, J., Kaur, J., Bartlett, A., Borkenhagen, L., & Loprinzi, C. (1999). Quality of life in hospice patients: A pilot study. *Psychosomatics, 40,* 309–313.

Briggs, R. (1990). Biological aging. In J. Bond & P. Coleman (Eds.), *Aging in society* (pp. 48–61). London: Sage.

Brock, D. B., Guralnik, J. M., & Brody, J. A. (1990). Demography and the epidemiology of aging in the United States. In E. L. Schneider & J. W. Rowe (Eds.), *Handbook of the biology of aging* (3rd ed., pp. 3–23). San Diego, CA: Academic Press.

Brockington, I. (1996). *Motherhood and mental health.* Oxford, England: Oxford University Press.

Brody, E. M., Litvin, S. J., Albert, S. M., & Hoffman, C. J. (1994). Marital status of daughters and patterns of parent care. *Journals of Gerontology: Social Sciences, 49,* S95–103.

Brody, E. M., Litvin, S. J., Hoffman, C., & Kleban, M. H. (1992). Differential effects of daughters' marital status on their parent care experiences. *The Gerontologist, 32,* 58–67.

Brody, G., Kim, S., Murry, V., & Brown, A. (2003). Longitudinal direct and indirect pathways linking older sibling competence to the development of younger sibling competence. *Developmental Psychology, 39,* 618–628.

Brody, G. H., Stoneman, Z., & Flor, D. (1995). Linking family processes and academic competence among rural African American youths. *Journal of Marriage & the Family, 47,* 567–579.

Brody, J. E. (1994, April 20). Making a strong case for antioxidants. *New York Times,* p. B9.

Brody, J. E. (1995, October 4). Personal health. *New York Times,* p. B7.

Brody, J. E. (1996, February 28). Good habits outweigh genes as key to a healthy old age. *New York Times,* p. B9.

Brody, N. (1992). *Intelligence* (2nd ed.). San Diego, CA: Academic Press.

Bronfenbrenner, U. (1979). *The ecology of human development.* Cambridge, MA: Harvard University Press.

Bronfenbrenner, U. (1989). Ecological systems theory. *Annals of Child Development, 6,* 187–249.

Bronfenbrenner, U. (1993). The ecology of cognitive development: Research models and fugitive findings. In R. H. Wozniak and K. W. Fischer (Eds.), *Development in context: Acting and thinking in specific environments.* Hillsdale, NJ: Erlbaum.

Bronson, G. W. (1994). Infants' transitions toward adult-like scanning. *Child development, 65,* 1253–1261.

Brook, J., Whiteman, M., Finch, S., & Cohen, P. (2000). Longitudinally foretelling drug use in the late twenties: Adolescent personality and social-environmental antecedents. *Journal of Genetic Psychology, 161,* 37–51.

Brooks-Gunn, J. (1987). Pubertal processes and girls' psychological adaptation. In R. M. Lerner & T. T. Foch (Eds.), *Biological-psychosocial interactions in early adolescence* (pp. 123–154). Hillsdale, NJ: Erlbaum.

Brooks-Gunn, J. (1995). Children in families in communities: Risk and intervention in the Bronfenbrenner tradition. In P. Moen, G. H. Elder, Jr., & K. Lüscher (Eds.), *Examining lives in context: Perspectives on the ecology of human development* (pp. 467–519). Washington, DC: American Psychological Association.

Brooks-Gunn, J., Guo, G., & Furstenberg, F. F., Jr. (1993). Who drops out of and who continues beyond high school? A 20-year follow-up of black urban youth. *Journal of Research on Adolescence, 3,* 271–294.

Brooks-Gunn, J., & Reiter, E. O. (1990). The role of pubertal processes. In S. S. Feldman & G. R. Elliott (Eds.), *At the threshold: The developing adolescent* (pp. 16–53). Cambridge, MA: Harvard University Press.

Brooks-Gunn, J., & Warren, M. P. (1985). The effects of delayed menarche in different contexts: Dance and nondance students. *Journal of Youth & Adolescence, 13,* 285–300.

Brown, A., & Day, J. (1983). Macrorules for summarizing text: The development of expertise. *Journal of Verbal Learning & Verbal Behavior, 22,* 1–14.

Brown, A. S., Jones, E. M., & Davis, T. L. (1995). Age differences in conversational source monitoring. *Psychology & Aging, 10,* 111–122.

Brown, B. B. (1990). Peer groups and peer cultures. In S. S. Feldman & G. R. Elliott (Eds.), *At the threshold: The developing adolescent* (pp. 171–196). Cambridge, MA: Harvard University Press.

Brown, B. B., Dolcini, M. M., & Leventhal, A. (1995, March). *The emergence of peer crowds: Friend or foe to adolescent health?* Paper presented at the biennial meetings of the Society for Research in Child Development, Indianapolis, IN.

Brown, B. B., & Huang, B. (1995). Examining parenting practices in different peer contexts: Implications for adolescent trajectories. In L. J. Crockett & A. C. Crouter (Eds.), *Pathways through adolescence* (pp. 151–174). Mahwah, NJ: Erlbaum.

Brown, B. B., Mory, M. S., & Kinney, D. (1994). Casting adolescent crowds in a relational perspective: Caricature, channel, and context. In R. Montemayor, G. R. Adams, & T. P. Gullotta (Eds.), *Personal relationships during adolescence* (pp. 123–167). Thousand Oaks, CA: Sage.

Brown, C. (1997). Sex differences in the career development of urban African American adolescents. *Journal of Career Development, 23,* 295–304.

Brown, G., & Dixson, A. (2000). The development of behavioral sex differences in infant rhesus macaques. *Primates, 41,* 63–77.

Brown, G. W. (1989). Life events and measurement. In G. W. Brown & T. O. Harris (Eds.), *Life events and illness* (pp. 3–45). New York: Guilford Press.

Brown, G. W. (1993). Life events and affective disorder: Replications and limitations. *Psychosomatic Medicine, 55,* 248–259.

Brown, G. W., & Harris, T. (1978). *Social origins of depression.* New York: Free Press.

Brown, J., Bakeman, R., Coles, C., Sexson, W., & Demi, A. (1998). Maternal drug use during pregnancy: Are preterm and full-term infants affected differently? *Developmental Psychology, 34,* 540–554.

Brown, L. (2000). *Helicobacter pylori:* Epidemiology and routes of transmission. *Epidemiology Review, 22,* 283–297.

Brown, R. (1973). *A first language: The early stages.* Cambridge, MA: Harvard University Press.

Brown, R., & Bellugi, U. (1964). Three processes in the acquisition of syntax. *Harvard Educational Review, 334,* 133–151.

Brown, S. (2003). Relationship quality dynamics of cohabiting unions. *Journal of Family Issues, 24,* 583–601.

Brown, S., & Booth, A. (1996). Cohabitation versus marriage: A comparison of relationship quality. *Journal of Marriage & the Family, 58,* 668–678.

Brown, W., Basil, M., & Bocarnea, M. (2003). Social influence of an international celebrity: Responses to the death of Princess Diana. *Journal of Communication, 53,* 587–605.

Brownell, C. A. (1990). Peer social skills in toddlers: Competencies and constraints illustrated by same-age and mixed-age interaction. *Child Development, 61,* 836–848.

Bruer, J. (1999). *The myth of the first three years.* New York: Free Press.

Bryant, P., MacLean, M., & Bradley, L. (1990). Rhyme, language, and children's reading. *Applied Psycholinguistics, 11,* 237–252.

Bryant, P. E., MacLean, M., Bradley, L. L., & Crossland, J. (1990). Rhyme and alliteration, phoneme detection, and learning to read. *Developmental Psychology, 26,* 429–438.

Bryant, S., & Rakowski, W. (1992). Predictors of mortality among elderly African-Americans. *Research on Aging, 14,* 50–67.

Buchanan, C. M., Maccoby, E. E., & Dornbusch, S. M. (1991). Caught between parents: Adolescents' experience in divorced homes. *Child Development, 62,* 1008–1029.

Buchbinder, E., & Eisikovits, Z. (2003). Battered women's entrapment in shame: A phenomenological study. *American Journal of Orthopsychiatry, 73,* 355–366.

Buchner, D. M., Beresford, S. A. A., Larson, E. B., LaCroix, A. Z., & Wagner, E. H. (1992). Effects of physical activity on health status in older adults II: Intervention studies. *Annual Review of Public Health, 13,* 469–488.

Bugental, D., & Happaney, K. (2004). Predicting infant maltreatment in low-income families: The interactive effects of maternal attributions and child status at birth. *Developmental Psychology, 40,* 234–243.

Buhrmester, D. (1992). The developmental courses of sibling and peer relationships. In F. Boer & J. Dunn (Eds.), *Children's sibling relationships: Developmental and clinical issues.* Hillsdale, NJ: Erlbaum.

Buhrmester, D., & Furman, W. (1990). Perceptions of sibling relationships during middle childhood and adolescence. *Child Development, 61,* 1387–1398.

Bukowski, W., Sippola, L., & Hoza, B. (1999). Same and other: Interdependency between participation in same- and other-sex friendships. *Journal of Youth & Adolescence, 28,* 439–459.

Bulcroft, R. A., & Bulcroft, K. A. (1991). The nature and functions of dating in later life. *Research on Aging, 13,* 244–260.

Bulkeley, W. (1998, September 16). Education: Kaplan plans a law school via the Web. *Wall Street Journal,* p. B1.

Bullock, M., & Lütkenhaus, P. (1990). Who am I? Self-understanding in toddlers. *Merrill-Palmer Quarterly, 36,* 217–238.

Bumpass, L. L., & Aquilino, W. S. (1995). *A social map of midlife: Family and work over the middle life course.* Report of the MacArthur Foundation research network on successful midlife development, Vero Beach, FL.

Bureau of the Census. (2003). *2002 American Community Survey.* Retrieved June 18, 2004, from http://www.census.gov/acs/www/index.html.

Burgess, N. J. (1995). Looking back, looking forward: African American families in sociohistorical perspective. In B. B. Ingoldsby & S. Smith (Eds.), *Families in multicultural perspective* (pp. 321–334). New York: Guilford Press.

Burgess, S. (1997). The role of shared reading in the development of phonological awareness: A longitudinal study of middle to upper class children. *Early Child Development & Care, 127/128,* 191–199.

Burke, L., & Follingstad, D. (1999). Violence in lesbian and gay relationships: Theory, prevalence, and correlational factors. *Clinical Psychology Review, 19,* 487–512.

Burkham, D., Lee, V., & Smerdon, B. (1997). Gender and science learning early in high school: Subject matter and laboratory experiences. *American Educational Research Journal, 34,* 297–332.

Burkhauser, R. V., Butrica, B. A., & Wasylenko, M. J. (1995). Mobility patterns of older home owners. *Research on Aging, 17,* 363–384.

Burley, R., Turner, L., & Vitulli, W. (1999). The relationship between goal orientation and age among adolescents and adults. *Journal of Genetic Psychology, 160,* 84–88.

Burn, S., O'Neil, A., & Nederend, S. (1996). Childhood tomboyishness and adult androgeny. *Sex Roles, 34,* 419–428.

Burnett, J. W., Anderson, W. P., & Heppner, P. P. (1995). Gender roles and self-esteem: A consideration of environmental factors. *Journal of Counseling & Development, 73,* 323–326.

Burnham, H., & Hogervorst, E. (2004). Recognition of facial expressions of emotion by patients with dementia of the Alzheimer type. *Dementia & Geriatric Cognitive Disorders, 18,* 75–79.

Burns, A. (1992). Mother-headed families: An international perspective and the case of Australia. *Social Policy Report, Society for Research in Child Development, 6,* 1–22.

Burton, L. (1992). Black grandparents rearing children of drug-addicted parents: Stressors, outcomes, and social service needs. *Gerontologist, 31,* 744–751.

Bus, A., & van IJzendoorn, M. (1999). Phonological awareness and early reading: A meta-analysis of experimental training studies. *Journal of Educational Psychology, 91,* 403–414.

Busch, C. M., Zonderman, A. B., & Costa, P. T., Jr. (1994). Menopausal transition and psychological distress in a nationally representative sample: Is menopause associated with psychological distress? *Journal of Aging & Health, 6,* 209–228.

Buss, A. (1989). Temperaments as personality traits. In G. A. Kohnstamm, J. E. Bates, & M. K. Rothbart (Eds.), *Temperament in childhood* (pp. 49–58). Chichester, England: Wiley.

Buss, A. H., & Plomin, R. (1984). *Temperament: Early developing personality traits.* Hillsdale, NJ: Erlbaum.

Buss, A. H., & Plomin, R. (1986). The EAS approach to temperament. In R. Plomin & J. Dunn (Eds.), *The study of temperament: Changes, continuities and challenges* (pp. 67–80). Hillsdale, NJ: Erlbaum.

Buss, D. (1999). *Evolutionary psychology.* Boston: Allyn & Bacon.

Buss, D., Abbott, M., Algleitner, A., Ahserian, A., Biaggio, A., et al. (1990). International preferences in selecting mates: A study of 37 cultures. *Journal of Cross-Cultural Psychology, 21,* 5–47.

Buss, D., & Schmitt, D. (1993). Sexual strategies theory: An evolutionary perspective on human mating. *Psychological Review, 100,* 204–232.

Bussey, K., & Bandura, A. (1992). Self-regulation mechanisms governing gender development. *Child Development, 63,* 1236–1250.

Bussing, R., Zima, B., Gary, F., & Garvan, C. (2002). Use of complementary and alternative medicine for symptoms of attention-deficit hyperactivity disorder. *Psychiatric Services, 53,* 1096–1102.

Butters, M., Whyte, E., Nebes, R., Begley, A., Dew, M., Mulsant, B., Zmuda, M., Bhalla, R., Meltzer, C., Pollock, B., Reynolds, C., & Becker, J. (2004). Nature and determinants of neuropsychological functioning in late-life depression. *Archives of General Psychiatry, 61,* 587–595.

Buzi, R., Roberts, R., Ross, M., Addy, R., & Markham, C. (2003). The impact of a history of sexual abuse on high-risk sexual behaviors among females attending alternative schools. *Adolescence, 38,* 595–605.

Byrne, G., & Raphael, B. (1999). Depressive symptoms and depressive episodes in recently widowed older men. *International Psychogeriatrics, 11,* 67–74.

Byrne, G., Raphael, G., & Arnold, E. (1999). Alcohol consumption and psychological distress in recently widowed older men. *Australian & New Zealand Journal of Psychiatry, 33,* 740–747.

Byrne, M. (1998). Taking a computational approach to aging: The SPAN theory of working memory. *Psychology & Aging, 13,* 309–322.

Cahn, D., Marcotte, A., Stern, R., Arruda, J., Akshoomoff, N., & Leshko, I. (1966). The Boston Qualitative Scoring System for the Rey-Osterrieth Complex Figure: A study of children with attention deficit hyperactivity disorder. *Clinical Neuropsychologist, 10,* 397–406.

Cairns, R. B., & Cairns, B. D. (1994). *Lifelines and risks: Pathways of youth in our time.* Cambridge, England: Cambridge University Press.

Calkins, S., Dedmon, S., Gill, K., Lomax, L., & Johnson, L. (2002). Frustration in infancy: Implications for emotion regulation, physiological processes, and temperament. *Infancy, 3,* 175–197.

Callaghan, T. (1999). Early understanding and production of graphic symbols. *Child Development, 70,* 1314–1324.

Callaghan, T., & Rankin, M. (2002). Emergence of graphic symbol functioning and the question of domain specificity: A longitudinal training study. *Child Development, 73,* 359–376.

Callahan, K., Rademacher, J., & Hildreth, B. (1998). The effect of parent participation in strategies to improve the homework performance of students who are at risk. *Remedial & Special Education, 19,* 131–141.

Camilleri, C., & Malewska-Peyre, H. (1997). Socialization and identity strategies. In J. Berry, P. Dasen, & T. Saraswathi (Eds.), *Handbook of cross-cultural psychology, Vol. 2: Basic processes and human development.* Boston: Allyn & Bacon.

Campbell, A., Shirley, L., & Candy, J. (2004). A longitudinal study of gender-related cognition and behaviour. *Developmental Science, 7,* 1–9.

Campbell, A., Shirley, L., & Caygill, L. (2002). Sex-typed preferences in three domains: Do two-year-olds need cognitive variables? *British Journal of Psychology, 93,* 203–217.

Campbell, F., Ramey, C., Pungello, E., Sparling, J., & Miller-Johnson, S. (2002). Early childhood education: Young adult outcomes from the Abecedarian Project. *Applied Developmental Science, 6,* 42–57.

Campbell, F. A., & Ramey, C. T. (1994). Effects of early intervention on intellectual and academic achievement: A follow-up study of children from low-income families. *Child Development, 65,* 684–698.

Campbell, L., Connidis, I., & Davies, L. (1999). Sibling ties in later life: A social network analysis. *Journal of Family Issues, 20,* 114–148.

Campbell, L., & Martin-Matthews, A. (2003). The gendered nature of men's filial care. *Journal of Gerontology, Series B: Psychological Sciences & Social Sciences, 58B,* S350–S358.

Campbell, S. B., Cohn, J. F., Flanagan, C., Popper, S., & Meyers, T. (1992). Course and correlates of postpartum depression during the transition to parenthood. *Development & Psychopathology, 4,* 29–47.

Campisi, J., Dimri, G., & Hara, E. (1996). Control of replicative senescence. In E. L. Schneider & J. W. Rowe (Eds.), *Handbook of the biology of aging* (4th ed., pp. 121–149). San Diego, CA: Academic Press.

Cao, L., Jiao, X., Zuzga, D., Liu, Y., Fong, D., Young, D., & During, M. (2004). VEGF links hippocampal activity with neurogenesis, learning and memory. *Nature Genetics, 36,* 827–835.

Caplan, G. (1964). *Principles of preventive psychiatry.* New York: Basic Books.

Capron, C., & Duyme, M. (1989). Assessment of effects of socio-economic status on IQ in a full cross-fostering study. *Nature, 340,* 552–554.

Capute, A. J., Palmer, F. B., Shapiro, B. K., Wachtel, R. C., Ross, A., & Accardo, P. J. (1984). Primitive reflex profile: A quantification of primitive reflexes in infancy. *Developmental Medicine & Child Neurology, 26,* 375–383.

Caputo, R. (1996). The effects of race and marital status on child support and work effort. *Journal of Sociology & Social Welfare, 23,* 51–68.

Cardon, R., & Fulker, D. (1991). Sources of continuity in infant predictors of later IQ. *Intelligence, 15,* 279–293.

Carey, R. G. (1974). Living until death: A program of service and research for the terminally ill. *Hospital Progress.* (Reprinted in E. Kübler-Ross [Ed.], *Death. The final stage of growth.* Englewood Cliffs, NJ: Prentice-Hall, 1975.)

Carey, S., & Bartlett, E. (1978). Acquiring a single new word. *Papers & Reports on Child Language Development, 15,* 17–29.

Carlson, E., Sampson, M., & Sroufe, A. (2003). Implications of attachment theory and research for developmental-behavioral pediatrics. *Journal of Developmental & Behavioral Pediatrics, 24,* 364–379.

Carlson, E., Sroufe, A., & Egeland, B. (2004). The construction of experience: A longitudinal study of representation and behavior. *Child Development, 75,* 66–83.

Carlson, E. A., & Sroufe, L. A. (1995). Contribution of attachment theory to developmental psychopathology. In D. Cicchetti & D. J. Conen (Eds.), *Developmental psychopathology, Vol. 1: Theory and methods* (pp. 581–617). New York: Wiley.

Carmeli, E., Reznick, A., Coleman, R., & Carmeli, V. (2000). Muscle strength and mass of lower extremities in relation to functional abilities in elderly adults. *Gerontology, 46,* 249–257.

Carnelley, K., Wortman, C., & Kessler, R. (1999). The impact of widowhood on depression: Findings from a prospective survey. *Psychological Medicine, 29,* 1111–1123.

Carnoy, M., Loeb, S., & Smith, T. (2001). *Do higher state test scores in Texas make for better high school outcomes?* Philadelphia, PA: Consortium for Policy Research in Education/University of Pennsylvania, #RR0047. Retrieved November 11, 2004, from http://www.cpre.org/publications/rr47.pdf.

Caron, A. J., & Caron, R. F. (1981). Processing of relational information as an index of infant risk. In S. Friedman & M. Sigman (Eds.), *Preterm birth and psychological development* (pp. 219–240). New York: Academic Press.

Carpenter, S. (2001). Teens' risky behavior is about more than race and family resources. *APA Monitor, 32,* 22–23.

Carr, S. (2000). As distance education comes of age, the challenge is keeping the students. *Chronicle of Higher Education, 46,* A39–A41.

Carroll, J., & Snowling, M. (2004). Language and phonological skills in children at high risk of reading difficulties. *Journal of Child Psychology & Psychiatry, 45,* 631–640.

Carson, D., Klee, T. & Perry, C. (1998). Comparisons of children with delayed and normal language at 24 months of age on measures of behavioral difficulties, social and cognitive development. *Infant Mental Health Journal, 19,* 59–75.

Carstensen, L. L. (1992). Social and emotional patterns in adulthood: Support for socioemotional selectivity theory. *Psychology & Aging, 7,* 331–338.

Carstensen, L. L., Gottman, J. M., & Levenson, R. W. (1995). Emotional behavior in long-term marriage. *Psychology & Aging, 10,* 149.

Carver, P., Egan, S., & Perry, D. (2004). Children who question their heterosexuality. *Developmental Psychology, 40,* 43–53.

Carver, R. P. (1990). Intelligence and reading ability in grades 2–12. *Intelligence, 14,* 449–455.

Casas, J. F., & Mosher, M. (1995, March). *Relational and overt aggression in preschool: "You can't come to my birthday party unless..."* Paper presented at the biennial meeting of the Society for Research in Child Development, Indianapolis, IN.

Casasola, M., & Cohen, L. (2000). Infants' association of linguistic labels with causal actions. *Developmental Psychology, 36,* 155–168.

Case, R. (1985). *Intellectual development: Birth to adulthood.* New York: Academic Press.

Case, R. (1991). Stages in the development of the young child's first sense of self. *Developmental Review, 11,* 210–230.

Case, R. (1992). *The mind's staircase: Exploring thought and knowledge.* Hillsdale, NJ: Erlbaum.

Case, R. (1997). The development of conceptual structures. In B. Damon (General Ed.) and D. Kuhn & R. S. Siegler (Series Eds.), *Handbook of child psychology, Vol. 2: Cognitive, language, and perceptual development.* New York: Wiley.

Case, R. B., Moss, A. J., Case, N., McDermott, M., & Eberly, S. (1992). Living alone after myocardial infarction: Impact on prognosis. *Journal of the American Medical Association, 267,* 515–519.

Cashon, C., & Cohen, L. (2000). Eight-month-old infants' perceptions of possible and impossible events. *Infancy, 1,* 429–446.

Caslyn, C., Gonzales, P., & Frase, M. (1999). *Highlights from the Third International Mathematics and Science Study.* Washington, DC: National Center for Education Statistics.

Casper, L., & Smith, K. (2002). Dispelling the myths: Self-care, class, and race. *Journal of Family Issues, 23,* 716–727.

Caspi, A. (2000). The child is father of the man: Personality continuities from childhood to adulthood. *Journal of Personality & Social Psychology, 78,* 158–172.

Caspi, A., & Elder, G. H., Jr. (1988). Childhood precursors of the life course: Early personality and life disorganization. In E. M. Hetherington, R. M. Lerner, & M. Perlmutter (Eds.), *Child development in life-span perspective* (pp. 115–142). Hillsdale, NJ: Erlbaum.

Caspi, A., Harrington, H., Milne, B., Amell, J., Theodore, R., & Moffitt, T. (2003). Children's behavioral styles at age 3 are linked to their adult personality traits at age 26. *Journal of Personality, 71,* 495–513.

Caspi, A., Henry, B., McGee, R. O., Moffitt, T. E., & Silva, P. A. (1995). Temperamental origins of child and adolescent behavior problems: From age three to age fifteen. *Child Development, 66,* 55–68.

Caspi, A., Lynam, D., Moffitt, T. E., & Silva, P. A. (1993). Unraveling girls' delinquency: Biological, dispositional, and contextual contributions to adolescent misbehavior. *Developmental Psychology, 29,* 19–30.

Cassidy, J., & Berlin, L. J. (1994). The insecure/ambivalent pattern of attachment: Theory and research. *Child Development, 65,* 971–991.

Cassileth, B. R., Walsh, W. P., & Lusk, E. J. (1988). Psychosocial correlates of cancer survival: A subsequent report 3 to 8 years after cancer diagnosis. *Journal of Clinical Oncology, 6,* 1753–1759.

Castellino, D., Lerner, J., Lerner, R., & von Eye, A. (1998). Maternal employment and education: Predictors of young adolescent career trajectories. *Applied Developmental Science, 2,* 114–126.

Castellsagué, X., Bosch, X., Muñoz, N., Meijer, C., Shah, K., Sanjosé, S., Eluf-Neto, J., Ngelangel, C., Chicareon, S., Smith, J., Herrero, R., Moreno, V., & Franceschi, F. (2002). Male circumcision, penile human papillomavirus infection, and cervical cancer in female partners. *New England Journal of Medicine, 346,* 1105–1112.

Castle, J., Groothues, C., Bredenkamp, D., Beckett, C., et al. (1999). Effects of qualities of early institutional care on cognitive attainment. *American Journal of Orthopsychiatry, 69,* 424–437.

Castle, N. (2003). Searching for and selecting a nursing facility. *Medical Care Research & Review, 60,* 223–247.

Cato, J., & Canetto, S. (2003). Attitudes and beliefs about suicidal behavior when coming out is the precipitant of the suicidal behavior. *Sex Roles, 49,* 497–505.

Catsambis, S. (1995). Gender, race, ethnicity, and science education in the middle grades. *Journal of Research in Science Teaching, 32,* 243–257.

Cattell, R. B. (1963). Theory of fluid and crystallized intelligence: A critical experiment. *Journal of Educational Psychology, 54,* 1–22.

Caughy, M. O., DiPietro, J. A., & Strobino, D. M. (1994). Day-care participation as a protective factor in the cognitive development of low-income children. *Child Development, 65,* 457–471.

Cauley, J. A., Seeley, D. G., Ensrud, K., Ettinger, B., Black, D., & Cummings, S. R. (1995). Estrogen replacement therapy and fractures in older women. *Annals of Internal Medicine, 122,* 9–16.

Cavanaugh, J., & Whitbourne, S. (1999). *Gerontology: An interdsiciplinary perspective.* New York: Oxford University Press.

Cavill, S., & Bryden, P. (2003). Development of handedness: Comparison of questionnaire and performance-based measures of preference. *Brain & Cognition, 53,* 149–151.

CBS News. (2004, April 29). *Utah C-section mom gets probation.* Retrieved September 21, 2004, from http://www.cbsnews.com/stories/2004/03/12/national/printable605537.shtml.

Ceci, S., & Bronfenbrenner, U. (1985). "Don't forget to take the cupcakes out of the oven": Prospective memory, strategic time-monitoring, and context. *Child Development, 56,* 152–164.

Ceci, S. J., & Bruck, M. (1993). Suggestibility of the child witness: A historical review and synthesis. *Psychological Bulletin, 113,* 403–439.

Cederblad, M., Hook, B., Irhammar, M., & Mercke, A. (1999). Mental health in international adoptees as teenagers and young adults: An epidemiological study. *Journal of Child Psychology & Psychiatry & Allied Disciplines, 40,* 1239–1248.

Cederblad, M., Pruksachatkunakorn, P., Boripunkul, T., Intraprasert, S., & Hook, B. (2003). Sense of coherence in a Thai sample. *Transcultural Psychiatry, 40,* 585–600.

Center for Education Reform. (1999). *Charter schools.* Retrieved February 29, 2000, from www.edreform.com.

Centers for Disease Control (CDC). (1994). Prevalence of adults with no known major risk factors for coronary heart disease—behavioral risk factor surveillance system, 1992. *Morbidity & Mortality Weekly Report, 43,* 61–69.

Centers for Disease Control. (1996, October 18). Population-based prevalence of perinatal exposure to cocaine—Georgia, 1994. *Morbidity & Mortality Weekly Report, 45,* 887.

Centers for Disease Control. (1998a). *National diabetes fact sheet.* Retrieved October 11, 2000, from http://www.cdc.gov.

Centers for Disease Control. (1998b). *The role of STD detection and treatment in HIV prevention.* Retrieved September 1, 2000, from http://www.cdc.gov.

Centers for Disease Control. (1998c). Single-year U.S. mortality rates. *National Vital Statistics Reports, 47,* 10, Table 3.

Centers for Disease Control. (1999a). AIDS surveillance report. *Morbidity & Mortality Weekly Report,* 11.

Centers for Disease Control. (1999b). *Syphilis fact sheet.* Retrieved September 1, 2000, from http://www.cdc.gov.

Centers for Disease Control. (2000a). *The burden of prostate cancer.* Retrieved October 4, 2000, from http://www.cdc.gov.

Centers for Disease Control. (2000b). *Some facts about genital herpes.* Retrieved September 1, 2000, from http://www.cdc.gov.

Centers for Disease Control. (2000c). Youth risk behavior surveillance—United States, 1999. *Morbidity & Mortality Weekly Report, 49,* 1–96.

Centers for Disease Control and Prevention. (2001). *Genital herpes.* Retrieved January 27, 2003, from http://www.cdc.gov/nchstp/dst/Fact_Sheets_facts_Gnital_Herpes_htm.

Centers for Disease Control and Prevention. (2003a). *About minority health.* Retrieved August 26, 2004, from http://www.cdc.gov/omy/AMH/AMH.htm.

Centers for Disease Control and Prevention. (2003b). *Sexually transmitted disease surveillance, 2002.* Retrieved August 18, 2004, from http://www.cdc.gov/std/stats/natoverview.htm.

Centers for Disease Control and Prevention. (2004). Surveillance summaries. *Morbidity & Mortality Weekly Report, 53,* 2–29.

Centers for Disease Control National Immunization Program. (2000, January 21). 2000 childhood immunization schedule. *Morbidity & Mortality Weekly Report, 49,* 35–38.

Centers for Medicare and Medicaid Services (CMS). (2004). *Health care industry market update.* Retrieved September 9, 2004, from http://www.ahca.org/research/cms_market_update_030520.pdf.

Century Foundation. (1998). *Social security reform: A Century Foundation guide to the issues.* Retrieved February 22, 2001, from www.tcf.org/publications/Basics.

Ceponiene, R., Kuchnerenko, E., Fellman, V., Renlund, M., Suominen, K., & Naeaetaenen, R. (2002). Event-related potential features indexing central auditory discrimination by newborns. *Cognitive Brain Research, 13,* 101–113.

Cernoch, J. M., & Porter, R. H. (1985). Recognition of maternal axillary odors by infants. *Child Development, 56,* 1593–1598.

Certain, L., & Kahn, R. (2002). Prevalence, correlates, and trajectory of television viewing among infants and toddlers. *Pediatrics, 109,* 634–642.

Chadwick, O., Taylor, E., Taylor, A., Heptinstall, E. et al., (1999). Hyperactivity and reading disability: A longitudinal study of the nature of the association. *Journal of Child Psychology & Psychiatry, 40,* 1039–1050.

Chan, R., Raboy, B., & Patterson, C. (1998). Psychosocial adjustment among children conceived via donor insemination by lesbian and heterosexual mothers. *Child Development, 69,* 443–457.

Chang, L., & Murray, A. (1995, March). *Math performance of 5- and 6-year-olds in Taiwan and the U.S.: Maternal beliefs, expectations, and tutorial assistance.* Paper presented at the biennial meetings of the Society for Research in Child Development, Indianapolis, IN.

Chang, L., Schwartz, D., Dodge, K., & McBride-Chang, C. (2003). Harsh parenting in relation to child emotion regulation and aggression. *Journal of Family Psychology, 17,* 598–606.

Chao, R. (1994). Beyond parental control and authoritarian parenting style: Understanding Chinese parenting through the cultural notion of training. *Child Development, 65,* 1111–1119.

Chapman, J., & Tunmer, W. (1997). A longitudinal study of beginning reading achievement and reading self-concept. *British Journal of Educational Psychology, 67,* 279–291.

Charlesworth, W. R. (1992). Darwin and developmental psychology: Past and present. *Developmental Psychology, 28,* 5–16.

Chase-Lansdale, P. L., Cherlin, A. J., & Kiernan, K. E. (1995). The long-term effects of parental divorce on the mental health of young adults: A developmental perspective. *Child Development, 66,* 1614–1634.

Chase-Lansdale, P. L., & Hetherington, E. M. (1990). The impact of divorce on life-span development: Short and long term effects. In P. B. Baltes, D. L. Featherman, & R. M. Lerner (Eds.), *Life-span development and behavior, Vol. 10* (pp. 107–151). Hillsdale, NJ: Erlbaum.

Chasseigne, G., Grau, S., Mullet, E., & Cama, V. (1999). How well do elderly people cope with uncertainty in a learning task? *Acta Psychologica, 103,* 229–238.

Chatlos, J. (1997). Substance use and abuse and the impact on academic difficulties. *Child & Adolescent Clinics of North America, 6,* 545–568.

Chatters, L. M. (1991). Physical health. In J. S. Jackson (Ed.), *Life in black America* (pp. 199–220). Newbury Park, CA: Sage.

Chavkin, N., Gonzalez, J., & Rader, R. (2000). A home-school program in a Texas-Mexico border school: Voices from parents, students, and school staff. *School Community Journal, 10,* 127–137.

Cheay, C., & Rubin, K. (2004). European American and mainland Chinese mothers' responses to aggression and social withdrawal in preschoolers. *International Journal of Behavioral Development, 28,* 83–94.

Cheitlin, M. (2003). Cardiovascular physiology: Changes with aging. *American Journal of Geriatric Cardiology, 12,* 9–13.

Chen, J., Bierhals, A., Prigerson, H., Kasl, S., Mazure, C., & Jacobs, S. (1999). Gender differences in the effects of bereavement-related psychological distress in health outcomes. *Psychological Medicine, 29,* 367–380.

Chen, S. (1997). Child's understanding of secret and friendship development. *Psychological Science (China), 20,* 545.

Chen, X., Rubin, K. H., & Li, Z. (1995). Social functioning and adjustment in Chinese children: A longitudinal study. *Developmental Psychology, 31,* 531–539.

Chen, X., Rubin, K. H., & Sun, Y. (1992). Social reputation and peer relationships in Chinese and Canadian children: A cross-cultural study. *Child Development, 63,* 1336–1343.

Chen, Z. (1999). Ethnic similarities and differences in the association of emotional autonomy and adolescent outcomes: Comparing Euro-American and Asian-American adolescents. *Psychological Reports, 84,* 501–516.

Chen-Hafteck, L. (1997). Music and language development in early childhood: Integrating past research in the two domains. *Early Child Development & Care, 130,* 85–97.

Cheour, M., Martynova, O., Naeaetaenen, R., Erkkola, R., Sillanpaeae, M., Kero, P., Raz, A., Kaipio, M., Hiltunen, J., Aaltonen, O., Savela, J., & Haemaelaeinen, H. (2002). Speech sounds learned by sleeping newborns. *Nature, 415,* 599–600.

Cherlin, A. (1992). *Marriage, divorce, remarriage,* Cambridge, MA: Harvard University Press.

Cherlin, A., Chase-Lansdale, P., & McRae, C. (1998). Effects of parental divorce on mental health throughout the life course. *American Sociological Review, 63,* 239–249.

Cherlin, A., & Furstenberg, F. F. (1986). *The new American grandparent.* New York: Basic Books.

Chess, S., & Thomas, A. (1984). *Origins and evolution of behavior disorders: Infancy to early adult life.* New York: Brunner/Mazel.

Cheung, C., Chan, W., Lee, T., Liu, S., & Leung, K. (2001). Structure of moral consciousness and moral intentions among youth in Hong Kong. *International Journal of Adolescence & Youth, 9,* 83–116.

Chi, M. T. (1978). Knowledge structure and memory development. In R. S. Siegler (Ed.), *Children's thinking: What develops?* (pp. 73–96). Hillsdale, NJ: Erlbaum.

Chiapin, G., DeAraujo, G., & Wagner, A. (1998). Mother-in-law and daughter-in-law: How is the relationship between these two women? *Psicologia: Reflexao e Critica, 11,* 541–550.

Chiappe, P., & Siegel, L. (1999). Phonological awareness and reading acquisition in English- and Punjabi-speaking Canadian children. *Journal of Educational Psychology, 91,* 20–28.

Chickering, A., & Reisser, L. (1993). *Education and identity* (2nd ed.). San Francisco: Jossey-Bass.

Chien, Y., Cheng, J., Liu, M., Yang, H., Hsu, M., Chen, C., & Yang, C. (2001). Serologic markers of Epstein-Barr virus infection and nasopharyngeal carcinoma in Taiwanese men. *New England Journal of Medicine, 345,* 1877–1882.

Chincotta, D., & Underwood, G. (1997). Estimates, language of schooling and bilingual digit span. *European Journal of Cognitive Psychology, 9,* 325–348.

Chiriboga, D. A. (1989). Mental health at the midpoint: Crisis, challenge, or relief? In S. Hunter & M. Sundel (Eds.), *Midlife myths: Issues, findings, and practice implications* (pp. 116–144). Newbury Park, CA: Sage.

Chism, M., & Satcher, J. (1998). African American students' perceptions toward faculty at historically Black colleges. *College Student Journal, 32,* 315–320.

Chlebowski, R., Hendrix, S., Langer, R., Stefanick, M., Gass, M., Lane, D., Rodabough, R., Gilligan, M., Cyr, M., Thomson, C., Khandekar, J., Petrovitch, H., & McTiernan, A. (2003). Influence of estrogen plus progestin on breast cancer and mammography in healthy postmenopausal women: The Women's Health Initiative randomized trial. *Journal of the American Medical Association, 289,* 3243–3253.

Choi, N. (2003). Nonmarried aging parents' and their adult children's characteristics associated with transitions into and out of intergenerational coresidence. *Journal of Gerontological Social Work, 40,* 7–29.

Choi, N. G. (1991). Racial differences in the determinants of living arrangements of widowed and divorced elderly women. *The Gerontologist, 31,* 496–504.

Choi, S. (2000). Caregiver input in English and Korean: Use of nouns and verbs in book-reading and toy-play contexts. *Journal of Children's Language, 27,* 69–96.

Chomsky, N. (1959). A review of B. F. Skinner's *Verbal Behavior. Language, 35,* 26–129.

Chopak, J., Vicary, J., & Crockett, L. (1998). Predicting alcohol and tobacco use in a sample of rural adolescents. *American Journal of Health Behavior, 22,* 334–341.

Chou, C., Chou, J., & Tyang, N. (1998, February 18–22). *An exploratory study of Internet addiction, usage, and communication pleasure.* Paper presented at the annual meeting of the Association for Educational Communications and Technology, St. Louis, MO. ERIC No. ED 416 838.

Chou, K., Chi, I., & Chow, N. (2004). Sources of income and depression in elderly Hong Kong Chinese: Mediating and moderating effects of social support and financial strain. *Aging & Mental Health, 8,* 212–221.

Chou, K., Chow, N., & Chi, I. (2003). Volunteering aspirations of Hong Kong Chinese soon-to-be-old adults. *Activities, Adaptation, & Aging, 27,* 79–96.

Chow, B., & McBride-Chang, C. (2003). Promoting language and literacy development through parent-child reading in Hong Kong preschoolers. *Early Education & Development, 14,* 233–248.

Christakis, D., Zimmerman, F., DiGiuseppe, D., & McCarty, C. (2004). Early television exposure and subsequent attentional problems in children. *Pediatrics, 113,* 708–713.

Christensen, C. (1997). Onset, rhymes, and phonemes in learning to read. *Scientific Studies of Reading, 1,* 341–358.

Christensen, H., Henderson, A., Griffiths, K., & Levings, C. (1997). Does aging inevitably lead to declines in cognitive performance? A longitudinal study of elite academics. *Personality & Individual Differences, 23,* 67–78.

Chronicle of Higher Education. (1997, August 29). *Almanac: Facts about the U.S., each of the 50 states, and D.C.* Washington, DC: Author.

Church, M., Eldis, F., Blakley, B., & Bawle, E. (1997) Hearing, language, speech, vestibular, and dento-facial disorders in fetal alcohol syndrome. *Alcoholism: Clinical & Experimental Research, 21,* 227–237.

Ciabattari, T. (2004). Cohabitation and housework: The effects of marital intentions. *Journal of Marriage & the Family, 66,* 118–125.

Ciancio, D., Sadovsky, A., Malabonga, V., Trueblood, L., et al. (1999). Teaching classification and seriation to preschoolers. *Child Study Journal, 29,* 193–205.

Cicchetti, D., Rogosch, F., Maughan, A., Toth, S., & Bruce, J. (2003). False belief understanding in maltreated children. *Development & Psychopathology, 15,* 1067–1091.

Cillessen, A., & Mayeux, L. (2004). From censure to reinforcement: Developmental changes in the association between aggression and social status. *Child Development, 75,* 147–163.

Cillessen, A. H. N., van IJzendoorn, H. W., van Lieshout, C. F. M., & Hartup, W. W. (1992). Heterogeneity among peer-rejected boys: Subtypes and stabilities. *Child Development, 63,* 893–905.

Claes, M. (1998). Adolescents' closeness with parents, siblings, and friends in three countries: Canada, Belgium, and Italy. *Journal of Youth & Adolescence, 27,* 165–184.

Clarke-Stewart, A. (1992). Consequences of child care for children's development. In A. Booth (Ed.), *Child care in the 1990s: Trends and consequences* (pp. 63–82). Hillsdale, NJ: Erlbaum.

Clarkson-Smith, L., & Hartley, A. A. (1990). The game of bridge as an exercise in working memory and reasoning. *Journals of Gerontology: Psychological Sciences, 45,* P233–238.

Clawson, R., & Choate, J. (1999). Explaining participation on a class newsgroup. *Social Science Computer Review, 17,* 455–459.

Clinkingbeard, C., Minton, B., Davis, J., & McDermott, K. (1999). Women's knowledge about menopause, hormone replacement therapy (HRT), and interactions with healthcare providers: An exploratory study. *Journal of Women's Health & Gender-Based Medicine, 8,* 1097–1102.

Cnattingius, S., Berendes, H. W., & Forman, M. R. (1993). Do delayed childbearers face increased risks of adverse pregnancy outcomes after the first birth? *Obstetrics & Gynecology, 81,* 512–516.

Cobb, K. (2000, September 3). Breaking in drivers: Texas could join states restricting teens in effort to lower rate of fatal accidents. *Houston Chronicle,* pp. A1, A20.

Coffey, C., Saxton, J., Ratcliff, G., Bryan, R., & Lucke, J. (1999). Relation of education to brain size in normal aging: Implications for the reserve hypothesis. *Neurology, 53,* 189–196.

Cohen, G. (2000). *The creative age: Awakening human potential in the second half of life.* New York: Avon Books.

Cohen, R. (2000, April 11). Horror expressed in Germany over Dutch euthanasia. *New York Times Online.* Retrieved April 17, 2001, from www.nytimes.com.

Cohen, S. (1991). Social supports and physical health: Symptoms, health behaviors, and infectious disease. In E. M. Cummings, A. L. Greene, & K. H. Karraker (Eds.), *Life-span developmental psychology: Perspectives on stress and coping* (pp. 213–234). Hillsdale, NJ: Erlbaum.

Cohen, Y. A. (1964). *The transition from childhood to adolescence.* Chicago: Aldine.

Coie, J. (1997, August). *Testing developmental theory of antisocial behavior with outcomes from the Fast Track Prevention Project.* Paper presented at the annual meeting of the American Psychological Association, Chicago.

Coie, J., Cillessen, A., Dodge, K., Hubbard, J., et al., (1999). It takes two to fight: A test of relational factors and a method for assessing aggressive dyads. *Developmental Psychology, 35,* 1179–1188.

Coie, J., Terry, R., Lenox, K., Lochman, J., & Hyman, C. (1995). Childhood peer rejection and aggression as predictors of stable patterns of adolescent disorder. *Development & Psychopathology, 7,* 697–713.

Coie, J. D., & Cillessen, A. H. N. (1993). Peer rejection: Origins and effects on children's development. *Current Directions in Psychological Science, 2,* 89–92.

Coiro, M. J. (1995, March). *Child behavior problems as a function of marital conflict and parenting.* Paper presented at the biennial meetings of the Society for Research in Child Development, Indianapolis, IN.

Coke, M. (1992). Correlates of life satisfaction among elderly African Americans. *Journals of Gerontology, 47,* P316–P320.

Colby, A., Kohlberg, L., Gibbs, J., & Lieberman, M. (1983). A longitudinal study of moral judgment. *Monographs of the Society for Research in Child Development, 48* (1–2, Serial No. 200).

Cole, D. A. (1991). Change in self-perceived competence as a function of peer and teacher evaluation. *Developmental Psychology, 27,* 682–688.

Cole, M. (1992). Culture in development. In M. H. Bornstein & M. E. Lamb (Eds.), *Developmental psychology: An advanced textbook* (pp. 731–789). Hillsdale, NJ: Erlbaum.

Cole, P., Martin, S., & Dennis, T. (2004). Emotion regulation as a scientific construct: Methodological challenges and directions for child development research. *Child Development, 75,* 317–333.

Coleman, J., Pratt, R., Stoddard, R., Gerstmann, D., & Abel, H. (1997). The effects of the male and female singing and speaking voices on selected physiological and behavioral measures of premature infants in the intensive care unit. *International Journal of Arts Medicine, 5,* 4–11.

Coleman, M., Ganong, L., Killian, T., & McDaniel, A. (1999). Child support obligations: Attitudes and rationale. *Journal of Family Issues, 20,* 46–68.

Coley, R., & Chase-Lansdale, L. (1998). Adolescent pregnancy and parenthood: Recent evidence and future directions. *American Psychologist, 53,* 152–166.

Collaer, M. L., & Hines, M. (1995). Human behavioral sex differences: A role for gonadal hormones during early development? *Psychological Bulletin, 118,* 55–107.

Collet, J. P., Burtin, P., Gillet, J., Bossard, N., Ducruet, T., & Durr, F. (1994). Risk of infectious diseases in children attending different types of daycare setting. Epicreche Research Group. *Respiration, 61,* 16–19.

Colombo, J. (1993). *Infant cognition: Predicting later intellectual functioning.* Newbury Park, CA: Sage.

Colonia-Willner, R. (1999). Investing in practical intelligence: Ageing and cognitive efficiency among executives. *International Journal of Behavioral Development, 23,* 591–614.

Colton, M., Buss, K., Mangelsdorf, S., Brooks, C., Sorenson, D., Stansbury, K., Harris, M., & Gunnar, M. (1992). *Relations between toddler coping strategies, temperament, attachment and adrenocortical stress responses.* Poster presented at the 8th International Conference on Infant Studies, Miami.

Commissaris, C., Ponds, R., & Jolles, J. (1998). Subjective forgetfulness in a normal Dutch population: Possibilities of health education and other interventions. *Patient Education & Counseling, 34,* 25–32.

Committee on Infectious Diseases (1996). Recommended childhood immunization schedule. *Pediatrics, 97,* 143–146.

Compas, B. E., Ey, S., & Grant, K. E. (1993). Taxonomy, assessment, and diagnosis of depression during adolescence. *Psychological Bulletin, 114,* 323–344.

Condry, J., & Condry, S. (1976). Sex differences: A study in the eye of the beholder. *Child Development, 47,* 812–819.

Conger, R. D., Patterson, G. R., & Ge, X. (1995). It takes two to replicate: A mediational model for the impact of parents' stress on adolescent adjustment. *Child Development, 66,* 80–97.

Connell, J., & Witt, J. (2004). Applications of computer-based instruction: Using specialized software to aid letter-name and letter-sound recognition. *Journal of Applied Behavior Analysis, 37,* 67–71.

Connidis, I. A. (1994). Sibling support in older age. *Journals of Gerontology: Social Sciences, 49,* S309–317.

Connidis, I. A., & Davies, L. (1992). Confidants and companions: Choices in later life. *Journals of Gerontology: Social Sciences, 47,* S115–122.

Connidis, I. A., & McMullin, J. A. (1993). To have or have not: Parent status and the subjective well-being of older men and women. *The Gerontologist, 33,* 630–636.

Connolly, K., & Dalgleish, M. (1989). The emergence of a tool-using skill in infancy. *Developmental Psychology, 25,* 894–912.

Cook, S., & Heppner, P. (1997). Coping control, problem-solving appraisal, and depressive symptoms during a farm crisis. *Journal of Mental Health Counseling, 19,* 64–77.

Coombs, R. H. (1991). Marital status and personal well-being: A literature review. *Family Relations, 40,* 97–102.

Cooper, A., Putnam, D., Planchon, L., & Boies, S. (1999). Online sexual compulsivity: Getting tangled in the net. *Sexual Addiction & Compulsivity, 6,* 79–104.

Cooper, R. P., & Aslin, R. N. (1994). Developmental differences in infant attention to the spectral properties of infant-directed speech. *Child Development, 65,* 1663–1677.

Coplan, R., Bowker, A., & Cooper, S. (2003). Parenting daily hassles, child temperament and social adjustment in preschool. *Early Childhood Research Quarterly, 18,* 376–395.

Corbet, A., Long, W., Schumacher, R., Gerdes, J., & Cotton, R. (1995). Double-blind developmental evaluation at 1-year corrected age of 597 premature infants with birth weights from 500 to 1350 grams enrolled in three placebo-controlled trials of prophylactic synthetic surfactant. *Journal of Pediatrics, 126,* S5–12.

Cordellan, W. (1990) Television and children: Towards the millennium. *Communication Research Trends, 10,* 1–20.

Cornelius, M., Goldschmidt, L., Day, N., & Larkby, C. (2002). Alcohol, tobacco and marijuana use among pregnant teenagers: 6-year follow-up of offspring growth effects. *Neurotoxicology & Teratology, 24,* 703–710.

Corr, C. A. (1991/1992). A task-based approach to coping with dying. *Omega, 24,* 81–94.

Corrada, M., Brookmeyer, R., & Kawas, C. (1995). Sources of variability in prevalence rates of Alzheimer's disease. *International Journal of Epidemiology, 24,* 1000–1005.

Corrado, M. (2002). Teaching wedding rules: How bridal workers negotiate control over their customers. *Journal of Contemporary Ethnography, 31,* 33–67.

Corsaro, W., Molinari, L., Hadley, K., & Sugioka, H. (2003). Keeping and making friends: Italian children's transition from preschool to elementary school. *Social Psychology Quarterly, 66,* 272–292.

Corso, J. F. (1987). Sensory-perceptual processes and aging. In K. W. Schaie (Ed.), *Annual review of gerontology & geriatrics, Vol. 7* (pp. 29–56). New York: Springer.

Corwin, J., Loury, M., & Gilbert, A. N. (1995). Workplace, age, and sex as mediators of olfactory function: Data from the National Geographic smell survey. *Journals of Gerontology: Psychological Sciences, 50B,* P179–186.

Cosden, M., & McNamara, J. (1997). Self-concept and perceived social support among college students with and without learning disabilities. *Learning Disability Quarterly, 20,* 2–12.

Costa, M., Reus, V., Wolkowitz, O., Manfredi, F., & Lieberman, M. (1999). Estrogen replacement therapy and cognitive decline in memory-impaired post-menopausal women. *Biological Psychiatry, 46,* 182–188.

Costa, P. T., Jr., & McCrae, R. R. (1980b). Still stable after all these years: Personality as a key to some issues in adulthood and old age. In P. B. Baltes & O. G. Brim, Jr. (Eds.), *Life-span development and behavior* (pp. 65–102). New York: Academic Press.

Costa, P. T., Jr., McCrae, R. R., Zonderman, A. B., Barbano, H. E., Lebowitz, B., & Larson, D. M. (1986). Cross-sectional studies of personality in a national sample: 2. Stability in neuroticism, extraversion, and openness. *Psychology & Aging, 1,* 144–149.

Cotman, C. W., & Neeper, S. (1996). Activity-dependent plasticity and the aging brain. In E. L. Schneider & J. W. Rowe (Eds.), *Handbook of the biology of aging* (4th ed., pp. 284–299). San Diego, CA: Academic Press.

Cotton, L., Bynum, D., & Madhere, S. (1997). Socialization forces and the stability of work values from late adolescence to early adulthood. *Psychological Reports, 80,* 115–124.

Coulthard, H., & Harris, G. (2003). Early food refusal: The role of maternal mood. *Journal of Reproductive & Infant Psychology, 21,* 335–345.

Coulton, C. J., Korbin, J. E., Su, M., & Chow, J. (1995). Community level factors and child maltreatment rates. *Child Development, 66,* 1262–1276.

Council on Basic Education. (1998). *Quality counts.* Retrieved October 21, 1998, from http://www.c-b-e.org.

Counts, D. R. (1976/1977). The good death in Kaliai: Preparation for death in western New Britain. *Omega, 7,* 367–372.

Courage, M., & Howe, M. (2002). From infant to child: The dynamics of cognitive change in the second year of life. *Psychological Bulletin, 128,* 250–277.

Court curbs drug tests during pregnancy. (2001, March 22). *New York Times Online.* Retrieved April 4, 2001, from www.nytimes.com/2001/03/22/politics/22SCOT.html.

Coury, D. (2002). Developmental & behavioral pediatrics. In A. Rudolph, R. Kamei, & K. Overby (Eds.), *Rudolph's fundamental of pediatrics* (3rd ed., pp. 110–124). New York: McGraw-Hill.

Cowan, B. R., & Underwood, M. K. (1995, March). *Sugar and spice and everything nice? A developmental investigation of social aggression among girls.* Paper presented at the biennial meetings of the Society for Research in Child Development, Indianapolis, IN.

Cowan, C. P., & Cowan, P. A. (1987). Men's involvement in parenthood: Identifying the antecedents and understanding the barriers. In P. W. Berman & F. A. Pedersen (Eds.), *Men's transitions to parenthood: Longitudinal studies of early family experience* (pp. 145–174). Hillsdale, NJ: Erlbaum.

Cox, M., Paley, B., Burchinal, M., & Payne, C. (1999). Marital perceptions and interactions across the transition to parenthood. *Journal of Marriage & the Family, 61,* 611–625.

Cramer, D. (1991). Type A behavior pattern, extraversion, neuroticism and psychological distress. *British Journal of Medical Psychology, 64,* 73–83.

Cramer, P. (2000). Defense mechanisms in psychology today. *American Psychologist, 55,* 637–646.

Crawley, A., Anderson, D., Wilder, A., Williams, M., & Santomero, A. (1999). Effects of repeated exposures to a single episode of the television program *Blue's Clues* on the viewing behaviors and comprehension of preschool children. *Educational Psychology, 91,* 630–638.

Creators, the. (2000, March/April). *Modern Maturity,* pp. 38–44.

Crehan, G. (2004). The surviving sibling: The effects of sibling death in childhood. *Psychoanalytic Psychotherapy, 18,* 202–219.

Crick, N., & Dodge, K. (1994). A review and reformulation of social information processing mechanisms in children's social adjustment. *Psychological Bulletin, 115,* 74–101.

Crick, N., & Dodge, K. (1996). Social information-processing mechanisms in reactive and proactive aggression. *Child Development, 67,* 993–1002.

Crick, N., & Ladd, G. (1993). Children's perceptions of their peer experiences: Attributions, loneliness, social anxiety, and social avoidance. *Developmental Psychology, 29,* 244–254.

Crick, N. R., & Grotpeter, J. K. (1995). Relational aggression, gender, and social-psychological adjustment. *Child Development, 66,* 710–722.

Crimmins, E. M., & Ingegneri, D. G. (1990). Interaction and living arrangements of older parents and their children. *Research on Aging, 12,* 3–35.

Crittenden, P. (2000). Introduction. In P. Crittenden & A. Claussen (Eds.), *The organisation of attachment relationships: Maturation, culture and context.* Cambridge, UK: Cambridge University Press.

Crittenden, P. M. (1992). Quality of attachment in the preschool years. *Development & Psychopathology, 4,* 209–241.

Crittenden, P. M., Partridge, M. F., & Claussen, A. H. (1991). Family patterns of relationship in normative and dysfunctional families. *Development & Psychopathology, 3,* 491–512.

Crockenberg, S. (2003). Rescuing the baby from the bathwater: How gender and temperament (may) influence how child care affects child development. *Child Development, 74,* 1034–1038.

Crockenberg, S., & Litman, C. (1990). Autonomy as competence in 2-year-olds: Maternal correlates of child defiance, compliance, and self-assertion. *Developmental Psychology, 26,* 961–971.

Crockett, D. (2003). Critical issues children face in the 2000s. *School Psychology Quarterly, 18,* 446–453.

Crone, D., & Whitehurst, G. (1999). Age and schooling effects on emergent literacy and early reading skills. *Journal of Educational Psychology, 91,* 594–603.

Crook, C. (1987). Taste and olfaction. In P. Salapatek & L. Cohen (Eds.), *Handbook of infant perception, Vol. 1: From sensation to perception* (pp. 237–264). Orlando, FL: Academic Press.

Crouter, A. C., & McHale, S. M. (1993). Familial economic circumstances: Implications for adjustment and development in early adolescence. In

R. M. Lerner (Ed.), *Early adolescence. Perspectives on research, policy, and intervention* (pp. 71–91). Hillsdale, NJ: Erlbaum.

Crowell, J. A., & Waters, E. (1995, March). *Is the parent-child relationship a prototype of later love relationships? Studies of attachment and working models of attachment.* Paper presented at the biennial meeting of the Society for Research in Child Development, Indianapolis, IN.

Crowley, B., Hayslip, B., & Hobdy, J. (2003). Psychological hardiness and adjustment to life events in adulthood. *Journal of Adult Development, 10,* 237–248.

Crystal, S., Shae, D., & Krishnaswami, S. (1992). Educational attainment, occupational history, and stratification: Determinants of later-life economic outcomes. *Journals of Gerontology: Social Sciences, 47,* S213–221.

Csikszentmihalyi, M., & Rathunde, K. (1990). The psychology of wisdom: An evolutionary interpretation. In R. Sternberg (Ed.), *Wisdom: Its nature, origins, and development* (pp. 25–51). Cambridge, England: Cambridge University Press.

Cuba, L., & Longino, C. F., Jr. (1991). Regional retirement migration: The case of Cape Cod. *Journals of Gerontology: Social Sciences, 46,* S33–42.

Cumming, E. (1975). Engagement with an old theory. *International Journal of Aging & Human Development, 6,* 187–191.

Cumming, E., & Henry, W. E. (1961). *Growing old.* New York: Basic Books.

Cummings, E. M., & Davies, P. T. (1994). Maternal depression and child development. *Journal of Child Psychology & Psychiatry, 35,* 73–112.

Cummings, E. M., Hollenbeck, B., Iannotti, R., Radke-Yarrow, M., & Zahn-Waxler, C. (1986). Early organization of altruism and aggression: Developmental patterns and individual differences. In C. Zahn-Waxler, E. M. Cummings, & R. Iannotti (Eds.), *Altruism and aggression* (pp. 165–188). Cambridge, England: Cambridge University Press.

Cunningham, L. (1996). *Grief and the adolescent.* Newhall, CA: TeenAge Grief, Inc.

Cunningham, M., Swanson, D., Spencer, M., & Dupree, D. (2003). The association of physical maturation with family hassles among African American adolescent males. *Cultural Diversity & Ethnic Minority Psychology, 9,* 276–288.

Cunningham, W. R., & Haman, K. L. (1992). Intellectual functioning in relation to mental health. In J. E. Birren, R. B. Sloane, & G. D. Cohen (Eds.), *Handbook of mental health and aging* (2nd ed., pp. 340–355). San Diego, CA: Academic Press.

Curran, S., McLanahan, S., & Knab, J. (2003). Does remarriage expand perceptions of kinship support among the elderly? *Social Science Research, 32,* 171–190.

Curry, C. (2002). An approach to clinical genetics. In A. Rudolph, R. Kamei, & K. Overby (Eds.), *Rudolph's fundamentals of pediatrics.* (pp. 184–220). New York: McGraw-Hill.

Curyto, K., Chapleski, E., & Lichtenberg, P. (1999). Prediction of the presence and stability of depression in the Great Lakes Native American elderly. *Journal of Mental Health & Aging, 5,* 323–340.

Cushner, K., McClelland, A., & Safford, P. (1992). *Human diversity in education.* New York: McGraw-Hill.

Cutchin, M., Owen, S., & Chang, P. (2003). Becoming "at home" in assisted living residences: Exploring place integration processes. *Journals of Gerontology, Series B: Psychological & Social Sciences, 58B,* S234–S243.

Cuvo, A. (1974). Incentive level influence on overt rehearsal and free recall as a function of age. *Journal of Experimental Child Psychology, 18,* 167–181.

Czaja, S., & Sharit, J. (1998). Age differences in attitudes toward computers. *Journals of Gerontology, Series B: Psychological Sciences & Social Sciences, 53B,* P329–P340.

Czaja, S., Sharit, J., Nair, S., & Rubert, M. (1998). Understanding sources of user variability in computer-based data entry performance. *Behaviour & Information Technology, 17,* 282–293.

Da Costa, D., Larouche, J., Dritsa, M., & Brender, W. (2000). Psychosocial correlates of prepartum and postpartum depressed mood. *Journal of Affective Disorders, 59,* 31–40.

Daire, A. (2004). Investigating caregiver distress with the Parental Bonding Instrument (PBI). *Dementia: The International Journal of Social Research & Practice, 3,* 83–94.

D'Alton, M. E., & DeCherney, A. H. (1993). Prenatal diagnosis. *New England Journal of Medicine, 328,* 114–118.

Daly, L. E., Kirke, P. N., Molloy, A., Weir, D. G., & Scott, J. M. (1995). Folate levels and neural tube defects: Implications for prevention. *Journal of the American Medical Association, 274,* 1698–1702.

Daly, M., & Wilson, M. (1996). Violence against stepchildren. *Current Directions in Psychological Science, 5,* 77–81.

Daly, S., & Glenwick, D. (2000). Personal adjustment and perceptions of grandchild behavior in custodial grandmothers. *Journal of Clinical Child Psychology, 29*, 108–118.

Dammeijer, P., Schlundt, B., Chenault, M., Manni, J., & Anteunis, l. (2002). Effects of early auditory deprivation and stimulation on auditory brainstem responses in the rat. *Acta Oto-Laryngologica, 122*, 703–708.

Damon, W. (1977). *The social world of the child.* San Francisco: Jossey-Bass.

Damon, W. (1983). The nature of social-cognitive change in the developing child. In W. F. Overton (Ed.), *The relationship between social and cognitive development* (pp. 103–142). Hillsdale, NJ: Erlbaum.

Damon, W., & Hart, D. (1988). *Self understanding in childhood and adolescence.* New York: Cambridge University Press.

Danby, S., & Baker, C. (1998). How to be masculine in the block area. *Childhood: A Global Journal of Child Research, 5*, 151–175.

Darlington, R. B. (1991). The long-term effects of model preschool programs. In L. Okagaki & R. J. Sternberg (Eds.), *Directors of development* (pp. 203–215). Hillsdale, NJ: Erlbaum.

Datta, P., Poortinga, Y., & Marcoen, A. (2003). Parent care by Indian and Belgian caregivers in their roles of daughter/daughter-in-law. *Journal of Cross-Cultural Psychology, 34*, 736–749.

Davenport, E. (1992). *The making of minority scientists and engineers.* Invited address presented at the annual meeting of the American Educational Research Association, San Francisco, CA.

Davenport, E., Davison, M., Kuang, H., Ding, S., Kim, S., & Kwak, N. (1998). High school mathematics course-taking by gender and ethnicity. *American Educational Research Journal, 35*, 497–514.

Davey, F. (1998). Young women's expected and preferred patterns of employment and child care. *Sex Roles, 38*, 95–102.

Davey, M., Fish, L., Askew, J., & Robila, M. (2003). Parenting practices and the transmission of ethnic identity. *Journal of Marital & Family Therapy, 29*, 195–208.

Davidson, R. (1994). Temperament, affective style, and frontal lobe asymmetry. In G. Dawson & K. Fischer (Eds.), *Human behavior and the developing brain.* New York: Guilford Press.

Davies, L. (2003). Singlehood: Transitions within a gendered world. *Canadian Journal on Aging, 22*, 343–352.

Davies, P., & Rose, J. (1999). Assessment of cognitive development in adolescents by means of neuropsychological tasks. *Developmental Neuropsychology, 15*, 227–248.

Davis, D. L., Dinse, G. E., & Hoel, D. G. (1994). Decreasing cardiovascular disease and increasing cancer among whites in the United States from 1973 through 1987. *Journal of the American Medical Association, 271*, 431–437.

Dawber, T. R., Kannel, W. B., & Lyell, L. P. (1963). An approach to longitudinal studies in a community: The Framingham study. *Annals of the New York Academy of Science, 107*, 539–556.

Dawson, D. (2000). Alcohol consumption, alcohol dependence, and all-cause mortality. *Alcoholism: Clinical & Experimental Research, 24*, 72–81.

Dawson, D. A. (1991). Family structure and children's health and well-being: Data from the 1988 National Health Interview Survey on child health. *Journal of Marriage & the Family, 53*, 573–584.

Dawson, J., & Langan, P. (1994). *Murder in families.* Washington, DC: U.S. Department of Justice.

Dawson, T. (2002). New tools, new insights: Kohlberg's moral judgement stages revisited. *International Journal of Behavioral Development, 26*, 154–166.

Deakin, J., Aitken, M., Robbins, T., & Sahakian, B. (2004). Risk taking during decision-making in normal volunteers changes with age. *Journal of the International Neuropscyhological Society, 10*, 590–598.

DeAngelis, T. (1997). When children don't bond with parents. *Monitor of the American Psychological Association, 28* (6) 10–12.

Deater-Deckard, K., & Dodge, K. A. (1997). Externalizing behavior problems and discipline revisited: Nonlinear effects and variation by culture, context, and gender. *Psychological Inquiry, 8*, 161–175.

Deater-Deckard, K., Dodge, K. A., Bates, J. E., & Pettit, G. S. (1996). Physical discipline among African American and European American mothers: Links to children's externalizing behaviors. *Developmental Psychology, 32*, 1065–1072.

Deater-Deckard, K., Lansford, J., Dodge, K., Pettit, G., & Bates, J. (2003). The development of attitudes about physical punishment: An 8-year longitudinal study. *Journal of Family Psychology, 17*, 351–360.

DeCasper, A., & Fifer, W. (1980). Of human bonding: Newborns prefer their mothers' voices. *Science, 208*, 1174–1176.

DeCasper, A. J., Lecaneut, J., Busnel, M., Granier-DeFerre, C., & Maugeais, R. (1994). Fetal reactions to recurrent maternal speech. *Infant Behavior & Development, 17*, 159–164.

DeCasper, A. J., & Spence, M. J. (1986). Prenatal maternal speech influences newborns' perception of speech sounds. *Infant Behavior and Development, 9*, 133–150.

Deci, E., Koestner, R., & Ryan, R. (1999). A meta-analytic review of experiments examining the effects of extrinsic rewards on intrinsic motivation. *Psychological Bulletin, 125*, 627–668.

Deeg, D. J. H., Kardaun, W. P. F., & Fozard, J. L. (1996). Health, behavior, and aging. In J. E. Birren & K. W. Schaie (Eds.), *Handbook of the psychology of aging* (4th ed., pp. 129–149). San Diego, CA: Academic Press.

Degirmencioglu, S., Urberg, K., & Tolson, J. (1998). Adolescent friendship networks: Continuity and change over the school year. *Merrill-Palmer Quarterly, 44*, 313–337.

de Graaf, C., Polet, P., & van Staveren, W. A. (1994). Sensory perception and pleasantness of food flavors in elderly subjects. *Journals of Gerontology: Psychological Sciences, 49*, P93–99.

de Haan, M., Luciana, M., Maslone, S. M., Matheny, L. S., & Richards, M. L. M. (1994). Development, plasticity, and risk: Commentary on Huttenlocher, Pollit and Gorman, and Gottesman and Goldsmith. In C. A. Nelson (Ed.), *The Minnesota Symposia on Child Psychology, Vol. 27* (pp. 161–178). Hillsdale, NJ: Erlbaum.

De Jong, G. F., Wilmoth, J. M., Angel, J. L., & Cornwell, G. T. (1995). Motives and the geographic mobility of very old Americans. *Journals of Gerontology: Social Sciences, 50B*, S395–404.

de Jong, M., & Bus, A. (2002). Quality of book-reading matters for emergent readers: An experiment with the same book in a regular or electronic format. *Journal of Educational Psychology, 94*, 144–155.

Dekovic, M., & Meeus, W. (1997). Peer relations in adolescence: Effects of parenting and adolescents' self-concept. *Journal of Adolescence, 20*, 163–176.

Dekovic, M., Noom, M., & Meeus, W. (1997). Expectations regarding development during adolescence: Parental and adolescent perceptions. *Journal of Youth & Adolescence, 26*, 253–272.

de Lacoste, M., Horvath, D., & Woodward, J. (1991). Possible sex differences in the developing human fetal brain. *Journal of Clinical & Experimental Neuropsychology, 13*, 831.

del Barrio, V., Moreno-Rosset, C., Lopez-Martinez, R., & Olmedo, M. (1997). Anxiety, depression and personality structure. *Personality & Individual Differences, 23*, 327–335.

Dellatolas, G., de Agostini, M., Curt, F., Kremin, H., Letierce, A., Maccario, J., & Lellouch, J. (2003). Manual skill, hand skill asymmetry, and cognitive performances in young children. *Laterality: Asymmetries of Body, Brain & Cognition, 8*, 317–338.

DeLoache, J., Pierroutsakos, S., & Uttal, D. (2003). The origins of pictorial competence. *Current Directions in Psychological Science, 12*, 114–118.

DeLoache, J. S. (1995). Early understanding and use of symbols: The model model. *Current Directions in Psychological Science, 4*, 109–113.

DeMaris, A., & Rao, K. V. (1992). Premarital cohabitation and subsequent marital stability in the United States: A reassessment. *Journal of Marriage & the Family, 54*, 178–190.

DeMars, C. (2000). Test stakes and item format interactions. *Applied Measurement in Education, 13*, 55–77.

Demb, H., & Chang, C. (2004). The use of psychostimulants in children with disruptive behavior disorders and developmental disabilities in a community setting. *Mental Health Aspects of Developmental Disabilities, 7*, 26–36.

Dempster, F. (1981). Memory span: Sources of individial and developmental differences. *Psychological Bulletin, 89*, 63–100.

DeMulder, E., Denham, S., Schmidt, M., & Mitchell, J. (2000). Q-sort assessment of attachment security during the preschool years: Links from home to school. *Developmental Psychology, 36*, 274–282.

Denham, S., Blair, K., DeMulder, E., Levitas, J., Sawyer, K., Auerbach-Major, S., & Queenan, P. (2003). Preschool emotional competence: Pathway to social competence. *Child Development, 74*, 238–256.

Denham, S., Caverly, S., Schmidt, M., Blair, K., DeMulder, E., Caal, S., Hamada, H., & Mason, T. (2002). Preschool understanding of emotions: Contributions to classroom anger and aggression. *Journal of Child Psychology, 43*, 901–916.

Dennerstein, L., Dudley, E., & Guthrie, J. (2002). Empty nest or revolving door? A prospective study of women's quality of life in midlife during the phase of children leaving and re-entering the home. *Psychological Medicine, 32*, 545–550.

Dennerstein, L., Lehert, P., Burger, H., & Dudley, E. (1999). Mood and the menopausal transition. *Journal of Nervous & Mental Disease, 187*, 685–691.

Dennerstein, L., Lehert, P., & Guthrie, J. (2002). The effects of the menopausal transition and biopsychosocial factors on well-being. *Archives of Women's Mental Health, 5,* 15–22.

Denney, N. W. (1982). Aging and cognitive changes. In B. B. Wolman (Ed.), *Handbook of developmental psychology* (pp. 807–827). Englewood Cliffs, NJ: Prentice-Hall.

Denney, N. W. (1984). Model of cognitive development across the life span. *Developmental Review, 4,* 171–191.

Dennis, W. (1960). Causes of retardation among institutional children: Iran. *Journal of Genetic Psychology, 96,* 47–59.

Den Ouden, L., Rijken, M., Brand, R., Verloove-Vanhorick, S. P., & Ruys, J. H. (1991). Is it correct to correct? Developmental milestones in 555 "normal" preterm infants compared with term infants. *Journal of Pediatrics, 118,* 399–404.

Depressed elderly react best to a mix of drugs and psychotherapy. (1999, March). *APA Monitor Online.* Retrieved February 7, 2001, from www.apa.org/monitor/ mar99/depress.html.

DeRegnier, R., Wewerka, S., Georgieff, M., Mattia, F., & Nelson, C. (2002). Influences of postconceptional age and postnatal experience on the development of auditory recognition memory in the newborn infant. *Developmental Psychobiology, 41,* 215–225.

DeSpelder, L. A., & Strickland, A. L. (1983). *The last dance: Encountering death and dying.* Palo Alto, CA: Mayfield.

Dessens, A., Cohen-Kettenis, P., Mellenbergh, G., van de Poll, N., Koppe, J., & Boer, K. (1999). Prenatal exposure to anticonvulsants and psychosexual development. *Archives of Sexual Behavior, 28,* 31–44.

Detchant, Lord Walton. (1995). Dilemmas of life and death: Part one. *Journal of the Royal Society of Medicine, 88,* 311–315.

Deter, H., & Herzog, W. (1994). Anorexia nervosa in a long-term perspective: Results of the Heidelberg-Mannheim study. *Psychosomatic Medicine, 56,* 20–27.

de Villiers, P. A., & de Villiers, J. G. (1992). Language development. In M. H. Bornstein & M. E. Lamb (Eds.), *Developmental psychology: An advanced textbook* (3rd ed., pp. 337–418). Hillsdale, NJ: Erlbaum.

Dezoete, J., MacArthur, B., & Tuck, B. (2003). Prediction of Bayley and Stanford-Binet scores with a group of very low birthweight children. *Child: Care, Health, & Development, 29,* 367–372.

Dgnelie, G., Zorge, I., & McDonald, T. (2000). Lutein improves visual function in some patients with retinal degeneration: A pilot study via the Internet. *Journal of the American Optometric Association, 71,* 147–164.

Diagram Group (1977). *Child's body.* New York: Paddington.

Diamond, A. (1991). Neuropsychological insights into the meaning of object concept development. In S. Carey & R. Gelman (Eds.), *The epigenesis of mind: Essays on biology and cognition* (pp. 67–110). Hillsdale, NJ: Erlbaum.

Dick, D., Rose, R., Viken, R., & Kaprio, J. (2000). Pubertal timing and substance use: Associations between and within families across late adolescence. *Developmental Psychology, 36,* 180–189.

Diehl, L., Vicary, J., & Deike, R. (1997). Longitudinal trajectories of self-esteem from early to middle adolescence and related psychosocial variables among rural adolescents. *Journal of Research on Adolescence, 7,* 393–411.

Diener, M., & Kim, D. (2004). Maternal and child predictors of preschool children's social competence. *Journal of Applied Developmental Psychology, 25,* 3–24.

Diesendruck, G., & Shatz, M. (2001). Two-year-olds' recognition of hierarchies: Evidence from their interpretation of the semantic relation between object labels. *Cognitive Development, 16,* 577–594.

Dietz, B., Carrozza, M., & Ritchey, P. (2003). Does financial self-efficacy explain gender differences in retirement saving strategies? *Journal of Women & Aging, 15,* 83–96.

Digman, J. M. (1990). Personality structure: Emergence of the five-factor model. *Annual Review of Psychology, 41,* 417–440.

DiMario, F. (2002). The nervous system. In A. Rudolph, R. Kamei, & K. Overby (Eds.), *Rudolph's fundamental of pediatrics* (3rd ed., pp. 796–846). New York: McGraw-Hill.

D'Imperio, R., Dubow, E., & Ippolito, M. (2000). Resilient and stress-affected adolescents in an urban setting. *Journal of Clinical Child Psychology, 29,* 129–142.

Dindia, K., & Allen, M. (1992). Sex differences in self-disclosure: A meta-analysis. *Psychological Bulletin, 112,* 106–124.

Dion, M., Braver, S., Wolchik, S., & Sandler, I. (1997). Alcohol abuse and psychopathic deviance in noncustodial parents as predictors of child support payment and visitation. *American Journal of Orthopsychiatry, 67,* 70–79.

DiPietro, J., Hodgson, D., Costigan, K., Hilton, S., & Johnson, T. (1996). Fetal neurobehavioral development. *Child Development, 67,* 2553–2567.

DiPietro, J., Hodgson, D., Costigan, K., & Johnson, T. (1996). Fetal antecedents of infant temperament. *Child Development, 67,* 2568–2583.

Dishion, T. J., French, D. C., & Patterson, G. R. (1995). The development and ecology of antisocial behavior. In D. Cicchetti & D. J. Cohen (Eds.), *Developmental psychopathology, Vol. 2: Risk, disorder, and adaptation* (pp. 421–471). New York: Wiley.

Dishion, T. J., Patterson, G. R., Stoolmiller, M., & Skinner, M. L. (1991). Family, school, and behavioral antecedents to early adolescent involvement with antisocial peers. *Developmental Psychology, 27,* 172–180.

Dittmann-Kohli, F., Lachman, M. E., Kliegl, R., & Baltes, P. B. (1991). Effects of cognitive training and testing on intellectual efficacy beliefs in elderly adults. *Journals of Gerontology: Psychological Sciences, 46,* P162–164.

Dobson, A., Brown, W., Ball, J., Powers, J., & McFadden, M. (1999). Women drivers' behaviour, socio-demographic characteristics and accidents. *Accident Analysis & Prevention, 31,* 525–535.

Dockett, S., & Smith, I. (1995, March). *Children's theories of mind and their involvement in complex shared pretense.* Paper presented at the biennial meetings of the Society for Research in Child Development, Indianapolis, IN.

Doctoroff, S. (1997). Sociodramatic script training and peer role prompting: Two tactics to promote and sociodramatic play and peer interaction. *Early Child Development & Care, 136,* 27–43.

Dodge, K. (1993). Social-cognitive mechanisms in the development of conduct disorder and depression. *Annual Review of Psychology, 44,* 559–584.

Dodge, K. (1997, April). *Testing developmental theory through prevention trials.* Paper presented at the biennial meeting of the Society for Research on Child Development. Washington, DC.

Dodge, K. A., Pettit, G. S., & Bates, J. E. (1994). Socialization mediators of the relation between socioeconomic status and child conduct problems. *Child Development, 65,* 649–665.

Doh, H., & Falbo, T. (1999). Social competence, maternal attentiveness, and overprotectiveness: Only children in Korea. *International Journal of Behavioral Development, 23,* 149–162.

Dollard, J., Doob, L. W., Miller, N. E., Mowrer, O. H., & Sears, R. R. (1939). *Frustration and aggression.* New Haven, CT: Yale University Press.

Donnerstein, E., Slaby, R. G., & Eron, L. D. (1994). The mass media and youth aggression. In L. D. Eron, J. H. Gentry, & P. Schlegel (Eds.), *Reason to hope: A psychosocial perspective on violence and youth* (pp. 219–250). Washington, DC: American Psychological Association.

Donohew, R., Hoyle, R., Clayton, R., Skinner, W., Colon, S., & Rice, R. (1999). Sensation seeking and drug use by adolescents and their friends: Models for marijuana and alcohol. *Journal of Studies on Alcohol, 60,* 622–631.

Dorn, L., Dahl, R., Williamson, D., Birmaher, B., Axelson, D., Perel, J., Stull, S., & Ryan, N. (2003). Developmental markers in adolescence: Implications for studies of pubertal processes. *Journal of Youth & Adolescence, 32,* 315–324.

Dornbusch, S. M., Ritter, P. L., Liederman, P. H., Roberts, D. F., & Fraleigh, M. J. (1987). The relation of parenting style to adolescent school performance. *Child Development, 58,* 1244–1257.

Doty, R. L., Shaman, P., Appelbaum, S. L., Bigerson, R., Sikorski, L., & Rosenberg, L. (1984). Smell identification ability: Changes with age. *Science, 226,* 1441–1443.

Downe-Wamboldt, B., & Tamlyn, D. (1997). An international survey of death education trends in faculties of nursing and medicine. *Death Studies, 21,* 177–188.

Doyle, A. B., & Aboud, F. E. (1995). A longitudinal study of white children's racial prejudice as a social-cognitive development. *Merrill-Palmer Quarterly, 41,* 209–228.

Draper, B., Gething, L., Fethney, J., & Winfield, S. (1999). The Senior Psychiatrist Survey III: Attitudes towards personal ageing, life experiences and psychiatric practice. *Australian & New Zealand Journal of Psychiatry, 33,* 717–722.

Dreher, G. F., & Bretz, R. D., Jr. (1991). Cognitive ability and career attainment: Moderating effects of early career success. *Journal of Applied Psychology, 76,* 392–397.

Drevets, W., Price, J., Simpson, J., Todd, R., Reich, T., Vannier, M., & Raichle, M. (1997). Subgenual prefrontal cortex abnormalities in mood disorders. *Nature, 386,* 824–827.

Driscoll, A., & Nagel, N. (1999). *Early childhood education: Birth-8.* Needham Heights, MA: Allyn & Bacon.

Drobnic, S., Blossfeld, H., & Rohwer, G. (1999). Dynamics of women's employment patterns over the family life course: A comparison of the United States and Germany. *Journal of Marriage & the Family, 61,* 133–146.

Droege, K., & Stipek, D. (1993). Children's use of dispositions to predict class-mates' behavior. *Developmental Psychology, 29,* 646–654.

Drum, P. (1985). Retention of text information by grade, ability and study. *Discourse Processes, 8,* 21–52.

Due, P., Holstein, B., Lund, R., Modvig, J., & Avlund, K. (1999). Social relations: Network, support and relational strain. *Social Science & Medicine, 48,* 661–673.

Duffy, F. (1994). The role of quantified electroencephalography in psychological research. In K. Fischer & G. Dawson (Eds.), *Human behavior and the developing brain* (pp. 93–136). New York: Guilford Press.

Duka, T., Tasker, R., & McGowan, J. (2000). The effects of 3-week estrogen hormone replacement on cognition in elderly healthy females. *Psychopharmacology, 149,* 129–139.

Duke, P. M., Carlsmith, J. M., Jennings, D., Martin, J. A., Dornbusch, S. M., Gross, R. T., & Siegel-Gorelick, B. (1982). Educational correlates of early and late sexual maturation in adolescence. *Journal of Pediatrics, 100,* 633–637.

Duncan, M., Stayton, C., & Hall, C. (1999). Police reports on domestic incidents involving intimate partners: Injuries and medical help-seeking. *Women & Health, 30,* 1–13.

Dunn, J. (1994). Experience and understanding of emotions, relationships, and membership in a particular culture. In P. Ekman & R. J. Davidson (Eds.), *The nature of emotion: Fundamental questions* (pp. 352–355). New York: Oxford University Press.

Dunphy, D. C. (1963). The social structure of urban adolescent peer groups. *Sociometry, 26,* 230–246.

Dura, J. R., & Kiecolt-Glaser, J. K. (1991). Family transitions, stress, and health. In P. A. Cowan & M. Hetherington (Eds.), *Family transitions* (pp. 59–76). Hillsdale, NJ: Erlbaum.

Durlak, J. A. (1972). Relationship between attitudes toward life and death among elderly women. *Developmental Psychology, 8,* 146.

Dush, C., Cohan, C., & Amato, P. (2003). The relationship between cohabitation and marital quality and stability: Change across cohorts? *Journal of Marriage & the Family, 65,* 539–549.

Dutch Senate OKs doctor-assisted suicide. (2001, April 11). *Houston Chronicle,* p. 16A.

Duursma, S. A., Raymakers, J. A., Boereboom, F. T. J., & Scheven, B. A. A. (1991). Estrogen and bone metabolism. *Obstetrical & Gynecological Survey, 47,* 38–44.

Duvall, E. M. (1962). *Family development.* New York: Lippincott.

Duvall, S., Delquadri, J., & Ward, D. (2004). A preliminary investigation of the effectiveness of homeschool instructional environments for students with attention-deficit/hyperactivity disorder. *School Psychology Review, 33,* 140–158.

Dwyer, J., Allayee, H., Dwyer, K., Fan, J., Wu, H., Mar, R., Lusis, A., & Mehrabian, M. (2004). Arachidonate 5-lipoxygenase promoter genotype, dietary arachidonic acid, and atherosclerosis. *New England Journal of Medicine, 350,* 29–37.

Dyck, J., Gee, N., & Smither, J. (1998). The changing construct of computer anxiety for younger and older adults. *Computers in Human Behavior, 14,* 61–77.

Dyregrov, A., Gjestad, R., Bie Wikander, A., & Vigerust, S. (1999). Reactions following the sudden death of a classmate. *Scandinavian Journal of Psychology, 40,* 167–176.

Eagly, A., & Wood, W. (1999). The origins of sex differences in human behavior: Evolved dispositions versus social roles. *American Psychologist, 54,* 408–423.

Eames, M., Ben-Schlomo, Y., & Marmot, M. G. (1993). Social deprivation and premature mortality: Regional comparison across England. *British Medical Journal, 307,* 1097–1102.

Earles, J. L., & Salthouse, T. A. (1995). Interrelations of age, health, and speed. *Journals of Gerontology: Psychological Sciences, 50B,* P33–41.

Eccles, J., Barber, B., & Jozefowicz, D. (1998). Linking gender to educational, occupational, and recreational choices: Applying the Eccles et al. model of achievement-related choices. In W. B. Swann, Jr., J. H. Langlois, & L. A. Gibert (Eds.), *Sexism and stereotypes in modern society: The gender science of Janet Spence* (pp. 153–192). Washington, DC: APA Press.

Eccles, J., Jacobs, J., & Harold, R. (1990). Gender role stereotypes, expectancy effects, and parents' socialization of gender differences. *Journal of Social Issues, 46,* 183–201.

Echt, K., Morrell, R., & Park, D. (1998). Effects of age and training formats on basic computer skill acquisition in older adults. *Educational Gerontology, 24,* 3–25.

Eckensberger, E., & Zimba, R. (1997). The development of moral judgment. In J. Berry, P. Dasen, & T. Saraswathi (Eds.), *Handbook of cross-cultural psychology, Vol. 2.* (pp. 299–328). Boston: Allyn & Bacon.

Education Commission of the States (ECS). (2004). *ECS report to the nation: State implementation of the No Child Left Behind Act.* Retrieved September 21, 2004, from http://www.ecs.org/ecsmain.asp?page=/html/special/nclb/reporttothenation/reporttothenation.htm.

Education Trust. (1996). *Education watch: The 1996 Education Trust state and national data book.* Washington, DC: Author.

Edwards, J. N. (1969). Familial behavior as social exchange. *Journal of Marriage & the Family, 31,* 518–526.

Egan, S. K., & Perry, D. G. (1998). Does low self-regard invite victimization? *Developmental Psychology, 34,* 299–309.

Eichorn, D. H., Clausen, J. A., Haan, N., Honzik, M. P., & Mussen, P. H. (Eds.). (1981). *Present and past in middle life.* New York: Academic Press.

Einerson, M. (1998). Fame, fortune, and failure: Young girls' moral language surrounding popular culture. *Youth & Society, 30,* 241–257.

Eisenberg, N. (1992). *The caring child.* Cambridge, MA: Harvard University Press.

Eisenberg, N. (2000). Emotion, regulation, and moral development. *Annual Review of Psychology, 51,* 665–697.

Eisenberg, N., Fabes, R. A., Murphy, B., Karbon, M., Smith, M., & Maszk, P. (1996). The relations of children's dispositional empathy-related responding to their emotionality, regulation, and social functioning. *Developmental Psychology, 32,* 195–209.

Eisenberg, N., Fabes, R. A., Murphy, B., Maszk, P., Smith, M., & Karbon, M. (1995). The role of emotionality and regulation in children's social functioning: A longitudinal study. *Child Development, 66,* 1360–1384.

Eisenberg, N., Guthrie, I., Murphy, B., Shepard, S., et al. (1999). Consistency and development of prosocial dispositions: A longitudinal study. *Child Development, 70,* 1360–1372.

Eisenberger, N. (2003). Does rejection hurt? An fMRI study of social exclusion. *Science, 302,* 290–292.

Eisenberger, R., Pierce, W., & Cameron, J. (1999). Effects of reward on intrinsic motivation-negative, neutral, and positive: Comment on Deci, Koestner, and Ryan. *Psychological Bulletin, 125,* 677–691.

Elbedour, S., Baker, A., & Charlesworth, W. (1997). The impact of political violence on moral reasoning in children. *Child Abuse & Neglect, 21,* 1053–1066.

Elder, G. H., Jr. (1974). *Children of the Great Depression.* Chicago: University of Chicago Press.

Elder, G. H., Jr. (1978). Family history and the life course. In T. Hareven (Ed.), *Transitions: The family and the life course in historical perspective* (pp. 17–64). New York: Academic Press.

Elder, G. H., Jr., & Caspi, A. (1988). Economic stress in lives: Developmental perspectives. *Journal of Social Issues, 44,* 25–45.

Elder, G. H., Jr., Liker, J. K., & Cross, C. E. (1984). Parent-child behavior in the Great Depression: Life course and intergenerational influences. In P. B. Baltes & O. G. Brim, Jr. (Eds.), *Life-span development and behavior, Vol. 6* (pp. 111–159). New York: Academic Press.

Eley, T., Liang, H., Plomin, R., Sham, P., Sterne, A., Williamson, R., & Purcell, S. (2004). Parental familial vulnerability, family environment, and their interactions as predictors of depressive symptoms in adolescents. *Journal of the American Academy of Child Psychiatry, 43,* 298–306.

Elizur, Y., & Mintzer, A. (2003). Gay males' intimate relationship quality: The roles of attachment security, gay identity, social support, and income. *Personal Relationships, 10,* 411–435.

Elkind, D. (1967). Egocentrism in adolescence. *Child Development, 38,* 1025–1033.

Ellenbogen, S., & Chamberland, C. (1997). The peer relations of dropouts: A comparative study of at-risk and not at-risk youths. *Journal of Adolescence, 20,* 355–367.

Ellickson, P., Martino, S., & Collins, R. (2004). Marijuana use from adolescence to young adulthood: Multiple developmental trajectories and their associated outcomes. *Health Psychology, 23,* 299–307.

Elliot, A., & Hall, N. (1997). The impact of self-regulatory teaching strategies on "at-risk" preschoolers' mathematical learning in a computer-mediated environment. *Journal of Computing in Childhood Education, 8,* 187–198.

Elliott, D., Mok, D., & Briere, J. (2004). Adult sexual assault: Prevalence, symptomatology, and sex differences in the general population. *Journal of Traumatic Stress, 17,* 203–211.

Ellis, R., & Allaire, J. (1999). Modeling computer interest in older adults: The role of age, education, computer knowledge, and computer anxiety. *Human Factors, 41,* 345–355.

Ellsworth, C. P., Muir, D. W., & Hains, S. M. J. (1993). Social competence and person-object differentiation: An analysis of the still-face effect. *Developmental Psychology, 29,* 63–73.

Emanuel, E., Fairclough, D., Clarridge, B., Blum, D., Bruera, E., Penley, W., Schnipper, L., & Mayer, R. (2000). Attitudes and practices of U. S. oncologists regarding euthanasia and physician-assisted suicide. *Annals of Internal Medicine, 133,* 527–532.

Emde, R. N., Plomin, R., Robinson, J., Corley, R., DeFries, J., Fulker, D. W., Reznick, J. S., Campos, J., Kagan, J., & Zahn-Waxler, C. (1992). Temperament, emotion, and cognition at fourteen months: The MacArthur longitudinal twin study. *Child Development, 63,* 1437–1455.

Emery, C. F., & Gatz, M. (1990). Psychological and cognitive effects of an exercise program for community-residing older adults. *The Gerontologist, 30,* 184–192.

Emery, R., & Laumann-Billings, L. (1998). An overview of the nature, causes, and consequences of abusive family relationships: Toward differentiating maltreatment and violence. *American Psychologist, 53,* 121–135.

Engle, P., & Breaux, C. (1998). Fathers' involvement with children: Perspectives from developing countries. *Society for Research in Child Development Social Policy Report, 12,* 1–21.

Ensign, J. (1998). *Defying the stereotypes of special education: Homeschool students.* Paper presented at the annual meeting of the American Education Research Association, San Diego, CA.

Entwisle, D. R. (1990). Schools and the adolescent. In S. S. Feldman & G. R. Elliott (Eds.), *At the threshold: The developing adolescent* (pp. 197–224). Cambridge, MA: Harvard University Press.

Entwisle, D. R., & Alexander, K. L. (1990). Beginning school math competence: Minority and majority comparisons. *Child Development, 61,* 454–471.

Ericsson, K. A. (1990). Peak performance and age: An examination of peak performance in sports. In P. Baltes & M. M. Baltes (Eds.), *Successful aging* (pp. 164–196). Cambridge, MA: Cambridge University Press.

Ericsson, K. A., & Crutcher, R. J. (1990). The nature of exceptional performance. In P. B. Baltes, D. L. Featherman, & R. M. Lerner (Eds.), *Life-span development and behavior, Vol. 10* (pp. 188–218). Hillsdale, NJ: Erlbaum.

Erikson, E. H. (1950). *Childhood and society.* New York: Norton.

Erikson, E. H. (1959). *Identity and the life cycle.* New York: Norton (reissued, 1980).

Erikson, E. H. (1963). *Childhood and society* (2nd ed.). New York: Norton.

Erikson, E. H. (1980a). *Identity and the life cycle.* New York: Norton (originally published 1959).

Erikson, E. H. (1980b). Themes of adulthood in the Freud-Jung correspondence. In N. J. Smelser & E. Erikson (Eds.), *Themes of work and love in adulthood* (pp. 43–76). Cambridge, MA: Harvard University Press.

Erikson, E. H. (1982). *The life cycle completed.* New York: Norton.

Erikson, E. H., Erikson, J. M., & Kivnick, H. Q. (1986). *Vital involvement in old age.* New York: Norton.

Eron, L. D. (1987). The development of aggressive behavior from the perspective of a developing behaviorism. *American Psychologist, 42,* 435–442.

Eron, L. D., Huesmann, L. R., & Zelli, A. (1991). The role of parental variables in the learning of aggression. In D. J. Pepler & K. H. Rubin (Eds.), *The development and treatment of childhood aggression* (pp. 169–188). Hillsdale, NJ: Erlbaum.

Escorihuela, R. M., Tobena, A., & Fernández-Teruel, A. (1994). Environmental enrichment reverses the detrimental action of early inconsistent stimulation and increases the beneficial effects of postnatal handling on shuttlebox learning in adult rats. *Behavioral Brain Research, 61,* 169–173.

Eskes, T. K. A. B. (1992). Home deliveries in the Netherlands-perinatal mortality and morbidity. *International Journal of Gynecology & Obstetrics, 38,* 161–169.

Eslea, M., Menesini, E., Morita, Y., O'Moore, M., Mora-Merchan, J., Pereira, B., & Smith, P. (2004). Friendship and loneliness among bullies and victims: Data from seven countries. *Aggressive Behavior, 30,* 71–83.

Esposito, K., Giugliano, F., Di Palo, C., Giugliano, G., Marfella, R., D'Andrea, F., D' Armiento, M., & Giugliano, D. (2004). Effect of lifestyle changes on erectile dysfunction in obese men: A randomized controlled trial. *Journal of the American Medical Association, 291,* 2978–2984.

Espy, K., Stalets, M., McDiarmid, M., Senn, T., Cwik, M., & Hamby, A. (2002). Executive functions in preschool children born preterm: Application of cognitive neuroscience paradigms. *Child Neuropsychology, 8,* 83–92.

Etaugh, C., & Liss, M. (1992). Home, school, and playroom: Training grounds for adult gender roles. *Sex Roles, 26,* 129–147.

Ethington, C. (1991). A test of a model of achievement behaviors. *American Educational Research Journal, 28,* 155–172.

Evans, G. (2004). The environment of childhood poverty. *American Psychologist, 59,* 77–92.

Evans, R., & Erikson, E. (1967). *Dialogue with Erik Erikson.* New York: Harper & Row.

Evans, R. I. (1969). *Dialogue with Erik Erikson.* New York: Dutton.

Ewald, P. (2000). *Plague time.* New York: Free Press.

Ex, C., & Janssens, J. (1998). Maternal influences on daughters' gender role attitudes. *Sex Roles, 38,* 171–186.

Eyetsemitan, F. (1998). Stifled grief in the workplace. *Death Studies, 22,* 469–479.

Fabes, R. A., Knight, G. P., & Higgins, D. A. (1995, March). *Gender differences in aggression: A meta-analytic reexamination of time and age effects.* Paper presented at the biennial meetings of the Society for Research in Child Development, Indianapolis, IN.

Fabi, M. (2004). Cybersex: The dark side of the force. *International Journal of Applied Psychoanalytic Studies, 1,* 208–209.

Fagan, J. (2000). A theory of intelligence as processing: Implications for society. *Psychology, Public Policy, & Law, 6,* 168–179.

Fagan, J., & Holland, C. (2002). Equal opportunity and racial differences in IQ. *Intelligence, 30,* 361–387.

Fagan, J. F., & Detterman, D. K. (1992). The Fagan Test of Infant Intelligence: A technical summary. *Journal of Applied Developmental Psychology, 13,* 173–193.

Fagan, J. F., & Singer, L. T. (1983). Infant recognition memory as a measure of intelligence. In L. P. Lipsett (Ed.), *Advances in infancy research, Vol. 2* (pp. 31–78). Norwood, NJ: Ablex.

Fagard, J., & Jacquet, A. (1989). Onset of bimanual coordination and symmetry versus asymmetry of movement. *Infant Behavior & Development, 12,* 229–235.

Fagot, B. I., & Hagan, R. (1991). Observations of parent reactions to sex-stereotyped behaviors: Age and sex effects. *Child Development, 62,* 617–628.

Fagot, B. I., & Leinbach, M. D. (1989). The young child's gender schema: Environmental input, internal organization. *Child Development, 60,* 663–672.

Fagot, B. I., & Leinbach, M. D. (1993). Gender-role development in young children: From discrimination to labeling. *Developmental Review, 13,* 205–224.

Fagot, B. I., Leinbach, M. D., & O'Boyle, C. (1992). Gender labeling, gender stereotyping, and parenting behaviors. *Developmental Psychology, 28,* 225–230.

Fahle, M., & Daum, I. (1997). Visual learning and memory as functions of age. *Neuropsychologia, 35,* 1583–1589.

Fahrenfort, J., Jacobs, E., Miedema, S., & Schweizer, A. (1996). Signs of emotional disturbance three years after early hospitalization. *Journal of Pediatric Psychology, 21,* 353–366.

FairTest. (2004). *No Child Left Behind after two years: A track record of failure.* Retrieved September 21, 2004, from http://www.fairtest.org/nclb%20flaw%20fact%20sheet%201-7-04.html.

Falbo, T. (1992). Social norms and one-child family: Clinical and policy limitations. In F. Boer & J. Dunn (Eds.), *Children's sibling relationships* (pp. 71–82). Hillsdale, NJ: Erlbaum.

Fallis, R., & Opotow, S. (2003). Are students failing school or are schools failing students? Class cutting in high school. *Journal of Social Issues, 59,* 103–119.

Fantuzzo, J., Coolahan, K., & Mendez, J. (1998). Contextually relevant validation of peer play constructs with African American Head Start children: Penn Interactive Peer Play Scale. *Early Childhood Research Quarterly, 13,* 411–431.

Fantuzzo, J., Sekino, Y., & Cohen, H. (2004). An examination of the contributions of interactive peer play to salient classroom competencies for urban Head Start children. *Psychology in the Schools, 41,* 323–336.

Fantz, R. L. (1956). A method for studying early visual development. *Perceptual & Motor Skills, 6,* 13–15.

Farmer, T., Estell, D., Leung, M., Trott, H., Bishop, J., & Cairns, B. (2003). Individual characteristics, early adolescent peer affiliations, and school dropout: An examination of aggressive and popular group types. *Journal of School Psychology, 41,* 217–232.

Farnham-Diggory, S. (1992). *The learning-disabled child.* Cambridge, MA: Harvard University Press.

Farrar, M. J. (1992). Negative evidence and grammatical morpheme acquisition. *Developmental Psychology, 28,* 90–98.

Farrell, M. P., & Rosenberg, S. D. (1981). *Men at midlife.* Boston: Auburn House.

Farrington, D. P. (1991). Childhood aggression and adult violence: Early precursors and later life outcomes. In D. J. Pepler & K. H. Rubin (Eds.), *The development and treatment of childhood aggression* (pp. 5–30). Hillsdale, NJ: Erlbaum.

Farver, J. (1996). Aggressive behavior in preschoolers' social networks: Do birds of a feather flock together? *Early Childhood Research Quarterly, 11,* 333–350.

Farver, J., Bhadha, B., & Narang, S. (2002). Acculturation and psychological functioning in Asian Indian adolescents. *Social Development, 11,* 11–29.

Fathers' Rights Coalition. (1999). *Statistics on a fatherless America.* Retrieved December 6, 1999, from www.fathersrc.com.

Fearon, I., Hains, S., Muir, D., & Kisilevsky, B. (2002). Development of tactile responses in human preterm and full-term infants from 30 to 40 weeks postconceptional age. *Infancy, 3,* 31–51.

Federal Interagency Forum on Aging-Related Statistics (FIFARS). (2000). *Older Americans 2000: Key indicators of well-being.* Retrieved February 7, 2001, from http://www.agingstats.gov/chartbook2000.

Federal Interagency Forum on Child and Family Statistics (FIFCFS). (2000). *America's children: Key national indicators of well-being 2000.* Washington, DC: Author.

Feeney, J. A. (1994). Attachment style, communication patterns, and satisfaction across the life cycle of marriage. *Personal Relationships, 1,* 333–348.

Fein, J., Durbin, D., & Selbst, S. (2002). Injuries & emergencies. In A. Rudolph, R. Kamei, & K. Overby (Eds.), *Rudolph's fundamentals of pediatrics,* (3rd ed., pp. 390–436). New York: McGraw-Hill.

Feiring, C. (1999). Other-sex friendship networks and the development of romantic relationships in adolescence. *Journal of Youth & Adolescence, 28,* 495–512.

Feld, S., & George, L. K. (1994). Moderating effects of prior social resources on the hospitalizations of elders who become widowed. *Aging & Health, 6,* 275–295.

Feldman, R. (2003). Paternal socio-psychological factors and infant attachment: The mediating role of synchrony in father-infant interactions. *Infant Behavior & Development, 25,* 221–236.

Feldman, R., & Eidelman, A. (2003). Skin-to-skin contact (kangaroo care) accelerates autonomic and neurobehavioural maturation in preterm infants. *Developmental Medicine & Child Neurology, 45,* 274–281.

Fenn, D., & Ganzini, L. (1999). Attitudes of Oregon psychologists toward physician-assisted suicide and the Oregon Death With Dignity Act. *Professional Psychology: Research & Practice, 30,* 235–244.

Fenson, L., Dale, P. S., Reznick, J. S., Bates, E., Thal, D. J., & Pethick, S. J. (1994). Variability in early communicative development. *Monographs of the Society for Research in Child Development, 59* (5, Serial No. 242).

Fergusson, D. M., Horwood, L. J., & Lynskey, M. T. (1993). Maternal smoking before and after pregnancy: Effects on behavioral outcomes in middle childhood. *Pediatrics, 92,* 815–822.

Fernald, A., & Kuhl, P. (1987). Acoustic determinants of infant preference for motherese speech. *Infant Behavior & Development, 10,* 279–293.

Fernandez, M. (1997). Domestic violence by extended family members in India. *Journal of Interpersonal Violence, 12,* 433–455.

Fiatarone, M. A., & Evans, W. J. (1993). The etiology and reversibility of muscle dysfunction in the aged. *Journals of Gerontology, 48* (Special Issue), 77–83.

Field, T. (1995). Psychologically depressed parents. In M. H. Bornstein (Ed.), *Handbook of parenting, Vol. 4: Applied and practical parenting* (pp. 85–99). Mahwah, NJ: Erlbaum.

Field, T. M. (1977). Effects of early separation, interactive deficits, and experimental manipulations on infant-mother face-to-face interaction. *Child Development, 48,* 763–771.

Fielding-Barnsley, R., & Purdie, N. (2003). Early intervention in the home for children at risk of reading failure. *Support for Learning, 18,* 77–82.

Fields, R. B. (1992). Psychosocial response to environment change. In V. B. Van Hasselt & M. Hersen (Eds.), *Handbook of social development: A lifespan perspective* (pp. 503–544). New York: Plenum.

Findling, R., Feeny, N., Stansbrey, R., Delporto-Bedoya, D., & Demeter, C. (2004). Special articles: Treatment of mood disorders in children and adolescents: Somatic treatment for depressive illnesses in children and adolescents. *Psychiatric Clinics of North America, 27,* 113–137.

Fischer, K., & Rose, S. (1994). Dynamic development of coordination of components in brain and behavior: A framework for theory and research. In K. Fischer & G. Dawson (Eds.), *Human behavior and the developing brain* (pp. 3–66). New York: Guilford Press.

Fischer, K. W., & Bidell, T. (1991). Constraining nativist inferences about cognitive capacities. In S. Carey & R. Gelman (Eds.), *The epigenesis of mind: Essays on biology and cognition* (pp. 199–236). Hillsdale, NJ: Erlbaum.

Fischer, L., Wei, F., Solberg, L., Rush, W., & Heinrich, R. (2003). Treatment of elderly and other adult patients for depression in primary care. *Journal of the American Geriatrics Society, 51,* 1554–1562.

Fish, M., Stifter, C. A., & Belsky, J. (1991). Conditions of continuity and discontinuity in infant negative emotionality: Newborn to five months. *Child Development, 62,* 1525–1537.

Fisher, B., & Specht, D. (1999). Successful aging and creativity in later life. *Journal of Aging Studies, 13,* 457–472.

Fisher, C. (2000). Mood and emotions while working: Missing pieces of job satisfaction? *Journal of Organizational Behavior, 21,* 185–202.

Fisher, J., Feekery, C., & Rowe-Murray, H. (2002). Nature, severity and correlates of psychological distress in women admitted to a private mother-baby unit. *Journal of Paediatrics & Child Health, 38,* 140–145.

Fitzgerald, B. (1999). Children of lesbian and gay parents: A review of the literature. *Marriage & Family Review, 29,* 57–75.

Fitzgerald, D., & White, K. (2003). Linking children's social worlds: Perspective-taking in parent-child and peer contexts. *Social Behavior & Personality, 31,* 509–522.

Fitzpatrick, J. L., & Silverman, T. (1989). Women's selection of careers in engineering: Do traditional-nontraditional differences still exist? *Journal of Vocational Behavior, 34,* 266–278.

Flannery, D., Vazsonyi, A., Embry, D., Powell, K., Atha, H., Vesterdal, W., & Shenyang, G. (2000, August). *Longitudinal effectiveness of the Peace-Builders' universal school-based violence prevention program.* Paper presented at the annual meeting of the American Psychological Association, Washington, DC.

Flannery, D. J., Montemayor, R., & Eberly, M. B. (1994). The influence of parent negative emotional expression on adolescents' perceptions of their relationships with their parents. *Personal Relationships, 1,* 259–274.

Flavell, J. H. (1985). *Cognitive development* (2nd ed.). Englewood Cliffs, NJ: Prentice-Hall.

Flavell, J. H. (1986). The development of children's knowledge about the appearance-reality distinction. *American Psychologist, 41,* 418–425.

Flavell, J. H. (1993). Young children's understanding of thinking and consciousness. *Current Directions in Psychological Science, 2,* 40–43.

Flavell, J. H., Everett, B. A., Croft, K., & Flavell, E. R. (1981). Young children's knowledge about visual perception: Further evidence for the Level 1–Level 2 distinction. *Developmental Psychology, 17,* 99–103.

Flavell, J. H., Green, F. L., & Flavell, E. R. (1990). Developmental changes in young children's knowledge about the mind. *Cognitive Development, 5,* 1–27.

Flavell, J. H., Green, F. L., Wahl, K. E., & Flavell, E. R. (1987). The effects of question clarification and memory aids on young children's performance on appearance-reality tasks. *Cognitive Development, 2,* 127–144.

Flavell, J. H., Zhang, X.-D., Zou, H., Dong, Q., & Qi, S. (1983). A comparison of the appearance-reality distinction in the People's Republic of China and the United States. *Cognitive Psychology, 15,* 459–466.

Fleeson, W., & Heckhausen, J. (1997). More or less "me" in past, present, and future: Perceived lifetime personality during adulthood. *Psychology & Aging, 12,* 125–136.

Flowers, L., & Pascarella, E. (1999). Cognitive effects of college racial composition on African American students after 3 years of college. *Journal of College Student Development, 40,* 669–677.

Floyd, F., Stein, T., Harter, K., Allison, A., et al. (1999). Gay, lesbian, and bisexual youths: Separation-individuation, parental attitudes, identity consolidation, and well-being. *Journal of Youth & Adolescence, 28,* 705–717.

Flynn, J. (1999). Searching for justice: The discovery of IQ gains over time. *American Psychologist, 54,* 5–20.

Flynn, J. (2003). Movies about intelligence: The limitations of g. *Current Directions in Psychological Science, 12,* 95–99.

Fokin, V., Ponomareva, N., Androsova, L., & Gavrilova, S. (1997). Interhemispheric asymmetry and neuroimmune modulation in normal aging and Alzheimer's dementias. *Human Physiology, 23,* 284–288.

Foley, D., Monjan, A., Izmirlian, G., Hays, J., & Blazer, D. (1999). Incidence and remission of insomnia among elderly adults in a biracial cohort. *Sleep, 22* (Supplement 2), S373–S378.

Folkman, S., & Lazarus, R. (1980). An analysis of coping in a middle-aged community sample. *Journal of Personality and Social Psychology, 70,* 336–348.

Folven, R. J., & Bonvillian, J. D. (1991). The transition from nonreferential to referential language in children acquiring American Sign Language. *Developmental Psychology, 27,* 806–816.

Fonda, S., Clipp, E., & Maddox, G. (2002). Patterns in functioning among residents of an affordable assisted living housing facility. *Gerontologist, 42,* 178–187.

Fordham, K., & Stevenson-Hinde, J. (1999). Shyness, friendship quality, and adjustment during middle childhood. *Journal of Child Psychology & Psychiatry & Allied Disciplines, 40,* 757–768.

Forsell, Y., & Winblad, B. (1999). Incidence of major depression in a very elderly population. *Journal of Geriatric Psychiatry, 14,* 368–372.

Forte, C., & Hansvick, C. (1999). Applicant age as a subjective employability factor: A study of workers over and under age fifty. *Journal of Employment Counseling, 36,* 24–34.

Foster, T. (2003). Suicide note themes and suicide prevention. *International Journal of Psychiatry in Medicine, 33,* 323–331.

Foulder-Hughes, L., & Cooke, L. (2003a). Do mainstream schoolchildren who were born preterm have motor problems? *British Journal of Occupational Therapy, 66,* 9–16.

Foulder-Hughes, L., & Cooke, R. (2003b). Motor, cognitive, and behavioural disorders in children born very preterm. *Developmental Medicine & Child Neurology, 45,* 97–103.

Fouquereau, E., & Baudoin, C. (2002). The Marital Satisfaction Questionnaire for Older Persons: Factor structure in a French sample. *Social Behavior & Personality, 30,* 95–104.

Fourn, L., Ducic, S., & Seguin, L. (1999). Smoking and intrauterine growth retardation in the Republic of Benin. *Journal of Epidemiology & Community Health, 53,* 432–433.

Foust, M. (2004, August 21). Party platforms tell voters how Republicans, Democrats differ. *Baptist Press.* Retrieved September 25, 2004, from http://www.bpnews.net/bpnews.asp?ID=18981.

Fox, N., Henderson, H., Rubin, K., Calkins, S., & Schmidt, L. (2001). Continuity and discontinuity of behavioral inhibition and exuberance: Psychophysiological and behavioral influences across the first four years of life. *Child Development, 72,* 1–21.

Fox, N. A., Kimmerly, N. L., & Schafer, W. D. (1991). Attachment to mother/attachment to father: A meta-analysis. *Child Development, 62,* 210–225.

Fozard, J. L. (1990). Vision and hearing in aging. In J. E. Birren & K. W. Schaie (Eds.), *Handbook of the psychology of aging* (3rd ed., pp. 150–171). San Diego, CA: Academic Press.

Fozard, J. L., Metter, E. J., & Brant, L. J. (1990). Next steps in describing aging and disease in longitudinal studies. *Journals of Gerontology: Psychological Sciences, 45,* P116–127.

Franche, R., & Bulow, C. (1999). The impact of a subsequent pregnancy on grief and emotional adjustment following a perinatal loss. *Infant Mental Health Journal, 20,* 175–187.

Francis, L. (1997). Ideology and interpersonal emotion management: Redefining identity in two support groups. *Social Psychology Quarterly, 60,* 153–171.

Francis, P. L., Self, P. A., & Horowitz, F. D. (1987). The behavioral assessment of the neonate: An overview. In J. D. Osofsky (Ed.), *Handbook of infant development* (2nd ed., pp. 723–779). New York: Wiley-Interscience.

Francis-Smythe, J., & Smith, P. (1997). The psychological impact of assessment in a development center. *Human Relations, 50,* 149–167.

Franco, N., & Levitt, M. (1998). The social ecology of middle childhood: Family support, friendship quality, and self-esteem. *Family Relations: Interdisciplinary Journal of Applied Family Studies, 47,* 315–321.

Fraser, A. M., Brockert, J. E., & Ward, R. H. (1995). Association of young maternal age with adverse reproductive outcomes. *New England Journal of Medicine, 332,* 1113–1117.

Fredriksen, K., Rhodes, J., Reddy, R., & Way, N. (2004). Sleepless in Chicago: Tracking the effects of adolescent sleep loss during the middle school years. *Child Development, 75,* 84–95.

Freeman, E., Sammel, M., Liu, L., García, C., Nelson, D., & Hollander, L. (2004). Hormones and menopausal status as predictors of depression in women in transition to menopause. *Archives of General Psychiatry, 61,* 62–70.

Freeman, E. W., & Rickels, K. (1993). *Early childbearing: Perspectives of black adolescents on pregnancy, abortion, and contraception.* Newbury Park, CA: Sage.

Frey, K. S., & Ruble, D. N. (1992). Gender constancy and the "cost" of sex-typed behavior: A test of the conflict hypothesis. *Developmental Psychology, 28,* 714–721.

Frick, P., Christian, R., & Wooton, J. (1999). Age trends in association between parenting practices and conduct problems. *Behavior Modification, 23,* 106–128.

Friedman, H. S., Hawley, P. H., & Tucker, J. S. (1994). Personality, health, and longevity. *Current Directions in Psychological Science, 3,* 37–41.

Friedman, M., & Rosenman, R. H. (1974). *Type A behavior and your heart.* New York: Knopf.

Frieswijk, N., Buunk, B., Steverink, N., & Slaets, J. (2004). The effect of social comparison information on the life satisfaction of frail older persons. *Psychology & Aging, 19,* 183–190.

Frisch, A., Laufer, N., Danziger, Y., Michaelovsky, E., Leor, S., Carel, C., Stein, D., Fenig, S., Mimouni, M., Apter, A., & Weizman, A. (2001). Association of anorexia nervosa with the high activity allele of the COMT gene: A family-based study in Israeli patients. *Molecular Psychiatry, 6,* 243–245.

Frisch, M., Glimelius, B., van den Brule, A., Wohlfahrt, J., Meijer, C., Walboomers, J., Goldman, S., Svensson, C., Hans-Olov, A., & Melbye, M. (1997). Sexually transmitted infection as a cause of anal cancer. *New England Journal of Medicine, 337,* 1350–1358.

Fuchs, L., Fuchs, D., Karns, K., Hamlett, C., Dutka, S., & Katsaroff, M. (2000). The importance of providing background information on the structure and scoring of performance assessments. *Applied Measurement in Education, 13,* 134.

Fuller, T. L., & Fincham, F. D. (1995). Attachment style in married couples: Relation to current marital functioning, stability over time, and method of assessment. *Personal Relationships, 2,* 17–34.

Fung, H. (1999). Becoming a moral child: The socialization of shame among young Chinese children. *Ethos, 27,* 180–209.

Funk, J., Baldacci, H., Pasold, T., & Baumgardner, J. (2004). Violence exposure in real-life, video games, television, movies, and the Internet: Is there desensitization? *Journal of Adolescence, 27,* 23–39.

Funk, J., & Buchman, D. (1999). Playing violent video and computer games and adolescent self-concept. *Journal of Communication, 46,* 19–32.

Funk, J., Buchman, D., Jenks, J., & Bechtoldt, H. (2003). Playing violent video games, desensitization, and moral evaluation in children. *Journal of Applied Developmental Psychology, 24,* 413–436.

Funk, J., Buchman, D., Myers, B., & Jenks, J. (2000, August). *Asking the right questions in research on violent electronic games.* Paper presented at the annual meeting of the American Psychological Association, Washington, DC.

Furnham, A. (1999). Economic socialization: A study of adults' perceptions and uses of allowances (pocket money) to educate children. *British Journal of Developmental Psychology, 17,* 585–604.

Furrow, D., & Nelson, K. (1984). Environmental correlates of individual differences in language acquisition. *Journal of Child Language, 11,* 523–534.

Furstenberg, F., & Harris, J. (1992). When fathers matter/why fathers matter: the impact of paternal involvement on the offspring of adolescent mothers. In R. Lerman & T. Ooms (Eds.), *Young unwed fathers.* Philadelphia: Temple University Press.

Furstenberg, F. F., Jr., & Cherlin, A. J. (1991). *Divided families: What happens to children when parents part.* Cambridge, MA: Harvard University Press.

Gaillard, W., Hertz-Pannier, L., Mott, S., Barnett, A., LeBihan, D., & Theodore, W. (2000). Functional anatomy of cognitive development: fMRI of verbal fluency in children and adults. *Neurology, 54,* 180–185.

Gainey, R., Catalano, R., Haggerty, K., & Hoppe, M. (1997). Deviance among the children of heroin addicts in treatment: Impact of parents and peers. *Deviant Behavior, 18,* 143–159.

Galambos, N., & Maggs, J. (1991). Out-of-school care of young adolescents and self-reported behavior. *Developmental Psychology, 27,* 644–655.

Galanaki, E. (2004). Teachers and loneliness: The children's perspective. *School Psychology International, 25,* 92–105.

Galassi, J., Gulledge, S., & Cox, N. (1997). Middle school advisories: Retrospect and prospect. *Review of Educational Research, 67,* 301–338.

Gallagher, A., Frith, U., & Snowling, M. (2000). Precursors of literacy delay among children at genetic risk of dyslexia. *Journal of Child Psychology & Psychiatry & Allied Disciplines, 41,* 202–213.

Gallagher, S. K. (1994). Doing their share: Comparing patterns of help given by older and younger adults. *Journal of Marriage & the Family, 56,* 567–578.

Gallagher, W. (1993, May). Midlife myths. *The Atlantic Monthly,* pp. 51–68.

Gallagher-Thompson, D., Futterman, A., Farberow, N., Thompson, L. W., & Peterson, J. (1993). The impact of spousal bereavement on older widows and widowers. In M. S. Stroebe, W. Stroebe, & R. O. Hansson (Eds.), *Handbook of bereavement: Theory, research, and intervention* (pp. 227–239). Cambridge, England: Cambridge University Press.

Gallagher-Thompson, D., Tazeau, Y., & Basilio L. (1997). The relationships of dimensions of acculturation to self-reported depression in older Mexican-American women. *Journal of Clinical Geropsychology, 3,* 123–137.

Gallo, W., Bradley, E., Siegel, M., & Kasl, S. (2000). Health effects of involuntary job loss among older workers: Findings from the health and retirement survey. *Journals of Gerontology, Series B: Psychological Sciences & Social Sciences, 55B,* S131–S140.

Galloway, J., & Thelen, E. (2004). Feet first: Object exploration in young infants. *Infant Behavior & Development, 27,* 107–112.

Gambert, S. R., Schultz, B. M., & Hamdy, R. C. (1995). Osteoporosis: Clinical features, prevention, and treatment. *Endocrinology and Metabolism Clinics of North America, 24,* 317–371.

Gamoran, A., Porter, A., Smithson, J., & White, P. (1997). Upgrading high school mathematics instruction: Improving learning opportunities for low-achieving, low-income youth. *Educational Evaluation & Policy Analysis, 19,* 325–338.

Gana, K., Alaphilippe, D., & Bailly, N. (2004). Positive illusions and mental and physical health in later life. *Aging & Mental Health, 8,* 58–64.

Ganchrow, J. R., Steiner, J. E., & Daher, M. (1983). Neonatal facial expressions in response to different qualities and intensities of gustatory stimuli. *Infant Behavior & Development, 6,* 189–200.

Gannon, L., & Stevens, J. (1998). Portraits of menopause in the mass media. *Women & Health, 27,* 1–15.

Ganong, L., & Coleman, M. (1994). *Remarried family relationships.* Thousand Oaks, CA: Sage Publications.

Garbarino, J., Dubrow, N., Kostelny, K., & Pardo, C. (1992). *Children in danger: Coping with the consequences of community violence.* San Francisco: Jossey-Bass.

Garcia, G., & Miller, R. (2001). Single-cell analyses reveal two defects in peptide-specific activation of naive T cells from aged mice. *Journal of Immunology, 166,* 3151–3157.

Gardiner, M., Luszcz, M., & Bryan, J. (1997). The manipulation and measurement of task-specific memory self-efficacy in younger and older adults. *International Journal of Behavioral Development, 21,* 209–227.

Gardner, H. (1983). *Frames of mind: The theory of multiple intelligence.* New York: Basic Books.

Garfield, P., Kent, A., Paykel, E., Creighton, F., & Jacobson, R. (2004). Outcome of postpartum disorders: A 10 year follow-up of hospital admissions. *Acta Psychiatrica Scandinavica, 109,* 434–439.

Garland, A. F., & Zigler, E. (1993). Adolescent suicide prevention: Current research and social policy implications. *American Psychologist, 48,* 169–182.

Garmezy, N. (1993). Vulnerability and resilience. In D. C. Funder, R. D. Parke, C. Tomlinson-Keasey, & K. Widaman (Eds.), *Studying lives through time: Personality and development* (pp. 377–398). Washington, DC: American Psychological Association.

Garmezy, N., & Rutter, M. (Eds.). (1983). *Stress, coping, and development in children.* New York: McGraw-Hill.

Garnier, H., Stein, J., & Jacobs, J. (1997). The process of dropping out of high school: A 19-year perspective. *American Educational Research Journal, 34,* 395–419.

Garrison, R. J., Gold, R. S., Wilson, P. W. F., & Kannel, W. B. (1993). Educational attainment and coronary heart disease risk: The Framingham offspring study. *Preventive Medicine, 22,* 54–64.

Gartstein, M., & Rothbart, M. (2003). Studying infant temperament via the revised infant behavior questionnaire. *Infant Behavior & Development, 26,* 64–86.

Gary, J., Kling, B., & Dodd, B. (2004). A program for counseling and campus support services for African American and Latino adult learners. *Journal of College Counseling, 7,* 18–23.

Gathercole, S., Pickering, S., Ambridge, B., & Wearing, H. (2004). The structure of working memory from 4 to 15 years of age. *Developmental Psychology, 40,* 177–190.

Gatz, M., Kasl-Godley, J. E., & Karel, M. J. (1996). Aging and mental disorders. In J. E. Birren & K. W. Schaie (Eds.), *Handbook of the psychology of aging* (4th ed., pp. 365–381). San Diego, CA: Academic Press.

Gauntlett-Gilbert, J., Keegan, A., & Petrak, J. (2004). Drug-facilitated sexual assault: Cognitive approaches to treating the trauma. *Behavioral & Cognitive Psychotherapy, 32,* 211.

Gaziano, J. M., & Hennekens, C. H. (1995). Dietary fat and risk of prostate cancer. *Journal of the National Cancer Institute, 87,* 1427–1428.

Ge, X., & Conger, R. (1999). Adjustment problems and emerging personality characteristics from early to late adolescence. *American Journal of Community Psychology, 27,* 429–459.

Geary, D., Lin, F., Chen, G., Saults, S., et al. (1999). Contributions of computational fluency to cross-national differences in arithmetical reasoning abilities. *Journal of Educational Psychology, 91,* 716–719.

Geary, D. C., Bow-Thomas, C. C., Fan, L., & Siegler, R. S. (1993). Even before formal instruction, Chinese children outperform American children in mental addition. *Cognitive Development, 8,* 517–529.

Gee, C., & Rhodes, J. (1999). Postpartum transitions in adolescent mothers' romantic and maternal relationships. *Merrill-Palmer Quarterly, 45,* 512–532.

Gee, C., & Rhodes, J. (2003). Adolescent mothers' relationship with their children's biological fathers: Social support, social strain and relationship continuity. *Journal of Family Psychology, 17,* 370–383.

Gelman, R. (1972). Logical capacity of very young children: Number invariance rules. *Child Development, 43,* 75–90.

Gentile, D., Lynch, P., Linder, J., & Walsh, D. (2004). The effects of violent video game habits on adolescent hostility, aggressive behaviors, and school performance. *Journal of Adolescence, 27,* 5–22.

George, L. K. (1990). Social structure, social processes, and social-psychological states. In R. H. Binstock & L. K. George (Eds.), *Handbook of aging and the social sciences* (3rd ed., pp. 186–204). San Diego, CA: Academic Press.

George, L. K. (1993). Sociological perspectives on life transitions. *Annual Review of Sociology, 19,* 353–373.

Georgieff, M. K. (1994). Nutritional deficiencies as developmental risk factors: Commentary on Pollitt and Gorman. In C. A. Nelson (Ed.), *The Minnesota Symposia on Child Development, Vol. 27* (pp. 145–159). Hillsdale, NJ: Erlbaum.

Gerbner tackles "fairness." (1997, February 24). *Electronic media.* Retrieved January 15, 2001, from www.mediascope.org/pubs/ibriefs/dft.html.

Gerhardstein, P., Liu, J., & Rovee-Collier, C. (1998). Perceptual constraints on infant memory retrieval. *Journal of Experimental Child Psychology, 69,* 109–131.

Gershoff, E. (2002). Corporal punishment by parents and associated child behaviors and experiences: A meta-analytic and theoretical review. *Psychological Bulletin, 128,* 539–579.

Gerwood, J., LeBlanc, M., & Piazza, N. (1998). The Purpose-in-Life Test and religious denomination: Protestant and Catholic scores in an elderly population. *Journal of Clinical Psychology, 54,* 49–53.

Gesell, A. (1925). *The mental growth of the preschool child.* New York: Macmillan.

Gesser, G., Wong, P. T. P., & Reker, G. T. (1987/1988). Death attitudes across the life-span: The development and validation of the death attitude profile (DAP). *Omega, 18,* 113–128.

Giambra, L. M., Arenberg, D., Zonderman, A. B., Kawas, C., & Costa, P. T., Jr. (1995). Adult life span changes in immediate visual memory and verbal intelligence. *Psychology & Aging, 10,* 123–139.

Gibbs, R., & Beitel, D. (1995). What proverb understanding reveals about how people think. *Psychological Bulletin, 118,* 133–154.

Gibson, D. R. (1990). Relation of socioeconomic status to logical and sociomoral judgment of middle-aged men. *Psychology & Aging, 5,* 510–513.

Gibson, E. J., & Walk, R. D. (1960). The "visual cliff." *Scientific American, 202,* 80–92.

Gilbertson, M., & Bramlett, R. (1998). Phonological awareness screening to identify at-risk readers: Implications for practitioners. *Language, Speech, & Hearing Services in Schools, 29,* 109–116.

Gill, T., Baker, D., Gottschalk, M., Peduzzi, P., Allore, H., & Byers, A. (2002). A program to prevent functional decline in physically frail, elderly persons who live at home. *Medical Care Research & Review, 60,* 223–247.

Gilligan, C. (1982). *In a different voice: Psychological theory and women's development.* Cambridge, MA: Harvard University Press.

Gilligan, C., & Wiggins, G. (1987). The origins of morality in early childhood relationships. In J. Kagan & S. Lamb (Eds.), *The emergence of morality in young children* (pp. 277–307). Chicago: University of Chicago Press.

Gilman, E. A., Cheng, K. K., Winter, H. R., & Scragg, R. (1995). Trends in rates and seasonal distribution of sudden infant deaths in England and Wales, 1988–1992. *British Medical Journal, 30,* 631–632.

Gladue, B. A. (1994). The biopsychology of sexual orientation. *Current Directions in Psychological Science, 3,* 150–154.

Glaser, D. (2000). Child abuse and neglect and the brain-a review. *Journal of Child Psychology & Psychiatry & Allied Disciplines, 41,* 97–116.

Glaser, R., Kiecolt-Glaser, J. K., Bonneau, R. H., Malarkey, W., Kennedy, S., & Hughes, J. (1992). Stress-induced modulation of the immune response to recombinant hepatitis B vaccine. *Psychosomatic Medicine, 54,* 22–29.

Glass, J., & Jolly, G. (1997). Satisfaction in later life among women 60 or over. *Educational Gerontology, 23,* 297–314.

Glass, J., & Kilpatrick, B. (1998). Gender comparisons of baby boomers and financial preparation for retirement. *Educational Gerontology, 24,* 719–745.

Glass, S. (1998). Shared vows. *Psychology Today, 31*, 34.

Glazer, H. (1998). Expressions of children's grief: A qualitative study. *International Journal of Play Therapy, 7*, 51–65.

Gleason, K., Jensen-Campbell, L., & Richardson, D. (2004). Agreeableness as a predictor of aggression in adolescence. *Aggressive Behavior, 30*, 43–61.

Gledhill, L., (1997, March 18). Deadbeat dads. *Missouri Digital News.* Retrieved December 6, 1999, from www.mdn.com.

Gleitman, L. R., & Gleitman, H. (1992). A picture is worth a thousand words, but that's the problem: The role of syntax in vocabulary acquisition. *Current Directions in Psychological Science, 1*, 31–35.

Glenn, N. D. (1990). Quantitative research on marital quality in the 1980s: A critical review. *Journal of Marriage & the Family, 52*, 818–831.

Glenn, N. D., & Weaver, C. N. (1985). Age, cohort, and reported job satisfaction in the United States. In A. S. Blau (Ed.), *Current perspectives on aging and the life cycle. A research annual, Vol. 1: Work, retirement and social policy* (pp. 89–110). Greenwich, CT: JAI Press.

Gloger-Tippelt, G., & Huerkamp, M. (1998). Relationship change at the transition to parenthood and security of infant-mother attachment. *International Journal of Behavioral Development, 23*, 633–655.

Gnepp, J., & Chilamkurti, C. (1988). Children's use of personality attributions to predict other people's emotional and behavioral reactions. *Child Development, 50*, 743–754.

Gohm, C., Humphreys, L., & Yao, G. (1998). Underachievement among spatially gifted students. *American Educational Research Journal, 35*, 515–531.

Gold, D. (1996). Continuities and discontinuities in sibling relationships across the life span. In V. I. Bengtson (Ed.), *Adulthood and aging: Research on continuities and discontinuities.* New York: Springer.

Gold, D. P., Andres, D., Etezadi, J., Arbuckle, T., Schwartzman, A., & Chaikelson, J. (1995). Structural equation model of intellectual change and continuity and predictors of intelligence in older men. *Psychology & Aging, 10*, 294–303.

Goldberg, A. P., Dengel, D. R., & Hagberg, J. M. (1996). Exercise physiology and aging. In E. L. Schneider & J. W. Rowe (Eds.), *Handbook of the biology of aging* (4th ed., pp. 331–354). San Diego, CA: Academic Press.

Goldberg, A. P., & Hagberg, J. M. (1990). Physical exercise in the elderly. In E. R. Schneider & J. W. Rowe (Eds.), *Handbook of the biology of aging* (3rd ed., pp. 407–428). San Diego, CA: Academic Press.

Goldberg, W. A. (1990). Marital quality, parental personality, and spousal agreement about perceptions and expectations for children. *Merrill-Palmer Quarterly, 36*, 531–556.

Goldfield, B. A. (1993). Noun bias in maternal speech to one-year-olds. *Journal of Child Language, 20*, 85–99.

Goldfield, B. A., & Reznick, J. S. (1990). Early lexical acquisition: Rate, content, and the vocabulary spurt. *Journal of Child Language, 17*, 171–183.

Golding, J., Emmett, P., & Rogers, I. (1997a). Does breast feeding protect against non-gastric infections? *Early Human Development, 49* (Supp.), S105–S120.

Goldin-Meadow, S. (2002). Constructing communication by hand. *Cognitive Development, 17*, 1385–1405.

Golding, J., Emmett, P., & Rogers, I. (1997b). Gastroenteritis, diarrhea and breast feeding. *Early Human Development, 49* (Supp.), S83–S103.

Goldsmith, H., & Alansky, J. (1987). Maternal and infant temperamental predictors of attachment: A meta-analytic review. *Journal of Consulting & Clinical Psychology, 55*, 805–806.

Goldsmith, H. H., Buss, K. A., & Lemery, K. S. (1995, March). *Toddler and childhood temperament: Expanded content, stronger genetic evidence, new evidence for the importance of environment.* Paper presented at the biennial meetings of the Society for Research in Child Development, Indianapolis, IN.

Goleman, D. (1995). *Emotional intelligence.* New York: Bantam.

Golinkoff, R. M., Mervis, C. B., & Hirsh-Pasek, K. (1994). Early object labels: The case for lexical principles. *Journal of Child Language, 21*, 125–155.

Gollan, T., & Silverberg, N. (2001). Tip-of-the-tongue states in Hebrew-English bilinguals. *Bilingualism: Language & Cognition, 4*, 63–83.

Golombok, S., & Fivush, R. (1994). *Gender development.* Cambridge, England: Cambridge University Press.

Golombok, S., & Tasker, F. (1996). Do parents influence the sexual orientation of their children? Findings from a longitudinal study of lesbian families. *Developmental Psychology, 32*, 3–11.

Gomez, R., Bounds, J., Holmberg, K., Fullarton, C., & Gomez, A. (1999). Effects of neuroticism and avoidant coping style on maladjustment during early adolescence. *Personality & Individual Differences, 26*, 305–319.

Gomez, R., Holmberg, K., Bounds, J., Fullarton, C., & Gomez, A. (1999). Neuroticism and extraversion as predictors of coping styles during early adolescence. *Personality & Individual Differences, 27*, 3–17.

Gonzales, N., Dumka, L., Deardorff, J., Carter, S., & McCray, A. (2004). Preventing poor mental health and school dropout of Mexican American adolescents following the transition to junior high school. *Journal of Adolescent Research, 19*, 113–131.

Gonzalez, J., & Valle, I. (2000). Word identification and reading disorders in the Spanish language. *Journal of Learning Disabilities, 33*, 44–60.

Good, T. L., & Weinstein, R. S. (1986). Schools make a difference: Evidence, criticisms, and new directions. *American Psychologist, 41*, 1090–1097.

Goodenough, F. L. (1931). *Anger in young children.* Minneapolis: University of Minnesota Press.

Goodman, C., & Silverstein, M. (2002). Grandmothers raising grandchildren: Family structure and well-being in culturally diverse families. *Gerontologist, 42*, 676–689.

Goodsitt, J. V., Morse, P. A., Ver Hoeve, J. N., & Cowan, N. (1984). Infant speech recognition in multisyllabic contexts. *Child Development, 55*, 903–910.

Goossens, L., Beyers, W., Emmen, M., & van Aken, M. (2002). The imaginary audience and personal fable: Factor analyses and concurrent validity of the "New Look" measures. *Journal of Research on Adolescence, 12*, 193–215.

Goossens, R., & van IJzendoorn, M. (1990). Quality of infants' attachments to professional caregivers: Relation to infant-parent attachment and day-care characteristics. *Child Development, 61*, 832–837.

Gopnik, A., & Astington, J. W. (1988). Children's understanding of representational change and its relation to the understanding of false belief and the appearance-reality distinction. *Child Development, 59*, 26–37.

Gopnik, A., & Wellman, H. M. (1994). The theory theory. In L. A. Hirschfeld & S. A. Gelman (Eds.), *Mapping the mind* (pp. 257–293). Cambridge, England: Cambridge University Press.

Gordon, G. S., & Vaughan, C. (1986). Calcium and osteoporosis. *Journal of Nutrition, 116*, 319–322.

Gossett, B., Cuyjet, M., & Cockriel, I. (1998). African Americans' perception of marginality in the campus culture. *College Student Journal, 32*, 22–32.

Gothelf, D., Apter, A., Brand-Gothelf, A., Offer, N., Ofek, H., Tyano, S., & Pfeffer, C. (1998). Death concepts in suicidal adolescents. *Journal of the American Academy of Child & Adolescent Psychiatry, 37*, 1279–1286.

Gottlob, L., & Madden, D. (1999). Age differences in the strategic allocation of visual attention. *Journals of Gerontology: Series B: Psychological Sciences & Social Sciences, 54B*, P165–P172.

Gottman, J. M. (1986). The world of coordinated play: Same- and cross-sex friendship in young children. In J. M. Gottman & J. G. Parker (Eds.), *Conversations of friends: Speculations on affective development* (pp. 139–191). Cambridge, England: Cambridge University Press.

Gottman, J. M. (1994). *Why marriages succeed or fail.* New York: Simon & Schuster.

Gould, E., Reeves, A., Graziano, M., & Gross, C. (1999). Neurogenesis in the neocortex of adult primates. *Science, 286*, 548–552.

Graber, J. A., Brooks-Gunn, J., Paikoff, R. L., & Warren, M. P. (1994). Prediction of eating problems: An 8-year study of adolescent girls. *Developmental Psychology, 30*, 823–834.

Grabowski, L., Call, K., & Mortimer, J. (2001). Global and economic self-efficacy in the educational attainment process. *Social Psychology Quarterly, 64*, 164–197.

Grady, D., Herrington, D., Bittner, V., Blumenthal, R., Davidson, M., Hlatky, M., Hsia, J., Hulley, S., Herd, A., Khan, S., Newby, K., Waters, D., Vittinghoff, E., & Wenger, N. (2002). Cardiovascular disease outcomes during 6.8 years of hormone therapy: Heart and estrogen/progestin replacement study follow-up (HERS II). *Journal of the American Medical Association, 288*, 49–57.

Graham, J., Cohen, R., Zbikowski, S., & Secrist, M. (1998). A longitudinal investigation of race and sex as factors in children's classroom friendship choices. *Child Study Journal, 28*, 245–266.

Graham, S., & Harris, K. (1997). It can be taught, but it does not develop naturally: Myths and realities in writing instruction. *School Psychology Review, 26*, 414–424.

Gralinski, J. H., & Kopp, C. B. (1993). Everyday rules for behavior: Mothers' requests to young children. *Developmental Psychology, 29*, 573–584.

Graves, S. (1993). Television, the portrayal of African Americans, and the development of children's attitudes. In G. L. Berry & J. K. Asamen (Eds.), *Children and television: Images in a changing sociocultural world.* Newbury Park, CA: Sage.

Gray, A., Berlin, J. A., McKinlay, J. B., & Longcope, C. (1991). An examination of research design effects on the association of testosterone and male aging: Results of a meta-analysis. *Journal of Clinical Epidemiology, 44,* 671–684.

Graziano, A. M., Hamblen, J. L., & Plante, W. A. (1996). Sububusive violence in child rearing in middle-class American families. *Pediatrics, 98,* 845–848.

Green, R. (2004). Risk and resilience in lesbian and gay couples: Comment on Solomon, Rothblum, & Balsam. *Journal of Family Psychology, 18,* 290–292.

Green, S. (2001). Systemic vs. individualistic approaches to bullying. *Journal of the American Medical Association, 286,* 787.

Green, S., Pring, L., & Swettenham, J. (2004). An investigation of first-order false belief understanding of children with congenital profound visual impairment. *British Journal of Developmental Psychology, 22,* 1–17.

Greenberg, J., Lewis, S., & Dodd, D. (1999). Overlapping addictions and self-esteem among college men and women. *Addictive Behaviors, 24,* 565–571.

Greenberg, M. T., Siegel, J. M., & Leitch, C. J. (1983). The nature and importance of attachment relationships to parents and peers during adolescence. *Journal of Youth & Adolescence, 12,* 373–386.

Greenberg, M. T., Speltz, M. L., & DeKlyen, M. (1993). The role of attachment in the early development of disruptive behavior problems. *Development & Psychopathology, 5,* 191–213.

Greenberger, E., & Steinberg, L. (1986). *When teenagers work: The psychological and social costs of adolescent employment.* New York: Basic Books.

Greene, K., Krcmar, M., Rubin, D., Walters, L., & Hale, J. (2002). Elaboration in processing adolescent health messages: The impact of egocentrism and sensation seeking on message processing. *Journal of Communication, 52,* 812–831.

Greenfield, P. (1994). Video games as cultural artifacts. *Journal of Applied Developmental Psychology, 15,* 3–12.

Greenfield, P., Brannon, C., & Lohr, D. (1994). Two-dimensional representation of movement through three-dimensional space: The role of video game expertise. *Journal of Applied Developmental Psychology, 15,* 87–104.

Greenhaus, J., Collins, K., Singh, R., & Parasuraman, S. (1997). Work and family influences on departure from public accounting. *Journal of Vocational Behavior, 50,* 249–270.

Greenspan, S., Resnick, N., & Parker, R. (2003). Combination therapy with hormone replacement and alendronate for prevention of bone loss in elderly women: A randomized controlled trial. *Journal of the American Medical Association, 289,* 2525–2533.

Greer, D. S., Mor, V., Morris, J. N., Sherwood, S., Kidder, D., & Birnbaum, H. (1986). An alternative in terminal care: Results of the National Hospice Study. *Journal of Chronic Diseases, 39,* 9–26.

Greer, S. (1991). Psychological response to cancer and survival. *Psychological Medicine, 21,* 43–49.

Greer, S., Morris, T., & Pettingale, K. W. (1979). Psychological response to breast cancer: Effect on outcome. *Lancet,* 785–787.

Gregg, V., Gibbs, J. C., & Basinger, K. S. (1994). Patterns of developmental delay in moral judgment by male and female delinquents. *Merrill-Palmer Quarterly, 40,* 538–553.

Greider, L. (2000, March/April). How not to be a monster-in-law. *Modern Maturity, 43* (2), 56–59, 81.

Griffith, J. (1998). The relation of school structure and social environment to parent involvement in elementary schools. *Elementary School Journal, 99,* 53–80.

Griffiths, M. (1999). Internet addiction: Fact or fiction? *Psychologist, 12,* 246–250.

Griffiths, M. (2003). Internet gambling: Issues, concerns, and recommendations. *CyberPsychology, 6,* 557–568.

Grohol, J. (1999). *Internet Addiction Guide.* Retrieved February 3, 2000, from http://www.psychcentral.com/netaddiction.

Grolnick, W. S., & Slowiaczek, M. L. (1994). Parents' involvement in children's schooling: A multidimensional conceptualization and motivational model. *Child Development, 65,* 237–252.

Groome, L., Mooney, D., Holland, S., Smith, L., Atterbury, J., & Dykman, R. (1999). Behavioral state affects heart rate response to low-intensity sound in human fetuses. *Early Human Development, 54,* 39–54.

Gross, J., Carstensen, L., Pasupathi, M., Tsai, J., Gostestam-Skorpen, C., & Hsu, A. (1997). Emotion and aging: Experience, expression, and control. *Psychology & Aging, 12,* 590–599.

Grossman, A., Daugelli, A., & Hershberger, S. (2000). Social support networks of lesbian, gay, and bisexual adults 60 years of age and older. *Journals of Gerontology, Series B: Psychological Sciences & Social Sciences, 55B,* P171–P179.

Grossmann, K., Grossmann, K. E., Spangler, G., Suess, G., & Unzner, L. (1985). Maternal sensitivity and newborns' orientation responses as related to quality of attachment in northern Germany. *Monographs of the Society of Research in Child Development, 50* (1–2, Serial No. 209), 233–256.

Grusec, J. (1992). Social learning theory and developmental psychology: The legacies of Robert Sears and Albert Bandura. *Developmental Psychology, 28,* 776–786.

Guerin, D. W., & Gottfried, A. W. (1994a). Developmental stability and change in parent reports of temperament: A ten-year longitudinal investigation from infancy through preadolescence. *Merrill-Palmer Quarterly, 40,* 334–355.

Guerin, D. W., & Gottfried, A. W. (1994b). Temperamental consequences of infant difficultness. *Infant Behavior & Development, 17,* 413–421.

Guesry, P. (1998). The role of nutrition in brain development. *Preventive Medicine, 27,* 189–194.

Gullotta, T., Adams, G., & Montemayor, R. (1993). *Adolescent sexuality.* Newbury Park, CA: Sage.

Gunnar, M., Sebanc, A., Tout, K., Donzella, B., & Van Dulmen, M. (2003). Peer rejection, temperament, and cortisol activity in preschoolers. *Developmental Psychobiology, 43,* 346–358.

Gunnar, M. R. (1994). Psychoendocrine studies of temperament and stress in early childhood: Expanding current models. In J. E. Bates & T. D. Wachs (Eds.), *Temperament: Individual differences at the interface of biology and behavior* (pp. 175–198). Washington, DC: American Psychological Association.

Gunter, T., Jackson, J., & Mulder, G. (1998). Priming and aging: An electrophysiological investigation of N400 and recall. *Brain & Language, 65,* 333–355.

Gunther, M. (1955). Instinct and the learning couple. *Lancet, 1,* 575.

Gunther, M. (1961). Infant behavior at the breast. In B. Foss (Ed.), *Determinants of infant behavior* (pp. 37–44). London: Methuen.

Guo, S. F. (1993). Postpartum depression. *Chung-Hua Fu Chan Ko Tsa Chi, 28,* 532–533, 569.

Gur, R., Gunning-Dixon, F., Bilker, W., & Gur, R. (2002). Sex differences in temporo-limbic and frontal brain volumes of healthy adults. *Cerebral Cortex, 12,* 998–1003.

Gur, R. C., Turetsky, B., Matsui, M., Yan, M., Bilker, W., Hughett, P., & Gur, R. E. (1999). Sex differences in brain gray and white matter in healthy young adults: Correlations with cognitive performance. *Journal of Neuroscience, 19,* 4065–4072.

Guralnik, J. M., & Kaplan, G. A. (1989). Predictors of healthy aging: Prospective evidence from the Alameda County Study. *American Journal of Public Health, 79,* 703–708.

Guralnik, J. M., Land, K. C., Blazer, D., Fillenbaum, G. G., & Branch, L. G. (1993). Educational status and active life expectancy among older blacks and whites. *New England Journal of Medicine, 329,* 110–116.

Guralnik, J. M., & Paul-Brown, D. (1984). Communicative adjustments during behavior-request episodes among children at different developmental levels. *Child Development, 55,* 911–919.

Guralnik, J. M., Simonsick, E. M., Ferrucci, L., Glynn, R. J., Berkman, L. F., Blazer, D. G., Scherr, P. A., & Wallace, R. B. (1994). A short physical performance battery assessing lower extremity function: Association with self-reported disability and prediction of mortality and nursing home admission. *Journals of Gerontology: Medical Sciences, 49,* M85–94.

Gurland, B., Wilder, D., Lantiga, R., Stern, Y., Chen, J., Killeffer, E., & Mayeux, R. (1999). Rates of dementia in three ethnoracial groups. *International Journal of Geriatric Psychiatry, 14,* 481–493.

Gurnáková, J., & Kusá, D. (2004). Gender self-concept in personal theories of reality. *Studia Psychologica, 46,* 49–61.

Guse, L., & Masesar, M. (1999). Quality of life and successful aging in long-term care: Perceptions of residents. *Issues in Mental Health Nursing, 20,* 527–539.

Gustafson, S. B., & Magnusson, D. (1991). *Female life careers: A pattern approach.* Hillsdale, NJ: Erlbaum.

Guzzetti, B., & Williams, W. (1996). Gender, text, and discussion: Examining intellectual safety in the science classroom. *Journal of Research in Science Teaching, 33,* 5–20.

Gzesh, S. M., & Surber, C. F. (1985). Visual perspective-taking skills in children. *Child Development, 56,* 1204–1213.

Haan, N. (1981). Common dimensions of personality development: Early adolescence to middle life. In D. H. Eichorn, J. A. Clausen, N. Haan, M. P. Honzik, & P.H. Mussen (Eds.), *Present and past in middle life.* New York: Academic Press.

Haan, N., Millsap, R., & Hartka, E. (1986). As time goes by: Change and stability in personality over fifty years. *Psychology & Aging, 1,* 220–232.

Hack, M., Taylor, C. B. H., Klein, N., Eiben, R., Schatschneider, C., & Mercuri-Minich, N. (1994). School-age outcomes in children with birth weights under 750 g. *New England Journal of Medicine, 331,* 753–759.

Hagan, J. (1997). Defiance and despair: Subcultural and structural linkages between delinquency and despair in the life course. *Social Forces, 76,* 119–134.

Hagekull, B., & Bohlin, G. (2003). Early temperament and attachment as predictors of the Five Factor Model of personality. *Attachment & Human Development, 5,* 2–18.

Hagestad, G. O. (1984). The continuous bond: A dynamic, multigenerational perspective on parent-child relations between adults. In M. Perlmutter (Ed.), *Minnesota Symposia on Child Psychology* (pp. 129–158). Hillsdale, NJ: Erlbaum.

Hagestad, G. O. (1985). Continuity and connectedness. In V. L. Bengtson (Ed.), *Grandparenthood* (pp. 31–38). Beverly Hills, CA: Sage.

Hagestad, G. O. (1986). Dimensions of time and the family. *American Behavioral Scientist, 29,* 679–694.

Hagestad, G. O. (1990). Social perspectives on the life course. In R. H. Binstock & L. K. George (Eds.), *Handbook of aging and the social sciences* (3rd ed., pp. 151–168). San Diego, CA: Academic Press.

Haier, R. J., Chueh, D., Touchette, P., Lott, I., Buchsbaum, M. S., MacMillan, D., Sandman, C., LaCasse, L., & Sosa, E. (1995). Brain size and cerebral glucose metabolic rate in nonspecific mental retardation and Down syndrome. *Intelligence, 20,* 191–210.

Haight, W., Wang, X., Fung, H., Williams, K., et al. (1999). Universal, developmental, and variable aspects of young children's play. *Child Development, 70,* 1477–1488.

Hakansson, G., Salameh, E., & Nettelbladt, U. (2003). Measuring language development in bilingual children: Swedish-Arabic children with and without language impairment. *Linguistics, 41,* 255–288.

Haley, W. E., West, C. A. C., Wadley, V. G., Ford, G. R., White, F. A., Barrett, J. J., Harrell, L. E., & Roth, D. L. (1995). Psychological, social, and health impact of caregiving: A comparison of black and white dementia family caregivers and noncaregivers. *Psychology & Aging, 10,* 540–552.

Halford, G. S., Maybery, M. T., O'Hare, A. W., & Grant, P. (1994). The development of memory and processing capacity. *Child Development, 65,* 1338–1356.

Hall, D. R., & Zhao, J. Z. (1995). Cohabitation and divorce in Canada: Testing the selectivity hypothesis. *Journal of Marriage & the Family, 57,* 421–427.

Hall, D. T. (1972). A model of coping with role conflict: The role behavior of college educated women. *Administrative Science Quarterly, 17,* 471–486.

Hall, D. T. (1975). Pressures from work, self, and home in the life stages of married women. *Journal of Vocational Behavior, 6,* 121–132.

Hall, G. (2003, September). Primary elective C-section up 20% from 1999 to 2001. *OB/GYN News.* Retrieved April 1, 2004, from http://www.imng.com.

Halle, T. (1999). Implicit theories of social interactions: Children's reasoning about the relative importance of gender and friendship in social partner choices. *Merrill-Palmer Quarterly, 45,* 445–467.

Hallfrisch, J., Muller, D., Drinkwater, D., Tobin, J., & Adres, R. (1990). Continuing diet trends in men: The Baltimore Longitudinal Study of Aging. *Journals of Gerontology: Medical Sciences, 45,* M186–191.

Hallmark Corporation. (2004). *Wedding facts.* Retrieved August 24, 2004, from http://pressroom.hallmark.com/wedding_facts.html.

Hallstrom, T., & Samuelsson, S. (1985). Mental health in the climacteric: The longitudinal study of women in Gothenberg. *Acta Obstetrics Gynecology Scandanavia, 130* (Suppl), 13–18.

Halpern, C. T., Udry, J. R., Campbell, B., & Suchindran, C. (1993). Testosterone and pubertal development as predictors of sexual activity: A panel analysis of adolescent males. *Psychosomatic Medicine, 55,* 436–447.

Halpern, D. (1997). Sex differences in intelligence: Implications for education. *American Psychologist, 52,* 1091–1102.

Halpern, D. F. (1986). *Sex differences in cognitive abilities.* Hillsdale, NJ: Erlbaum.

Hamberger, K., & Minsky, D. (2000, August). *Evaluation of domestic violence training programs for health care professionals.* Paper presented at the annual meeting of the American Psychological Association. Washington, DC.

Hamilton, C. E. (1995, March). *Continuity and discontinuity of attachment from infancy through adolescence.* Paper presented at the biennial meetings of the Society for Research in Child Development, Indianapolis, IN.

Hammond, M., Landry, S., Swank, P., & Smith, K. (2000). Relation of mothers' affective development history and parenting behavior: Effects on infant medical risk. *American Journal of Orthopsychiatry, 70,* 95–103.

Handley-Derry, M., Low, J., Burke, S., Waurick, M., Killen, H., & Derrick, E. (1997). Intrapartum fetal asphyxia and the occurrence of minor deficits in 4- to 8-year-old children. *Developmental Medicine & Child Neurology, 39,* 508–514.

Hanna, E., & Meltzoff, A. N. (1993). Peer imitation by toddlers in laboratory, home, and day-care contexts: Implications for social learning and memory. *Developmental Psychology, 29,* 701–710.

Hanninen, T., Koivisto, K., Reinikainen, K., Helkala, E., Soininen, H., Mykkanen, L., Laakso, M., & Riekkinen, P. (1996). Prevalence of ageing-associated cognitive decline in an elderly population. *Age & Ageing, 25,* 201–205.

Hansen, M., Kurinczuk, J., Bower, C., & Webb, S. (2002). The risk of major birth defects after intracytoplasmic sperm injection and in vitro fertilization. *New England Journal of Medicine, 346,* 725–730.

Hardy, M. A., & Hazelrigg, L. E. (1993). The gender of poverty in an aging population. *Research on Aging, 15,* 243–278.

Hardy, M. A., & Quadagno, J. (1995). Satisfaction with early retirement: Making choices in the auto industry. *Journals of Gerontology: Social Sciences, 50B,* S217–228.

Haring, M., Hewitt, P., & Flett, G. (2003). Perfectionism, coping, and quality of intimate relationships. *Journal of Marriage & the Family, 65,* 143–158.

Harkness, S. (1998). Time for families. *Anthropology Newsletter, 39,* 1, 4.

Harkness, S., & Super, C. M. (1985). The cultural context of gender segregation in children's peer groups. *Child Development, 56,* 219–224.

Harland, P., Reijneveld, S., Brugman, E., Verloove-Vanhorick, S., & Verhulst, F. (2002). Family factors and life events as risk factors for behavioral and emotional problems in children. *European Child & Adolescent Psychiatry, 11,* 176–184.

Harlow, H., & Zimmerman, R. (1959). Affectional responses in the infant monkey. *Science, 130,* 421–432.

Harris, B., Lovett, L., Newcombe, R. G., Read, G. F., Walker, R., & Riad-Fahmy, D. (1994). Maternity blues and major endocrine changes: Cardiff puerperal mood and hormone study II. *British Medical Journal, 308,* 949–953.

Harris, P. L. (1989). *Children and emotion: The development of psychological understanding.* Oxford: Blackwell.

Harris, R. L., Ellicott, A. M., & Holmes, D. S. (1986). The timing of psychosocial transitions and changes in women's lives: An examination of women aged 45 to 60. *Journal of Personality & Social Psychology, 51,* 409–416.

Harrison, A., Wilson, M., Pine, C., Chan, S., & Buriel, R. (1990). Family ecologies of ethnic minority children. *Child Development, 61,* 347–362.

Harrist, A., Zaia, A., Bates, J., Dodge, K., & Pettit, G. (1997). Subtypes of social withdrawal in early childhood: Sociometric status and social-cognitive differences across four years. *Child Development, 68,* 278–294.

Hart, B., & Risley, T. R. (1995). *Meaningful differences in the everyday experience of young American children.* Baltimore: Paul H. Brookes.

Hart, C., Olsen, S., Robinson, C., & Mandleco, B. (1997). The development of social and communicative competence in childhood: Review and a model of personal, familial, and extrafamilial processes. *Communication Yearbook, 20,* 305–373.

Hart, D., Mele-McCarthy, J., Pasternack, R., Zimbrich, K., & Parker, D. (2004). Community college: A pathway to success for youth with learning, cognitive, and intellectual disabilities in secondary settings. *Education & Training in Developmental Disabilities, 39,* 54–66.

Hart, S., Jones, N., Field, T., & Lundy, B. (1999). One-year-old infants of intrusive and withdrawn depressed mothers. *Child Psychiatry & Human Development, 30,* 111–120.

Harter, S. (1987). The determinations and mediational role of global self-worth in children. In N. Eisenberg (Ed.), *Contemporary topics in developmental psychology* (pp. 219–242). New York: Wiley-Interscience.

Harter, S. (1990). Processes underlying adolescent self-concept formation. In R. Montemayor, G. R. Adams, & T. P. Gullotta (Eds.), *From childhood to adolescence: A transitional period?* (pp. 205–239). Newbury Park, CA: Sage.

Harter, S., & Monsour, A. (1992). Developmental analysis of conflict caused by opposing attributes in the adolescent self-portrait. *Developmental Psychology, 28,* 251–260.

Harton, H., & Latane, B. (1997). Social influence and adolescent lifestyle attitudes. *Journal of Research on Adolescence, 7,* 197–220.

Hartup, W. W. (1974). Aggression in childhood: Developmental perspectives. *American Psychologist, 29,* 336–341.

Hartup, W. W. (1996). The company they keep: Friendships and their developmental significance. *Child Development, 67,* 1–13.

Harvey, R., Fletcher, J., & French, D. (2001). Social reasoning: A source of influence on aggression. *Clinical Psychology Review, 21,* 447–469.

Harwood, D., Barker, W., Ownby, R., Bravo, M., Aguero, H., & Duara, R. (2000). Depressive symptoms in Alzheimer's disease: An examination among community-dwelling Cuban American patients. *American Journal of Geriatric Psychiatry, 8,* 84–91.

Hashima, P. Y., & Amato, P. R. (1994). Poverty, social support, and parental behavior. *Child Development, 65,* 394–403.

Hatano, G. (1990). Toward the cultural psychology of mathematical cognition: Commentary. In H. Stevenson & S. Lee (Eds.), *Contexts of achievement. Monographs of the Society for Research in Child Development, 55* (12, Serial No. 221), 108–115.

Hatchett, S. J., Cochran, D. L., & Jackson, J. S. (1991). Family life. In J. S. Jackson (Ed.), *Life in black America.* Newbury Park, CA: Sage.

Hatchett, S. J., & Jackson, J. S. (1993). African American extended kin systems: An assessment. In H. P. McAdoo (Ed.), *Family ethnicity: Strength in diversity* (pp. 90–108). Newbury Park, CA: Sage.

Hausman, P. B., & Weksler, M. E. (1985). Changes in the immune response with age. In C. E. Finch & E. L. Schneider (Eds.), *Handbook of the biology of aging* (2nd ed., pp. 414–432). New York: Van Nostrand Reinhold.

Hawkins, H. L., Kramer, A. F., & Capaldi, D. (1992). Aging, exercise, and attention. *Psychology & Aging, 7,* 643–653.

Hay, D., Payne, A., & Chadwick, A. (2004). Peer relations in childhood. *Journal of Child Psychology & Psychiatry & Allied Disciplines, 45,* 84–108.

Hayes, M., Parker, K., Sallinen, B., & Davare, A. (2001). Bedsharing, temperament, and sleep disturbance in early childhood. *Sleep: Journal of Sleep & Sleep Disorders Research, 24,* 657–662.

Hayflick, L. (1977). The cellular basis for biological aging. In C. E. Finch & L. Hayflick (Eds.), *Handbook of the biology of aging* (pp. 159–186). New York: Van Nostrand Reinhold.

Hayflick, L. (1987). Origins of longevity. In H. R. Warner, R. N. Butler, R. L. Sprott, & E. L. Schneider (Eds.), *Aging, Vol. 31. Modern biological theories of aging* (pp. 21–34). New York: Raven Press.

Hayflick, L. (1994). *How and why we age.* New York: Ballantine Books.

Hayne, H., Herbert, J., & Simcock, G. (2003). Imitation from television by 24- and 30-month-olds. *Developmental Science, 6,* 254–261.

Hayne, H., & Rovee-Collier, C. (1995). The organization of reactivated memory in infancy. *Child Development, 66,* 893–906.

Hayward, M. D., Friedman, S., & Chen, H. (1996). Race inequities in men's retirement. *Journals of Gerontology: Social Sciences, 51B,* S1–10.

Hayward, M. D., & Hardy, M. A. (1985). Early retirement processes among older men: Occupational differences. *Research on Aging, 7,* 491–518.

Hazan, C., Hutt, M., Sturgeon, J., & Bricker, T. (1991, April). *The process of relinquishing parents as attachment figures.* Paper presented at the biennial meetings of the Society for Research in Child Development, Seattle, WA.

Hazan, C., & Shaver, P. (1987). Romantic love conceptualized as an attachment process. *Journal of Personality & Social Psychology, 52,* 511–524.

Hazelrigg, L. E., & Hardy, M. A. (1995). Older adult migration to the sunbelt: Assessing income and related characteristics of recent migrants. *Research on Aging, 17,* 109–234.

Hazuda, H., Wood, R., Lichtenstein, M., & Espino, D. (1998). Sociocultural status, psychosocial factors, and cognitive functional limitation in elderly Mexican Americans: Findings from the San Antonio Longitudinal Study of Aging. *Journal of Gerontological Social Work, 30,* 99–121.

He, Y., Colantonio, A., & Marshall, V. (2003). Later-life career disruption and self-rated health: An analysis of General Social Survey data. *Canadian Journal on Aging, 22,* 45–57.

Healy, J. (2004). Early television and subsequent attention problems in children. *Pediatrics, 113,* 917–918.

Heckhausen, J., & Brim, O. (1997). Perceived problems for self and others: Self-protection by social downgrading throughout adulthood. *Psychology & Aging, 12,* 610–619.

Heidelise, A., Duffy, F., McAnulty, G., Rivkin, M., Vajapeyam, S., Mulkern, R., Warfield, S., Huppi, P., Butler, S., Conneman, N., Fischer, C., & Eichenwald, E. (2004). Early experience alters brain function and structure. *Pediatrics, 113,* 846–857.

Heinicke, C., Goorsky, M., Moscov, S., Dudley, K., Gordon, J., Schneider, C., & Guthrie, D. (2000). Relationship-based intervention with at-risk mothers: Factors affecting variations in outcome. *Infant Mental Health Journal, 21,* 133–155.

Heinonen, K., Raikkonen, K., & Keltikangas-Jarvinen, L. (2003). Maternal perceptions and adolescent self-esteem: A six-year longitudinal study. *Adolescence, 38,* 669–687.

Hellinghausen, M. (1999, April 29). Miracle birth: Nurses recount unforgettable arrival of the Houston octuplets. *Nurse Week/Health Week.* Retrieved March 6, 2001, from http://www.nurseweek.com.

Helme, R. (1998). Pain in the elderly. *Australasian Journal on Aging, 17,* 33–35.

Helson, R., & Klohnen, D. (1998). Affective coloring of personality from young adulthood to midlife. *Personality & Social Psychology Bulletin, 24,* 241–252.

Helson, R., Mitchell, V., & Moane, G. (1984). Personality and patterns of adherence and nonadherence to the social clock. *Journal of Personality & Social Psychology, 46,* 1079–1096.

Henderson, H., Marshall, P., Fox, N., & Rubin, K. (2004). Psychophysiological and behavioral evidence for varying forms and functions of nonsocial behavior in preschoolers. *Child Development, 75,* 236–250.

Henry, B., Caspi, A., Moffitt, T., Harrington, H., et al. (1999). Staying in school protects boys with poor self-regulation in childhood from later crime: A longitudinal study. *International Journal of Behavioral Development, 23,* 1049–1073.

Henry, B., Caspi, A., Moffitt, T., & Silva, P. (1996). Temperamental and familial predictors of violent and nonviolent criminal convictions: Age 3 to age 18. *Developmental Psychology, 32,* 614–623.

Henry, J., MacLeod, M., Phillips, L., & Crawford, J. (2004). A meta-analytic review of prospective memory and aging. *Psychology & Aging, 19,* 27–39.

Henry J. Kaiser Family Foundation. (1999). *Sex on TV.* Washington, DC: Author.

Heppner, M., Fuller, B., & Multon, K. (1998). Adults in involuntary career transition: An analysis of the relationship between the psychological and career domains. *Journal of Career Assessment, 6,* 329–346.

Hermes, S., & Keel, P. (2003). The influence of puberty and ethnicity on awareness and internalization of the thin ideal. *International Journal of Eating Disorders, 33,* 465–467.

Hernandez, D. (1997). Child development and the social demography of childhood. *Child Development, 68,* 149–169.

Herrenkohl, E., Herrenkohl, R., Egolf, B., & Russo, M. (1998). The relationship between early maltreatment and teenage parenthood. *Journal of Adolescence, 21,* 291–303.

Hertenstein, M., & Campos, J. (2004). The retention effects of an adult's emotional displays on infant behavior. *Child Development, 75,* 595–613.

Hertzog, C., Dixon, R., Hultsch, D., & MacDonald, S. (2003). Latent change models of adult cognition: Are changes in processing speed and working memory associated with changes in episodic memory? *Psychology & Aging, 18,* 755–769.

Herzog, A. R., House, J. S., & Morgan, J. N. (1991). Relation of work and retirement to health and well-being in older age. *Psychology & Aging, 6,* 202–211.

Hess, E. H. (1972). "Imprinting" in a natural laboratory. *Scientific American, 227,* 24–31.

Hess, T., Bolstad, C., Woodburn, S., & Auman, C. (1999). Trait diagnosticity versus behavioral consistency as determinants of impression change in adulthood. *Psychology & Aging, 14,* 77–89.

Hesser, A., Cregler, L., & Lewis, L. (1998). Predicting the admission into medical school of African American college students who have participated in summer academic enrichment programs. *Academic Medicine, 73,* 187–191.

Hester, R., Kinsella, G., & Ong, B. (2004). Effect of age on forward and backward span tasks. *Journal of the International Neuropsychological Society, 10,* 475–481.

Hetherington, E., Bridges, M., & Insabella, G. (1998). What matters? What does not?: Five perspectives on the association between marital transitions and children's adjustment. *American Psychologist, 53,* 167–184.

Hetherington, E., Henderson, S., Reiss, D., Anderson, E., et al. (1999). Adolescent siblings in stepfamilies: Family functioning and adolescent adjustment. *Monographs of the Society for Research in Child Development, 64,* 222.

Hetherington, E. M. (1991a). Presidential address: Families, lies, and videotapes. *Journal of Research on Adolescence, 1,* 323–348.

Hetherington, E. M. (1991b). The role of individual differences and family relationships in children's coping with divorce and remarriage. In P. A. Cowen & M. Hetherington (Eds.), *Family transitions* (pp. 165–194). Hillsdale, NJ: Erlbaum.

Hetherington, E. M., & Clingempeel, W. G. (1992). Coping with marital transitions: A family systems perspective. *Monographs of the Society for Research in Child Development, 57* (2–3, Serial No. 227).

Hetherington, E. M., & Stanley-Hagan, M. M. (1995). Parenting in divorced and remarried families. In M. H. Bornstein (Ed.), *Handbook of parenting, Vol. 3: Status and social conditions of parenting* (pp. 233–254). Mahwah, NJ: Erlbaum.

Heun, R., & Bonsignore, M. (2004). No evidence for a genetic relationship between Alzheimer's disease and longevity. *Dementia & Geriatric Cognitive Disorders, 18*, 1–5.

Hicks, D., & Gwynne, M. (1996). *Cultural anthropology.* New York: Harper-Collins.

Higgins, C., Duxbury, L., & Lee, C. (1994). Impact of life-cycle stage and gender on the ability to balance work and family responsibilities. *Family Relations, 43*, 144–150.

Hill, C. (1999). Fusion and conflict in lesbian relationships. *Feminism & Psychology, 9*, 179–185.

Hill, J., Brooks–Gunn, J., & Waldfogel, J. (2003). Sustained effects of high participation in an early intervention for low-birth-weight premature infants. *Developmental Psychology, 39*, 730–744.

Hill, R. D., Storandt, M., & Malley, M. (1993). The impact of long-term exercise training on psychological function in older adults. *Journals of Gerontology: Psychological Sciences, 48*, P12–17.

Hillen, T., Davies, S., Rudd, A., Kieselbach, T., & Wolfe, C. (2003). Self ratings of health predict functional outcome and recurrence free survival after stroke. *Journal of Epidemiology & Community Health, 57*, 960–966.

Himes, C. L. (1994). Parental caregiving by adult women. *Research on Aging, 16*, 191–211.

Hinde, R. A., Titmus, G., Easton, D., & Tamplin, A. (1985). Incidence of "friendship" and behavior toward strong associates versus nonassociates in preschoolers. *Child Development, 56*, 234–245.

Hinden, S. (2000). Computer age brings wide new world to golden age. *Washington Post Online.* Retrieved March 19, 2000, from www.washingtonpost.com.

Hinton, J. (1975). The influence of previous personality on reactions to having terminal cancer. *Omega, 6*, 95–111.

Hirdes, J. P., & Strain, L. A. (1995). The balance of exchange in instrumental support with network members outside the household. *Journals of Gerontology: Social Sciences, 50B*, S134–142.

Ho, C., & Bryant, P. (1997). Learning to read Chinese beyond the logographic phase. *Reading Research Quarterly, 32*, 276–289.

Hobbs, J., & Ferth, P. (1993). *The Bounty pregnancy guide.* New York: Bounty Health Care Publishing.

Hoch, C. C., Buysse, D. J., Monk, T. H., & Reynolds, C. F. I. (1992). Sleep disorders and aging. In J. E. Birren, R. B. Sloane, & G. D. Cohen (Eds.), *Handbook of mental health and aging* (2nd ed., pp. 557–582). San Diego, CA: Academic Press.

Hodges, E. V. E., Malone, M. J., & Perry, D. G. (1997). Individual risk and social risk as interacting determinants of victimization in the peer group. *Developmental Psychology, 33*, 1032–1039.

Hoeksma, J., Oosterlaan, J., & Schipper, E. (2004). Emotion regulation and the dynamics of feelings: A conceptual and methodological framework. *Child Development, 75*, 354–360.

Hoffman, H. J., & Hillman, L. S. (1992). Epidemiology of the sudden infant death syndrome: Maternal, neonatal, and postneonatal risk factors. *Clinics in Perinatology, 19*(4), 717–737.

Hoffman, M. (1970). Moral development. In P. Mussen (Ed.), *Carmichael's manual of child psychology, Vol. 2.* New York: Wiley.

Hoffman, M. (1988). Moral development. In M. Bornstein & M. Lamb (Eds.), *Developmental psychology: An advanced textbook* (2nd ed., pp. 497–548). Hillsdale, NJ: Erlbaum.

Hoffman, M. L. (1982). Development of prosocial motivation: Empathy and guilt. In N. Eisenberg (Ed.), *The development of prosocial behavior* (pp. 281–314). New York: Academic Press.

Hoffnung, M. (2004). Wanting it all: Career, marriage, and motherhood during college-educated women's 20s. *Sex Roles, 50*, 711–723.

Hogan, T. D., & Steinnes, D. N. (1994). Toward an understanding of elderly seasonal migration using origin-based household data. *Research on Aging, 16*, 463–475.

Holden, G. W., Coleman, S. M., & Schmidt, K. L. (1995). Why 3-year-old children get spanked: Parent and child determinants as reported by college-educated mothers. *Merrill-Palmer Quarterly, 41*, 431–452.

Holden, K. C., & Smock, P. J. (1991). The economic costs of marital dissolution: Why do women bear a disproportionate cost? *Annual Review of Sociology, 17*, 51–78.

Holland, J. L. (1973). *Making vocational choices: A theory of careers.* Englewood Cliffs, NJ: Prentice-Hall.

Holland, J. L. (1992). *Making vocational choices: A theory of vocational personalities and work environments* (2nd ed.). Odessa, FL: Psychological Assessment Resources.

Hollander, J. (2004). "I Can Take Care of Myself": The impact of self-defense training on women's lives. *Violence Against Women, 10*, 205–235.

Holmbeck, G. N., & Hill, J. P. (1991). Conflictive engagement, positive affect, and menarche in families with seventh-grade girls. *Child Development, 62*, 1030–1048.

Holstein, M., & Minkler, M. (2003). Self, society, and the "new gerontology." *Gerontologist, 43*, 787–796.

Honzik, M. P. (1986). The role of the family in the development of mental abilities: A 50-year study. In N. Datan, A. L. Greene, & H. W. Reese (Eds.), *Life-span developmental psychology: Intergenerational relations* (pp. 185–210). Hillsdale, NJ: Erlbaum.

Hood, M., & Ellison, R. (2003). Television viewing and change in body fat from preschool to early adolescence: The Framingham Children's Study. *International Journal of Obesity & Related Metabolic Disorders, 27*, 827–833.

Horan, W., Pogge, D., Borgaro, S., & Stokes, J. (1997). Learning and memory in adolescent psychiatric inpatients with major depression: A normative study of the California Verbal Learning Test. *Archives of Clinical Neuropsychology, 12*, 575–584.

Horn, J. L. (1982). The aging of human abilities. In B. B. Wolman (Ed.), *Handbook of developmental psychology* (pp. 847–870). Englewood Cliffs, NJ: Prentice-Hall.

Horn, J. L., & Donaldson, G. (1980). Cognitive development in adulthood. In O. G. Brim, Jr. & J. Kagan (Eds.), *Constancy and change in human development* (pp. 415–529). Cambridge, MA: Harvard University Press.

Horn, L., & Bertold, J. (1999). *Students with disabilities in post-secondary education: A profile of preparation, participation, and outcomes.* Washington, DC: National Center for Educational Statistics. Retrieved August 23, 2000, from http://www.nces.ed.gov.

Horn, L., & Premo, M. (1995). *Profile of undergraduates in U.S. postsecondary education institutions.* Washington DC: U.S. Department of Education.

Hornbrook, M. C., Stevens, V. J., & Wingfield, D. J. (1994). Preventing falls among community-dwelling older persons: Results from a randomized trial. *The Gerontologist, 34*, 16–23.

Horner, K. W., Rushton, J. P., & Vernon, P. A. (1986). Relation between aging and research productivity of academic psychologists. *Psychology & Aging, 1*, 319–324.

Hornik, M. (1998). Physician-assisted suicide and euthanasia's impact on the frail elderly: A social worker's response. *Journal of Long Term Home Health Care: The Pride Institute Journal, 17*, 34–41.

Horowitz, A., McLaughlin, J., & White, H. (1998). How the negative and positive aspects of partner relationships affect the mental health of young married people. *Journal of Health & Social Behavior, 39*, 124–136.

Horowitz, F. D. (1990). Developmental models of individual differences. In J. Colombo & J. Fagen (Eds.), *Individual differences in infancy: Reliability, stability, prediction* (pp. 3–18). Hillsdale, NJ: Erlbaum.

Houck, G., & Lecuyer-Maus, E. (2004). Maternal limit setting during toddlerhood, delay of gratification and behavior problems at age five. *Infant Mental Health Journal, 25*, 28–46.

House, J. A., Kessler, R. C., & Herzog, A. R. (1990). Age, socioeconomic status, and health. *The Milbank Quarterly, 68*, 383–411.

House, J. S., Kessler, R. C., Herzog, A. R., Mero, R. P., Kinney, A. M., & Breslow, M. J. (1992). Social stratification, age, and health. In K. W. Schaie, D. Blazer, & J. M. House (Eds.), *Aging, health behaviors, and health outcomes* (pp. 1–32). Hillsdale, NJ: Erlbaum.

Houseknecht, S. K. (1987). Voluntary childlessness. In M. B. Sussman & S. K. Steinmetz (Eds.), *Handbook of marriage and the family* (pp. 369–395). New York: Plenum.

Houston, D., & Jusczyk, P. (2003). Infants' long-term memory for the sound patterns of words and voices. *Journal of Experimental Psychology: Human Perception & Performance, 29*, 1143–1154.

Hovell, M., Blumberg, E., Sipan, C., Hofstetter, C., Burkham, S., Atkins, C., & Felice, M. (1998). Skills training for pregnancy and AIDS prevention in Anglo and Latino youth. *Journal of Adolescent Health, 23*, 139–149.

Hovell, M., Sipan, C., Blumberg, E., Atkins, C., Hofstetter, C. R., & Kreitner, S. (1994). Family influences on Latino and Anglo adolescents' sexual behavior. *Journal of Marriage & the Family, 56*, 973–986.

Howe, D., & Fearnley, S. (2003). Disorders of attachment in adopted and fostered children: Recognition and treatment. *Clinical Child Psychology & Psychiatry, 8*, 369–387.

Howes, C. (1983). Patterns of friendship. *Child Development, 54*, 1041–1053.

Howes, C. (1987). Social competence with peers in young children: Developmental sequences. *Developmental Review, 7*, 252–272.

Howes, C., & Matheson, C. C. (1992). Sequences in the development of competent play with peers: Social and pretend play. *Developmental Psychology, 28*, 961–974.

Howes, C., Phillips, D. A., & Whitebook, M. (1992). Thresholds of quality: Implications for the social development of children in center-based child care. *Child Development, 63*, 449–460.

Hoyert, D. L. (1991). Financial and household exchanges between generations. *Research on Aging, 13*, 205–225.

Hoyert, D. L., & Seltzer, M. M. (1992). Factors related to the well-being and life activities of family caregivers. *Family Relations, 41*, 74–81.

Hu, F., Li, T., Colditz, G., Willet, W., & Manson, J. (2003). Television watching and other sedentary behavior in relation to risk of obesity and type 2 diabetes mellitus in women. *Journal of the American Medical Association, 289*, 1785–1791.

Huang, H., & Hanley, J. (1997). A longitudinal study of phonological awareness, visual skills, and Chinese reading acquisition among first-graders in Taiwan. *International Journal of Behavioral Development, 20*, 249–268.

Hubel, D. H., & Weisel, T. N. (1963). Receptive fields of cells in striate cortex of very young, visually inexperienced kittens. *Journal of Neurophysiology, 26*, 994–1002.

Hudziak, J., van Beijsterveldt, C., Bartels, M., Rietveld, M., Rettew, D., Derks, E., & Boomsma, D. (2003). Individual differences in aggression: Genetic analyses by age, gender, and informant in 3-, 7-, and 10-year-old Dutch twins. *Behavior Genetics, 33*, 575–589.

Huesmann, L. R., Lagerspetz, K., & Eron, L. D. (1984). Intervening variables in the television violence-aggression relation: Evidence from two countries. *Developmental Psychology, 20*, 746–775.

Huffman, L. C., Bryan, Y. E., Pedersen, F. A., Lester, B. M., Newman, J. D., & del Carmen, R. (1994). Infant cry acoustics and maternal ratings of temperament. *Infant Behavior & Development, 17*, 45–53.

Hulbert, A. (2003). *Raising America: Experts, parents, and a century of advice about children.* New York: Alfred A. Knopf.

Hulley, S., Furberg, C., Barrett-Connor, E., Cauley, J., Grady, D., Haskell, W., Knopp, R., Lowery, M., Satterfield, S., Schrott, H., Vittinghoff, E., & Hunninghake, D. (2002). Noncardiovascular disease outcomes during 6.8 years of hormone therapy: Heart and estrogen/progestin replacement study follow-up (HERS II). *Journal of the American Medical Association, 288*, 58–64.

Hultsch, D., Hertzog, C., Small, B., & Dixon, R. (1999). Use it or lose it: Engaged lifestyle as a buffer of cognitive decline in aging? *Psychology & Aging, 14*, 245–263.

Hultsch, D. F., Hertzog, C., Small, B. J., McDonald-Miszczak, L., & Dixon, R. A. (1992). Short-term longitudinal change in cognitive performance in later life. *Psychology & Aging, 7*, 571–584.

Hummert, M., Garstka, T., & Shaner, J. (1997). Stereotyping of older adults: The role of target facial cues and perceiver characteristics. *Psychology & Aging, 21*, 107–114.

Humphreys, A., & Smith, P. (1987). Rough and tumble, friendship, and dominance in school children: Evidence for continuity and change with age. *Child Development, 58*, 201–212.

Hunfeld, J., Tempels, A., Passchier, J., Hazebroek, F., et al. (1999). Parental burden and grief one year after the birth of a child with a congenital anomaly. *Journal of Pediatric Psychology, 24*, 515–520.

Hunter, D. J., Spiegelman, D., Adami, H., Beeson, L., van den Brandt, P. A., Folsom, A. R., Fraser, G. E., Goldbohm, A., Graham, S., Howe, G. R., Kushi, L. H., Marshall, J. R., McDermott, A., Miller, A. B., Speizer, F. E., Wolk, A., Yuan, S., & Willett, W. (1996). Cohort studies of fat intake and the risk of breast cancer-a pooled analysis. *New England Journal of Medicine, 334*, 356–361.

Hunter, S., & Sundel, M. (1989). *Midlife myths: Issues, findings, and practice implications.* Newbury Park, CA: Sage.

Hurwitz, E., Gunn, W. J., Pinsky, P. F., & Schonberger, L. B. (1991). Risk of respiratory illness associated with day-care attendance: A nationwide study. *Pediatrics, 87*, 62–69.

Husaini, B., Blasi, A., & Miller, O. (1999). Does public and private religiosity have a moderating effect on depression? A bi-racial study of elders in the American South. *International Journal of Aging & Human Development, 48*, 63–72.

Huth-Bocks, A., Levendosky, A., Bogat, G., & von Eye, A. (2004). The impact of maternal characteristics and contextual variables on infant-mother attachment. *Child Development, 75*, 480–496.

Hutt, S. J., Lenard, H. G., & Prechtl, H. F. R. (1969). Psychophysiological studies in newborn infants. In L. P. Lipsitt & H. W. Reese (Eds.), *Advances in child development and behavior, Vol. 4* (pp. 128–173). New York: Academic Press.

Huttenlocher, J. (1995, April). *Children's language in relation to input.* Paper presented at the biennial meetings of the Society for Research in Child Development, Indianapolis, IN.

Huttenlocher, P. R. (1994). Synaptogenesis, synapse elimination, and neural plasticity in human cerebral cortex. In C. A. Nelson (Ed.), *The Minnesota Symposia on Child Psychology, Vol. 27* (pp. 35–54). Hillsdale, NJ: Erlbaum.

Hyde, J., Fennema, E., & Lamon, S. (1990). Gender differences in mathematics performance: A meta-analysis. *Psychological Bulletin, 107*, 139–155.

Hyun, O., Lee, W., Yoo, A., Cho, B., Yoo, K., Miller, B., Schvaneveldt, J., & Lau, S. (2002). Social support for two generations of new mothers in selected populations in Korea, Hong Kong, and the United States. *Journal of Comparative Family Studies, 33*, 515–527.

Idler, E., & Kasl, S. (1997a). Religion among disabled and nondisabled persons I: Cross-sectional patterns in health practices, social activities, and well-being. *Journals of Gerontology, Series B: Psychological Sciences & Social Sciences, 52B*, S294–S305.

Idler, E., & Kasl, S. (1997b). Religion among disabled and nondisabled persons II: Attendance at religious services as a predictor of the course of disability. *Journals of Gerontology, Series B: Psychological Sciences & Social Sciences, 52B*, S306–S316.

Iecovich, E., & Lankri, M. (2002). Title attitudes of elderly persons towards receiving financial support from adult children. *Journal of Aging Studies, 16*, 121–133.

Ingersoll-Dayton, B., Neal, M., Ha, J., & Hammer, L. (2003). Collaboration among siblings providing care for older parents. *Journal of Gerontological Social Work, 40*, 51–66.

Ingoldsby, E., Shaw, D., Owens, E., & Winslow, E. (1999). A longitudinal study of interparental conflict, emotional and behavioral reactivity, and preschoolers' adjustment problems among low-income families. *Journal of Abnormal Child Psychology, 27*, 343–356.

Ingram, D. (1981). Early patterns of grammatical development. In R. E. Stark (Ed.), *Language behavior in infancy and early childhood* (pp. 327–358). New York: Elsevier North-Holland.

Ingrassia, M. (1993, August 2). Daughters of Murphy Brown. *Newsweek*, 58–59.

Inhelder, B., & Piaget, J. (1958). *The growth of logical thinking from childhood to adolescence.* New York: Basic Books.

Inkeles, A., & Usui, C. (1989). Retirement patterns in cross-national perspective. In D. I. Kertzer & K. W. Schaie (Eds.), *Age structuring in comparative perspective* (pp. 227–262). Hillsdale, NJ: Erlbaum.

Insabella, G. M. (1995, March). *Varying levels of exposure to marital conflict: Prediction of adolescent adjustment across intact families and stepfamilies.* Paper presented at the biennial meetings of the Society for Research in Child Development, Indianapolis, IN.

Interactive Digital Software Association. (1998). *Deep impact: How does the interactive entertainment industry affect the U.S. economy?* Retrieved from http://www.idsa.com.

Irwin, M., & Pike, J. (1993). Bereavement, depressive symptoms, and immune function. In M. S. Stroebe, W. Stroebe, & R. O. Hansson (Eds.), *Handbook of bereavement: Theory, research, and intervention* (pp. 160–171). Cambridge, England: Cambridge University Press.

Isabella, R. A. (1995). The origins of infant-mother attachment: Maternal behavior and infant development. *Annals of Child Development, 10*, 57–81.

Isaksson, K., Johansson, G., Bellaagh, K., & Sjöberg, A. (2004). Work values among the unemployed: Changes over time and some gender differences. *Scandinavian Journal of Psychology, 45*, 207–214.

Itier, R., & Taylor, M. (2004). Face inversion and contrast-reversal effects across development: In contrast to the expertise theory. *Developmental Science, 7*, 246–260.

Iversen, L., & Sabroe, S. (1988). Psychological well-being among unemployed and employed people after a company closedown: A longitudinal study. *Journal of Social Issues, 44*, 141–152.

Ivy, G. O., MacLeod, C. M., Petit, T. L., & Marcus, E. J. (1992). A physiological framework for perceptual and cognitive changes in aging. In F. I. M. Craik & T. A. Salthouse (Eds.), *The handbook of aging and cognition* (pp. 273–314). Hillsdale, NJ: Erlbaum.

Iwashyna, T., & Christakis, N. (2003). Marriage, widowhood, and health-care use. *Social Science & Medicine, 57*, 2137–2147.

Izard, C. E., Fantauzzo, C. A., Castle, J. M., Haynes, O. M., Rayias, M. F., & Putnam, P. H. (1995). The ontogeny and significance of infants' facial expressions in the first 9 months of life. *Developmental Psychology, 31*, 997–1013.

Izard, C. E., & Harris, P. (1995). Emotional development and developmental psychopathology. In D. Cicchetti & D. J. Cohen (Eds.), *Developmental psychopathology, Vol. 1: Theory and methods* (pp. 467–503). New York: Wiley.

Jackson, D., & Tein, J. (1998). Adolescents' conceptualization of adult roles: Relationships with age, gender, work goal, and maternal employment. *Sex Roles, 38,* 987–1008.

Jackson, D. J., Longino, C. F., Jr. , Zimmerman, R. S., & Bradsher, J. E. (1991). Environmental adjustments to declining functional ability: Residential mobility and living arrangements. *Research on Aging, 13,* 289–309.

Jackson, L., & Bracken, B. (1998). Relationship between students' social status and global and domain-specific self-concepts. *Journal of School Psychology, 36,* 233–246.

Jacobs, J., Finken, L., Griffin, N., & Wright, J. (1998). The career plans of science-talented rural adolescent girls. *American Educational Research Journal, 35,* 681–704.

Jacobs, S. C., Kosten, T. R., Kasl, S. V., Ostfeld, A. M., Berkman, L., & Charpentier, P. (1987/1988). Attachment theory and multiple dimensions of grief. *Omega, 18,* 41–52.

Jacobsen, T., & Hofmann, V. (1997). Children's attachment representations: Longitudinal relations to school behavior, and academic competency in middle childhood and adolescence. *Developmental Psychology, 33,* 703–710.

Jacobsen, T., Husa, M., Fendrich, M., Kruesi, M., & Ziegenhain, U. (1997). Children's ability to delay gratification: Longitudinal relations to mother-child attachment. *Journal of Genetic Psychology, 158,* 411–426.

Jacoby, S. (2000, July/August). The fine art of grandparenting. *AARP Bulletin, 413,* 23.

Jadack, R. A., Hyde, J. S., Moore, C. F., & Keller, M. L. (1995). Moral reasoning about sexually transmitted diseases. *Child Development, 66,* 167–177.

Jahnke, H. C., & Blanchard-Fields, F. (1993). A test of two models of adolescent egocentrism. *Journal of Youth & Adolescence, 22,* 313–326.

Jain, T., Harlow, B., & Hornstein, M. (2002). Insurance coverage and outcomes of in vitro fertilization. *New England Journal of Medicine, 347,* 661–666.

Jain, T., Missmer, S., & Hornstein, M. (2004). Trends in embryo-transfer practice and in outcomes of the use of assisted reproductive technology in the United States. *New England Journal of Medicine, 350,* 1639–1645.

Jambunathan, S., & Burts, D. (2003). Comparison of perception of self-competence among five ethnic groups of preschoolers in the U.S. *Early Childhood Education, 173,* 651–660.

James, S. A., Keenan, N. L., & Browning, S. (1992). Socioeconomic status, health behaviors, and health status among blacks. In K. W. Schaie, D. Blazer, & J. M. House (Eds.), *Aging, health behaviors, and health outcomes* (pp. 39–57). Hillsdale, NJ: Erlbaum.

Janosz, M., Le Blanc, M., Boulerice, B., & Tremblay, R. (2000). Predicting different types of school dropouts: A typological approach with two longitudinal samples. *Journal of Educational Psychology, 92,* 171–190.

Janssen, T., & Carton, J. (1999). The effects of locus of control and task difficulty on procrastination. *Journal of Genetic Psychology, 160,* 436–442.

Japan Times. (2003, May 15). *ADHD girl's mother files petition.* Retrieved April 10, 2004, from http://japantimes.co.jp.

Jarolmen, J. (1998). A comparison of the grief reaction of children and adults: Focusing on pet loss and bereavement. *Omega, 37,* 133–150.

Javo, C., Ronning, J., Heyerdahl, S., & Rudmin, F. (2004). Parenting correlates of child behavior problems in a multiethnic community sample of preschool children in northern Norway. *European Child & Adolescent Psychiatry, 13,* 8–18.

Jendrek, M. (1993). Grandparents who parent their grandchildren: Effects on lifestyle. *Journal of Marriage & the Family, 55,* 609–621.

Jenkins, J. & Buccioni, J. (2000). Children's understanding of marital conflict and the marital relationship. *Journal of Child Psychology & Psychiatry & Allied Disciplines, 41,* 161–168.

Jenkins, J. M., & Astington, J. W. (1996). Cognitive factors and family structure associated with theory of mind development in young children. *Developmental Psychology, 32,* 70–78.

Jenkins, L., Myerson, J., Hale, S., & Fry, A. (1999). Individual and developmental differences in working memory across the life span. *Psychonomic Bulletin & Review, 6,* 28–40.

Jensen, A., & Whang, P. (1994). Speed of accessing arithmetic facts in long-term memory: A comparison of Chinese-American and Anglo-American children. *Contemporary Educational Psychology, 19,* 1–12.

Jensen, K. (2003). Bioidentical hormone replacement therapy: Theory and evidence. *Saskatchewan Drug Information Service News, 20.* Retrieved

August 27, 2004, from http://www.usask.ca/pharmacy-nutrition/services/read.php?id=11.

Jensen-Campbell, L., Gleason, K., Adams, R., & Malcolm, K. (2003). Interpersonal conflict, agreeableness, and personality development. *Journal of Personality, 71,* 1059–1085.

Jerrome, D. (1990). Intimate relationships. In J. Bond & P. Coleman (Eds.), *Aging in society* (pp. 181–208). London: Sage.

Jessor, R. (1992). Risk behavior in adolescence: A psychosocial framework for understanding and action. *Developmental Review, 12,* 374–390.

Jette, A. M. (1996). Disability trends and transitions. In R. H. Binstock & L. K. George (Eds.), *Handbook of aging and the social sciences* (4th ed., pp. 94–116). San Diego, CA: Academic Press.

Jimerson, S. (1999). On the failure of failure: Examining the association between early grade retention and educational and employment outcomes during late adolescence. *Journal of School Psychology, 37,* 243–272.

Jin, Y., Jing, J., Morinaga, R., Miki, K., Su, X., & Chen, X. (2002). A comparative study of theory of mind in Chinese and Japanese children. *Chinese Mental Health Journal, 16,* 446–448.

Johansson, B., Hofer, S., Allaire, J., Maldonado-Molina, M., Piccinin, A., Berg, S., Pedersen, N., & McClearn, G. (2004). Change in cognitive capabilities in the oldest old: The effects of proximity to death in genetically related individuals over a 6-year period. *Psychology & Aging, 19,* 145–156.

John, O. P., Caspi, A., Robins, R. W., Moffitt, T. E., & Stouthamer-Loeber, M. (1994). The "little five": Exploring the nomological network of the five-factor model of personality in adolescent boys. *Child Development, 65,* 160–178.

Johnson, C. L., & Barer, B. M. (1990). Families and networks among older inner-city blacks. *The Gerontologist, 30,* 726–733.

Johnson, E., & Breslau, N. (2000). Increased risk of learning disabilities in low birth weight boys at age 11 years. *Biological Psychiatry, 47,* 490–500.

Johnson, H., Nusbaum, B., Bejarano, A., & Rosen, T. (1999). An ecological approach to development in children with prenatal drug exposure. *American Journal of Orthopsychiatry, 69,* 448–456.

Johnson, J., Vogt, B., Kim, R., Cotman, C., & Head, E. (2004). Isolated executive impairment and associated frontal neuropathology. *Dementia & Geriatric Cognitive Disorders, 17,* 360–367.

Johnston, C. (1996). Interactive storybook software: Effects on verbal development in kindergarten children. *Early Child Development & Care, 132,* 33–44.

Jones, M., & Wheatley, J. (1990). Gender differences in teacher-student interactions in science classrooms. *Journal of Research in Science Teaching, 27,* 861–874.

Jones, M. C. (1924). A laboratory study of fear: The case of Peter. *Pedagogical Seminary, 31,* 308–315.

Jonsson, P. (2003). The new face of homeschooling. *Christian Science Monitor Online.* Retrieved June 23, 2004, from http://www.csmonitor.com/2003/0429/p01s01-ussc.html.

Jorgenson, S. (1993). Adolescent pregnancy and parenting. In T. Gullotta, G. Adams, & R. Montemayor (Eds.), *Adolescent sexuality* (pp. 103–140). Thousand Oaks, CA: Sage Publications.

Jorm, A., Christensen, H., Henderson, A., Jacomb, P., Korten, A., & Mackinnon, A. (1998). Factors associated with successful aging. *Journal of Aging, 17,* 33–37.

Joseph, K., Young, D., Dodds, L., O'Connell, C., Allen, V., Chandra, S., & Allen, A. (2003). Changes in maternal characteristics and obstetric practice and recent increases in primary cesarean delivery. *Obstetrics and Gynecology, 102,* 791–800.

Joseph, R. (2000). Fetal brain behavior and cognitive development. *Developmental Review, 20,* 81–98.

Joshi, M. S., & MacLean, M. (1994). Indian and English children's understanding of the distinction between real and apparent emotion. *Child Development, 65,* 1372–1384.

Josse, D., Thibault, H., Bourdais, C., Mirailles, P., Pireyre, E., Surgal, L., Gerboin-Reyrolles, P., & Chauliac, M. (1999). Iron deficiency and psychomotor development in young children in a child health centre: Assessment with revised version of the Brunet-Lezine scale. *Approche Neuropsychologique des Apprentissages chez l'Enfant, 11,* 21–27.

Joung, I. M. A., Stronks, K., van de Mheen, H., & Mackenbach, J. P. (1995). Health behaviours explain part of the differences in self reported health associated with partner/marital status in The Netherlands. *Journal of Epidemiology & Community Health, 49,* 482–488.

Juan, E., Blascao, T., Font, A., Doval, E., Sanz, A., Maroto, P., & Pallares, C. (2003). Perception of control and survival in patients with advanced lung cancer referred for palliative treatment. *Ansiedad y Estres, 9,* 1–5.

Judge, T., Bono, J., & Locke, E. (2000). Personality and job satisfaction: The mediating role of job characteristics. *Journal of Applied Psychology, 85,* 237–249.

Juffer, F., Hoksbergen, R., Riksen-Walraven, J., & Kohnstamm, G. (1997). Early intervention in adoptive families: Supporting maternal sensitive responsiveness, infant-mother attachment, and infant competence. *Journal of Child Psychology & Psychiatry & Allied Disciplines, 38,* 1039–1050.

Juffer, F., & Rosenboom, L., (1997). Infant mother attachment of internationally adopted children in the Netherlands. *International Journal of Behavioral Development, 20,* 93–107.

Jusczyk, P., & Hohne, E. (1997). Infants' memory for spoken words. *Science, 277.*

Jusczyk, P., Houston, D., & Newsome, M. (1999). The beginnings of word segmentation in English-learning infants. *Cognitive Psychology, 39,* 159–207.

Jussim, L., & Eccles, J. (1992). Teacher expectations II: Construction and reflection of student achievement. *Journal of Personality & Social Psychology, 63,* 947–961.

Jutras, S., & Lavoie, J. (1995). Living with an impaired elderly person: The informal caregiver's physical and mental health. *Journal of Aging & Health, 7,* 46–73.

Kagan, J. (1989). *Unstable ideas: Temperament, cognition, and self.* Cambridge, MA: Harvard University Press.

Kagan, J. (1994). *Galen's prophecy.* New York: Basic Books.

Kagan, J., Reznick, J. S., & Snidman, N. (1990). The temperamental qualities of inhibition and lack of inhibition. In M. Lewis & S. M. Miller (Eds.), *Handbook of developmental psychopathology* (pp. 219–226). New York: Plenum.

Kagan, J., Snidman, N., & Arcus, D. (1993). On the temperamental categories of inhibited and uninhibited children. In K. H. Rubin & J. B. Asendorpf (Eds.), *Social withdrawal, inhibition, and shyness in childhood* (pp. 19–28). Hillsdale, NJ: Erlbaum.

Kahana-Kalman, R., & Walker-Andrews, A. (2001). The role of person familiarity in young infants' perception of emotional expressions. *Child Development, 72,* 352–369.

Kahn, S. B., Alvi, S., Shaukat, N., Hussain, M. A., & Baig, T. (1990). A study of the validity of Holland's theory in a non-Western culture. *Journal of Vocational Behavior, 36,* 132–146.

Kail, R. (1990). *The development of memory in children* (3rd ed.). New York: Freeman.

Kail, R. (1991). Processing time declines exponentially during childhood and adolescence. *Developmental Psychology, 27,* 259–266.

Kail, R. (1997). Processing time, imagery, and spatial memory. *Journal of Experimental Child Psychology, 64,* 67–78.

Kail, R., & Hall, L. (1999). Sources of developmental change in children's word-problem performance. *Journal of Educational Psychology, 91,* 660–668.

Kail, R., & Hall, L. K. (1994). Processing speed, naming speed, and reading. *Developmental Psychology, 30,* 949–954.

Kales, H., Blow, F., Bingham, R., Copeland, L. & Mellow, A. (2000, June). Race and inpatient psychiatric diagnoses among elderly veterans. *Psychiatric Services Journal, 51,* 795–800.

Kalish, R. A. (1985). The social context of death and dying. In R. H. Binstock & E. Shanas (Eds.), *Handbook of aging and the social sciences* (2nd ed., pp. 149–170). New York: Van Nostrand Reinhold.

Kalish, R. A., & Reynolds, D. K. (1976). *Death and ethnicity: A psychocultural study.* Los Angeles: University of Southern California Press (reprinted 1981, Baywood Publishing Co, Farmingdale, NJ).

Kallman, D. A., Plato, C. C., & Tobin, J. D. (1990). The role of muscle loss in the age-related decline of grip strength: Cross-sectional and longitudinal perspectives. *Journals of Gerontology: Medical Sciences, 45,* M82–88.

Kalmijn, M. (2003). Shared friendship networks and the life course: An analysis of survey data on married and cohabiting couples. *Social Networks, 25,* 231–249.

Kalmuss, D. (2004). Nonviolational sex and sexual health. *Archives of Sexual Behavior, 33,* 197–209.

Kaltiala-Heino, R., Kosunen, E., & Rimpela, M. (2003). Pubertal timing, sexual behaviour and self-reported depression in middle adolescence. *Journal of Adolescence, 26,* 531–545.

Kamo, Y., Ries, L. M., Farmer, Y. M., Nickinovich, D. G., & Borgatta, E. F. (1991). Status attainment revisited. The National Survey of Families and Households. *Research on Aging, 13,* 124–143.

Kandel, D. B., & Wu, P. (1995). The contributions of mothers and fathers to the intergenerational transmission of cigarette smoking in adolescence. *Journal of Research on Adolescence, 5,* 225–252.

Kane, C. (1998). Differences in family of origin perceptions among African American, Asian American and Hispanic American college students. *Journal of Black Studies, 29,* 93–105.

Kane, R. L., & Kane, R. A. (1990). Health care for older people: Organizational and policy issues. In R. H. Binstock & L. K. George (Eds.), *Handbook of aging and the social sciences* (3rd ed., pp. 415–437). San Diego, CA: Academic Press.

Kane, R. L., Klein, S. J., Bernstein, L., Rothenberg, R., & Wales, J. (1985). Hospice role in alleviating the emotional stress of terminal patients and their families. *Medical Care, 23,* 189–197.

Kane, R. L., Wales, J., Bernstein, L., Leibowitz, A., & Kaplan, S. (1984). A randomized controlled trial of hospice care. *Lancet,* 890–894.

Kane, T., Staiger, P., & Ricciardelli, L. (2000). Male domestic violence: Attitudes, aggression and interpersonal dependency. *Journal of Interpersonal Violence, 15,* 16–29.

Kann, L., Warren, C. W., Harris, W. A., Collins, J. L., Douglas, K. A., Collins, M. E., Williams, B. I., Ross, J. G., & Kolbe, L. J. (1995). Youth risk behavior surveillance-United States, 1993. *Morbidity & Mortality Weekly Reports, 44* (SS 1), 1–55.

Kannel, W. B., & Gordon, T. (1980). Cardiovascular risk factors in the aged: The Framingham study. In S. G. Haynes & M. Feinleib (Eds.), *Second conference on the epidemiology of aging,* U.S. Department of Health and Human Services NIH Publication No. 80–969 (pp. 65–89). Washington, DC: U.S. Government Printing Office.

Kaplan, G. A. (1992). Health and aging in the Alameda County study. In K. W. Schaie, D. Blazer, & J. M. House (Eds.), *Aging, health behaviors, and health outcomes* (pp. 69–88). Hillsdale, NJ: Erlbaum.

Kaplan, H., & Sadock, B. (1991). *Synopsis of psychiatry* (6th ed.). Baltimore, MD: Williams & Wilkins.

Kaplan, P., Bachorowski, J., Smoski, M., & Zinser, M. (2001). Role of clinical diagnosis and medication use in effects of maternal depression on infant-directed speech. *Infancy, 2,* 537–548.

Kaplan, R. M. (1985). The controversy related to the use of psychological tests. In B. B. Wolman (Ed.), *Handbook of intelligence: Theories, measurements, and applications* (pp. 465–504). New York: Wiley.

Karmiloff-Smith, A. (1991). Beyond modularity: Innate constraints and developmental change. In S. Carey & R. Gelman (Eds.), *The epigenesis of mind: Essays on biology and cognition* (pp. 171–197). Hillsdale, NJ: Erlbaum.

Kaslow, F. (2004). Death of one's partner: The anticipation and the reality. *Professional Psychology: Research & Practice, 35,* 227–233.

Katz, P., & Bartone, P. (1998). Mourning, ritual and recovery after an airline tragedy. *Omega, 36,* 193–200.

Katz, P. A., & Ksansnak, K. R. (1994). Developmental aspects of gender role flexibility and traditionality in middle childhood and adolescence. *Developmental Psychology, 30,* 272–282.

Katz, R., & Wertz, R. (1997). The efficacy of computer-provided reading treatment for chronic aphasic adults. *Journal of Speech & Hearing Research, 40,* 493–507.

Kaufman, G., & Elder, G. (2003). Grandparenting and age identity. *Journal of Aging Studies, 17,* 269–282.

Kaufman, M. (1997). The teratogenic effects of alcohol following exposure during pregnancy, and its influence on the chromosome constitution of the pre-ovulatory egg. *Alcohol & Alcoholism, 32,* 113–128.

Keech, R. (2002). Ophthalmology. In A. Rudolph, R. Kamei, & K. Overby (Eds.), *Rudolph's fundamental of pediatrics* (3rd ed., pp. 847–862). New York: McGraw-Hill.

Keefe, S. E. (1984). Real and ideal extended familism among Mexican Americans and Anglo Americans: On the meaning of "close" family ties. *Human Organization, 43,* 65–70.

Keen, R. (2003). Representation of objects and events: Why do infants look so smart and toddlers look so dumb? *Current Directions in Psychological Science, 12,* 79–83.

Keene, J., Hope, T., Rogers, P., & Elliman, N. (1998). An investigation of satiety in ageing, dementia, and hyperphagia. *International Journal of Eating Disorders, 23,* 409–418.

Keith, P. M. (1981/1982). Perception of time remaining and distance from death. *Omega, 12,* 307–318.

Kellehear, A., & Lewin, T. (1988/1989). Farewells by the dying: A sociological study. *Omega, 19,* 275–292.

Kelleher, C., Friel, S., Gabhainn, S., & Tay, J. (2003). Socio-demographic predictors of self-rated health in the Republic of Ireland: Findings from the National Survey on Lifestyle, Attitudes, and Nutrition, SLAN. *Social Science & Medicine, 57,* 477–486.

Kelley, M. L., Sanches-Hucles, J., & Walker, R. R. (1993). Correlates of disciplinary practices in working- to middle-class African-American mothers. *Merrill-Palmer Quarterly, 39,* 252–264.

Kemmelmeier, M., Wieczorkowska, G., Erb, H., & Burnstein, E. (2002). Individualism, authoritarianism, and attitudes toward assisted death: Cross-cultural, cross-regional, and experimental evidence. *Journal of Applied Social Psychology, 32,* 60–85.

Kendall-Tackett, K., Williams, L., & Finkelhor, D. (1993). Impact of sexual abuse on children: A review and synthesis of recent empirical studies. *Psychological Bulletin, 113,* 164–180.

Kendler, K., Kessler, R., Walters, E., MacLean, C., Neale, M., Health, A., & Eaves, L. (1995). Stressful life events, genetic liability, and onset of an episode of major depression in women. *American Journal of Psychiatry, 152,* 833–842.

Kennedy, K., Nowak, S., Raghuraman, R., Thomas, J., & Davis, S. (2000). Academic dishonesty and distance learning: Student and faculty views. *College Student Journal, 34,* 309–314.

Kent, L., Doerry, U., Hardy, E., Parmar, R., Gingell, K., Hawai, Z., Kirley, A., Lowe, N., Fitzgerald, M., Gill, M., & Craddock, N. (2002). Evidence that variation at the serotonin transporter gene influences susceptibility to attention deficit hyperactivity disorder (ADHD): Analysis and pooled analysis. *Molecular Psychiatry, 7,* 908–912.

Kercsmar, C. (1998). The respiratory system. In R. Behrman & R. Kliegman (Eds.), *Nelson essentials of pediatrics* (3rd ed). Philadelphia: W. B. Saunders.

Kerns, K., Don, A., Mateer, C., & Streissguth, A. (1997). Cognitive deficits in nonretarded adults with fetal alcohol syndrome. *Journal of Learning Disabilities, 30,* 685–693.

Kerpelman, J., & Schvaneveldt, P. (1999). Young adults' anticipated identity importance of career, marital, and parental roles: Comparisons of men and women with different role balance orientations. *Sex Roles, 41,* 189–217.

Keskinen, E., Ota, H., & Katila, A. (1998). Older drivers fail in intersections: Speed discrepancies between older and younger male drivers. *Accident Analysis & Prevention, 30,* 323–330.

Kessler, R., McGonagle, K., Zhao, S., Nelson, C., Hughes., M., Eshleman, S., Wittchen, H., & Kendler, K. (1994). Lifetime and 12-month prevalence of DSM-III-R psychiatric disorders in the United States: Results from the National Comorbidity Survey. *American Journal of Psychiatry, 51,* 8–19.

Kessler, R. C., Foster, C., Webster, P. S., & House, J. S. (1992). The relationship between age and depressive symptoms in two national surveys. *Psychology & Aging, 7,* 119–126.

Kessler, R. C., Turner, J. B., & House, J. S. (1988). Effects of unemployment on health in a community survey: Main, modifying, and mediating effects. *Journal of Social Issues, 44,* 69–85.

Kesteloot, H., Lesaffre, E., & Joossens, J. V. (1991). Dairy fat, saturated animal fat, and cancer risk. *Preventive Medicine, 20,* 226–236.

Khlat, M., Sermet, C., & Le Pape, A. (2000). Women's health in relation with their family and work roles: France in the early 1990s. *Social Science & Medicine, 50,* 1807–1825.

Kiecolt-Glaser, J. (2000, August). *Friends, lovers, relaxation, and immunity: How behavior modifies health. Cortisol and the language of love: Text analysis of newlyweds' relationship stories.* Paper presented at the annual meeting of the American Psychological Association. Washington, DC.

Kiecolt-Glaser, J. K., & Glaser, R. (1995). Measurement of immune response. In S. Cohen, R. C. Kessler, & L. U. Gordon (Eds.), *Measuring stress: A guide for health and social scientists* (pp. 213–229). New York: Oxford University Press.

Kiecolt-Glaser, J. K., Glaser, R., Suttleworth, E. E., Dyer, C. S., Ogrocki, P., & Speicher, C. E. (1987). Chronic stress and immunity in family caregivers of Alzheimer's disease patients. *Psychosomatic Medicine, 49,* 523–535.

Kilbride, H., Castor, C., Hoffman, E., & Fuger, K. (2000). Thirty-six month outcome of prenatal cocaine exposure for term or near-term infants: Impact of early case management. *Journal of Developmental Pediatrics, 21,* 19–26.

Kilic, C., & Ulusoy, M. (2003). Psychological effects of the November 1999 earthquake in Turkey: An epidemiological study. *Psychiatrica Scandinavica, 108,* 232–238.

Kilpatrick, S. J., & Laros, R. K. (1989). Characteristics of normal labor. *Obstetrics & Gynecology, 74,* 85–87.

Kim, J., Hetherington, E., & Reiss, D. (1999). Associations among family relationships, antisocial peers, and adolescents' externalizing behaviors: Gender and family type differences. *Child Development, 70,* 1209–1230.

Kim, S. (1997). Relationships between young children's day care experience and their attachment relationships with parents and socioemotional behavior problems. *Korean Journal of Child Studies, 18,* 5–18.

Kimm, S., Glynn, N., Kriska, A., Barton, B., Kronsberg, S., Daniels, S., Crawford, P., Sabry, A., & Liu, K. (2002). Decline in physical activity in black girls and white girls during adolescence. *New England Journal of Medicine, 347,* 709–715.

Kinney, D. A. (1993). From "nerds" to "normals": Adolescent identity recovery within a changing social system. *Sociology of Education, 66,* 21–40.

Kinzl, J., Mangweth, B., Traweger, C., & Biebl, W. (1996). Sexual dysfunction in males: Significance of adverse childhood experiences. *Child Abuse & Neglect, 20,* 759–766.

Kirby, P., Biever, J., Martinez, I., & Gomez, J. (2004). Adults returning to school: The impact on family and work. *Journal of Psychology: Interdisciplinary & Applied, 138,* 65–76.

Kirk, S., Gallagher, J., & Anastasiow, N. (1993). *Educating exceptional children* (7th ed.). Boston: Houghton Mifflin.

Kirkcaldy, B., Siefen, G., Surall, D., & Bischoff, R. (2004). Predictors of drug and alcohol abuse among children and adolescents. *Personality & Individual Differences, 36,* 247–265.

Kitson, G. C. (1992). *Portrait of divorce: Adjustment to marital breakdown.* New York: Guilford Press.

Kitzan, L., Ferraro, F., Petros, T., & Ludorf, M. (1999). The role of vocabulary ability during visual word recognition in younger and older adults. *Journal of General Psychology, 126,* 6–16.

Kivett, V. R. (1991). Centrality of the grandfather role among older rural black and white men. *Journals of Gerontology: Social Sciences, 46,* S250–258.

Klaczynski, P., Fauth, J., & Swanger, A. (1998). Adolescent identity: Rational vs. experiential processing, formal operations, and critical thinking beliefs. *Journal of Youth & Adolescence, 27,* 185–207.

Klahr, D. (1992). Information-processing approaches to cognitive development. In M. H. Bernstein & M. E. Lamb (Eds.), *Developmental psychology: An advanced textbook* (3rd ed., pp. 273–335). Hillsdale, NJ: Erlbaum.

Klaiber, E., Broverman, D., Vogel, W., Peterson, L., & Snyder, M. (1997). Relationships of serum estradiol levels, menopausal duration, and mood during hormonal replacement therapy. *Psychoneuroendocrinology, 22,* 549–558.

Klebanov, P. K., Brooks-Gunn, J., Hofferth, S., & Duncan, G. J. (1995, March). *Neighborhood resources, social support and maternal competence.* Paper presented at the biennial meetings of the Society for Research in Child Development, Indianapolis, IN.

Kleemeier, R. W. (1962). Intellectual changes in the senium. *Proceedings of the Social Statistics Section of the American Statistics Association, 1,* 290–295.

Klein, A., & Swartz, S. (1996). *Reading Recovery in California: Program overview.* San Francisco: San Francisco Unified School District.

Klenow, D. J., & Bolin, R. C. (1989/1990). Belief in an afterlife: A national survey. *Omega, 20,* 63–74.

Kletzky, O. A., & Borenstein, R. (1987). Vasomotor instability of the menopause. In D. R. Mishell, Jr. (Ed.), *Menopause: Physiology and pharmacology.* (pp. 53–66). Chicago: Year Book Medical Publishers.

Kliegl, R., Smith, J., & Baltes, P. B. (1989). Testing-the-limits and the study of adult age differences in cognitive plasticity of a mnemonic skill. *Developmental Psychology, 25,* 247–256.

Kliegl, R., Smith, J., & Baltes, P. B. (1990). On the locus and process of magnification of age differences during mnemonic training. *Developmental Psychology, 26,* 894–904.

Kliegman, R. (1998). Fetal and neonatal medicine. In R. Behrman & R. Kliegman (Eds.), *Nelson essentials of pediatrics* (3rd ed., pp. 167–225). Philadelphia: W. B. Saunders.

Kline, D. W., Kline, T. J. B., Fozard, J. L., Kosnik, W., Schieber, F., & Sekuler, R. (1992). Vision, aging, and driving: The problem of older drivers. *Journals of Gerontology: Psychological Sciences, 47,* P27–34.

Kline, D. W., & Scialfa, C. T. (1996). Visual and auditory aging. In J. E. Birren & K. W. Schaie (Eds.), *Handbook of the psychology of aging* (4th ed., pp. 181–203). San Diego, CA: Academic Press.

Kline, G., Stanley, S., Markman, H., & Olmos-Gallo, P. (2004). Timing is everything: Pre-engagement cohabitation and increased risk for poor marital outcomes. *Journal of Family Psychology, 18,* 311–318.

Klonoff-Cohen, H. D., Edelstein, S. L., Lefkowitz, E. S., Srinivasan, I. P., Kaegi, D., Chang, J. C., & Wiley, K. J. (1995). The effect of passive smoking and tobacco exposure through breast milk on sudden infant death syndrome. *Journal of the American Medical Association, 273,* 795–798.

Knox, D. (1998). *The divorced dad's survival book: How to stay connected to your kids.* New York: Insight.

Knox, D., Zusman, M., McGinty, K., & Abowitz, D. (2003). Weddings: Some data on college student perceptions. *College Student Journal, 37,* 197–200.

Kochanek, K., & Martin, J. (2004). *Supplemental analyses of recent trends in infant mortality.* Retrieved April 13, 2004, from http://www.cdc.gov.

Kochanek, K., & Smith, B. (2004). Deaths: Preliminary data for 2002. *National Vital Statistics Report: Volume 52.* Hyattsville, Maryland: National Center for Health Statistics. Retrieved April 13, 2004, from http://www.cdc.gov.

Kochanska, G. (1997a). Multiple pathways to conscience for children with different temperaments: From toddlerhood to age 5. *Developmental Psychology, 33,* 228–240.

Kochanska, G. (1997b). Mutually responsive orientation between mothers and their young: Implications for early socialization. *Child Development, 68,* 94–112.

Kochanska, G., Casey, R., & Fukumoto, A. (1995). Toddlers' sensitivity to standard violations. *Child Development, 66,* 643–656.

Kochanska, G., Murray, K., & Coy, K. (1997). Inhibitory control as a contributor to conscience in childhood: From toddler to early school age. *Child Development, 68,* 263–277.

Kochanska, G., Murray, K., Jacques, T., Koenig, A., Vandegeest, K. (1996). Inhibitory control in young children and its role in emerging internalization. *Child Development, 67,* 490–507.

Kochenderfer, B. J., & Ladd, G. W. (1996). Peer victimization: Cause or consequence of school maladjustment. *Child Development, 67,* 1305–1317.

Kocsis, J. (1998). Geriatric dysthymia. *Journal of Clinical Psychiatry, 59,* 13–15.

Koenig, A., Cicchetti, D., & Rogosch, F. (2004). Moral development: The association between maltreatment and young children's prosocial behaviors and moral transgressions. *Social Development, 13,* 97–106.

Koenig, H., George, L., Hays, J., Larson, D., Cohen, H., & Blazer, D. (1998). The relationship between religious activities and blood pressure in older adults. *International Journal of Psychiatry in Medicine, 28,* 189–213.

Koeppe, R. (1996). Language differentiation in bilingual children: The development of grammatical and pragmatic competence. *Linguistics, 34,* 927–954.

Kohlberg, L. (1964). Development of moral character and moral ideology. In M. L. Hoffman & L. W. Hoffman (Eds.), *Review of child development research, Vol. 1* (pp. 283–332). New York: Russell Sage Foundation.

Kohlberg, L. (1966). A cognitive-developmental analysis of children's sex-role concepts and attitudes. In E. E. Maccoby (Ed.), *The development of sex differences* (pp. 82–172). Stanford, CA: Stanford University Press.

Kohlberg, L. (1976). Moral stages and moralization: The cognitive developmental approach. In T. Lickona (Ed.), *Moral development and behavior: Theory, research, and social issues* (pp. 31–53). New York: Holt.

Kohlberg, L. (1981). *Essays on moral development, Vol. 1: The philosophy of moral development.* New York: Harper & Row.

Kohlberg, L., & Elfenbein, D. (1975). The development of moral judgments concerning capital punishment. *American Journal of Orthopsychiatry, 54,* 614–640.

Kohlberg, L., Levine, C., & Hewer, A. (1983). *Moral stages: A current formulation and a response to critics.* Basel, Switzerland: S. Karger.

Kohlberg, L., & Ullian, D. Z. (1974). Stages in the development of psychosexual concepts and attitudes. In R. C. Friedman, R. M. Richart, & R. L. Vande Wiele (Eds.), *Sex differences in behavior* (pp. 209–222). New York: Wiley.

Kohli, M. (1994). Work and retirement: A comparative perspective. In M. W. Riley, R. L. Kahn, & A. Foner (Eds.), *Age and structural lag* (pp. 80–106). New York: Wiley-Interscience.

Kolata, G. (1996, February 27). New era of robust elderly belies the fears of scientists. *New York Times,* A1, B10.

Kolder, V., Gallagher, J., & Parsons, M. (1987). Court-ordered obstetrical interventions. *New England Journal of Medicine, 316,* 1192–1196.

Koskinen, P., Blum, I., Bisson, S., Phillips, S., et al. (2000). Book access, shared reading, and audio models: The effects of supporting the literacy learning of linguistically diverse students in school and at home. *Journal of Educational Psychology, 92,* 23–36.

Kost, K. (1997). The effects of support on the economic well-being of young fathers. *Families in Society, 78,* 370–382.

Kostanski, M., & Gullone, E. (1999). Dieting and body image in the child's world: Conceptualization and behavior. *Journal of Genetic Psychology, 160,* 488–499.

Kozma, A., Stones, M. J., & Hannah, T. E. (1991). Age, activity, and physical performance: An evaluation of performance models. *Psychology & Aging, 6,* 43–49.

Kozu, J. (1999). Domestic violence in Japan. *American Psychologist, 54,* 50–54.

Krause, N., Ingersoll-Dayton, B., Liang, J., & Sugisawa, H. (1999). Religion, social support, and health among the Japanese elderly. *Journal of Health Behavior & Health Education, 40,* 405–421.

Krause, N., Jay, G., & Liang, J. (1991). Financial strain and psychological well-being among the American and Japanese elderly. *Psychology & Aging, 6,* 170–181.

Kraut, R., Patterson, M., Lundmark, V., Kiesler, S., Mukophadhyay, T., & Schertis, W. (1998). Internet paradox: A social technology that reduces social involvement and psychological well-being? *American Psychologist, 53,* 1017–1031.

Kreijkamp-Kaspers, S., Kok, L., Grobbee, D., de Haan, E., Aleman, A., Lampe, J., & van der Schouw, Y. (2004). Effect of soy protein containing isoflavones on cognitive function, bone mineral density, and plasma lipids in postmenopausal women: A randomized controlled trial. *Journal of the American Medical Association, 292,* 65–74.

Kressley, K., & Huebschmann, M. (2002). The 21st century campus: Gerontological perspectives. *Educational Gerontology, 28,* 835–851.

Kronenberg, F. (1994). Hot flashes: Phenomenology, quality of life, and search for treatment options. *Experimental Gerontology, 29,* 319–336.

Krueger-Lebus, S., & Rauchfleisch, U. (1999). Level of contentment in lesbian partnerships with and without children. *System Familie, 12,* 74–79.

Kübler-Ross, E. (1969). *On death and dying.* New York: Macmillan.

Kübler-Ross, E. (1974). *Questions and answers on death and dying.* New York: Macmillan.

Kuebli, J., Butler, S., & Fivush, R. (1995). Mother-child talk about past emotions: Relationships of maternal language and child gender over time. *Cognition & Emotion, 9,* 265–283.

Kuhl, P. L., & Meltzoff, A. N. (1984). The intermodal representation of speech in infants. *Infant Behavior & Development, 7,* 361–381.

Kuhn, D. (1992). Cognitive development. In M. H. Bornstein & M. E. Lamb (Eds.), *Developmental psychology: An advanced textbook* (3rd ed., pp. 211–272). Hillsdale, NJ: Erlbaum.

Kuhn, D., Kohlberg, L., Languer, J., & Haan, N. (1977). The development of formal operations in logical and moral judgment. *Genetic Psychology Monographs, 95,* 97–188.

Kunkel, S. R., & Applebaum, R. A. (1992). Estimating the prevalence of long-term disability for an aging society. *Journals of Gerontology: Social Sciences, 47,* S253–260.

Kunnen, E., & Steenbeek, H. (1999). Differences in problems of motivation in different special groups. *Child: Care, Health & Development, 25,* 429–446.

Kupersmidt, J. B., Griesler, P. C., DeRosier, M. E., Patterson, C. J., & Davis, P. W. (1995). Childhood aggression and peer relations in the context of family and neighborhood factors. *Child Development, 66,* 360–375.

Kurdek, L. (1997). Relation between neuroticism and dimensions of relationship commitment: evidence from gay, lesbian, and heterosexual couples. *Journal of Family Psychology, 11,* 109–124.

Kurdek, L. (1998). Relationship outcomes and their predictors: longitudinal evidence from heterosexual married, gay cohabiting, and lesbian cohabiting couples. *Journal of Marriage & the Family, 60,* 553–568.

Kurdek, L. (2000). The link between sociotropy/autonomy and dimensions of relationship commitment: Evidence from gay and lesbian couples. *Personal Relationships, 7,* 153–164.

Kurdek, L. A. (1995a). Developmental changes in relationship quality in gay and lesbian cohabiting couples. *Developmental Psychology, 31,* 86–94.

Kurdek, L. A. (2003). Differences between gay and lesbian cohabiting couples. *Journal of Social & Personal Relationships, 20,* 411–436.

Kurdek, L. A., & Fine, M. A. (1994). Family acceptance and family control as predictors of adjustment in young adolescents: Linear, curvilinear, or interactive effects? *Child Development, 65,* 1137–1146.

Kurz, A., Erkinjuntti, T., Small, G., Lilienfeld, S., & Damaraju, C. (2003). Long-term safety and cognitive effects of galantamine in the treatment of probable vascular dementia or Alzheimer's disease with cerebrovascular disease. *European Journal of Neurology, 10,* 633–640.

Kuttler, A., LaGreca, A., & Prinstein, M. (1999). Friendship qualities and social-emotional functioning of adolescents with close, cross-sex friendships. *Journal of Research on Adolescence, 9,* 339–366.

Kyriacou, D., Anglin, D., Taliaferro, E., Stone, S., Tubb, T., Linden, J., Muelleman, R., Barton, E., & Kraus, J. (1999). Risk factors for injury to women from domestic violence. *New England Journal of Medicine, 341,* 1892–1898.

Laakso, M., Vaurio, O., Savolainen, L., Repo, E., Soininen, H., Aronen, H., & Tiihonen, J. (2000). A volumetric MRI study of the hippocampus in type 1 and 2 alcoholism. *Behavioral Brain Research, 109,* 177–186.

Labouvie-Vief, G. (1980). Beyond formal operations: Uses and limits of pure logic in life-span development. *Human Development, 23,* 141–161.

Labouvie-Vief, G. (1990). Modes of knowledge and the organization of development. In M. L. Commons, C. Armon, L. Kohlberg, F. A. Richards, T. A. Grotzer, & J. D. Sinnott (Eds.), *Adult development: Vol. 2. Models and methods in the study of adolescent and adult thought* (pp. 43–62). New York: Praeger.

Lacey, J., Mink, P., Lubin, J., Sherman, M., Troisi, R., Hartge, P., Schatzkin, A., & Schairer, C. (2002). Menopausal hormone replacement therapy and risk of ovarian cancer. *Journal of the American Medical Association, 288,* 334–341.

Lachman, M., & Weaver, S. (1998). Sociodemographic variations in the sense of control by domain: Findings from the MacArthur studies of midlife. *Psychology & Aging, 13,* 553–562.

Ladd, G., & Troop-Gordon, W. (2003). The role of chronic peer difficulties in the development of children's psychological adjustment problems. *Child Development, 74,* 1344–1367.

La Freniere, P., Strayer, F. F., & Gauthier, R. (1984). The emergence of same-sex affiliative preferences among preschool peers. A developmental/ethological perspective. *Child Development, 55,* 1958–1965.

Lafuente, M., Grifol, R., Segarra, J., Soriano, J., Gorba, M., & Montesinos, A. (1997). Effects of the Firstart method of prenatal stimulation on psychomotor development: The first six months. *Pre- & Peri-Natal Psychology Journal, 11,* 151–162.

Laguna, K., & Babcock, R. (1997). Computer anxiety in young and older adults: Implications for human-computer interactions in older populations. *Computers in Human Behavior, 13,* 317–326.

Laird, R., Pettit, G., Dodge, K., & Bates, J. (1999). Best friendships, group relationships, and antisocial behavior in early adolescence. *Journal of Early Adolescence, 19,* 413–437.

Lakatos, K., Nemoda, Z., Birkas, E., Ronai, Z., Kovacs, E., Ney, K., Toth, I., Sasvari-Szekely, M., & Gervai, J. (2003). Association of D4 dopamine receptor gene and serotonin transporter promoter polymorphisms with infants' response to novelty. *Molecular Psychiatry, 8,* 90–97.

Lakatta, E. G. (1990). Heart and circulation. In E. L. Schneider & J. W. Rowe (Eds.), *Handbook of the biology of aging* (3rd ed., pp. 181–217). San Diego, CA: Academic Press.

Lam, R., Pacala, J., & Smith, S. (1997). Factors related to depressive symptoms in an elderly Chinese American sample. *Gerontologist, 17,* 57–70.

Lamb, M. (1997). *The role of father in child development* (3rd ed.). New York: Wiley.

Lamb, M. E. (1981). The development of father-infant relationships. In M. E. Lamb (Ed.), *The role of the father in child development* (2nd ed., pp. 459–488). New York: Wiley.

Lamb, M. E., Sternberg, K. J., & Prodromidis, M. (1992). Nonmaternal care and the security of infant-mother attachment: A reanalysis of the data. *Infant Behavior & Development, 15,* 71–83.

Lamborn, S. D., Mounts, N. S., Steinberg, L., & Dornbusch, S. M. (1991). Patterns of competence and adjustment among adolescents from authoritative, authoritarian, indulgent, and neglectful families. *Child Development, 62,* 1049–1065.

Lampard, R., & Peggs, K. (1999). Repartnering: The relevance of parenthood and gender to cohabitation and remarriage among the formerly married. *British Journal of Sociology, 50,* 443–465.

Landolt, M., & Dutton, D. (1997). Power and personality: An analysis of gay male intimate abuse. *Sex Roles, 37,* 335–359.

Landry, S., Smith, K., Miller-Loncar, C., & Swank, P. (1997). Predicting cognitive-linguistic and social growth curves from early maternal behaviors in children at varying degrees of biologic risk. *Developmental Psychology, 33,* 1040–1053.

Landry, S., Smith, K., Swank, P., Assel, M., & Vellet, S. (2001). Does early responsive parenting have a special importance for children's development or is consistency across early childhood necessary? *Developmental Psychology, 37,* 387–403.

Landry, S. H., Garner, P. W., Swank, P. R., & Baldwin, C. D. (1996). Effects of maternal scaffolding during joint toy play with preterm and full-term infants. *Merrill-Palmer Quarterly, 42,* 177–199.

Langlois, J. H., Ritter, J. M., Roggman, L. A., & Vaughn, L. S. (1991). Facial diversity and infant preferences for attractive faces. *Developmental Psychology, 27,* 79–84.

Langlois, J. H., Roggman, L. A., Casey, R. J., Ritter, J. M., Rieser-Danner, L. A., & Jenkins, V. Y. (1987). Infant preferences for attractive faces: Rudiments of a stereotype? *Developmental Psychology, 23,* 363–369.

Langlois, J. H., Roggman, L. A., & Rieser-Danner, L. A. (1990). Infants' differential social responses to attractive and unattractive faces. *Developmental Psychology, 26,* 153–159.

Lansdown, R., & Benjamin, G. (1985). The development of the concept of death in children aged 5–9 years. *Child: Care, Health & Development, 11,* 13–30.

Lapsley, D. K. (1993). Toward an integrated theory of adolescent ego development: The "new look" at adolescent egocentrism. *American Journal of Orthopsychiatry, 63,* 562–571.

Lapsley, D. K., & Murphy, M. N. (1985). Another look at the theoretical assumptions of adolescent egocentrism. *Developmental Review, 5,* 201–217.

Larson, R. (2000). Toward a psychology of positive youth development. *American Psychologist, 55,* 170–183.

Larson, R., Mannell, R., & Zuzanek, J. (1986). Daily well-being of older adults with friends and family. *Psychology & Aging, 1,* 117–126.

Larson, R., & Verma, S. (1999). How children and adolescents spend time across the world: Work, play, and developmental opportunities. *Psychological Bulletin, 125,* 701–736.

LaSala, M. (2001). Monogamous or not: Understanding and counseling gay male couples. *Families in Society, 82,* 605–611.

Laso, F., Iglesias-Osma, C., Ciudad, J., Lopez, A., Pastor, I., & Orfao, A. (1999). Chronic alcoholism is associated with an imbalanced production of the Th-a/Th-2 cytokines by peripheral blood T cells. *Alcoholism: Clinical & Experimental Research, 23,* 1306–1311.

Lau, A., Uba, A., & Lehman, D. (2002). Infectious diseases. In A. Rudolph, R. Kamei, & K. Overby (Eds.), *Rudolph's fundamental of pediatrics* (3rd ed., pp. 289–399). New York: McGraw-Hill.

Laub, J. H., & Sampson, R. J. (1995). The long-term effect of punitive discipline. In J. McCord (Ed.), *Coercion and punishment in long-term perspectives* (pp. 247–258). Cambridge, England: Cambridge University Press.

Laumann, E. O., Gagnon, J. H., Michael, R. T., & Michaels, S. (1994). *The social organization of sexuality: Sexual practices in the United States.* Chicago: University of Chicago Press.

Laursen, B. (1995). Conflict and social interaction in adolescent relationships. *Journal of Research on Adolescence, 5,* 55–70.

Lawlor, S., & Choi, P. (1998). The generation gap in menstrual cycle attributions. *British Journal of Health Psychology, 3,* 257–263.

Lawrence, R. H., Bennett, J. M., & Markides, K. S. (1992). Perceived intergenerational solidarity and psychological distress among older Mexican Americans. *Journals of Gerontology: Social Sciences, 47,* S55–65.

Lawrence, V., Houghton, S., Douglas, G., Durkin, K., Whiting, K., & Tannock, R. (2004). Children with ADHD: Neuropsychological testing and real-world activities. *Journal of Attention Disorders, 7,* 137–149.

Lawson, E., & Thompson, A. (1996). Black men's perceptions of divorce-related stressors and strategies for coping with divorce. *Journal of Family Issues, 17,* 249–273.

Lawton, L., Silverstein, M., & Bengtson, V. (1994). Affection, social contact, and geographic distance between adult children and their parents. *Journal of Marriage & the Family, 56,* 57–68.

Lawton, M. P. (1985). Housing and living environments of older people. In R. H. Binstock & E. Shanas (Eds.), *Aging and the social sciences* (2nd ed., pp. 450–478). New York: Van Nostrand Reinhold.

Lawton, M. P. (1990). Residential environment and self-directedness among older people. *American Psychologist, 45,* 638–640.

Layton, L., Deeny, K., Tall, G., & Upton, G. (1996). Researching and promoting phonological awareness in the nursery class. *Journal of Research in Reading, 19,* 1–13.

Leaper, C. (1991). Influence and involvement in children's discourse: Age, gender, and partner effects. *Child Development, 62,* 797–811.

Lederer, J. (2000). Reciprocal teaching of social studies in inclusive elementary classrooms. *Journal of Learning Disabilities, 33,* 91–106.

Lederman, R., & Mian, T. (2003). The Parent-Adolescent Relationship Education (PARE) program: A curriculum for prevention of STDs and pregnancy in middle school youth. *Behavioral Medicine, 29,* 33–41.

Lee, G. R., Dwyer, J. W., & Coward, R. T. (1993). Gender differences in parent care: Demographic factors and same-gender preferences. *Journals of Gerontology: Social Sciences, 48,* S9–16.

Lee, G. R., Seccombe, K., & Shehan, C. L. (1991). Marital status and personal happiness: An analysis of trend data. *Journal of Marriage & the Family, 53,* 839–844.

Lee, I., Manson, J. E., Hennekens, C. H., & Paffenbarger, R. S., Jr. (1993). Body weight and mortality; A 27-year follow-up of middle-aged men. *Journal of the American Medical Association, 270,* 2823–2828.

Lee, I.-M., Hsieh, C., & Paffenbarger, R. S. (1995). Exercise intensity and longevity in men. *Journal of the American Medical Association, 273,* 1179–1184.

Lee, J. (1996). *What your doctor may not tell you about menopause.* New York: Warner Books.

Lee, M., Law, C., & Tam, K. (1999). Parenthood and life satisfaction: A comparison of single and dual-parent families in Hong Kong. *International Social Work, 42,* 139–162.

Lee, S. & Keith, P. (1999). The transition to motherhood of Korean women. *Journal of Comparative Family Studies, 30,* 453–470.

Lee, V. E., Burkham, D. T., Zimiles, H., & Ladewski, B. (1994). Family structure and its effect on behavioral and emotional problems in young adolescents. *Journal of Research on Adolescence, 4,* 405–437.

Leff, M., Moolchan, E., Cookus, B., Spurgeon, L., Evans, L., London, E., Kimes, A., Schroeder, J., & Ernst, M. (2003). Predictors of smoking initiation among at risk youth: A controlled study. *Journal of Child & Adolescent Substance Abuse, 13,* 59–76.

Legerstee, M., Pomerleau, A., Malcuit, G., & Feider, H. (1987). The development of infants' responses to people and a doll: Implications for research in communication. *Infant Behavior & Development, 10,* 81–95.

Lehman, D., & Nisbett, R. (1990). A longitudinal study of the effects of undergraduate training on reasoning. *Developmental Psychology, 26,* 952–960.

Lehman, H. C. (1953). *Age and achievement.* Princeton, NJ: Princeton University Press.

Lehr, U. (1982). Hat die Grosfamilie heute noch eine Chance? [Does the extended family have a chance these days?]. *Der Deutsche Artz, 18 Sonderdruck.*

Leigh, G. K. (1982). Kinship interaction over the family life span. *Journal of Marriage & the Family, 44,* 197–208.

Lemaire, P., & Lecacheur, M. (2004). Five-rule effects in young and older adults' arithmetic: Further evidence for age-related differences in strategy selection. *Current Psychology Letters: Behavior, Brain, & Cognition, 12.* Retrieved from http://cpl.revues.org/document412.html.

Lenhardt, A., & McCourt, B. (2000). Adolescent unresolved grief in response to the death of a mother. *Professional School Counseling, 3,* 189–196.

Leo, R., Narayan, D., Sherry, C., Michalek, C., et al. (1997). Geropsychiatric consultation for African-American and Caucasian patients. *General Hospital Psychiatry, 19,* 216–222.

Leong, F., Austin, J., Sekaran, U., & Komarraju, M. (1998). An evaluation of the cross-cultural validity of Holland's theory: Career choices by workers in India. *Journal of Vocational Behavior, 52,* 441–455.

Lester, D. (1990). The Collett-Lester fear of death scale: The original version and a revision. *Death Studies, 14,* 451–468.

Leve, L. D., & Fagot, B. I. (1995, April). *The influence of attachment style and parenting behavior on children's prosocial behavior with peers.* Paper presented at the biennial meetings of the Society for Research in Child Development, Indianapolis, IN.

Levenson, R. W., Carstensen, L. L., & Gottman, J. M. (1993). Long-term marriage: Age, gender, and satisfaction. *Psychology & Aging, 8,* 301–313.

Leviatan, U. (1999). Contribution of social arrangements to the attainment of successful aging: The experience of the Israeli kibbutz. *Journals of Gerontology, Series B: Psychological Sciences & Social Sciences, 54B,* P205–P213.

Levine, J., Pollack, H., & Comfort, M. (2001). Academic and behavioral outcomes among the children of young mothers. *Journal of Marriage & Family, 63,* 355–369.

Levine, L., & Bluck, S. (1997). Experienced and remembered emotional intensity in older adults. *Psychology & Aging, 12,* 514–523.

Levinson, D. J. (1978). *The seasons of a man's life.* New York: Knopf.

Levinson, D. J. (1986). A conception of adult development. *American Psychologist, 41,* 3–13.

Levinson, D. J. (1990). A theory of life structure development in adulthood. In C. N. Alexander & E. J. Langer (Eds.), *Higher stages of human development* (pp. 35–54). New York: Oxford University Press.

Levitt, M. J., Guacci-Franco, N., & Levitt, J. L. (1993). Convoys of social support in childhood and early adolescence: Structure and function. *Developmental Psychology, 29,* 811–818.

Levitt, M. J., Weber, R. A., & Guacci, N. (1993). Convoys of social support: An intergenerational analysis. *Psychology & Aging, 8,* 323–326.

Levorato, M., & Donati, V. (1999). Conceptual and lexical knowledge of shame in Italian children and adolescents. *International Journal of Behavioral Development, 23,* 873–898.

Levy, G. D., & Fivush, R. (1993). Scripts and gender: A new approach for examining gender-role development. *Developmental Review, 13,* 126–146.

Levy, L. H., Martinkowski, K. S., & Derby, J. F. (1994). Differences in patterns of adaptation in conjugal bereavement: Their sources and potential significance. *Omega, 29,* 71–87.

Levy-Shiff, R., Vakil, E., Dimitrovsky, L., Abramovitz, M., Shahar, N., Har-Even, D., Gross, S., Lerman, M., Levy, I., Sirota, L., & Fish, B. (1998). Medical, cognitive, emotional, and behavioral outcomes in school-age children conceived by in-vitro fertilization. *Journal of Clinical Child Psychology, 27,* 320–329.

Lewald, J. (2004). Gender-specific hemispheric asymmetry in auditory space perception. *Cognitive Brain Research, 19,* 92–99.

Lewis, C., & Lamb, M. E. Fathers' influences on children's development: The evidence from two-parent families. *European Journal of Psychology of Education, 18,* 211–228.

Lewis, C. C. (1981). How adolescents approach decisions: Changes over grades seven to twelve and policy implications. *Child Development, 52,* 538–544.

Lewis, J., Malow, R., & Ireland, S. (1997). HIV/AIDS in heterosexual college students: A review of a decade of literature. *Journal of American College Health, 45,* 147–158.

Lewis, M. (1990). Social knowledge and social development. *Merrill-Palmer Quarterly, 36,* 93–116.

Lewis, M. (1991). Ways of knowing: Objective self-awareness of consciousness. *Developmental Review, 11,* 231–243.

Lewis, M., Allesandri, S. M., & Sullivan, M. W. (1992). Differences in shame and pride as a function of children's gender and task difficulty. *Child Development, 63,* 630–638.

Lewis, M., & Brooks, J. (1978). Self-knowledge and emotional development. In M. Lewis & L. A. Rosenblum (Eds.), *The development of affect* (pp. 205–226). New York: Plenum.

Lewis, M., Sullivan, M. W., Stanger, C., & Weiss, M. (1989). Self development and self-conscious emotions. *Child Development, 60,* 146–156.

Lewis, M. D. (1993). Early socioemotional predictors of cognitive competence at 4 years. *Developmental Psychology, 29,* 1036–1045.

Li, L., & Seltzer, M. (2003). Parent care, intergenerational relationship quality, and mental health of adult daughters. *Research on Aging, 25,* 484–504.

Li, S., Lindenberger, B., Aschersleben, G., Prinz, W., & Baltes, P. (2004). Transformations in the couplings among intellectual abilities and constituent cognitive processes across the life span. *Psychological Science, 15,* 155–163.

Li, S., Lindenberger, U., Hommel, B., Aschersleben, G., Prinz, W., & Baltes, P. (2004). Transformations in the couplings among intellectual abilities and constituent cognitive processes across the life span. *Psychological Science, 15,* 155–163.

Lickona, T. (1978). Moral development and moral education. In J. M. Gallagher & J. J. A. Easley (Eds.), *Knowledge and development, Vol. 2* (pp. 21–74). New York: Plenum.

Lickona, T. (1983). *Raising good children.* New York: Bantam Books.

Lieberman, M., Doyle, A., & Markiewicz, D. (1995, March). *Attachment to mother and father: Links to peer relations in children.* Paper presented at the biennial meetings of the Society for Research in Child Development, Indianapolis, IN.

Lieberman, M., Doyle, A., & Markiewicz, D. (1999). Developmental patterns in security of attachment to mother and father in late childhood and early adolescence: Associations with peer relations. *Child Development, 70,* 202–213.

Lieberman, M. A. (1965). Psychological correlates of impending death: Some preliminary observations. *Journal of Gerontology, 20,* 182–190.

Lieberman, M. A., & Coplan, A. S. (1970). Distance from death as a variable in the study of aging. *Developmental Psychology, 2,* 71–84.

Liem, R., & Liem, J. H. (1988). Psychological effects of unemployment on workers and their families. *Journal of Social Issues, 44,* 87–105.

Light, L. L. (1991). Memory and aging: Four hypotheses in search of data. *Annual Review of Psychology, 42,* 333–376.

Lillard, A. (1998). Ethnopsychologies: Cultural variations in theories of mind. *Psychological Bulletin, 123,* 3–32.

Lillard, A. S., & Flavell, J. H. (1992). Young children's understanding of different mental states. *Developmental Psychology, 28,* 626–634.

Lim, K. O., Zipursky, R. B., Watts, M. C., & Pfefferbaum, A. (1992). Decreased gray matter in normal aging: An in vivo magnetic resonance study. *Journals of Gerontology: Biological Sciences, 47,* B26–30.

Lim, V. (2003). An empirical study of older workers' attitudes towards the retirement experience. *Employee Relations, 25,* 330–346.

Lima, S. D., Hale, S., & Myerson, J. (1991). How general is general slowing? Evidence from the lexical domain. *Psychology & Aging, 6,* 416–425.

Lin, A. (2003). Factors related to attitudes toward death among American and Chinese older adults. *Omega, 47,* 3–23.

Lin, C., Hsiao, C., & Chen, W. (1999). Development of sustained attention assessed using the Continuous Performance Test among children 6–15 years of age. *Journal of Abnormal Child Psychology, 27,* 403–412.

Lincourt, A., Rybash, J., & Hoyer, W. (1998). Aging, working memory, and the development of instance-based retrieval. *Brain & Cognition, 37,* 100–102.

Lindahl, K., Clements, M., & Markman, H. (1997). Predicting marital and parent functioning in dyads and triads: A longitudinal investigation of marital processes. *Journal of Family Psychology, 11,* 139–151.

Lindgren, C., Connelly, C., & Gaspar, H. (1999). Grief in spouse and children caregivers of dementia patients. *Western Journal of Nursing Research, 21,* 521–537.

Lindo, G., & Nordholm, L. (1999). Adaptation strategies, well-being, and activities of daily living among people with low vision. *Journal of Visual Impairment & Blindness, 93,* 434–446.

Lindsay, D. S., & Read, J. D. (1994). Psychotherapy and memory of childhood sexual abuse: A cognitive perspective. *Applied Cognitive Psychology, 8,* 281–338.

Lindsay, R. (1985). The aging skeleton. In M. R. Haug, A. B. Ford, & M. Sheafor (Eds.), *The physical and mental health of aged women* (pp. 65–82). New York: Springer.

Lindstrom, T. (1997). Immunity and somatic health in bereavement. A prospective study of 39 Norwegian widows. *Omega, 35,* 231–241.

Lineweaver, T., & Hertzog, C. (1998). Adults' efficacy and control beliefs regarding memory and aging: Separating general from personal beliefs. *Aging, Neuropsychology, & Cognition, 5,* 264–296.

Linnet, K., Dalsgaard, S., Obel, C., Wisborg, K., Henriksen, T., Rodriquez, A., Kotimaa, A., Moilanen, I., Thomsen, P., Olsen, J., & Jarvelin, M. (2003). Maternal lifestyle factors in pregnancy risk of attention deficit hyperactivity disorder and associated behaviors: Review of the current evidence. *American Journal of Psychiatry, 160,* 1028–1040.

Lissner, L., Bengtsson, C., Björkelund, C., & Wedel, H. (1996). Physical activity levels and changes in relation to longevity: A prospective study of Swedish women. *American Journal of Epidemiology, 143,* 54–62.

Litwak, E., & Longino, C. F., Jr. (1987). Migration patterns among the elderly: A developmental perspective. *The Gerontologist, 27,* 266–272.

Livesley, W. J., & Bromley, D. B. (1973). *Person perception in childhood and adolescence.* London: Wiley.

Lobel, T., Slone, M., & Winch, G. (1997). Masculinity, popularity, and self-esteem among Israeli preadolescent girls. *Sex Roles, 36,* 395–408.

Loeb, S., Fuller, B., Kagan, S., & Carrol, B. (2004). Child care in poor communities: Early learning effects of type, quality, and stability. *Child Development, 75,* 47–65.

Loehlin, J. C., Horn, J. M., & Willerman, L. (1994). Differential inheritance of mental abilities in the Texas Adoption Project. *Intelligence, 19,* 325–336.

Lohan, J., & Murphy, S. (2001/2002). Parents' perceptions of adolescent sibling grief responses after an adolescent or young adult child's sudden, violent death. *Omega, 44,* 195–213.

Longino, C. F., Jr. (1990). Geographical distribution and migration. In R. H. Binstock & L. K. George (Eds.), *Handbook of aging and the social sciences* (3rd ed., pp. 45–63). San Diego, CA: Academic Press.

Longino, C. F., Jr., Jackson, D. J., Zimmerman, R. S., & Bradsher, J. E. (1991). The second move: Health and geographic mobility. *Journals of Gerontology: Social Sciences, 46,* S218–224.

Loonsbury, J. (1992). Interdisciplinary instruction: A mandate for the nineties. In J. Loonsbury (Ed.), *Connecting the curriculum through interdisciplinary instruction.* Columbus, OH: National Middle School Association.

Lopez-Alarcon, M., Villapando, S., & Fajardo, A. (1997). Breast-feeding lowers the frequency and duration of acute respiratory infection and diarrhea in infants under six months of age. *Journal of Nutrition, 127,* 436–443.

Love, J., Harrison, L., Sagi-Schwartz, A., van IJzendoorn, M., Ross, C., Ungerer, J., Raikes, H., Brady-Smith, C., Boller, K., Brooks-Gunn, J., Constantine, J., Kisker, E., Paulsell, D., & Chazan-Cohen, R. (2003). Child care quality matters: How conclusions may vary with context. *Child Development, 74,* 1021–1033.

Lowenstein, D., Acevedo, A., Czaja, S., & Duara, R. (2004). Cognitive rehabilitation of mildly impaired Alzheimer disease patients on cholinesterase inhibitors. *American Journal of Geriatric Psychiatry, 12,* 395–402.

Lubinski, D., & Benbow, C. P. (1992). Gender differences in abilities and preferences among the gifted: Implications for the math-science pipeline. *Current Directions in Psychological Science, 1,* 61–66.

Lundh, W., & Gyllang, C. (1993). Use of the Edinburgh Postnatal Depression Scale in some Swedish child health care centres. *Scandinavian Journal of Caring Sciences, 7,* 149–154.

Luster, T., Boger, R., & Hannan, K. (1993). Infant affect and home environment. *Journal of Marriage & the Family, 55,* 651–661.

Luster, T., & McAdoo, H. (1996). Family and child influences on educational attainment: A secondary analysis of the High/Scope Perry Preschool data. *Developmental Psychology, 32,* 26–39.

Luster, T., & McAdoo, H. P. (1995). Factors related to self-esteem among African American youths: A secondary analysis of the High/Scope Perry Preschool data. *Journal of Research on Adolescence, 5,* 451–467.

Lutfey, K., & Maynard, D. (1998). Bad news in oncology: How physician and patient talk about death and dying without using those words. *Social Psychology Quarterly, 61,* 321–341.

Luthar, S. S., & Zigler, E. (1992). Intelligence and social competence among high-risk adolescents. *Development & Psychopathology, 4,* 287–299.

Lyons, N. P. (1983). Two perspectives: On self, relationships, and morality. *Harvard Educational Review, 53,* 125–145.

Lytle, M., Bilt, J., Pandav, R., Dodge, H., & Ganguli, M. (2004). Exercise level and cognitive decline: The MoVIES project. *Alzheimer Disease & Associated Disorders, 18,* 57–64.

Lytton, H., & Romney, D. M. (1991). Parents' differential socialization of boys and girls: A meta-analysis. *Psychological Bulletin, 109,* 267–296.

Ma, H. (2003). The relation of moral orientation and moral judgment to prosocial and antisocial behaviour of Chinese adolescents. *International Journal of Psychology, 38,* 101–111.

Ma, H., Shek, D., Cheung, P., & Oi Bun Lam, C. (2000). Parental, peer and teacher influences on the social behavior of Hong Kong Chinese adolescents. *Journal of Genetic Psychology, 161,* 65–78.

Maas, H. S., & Kuypers, J. A. (1974). *From thirty to seventy.* San Francisco: Jossey-Bass.

Maccoby, E., & Jacklin, C. (1974). *The psychology of sex differences.* Stanford, CA: Stanford University Press.

Maccoby, E., & Lewis, C. (2003). Less day care or different day care? *Child Development, 74,* 1069–1075.

Maccoby, E. E. (1980). *Social development: Psychological growth and the parent-child relationship.* New York: Harcourt Brace Jovanovich.

Maccoby, E. E. (1984). Middle childhood in the context of the family. In W. A. Collins (Ed.), *Development during middle childhood: The years from six to twelve* (pp. 184–239). Washington, DC: National Academy Press.

Maccoby, E. E. (1988). Gender as a social category. *Developmental Psychology, 24,* 755–765.

Maccoby, E. E. (1990). Gender and relationships: A developmental account. *American Psychologist, 45,* 513–520.

Maccoby, E. E. (1995). The two sexes and their social systems. In P. Moen, G. H. Elder, Jr., & K. Lüscher (Eds.), *Examining lives in context: Perspectives on the ecology of human development* (pp. 347–364). Washington, DC: American Psychological Association.

Maccoby, E. E., & Jacklin, C. N. (1987). Gender segregation in childhood. In H. W. Reese (Ed.), *Advances in child development and behavior, Vol. 20* (pp. 239–288). Orlando, FL: Academic Press.

Maccoby, E. E., & Martin, J. A. (1983). Socialization in the context of the family: Parent-child interaction. In E. M. Hetherington (Ed.), *Handbook of child psychology: Socialization, personality, & social development, Vol. 4* (pp. 1–102). New York: Wiley.

MacDonald, S., Hultsch, D., Strauss, E., & Dixon, R. (2003). Age-related slowing of digit symbol substitution revisited: What do longitudinal age changes reflect? *Journals of Gerontology, Series B: Psychological Sciences & Social Sciences, 58B,* P187–P194.

MacDorman, M., & Atkinson, J. (1999, July 30). Infant mortality statistics from the 1997 period. Linked birth/infant death data set. *National Vital Statistics Reports, 47* (23), 1–24.

MacIver, D. J., Reuman, D. A., & Main, S. R. (1995). Social structuring of the school: Studying what is, illuminating what could be. *Annual Review of Psychology, 46,* 375–400.

Macrae, C., & Bodenhausen, G. (2000). Social cognition: Thinking categorically about others. *Annual Review of Psychology, 51,* 93–120.

MacRae, H. (1992). Fictive kin as a component of the social networks of older people. *Research on Aging, 14,* 226–247.

Madan-Swain, A., Brown, R., Foster, M., Verga, R., et al. (2000). Identity in adolescent survivors of childhood cancer. *Journal of Pediatric Psychology, 25,* 105–115.

Madden, D. J. (1992). Four to ten milliseconds per year: Age-related slowing of visual word identification. *Journals of Gerontology: Psychological Sciences, 47,* P59–68.

Madison, C., Johnson, J., Seikel, J., Arnold, M., & Schultheis, L. (1998). Comparative study of the phonology of preschool children prenatally exposed to cocaine and multiple drugs and non-exposed children. *Journal of Communication Disorders, 31,* 231–244.

Magarey, A., Daniels, l., Boulton, T., & Cockington, R. (2003). Predicting obesity in early adulthood from childhood and parental obesity. *International Journal of Obesity & Related Metabolic Disorders, 27,* 505–513.

Maguire, M., & Dunn, J. (1997). Friendships in early childhood and social understanding. *International Journal of Behavioral Development, 21,* 669–686.

Maier, S. F., Watkins, L. R., & Fleshner, M. (1994). The interface between behavior, brain, and immunity. *American Psychologist, 49,* 1004–1017.

Main, M., & Hesse, E. (1990). Parents' unresolved traumatic experiences are related to infant disorganized attachment status: Is frightened and/or frightening parental behavior the linking mechanism? In M. T. Greenberg, D. Cicchetti, & E. M. Cummings (Eds.), *Attachment in the preschool years: Theory, research, and intervention* (pp. 161–182). Chicago: University of Chicago Press.

Main, M., & Solomon, J. (1990). Procedures for identifying infants as disorganized/disoriented during the Ainsworth Strange Situation. In M. T. Greenberg, D. Cicchetti, & E. M. Cummings (Eds.), *Attachment in the preschool years: Theory, research, and intervention* (pp. 121–160). Chicago: University of Chicago Press.

Mainemer, H., Gilman, L., & Ames, E. (1998). Parenting stress in families adopting children from Romanian orphanages. *Journal of Family Issues, 19,* 164–180.

Maitel, S., Dromi, E., Sagi, A., & Bornstein, M. (2000). The Hebrew Communicative Development Inventory: Language-specific properties and cross-linguistic generalizations. *Journal of Child Language, 27,* 43–67.

Maki, P., Veijola, J., Rantakallio, P., Jokelainen, J., Jones, P., & Isohanni, M. (2004). Schizophrenia in the offspring of antenatally depressed mothers: A 31-year follow-up of the Northern Finland 1966 Birth Cohort. *Schizophrenia Research, 66,* 79–81.

Malabonga, V., & Pasnak, R. (2002). Hierarchical categorization by bilingual Latino children: Does a basic-level bias exist? *Genetic, Social, & General Psychology Monographs, 128,* 409–441.

Malina, R. M. (1982). Motor development in the early years. In S. G. Moore & C. R. Cooper (Eds.), *The young child: Reviews of research, Vol. 3* (pp. 211–232). Washington, DC: National Association for the Education of Young Children.

Malina, R. M. (1990). Physical growth and performance during the transition years. In R. Montemayor, G. R. Adams, & T. P. Gullotta (Eds.), *From childhood to adolescence: A transitional period?* (pp. 41–62). Newbury Park, CA: Sage.

Malinosky-Rummell, R., & Hansen, D. (1993). Long-term consequences of childhood physical abuse. *Psychological Bulletin, 114,* 68–79.

Malkinson, R., & Bar-Tur, L., (1999). The aging of grief in Israel: A perspective of bereaved parents. *Death Studies, 23,* 413–431.

Mallet, P., Apostolidis, T., & Paty, B. (1997). The development of gender schemata about heterosexual and homosexual others during adolescence. *Journal of General Psychology, 124,* 91–104.

Malo, J., & Tremblay, R. (1997). The impact of parental alcoholism and maternal social position on boys' school adjustment, pubertal maturation and sexual behavior: A test of two competing hypotheses. *Journal of Child Psychology & Psychiatry & Allied Disciplines, 38,* 187–197.

Manson, J., Greenland, P., LaCroix, A., Stefanick, M., Mouton, C., Oberman, A., Perri, M., Sheps, D., Pettinger, M., & Siscovick, D. (2002). Walking compared with vigorous exercise for the prevention of cardiovascular events in women. *New England Journal of Medicine, 347,* 716–725.

Manson, J. E., Willett, W. C., Stampfer, M. J., Colditz, G. A., Hunter, D. J., Hankinson, S. E., Hennekens, C. H., & Speizer, F. E. (1995). Body weight and mortality among women. *New England Journal of Medicine, 333,* 677–685.

Manton, K. G., Stallard, E., & Liu, K. (1993). Forecasts of active life expectancy: Policy and fiscal implications. *Journals of Gerontology, 48* (Special Issue), 11–26.

Mäntylä, T. (1994). Remembering to remember: Adult age differences in prospective memory. *Journals of Gerontology: Psychological Sciences, 49,* P276–282.

Mao, H. (2003). The relationship between voluntary employer changes and perceived job stress in Taiwan. *International Journal of Stress Management, 10,* 75–85.

Maratsos, M. (1983). Some current issues in the study of the acquisition of grammar. In J. H. Flavell & E. M. Markman (Eds.), *Handbook of child psychology: Cognitive development* (pp. 707–786). New York: Wiley.

Maratsos, M. (1998). The acquisition of grammar. In W. Damon (Ed.), *Handbook of child psychology, Vol. 2: Cognition, perception, and language* (5th ed., pp. 421–466). New York: Wiley.

Maratsos, M. (2000). More overregularizations after all: New data and discussion of Marcus, Pinker, Ullman, Hollander, Rosen, & Xu. *Journal of Child Language, 27,* 183–212.

March of Dimes. (2004). *Environmental risks and pregnancy.* Retrieved September, 21, 2004, from http://www.marchofdimes.com/professionals/681_9146.asp.

Marcia, J. (2002). Identity and psychosocial development in adulthood. *Identity, 2,* 7–28.

Marcia, J. E. (1966). Development and validation of ego identity status. *Journal of Personality & Social Psychology, 3,* 551–558.

Marcia, J. E. (1980). Identity in adolescence. In J. Adelson (Ed.), *Handbook of adolescent psychology* (pp. 159–187). New York: Wiley.

Marcovitch, S., Goldberg, S., Gold, A., & Washington, J. (1997). Determinants of behavioural problems in Romanian children adopted in Ontario. *International Journal of Behavioral Development, 20,* 17–31.

Marcus, D. E., & Overton, W. F. (1978). The development of cognitive gender constancy and sex role preferences. *Child Development, 49,* 434–444.

Marcus, R. F. (1986). Naturalistic observation of cooperation, helping, and sharing and their association with empathy and affect. In C. Zahn-Waxler, E. M. Cummings, & R. Iannotti (Eds.), *Altruism and aggression: Biological and social origins* (pp. 256–279). Cambridge, England: Cambridge University Press.

Marean, G. C., Werner, L. A., & Kuhl, P. K. (1992). Vowel categorization by very young infants. *Developmental Psychology, 28,* 396–405.

Margolin, G., & Gordis, E. (2000). The effects of family and community violence on children. *Annual Review of Psychology, 51,* 445–479.

Markey, C., Markey, P., & Tinsley, B. (2003). Personality, puberty, and preadolescent girls' risky behaviors: Examining the predictive value of the Five-Factor Model of personality. *Journal of Research in Personality, 37,* 405–419.

Markey, P., Markey, C., & Tinsley, B. (2004). Children's behavioral manifestations of the five-factor model of personality. *Personality & Social Psychology Bulletin, 30,* 423–432.

Markides, K. S., & Lee, D. J. (1991). Predictors of health status in middle-aged and older Mexican Americans. *Journals of Gerontology: Social Sciences, 46,* S243–249.

Markman, E. M. (1992). Constraints on word learning: Speculations about their nature, origins, and domain specificity. In M. R. Gunnar & M. Maratsos (Eds.), *Minnesota Symposia on Child Psychology, Vol. 25* (pp. 59–101). Hillsdale, NJ: Erlbaum.

Marks, N., & Lamberg, J. (1998). Marital status continuity and change among young and midlife adults. *Journal of Family Issues, 19,* 652–686.

Marsh, H., Craven, R., & Debus, R. (1999). Separation of competency and affect components of multiple dimensions of academic self-concept: A developmental perspective. *Merrill-Palmer Quarterly, 45,* 567–601.

Marsh, H., & Yeung, A. (1997). Coursework selection: Relations to academic self-concept and achievement. *American Educational Research Journal, 34,* 691–720.

Marsh, H., & Yeung, A. (1998). Longitudinal structural equation models of academic self-concept and achievement: Gender differences in the development of math and English constructs. *American Educational Research Journal, 35,* 705–738.

Marshall, N., Coll, C., Marx, F., McCartney, K., Keefe, N., & Ruh, J. (1997). After-school time and children's behavioral adjustment. *Merrill-Palmer Quarterly, 43,* 497–514.

Marshall, V. W. (1975). Age and awareness of finitude in developmental gerontology. *Omega, 6,* 113–129.

Marshall, V. W. (1996). The state of theory in aging and the social sciences. In R. H. Binstock & L. K. George (Eds.), *Handbook of aging and the social sciences* (4th ed., pp. 12–30). San Diego, CA: Academic Press.

Marshall, V. W., & Levy, J. A. (1990). Aging and dying. In R. H. Binstock & L. K. George (Eds.), *Handbook of aging and the social sciences* (3rd ed., pp. 245–260). San Diego, CA: Academic Press.

Marsiglio, W., & Donnelly, D. (1991). Sexual relations in later life: A national study of married persons. *Journals of Gerontology: Social Sciences, 46,* S338–344.

Martin, C. L. (1991). The role of cognition in understanding gender effects. In H. W. Reese (Ed.), *Advances in child development and behavior, Vol. 23* (pp. 113–150). San Diego, CA: Academic Press.

Martin, C. L. (1993). New directions for investigating children's gender knowledge. *Developmental Review, 13,* 184–204.

Martin, C. L., & Halverson, C. F., Jr. (1981). A schematic processing model of sex typing and stereotyping in children. *Child Development, 52,* 1119–1134.

Martin, C. L., & Little, J. K. (1990). The relation of gender understanding to children's sex-typed preferences and gender stereotypes. *Child Development, 61,* 1427–1439.

Martin, C. L., Wood, C. H., & Little, J. K. (1990). The development of gender stereotype components. *Child Development, 61,* 1891–1904.

Martin, J. (1995). Birth characteristics for Asian or Pacific Islander subgroups, 1992. *Monthly Vital Statistics Report, 43* (10, Supplement).

Martin, J., & D'Augelli, A. (2003). How lonely are gay and lesbian youth? *Psychological Reports, 93,* 486.

Martin, J., & Nguyen, D. (2004). Anthropometric analysis of homosexuals and heterosexuals: Implications for early hormone exposure. *Hormones & Behavior, 45,* 31–39.

Martin, R., Annis, S., Darling, L., Wadley, V., Harrell, L., & Marson, D. (2003). Loss of calculation abilities in patients with mild and moderate Alzheimer disease. *Archives of Neurology, 60,* 1585–1589.

Martin, R., Noyes, J., Wisenbaker, J. & Huttunen, M. (1999). Prediction of early childhood negative emotionality and inhibition from maternal distress during pregnancy. *Merrill-Palmer Quarterly, 45,* 370–391.

Martin, R. P., Wisenbaker, J., & Huttunen, M. (1994). Review of factor analytic studies of temperament measures based on the Thomas-Chess structural model: Implications for the Big Five. In C. F. Halverson, Jr., G. A. Kohnstamm, & R. P. Martin (Eds.), *The developing structure of temperament and personality from infancy to adulthood* (pp. 157–172). Hillsdale, NJ: Erlbaum.

Martinez-Schallmoser, L., Telleen, S., & MacMullen, N. (2003). Effect of social support and acculturation on postpartum depression in Mexican American women. *Journal of Transcultural Nursing, 14,* 329–338.

Martorano, S. C. (1977). A developmental analysis of performance on Piaget's formal operations tasks. *Developmental Psychology, 13,* 666–672.

Maruyama, M., Arai, H., Ootsuki, M., Okamura, N., Matsui, T., Sasaki, H., Yamazaki, T., & Kaneta, T. (2003). Biomarkers in subjects with amnestic mild cognitive impairment. *Journal of the American Geriatrics Society, 51,* 1671–1672.

Marx, G. (1987). *Groucho and me.* New York: AMS Press.

Masataka, N. (1999). Preference for infant-directed singing in 2-day-old hearing infants of deaf parents. *Developmental Psychology, 35,* 1001–1005.

Mascolo, M. F., & Fischer, K. W. (1995). Developmental transformations in appraisals for pride, shame, and guilt. In J. P. Tangney & K. W. Fischer (Eds.), *Self-conscious emotions: The psychology of shame, guilt, embarrassment, and pride* (pp. 64–113). New York: Guilford Press.

Mason, M., & Chuang, S. (2001). Culturally-based after-school arts programming for low-income urban children: Adaptive and preventive effects. *Journal of Primary Prevention, 22,* 45–54.

Massachusetts Department of Education. (2000). *Charter school initiative.* Retrieved February 29, 2000, from http://www.doe.mass.edu/cs.

Mast, B., Azar, A., MacNeill, S., & Lichtenberg, P. (2004). Depression and activities of daily living predict rehospitalization within 6 months of discharge from geriatric rehabilitation. *Rehabilitation Psychology, 49,* 219–223.

Masten, A., & Coatsworth, D. (1998). The development of competence in favorable and unfavorable environments: Lessons from research on successful children. *American Psychologist, 53,* 205–220.

Masten, A. S., Best, K. M., & Garmezy, N. (1990). Resilience and development: Contributions from the study of children who overcome adversity. *Development & Psychopathology, 2,* 425–444.

Masur, E., & Rodemaker, J. (1999). Mothers' and infants' spontaneous vocal, verbal, and action imitation during the second year. *Merrill-Palmer Quarterly, 45,* 392–412.

Maszk, P., Eisenberg, N., & Guthrie, I. (1999). Relations of children's social status to their emotionality and regulation: A short-term longitudinal study. *Merrill-Palmer Quarterly, 454,* 468–492.

Mathew, A., & Cook, M. (1990). The control of reaching movements by young infants. *Child Development, 61,* 1238–1257.

Matthews, K. A., Wing, R. R., Kuller, L. H., Meilahn, E. N., Kelsey, S. F., Costello, E. J., & Caggiula, A. W. (1990). Influences of natural menopause on psychological characteristics and symptoms of middle-aged healthy women. *Journal of Consulting & Clinical Psychology, 58,* 345–351.

Mattson, S., & Riley, E. (1999). Implicit and explicit memory functioning in children with heavy prenatal alcohol exposure. *Journal of the International Neuropsychological Society, 5,* 462–471.

Mattson, S., Riley, E., Gramling, L., Delis, D., & Jones, K. (1998). Neuropsychological comparison of alcohol-exposed children with or without physical features of fetal alcohol syndrome. *Neuropsychology, 12,* 146–153.

Mature Market Institute. (2003a). *The MetLife market survey of assisted living costs.* Retrieved September 9, 2004, from http://www.metlife.com/WPSAssets/16670870001065792597V1F2003%20Assisted%20Living%20Survey.pdf.

Mature Market Institute. (2003b). *The MetLife market survey of nursing home and home health care costs.* Retrieved September 9, 2004, from http://www.bjfim.com/pdf/2003%20MetLife%20Cost%20Survey.pdf.

Mature Market Institute. (2004). *The future of retirement living.* Retrieved September 9, 2004, from www.metlife.com/WPSAssets/18620262201089823697V1FFuture%20of%20Retirement%20Living.pdf.

Maughan, B., Pickles, A., & Quinton, D. (1995). Parental hostility, childhood behavior, and adult social functioning. In J. McCord (Ed.), *Coercion and punishment in long-term perspectives* (pp. 34–58). Cambridge, England: Cambridge University Press.

Maurer, D., & Maurer, C. (1988). *The world of the newborn.* New York: Basic Books.

Mayes, L., Cicchetti, D., Acharyya, S., & Zhang, H. (2003). Developmental trajectories of cocaine-and-other-drug-exposed and non-cocaine-exposed children. *Journal of Developmental & Behavioral Pediatrics, 24,* 323–335.

Mayeux, L., & Cillissen, A. (2003). Development of social problem solving in early childhood: Stability, change, and associations with social competence. *Journal of Genetic Psychology, 164,* 153–173.

Maylor, D., Vousden, J., & Brown, D. (1999). Adult age differences in short-term memory for serial order: Data and a model. *Psychology & Aging, 14,* 572–594.

Maylor, E. (1998). Changes in event-based prospective memory across adulthood. *Aging, Neuropsychology, & Cognition, 5,* 107–128.

Maylor, E. A. (1993). Aging and forgetting in prospective and retrospective memory tasks. *Psychology & Aging, 8,* 420–428.

Mayringer, H., & Wimmer, H. (2000). Pseudoname learning by German-speaking children with dyslexia: Evidence for a phonological learning deficit. *Journal of Experimental Child Psychology, 75,* 116–133.

Mayseless, O., Wiseman, H., & Hai, I. (1998). Adolescents' relationships with father, mother, and same-gender friend. *Journal of Adolescent Research, 13,* 101–123.

McAdams, D., Hart, H., & Maruna, S. (1998). The anatomy of generativity. In D. P. McAdams & E. de St. Aubin (Eds.), *Generativity and adult development: How and why we care about the next generation* (pp. 7–44). Washington, DC: American Psychological Association.

McAllister, D., Kaplan, B., Edworthy, S., Martin, L., et al. (1997). The influence of systemic lupus erythematosus on fetal development: Cognitive, behavioral, and health trends. *Journal of the International Neurological Society, 3,* 370–376.

McAuley, E. (1993). Self-efficacy, physical activity, and aging. In J. R. Kelly (Ed.), *Activity and aging. Staying involved in late life* (pp. 187–205). Newbury Park, CA: Sage.

McBride-Chang, C. (1998). The development of invented spelling. *Early Education & Development, 9,* 147–160.

McBride-Chang, C., & Ho, C. (2000). Developmental issues in Chinese children's character acquisition. *Journal of Educational Psychology, 92,* 50–55.

McBride-Chang, C., Shu, H., Zhou, C., & Wagner, R. (2004). Morphological awareness uniquely predicts young children's Chinese character recognition. *Journal of Educational Psychology, 96,* 743–751.

McCall, B., Cavanaugh, M., Arvey, R., & Taubman, P. (1997). Genetic influences on job and occupational switching. *Journal of Vocational Behavior, 50,* 60–77.

McCall, R. B. (1993). Developmental functions for general mental performance. In D. K. Detterman (Ed.), *Current topics in human intelligence, Vol. 3: Individual differences and cognition* (pp. 3–30). Norwood, NJ: Ablex.

McClun, L., & Merrell, K. (1998). Relationship of perceived parenting styles, locus of control orientation, and self-concept among junior high age students. *Psychology in the Schools, 35,* 381–390.

McClure, E. (2000). A meta-analytic review of sex differences in facial expression processing and their development in infants, children, and adolescents. *Psychological Bulletin, 126,* 242–453.

McCoy, N. (1998). Methodological problems in the study of sexuality and the menopause. *Maturitas, 29,* 51–60.

McCrae, R., Costa, P., Ostendord, F., & Angleitner, A. (2000). Nature over nurture: Temperament, personality, and life span development. *Journal of Personality & Social Psychology, 78,* 173–186.

McCrae, R. R., & Costa, P. T., Jr. (1984). *Emerging lives, enduring dispositions: Personality in adulthood.* Boston: Little, Brown.

McCrae, R. R., & Costa, P. T., Jr. (1994). The stability of personality: Observations and evaluations. *Current Directions in Psychological Science, 3,* 173–175.

McCrae, R. R., & John, O. P. (1992). An introduction to the Five-Factor Model and its applications. *Journal of Personality, 60,* 175–215.

McCullough, M. (1998, December 22). Birth of octuplets worries infertility specialists. *Seattle Times.* Retrieved March 6, 2001, from http://www.seattletimes.com.

McCune, L. (1995). A normative study of representational play at the transition to language. *Developmental Psychology, 31,* 198–206.

McDonald, L. (2004, April 28). China may grow old before it gets rich. *Sydney Morning Herald.* Retrieved September 10, 2004, from http://www.smh.com.au/articles/2004/04/27/1082831569621.html?from=storyrhs&oneclick=true.

McDonald, P. L., & Wanner, R. A. (1990). *Retirement in Canada.* Toronto: Butterworths.

McDonough, C., Horgan, A., Codd, M., & Casey, P. (2000). Gender differences in the results of the final medical examination at University College Dublin. *Medical Education, 34,* 30–34.

McElree, B., Jia, G., & Litvak, A. (2000). The time course of conceptual processing in three bilingual populations. *Journal of Memory & Language, 42,* 229–254.

McEvoy, G. M., & Cascio, W. F. (1989). Cumulative evidence of the relationship between employee age and job performance. *Journal of Applied Psychology, 74,* 11–17.

McFadden, D. (1998). Sex differences in the auditory system. *Developmental Neuropsychology, 14,* 261–298.

McFalls, J. A., Jr. (1990). The risks of reproductive impairment in the later years of childbearing. *Annual Review of Sociology, 16,* 491–519.

McFayden-Ketchumm, S., Bates, J., Dodge, K., & Pettit, G. (1996). Patterns of change in early childhood aggressive-disruptive behavior: Gender differences in predictions from early coercive and affectionate mother-child interactions. *Child Development, 67,* 2417–2433.

McGrath, M., & Sullivan, M. (2002). Birth weight, neonatal morbidities, and school age outcomes in full-term and preterm infants. *Issues in Comprehensive Pediatric Nursing, 25,* 231–254.

McHale, S., Crouter, A., & Tucker, C. (1999). Family context and gender role socialization in middle childhood: Comparing girls to boys and sisters to brothers. *Child Development, 70,* 990–1004.

McIntosh, B. R., & Danigelis, N. L. (1995). Race, gender, and the relevance of productive activity for elders' affect. *Journals of Gerontology: Social Sciences, 50B,* S229–239.

McKinlay, J. B., McKinlay, S. M., & Brambilla, D. J. (1987). Health status and utilization behavior associated with menopause. *American Journal of Epidemiology, 125,* 110–121.

McKitrick, L., Friedman, L., Thompson, L., Gray, C., & Yesavage, J. (1997). Feasibility and psychometric description of a paced auditory serial addition task adapted for older adults. *Journal of Clinical Geropsychology, 3,* 57–71.

McLanahan, S., & Sandefur, G. (1994). *Growing up with a single parent: What hurts, what helps.* Cambridge, MA: Harvard University Press.

McLoyd, V. (1998). Socioeconomic disadvantage and child development. *American Psychologist, 53,* 185–204.

McLoyd, V., & Wilson, L. (1991). The strain of living poor: Parenting, social support, and child mental health. In A. C. Huston (Ed.), *Children in poverty: Child development and public policy* (pp. 105–135). Cambridge, England: Cambridge University Press.

McLoyd, V. C. (1990). The impact of economic hardship on black families and children: Psychological distress, parenting, and socioemotional development. *Child Development, 61,* 311–346.

McLoyd, V. C., Jayaratne, T. E., Ceballo, R., & Borquez, J. (1994). Unemployment and work interruption among African American single mothers: Effects on parenting and adolescent socioemotional functioning. *Child Development, 65,* 562–589.

McMahon, R. (1997, April). *Prevention of antisocial behavior: Initial findings from the Fast Track Project.* Symposium presented at the annual meeting of the society for Research in Child Development, Washington, DC.

McMaster, F., & Kusumaker, V. (2004). MRI study of the pituitary gland in adolescent depression. *Journal of Psychiatric Research, 38,* 231–236.

McNeal, C., & Amato, P. (1998). Parents' marital violence: Long-term consequences for children. *Journal of Family Issues, 19,* 123–139.

Mead, S., & Fisk, A. (1998). Measuring skill acquisition and retention with an ATM simulator: The need for age-specific training. *Human Factors, 40,* 516–523.

Mediascope Press. (1999a). *Media use in America/Issue Brief Series.* Studio City, CA: Mediascope Inc.

Mediascope Press. (1999b). *The social effects of electronic interactive games: An annotated bibliography.* Studio City, CA: Mediascope Inc.

Mediascope Press. (1999c). *Substance use in popular movies and music/Issue Brief Series.* Studio City, CA: Mediascope Inc.

Mediascope Press. (2000). *Teens, sex and the media/Issue Brief Series.* Studio City, CA: Mediascope Inc.

Medvedova, L. (1998). Personality dimensions—"little five"—and their relationships with coping strategies in early adolescence. *Studia Psychologica, 40,* 261–265.

Meeks, S. (1997). Illnesses in late life: Short-term course of mental illness in middle age and late life. *International Psychogeriatrics, 9,* 343–358.

Meeus, W., Dekovic, M., & Iedema, J. (1997). Unemployment and identity in adolescence: A social comparison perspective. *Career Development Quarterly, 45,* 369–380.

Mehta, K. (1997). The impact of religious beliefs and practices on aging: A cross-cultural comparison. *Journal of Aging Studies, 11,* 101–114.

Mehta, M., Goodyer, I., & Sahakian, B. (2004). Methylphenidate improves working memory and set-shifting in AD/HD: Relationships to baseline memory capacity. *Journal of Child Psychology & Psychiatry & Allied Disciplines, 45,* 293–305.

Meisenhelder, J., & Chandler, E. (2000). Faith, prayer, and health outcomes in elderly Native Americans. *Clinical Nursing Research, 9,* 191–203.

Melby, J. N., & Conger, R. D. (1996). Parental behaviors and adolescent academic performance: A longitudinal analysis. *Journal of Research on Adolescence, 6,* 113–137.

Melot, A., & Houde, O. (1998). Categorization and theories of mind: The case of the appearance/reality distinction. *Cahiers de Psychologie Cognitive/Current Psychology of Cognition, 17,* 71–93.

Melson, G., Peet, S., & Sparks, C. (1991). Children's attachments to their pets: Links to socioemotional development. *Children's Environmental Quarterly, 8,* 55–65.

Meltzoff, A. N. (1988). Infant imitation and memory: Nine-month-olds in immediate and deferred tasks. *Child Development, 59,* 217–225.

Meltzoff, A. N. (1995). Understanding the intentions of others: Re-enactment of intended acts by 18-month-old children. *Developmental Psychology, 31,* 838–850.

Meltzoff, A. N., & Moore, M. K. (1977). Imitation of facial and manual gestures by human neonates. *Science, 198,* 75–78.

Menaghan, E. G., & Lieberman, M. A. (1986). Changes in depression following divorce: A panel study. *Journal of Marriage & the Family, 48,* 319–328.

Menesini, E., Sanchez, V., Fonzi, A., Ortega, R., Costabile, A., & Lo Feudo, G. (2003). Moral emotions and bullying: A cross-national comparison of differences between bullies, victims and outsiders. *Aggressive Behavior, 29,* 515–530.

Meredith, K., & Rassa, G. (1999). Aligning the levels of awareness with the stages of grieving. *Journal of Cognitive Rehabilitation, 17,* 10–12.

Merikangas, K. R., & Angst, J. (1995). The challenge of depressive disorders in adolescence. In M. Rutter (Ed.), *Psychosocial disturbances in young people: Challenges for prevention* (pp. 131–165). Cambridge, England: Cambridge University Press.

Meritesacker, B., Bade, U., Haverkock, A., & Pauli-Pott, U. (2004). Predicting maternal reactivity/sensitivity: The role of infant emotionality, maternal depressiveness/anxiety, and social support. *Infant Mental Health Journal, 25,* 47–61.

Merrick, J., & Morad, M. (2002). Adolescent pregnancy in Israel. *International Journal of Adolescent Medicine, 14,* 161–164.

Merrill, D. M., & Mor, V. (1993). Pathways to hospital death among the oldest old. *Journal of Aging & Health, 5,* 516–535.

Meyer, D., & Bartfield, J. (1996). Compliance with child support orders in divorce cases. *Journal of Marriage & the Family, 58,* 201–212.

Meyer, D. & Bartfield, J. (1998). Patterns of child support compliance in Wisconsin. *Journal of Marriage & the Family, 60,* 309–318.

Meyer, M. (1998). Perceptual differences in fetal alcohol syndrome affect boys performing a modeling task. *Perceptual & Motor Skills, 87,* 784–786.

Meyer-Bahlburg, H. F. L., Ehrhardt, A. A., Rosen, L. R., Gruen, R. S., Veridiano, N. P., Vann, F. H., & Neuwalder, H. F. (1995). Prenatal estrogens and the development of homosexual orientation. *Developmental Psychology, 31,* 12–21.

Michael, R. T., Gagnon, J. H., Laumann, E. O., & Kolata, G. (1994). *Sex in America.* Boston: Little, Brown.

Microsoft launches Web site for seniors and a major grant to SeniorNet—two more steps toward closing the "digital divide." (1998, October 1). *Microsoft News.* Retrieved February 16, 2001, from http://www.microsoft.com/presspass.

Miech, R., & Shanahan, M. (2000). Socioeconomic status and depression over the life course. *Journal of Health & Social Behavior, 41,* 162–176.

Miliotis, D., Sesma, A., & Masten, A. (1999). Parenting as a protective process for school success in children from homeless families. *Early Education & Development, 10,* 111–133.

Miller, B., Benson, B., & Galbraith, K. (2001). Family relationships and adolescent pregnancy risk: A research synthesis. *Developmental Review, 21,* 1–38.

Miller, B., Norton, M., Curtis, T., Hill, E., Schvaneveldt, P., & Young, M. (1998). The timing of sexual intercourse among adolescents: Family, peer, and other antecedents: Erratum. *Youth & Society, 29,* 390.

Miller, B. C., & Moore, K. A. (1990). Adolescent sexual behavior, pregnancy, and parenting: Research through the 1980s. *Journal of Marriage & the Family, 52,* 1025–1044.

Miller, P., Eisenberg, N., Fabes, R., & Shell, R. (1996). Relations of moral reasoning and vicarious emotion to young children's prosocial behavior toward peers and adults. *Developmental Psychology, 29,* 3–18.

Miller, P., Wang, S., Sandel, T., & Cho, G. (2002). Self-esteem as folk theory: A comparison of European American and Taiwanese mothers' beliefs. *Science & Practice, 2,* 209–239.

Miller, R. A. (1990). Aging and the immune response. In E. L. Schneider & J. W. Rowe (Eds.), *Handbook of the biology of aging* (3rd ed., pp. 157–180). San Diego, CA: Academic Press.

Miller, T. (1996, July). Segmenting the Internet. *American Demographics.* Retrieved March 21, 2000, from http://www.americandemographics.com.

Miller, T. Q., Smith, T. W., Turner, C. W., Guijarro, M. L., & Hallet, A. J. (1996). A meta-analytic review of research on hostility and physical health. *Psychological Bulletin, 119,* 322–348.

Miller, T. Q., Turner, C. W., Tindale, R. S., Posavac, E. J., & Dugoni, B. L. (1991). Reasons for the trend toward null findings in research on Type A behavior. *Psychological Bulletin, 110,* 469–495.

Mills, D., Coffey-Corina, S., & Neville, H. (1994). Variability in cerebral organization during primary language acquisition. In G. Dawson & K. Fischer (Eds.) *Human behavior and the developing brain.* New York: Guilford Press.

Min, J. (2004, August 31). South Korea to introduce filial piety bill. *Straits Times Interactive.* Retrieved September 10, 2004, from http://straitstimes.asia1.com.sg/eyeoneastasia/story/0,4395,270186,00.html.

Minkler, M., & Fadem, P. (2002). "Successful aging": A disability perspective. *Journal of Disability Policy Studies, 12,* 229–235.

Minty, B. (1999). Outcomes in long-term foster family care. *Journal of Child Psychology & Psychiatry & Allied Disciplines, 40,* 991–999.

Mischel, W. (1966). A social learning view of sex differences in behavior. In E. E. Maccoby (Ed.), *The development of sex differences* (pp. 56–81). Stanford, CA: Stanford University Press.

Mischel, W. (1970). Sex typing and socialization. In P. H. Mussen (Ed.), *Carmichael's manual of child psychology, Vol. 2* (pp. 3–72). New York: Wiley.

Mitchell, A. (2002). Infertility treatment: More risks and challenges. *New England Journal of Medicine, 346,* 769–770.

Mitchell, C. M., O'Nell, T. D., Beals, J., Dick, R. W., Keane, E., & Manson, S. M. (1996). Dimensionality of alcohol use among American Indian adolescents: Latent structure, construct validity, and implications for developmental research. *Journal of Research on Adolescence, 6,* 151–180.

Mitchell, P. R., & Kent, R. D. (1990). Phonetic variation in multisyllable babbling. *Journal of Child Language, 17,* 247–265.

Mizuta, I., Zahn-Waxler, C., Cole, P., & Hiruma, N. (1996). A cross-cultural study of preschoolers' attachment: Security and sensitivity in Japanese and U.S. dyads. *International Journal of Behavioral Development, 19,* 141–159.

Moen, P. (1991). Transitions in mid-life: Women's work and family roles in the 1970s. *Journal of Marriage & the Family, 53,* 135–150.

Moen, P. (1996). Gender, age, and the life course. In R. H. Binstock & L. K. George (Eds.), *Handbook of aging and the social sciences* (4th ed., pp. 171–187). San Diego, CA: Academic Press.

Moen, P., & Erickson, M. A. (1995). Linked lives: A transgenerational approach to resilience. In P. Moen, G. H. Elder, Jr., & K. Lüscher (Eds.), *Examining lives in context: Perspectives on the ecology of human development* (pp. 169–210). Washington, DC: American Psychological Association.

Moffitt, T. E. (1993). Adolescence-limited and life-course-persistent antisocial behavior: A developmental taxonomy. *Psychology Review, 100,* 674–701.

Mohanty, A. & Perregaux, C. (1997). Language acquisition and bilingualism. In J. Berry, P. Dasen, & T. Saraswath (Eds.), *Handbook of cross-cultural psychology, Vol. 2.* Boston: Allyn & Bacon.

Mohsin, M., Wong, F., Bauman, A., & Bai, J. (2003). Maternal and neonatal factors influencing premature birth and low birth weight in Australia. *Journal of Biosocial Science, 35,* 161–174.

Monarch, E., Saykin, A., & Flashman, L. (2004). Neuropsychological impairment in borderline personality disorder. *Psychiatric Clinics of North America, 27,* 67–82.

Monk, C., Webb, S., & Nelson, C. (2001). Prenatal neurobiological development: Molecular mechanisms and anatomical change. *Developmental Neuropsychology, 19,* 211–236.

Monroy, T. (2000, March 15). Boomers alter economics. *Interactive Week.* Retrieved March 21, 2000, from http://www.ZDNet.com.

Monson, R. (1997). State-ing sex and gender: Collecting information from mothers and fathers in paternity cases. *Gender & Society, 11,* 279–295.

Montemayor, R., & Eisen, M. (1977). The development of self-conceptions from childhood to adolescence. *Developmental Psychology, 13,* 314–319.

Montemurro, B. (2002). "You go 'cause you have to": The bridal shower as a ritual of obligation. *Symbolic Interaction, 25,* 67–92.

Montgomery, M., & Sorel, G. (1998). Love and dating experience in early and middle adolescence: Grade and gender comparisons. *Journal of Adolescence, 21,* 677–689.

Moody, E. (1997). Lessons from pair counseling with incarcerated juvenile delinquents. *Journal of Addictions & Offender Counseling, 18,* 10–25.

Moon, C., & Fifer, W. P. (1990). Syllables as signals for 2-day-old infants. *Infant Behavior & Development, 13,* 377–390.

Mooney, L., Knox, D., & Schacht, C. (2000a). *Social problems.* Belmont, CA: Wadsworth.

Mooney, L., Knox, D., & Schacht, C. (2000b). *Understanding social problems* (2nd ed.). Thousand Oaks, CA: Wadsworth.

Moore, C., Barresi, J., & Thompson, C. (1998). The cognitive basis of future-oriented prosocial behavior. *Social Development, 7,* 198–218.

Moore, K. L. (1998). *The developing human: Clinically oriented embryology* (6th ed.). Philadelphia: Saunders.

Moore, K. L., & Persaud, T. V. N. (1993). *The developing human: Clinically oriented embryology* (5th ed.). Philadelphia: Saunders.

Mor, V. (1987). *Hospice care systems: Structure, process, costs, and outcome.* New York: Springer.

Mor, V., Greer, D. S., & Kastenbaum, R. (Eds.). (1988). *The hospice experiment.* Baltimore, MD: Johns Hopkins University Press.

Morfei, M., Hooker, K., Carpenter, J., Mix, C., & Blakeley, E. (2004). Agentic and communal generative behavior in four areas of adult life: Implications for psychological well-being. *Adult Development, 11,* 55–58.

Morgan, B., Finan, A., Yarnold, R., Petersen, S., Horsfield, M., Rickett, A., & Wailoo, M. (2002). Assessment of infant physiology and neuronal development using magnetic resonance imaging. *Child: Care, Health, & Development, 28,* 7–10.

Morgan, C., Covington, J., Geisler, M., Polich, J., & Murphy, C. (1997). Olfactory event-related potentials: Older males demonstrate the greatest deficits. *Electroencephalography & Clinical Neurophysiology, 104,* 351–358.

Morgan, D. G. (1992). Neurochemical changes with aging: Predisposition towards age-related mental disorders. In J. E. Birren, R. B. Sloane, & G. D. Cohen (Eds.), *Handbook of mental health and aging* (2nd ed., pp. 175–200). San Diego, CA: Academic Press.

Morgan, J. L. (1994). Converging measures of speech segmentation in preverbal infants. *Infant Behavior & Development, 17,* 389–403.

Morgan, L. A. (1991). *After marriage ends: Economic consequences for midlife women.* Newbury Park, CA: Sage.

Mork, J., Lie, K., Glattre, E., Clark, S., Hallmans, G., Jellum, E., Koskela, P., Moller, B., Pukkala, E., Schiller, J., Wang, Z., Youngman, L., Lehtinen, M., & Dillner, J. (2001). Human papillomavirus infection as a risk factor for squamous-cell carcinoma of the head and neck. *New England Journal of Medicine, 344,* 1125–1131.

Morris, D., & Langer, G. (2004, January 21). *Same-sex marriage: Most oppose it, but balk at amending Constitution.* Retrieved November 20, 2004, from http://www.abcnews.go.com/sections/us/Relationships/same_sex_marriage_poll_040121.htm.

Morris, D. L., Kritchevsky, S. B., & Davis, C. E. (1994). Serum carotenoids and coronary heart disease. The Lipid Research Clinics Coronary Primary Prevention Trial and Follow-up Study. *Journal of the American Medical Association, 272,* 1439–1441.

Morrison, D. R., & Cherlin, A. J. (1995). The divorce process and young children's well-being: A prospective analysis. *Journal of Marriage & the Family, 57,* 800–812.

Morrison, N. A., Qi, J. C., Tokita, A., Kelly, P. J., Crofts, L., Nguyen, T. V., Sambrook, P. N., & Eisman, J. A. (1994). Prediction of bone density from vitamin D receptor alleles. *Nature, 367,* 284–287.

Morrissette, P. (1999). Post-traumatic stress disorder in child sexual abuse: Diagnostic and treatment considerations. *Child & Youth Care Forum, 28,* 205–219.

Morrongiello, B. A. (1988). Infants' localization of sounds along the horizontal axis: Estimates of minimum audible angle. *Developmental Psychology, 24,* 8–13.

Morrongiello, B. A., Fenwick, K. D., & Chance, G. (1990). Sound localization acuity in very young infants: An observer-based testing procedure. *Developmental Psychology, 24,* 75–84.

Morrow, D., Menard, W., Ridolfo, H., Stine-Morrow, E., Teller, T., & Bryant, D. (2003). Expertise, cognitive ability, and age effects on pilot communication. *International Journal of Aviation Psychology, 13,* 345–371.

Morse, P. A., & Cowan, N. (1982). Infant auditory and speech perception. In T. M. Field, A. Houston, H. C. Quay, L. Troll, & G. E. Finley (Eds.), *Review of human development* (pp. 32–61). New York: Wiley.

Mortimer, J., & Harley, C. (2002). The quality of work and youth mental health. *Work & Occupations, 29,* 166–197.

Mortimer, J., Zimmer-Gembeck, M., Holmes, M., & Shanahan, M. (2002). The process of occupational decision making: Patterns during the transition to adulthood. *Journal of Vocational Behavior, 61,* 439–465.

Mortimer, J. T., & Finch, M. D. (1996). Work, family, and adolescent development. In J. T. Mortimer & M. D. Finch (Eds.), *Adolescents, work, and family: An intergenerational developmental analysis* (pp. 1–24. Thousand Oaks, CA: Sage.

Mortimer, J. T., Finch, M. D., Dennehy, K., Lee, C., & Beebe, T. (1995, March). *Work experience in adolescence.* Paper presented at the biennial meetings of the Society for Research in Child Development, Indianapolis, IN.

Mosher, W. D. (1987). Infertility: Why business is booming. *American Demography,* June, 42–43.

Mosher, W. D., & Pratt, W. F. (1987). Fecundity, infertility, and reproductive health in the United States, 1982. *Vital Health Statistics, 23 (14).*

Mott, J., Crowe, P., Richardson, J., & Flay, B. (1999). After-school supervision and adolescent cigarette smoking: Contributions of the setting and intensity of after-school self-care. *Journal of Behavioral Medicine, 22,* 35–58.

Mounts, N. S., & Steinberg, L. (1995). An ecological analysis of peer influence on adolescent grade point average and drug use. *Developmental Psychology, 31,* 915–922.

Mueller, K., & Yoder, J. (1999). Stigmatization of non-normative family size status. *Sex Roles, 41,* 901–919.

Mueller, U., Overton, W., & Reene, K. (2001). Development of conditional reasoning: A longitudinal study. *Journal of Cognition & Development, 2,* 27–49.

Mullins, L. C., & Mushel, M. (1992). The existence and emotional closeness of relationships with children, friends, and spouses. The effect on loneliness among older persons. *Research on Aging, 14,* 448–470.

Mumme, D., & Fernald, A. (2003). The infant as onlooker: Learning from emotional reactions observed in a television scenario. *Child Development, 74,* 221–237.

Mundy, G. R. (1994). Boning up on genes. *Nature, 367,* 216–217.

Munroe, R. H., Shimmin, H. S., & Munroe, R. L. (1984). Gender understanding and sex role preference in four cultures. *Developmental Psychology, 20,* 673–682.

Murnen, S., Smolak, L., Mills, J., & Good, L. (2003). Thin, sexy women and strong, muscular men: Grade-school children's responses to objectified images of women and men. *Sex Roles, 49,* 427–437.

Murphy, K., Hanrahan, P., & Luchins, D. (1997). A survey of grief and bereavement in nursing homes: The importance of hospice grief and bereavement for the end-stage Alzheimer's disease patient and family. *Journal of the American Geriatrics Society, 45,* 1104–1107.

Murphy, S., Braun, T., Tillery, L., Cain, K., Johnson, L., & Beaton, R. (1999). PTSD among bereaved parents following the violent deaths of their 12- to 28-year-old children: A longitudinal prospective analysis. *Journal of Traumatic Stress, 12,* 273–291.

Murphy, S., Johnson, L., & Lohan, J. (2003). Finding meaning in a child's violent death: A five-year provective analysis of parents' personal narratives and empirical data. *Death Studies, 27,* 381–404.

Murphy, S. O. (1993, April). *The family context and the transition to siblinghood: Strategies parents use to influence sibling-infant relationships.* Paper presented at the biennial meetings of the Society for Research in Child Development, New Orleans, LA.

Murray, B. (1998, June). Dipping math scores heat up debate over math teaching. *APA Monitor, 29,* 34–35.

Murray, J. P. (1980). *Television and youth: 25 years of research and controversy.* Stanford, CA: The Boys Town Center for the Study of Youth Development.

Murray, L., Sinclair, D., Cooper, P., Ducournau, P., et al. (1999). The socioemotional development of 5-year-old children of postnatally depressed mothers. *Journal of Child Psychology & Psychiatry & Allied Disciplines, 40,* 1259–1271.

Murrell, S. A., & Himmelfarb, S. (1989). Effects of attachment bereavement and pre-event conditions on subsequent depressive symptoms in older adults. *Psychology & Aging, 4,* 166–172.

Murry, V. (1997). The impact of sexual activity and fertility timing on African American high school graduates' later life experiences. *Families in Society, 78,* 383–392.

Murstein, B. I. (1986). *Paths to marriage.* Beverly Hills, CA: Sage.

Musick, M., Koenig, H., Hays, J., & Cohen, H. (1998). Religious activity and depression among community-dwelling elderly persons with cancer: The moderating effect of race. *Journals of Gerontology, Series B: Psychological Sciences & Social Sciences, 53B,* S218–S227.

Mutch, L., Leyland, A., & McGee, A. (1993). Patterns of neuropsychological function in a low-birth-weight population. *Developmental Medicine & Child Neurology, 35,* 943–956.

Muthesius, D. (1997). Reminiscence and the relationship between young and old. *Zeitschrift fuer Gerontologie und Geriatrie, 30,* 354–361.

Muzi, M. (2000). *The experience of parenting.* Upper Saddle River, NJ: Prentice Hall.

Mwamwenda, T. (1999). Undergraduate and graduate students' combinatorial reasoning and formal operations. *Journal of Genetic Psychology, 160,* 503–506.

Nachmias, M. (1993, April). *Maternal personality relations with toddler's attachment classification, use of coping strategies, and adrenocortical stress response.* Paper presented at the biennial meetings of the Society for Research in Child Development, New Orleans, LA.

Nagamine, S. (1999). Interpersonal conflict situations: Adolescents' negotiation processes using an interpersonal negotiation strategy model: Adolescents' relations with their parents and friends. *Japanese Journal of Educational Psychology, 47,* 218–228.

Nagumey, A., Reich, J., & Newsom, J. (2004). Gender moderates the effects of independence and dependence desires during the social support process. *Psychology & Aging, 19,* 215–218.

Nagy, W., Berninger, V., Abbott, R., Vaughan, K., & Vermeulen, K. (2004). Relationship of morphology and other language skills to literacy skills in at-risk second-grade readers and at-risk fourth-grade writers. *Journal of Educational Psychology, 96,* 730–742.

Narvaez, D. (1998). The influence of moral schemas on the reconstruction of moral narratives in eighth graders and college students. *Journal of Educational Psychology, 90,* 13–24.

Nathanson, C. A., & Lorenz, G. (1982). Women and health: The social dimensions of biomedical data. In J. Z. Giele (Ed.), *Women in the middle years* (pp. 37–88). New York: Wiley.

National Abortion and Reproductive Rights Action League. (1997). *Limitations on the rights of pregnant women.* Retrieved March 5, 2001, from http://www.naral.org/publications/facts.

National Center for Chronic Disease Prevention and Health Promotion. (2000). *Obesity epidemic increases dramatically in the United States.* Retrieved August 23, 2000, from http://www.cdc.gov.

National Center for Education Statistics (NCES). (1997). *Condition of education/1997.* Washington, DC: U.S. Department of Education.

National Center for Education Statistics. (1998). *Digest of educational statistics.* Washington, DC: Author.

National Center for Education Statistics. (2000). *How many students with disabilities receive services?* Retrieved August 23, 2000, from http://www.nces.ed.gov.

National Center for Education Statistics. (2002). *Distance education at degree-granting postsecondary institutions: 2000–2001.* Retrieved August 18, 2004, from http://nces.ed.gov/surveys/peqis/publications/2003017/index.asp.

National Center for Education Statistics. (2003a). *The nation's report card: Mathematics highlights 2003.* Washington, DC: U. S. Department of Education, NCES 2004–451.

National Center for Education Statistics. (2003b). *The nation's report card: Reading highlights 2003.* Washington, DC: U.S. Department of Education, NCES 2004–452.

National Center for Education Statistics. (2003c). *The condition of education 2003.* Retrieved August 18, 2004, from http://nces.ed.gov/pubs2003/2003067.pdf.

National Center for Education Statistics. (2004a). *Average mathematics scale scores for 4th- and 8th-graders: Selected years 1990–2003.* Retrieved November 11, 2004, from http://nces.ed.gov/programs/coe/2004/charts/chart11.asp.

National Center for Education Statistics (2004b). *Average reading scale scores for 4th- and 8th-graders: Selected years 1992–2003.* Retrieved November 11, 2004, from http://nces.ed.gov/programs/coe/2004/charts/chart09.asp.

National Center for Health Statistics (NCHS). (1996). Guidelines for school health programs to promote lifelong healthy eating. *Morbidity & Mortality Weekly Report, 45,* 1–33.

National Center for Health Statistics. (1997). *Vital statistics of the United States.* Washington, DC: U.S. Government Printing Office.

National Center for Health Statistics. (1999, September 14). Trends in twin and triplet births: 1980–1997. *National Vital Statistics Reports.*

National Center for Health Statistics. (2000a). *CDC growth charts.* Retrieved August 23, 2000, from http://www.cdc.gov/nchs.

National Center for Health Statistics. (2000b). *Health, United States 2000 with adolescent chart book.* Retrieved August 24, 2004, from http://www.cdc.gov/nchs/products/pubs/pubd/hus/hestatus.htm.

National Center for Health Statistics. (2003). *Births: Final data for 2002.* Retrieved June 18, 2004, from http://www.cdc.gov/nchs/pressroom/3facts/teenbirth.htm.

National Center for Injury Prevention and Control (NCIPC). (2000). *Fact book for the year 2000.* Washington, DC: Author.

National Clearinghouse for English Language Acquisition and Language Instruction Educational Programs (NCELA). (2002). *The growing numbers of limited English proficient students.* Retrieved June 23, 2004, from http://www.ncela.gwu.edu/policy/states/stateposter.pdf.

National Institute of Child Health and Human Development (NICHD) Early Child Care Research Network. (1998). The effects of infant child care on mother-infant attachment security: Results of the NICHD study of early child care. *Child Development, 68,* 860–879.

National Institute of Child Health and Human Development Early Child Care Research Network. (1999). Chronicity of maternal depressive symptoms, maternal sensitivity, and child functioning at 36 months. *Developmental Psychology, 35,* 1297–1310.

National Institute of Child Health and Human Development Early Child Care Research Network. (2003). Does amount of time spent in child care predict socioemotional adjustment during the transition to kindergarten? *Child Development, 74,* 976–1005.

National Institute of Child Health and Human Development Early Child Care Research Network. (2004a). Affect dysregulation in the mother-child relationship in the toddler years: Antecedents and consequences. *Development & Psychopathology, 16,* 43–68.

National Institute of Child Health and Human Development (NCIHD) Early Child Care Research Network. (2004b). Are child developmental outcomes related to before- and after-school care arrangements? Results from the NICHD Study of Early Child Care. *Child Development, 75,* 280–295.

National Institute on Aging (NIA). (2000a). *Depression: A serious but treatable illness.* Retrieved February 7, 2001, from http://www.nih.gov/nia.

National Institute on Aging. (2000b). *Sexuality in later life.* Retrieved February 7, 2001, from http://www.nih.gov/nia.

National Institutes of Health (NIH). (2003). *HIV/AIDS statistics.* Retrieved November 11, 2003, from http://www.niaid.nih.gov/factsheets/aidsstat.htm.

National Institutes of Health. (2004). *Stem cell basics.* Retrieved September 24, 2004, from http://stemcells.nih.gov/info/basics/basics4.asp.

National Science Foundation. (1996). *Women, minorities, and persons with disabilities in science and engineering.* Washington, DC: Author.

Naude, H., & Pretorius, E. (2003). Investigating the effects of asthma medication on the cognitive and psychosocial functioning of primary school children with asthma. *Early Child Development & Care, 173,* 699–709.

Neill, M. (1998). *High stakes tests do not improve student learning.* Retrieved October 21, 1998, from http://www.fairtest.org.

Neill, M. (2000). Too much harmful testing? *Educational Measurement: Issues & Practice, 16,* 57–58.

Neimeyer, R., Prigerson, H., & Davies, B. (2002). Mourning and meaning. *American Behavioral Scientist, 46,* 235–251.

Neimeyer, R. A., & Chapman, K. M. (1980/1981). Self/ideal discrepancy and fear of death: The test of an existential hypothesis. *Omega, 11,* 233–239.

Neisser, U., Boodoo, G., Bouchard, T. J., Jr., Boykin, A. W., Brody, N., Ceci, S. J., Halpern, D. F., Loehlin, J. C., Perloff, R., Sternberg, R. J., & Urbina, S. (1996). Intelligence: Knowns and unknowns. *American Psychologist, 51,* 77–101.

Neisser, U., & Harsch, N. (1992). Phantom flashbulbs: False recollections of hearing the news about Challenger. In E. Winograd & U. Neisser (Eds.), *Affect and accuracy in recall: Studies of "flashbulb" memories* (pp. 9–31). New York: Cambridge University Press.

Neitzel, C., & Stright, A. (2003). Mothers' scaffolding of children's problem solving: Establishing a foundation of academic self-regulatory competence. *Journal of Family Psychology, 17,* 147–159.

Nelson, E. A., & Dannefer, D. (1992). Aged heterogeneity: Fact or fiction? The fate of diversity in gerontological research. *The Gerontologist, 32,* 17–23.

Nelson, H. (2004). Commonly used types of postmenopausal estrogen for treatment of hot flashes: Scientific review. *Journal of the American Medical Association, 291,* 1610–1620.

Nelson, H., Humphrey, L., Nygren, P., Teutsch, S., & Allan, J. (2002). Postmenopausal hormone replacement therapy: Scientific review. *Journal of the American Medical Association, 288,* 872–881.

Nelson, K. (1973). Structure and strategy in learning to talk. *Monographs of the Society for Research in Child Development, 38* (Serial No. 149).

Nelson, K. (1977). Facilitating children's syntax acquisition. *Developmental Psychology, 13,* 101–107.

Nelson, M. E., Fiatarone, M. A., Morganti, C. M., Trice, I., Greenberg, R. A., & Evans, W. J. (1994). Effects of high-intensity strength training on multiple risk factors for osteoporotic fractures. *Journal of the American Medical Association, 272,* 1909–1914.

Nelson, S. (1980). Factors influencing young children's use of motives and outcomes as moral criteria. *Child Development, 51,* 823–829.

Neshat-Doost, H., Taghavi, M., Moradi, A., Yule, W., & Dalgleish, T. (1998). Memory for emotional trait adjectives in clinically depressed youth. *Journal of Abnormal Psychology, 107,* 642–650.

Neugarten, B. L. (1970). Dynamics of transition of middle age to old age. *Journal of Geriatric Psychiatry, 4,* 71–87.

Neugarten, B. L. (1979). Time, age, and the life cycle. *American Journal of Psychiatry, 136,* 887–894.

Neugebauer, R., Hoek, H., & Susser, E. (1999). Prenatal exposure to wartime famine and development of antisocial personal disorder in early adulthood. *Journal of the American Medical Association, 282,* 455–462.

New Zealand Ministry of Education. (2003). *Homeschooling in 2003.* Retrieved June 23, 2004, from http://www.minedu.govt.nz/index.cfm?layout=document&documentid=6893&indexid=6852&indexparentid=5611.

Newcomb, A. F., & Bagwell, C. L. (1995). Children's friendship relations: A meta-analytic review. *Psychological Bulletin, 117,* 306–347.

Newcomb, A. F., Bukowski, W. M., & Pattee, L. (1993). Children's peer relations: A meta-analytic review of popular, rejected, neglected, controversial, and average sociometric status. *Psychological Bulletin, 113,* 99–128.

Newman, D., Caspi, A., Moffitt, T., & Silva, P. (1997). Antecedents of adult interpersonal functioning: Effects of individual differences in age 3 temperament. *Developmental Psychology, 33,* 206–217.

Ng, A., Ying, P., Phillips, D., & Lee, W. (2002). Persistence and challenges to filial piety and informal support of older persons in a modern Chinese society: A case study in Tuen Mun, Hong Kong. *Journal of Aging Studies, 16,* 135–153.

Ni, Y. (1998). Cognitive structure, content knowledge, and classificatory reasoning. *Journal of Genetic Psychology, 159,* 280–296.

Nicholson, J. (1998). Inborn errors of metabolism. In R. Behrman & R. Kliegman (Eds.), *Nelson essentials of pediatrics* (3rd ed., pp. 147–166). Philadelphia: W. B. Saunders.

Niedzwienska, A. (2003). Misleading postevent information and flashbulb memories. *Memory, 11,* 549–558.

Nightingale, E. O., & Goodman, M. (1990). *Before birth. Prenatal testing for genetic disease.* Cambridge, MA: Harvard University Press.

Nijhuis, J. (2003). Fetal behavior. *Neurobiology of Aging, 24,* S41–S46.

Nilsson, E., Gillberg, C., Gillberg, I., & Rastam, M. (1999). Ten-year follow-up of adolescent-onset anorexia nervosa: Personality disorders. *Journal of the American Academy of Child & Adolescent Psychiatry, 38,* 1389–1395.

Rosenthal, J., Rodewald, L., McCauley, M., Berman, S., Irigoyen, M., Sawyer, M., Yusuf, H., Davis, R., & Kalton, G. (2004). Immunization coverage levels among 19- to 35-month-old children in 4 diverse, medically underserved areas of the United States. *Pediatrics, 113,* e296–e302.

Rosenthal, R. (1994). Interpersonal expectancy effects: A 30-year perspective. *Current Directions in Psychological Science, 3,* 176–179.

Rosenthal, S., Lewis, L., Succop, P., & Burklow, K. (1997). Adolescent girls' perceived prevalence of sexually transmitted diseases and condom use. *Journal of Developmental & Behavioral Pediatrics, 18,* 158–161.

Rosow, I. (1985). Status and role change through the life cycle. In R. H. Binstock & E. Shanas (Eds.), *Handbook of aging and the social sciences* (2nd ed.) (pp. 62–93). New York: Van Nostrand Reinhold.

Ross, C. E. (1995). Reconceptualizing marital status as a continuum of social attachment. *Journal of Marriage & the Family, 57,* 129–140.

Ross, R. K., Paganini-Hill, A., Mack, T. M., & Henderson, B. E. (1987). Estrogen use and cardiovascular disease. In D. R. Mishell, Jr. (Ed.), *Menopause: Physiology and pharmacology* (pp. 209–224). Chicago: Year Book Medical Publishers.

Rossman, I. (1980). Bodily changes with aging. In E. W. Busse & D. G. Blazer (Eds.), *Handbook of geriatric psychiatry* (pp. 125–146). New York: Van Nostrand Reinhold.

Rossow, I., & Amundsen, A. (1997). Alcohol abuse and mortality: A 40-year prospective study of Norwegian conscripts. *Social Science & Medicine, 44,* 261–267.

Rostosky, S., Owens, G., & Zimmerman, R., & Riggle, E. D. (2003). Associations among sexual attraction status, school belonging, and alcohol and marijuana use in rural high school students. *Journal of Adolescence, 26,* 741–751.

Roth, M. (2003). Validation of the Arnett Inventory of Sensation Seeking (AISS): Efficiency to predict the willingness towards occupational change, and affection by social desirability. *Personality & Individual Differences, 35,* 1307–1314.

Rothbard, J. C., & Shaver, P. R. (1994). Continuity of attachment across the life span. In M. B. Sperling & W. H. Berman (Eds.), *Attachment in adults. Clinical and developmental perspectives* (pp. 31–71). New York: Guilford Press.

Rothbart, M., Ahadi, S., & Evans, D. (2000). Temperament and personality: Origins and outcomes. *Journal of Personality & Social Psychology, 78,* 122–135.

Rothbart, M. K., Derryberry, D., & Posner, M. I. (1994). A psychobiological approach to the development of temperament. In J. E. Bates & T. D. Wachs (Eds.), *Temperament. Individual differences at the interface of biology and behavior* (pp. 83–116). Washington, DC: American Psychological Association.

Roux, A., Merkin, S., Arnett, D., Chambless, L., Massing, M., Nieto, J., Sorlie, P., Szklo, M., Tyroler, H., & Watson, R. (2001). Neighborhood of residence and incidence of coronary heart disease. *New England Journal of Medicine, 345,* 99–106.

Rovee-Collier, C. (1993). The capacity for long-term memory in infancy. *Current Directions in Psychological Science, 2,* 130–135.

Rowe, D. (2002). IQ, birth weight, and number of sexual partners in White, African American, and mixed race adolescents. *Population & Environment: A Journal of Interdisciplinary Studies, 23,* 513–524.

Rowe, J., & Kahn, R. (1997). Successful aging. *Gerontologist, 37,* 433–440.

Rowe, J., & Kahn, R. (1998). *Successful aging.* New York: Pantheon.

Rowland, D., & Tai, W. (2003). A review of plant-derived and herbal approaches to the treatment of sexual dysfunctions. *Journal of Sex & Marital Therapy, 29,* 185–205.

Rowley, S. (2000). Profiles of African American college students' educational utility and performance: A cluster analysis. *Journal of Black Psychology, 26,* 3–26.

Roy, E., Bryden, P., & Cavill, S. (2003). Hand differences in pegboard performance through development. *Brain & Cognition, 53,* 315–317.

Roy, P., Rutter, M., & Pickles, A. (2000). Institutional care: Risk from family background or pattern of rearing. *Journal of Child Psychology & Psychiatry & Allied Disciplines, 41,* 139–149.

Rubin, K., Burgess, K., Dwyer, K., & Hastings, P. (2003). Predicting preschoolers' externalizing behaviors from toddler temperament, conflict, and maternal negativity. *Developmental Psychology, 39,* 164–176.

Rubin, K., Burgess, K., & Hastings, P. (2002). Stability and social-behavioral consequences of toddlers' inhibited temperament and parenting behaviors. *Child Development, 73,* 483–495.

Rubin, K., Nelson, L., Hastings, P., & Asendorpt, J. (1999). The transaction between parents' perception of their children's shyness and their parenting styles. *International Journal of Behavioral Development, 23,* 937–958.

Rubin, K. H., Fein, G. G., & Vandenberg, B. (1983). Play. In E. M. Hetherington (Ed.), *Handbook of child psychology: Socialization, personality, and social development* (Vol. 4) (pp. 693–774). New York: Wiley.

Rubin, K. H., Hymel, S., Mills, R. S. L., & Rose-Krasnor, L. (1991). Conceptualizing different developmental pathways to and from social isolation in childhood. In D. Cicchetti & S. L. Toth (Eds.), *Internalizing and externalizing expressions of dysfunction: Rochester Symposium on Developmental Psychopathology* (Vol. 2) (pp. 91–122). Hillsdale, NJ: Erlbaum.

Rubin, S., & Schechter, N. (1997). Exploring the social construction of bereavement: Perceptions of adjustment and recovery in bereaved men. *American Journal of Orthopsychiatry, 67,* 279–289.

Rubinstein, R. L. (1986). *Singular paths: Old men living alone.* New York: Columbia University Press.

Ruble, D., & Dweck, C. (1995). Self-conceptions, person conceptions, and their development. In N. Eisenberg (Ed.), *Social development.* Thousand Oaks, CA: Sage.

Ruble, D. N. (1987). The acquisition of self-knowledge: A self-socialization perspective. In N. Eisenberg (Ed.), *Contemporary topics in developmental psychology* (pp. 243–270). New York: Wiley-Interscience.

Rudd, M., Viney, L., & Preston, C. (1999). The grief experienced by spousal caregivers of dementia patients: The role of place of care of patient and gender of caregiver. *International Journal of Aging & Human Development, 48,* 217–240.

Rushton, J., & Rushton, E. (2003). Brain size, IQ, and racial-group differences: Evidence from musculoskeletal traits. *Intelligence, 31,* 139–155.

Rushton, J., Skuy, M., & Fridjhon, P. (2003). Performance on Raven's Advanced Progressive Matrices by African, East Indian, and White engineering students in South Africa. *Intelligence, 31,* 123–137.

Rutter, M. (1983). School effects on pupil progress: Research findings and policy implications. *Child Development, 54,* 1–29.

Rutter, M. (1987). Continuities and discontinuities from infancy. In J. D. Osofsky (Ed.), *Handbook of infant development* (2nd ed.) (pp. 1256–1296). New York: Wiley-Interscience.

Rutter, M., Dunn, J., Plomin, R., Simonoff, E., Pickles, A., Maughan, B., Ormel, J., Meyer, J., & Eaves, L. (1997). Integrating nature and nurture: Implications of person-environment correlations and interactions for developmental psychopathology. *Development & Psychopathology, 9,* 335–364.

Ryff, C. (1984). Personality development from the inside: The subjective experience of change in adulthood and aging. In P. B. Baltes & O. G. Brim, Jr. (Eds.), *Life-span development and behavior* (pp. 244–281). Orlando, FL: Academic Press.

Ryff, C., & Heincke, S. G. (1983). The subjective organization of personality in adulthood and aging. *Journal of Personality & Social Psychology, 44,* 807–816.

Rys, G., & Bear, G. (1997). Relational aggression and peer relations: Gender and developmental issues. *Merrill-Palmer Quarterly, 43,* 87–106.

Saavedra, M., Ramirez, A., & Contreras, C. (1997). Interactive interviews between elders and children: A possible procedure for improving affective state in the elderly. *Psiquiatricay Psicologica de America Latina, 43,* 63–66.

Sabol, W., Coulton, C., & Korbin, J. (2004). Building community capacity for violence prevention. *Journal of Interpersonal Violence, 19,* 322–340.

Sacco, V., & Kennedy, L. (1996). *The criminal event.* Belmont, CA: Wadsworth.

Saewyc, E., Bearinger, L., Heinz, P., Blum, R., & Resnick, M. (1998). Gender differences in health and risk behaviors among bisexual and homosexual adolescents. *Journal of Adolescent Health, 23,* 181–188.

Safren, S., & Heimberg, R. (1999). Depression, hopelessness, suicidality, and related factors in sexual minority and heterosexual adolescents. *Journal of Consulting & Clinical Psychology, 67,* 859–866.

Sagi, A. (1990). Attachment theory and research from a cross-cultural perspective. *Human Development, 33,* 10–22.

Sagi, A., van IJzendoorn, M. H., & Koren-Karie, N. (1991). Primary appraisal of the Strange Situation: A cross-cultural analysis of preseparation episodes. *Developmental Psychology, 27,* 587–596.

Sagiv, M., Vogelaere, P., Soudry, M., & Shrsam, R. (2000). Role of physical activity training in attenuation of height loss. *Gerontology, 46,* 266–270.

Salthouse, T. (2004). What and when of cognitive aging. *Current Directions in Psychological Science, 13,* 140–144.

Salthouse, T., Atkinson, T., & Berish, D. (2003). Executive functioning as a potential mediator of age-related cognitive decline in normal adults. *Journal of Experimental Psychology: General, 132,* 566–594.

Salthouse, T. A. (1991). *Theoretical perspectives on cognitive aging.* Hillsdale, NJ: Erlbaum.

Salthouse, T. A. (1993). Speed mediation of adult age differences in cognition. *Developmental Psychology, 29,* 722–738.

Salthouse, T. A. (1996). General and specific speed mediation of adult age differences in memory. *Journals of Gerontology: Psychological Sciences, 51B,* P30–42.

Salthouse, T. A. (1998). Independence of age-related influences on cognitive abilities across the life span. *Developmental Psychology, 34,* 851–864.

Salthouse, T. A., & Czaja, S. (2000). Structural constraints on process explanations in cognitive aging. *Psychology & Aging, 15,* 44–55.

Salthouse, T. A., & Maurer, T. J. (1996). Aging, job performance, and career development. In J. E. Birren & K. W. Schaie (Eds.), *Handbook of the psychology of aging* (4th ed., pp. 353–364). San Diego, CA: Academic Press.

Saltz, R. (1979). Children's interpretation of proverbs. *Language Arts, 56,* 508–514.

Samaritans. (1998). *Media guidelines on portrayals of suicide.* Retrieved February 16, 2001, from http://www.mentalhelp.net/samaritans/medreport.htm.

Sammartino, F. J. (1987). The effect of health on retirement. *Social Security Bulletin, 50* (2), 31–47.

Sampson, R. J., & Laub, J. H. (1994). Urban poverty and the family context of delinquency: A new look at structure and process in a classic study. *Child Development, 65,* 523–540.

Samuels, S., & Flor, R. (1997). The importance of automaticity for developing expertise in reading. *Reading & Writing Quarterly: Overcoming Learning Difficulties, 13,* 107–121.

Sanders, C. M. (1989). *Grief: The mourning after.* New York: Wiley-Interscience.

Sandman, C., Wadhwa, P., Chicz-DeMet, A., Porto, M., & Garite, T. (1999). Maternal corticotropin-releasing hormone and habituation in the human fetus. *Developmental Psychobiology, 34,* 163–173.

Sandman, C., Wadhwa, P., Hetrick, W., Porto, M., & Peeke, H. (1997). Human fetal heart rate dishabituation between thirty and thirty-two weeks. *Child Development, 68,* 1031–1040.

Sandnabba, N., & Ahlberg, C. (1999). Parents' attitudes and expectations about children's cross-gender behavior. *Sex Roles, 40,* 249–263.

Sands, L. P., & Meredith, W. (1992). Blood pressure and intellectual functioning in late midlife. *Journals of Gerontology: Psychological Sciences, 47,* P81–84.

Sands, L. P., Terry, H., & Meredith, W. (1989). Change and stability in adult intellectual functioning assessed by Wechsler item responses. *Psychology & Aging, 4,* 79–87.

Sandson, T., Bachna, K., & Morin, M. (2000). Right hemisphere dysfunction in ADHD: Visual hemispatial inattention and clinical subtype. *Journal of Learning Disabilities, 33,* 83–90.

Sano, M., Ernesto, C., Thomas, R., Kauber, M., Schafer, K., Grundman, M., Woodbury, P., Growdon, J., Cotman, D., Pfeiffer, E., Schneider, L., & Thal, L. (1997). A controlled trial of selegiline, alpha-tocopherol, or both as treatment for Alzheimer's disease. *New England Journal of Medicine, 336,* 1216–1222.

Sanson, A., Hemphill, S., & Smart, D. (2004). Connections between temperament and social development: A review. *Social Development, 13,* 142–170.

Sanson, A., Pedlow, R., Cann, W., Prior, M., et al. (1996). Shyness ratings: Stability and correlates in early childhood. *International Journal of Behavioral Development, 19,* 705–724.

Sarason, B. R., Sarason, I. G., & Pierce, G. R. (1990). Traditional views of social support and their impact on assessment. In B. R. Sarason, I. G. Sarason, & G. R. Pierce (Eds.), *Social support: An interactional view* (pp. 9–25). New York: Wiley.

Sato, S., Shimonska, Y., Nakazato, K., & Kawaai, C. (1997). A life-span developmental study of age identity: Cohort and gender differences. *Japanese Journal of Developmental Psychology, 8,* 88–97.

Savage, M., & Holcomb, D. (1999). Adolescent female athletes' sexual risk-taking behaviors. *Journal of Youth & Adolescence, 28,* 583–594.

Savage, S., & Gauvain, M. (1998). Parental beliefs and children's everyday planning in European-American and Latino families. *Journal of Applied Developmental Psychology, 19,* 319–340.

Savin-Williams, R., & Ream, G. (2003). Suicide attempts among sexual-minority male youth. *Journal of Clinical Child & Adolescent Psychology, 32,* 509–522.

Saxon, T., Colombo, J., Robinson, E., & Frick, J. (2000). Dyadic interaction profiles in infancy and preschool intelligence. *Journal of School Psychology, 38,* 9–25.

Scarr, S. (1997). Why child care has little impact on most children's development. *Current Directions in Psychological Science, 6,* 143–147.

Scarr, S., & Eisenberg, M. (1993). Child care research: Issues, perspectives, and results. *Annual Review of Psychology, 44,* 613–644.

Scarr, S., & McCartney, K. (1983). How people make their own environments: A theory of genotype/environment effects. *Child Development, 54,* 424–435.

Scarr, S., & Weinberg, R. A. (1983). The Minnesota adoption studies: Genetic differences and malleability. *Child Development, 54,* 260–267.

Scarr, S., Weinberg, R. A., & Waldman, I. D. (1993). IQ correlations in transracial adoptive families. *Intelligence, 17,* 541–555.

Schaal, B., Marlier, L., & Soussignan, R. (1998). Olfactory function in the human fetus: Evidence from selective neonatal responsiveness to the odor of amniotic fluid. *Behavioral Neuroscience, 112,* 1438–1449.

Schadt, D. (1997). The relationship of type to developmental issues of midlife women: Implications for counseling. *Journal of Psychological Type, 43,* 12–21.

Schafer, J., Caetano, R., & Cunradi, C. (2004). The present study was designed to identify the impact of drinking problems. *Journal of Interpersonal Violence, 19,* 127–142.

Schaffer, H., & Emerson, P. (1964). The development of social attachments in infancy. *Monographs of the Society for Research in Child Development, 29* (3, Serial No. 94).

Schaie, K. W. (1983). The Seattle longitudinal study: A 21-year exploration of psychometric intelligence in adulthood. In K. W. Schaie (Ed.), *Longitudinal studies of adult psychological development* (pp. 64–135). New York: Guilford Press.

Schaie, K. W. (1989). The hazards of cognitive aging. *The Gerontologist, 29,* 484–493.

Schaie, K. W. (1990). Intellectual development in adulthood. In J. E. Birren & K. W. Schaie (Eds.), *Handbook of the psychology of aging* (3rd ed., pp. 291–309). San Diego, CA: Academic Press.

Schaie, K. W. (1993). The Seattle Longitudinal Studies of adult intelligence. *Current Directions in Psychological Science, 2,* 171–175.

Schaie, K. W. (1994). The course of adult intellectual development. *American Psychologist, 49,* 304–313.

Schaie, K. W. (1996). Intellectual development in adulthood. In J. E. Birren & K. W. Schaie (Eds.), *Handbook of the psychology of aging* (4th ed., pp. 266–286). San Diego, CA: Academic Press.

Schaie, K. W., & Hertzog, C. (1983). Fourteen-year cohort-sequential analyses of adult intellectual development. *Developmental Psychology, 19,* 531–543.

Schaie, K. W., & Willis, S. L. (1991). Adult personality and psychomotor performance: Cross-sectional and longitudinal analyses. *Journals of Gerontology: Psychological Sciences, 46,* P275–284.

Schaie, K. W., Nguyen, H., Willis, S., Dutta, R., & Yue, G. (2001). Environmental factors as a conceptual framework for examining cognitive performance in Chinese adults. *International Journal of Behavioral Development, 25,* 193–202.

Scharlach, A. E., & Fredricksen, K. I. (1994). Eldercare versus adult care. Does care recipient age make a difference? *Research on Aging, 16,* 43–68.

Schatschneider, C., Fletcher, J., Francis, D., Carlson, C., & Foorman, B. (2004). Kindergarten prediction of reading skills: A longitudinal comparative analysis. *Journal of Educational Psychology, 96,* 265–282.

Schatschneider, C., Francis, D., Foorman, B., Fletcher, J., & Mehta, P. (1999). The dimensionality of phonological awareness: An application of item response theory. *Journal of Educational Psychology, 91,* 439–449.

Scheibel, A. B. (1992). Structural changes in the aging brain. In J. E. Birren, R. B. Sloane, & G. D. Cohen (Eds.), *Handbook of mental health and aging* (2nd ed., pp. 147–174). San Diego, CA: Academic Press.

Scheibel, A. B. (1996). Structural and functional changes in the aging brain. In J. E. Birren & K. W. Schaie (Eds.), *Handbook of the psychology of aging* (4th ed., pp. 105–128). San Diego, CA: Academic Press.

Scheidt, R., Humpherys, D., & Yorgason, J. (1999). Successful aging: What's not to like? *Journal of Applied Gerontology, 18,* 277–282.

Scheier, M. F., Matthews, K. A., Owens, J. F., Magovern, G. J., Lefebvre, S., Abbott, R. A., & Carver, C. S. (1989). Dispositional optimism and recovery from coronary artery bypass surgery: The beneficial effects on physical and psychological well-being. *Journal of Personality & Social Psychology, 57,* 1024–1040.

Schieber, F. (1992). Aging and the senses. In J. E. Birren, R. B. Sloane, & G. D. Cohen (Eds.), *Handbook of mental health and aging* (2nd ed., pp. 252–306). San Diego, CA: Academic Press.

Schieve, L., Meikle, S., Ferre, C., Peterson, H., Jeng, G., & Wilcox, L. (2002). Low and very low birth weight in infants conceived with the use of assisted reproductive technology. *New England Journal of Medicine, 346,* 731–737.

Schieve, L., Peterson, H., Meikle, S., Jeng, G., Danel, I., Burnett, N., & Wilcox, L. (1999). Birth rates and multiple-birth risk using in vitro fertilization. *Journal of the American Medical Association, 282,* 1832–1838.

Schlyter, S. (1996). Bilingual children's stories: French passé composé/imparfait and their correspondences in Swedish. *Linguistics, 34,* 1059–1085.

Schmidt, M., DeMulder, E., & Denham, S. (2002). Kindergarten social-emotional competence: Developmental predictors and psychosocial implications. *Early Child Development & Care, 172,* 451–461.

Schmidt, P. (2000, January 21). Colleges prepare for the fallout from state testing policies. *Chronicle of Higher Education, 46,* A26–A28.

Schmitt, D., Shackelford, T., & Buss, D. (2001). Are men really more "oriented" toward short-term mating than women? A critical review of theory and research. *Psychology, Evolution, & Gender, 3,* 211–239.

Schmitt, K., & Anderson, D. (2002). Television and reality: Toddlers' use of visual information from video to guide behavior. *Media Psychology, 4,* 51–76.

Schmitt, N., Sacco, J., Ramey, S., Ramey, C., & Chan, D. (1999). Parental employment, school climate, and children's academic and social development. *Journal of Applied Psychology, 84,* 737–753.

Schmitz, S., Fulker, D., Plomin, R., Zahn-Waxler, C., Emde, R., & DeFries, J. (1999). Temperament and problem behavior during early childhood. *International Journal of Behavioral Development, 23,* 333–355.

Schnarch, D. (1997). Sex, intimacy, and the Internet. *Journal of Sex Education & Therapy, 22,* 15–20.

Schneider, B., Hieshima, J. A., Lee, S., & Plank, S. (1994). East-Asian academic success in the United States: Family, school, and community explanations. In P. M. Greenfield & R. R. Cocking (Eds.), *Cross-cultural roots of minority child development* (pp. 323–350). Hillsdale, NJ: Erlbaum.

Schneider, M. (2004). The intersection of mental and physical health in older Mexican Americans. *Hispanic Journal of Behavioral Sciences, 26,* 333–355.

Schoen, R., & Wooldredge, J. (1989). Marriage choices in North Carolina and Virginia, 1969–71 and 1979–81. *Journal of Marriage & the Family, 51,* 465–481.

Schoendorf, K. C., Hogue, C. J. R., Kleinman, J. C., & Rowley, D. (1992). Mortality among infants of black as compared with white college-educated parents. *New England Journal of Medicine, 326,* 1522–1526.

Schoendorf, K. C., & Kiely, J. L. (1992). Relationship of Sudden Infant Death Syndrome to maternal smoking during and after pregnancy. *Pediatrics, 90,* 905–908.

Scholle, S., Buranosky, R., Hanusa, B., Ranieri, L., Dowd, K., & Valappil, B. (2003). Routine screening for intimate partner violence in an obstetrics and gynecology clinic. *American Journal of Public Health, 93,* 1070–1072.

Schonert-Reichl, K. (1999). Relations of peer acceptance, friendship adjustment, and social behavior to moral reasoning during early adolescence. *Journal of Early Adolescence, 19,* 249–279.

Schothorst, P., & van Engeland, H. (1996). Long-term behavioral sequelae of prematurity. *Journal of the American Academy of Child & Adolescent Psychiatry, 35,* 175–183.

Schraf, M., & Hertz-Lazarowitz, R. (2003). Social networks in the school context: Effects of culture and gender. *Journal of Social & Personal Relationships, 20,* 843–858.

Schreiber, M., Lutz, K., Schweizer, A., Kalveram, K., & Jaencke, L., (1998). Development and evaluation of an interactive computer-based training as a rehabilitation tool for dementia. *Psychologische Reitraege, 40,* 85–102.

Schreiber, M., Schweizer, A., Lutz, K., Kalveram, K., & Jaencke, L. (1999). Potential of an interactive computer-based training in the rehabilitation of dementia. An initial study. *Neuropsychological Rehabilitation, 9,* 155–167.

Schroeder, D., & Salthouse, T. (2004). Age-related effects on cognition between 20 and 50 years of age. *Personality & Individual Differences, 36,* 393–404.

Schuler, M., & Nair, P. (1999). Frequency of maternal cocaine use during pregnancy and infant neurobehavioral outcome. *Journal of Pediatric Psychology, 24,* 511–514.

Schuler, M., Nair, P., & Black, M. (2002). Ongoing maternal drug use, parenting attitudes, and a home intervention: Effects on mother-child interaction at 18 months. *Journal of Developmental & Behavioral Pediatrics, 23,* 87–94.

Schultz, N. R., Jr., Elias, M. F., Robbins, M. A., Streeten, D. H. P., & Blakeman, N. (1986). A longitudinal comparison of hypertensives and normotensives on the Wechsler Adult Intelligence Scale: Initial findings. *Journal of Gerontology, 41,* 169–175.

Schulz, A. (1998). Navajo women and the politics of identities. *Social Problems, 45,* 336–355.

Schulz, J. H. (1995). *The economics of aging* (6th ed.). Westport, CT: Auburn House.

Schulz, R., & Curnow, C. (1988). Peak performance and age among superathletes: Track and field, swimming, baseball, tennis, and golf. *Journals of Gerontology: Psychological Sciences, 43,* P113–120.

Schulz, R., Visintainer, P., & Williamson, G. M. (1990). Psychiatric and physical morbidity effects of caregiving. *Journals of Gerontology: Psychological Sciences, 45,* 181–191.

Schulz, R., & Williamson, G. M. (1991). A 2-year longitudinal study of depression among Alzheimer's caregivers. *Psychology & Aging, 6,* 569–578.

Schuster, C. (1997). Condom use behavior: An assessment of United States college students' health education needs. *International Quarterly of Community Health Education, 17,* 237–254.

Schvaneveldt, P., Miller, B., Berry, E., & Lee, T. (2001). Academic goals, achievement, and age at first sexual intercourse: Longitudinal, bidirectional influences. *Adolescence, 36,* 767–787.

Schwartz, C., Snidman, N., & Kagan, J. (1996). Early childhood temperament as a determinant of externalizing behavior in adolescence. *Development & Psychopathology, 8,* 527–537.

Schwartz, D., Dodge, K. A., & Coie, J. D. (1993). The emergence of chronic peer victimization in boys' play groups. *Child Development, 64,* 1755–1772.

Schwartz, R. M., Anastasia, M. L., Scanlon, J. W., & Kellogg, R. J. (1994). Effect of surfactant on morbidity, mortality, and resource use in newborn infants weighing 500 to 1500 g. *New England Journal of Medicine, 330,* 1476–1480.

Schwebel, D., Rosen, C., & Singer, J. (1999). Preschoolers' pretend play and theory of mind: The role of jointly constructed pretence. *British Journal of Developmental Psychology, 17,* 333–348.

Schweizer, T., Schnegg, M., & Berzborn, S. (1998). Personal networks and social support in a multiethnic community of southern California. *Social Networks, 20,* 1–21.

Schwitzer, A., Griffin, O., Ancie, J., & Thomas, C. (1999). Social adjustment experiences of African American college students. *Journal of Counseling & Development, 77,* 189–197.

Scott, J. (1998). Hematology. In R. Behrman & R. Kliegman (Eds.), *Nelson essentials of pediatrics* (3rd ed., pp. 545–582). Philadelphia: W. B. Saunders.

Sebanc, A. (2003). The friendship features of preschool children: Links with prosocial behavior and aggression. *Social Development, 12,* 249–268.

Sedney, M. (1999). Children's grief narratives in popular films. *Omega, 39,* 314–324.

Segatto, B., & Di Filippo, L. (2003). Vita relazionale ed emozioni nelle coppie in fase di pensionamento e/o nido vuoto. *Eta Evolutiva, 74,* 5–20.

Sege, R. (2004). The multisite violence prevention project: A commentary from academic research. *American Journal of Preventive Medicine, 26,* 78–79.

Seidman, E., Allen, L., Aber, J. L., Mitchell, C., & Feinman, J. (1994). The impact of school transitions in early adolescence on the self-sytem and perceived social context of poor urban youth. *Child Development, 65,* 507–522.

Seifer, R., Schiller, M., Sameroff, A. J., Resnick, S., & Riordan, K. (1996). Attachment, maternal sensitivity, and infant temperament during the first year of life. *Developmental Psychology, 32,* 12–25.

Seligman, M. E. P. (1991). *Learned optimism.* New York: Knopf.

Sellers, A., Burns, W., & Guyrke, J. (2002). Differences in young children's IQs on the Wechsler Preschool and Primary Scale of Intelligence-Revised as a function of stratification variables. *Neuropsychology, 9,* 65–73.

Sellers, R., Chavous, T., & Cooke, D. (1998). Racial ideology and racial centrality as predictors of African American college students' academic performance. *Journal of Black Psychology, 24,* 8–27.

Selman, R. L. (1980). *The growth of interpersonal understanding.* New York: Academic Press.

Semrud-Clikeman, M., Nielsen, K., Clinton, A., Sylvester, L., et al. (1999). An intervention approach for children with teacher- and parent-identified attentional difficulties. *Journal of Learning Disabilities, 32,* 581–590.

Senchak, M., Leonard, K., & Greene, B. (1998). Alcohol use among college students as a function of their typical social drinking context. *Psychology of Addictive Behaviors, 12,* 62–70.

Serbin, L., Moskowitz, D. S., Schwartzman, A. E., & Ledingham, J. E. (1991). Aggressive, withdrawn, and aggressive/withdrawn children in adolescence: Into the next generation. In D. J. Pepler & K. H. Rubin (Eds.), *The development and treatment of childhood aggression* (pp. 55–70). Hillsdale, NJ: Erlbaum.

Serbin, L., Poulin-Dubois, D., Colbourne, K., Sen, M., & Eichstedt, J. (2001). Gender stereotyping in infancy: Visual preferences for and knowledge of gender-stereotyped toys in the second year. *International Journal of Behavioral Development, 25,* 7–15.

Serbin, L. A., Powlishta, K. K., & Gulko, J. (1993). The development of sex typing in middle childhood. *Monographs of the Society for Research in Child Development, 58* (2, Serial No. 232).

Serdula, M. K., Ivery, D., Coates, R. J., Freedman, D. S., Williamson, D. F., & Byers, T. (1993). Do obese children become obese adults? A review of the literature. *Preventive Medicine, 22,* 167–177.

Serpell, R., & Hatano, G. (1997). Education, schooling, and literacy. In J. Berry, P. Dasen, & T. Saraswathi (Eds.), *Handbook of cross-cultural psychology, Vol. 2: Basic processes and human development.* Needham Heights, MA: Allyn & Bacon.

Shaffer, D., Garland, A., Gould, M., Fisher, P., & Trautman, P. (1988). Preventing teenage suicide: A critical review. *Journal of the American Academy of Child & Adolescent Psychiatry, 27,* 675–687.

Shaffer, D., Garland, A., Vieland, V., Underwood, M., & Busner, C. (1991). The impact of curriculum-based suicide prevention programs for teenagers. *Journal of the American Academy of Child & Adolescent Psychiatry, 30,* 588–596.

Shannon, T. (2004). Stem cell research: How Catholic ethics guides us. *Catholic Update.* Retrieved September 25, 2004, from http://www.usccb.org/prolife/issues/bioethic/stemcelltest71801.htm.

Shapiro, E. (1983). Impending death and the use of hospitals by the elderly. *Journal of the American Geriatric Society, 31,* 348–351.

Shapiro, E. (2002). Family bereavement after collective trauma: Private suffering, public meanings, and cultural contexts. *Journal of Systemic Therapies, 21,* 81–92.

Share, D., & Leiken, M. (2004). Language impairment at school entry and later reading disability: Connections at lexical versus supralexical levels of reading. *Scientific Studies of Reading, 8,* 87–110.

Sharma, S., Monsen, R., & Gary, B. (1997). Comparison of attitudes toward death and dying among nursing majors and other college students. *Omega, 34,* 219–232.

Sharma, V., & Sharma, A. (1997). Adolescent boys in Gujrat, India: Their sexual behavior and their knowledge of acquired immunodeficiency syndrome and other sexually transmitted diseases. *Journal of Developmental & Behavioral Pediatrics, 18,* 399–404.

Shaw, D. S., Kennan, K., & Vondra, J. I. (1994). Developmental precursors of externalizing behavior: Ages 1 to 3. *Developmental Psychology, 30,* 355–364.

Shaw, R., Ryst, E., & Steiner, H. (1996). Temperament as a correlate of adolescent defense mechanisms. *Child Psychiatry & Human Development, 27,* 105–114.

Shelton, B. A., & John, D. (1993). Ethnicity, race, and difference: A comparison of White, Black, and Hispanic men's household labor time. In J. C. Hood (Ed.), *Men, work, and family* (pp. 131–150). Newbury Park, CA: Sage.

Shiner, R. (2000). Linking childhood personality with adaptation: Evidence for continuity and change across time into late adolescence. *Journal of Personality & Social Psychology, 78,* 310–325.

Shneidman, E. S. (1980). *Voices of death.* New York: Harper & Row.

Shneidman, E. S. (1983). *Deaths of man.* New York: Jason Aronson.

Shochat, L. (2003). *Our Neighborhood:* Using entertaining children's television to promote interethnic understanding in Macedonia. *Conflict Resolution Quarterly, 21,* 79–93.

Shock, N. W., Greulich, R. C., Andres, R., Arenberg, D., Costa, P. T., Jr., Lakatta, E. G., & Tobin, J. D. (1984). *Normal human aging: The Baltimore Longitudinal Study of Aging,* NIH Publication No. 84–2450, U.S. Department of Health and Human Services, National Institute on Aging. Washington, DC: U.S. Government Printing Office.

Shoda, Y., Mischel, W., & Peake, P. (1990). Predicting adolescent cognitive and self-regulatory competencies from preschool delay of gratification. *Developmental Psychology, 26,* 978–986.

Shonkoff, J. P. (1984). The biological substrate and physical health in middle childhood. In W. A. Collins (Ed.), *Development during middle childhood: The years from six to twelve* (pp. 24–69). Washington, DC: National Academy Press.

Shore, C. (1986). Combinatorial play, conceptual development, and early multiword speech. *Developmental Psychology, 22,* 184–190.

Shore, C. M. (1995). *Individual differences in language development.* Thousand Oaks, CA: Sage.

Shu, H., Anderson, R., & Wu, N. (2000). Phonetic awareness: Knowledge of orthography-phonology relationships in the character acquisition of Chinese children. *Journal of Educational Psychology, 92,* 56–62.

Shumaker, S., Legault, C., Rapp, S., Thal, L., Wallace, R., Ockene, J., Hendrix, S., Jones, B., Assaf, A., Jackson, R., Kotchen, J., Wassertheil-Smoller, S., & Wactawski-Wende, J. (2003). Estrogen plus progestin and the incidence of dementia and mild cognitive impairment in postmenopausal women:

The Women's Health Initiative memory study: A randomized controlled trial. *Journal of the American Medical Association, 289,* 2651–2662.

Sicotte, C., & Stemberger, R. (1999). Do children with PDDNOS have a theory of mind? *Journal of Autism & Developmental Disorders, 29,* 225–233.

Siegal, M. (1987). Are sons and daughters treated more differently by fathers than by mothers? *Developmental Review, 7,* 183–209.

Siegler, I. C. (1983). Psychological aspects of the Duke Longitudinal Studies. In K. W. Schaie (Ed.), *Longitudinal studies of adult psychological development* (pp. 136–190). New York: Guilford Press.

Siegler, R. S. (1976). Three aspects of cognitive development. *Cognitive Psychology, 8,* 431–520.

Siegler, R. S. (1978). The origins of scientific reasoning. In R. S. Siegler (Ed.), *Children's thinking: What develops?* (pp. 109–150). Hillsdale, NJ: Erlbaum.

Siegler, R. S. (1981). Developmental sequences within and between concepts. *Monographs of the Society for Research in Child Development, 46* (2, Serial No. 189).

Siegler, R. S. (1994). Cognitive variability: A key to understanding cognitive development. *Current Directions in Psychological Science, 3,* 1–5.

Sigman, M., Neumann, C., Carter, E., Cattle, D. J., D'Souza, S., & Bwibo, N. (1988). Home interactions and the development of Embu toddlers in Kenya. *Child Development, 59,* 1251–1261.

Sijuwade, P. (2003). A comparative study of family characteristics of Anglo American and Asian American high achievers. *Journal of Applied Social Psychology, 33,* 445–454.

Silbereisen, R. K., & Kracke, B. (1993). Variations in maturational timing and adjustment in adolescence. In S. Jackson & H. Rodrigues-Tomé (Eds.), *Adolescence and its social worlds* (pp. 67–94). Hove, England: Erlbaum.

Silver, M., Jilinskaia, E., & Perls, T. (2001). Cognitive functional status of age-confirmed centenarians in a population-based study. *Journals of Gerontology, Series B: Psychological Sciences & Social Sciences, 56B,* P134–P140.

Silver, M., Newell, K., Brady, C., Hedley-White, E., & Perls, T. (2002). Distinguishing between neurodegenerative disease and disease-free aging: Correlating neuropsychological evaluations and neuropathological studies in centenarians. *Psychosomatic Medicine, 64,* 493–501.

Silverstein, M., & Long, J. (1998). Trajectories of grandparents' perceived solidarity with adult grandchildren: A growth curve analysis over 23 years. *Journal of Marriage & the Family, 60,* 912–923.

Simkin, S., Hawton, K., Whitehead, L., Fagg, J., & Eagle, M. (1995). A study of the effects of television drama portrayal of paracetamol self-poisoning. *British Journal of Psychiatry, 167,* 754–759.

Simoneau, G. G., & Liebowitz, H. W. (1996). Posture, gait, and falls. In J. E. Birren & K. W. Schaie (Eds.), *Handbook of the psychology of aging* (4th ed., pp. 204–217). San Diego, CA: Academic Press.

Simons, R. L., Robertson, J. F., & Downs, W. R. (1989). The nature of the association between parental rejection and delinquent behavior. *Journal of Youth & Adolescence, 18,* 297–309.

Simons-Morton, B., Crump, A., Haynie, D., Saylor, K., Eitel, P., & Yu, K. (1999). Psychosocial, school, and parent factors associated with recent smoking among early-adolescent boys and girls. *Preventive Medicine, 28,* 138–148.

Simonton, D. (2000). Creativity: Cognitive, personal, developmental, and social aspects. *American Psychologist, 55,* 151–158.

Simonton, D. K. (1988). Age and outstanding achievement: What do we know after a century of research? *Psychological Bulletin, 104,* 251–267.

Simonton, D. K. (1991). Career landmarks in science: Individual differences and interdisciplinary contrasts. *Developmental Psychology, 27,* 119–130.

Sims, M., Hutchins, T., & Taylor, M. (1997). Conflict as social interaction: Building relationship skills in child care settings. *Child & Youth Care Forum, 26,* 247–260.

Singh, S., & Darroch, J. (2000). Adolescent pregnancy and childbearing: Levels and trends in industrialized countries. *Family Planning Perspectives, 32,* 14–23.

Skaalvik, E., & Valas, H. (1999). Relations among achievement, self-concept and motivation in mathematics and language arts: A longitudinal study. *Journal of Experimental Education, 67,* 135–149.

Skinner, B. F. (1953). *Science and human behavior.* New York: Macmillan.

Skinner, B. F. (1957). *Verbal behavior.* New York: Prentice Hall.

Skinner, B. F. (1980). The experimental analysis of operant behavior: A history. In R. W. Riebes & K. Salzinger (Eds.), *Psychology: Theoretical-historical perspectives.* New York: Academic Press.

Skoe, E., Hansen, K., Morch, W., Bakke, I., Hoffman, T., Larsen, B., & Aasheim, M. (1999). Care-based moral reasoning in Norwegian and Canadian early adolescents: A cross-national comparison. *Journal of Early Adolescence, 19,* 280–291.

Skwarchuk, S., & Anglin, J. (2002). Children's acquisition of the English cardinal number words: A special case of vocabulary development. *Journal of Educational Psychology, 97,* 107–125.

Slaby, R. G., & Frey, K. S. (1975). Development of gender constancy and selective attention to same-sex models. *Child Development, 46,* 849–856.

Slater, A. (1995). Individual differences in infancy and later IQ. *Journal of Child Psychology & Psychiatry, 36,* 69–112.

Slaughter, V., & Lyons, M. (2003). Learning about life and death in early childhood. *Cognitive Psychology, 46,* 1–30.

Slobin, D. I. (1985a). Introduction: Why study acquisition crosslinguistically? In D. I. Slobin (Ed.), *The crosslinguistic study of language acquisition, Vol. 1: The data* (pp. 3–24). Hillsdale, NJ: Erlbaum.

Slobin, D. I. (1985b). Crosslinguistic evidence for the language-making capacity. In D. I. Slobin (Ed.), *The crosslinguistic study of language acquisition, Vol. 2: Theoretical issues* (pp. 1157–1256). Hillsdale, NJ: Erlbaum.

Slobounov, S., Moss, S., Slobounova, E., & Newell, K. (1998). Aging and time to instability in posture. *Journals of Gerontology, Series A: Biological Sciences & Medical Sciences, 53A,* B71–B78.

Small, S. A., & Luster, T. (1994). Adolescent sexual activity: An ecological, risk-factor approach. *Journal of Marriage & the Family, 56,* 181–192.

Smeeding, T. M. (1990). Economic status of the elderly. In R. H. Binstock & L. K. George (Eds.), *Handbook of aging and the social sciences* (3rd ed., pp. 362–381). San Diego, CA: Academic Press.

Smetana, J., Schlagman, N., & Adams, P. (1993). Preschool children's judgments about hypothetical and actual transgressions. *Child Development, 64,* 202–214.

Smetana, J. G. (1990). Morality and conduct disorders. In M. Lewis & S. M. Miller (Eds.), *Handbook of developmental psychopathology* (pp. 157–180). New York: Plenum.

Smetana, J. G., Killen, M., & Turiel, E. (1991). Children's reasoning about interpersonal and moral conflicts. *Child Development, 62,* 629–644.

Smith, A., Lalonde, R., & Johnson, S. (2004). Serial migration and its implications for the parent-child relationship: A retrospective analysis of the experiences of the children of Caribbean immigrants. *Cultural Diversity & Ethnic Minority Psychology, 10,* 107–122.

Smith, C., Umberger, G., Manning, E., Sleven, J., Wekstein, D., Schmitt, F., Markesbery, W., & Zhang, Z. (1999). Critical decline in fine motor hand movements in human aging. *Neurology, 53,* 1458–1461.

Smith, D., & Moen, P. (2004). Retirement satisfaction for retirees and their spouses: Do gender and the retirement decision-making process matter? *Journal of Family Issues, 25,* 262–285.

Smith, E., Gorman-Smith, D., Quinn, W., Rabiner, D., Tolan, P., & Winn, D. (2004). Community-based multiple family groups to prevent and reduce violent and aggressive behavior: The GREAT Families program. *American Journal of Preventive Medicine, 26,* 39–47.

Smith, E. L. (1982). Exercise for prevention of osteoporosis: A review. *Physician & Sportsmedicine, 10,* 72–83.

Smith, L., Fagan, J., & Ulvund, S. (2002). The relation of recognition memory in infancy and parental socioeconomic status to later intellectual competence. *Intelligence, 30,* 247–259.

Smith, M., Bibi, U., & Sheard, D. (2003). Misleading postevent information and flashbulb memories. *Memory, 11,* 549–558.

Smith, M., Sharit, J., & Czaja, S. (1999). Aging, motor control, and the performance of computer mouse tasks. *Human Factors, 41,* 389–396.

Smith, P., Smees, R., & Pellegrini, A. (2004). Play fighting and real fighting: Using video playback methodology with young children. *Aggressive Behavior, 30,* 164–173.

Smith, P., White, J., & Holland, L. (2003). A longitudinal perspective on dating violence among adolescent and college-age women. *American Journal of Public Health, 93,* 1104–1109.

Smith, S., Howard, J., & Monroe, A. (1998). An analysis of child behavior problems in adoptions in difficulty. *Journal of Social Service Research, 24,* 61–84.

Smith, W. (2004, January 19). Disabling assisted suicide: Why a deadly movement hasn't been contagious. *National Review Online.* Retrieved September 21, 2004, from http://www.nationalreview.com/script/printpage.asp?ref_/comment/smith200401190806.asp.

Smock, P. J. (1993). The economic costs of marital disruption for young women over the past two decades. *Demography, 30,* 353–371.

Smoll, F. L., & Schutz, R. W. (1990). Quantifying gender differences in physical performance: A developmental perspective. *Developmental Psychology, 26,* 360–369.

Snarey, J. (1995). In communitarian voice: The sociological expansion of Kohlbergian theory, research, and practice. In W. M. Kurtines & J. L.

Gerwitz (Eds.), *Moral development: An introduction* (pp. 109–134). Boston: Allyn & Bacon.

Snarey, J., Son, L., Kuehne, V. S., Hauser, S., & Vaillant, G. (1987). The role of parenting in men's psychosocial development: A longitudinal study of early adulthood infertility and midlife generativity. *Developmental Psychology, 23,* 593–603.

Snarey, J. R. (1985). Cross-cultural universality of social-moral development: A critical review of Kohlbergian research. *Psychological Bulletin, 97,* 202–232.

Snarey, J. R., Reimer, J., & Kohlberg, L. (1985). Development of social-moral reasoning among kibbutz adolescents: A longitudinal cross-sectional study. *Developmental Psychology, 21,* 3–17.

Snow, C. E. (1997, April). *Cross-domain connections and social class differences: Two challenges to nonenvironmentalist views of language development.* Paper presented at the biennial meetings of the Society for Research in Child Development, Washington, DC.

Snyder, C. (1997). Unique invulnerability: A classroom demonstration in estimating personal mortality. *Teaching of Psychology, 24,* 197–199.

Society for Assisted Reproductive Technology. (2004). *Guidelines on number of embryos transferred: Committee report.* Retrieved August 18, 2004, from http://www.sart.org.

Soken, N., & Pick. A. (1999). Infants' perception of dynamic affective expressions: Do infants distinguish specific expressions? *Child Development, 70,* 1275–1282.

Sola, A., Rogido, M., & Partridge, J. (2002). The perinatal period. In A. Rudolph, R. Kamei, & K. Overby (Eds.), *Rudolph's fundamental of pediatrics* (3rd ed., pp. 125–183). New York: McGraw-Hill.

Solano, L., Costa, M., Salvati, S., Coda, R., Aiuti, F., Mezzaroma, I., & Bertini, M. (1993). Psychosocial factors and clinical evolution in HIV-1 infection: A longitudinal study. *Journal of Psychosomatic Research, 37,* 39–51.

Soldo, B. J., Wolf, D. A., & Agree, E. M. (1990). Family, households, and care arrangements of frail older women: A structural analysis. *Journals of Gerontology: Social Sciences, 45,* S238–249.

Solomon, S., Rothblum, E., & Balsam, K. (2004). Pioneers in partnership: Lesbian and gay male couples in civil unions compared with those not in civil unions and married heterosexual siblings. *Journal of Family Psychology, 18,* 275–286.

Somers, M. D. (1993). A comparison of voluntarily childfree adults and parents. *Journal of Marriage & the Family, 55,* 643–650.

Sonneck, G., Etzersdorfer, E., & Nagel-Kuess, S. (1992). Subway suicide in Vienna (1980–1990): A contribution to the imitation effect in suicidal behavior. In P. Crepet, G. Ferrari, S. Platt, & M. Bellini (Eds.), *Suicidal behavior in Europe: Recent research findings.* Rome: Libbey.

Soori, H., & Bhopal, R. (2002). Parental permission for children's independent outdoor activities: Implications for injury prevention. *European Journal of Public Health, 12,* 104–109.

Sophian, C. (1995). Representation and reasoning in early numerical development: Counting, conservation, and comparisons between sets. *Child Development, 66,* 559–577.

Sorensen, E. (1997). A national profile of nonresident fathers and their ability to pay child support. *Journal of Marriage & the Family, 59,* 785–797.

Sorlie, P. D., Backlund, E., & Keller, J. B. (1995). U.S. mortality by economic, demographic, and social characteristics: The National Longitudinal Mortality Study. *American Journal of Public Health, 85,* 949–956.

Sotelo, M., & Sangrador, J. (1997). Psychological aspects of political tolerance among adolescents. *Psychological Reports, 81,* 1279–1288.

Sotelo, M., & Sangrador, J. (1999). Correlations of self-ratings of attitude towards violent groups with measures of personality, self-esteem, and moral reasoning. *Psychological Reports, 84,* 558–560.

Sowell, E., Peterson, B., Thompson, P., Welcome, S., Henkenius, A., & Toga, A. (2003). Mapping cortical change across the human life span. *Nature Neuroscience, 6,* 309–315.

Sparrow, P. R., & Davies, D. R. (1988). Effects of age, tenure, training, and job complexity on technical performance. *Psychology & Aging, 3,* 307–314.

Speece, M. W., & Brent, S. B. (1984). Children's understanding of death: A review of three components of a death concept. *Child Development, 55,* 1671–1686.

Speece, M. W., & Brent, S. B. (1992). The acquisition of a mature understanding of three components of the concept of death. *Death Studies, 16,* 211–229.

Spelke, E. S. (1979). Exploring audible and visible events in infancy. In A. D. Pick (Ed.), *Perception and its development: A tribute to Eleanor J. Gibson* (pp. 221–236). Hillsdale, NJ: Erlbaum.

Spelke, E. S. (1982). Perceptual knowledge of objects in infancy. In J. Mehler, E. C. T. Walker, & M. Garrett (Eds.), *Perspectives on mental representation* (pp. 409–430). Hillsdale, NJ: Erlbaum.

Spelke, E. S. (1985). Perception of unity, persistence, and identity: Thoughts on infants' conceptions of objects. In J. Mehler & R. Fox (Eds.), *Neonate cognition* (pp. 89–113). Hillsdale, NJ: Erlbaum.

Spelke, E. S. (1991). Physical knowledge in infancy: Reflections on Piaget's theory. In S. Carey & R. Gelman (Eds.), *The epigenesis of mind: Essays on biology and cognition* (pp. 133–169). Hillsdale, NJ: Erlbaum.

Spelke, E. S., & Owsley, C. J. (1979). Intermodal exploration and knowledge in infancy. *Infant Behavior & Development, 2,* 13–27.

Spelke, E. S., von Hofsten, C., & Kestenbaum, R. (1989). Object perception in infancy: Interaction of spatial and kinetic information for object boundaries. *Developmental Psychology, 25,* 185–196.

Spence, J. T., & Helmreich, R. L. (1978). *Masculinity and femininity.* Austin: University of Texas Press.

Spencer, M. B., & Dornbusch, S. M. (1990). Challenges in studying minority youth. In S. S. Feldman & G. R. Elliott (Eds.), *At the threshold: The developing adolescent* (pp. 123–146). Cambridge, MA: Harvard University Press.

Spenner, K. I. (1988). Occupations, work settings and the course of adult development: Tracing the implications of select historical changes. In P. B. Baltes, D. L. Featherman, & R. M. Lerner (Eds.), *Life-span development and behavior, Vol. 9* (pp. 244–288). Hillsdale, NJ: Erlbaum.

Spiegel, D., Bloom, J. R., Kraemer, H. C., & Gottheil, E. (1989, October 14). Effect of psychosocial treatment on survival of patients with metastatic breast cancer. *Lancet,* 888–901.

Spiers, P. S., & Guntheroth, W. G. (1994). Recommendations to avoid the prone sleeping position and recent statistics for Sudden Infant Death Syndrome in the United States. *Archives of Pediatric & Adolescent Medicine, 148,* 141–146.

Spitze, G. (1988). Women's employment and family relations: A review. *Journal of Marriage & the Family, 50,* 595–618.

Spitze, G., & Logan, J. (1990). More evidence on women (and men) in the middle. *Research on Aging, 12,* 182–198.

Sprang, G., & McNeil, J. (1998). Post-homicide reactions: Grief, mourning and post-traumatic stress disorder following a drunk driving fatality. *Omega, 37,* 41–58.

Spreen, O., Risser, A., & Edgell, D. (1995). *Developmental neuropsychology.* New York: Oxford University Press.

Sprigg, P. (2004). *Questions and answers: What's wrong with letting same-sex couples "marry"?* Retrieved September 24, 2004, from http://www.frc.org/get.cfm?i=IF03H01.

Srivastava, S., John, O., Gosling, S., & Potter, J. (2003). Development of personality in early and middle adulthood: Set like plaster or persistent change? *Journal of Personality and Social Psychology, 84,* 1041–1053.

Sroufe, L. A., Carlson, E., & Schulman, S. (1993). Individuals in relationships: Development from infancy through adolescence. In D. C. Funder, R. D. Parke, C. Tomlinson-Keasey, & K. Widaman (Eds.), *Studying lives through time: Personality and development* (pp. 315–342). Washington, DC: American Psychological Association.

St. James-Roberts, I., Bowyer, J., Varghese, S., & Sawdon, J. (1994). Infant crying patterns in Manila and London. *Child: Care, Health & Development, 20,* 323–337.

St. Pierre, T., Mark, M., Kaltreider, D., & Aikin, K. (1995). A 27-month evaluation of a sexual activity prevention program in boys and girls clubs across the nation. *Family Relations, 44,* 69–77.

Stack, S. (1992a). The effect of divorce on suicide in Finland: A time series analysis. *Journal of Marriage & the Family, 54,* 636–642.

Stack, S. (1992b). The effect of divorce on suicide in Japan: A time series analysis, 1950–1980. *Journal of Marriage & the Family, 54,* 327–334.

Stack, S., & Wasserman, I. (1993). Marital status, alcohol consumption, and suicide: An analysis of national data. *Journal of Marriage & the Family, 55,* 1018–1024.

Stadel, B. V., & Weiss, N. S. (1975). Characteristics of menopausal women: A survey of King and Pierce Counties in Washington, 1973–74. *American Journal of Epidemiology, 102,* 209–216.

Stallworth, J., & Lennon, J. (2003). An interview with Dr. Lester Breslow: A pioneer in chronic disease prevention and health behavior intervention shares insights from his professional and personal experiences. *American Journal of Public Health, 93,* 1803–1805.

Stambrook, M., & Parker, K. C. H. (1987). The development of the concept of death in childhood: A review of the literature. *Merrill-Palmer Quarterly, 33,* 133–158.

Stampfer, M. J., Colditz, G. A., Willett, W. C., Manson, J. E. Rosner, B., Speizer, F. E., & Hennekens, C. H. (1991). Postmenopausal estrogen therapy and cardiovascular disease: Ten-year follow-up from the Nurses' Health Study. *New England Journal of Medicine, 325,* 756–762.

Stampfer, M. J., Hennekins, C. H., Manson, J. E., Colditz, G. A., Rosner, B., & Willett, W. C. (1993). Vitamin E consumption and the risk of coronary disease in women. *New England Journal of Medicine, 328,* 1444–1449.

Stanford, E. P., Happersett, C. J., Morton, D. J., Molgaard, C. A., & Peddecord, K. M. (1991). Early retirement and functional impairment from a multiethnic perspective. *Research on Aging, 13,* 5–38.

Starfield, B. (1991). Childhood morbidity: Comparisons, clusters, and trends. *Pediatrics, 88,* 519–526.

Stattin, H., & Klackenberg-Larsson, I. (1993). Early language and intelligence development and their relationship to future criminal behavior. *Journal of Abnormal Psychology, 102,* 369–378.

Stearns, V., Beebe, K., Iyengar, M., & Dube, E. (2003). Paroxetine controlled release in the treatment of menopausal hot flashes: A randomized controlled trial. *Journal of the American Medical Association, 289,* 2827–2834.

Steele, J., & Mayes, S. (1995). Handedness and directional asymmetry in the long bones of the human upper limb. *International Journal of Osteoarchaeology, 5,* 39–49.

Steele, M., Hodges, J., Kaniuk, J., Hillman, S., & Henderson, K. (2003). Attachment representations and adoption: Associations between maternal states of mind and emotion narratives in previously maltreated children. *Journal of Child Psychotherapy, 29,* 187–205.

Steffens, D., Artigues, D., Ornstein, K., & Krishnan, K. (1997). A review of racial differences in geriatric depression: Implications for care and clinical research. *Journal of the National Medical Association, 89,* 731–736.

Stein, C., Wemmerus, V., Ward, M., Gaines, M., Freeberg, A., & Jewell, T. (1998). "Because they're my parents": An intergenerational study of felt obligation and parental caregiving. *Journal of Marriage & the Family, 60,* 611–622.

Stein, G. (2004). Improving our care at life's end: Making a difference. *Health & Social Work, 29,* 77–79.

Stein, K., Roeser, R., & Markus, H. (1998). Self-schemas and possible selves as predictors and outcomes of risky behaviors in adolescents. *Nursing Research, 47,* 96–106.

Steinberg, L. (1986). Latchkey children and susceptibility to peer pressure: An ecological analysis. *Developmental Psychology, 22,* 433–439.

Steinberg, L. (1990). Autonomy, conflict and harmony in the parent-adolescent relationship. In S. S. Feldman & G. R. Elliott (Eds.), *At the threshold: The developing adolescent* (pp. 255–276). Cambridge, MA: Harvard University Press.

Steinberg, L., Darling, N. E., Fletcher, A. C., Brown, B. B., & Dornbusch, S. M. (1995). Authoritative parenting and adolescent adjustment: An ecological journey. In P. Moen, G. H. Elder, Jr., & K. Lüscher (Eds.), *Examining lives in context: Perspectives on the ecology of human development* (pp. 423–466). Washington, DC: American Psychological Association.

Steinberg, L., Elmen, J. D., & Mounts, N. S. (1989). Authoritative parenting, psychosocial maturity, and academic success among adolescents. *Child Development, 60,* 1424–1436.

Steinberg, L., Fletcher, A., & Darling, N. (1994). Parental monitoring and peer influences on adolescent substance use. *Pediatrics, 93,* 1060–1064.

Steinberg, L., Lamborn, S. D., Darling, N., Mounts, N. S., & Dornbusch, S. M. (1994). Over-time changes in adjustment and competence among adolescents from authoritative, authoritarian, indulgent, and neglectful families. *Child Development, 65,* 754–770.

Steinberg, L., Lamborn, S. D., Dornbusch, S. M., & Darling, N. (1992). Impact of parenting practices on adolescent achievement: Authoritative parenting, school involvement, and encouragement to succeed. *Child Development, 63,* 1266–1281.

Steinberg, L., Mounts, N. S., Lamborn, S. D., & Dornbusch, S. D. (1991). Authoritative parenting and adolescent adjustment across varied ecological niches. *Journal of Research on Adolescence, 1,* 19–36.

Steiner, J. E. (1979). Human facial expressions in response to taste and smell stimulation. In H. W. Reese & L. P. Lipsitt (Eds.), *Advances in child development and behavior, Vol. 13* (pp. 257–296). New York: Academic Press.

Steinhauser, K., Christakis, N., Clipp, E., McNeilly, M., Grambow, S., Parker, J., & Tulsky, J. (2001). Preparing for the end of life: Preferences of patients, families, physicians, and other care providers. *Journal of Pain & Symptom Management, 22,* 727–737.

Sternberg, R. (1988). *The triarchic mind: A new theory of intelligence.* New York: Viking Press.

Sternberg, R. (2002). A broad view of intelligence: The theory of successful intelligence. *Consulting Psychology Journal: Practice and Research, 55,* 139–154.

Sternberg, R., Wagner, R., Williams, W., & Horvath, J. (1995). Testing common sense. *American Psychologist, 50,* 912–927.

Sternberg, R. J. (1987). Liking versus loving: A comparative evaluation of theories. *Psychological Bulletin, 102,* 331–345.

Sternberg, R. J. (1990). Wisdom and its relations to intelligence and creativity. In R. J. Sternberg (Ed.), *Wisdom: Its nature, origins, and development* (pp. 142–159). Cambridge, England: Cambridge University Press.

Sternberg, R. J., & Wagner, R. K. (1993). The g-ocentric view of intelligence and job performance is wrong. *Current Directions in Psychological Science, 2,* 1–5.

Stevens, J., & Choo, K. (1998). Temperature sensitivity of the body surface over the life span. *Somatosensory & Motor Research, 15,* 13–28.

Stevenson, H. (1994). Moving away from stereotypes and preconceptions: Students and their education in East Asia and the United States. In P. M. Greenfield & R. R. Cocking (Eds.), *Cross-cultural roots of minority child development* (pp. 315–322). Hillsdale, NJ: Erlbaum.

Stevenson, H. W., & Lee, S. (1990). Contexts of achievement: A study of American, Chinese, and Japanese children. *Monographs of the Society for Research in Child Development, 55* (1–2, Serial No. 221).

Stevenson, H. W., Lee, S., Chen, C., Lummis, M., Stigler, J., Fan, L., & Ge, F. (1990). Mathematics achievement of children in China and the United States. *Child Development, 61,* 1053–1066.

Stewart, A., & Ostrove, J. (1998). Women's personality in middle age: Gender, history, and midcourse corrections. *American Psychologist, 53,* 1185–1194.

Stewart, C. (2004). The physiology of stem cells: Potential for the elderly patient. *Journal of Musculoskeletal Neuron Interaction, 4,* 179–183.

Stewart, R. B., Beilfuss, M. L., & Verbrugge, K. M. (1995, March). *That was then, this is now: An empirical typology of adult sibling relationships.* Paper presented at the biennial meetings of the Society for Research in Child Development, Indianapolis, IN.

Stewart, S., Pearson, S., Luke, C., & Horowitz, J. (1998). Effects of home-based intervention on unplanned readmissions and out-of-hospital deaths. *Journal of the American Geriatrics Society, 46,* 174–180.

Stigler, J. W., Lee, S., & Stevenson, H. W. (1987). Mathematics classrooms in Japan, Taiwan, and the United States. *Child Development, 58,* 1272–1285.

Stigler, J. W., & Stevenson, H. W. (1991). How Asian teachers polish each lesson to perfection. *American Educator* (Spring), 12–20, 43–47.

Stipek, D., Gralinski, J., & Kopp, C. (1990). Self-concept development in the toddler years. *Developmental Psychology, 26,* 972–977.

Stolarova, M., Whitney, H., Webb, S., deRegnier, R., Georgieff, M., & Nelson, C. (2003). Electrophysiological brain responses of six-month-old low risk premature infants. *Infancy, 4,* 437–450.

Stoller, E. P., Forster, L. E., & Duniho, T. S. (1992). Systems of parent care within sibling networks. *Research on Aging, 14,* 28–49.

Stone, K., Karem, K., Sternberg, M., McQuillan, G., Poon, A., Unger, E., & Reeves, W. (2002). Seroprevalence of human papillomavirus type 16 infection in the United States. *Journal of Infectious Diseases, 186,* 1396–1402.

Stones, M. J., & Kozma, A. (1996). Activity, exercise, and behavior. In J. E. Birren & K. W. Schaie (Eds.), *Handbook of the psychology of aging* (4th ed., pp. 338–352). San Diego, CA: Academic Press.

Stormshak, E., Bierman, K., McMahon, R., Lengua, L., et al. (2000). Parenting practices and child disruptive behavior problems in early elementary school. *Journal of Clinical Child Psychology, 29,* 17–29.

Stoutjesdyk, D., & Jevne, R. (1993). Eating disorders among high performance athletes. *Journal of Youth and Adolescence, 22,* 271–282.

Strassberg, Z., Dodge, K. A., Pettit, G. S. & Bates, J. E. (1994). Spanking in the home and children's subsequent aggression toward kindergarten peers. *Development & Psychopathology, 6,* 445–461.

Straus, M. A. (1991a). Discipline and deviance: Physical punishment of children and violence and other crime in adulthood. *Social Problems, 38,* 133–152.

Straus, M. A. (1991b). New theory and old canards about family violence research. *Social Problems, 38,* 180–194.

Straus, M. A. (1995). Corporal punishment of children and adult depression and suicidal ideation. In J. McCord (Ed.), *Coercion and punishment in long-term perspectives* (pp. 59–77). Cambridge, England: Cambridge University Press.

Straus, M. A., & Donnelly, D. A. (1993). Corporal punishment of adolescents by American parents. *Youth & Society, 24,* 419–442.

Strawbridge, W. J., Camacho, T. C., Cohen, R. D., & Kaplan, G. A. (1993). Gender differences in factors associated with change in physical functioning in old age: A 6-year longitudinal study. *The Gerontologist, 33,* 603–609.

Strayer, F. F. (1980). Social ecology of the preschool peer group. In A. Collins (Ed.), *Minnesota symposia on child psychology, Vol. 13* (pp. 165–196). Hillsdale, NJ: Erlbaum.

Strayer, J., & Roberts, W. (2004). Empathy and observed anger and aggression in five-year-olds. *Social Development, 13,* 1–13.

Streissguth, A. P., Aase, J. M., Clarren, S. K., Randels, S. P., LaDue, R. A., & Smith, D. F. (1991). Fetal alcohol syndrome in adolescents and adults. *Journal of the American Medical Association, 265,* 1961–1967.

Streufert, S., Pogash, R., Piasecki, M., & Post, G. M. (1990). Age and management team performance. *Psychology & Aging, 5,* 551–559.

Striano, T., & Rochat, P. (1999). Developmental link between dyadic and triadic social competence in infancy. *British Journal of Developmental Psychology, 17,* 551–562.

Stroebe, M. (2002). Paving the way: From early attachment theory to contemporary bereavement research. *Mortality, 7,* 127–138.

Stroebe, M., van Son, M., Stroebe, W., Kleber, R., Schut, H., & van den Bout, J. (2000). On the classification and diagnosis of pathological grief. *Clinical Psychology Review, 20,* 57–75.

Stroebe, M. S., & Stroebe, W. (1993). The mortality of bereavement: A review. In M. S. Stroebe, W. Stroebe, & R. O. Hansson (Eds.), *Handbook of bereavement: Theory, research, and intervention* (pp. 175–195). Cambridge, England: Cambridge University Press.

Stroganova, T., Posikera, I., Pushina, N., & Orekhova, E. (2003). Lateralization of motor functions in early human ontogeny. *Human Physiology, 29,* 48–58.

Strom, R., & Strom, S. (1999). Establishing school volunteer programs. *Child & Youth Services, 20,* 175–188.

Students cite pregnancies as a reason to drop out. (1994, September 14). *New York Times,* p. B7.

Stull, D. E., & Hatch, L. R. (1984). Unravelling the effects of multiple life changes. *Research on Aging, 6,* 560–571.

Stunkard, A. J., Harris, J. R., Pedersen, N. L., & McClearn, G. E. (1990). The body-mass index of twins who have been reared apart. *New England Journal of Medicine, 322,* 1483–1487.

Sue, S., & Okazaki, S. (1990). Asian-American educational achievements: A phenomenon in search of an explanation. *American Psychologist, 45,* 913–920.

Sugisawa, H., Liang, J., & Liu, X. (1994). Social networks, social support, and mortality among older people in Japan. *Journals of Gerontology: Social Sciences, 49,* S3–13.

Sulkes, S. (1998). Developmental and behavioral pediatrics. In R. Behrman & R. Kliegman (Eds.), *Nelson essentials of pediatrics* (3rd ed., pp. 1–55). Philadelphia: W. B. Saunders.

Sullivan, K., Zaitchik, D., & Tager-Flusberg, H. (1994). Preschoolers can attribute second-order beliefs. *Developmental Psychology, 30,* 395–402.

Sullivan, M., Ormel, J., Kempen, G., & Tymstra, T. (1998). Beliefs concerning death, dying, and hastening death among older, functionally impaired Dutch adults: A one-year longitudinal study. *Journal of the American Geriatrics Society, 46,* 1251–1257.

Super, D. E. (1971). A theory of vocational development. In H. J. Peters & J. C. Hansen (Eds.), *Vocational guidance and career development* (pp. 111–122). New York: Macmillan.

Super, D. E. (1986). Life career roles: Self-realization in work and leisure. In D. T. H. &. Associates (Eds.), *Career development in organizations* (pp. 95–119). San Francisco: Jossey-Bass.

Suryadevara, V., Storey, S., Aronow, W., & Ahn, C. (2003). Association of abnormal serum lipids in elderly persons with atherosclerotic vascular disease and dementia, atherosclerotic vascular disease without dementia, dementia without atherosclerotic vascular disease, and no dementia or atherosclerotic vascular disease. *Journals of Gerontology, Series A: Biological Sciences & Medical Sciences, 58A,* 859–861.

Susman, E. J., Inoff-Germain, G., Nottelmann, E. D., Loriaux, D. L., Cutler, G. B., Jr., & Chrousos, G. P. (1987). Hormones, emotional dispositions, and aggressive attributes in young adolescents. *Child Development, 58,* 1114–1134.

Susser, E., & Lin, S. (1992). Schizophrenia after prenatal exposure to the Dutch hunger winter of 1944–45. *Archives of General Psychiatry, 49,* 983–988.

Sutton, P., & Munson, M. (2004). Births, marriages, divorces, and deaths: Provisional data for January 2004. *National Vital Statistics Reports; 53,* 1–6.

Svrakic, N., Svrakic, D., & Cloninger, C. (1996). A general quantitative theory of personality development: Fundamentals of a self-organizing psychobiological complex. *Development & Psychopathology, 8,* 247–272.

Swaim, K., & Bracken, B. (1997). Global and domain-specific self-concepts of a matched sample of adolescent runaways and nonrunaways. *Journal of Clinical Child Psychology, 26,* 397–403.

Swedo, S. E., Rettew, D. C., Kuppenheimer, M., Lum, D., Dolan, S., & Goldberger, E. (1991). Can adolescent suicide attempters be distinguished from at-risk adolescents? *Pediatrics, 88,* 620–629.

Sweeting, H., & West, P. (2002). Gender differences in weight related concerns in early to late adolescence. *Journal of Family Issues, 23,* 728–747.

Swendsen, J., & Mazure, C. (2000). Life stress as a risk factor for postpartum depression: Current research and methodological issues. *Clinical Psychology, 7,* 17–31.

Swensen, C. H., Eskew, R. W., & Kohlhepp, K. A. (1981). Stage of family life cycle, ego development, and the marriage relationship. *Journal of Marriage & the Family, 43,* 841–853.

Syme, S. L. (1990). Control and health: An epidemiological perspective. In J. Rodin, C. Schooler, & K. W. Schaie (Eds.), *Self directedness: Cause and effects throughout the life course* (pp. 213–229). Hillsdale, NJ: Erlbaum.

Tadmor, C. (2004). Preventive intervention for children with cancer and their families at the end-of-life. *Journal of Primary Prevention, 24,* 311–323.

Tait, M., Padgett, M. Y., & Baldwin, T. T. (1989). Job and life satisfaction: A reevaluation of the strength of the relationship and gender effects as a function of the date of the study. *Journal of Applied Psychology, 74,* 502–507.

Takahashi, K., Tamura, J., & Tokoro, M. (1997). Patterns of social relationships and psychological well-being among the elderly. *International Journal of Behavioral Development, 21,* 417–430.

Takata, T. (1999). Development process of independent and interdependent self-construal in Japanese culture: Cross-cultural and cross-sectional analyses. *Japanese Journal of Educational Psychology, 47,* 480–489.

Takei, W. (2001). How do deaf infants attain first signs? *Developmental Science, 4,* 71–78.

Takei, Y., & Dubas, J. S. (1993). Academic achievement among early adolescents: Social and cultural diversity. In R. M. Lerner (Ed.), *Early adolescence: Perspectives on research, policy, and intervention* (pp. 175–190). Hillsdale, NJ: Erlbaum.

Talan, J. (1998, October 28). Possible genetic link found for right-handedness, not for left. *Seattle Times.*

Talbott, M. (1998). Older widows' attitudes towards men and remarriage. *Journal of Aging Studies, 12,* 429–449.

Tamir, L. M. (1982). *Men in their forties: The transition to middle age.* New York: Springer.

Tani, F., Greenman, P., Schneider, B., & Fregoso, M. (2003). Bullying and the Big Five: A study of childhood personality and participant roles in bullying incidents. *School Psychology International, 24,* 131–146.

Tanner, J. M. (1978). *Fetus into man: Physical growth from conception to maturity.* Cambridge, MA: Harvard University Press.

Tanner, J. M. (1990). *Fetus into man: Physical growth from conception to maturity.* Cambridge, MA: Harvard University Press.

Tanner, J. M., Hughes, P. C. R., & Whitehouse, R. H. (1981). Radiographically determined widths of bone, muscle and fat in the upper arm and calf from 3–18 years. *Annals of Human Biology, 8,* 495–517.

Tan-Niam, C., Wood, D., & O'Malley, C. (1998). A cross-cultural perspective on children's theories of mind and social interaction. *Early Child Development & Care, 144,* 55–67.

Tanofsky-Kraff, M., Yanovski, S., Wilfley, D., Marmarosh, C., Morgan, C., & Yanovski, J. (2004). Eating-disordered behaviors, body fat, and psychopathology in overweight and normal-weight children. *Journal of Consulting and Clinical Psychology, 72,* 53–61.

Tapanya, S., Nicki, R., & Jarusawad, O. (1997). Worry and intrinsic/extrinsic religious orientation among Buddhist (Thai) and Christian (Canadian) elderly persons. *International Journal of Aging and Human Development, 44,* 73–83.

Tardif, T., & Wellman, H. (2000). Acquisition of mental state language in Mandarin- and Cantonese-speaking children. *Developmental Psychology, 36,* 25–43.

Tarter, R., Panzak, G., Switala, J., Lu, S., et al. (1997). Isokinetic muscle strength and its association with neuropsychological capacity in cirrhotic alcoholics. *Alcoholism: Clinical & Experimental Research, 21,* 191–196.

Tasbihsazan, R., Nettelbeck, T., & Kirby, N. (2003). Predictive validity of the Fagan Test of Infant Intelligence. *British Journal of Developmental Psychology, 21,* 585–597.

Taveras, E., Li, R., Grummer-Strawn, L., Richardson, M., Marshall, R., Rêgo, V., Miroshnik, I., & Lieu, T. (2004). Opinions and practices of clinicians associated with continuation of exclusive breastfeeding, *Pediatrics, 113,* e283–e290.

Taylor, J. A., & Danderson, M. (1995). A reexamination of the risk factors for the sudden infant death syndrome. *Journal of Pediatrics, 126,* 887–891.

Taylor, M., Cartwright, B. S., & Carlson, S. M. (1993). A developmental investigation of children's imaginary companions. *Developmental Psychology, 29,* 276–285.

Taylor, P. J., & Kopelman, M. D. (1984). Amnesia for criminal offenses. *Psychological Medicine, 14,* 481–588.

Taylor, R. D., & Roberts, D. (1995). Kinship support and maternal and adolescent well-being in economically disadvantaged African-American families. *Child Development, 66,* 1585–1597.

Taylor, R. J., Chatters, L. M., Tucker, M. B., & Lewis, E. (1990). Developments in research on black families: A decade review. *Journal of Marriage & the Family, 52,* 993–1014.

Taylor, W., Ayars, C., Gladney, A., Peters, R., Roy, J., Prokhorov, A., Chamberlain, R., & Gritz, E. (1999). Beliefs about smoking among adolescents: Gender and ethnic differences. *Journal of Child & Adolescent Substance Abuse, 8,* 37–54.

Teachman, J. (2003). Premarital sex, premarital cohabitation and the risk of subsequent marital dissolution among women. *Journal of Marriage & the Family, 65,* 444–455.

Temoshok, L. (1987). Personality, coping style, emotion and cancer: Towards an integrative model. *Cancer Surveys, 6,* 545–567.

Terashima, K., Mikami, A., Tachibana, N., Kumano-Go, T., Teshima, Y., Sugita, Y., & Takeda, M. (2004). Sleep characteristics of menopausal insomnia: A polysomnographic study. *Psychiatry & Clinical Neurosciences, 58,* 179–185.

Terman, L. (1916). *The measurement of intelligence.* Boston: Houghton Mifflin.

Terman, L., & Merrill, M. A. (1937). *Measuring intelligence: A guide to the administration of the new revised Stanford-Binet tests.* Boston: Houghton Mifflin.

Tershakovec, A. & Stallings, V. (1998). Pediatric nutrition and nutritional disorders. In R. Behrman & R. Kliegman (Eds.), *Nelson essentials of pediatrics* (3rd ed.). Philadelphia: W. B. Saunders.

Tervo, S., Kivipelto, M., Hänninen, T., Vanhanen, M., Hallikainen, M., Mannermaa, A., & Soininen, H. (2004). Incidence and risk factors for mild cognitive impairment: A population-based three-year follow-up study of cognitively healthy elderly subjects. *Dementia & Geriatric Cognitive Disorders, 17,* 196–203.

Tessier, R., Cristo, M., Velez, S., Giron, M., Line, N., Figueroa de Calume, Z., Ruiz-Palaez, J., & Charpak, N. (2003). Kangaroo mother care: A method for protecting high-risk low-birth-weight and premature infants against developmental delay. *Infant Behavior & Development, 26,* 384–397.

Teti, D. M., Gelfand, D. M., Messinger, D. S., & Isabella, R. (1995). Maternal depression and the quality of early attachment: An examination of infants, preschoolers, and their mothers. *Developmental Psychology, 31,* 364–376.

Thal, D., & Bates, E. (1990). Continuity and variation in early language development. In J. Colombo & J. Fagen (Eds.), *Individual differences in infancy: Reliability, stability, prediction* (pp. 359–385). Hillsdale, NJ: Erlbaum.

Thal, D., Tobias, S., & Morrison, D. (1991). Language and gesture in late talkers: A 1-year follow-up. *Journal of Speech & Hearing Research, 34,* 604–612.

Thapar, A., Fowler, T., Rice, F., Scourfield, J., van den Bree, M., Thomas, H., Harold, G., & Hay, D. (2003). Maternal smoking during pregnancy and attention deficit hyperactivity disorder symptoms in offspring. *American Journal of Psychiatry, 160,* 1985–1989.

Tharenou, P. (1999). Is there a link between family structures and women's and men's managerial career advancement? *Journal of Organizational Behavior, 20,* 837–863.

Tharp, R. G., & Gallimore, R. (1988). *Rousing minds to life.* New York: Cambridge University Press.

Thelen, E. (1995). Motor development: A new synthesis. *American Psychologist, 50,* 79–95.

Thelen, E., & Adolph, K. E. (1992). Arnold L. Gesell: The paradox of nature and nurture. *Developmental Psychology, 28,* 368–380.

Theriault, J. (1998). Assessing intimacy with the best friend and the sexual partner during adolescence: The PAIR-M inventory. *Journal of Psychology, 132,* 493–506.

Thobaben, M., & Duncan, R. (2003). Domestic elder abuse by health care providers. *Home Health Care Management & Practice, 15,* 168–169.

Thomas, A., & Chess, S. (1977). *Temperament and development.* New York: Brunner/Mazel.

Thomas, J., Yan, J., & Stelmach, G. (2000). Movement substructures change as a function of practice in children and adults. *Journal of Experimental Child Psychology, 75,* 228–244.

Thomas, L. (2003, June). Marriage insurance: Will you be married 'til death do you part? *The Washingtonian.* Retrieved August 24, 2004, from http://www.washingtonian.com/weddings/insurance.html.

Thomas, M. (1996). *Comparing theories of child development* (4th ed.). New York: Norton.

Thomas, M. (2000). *Comparing theories of development* (5th ed.). Pacific Grove, CA: Brooks/Cole.

Thomas, R. M. (Ed.). (1990). *The encyclopedia of human development and education: Theory, research, and studies.* Oxford, England: Pergamon Press.

Thompson, G., & Joshua-Shearer, M. (2002). In retrospect: What college undergraduates say about their high school education. *High School Journal, 85,* 1–15.

Thompson, L., Fagan, J., & Fulker, D. (1991). Longitudinal prediction of specific cognitive abilities from infant novelty preference. *Child Development, 62,* 530–538.

Thomson, E., & Colella, U. (1992). Cohabitation and marital stability: Quality or commitment? *Journal of Marriage & the Family, 54,* 259–267.

Thorn, A., & Gathercole, S. (1999). Language-specific knowledge and short-term memory in bilingual and non-bilingual children. *Quarterly Journal of Experimental Psychology: Human Experimental Psychology, 52A,* 303–324.

Thorne, B. (1986). Girls and boys together...but mostly apart: Gender arrangements in elementary schools. In W. W. Hartup & Z. Rubin (Eds.), *Relationships and development* (pp. 167–184). Hillsdale, NJ: Erlbaum.

Thornton, W., Douglas, G., & Houghton, S. (1999). Transition through stages of smoking: The effect of gender and self-concept on smoking behavior. (1999). *Journal of Adolescent Health, 25,* 284–289.

Thorpe, M., Pittenger, D., & Reed, B. (1999). Cheating the researcher: A study of the relation between personality measures and self-reported cheating. *College Student Journal, 33,* 49–59.

Thorslund, M., & Lundberg, O. (1994). Health and inequalities among the oldest old. *Journal of Aging & Health, 6,* 51–69.

Thorson, J. A., & Powell, F. C. (1990). Meanings of death and intrinsic religiosity. *Journal of Clinical Psychology, 46,* 379–390.

Thorson, J. A., & Powell, F. C. (1992). A revised death anxiety scale. *Death Studies, 16,* 507–521.

Tice, J., Ettinger, B., Ensrud, K., Wallace, R., Blackwell, T., & Cummings, S. (2003). Phytoestrogen supplements for the treatment of hot flashes: The isoflavone clover extract (ICE) study: A randomized controlled trial. *Journal of the American Medical Association, 290,* 207–214.

Tice, R. R., & Setlow, R. B. (1985). DNA repair and replication in aging organisms and cells. In C. E. Finch & E. L. Schneider (Eds.), *Handbook of the biology of aging* (2nd ed., pp. 173–224). New York: Van Nostrand Reinhold.

Tiedemann, J. (2000). Parents' gender stereotypes and teachers' beliefs as predictors of children's concept of their mathematical ability in elementary school. *Journal of Educational Psychology, 92,* 144–151.

Todd, R. D., Swarzenski, B., Rossi, P. G., & Visconti, P. (1995). Structural and functional development of the human brain. In D. Cicchetti & D. J. Cohen (Eds.), *Developmental psychopathology: Vol. 1. Theory and methods* (pp. 161–194). New York: Wiley.

Tokar, D., Fischer, A., & Subich, L. (1998). Personality and vocational behavior: A selective review of the literature, 1993–1997. *Journal of Vocational Behavior, 53,* 115–153.

Tolson, T., & Wilson, M. (1990). The impact of two- and three-generation black family structure on perceived family climate. *Child Development, 61,* 416–428.

Tomblin, J., Smith, E., & Zhang, X. (1997). Epidemiology of specific language impairment: Prenatal and perinatal risk factors. *Journal of Communication Disorders, 30,* 325–344.

Tomita, T., Ohta, Y., Ogawa, K., Sugiyama, H., Kagami, N., & Agari, I. (1997). Grief process and strategies of psychological helping: A review. *Japanese Journal of Counseling Science, 30,* 49–67.

Tomlinson-Keasey, C., Eisert, D. C., Kahle, L. R., Hardy-Brown, K., & Keasey, B. (1979). The structure of concrete operational thought. *Child Development, 50,* 1153–1163.

Toomela, A. (1999). Drawing development: Stages in the representation of a cube and a cylinder. *Child Development, 70,* 1141–1150.

Torgerson, D., & Bell-Syer, S. (2001). Hormone replacement therapy and prevention of nonvertebral fractures: A meta-analysis of randomized trials. *Journal of the American Medical Association, 285,* 2891–2897.

Torgerson, D., Thomas, R., Campbell, M., & Reid, D. (1997). Alcohol consumption and age of maternal menopause are associated with menopause onset. *Maturitas, 26,* 21–25.

Torgesen, J., Wagner, R., Rashotte, C., Rose, E., et al. (1999). Preventing reading failure in young children with phonological processing disabilities: Group and individual responses to instruction. *Journal of Educational Psychology, 91,* 594–603.

Tortora, G., & Grabowski, S. (1993). *Principles of anatomy and physiology.* New York: HarperCollins.

Townsend, G., & Belgrave, F. (2003). The influence of cultural and racial identification on the psychosocial adjustment of inner-city African American children in school. *American Journal of Community Psychology, 32,* 217–228.

Tracey, T. J., & Rounds, J. (1993). Evaluating Holland's and Gati's vocational-interest models: A structural meta-analysis. *Psychological Bulletin, 113,* 229–246.

Trainor, L., Clark, E., Huntley, A., & Adams, B. (1997). The acoustic basis of preferences for infant-directed singing. *Infant Behavior & Development, 20,* 383–396.

Trautner, H., Gervai, J., & Nemeth, R. (2003). Appearance-reality distinction and development of gender constancy understanding in children. *International Journal of Behavioral Development, 27,* 275–283.

Trehub, S., Unyk, A., Kamenetsky, S., Hill, D., et al. (1997). Mothers' and fathers' singing to infants. *Developmental Psychology, 33,* 500–507.

Trehub, S. E., Bull, D., & Thorpe, L. A. (1984). Infants' perception of melodies: The role of melodic contour. *Child Development, 55,* 821–830.

Trehub, S. E., & Rabinovitch, M. S. (1972). Auditory-linguistic sensitivity in early infancy. *Developmental Psychology, 6,* 74–77.

Trehub, S. E., Thorpe, L. A., & Morrongiello, B. A. (1985). Infants' perception of melodies: Changes in a single tone. *Infant Behavior & Development, 8,* 213–223.

Tremblay, R. E., Masse, L. C., Vitaro, F., & Dobkin, P. L. (1995). The impact of friends' deviant behavior on early onset of delinquency: Longitudinal data from 6 to 13 years of age. *Development and Psychopathology, 7,* 649–667.

Trentin, G. (2004). E-learning and the third age. *Journal of Computer Assisted Learning, 20,* 21–30.

Trichopoulou, A., Costacou, T., Bamia, C., & Trichopoulous, D. (2003). Adherence to a Mediterranean diet and survival in a Greek population. *New England Journal of Medicine, 348,* 2599–2608.

Trivers, R. (1972). Parental investment and sexual selection. In B. Campbell (Ed.), *Sexual selection and the descent of man: 1871–1971* (pp. 136–179). Chicago: Aldine.

Tronick, E. Z., Morelli, G. A., & Ivey, P. K. (1992). The Efe forager infant and toddler's pattern of social relationships: Multiple and simultaneous. *Developmental Psychology, 28,* 568–577.

Truluck, J., & Courtenay, B. (1999). Learning style preferences among older adults. *Educational Gerontology, 25,* 221–236.

Trusty, J. (1999). Effects of eighth-grade parental involvement on late adolescents' educational expectations. *Journal of Research & Development in Education, 32,* 224–233.

Tsang, P. (1998). Age, attention, expertise, and time-sharing performance. *Psychology & Aging, 13,* 323–347.

Tsang, W., & Hui-Chan, C. (2003). Effects of Tai Chi on joint proprioception and stability limits in elderly subjects. *Medicine & Science in Sports & Exercise, 35,* 1962–1971.

Tsitouridou, M., & Vryzas, K. (2003). Early childhood teachers' attitudes towards computer and information technology: The case of Greece. *Information Technology in Childhood Education Annual, 15,* 187–207.

Tsuya, N. O., & Martin, L. G. (1992). Living arrangements of elderly Japanese and attitudes toward inheritance. *Journals of Gerontology: Social Sciences, 47,* S45–54.

Tunstall-Pedoe, H., & Smith, W. C. S. (1990). Cholesterol as a risk factor for coronary heart disease. *British Medical Bulletin, 46,* 1075–1087.

Turic, D., Robinson, L., Duke, M., Morris, D. W., Webb, V., Hamshere, M., Milham, C., Hopkin, E., Pound, K., Fernando, S., Grierson, A., Easton, M., Williams, N., Van Den Bree, M., Chowdhury, R., Gruen, J., Krawczak, M., Owen, M. J., O'Donovan, M. C., & Williams, J. (2004). Linkage disequilibrium mapping provides further evidence of a gene for reading disability on chromosome 6p21.3–22. *Molecular Psychiatry, 8,* 176–185.

Turiel, E. (1983). *The development of social knowledge: Morality and convention.* New York: Cambridge University Press.

Turnage, B. (2004). African American mother-daughter relationships mediating daughter's self-esteem. *Child & Adolescent Social Work Journal, 21,* 155–173.

Turner, H. A., & Finkelhor, D. (1996). Corporal punishment as a stressor among youth. *Journal of Marriage & the Family, 58,* 155–166.

Twenge, J., Campbell, W., & Foster, C. (2003). Parenthood and marital satisfaction: A meta-analytic review. *Journal of Marriage & the Family, 65,* 574–583.

Twycross, R. G. (1996). Euthanasia: Going Dutch? *Journal of the Royal Society of Medicine, 89,* 61–63.

Tylka, T. (2004). The relation between body dissatisfaction and eating disorder symptomatology: An analysis of moderating variables. *Journal of Counseling Psychology, 51,* 178–191.

Udry, J. R., & Campbell, B. C. (1994). Getting started on sexual behavior. In A. S. Rossi (Ed.), *Sexuality across the life course* (pp. 187–208). Chicago: University of Chicago Press.

Uecker, A., & Nadel, L. (1996). Spatial locations gone awry: Object and spatial memory deficits in children with fetal alcohol syndrome. *Neuropsychologia, 34,* 209–223.

Uemura, N., Okamoto, S., Yamamoto, S., Matsumura, N., Yamaguchi, S., Yamakido, M., Taniyama, K., Sasaki, N., & Schlemper, R. (2001). *Heli-cobacter pylori* infection and the development of gastric cancer. *New England Journal of Medicine, 345,* 784–789.

Uhlenberg, P., Cooney, T., & Boyd, R. (1990). Divorce for women after midlife. *Journals of Gerontology: Social Sciences, 45,* S3–11.

Umberson, D. (1992). Relationships between adult children and their parents: Psychological consequences for both generations. *Journal of Marriage & the Family, 54,* 664–674.

Umetsu, D. (1998). Immunology and allergy. In R. Behrman & R. Kleigman (Eds.), *Nelson essentials of pediatrics* (3rd ed.). Philadelphia: W. B. Saunders.

Underwood, M. (1997). Peer social status and children's understanding of the expression and control of positive and negative emotions. *Merrill-Palmer Quarterly, 43,* 610–634.

Underwood, M. K., Coie, J. D., & Herbsman, C. R. (1992). Display rules for anger and aggression in school-age children. *Child Development, 63,* 366–380.

Underwood, M. K., Kupersmidt, J. B., & Coie, J. D. (1996). Childhood peer sociometric status and aggression as predictors of adolescent childbearing. *Journal of Research on Adolescence, 6,* 201–224.

Ungerer, J. A., & Sigman, M. (1984). The relation of play and sensorimotor behavior to language in the second year. *Child Development, 55,* 1448–1455.

United States Conference of Catholic Bishops. (2003). *Between man and woman: Questions and answers about marriage and same-sex unions.* Retrieved September 24, 2004, from http://www.usccb.org/laity/manandwoman.htm.

Uno, D., Florsheim, P., & Uchino, B. (1998). Psychosocial mechanisms underlying quality of parenting among Mexican-American and White adolescent mothers. *Journal of Youth & Adolescence, 27,* 585–605.

Updegraff, K., & Obeidallah, D. (1999). Young adolescents' patterns of involvement with siblings and friends. *Social Development, 8,* 52–69.

Upperman, P. U., & Church, A. T. (1995). Investigating Holland's typological theory with army occupational specialties. *Journal of Vocational Behavior, 47,* 61–75.

Urban, J., Carlson, E., Egeland, B., & Sroufe, L. A. (1991). Patterns of individual adaptation across childhood. *Development and Psychopathology, 3,* 445–460.

Urberg, K., Degirmencioglu, S., & Pilgrim, C. (1997). Close friend and group influence on adolescent cigarette smoking and alcohol use. *Developmental Psychology, 33,* 834–844.

Urberg, K., Degirmencioglu, S., & Tolson, J. (1998). Adolescent friendship selection and termination: The role of similarity. *Journal of Social & Personal Relationships, 15,* 703–710.

Urberg, K. A., Degirmencioglu, S. M., Tolson, J. M., & Halliday-Scher, K. (1995). The structure of adolescent peer networks. *Developmental Psychology, 31,* 540–547.

Urdan, T. (1997). Examining the relations among early adolescent students' goals and friends' orientation toward effort and achievement in school. *Contemporary Educational Psychology, 22,* 165–191.

U.S. Bureau of the Census. (1984). *Statistical abstract of the United States: 1984.* Washington, DC: U.S. Government Printing Office.

U.S. Bureau of the Census. (1990). *Statistical abstract of the United States: 1990.* Washington, DC: U.S. Government Printing Office.

U.S. Bureau of the Census. (1992). *Statistical abstract of the United States: 1992.* Washington, DC: U.S. Government Printing Office.

U.S. Bureau of the Census. (1994). *Statistical abstract of the United States: 1994.* Washington, DC: U.S. Government Printing Office.

U.S. Bureau of the Census. (1995a). *Sixty-five plus in the United States.* Statistical Brief. Washington, DC: U.S. Government Printing Office.

U.S. Bureau of the Census. (1995b). *Statistical abstract of the United States: 1995.* Washington, DC: U.S. Government Printing Office.

U.S. Bureau of the Census. (1996). *Statistical abstract of the United States: 1996.* Washington, DC: U.S. Government Printing Office.

U.S. Bureau of the Census. (1997). *Statistical abstract of the United States: 1997.* Washington, DC: U.S. Government Printing Office.

U.S. Bureau of the Census. (1998). *Statistical abstract of the United States: 1998.* Washington, DC: U.S. Government Printing Office.

U.S. Bureau of the Census. (1999). *Current population survey: March 1960 to 1999.* Washington, DC: U.S. Government Printing Office.

U.S. Bureau of the Census. (2000). Census brief: Women in the United States, a profile. Retrieved August 18, 2004, from http://www.census.gov.

U.S. Bureau of the Census. (2001). *Statistical abstract of the United States: 2001.* Washington, DC: U.S. Government Printing Office.

U.S. Bureau of the Census. (2002). *Statistival abstract of the United States: 2000.* Washington, DC: U.S. Government Printing Office.

U.S. Bureau of the Census. (2003a). *Statistical abstract of the United States: 2003.* Washington, DC: U.S. Government Printing Office.

U.S. Bureau of the Census. (2003b). *Married-couple and unmarried-partner households: 2000.* Retrieved August 18, 2004, from http://www.census.gov.

U.S. Department of Education. (1996). *Annual report to Congress on implementation of IDEA.* Washington, DC: U.S. Government Printing Office.

U.S. Department of Education. (2004). *No Child Left Behind: Introduction.* Retrieved September 21, 2004, from http://www.ed.gov/print/nclb/overview/intro/index.html.

U.S. Department of Health and Human Services. (1998a). *National initiative to eliminate racial and ethnic disparities in health: Cancer.* Retrieved October 11, 2000, from http:// www.raceandhealth.omhrc.gov.

U.S. Department of Health and Human Services. (1998b). *National initiative to eliminate racial and ethnic disparities in health: Cardiovascular disease.* Retrieved October 11, 2000, from http:// www.raceandhealth.omhrc.gov.

U.S. Department of Health and Human Services. (1998c). *National initiative to eliminate racial and ethnic disparities in health: Diabetes.* Retrieved October 11, 2000, from http://www.raceandhealth.omhrc.gov.

Ushikubo, M. (1998). A study of factors facilitating and inhibiting the willingness of the institutionalized disabled elderly for rehabilitation: A United States-Japanese comparison. *Journal of Cross-Cultural Gerontology, 13,* 127–157.

Vachon, M. (1998). Psychosocial needs of patients and families. *Journal of Palliative Care, 14,* 49–56.

Vaeisaenen, L. (1998). Family grief and recovery process when a baby dies. *Psychiatria Fennica, 29,* 163–174.

Vaillant, G. E. (1977). *Adaptation to life: How the best and brightest came of age.* Boston: Little, Brown.

Vaillant, G. E. (1991). The association of ancestral longevity with successful aging. *Journals of Gerontology: Psychological Sciences, 46,* P292–298.

Valdez-Menchaca, M. C., & Whitehurst, G. J. (1992). Accelerating language development through picture book reading: A systematic extension to Mexican day care. *Developmental Psychology, 28,* 1106–1114.

van Balen, F. (1998). Development of IVF children. *Developmental Review, 18,* 30–46.

van Beijsterveldt, C., Bartels, M., Hudziak, J., & Boomsma, D. (2003). Causes of stability of aggression from early childhood to adolescence: A longitudinal genetic analysis in Dutch twins. *Behavior Genetics, 33,* 591–605.

Van Boxtel, M., Paas, F., Houx, P., Adam, J., Teeken, J., & Jolles, J. (1997). Aerobic capacity and cognitive performance in a cross-sectional aging study. *Medicine & Science in Sports & Exercise, 29,* 1357–1365.

van den Boom, D. (1995). Do first-year intervention effects endure? Follow-up during toddlerhood of a sample of Dutch irritable infants. *Child Development, 66,* 1798–1816.

van den Boom, D. C. (1994). The influence of temperament and mothering on attachment and exploration: An experimental manipulation of sensitive responsiveness among lower-class mothers with irritable infants. *Child Development, 65,* 1457–1477.

Van den Broek, P., Lynch, J., Naslund, J., Ievers-Landis, C., & Verduin, K. (2004). The development of comprehension of main ideas in narratives: Evidence from the selection of titles. *Journal of Educational Psychology, 96,* 707–718.

van den Hoonaard, D. (1999). "No regrets": Widows' stories about the last days of their husbands' lives. *Journal of Aging Studies, 13,* 59–72.

van der Molen, M., Molenaar, P. (1994). Cognitive psychophysiology: A window to cognitive development and brain maturation. In G. Dawson & K. Fischer (Eds.), *Human behavior and the developing brain* (pp. 456–492). New York: Guilford Press.

Vandewater, E., Shim, M., & Caplovitz, A. (2004). Linking obesity and activity level with children's television and video game use. *Journal of Adolescence, 27*, 71–85.

van Doorn, C., Kasl, S., Beery, L., Jacobs, S., & Prigerson, H. (1998). The influence of marital quality and attachment styles on traumatic grief and depressive symptoms. *Journal of Nervous & Mental Disease, 186*, 566–573.

van Doornen, L., Snieder, H., & Boomsma, D. (1998). Serum lipids and cardiovascular reactivity to stress. *Biological Psychology, 47*, 279–297.

Van Dorn, R., & Williams, J. (2003). Correlates associated with escalation of delinquent behavior in incarcerated youths. *Social Work, 48*, 523–531.

Van Duuren, M., Kendell-Scott, L., & Stark, N. (2003). Early aesthetic choices: Infant preferences for attractive premature infant faces. *International Journal of Behavioral Development, 27*, 212–219.

van Grootheest, D., Beekman, A., van Groenou, M., & Deeg, D. (1999). Sex differences in depression after widowhood: Do men suffer more? *Social Psychiatry & Psychiatric Epidemiology, 34*, 391–398.

Van Hightower, N., & Gorton, J. (1998). Domestic violence among patients at two rural health care clinics: Prevalence and social correlates. *Public Health Nursing, 15*, 355–362.

van IJzendoorn, M. H. (1995). Adult attachment representations, parental responsiveness, and infant attachment: A meta-analysis on the predictive validity of the Adult Attachment Interview. *Psychological Bulletin, 117*, 387–403.

van IJzendoorn, M. H., Goldberg, S., Kroonenberg, P. M., & Frenkel, O. J. (1992). The relative effects of maternal and child problems on the quality of attachment: A meta-analysis of attachment in clinical samples. *Child Development, 63*, 840–858.

van IJzendoorn, M. H., & Kroonenberg, P. M. (1988). Cross-cultural patterns of attachment: A meta-analysis of the Strange Situation. *Child Development, 59*, 147–156.

Van Lange, P., DeBruin, E., Otten, W., & Joireman, J. (1997). Development of prosocial, individualistic, and competitive orientations: Theory and preliminary evidence. *Journal of Personality & Social Psychology, 73*, 733–746.

van Lieshout, C. F. M., & Haselager, G. J. T. (1994). The big five personality factors in Q-sort descriptions of children and adolescents. In C. F. Halverson, Jr., G. A. Kohnstamm, & R. P. Martin (Eds.), *The developing structure of temperament and personality from infancy to adulthood* (pp. 293–318). Hillsdale, NJ: Erlbaum.

Van Mierlo, J., & Van den Bulck, J. (2004). Benchmarking the cultivation approach to video game effects: A comparison of the correlates of TV viewing and game play. *Journal of Adolescence, 27*, 97–111.

Van Velsor, E., & O'Rand, A. M. (1984). Family life cycle, work career patterns, and women's wages at midlife. *Journal of Marriage & the Family, 46*, 365–373.

van Wel, F. (1994). "I count my parents among my best friends": Youths' bonds with parents and friends in the Netherlands. *Journal of Marriage & the Family, 56*, 835–843.

van Wormer, K., & McKinney, R. (2003). What schools can do to help gay/ lesbian/bisexual youth: A harm reduction approach. *Adolescence, 38*, 409–420.

Vartanian, L. (2000). Revisiting the imaginary audience and personal fable constructs of adolescent egocentrism: A conceptual review. *Adolescence, 35*, 639–661.

Vartanian, L. (2001). Adolescents' reactions to hypothetical peer group conversations: Evidence for an imaginary audience? *Adolescence, 36*, 347–380.

Vartanian, L. R. (1997). Separation-individuation, social support, and adolescent egocentrism: An exploratory study. *Journal of Early Adolescence, 17*, 245–270.

Vartanian, L. R., & Powlishta, K. K. (1996). A longitudinal examination of the social-cognitive foundations of adolescent egocentrism. *Journal of Early Adolescence, 16*, 157–178.

Vaughan, A., Mundy, P., Block, J., Burnette, C., Delgado, C., Gomez, Y., Meyer, J., Neal, A., & Pomares, Y. (2003). Child, caregiver, and temperament contributions to infant joint attention. *Infancy, 4*, 603–616.

Vaughn, B., Stevenson-Hinde, J., Waters, E., Kotsaftis, A., Lefever, G., Shouldice, A., Trudel, M., & Belsky, J. (1992). Attachment security and temperament in infancy and early childhood: Some conceptual clarification. *Developmental Psychology, 28*, 463–473.

Vega, W. A. (1990). Hispanic families in the 1980s: A decade of research. *Journal of Marriage & the Family, 52*, 1015–1024.

Venkatraman, M. M. (1995). A cross-cultural study of the subjective well-being of married elderly persons in the United States and India. *Journals of Gerontology: Social Sciences, 50B*, S35–44.

Ventura, S., Mosher, W., Curtin, S., Abma, J., & Henshaw, S. (2000). Trends in pregnancies and pregnancy rates by outcome: Estimates for the United States, 1976–1996. *Vital Health Statistics, 21* (56).

Verbrugge, L. M. (1989). Gender, aging, and health. In K. S. Markides (Ed.), *Aging and health* (pp. 23–78). Newbury Park, CA: Sage.

Verbrugge, L. M., Lepkowski, J. M., & Konkol, L. L. (1991). Levels of disability among U.S. adults with arthritis. *Journals of Gerontology: Social Sciences, 46*, S71–83.

Verbrugge, L. M., & Wingard, D. L. (1987). Sex differentials in health and mortality. *Women & Health, 12*, 103–145.

Vergano, D. (2004, April 25). Private stem cell research widens. *USA Today Online.* Retrieved September 25, 2004, from http://www.usatoday.com/ news/health/2004-04-25-stemcell-usat_x.htm.

Verhaeghen, P., & Marcoen, A. (1993). Memory aging as a general phenomenon: Episodic recall of older adults is a function of episodic recall of young adults. *Psychology & Aging, 8*, 380–388.

Verhaeghen, P., Marcoen, A., & Goossens, L. (1992). Improving memory performance in the aged through mnemonic training: A meta-analytic study. *Psychology & Aging, 7*, 242–251.

Verhaeghen, P., Marcoen, A., & Goossens, L. (1993). Facts and fiction about memory aging: A quantitative integration of research findings. *Journals of Gerontology: Psychological Sciences, 48*, P157–171.

Verhaeghen, P., & Salthouse, T. (1997). Meta-analyses of age-cognition relations in adulthood: Estimates of linear and nonlinear age effects and structural models. *Psychological Bulletin, 122*, 231–249.

Verhulst, F., & Versluis-Den Bieman, H. (1995). Development course of problem behaviors in adolescent adoptees. *Journal of the American Academy of Child & Adolescent Psychiatry, 34*, 151–159.

Veroff, J., Douvan, E., & Kulka, R. A. (1981). *The inner American: A self-portrait from 1957 to 1976.* New York: Basic Books.

Vig, E., & Pearlman, R. (2003). Quality of life while dying: A qualitative study of terminally ill older men. *Journal of the American Geriatrics Society, 51*, 1595–1601.

Vihko, R., & Apter, D. (1980). The role of androgens in adolescent cycles. *Journal of Steroid Biochemistry, 12*, 369–373.

Vikat, A., Rimpela, A., Kosunen, E., & Rimpela, M. (2002). Sociodemographic differences in the occurrence of teenage pregnancies in Finland in 1987–1998: A follow up study. *Journal of Epidemiology & Community Health, 56*, 659–670.

Vinokur, A. D., & van Ryn, M. (1993). Social support and undermining in close relationships: Their independent effects on the mental health of unemployed persons. *Journal of Personality & Social Psychology, 65*, 350–359.

Visscher, W., Feder, M., Burns, A., Brady, T., & Bray, R. (2003). The impact of smoking and other substance use by urban women on the birthweight of their infants. *Substance Use & Misuse, 38*, 1063–1093.

Vitaro, F., Tremblay, R., Kerr, M., Pagani, L., & Bukowski, W. (1997). Disruptiveness, friends' characteristics, and delinquency in early adolescence: A test of two competing models of development. *Child Development, 68*, 676–689.

Volz, J. (2000). Successful aging: The second 50. *Monitor, 31*, 24–28.

Voyer, D., Voyer, S., & Bryden, M. P. (1995). Magnitude of sex differences in spatial abilities: A meta-analysis and consideration of critical variables. *Psychological Bulletin, 117*, 250–270.

Vuchinich, S., Bank, L., & Patterson, G. R. (1992). Parenting, peers, and the stability of antisocial behavior in preadolescent boys. *Developmental Psychology, 28*, 510–521.

Vuorenkoski, L., Kuure, O., Moilanen, I., & Peninkilampi, V. (2000). Bilingualism, school achievement, and mental wellbeing: A follow-up study of return migrant children. *Journal of Child Psychology & Psychiatry & Allied Disciplines, 41*, 261–266.

Vygotsky, L. S. (1978). *Mind and society: The development of higher mental processes.* Cambridge, MA: Harvard University Press (original works published 1930, 1933, and 1935).

Waggoner, G. (2000). The new grandparents: What they buy, what they think. *Modern Maturity, 43*, 85, 91.

Waite, L. J. (1995). *Does marriage matter?* Presidential address to the Population Association of America, Chicago.

Walden, T. A. (1991). Infant social referencing. In J. Garber & K. A. Dodge (Eds.), *The development of emotion regulation and dysregulation* (pp. 69–88). Cambridge, England: Cambridge University Press.

Waldner-Haugrud, L., Gratch, L., & Magruder, B. (1997). Victimization and perpetration rates of violence in gay and lesbian relationships: Gender issues explored. *Violence & Victims, 12*, 173–184.

Walker, H., Messinger, D., Fogel, A., & Karns, J. (1992). Social and communicative development in infancy. In V. B. V. Hasselt & M. Hersen (Eds.), *Handbook of social development: A lifespan perspective* (pp. 157–181). New York: Plenum.

Walker, L. J. (1989). A longitudinal study of moral reasoning. *Child Development, 60,* 157–160.

Walker, L. J., de Vries, B., & Trevethan, S. D. (1987). Moral stages and moral orientations in real-life and hypothetical dilemmas. *Child Development, 58,* 842–858.

Walker-Andrews, A., & Kahana-Kalman, R. (1999). The understanding of pretence across the second year of life. *British Journal of Developmental Psychology, 17,* 523–536.

Walker-Andrews, A. S. (1997). Infants' perception of expressive behaviors: Differentiation of multimodal information. *Psychological Bulletin, 121,* 437–456.

Walker-Andrews, A. S., & Lennon, E. (1991). Infants' discrimination of vocal expressions: Contributions of auditory and visual information. *Infant Behavior & Development, 14,* 131–142.

Waller, A., Dennis, F., Brodie, J., & Cairns, A. (1998). Evaluating the use of TalksBac, a predictive communication device for nonfluent adults with aphasia. *International Journal of Language & Communication Disorders, 33,* 45–70.

Wallerstein, J., & Lewis, J. (1998). The long-term impact of divorce on children: A first report from a 25-year study. *Family & Conciliation Courts Review, 36,* 368–383.

Walls, C. T., & Zarit, S. H. (1991). Informal support from black churches and the well-being of elderly blacks. *The Gerontologist, 31,* 490–495.

Walton, G. E., & Bower, T. G. R. (1993). Amodal representation of speech in infants. *Infant Behavior & Development, 16,* 233–253.

Walton, G. E., Bower, N. J. A., & Bower, T. G. R. (1992). Recognition of familiar faces by newborns. *Infant Behavior & Development, 15,* 265–269.

Wang, C., & Chou, P. (1999). Risk factors for adolescent primigravida in Kaohsium county, Taiwan. *American Journal of Preventive Medicine, 17,* 43–47.

Wang, C., & Phinney, J. (1998). Differences in child rearing attitudes between immigrant Chinese mothers and Anglo-American mothers. *Early Development & Parenting, 7,* 181–189.

Wang, D., Kato, N., Inaba, Y., Tango, T., et al. (2000). Physical and personality traits of preschool children in Fuzhou, China: Only child vs. sibling. *Child: Care, Health & Development, 26,* 49–60.

Wang, Y., & Ollendick, T. (2001). A cross-cultural and developmental analysis of self-esteem in Chinese and Western children. *Clinical Child & Family Psychology Review, 4,* 253–271.

Warburton, J., Le Brocque, R., & Rosenman, L. (1998). Older people the reserve army of volunteers? An analysis of volunteerism among older Australians. *International Journal of Aging & Human Development, 46,* 229–245.

Ward, S. L., & Overton, W. F. (1990). Semantic familiarity, relevance, and the development of deductive reasoning. *Developmental Psychology, 26,* 488–493.

Wark, G. R., & Krebs, D. L. (1996). Gender and dilemma differences in real-life moral judgment. *Developmental Psychology, 32,* 220–230.

Warr, P., Jackson, P., & Banks, M. (1988). Unemployment and mental health: Some British studies. *Journal of Social Issues, 44,* 47–68.

Warren, S., Gunnar, M., Kagan, J., Anders, T., Simmens, S., Rones, M., Wease, S., Aron, E., Dahl, R., & Sroufe, A. (2003). Maternal panic disorder: Infant temperament, neurophysiology, and parenting behaviors. *Journal of the American Academy of Child & Adolescent Psychiatry, 42,* 814–825.

Wartner, U. B., Grossman, K., Fremmer-Bombik, E., & Suess, G. (1994). Attachment patterns at age six in south Germany: Predictability from infancy and implications for preschool behavior. *Child Development, 65,* 1014–1027.

Waskowic, T., & Chartier, B. (2003). Attachment and the experience of grief following the loss of a spouse. *Omega, 47,* 77–91.

Watamura, S., Donzella, B., Alwin, J., & Gunnar, M. (2003). Morning-to-afternoon increases in cortisol concentrations for infants and toddlers at child care: Age differences and behavioral correlates. *Child Development, 74,* 1006–1020.

Waters, E., Treboux, D., Crowell, J., Merrick, S., & Albersheim, L. (1995, March). *From the Strange Situation to the Adult Attachment Interview: A 20-year longitudinal study of attachment security in infancy and early adulthood.* Paper presented at the biennial meetings of the Society for Research in Child Development, Indianapolis, IN.

Watson, A., Nixon, C., Wilson, A., & Capage, L. (1999). Social interaction skills and theory of mind in young children. *Developmental Psychology, 35,* 386–391.

Watson, J. (1997). Grandmothering across the lifespan. *Journal of Gerontological Social Work, 28,* 45–62.

Watson, J. B. (1930). *Behaviorism.* New York: Norton.

Waxman, S. R., & Kosowski, T. D. (1990). Nouns mark category relations: Toddlers' and preschoolers' word-learning biases. *Child Development, 61,* 1461–1473.

Weaver, C., & Hinson, S. (2000). Job satisfaction of Asian Americans. *Psychological Reports, 86,* 586–594.

Weaver, D. A. (1994). The work and retirement decisions of older women: A literature review. *Social Security Bulletin, 57,* 3–24.

Weaver, J. (1999). Gerontology education: A new paradigm for the 21st century. *Educational Gerontology, 25,* 479–490.

Weaver, S., Clifford, E., Hay, D., & Robinson, J. (1997). Psychosocial adjustment to unsuccessful IVF and GIFT treatment. *Patient Education & Counseling, 31,* 7–18.

Webster, J., & McCall, M. (1999). Reminiscence functions across adulthood: A replication and extension. *Journal of Adult Development, 6,* 73–85.

Webster, M. L., Thompson, J. M., Mitchell, E. A., & Werry, J. S. (1994). Postnatal depression in a community cohort. *Australian & New Zealand Journal of Psychiatry, 28,* 42–49.

Webster-Stratton, C., & Reid, M. (2003). Treating conduct problems and strengthening social and emotional competence in young children: The Dina Dinosaur treatment program. *Journal of Emotional & Behavioral Disorders, 11,* 130–143.

Wechsler, H., Davenport, A., Dowdall, G., Moeykens, B., & Castillo, S. (1994). Health and behavioral consequences of binge drinking in college. *Journal of the American Medical Association, 272,* 1672–1677.

Wechsler, H., Dowdall, G., Maenner, G., Gledhill-Hoyt, J., & Lee, H. (1998). Changes in binge drinking and related problems among American college students between 1993 and 1997. *Journal of American College Health, 47,* 57–68.

Weeks, J. (2004). Same-sex partnerships. *Feminism & Psychology, 14,* 158–164.

Weimer, B., Kerns, K., & Oldenburg, C. (2004). Adolescents' interactions with a best friend: Associations with attachment style. *Journal of Experimental Psychology, 88,* 102–120.

Weinberg, R. A. (1989). Intelligence and IQ: Landmark issues and great debates. *American Psychologist, 44,* 98–104.

Weinberg, R. A., Scarr, S., & Waldman, I. D. (1992). The Minnesota transracial adoption study: A follow-up of IQ test performance. *Intelligence, 16,* 117–135.

Weinberger, J. (1996). A longitudinal study of children's early literacy experiences at home and later literacy development at home and school. *Journal of Research in Reading, 19,* 14–24.

Weindrich, D., Jennen-Steinmetz, C., Laucht, M., & Schmidt, M. (2003). Late sequelae of low birthweight: Mediators of poor school performance at 11 years. *Developmental Medicine & Child Neurology, 45,* 463–469.

Weinfield, N., & Egeland, B. (2004). Continuity, discontinuity, and coherence in attachment from infancy to late adolescence: Sequelae of organization and disorganization. *Attachment & Human Development, 6,* 73–97.

Weinstock, L. (1999). Gender differences in the presentation and management of social anxiety disorder. *Journal of Clinical Psychiatry, 60,* 9–13.

Weisburger, J. H., & Wynder, E. L. (1991). Dietary fat intake and cancer. *Hematology/Oncology Clinics of North America, 5,* 7–23.

Weisner, T., & Wilson-Mitchell, J. (1990). Nonconventional family lifestyles and sex typing in six-year olds. *Child Development, 62,* 1915–1933.

Weisse, C. S. (1992). Depression and immunocompetence: A review of the literature. *Psychological Bulletin, 111,* 475–489.

Welch, D. C., & West, R. L. (1995). Self-efficacy and mastery: Its application to issues of environmental control, cognition, and aging. *Developmental Review, 15,* 150–171.

Welch, M. (2004, February). Injustice by default: How the effort to catch "deadbeat dads" ruins innocent men's lives. *Reason Online.* Retrieved September 21, 2004, from http://reason.com/0402/fe.mw.injustice.shtml.

Welch-Ross, M. (1997). Mother-child participation in conversation about the past: Relationships to preschoolers' theory of mind. *Developmental Psychology, 33,* 618–629.

Welford, A. T. (1993). The gerontological balance sheet. In J. Cerella, J. Rybash, W. Hoyer, & M. L. Commons (Eds.), *Adult information processing: Limits on loss* (pp. 3–10). San Diego, CA: Academic Press.

Wellman, H., Cross, D., & Watson, J. (2001). Meta-analysis of theory-of-mind development: The truth about false belief. *Child Development, 72,* 655–684.

Wellman, H. M. (1982). The foundations of knowledge: Concept development in the young child. In S. G. Moore & C. C. Cooper (Eds.), *The young child: Reviews of research, Vol. 3* (pp. 115–134). Washington, DC: National Association for the Education of Young Children.

Wells, G., Malpass, R., Lindsay, R., Fisher, R., Turtle, J., & Fulero, S. (2000). From the lab to the police station. *American Psychologist, 55,* 581–598.

Wen, S. W., Goldenberg, R. L., Cutter, G. R., Hoffman, H. J., Cliver, S. P., Davis, R. O., & DuBard, M. D. (1990). Smoking, maternal age, fetal growth, and gestational age at delivery. *American Journal of Obstetrics & Gynecology, 162,* 53–58.

Wentzel, K. R., & Asher, S. R. (1995). The academic lives of neglected, rejected, popular, and controversial children. *Child Development, 66,* 754–763.

Werker, J. F., Pegg, J. E., & McLeod, P. J. (1994). A cross-language investigation of infant preference for infant-directed communication. *Infant Behavior & Development, 17,* 323–333.

Werner, E. E. (1995). Resilience in development. *Current Directions in Psychological Science, 4,* 81–85.

Werner, E. E., & Smith, R. S. (1992). *Overcoming the odds: High risk children from birth to adulthood.* Ithaca, NY: Cornell University Press.

Werner, L. A., & Gillenwater, J. M. (1990). Pure-tone sensitivity of 2- to 5-week-old infants. *Infant Behavior & Development, 13,* 355–375.

Wernet, S., Olliges, R., & Delicath, T. (2000). Postcourse evaluations of WebCT (web course tools) classes by social work students. *Research on Social Work Practice, 10,* 387–504.

Werth, J. (2000). End-of-life decisions for persons with AIDS. *American Psychological Association Public Interest Directorate.* Retrieved February 20, 2001, from http://www.apa.org/pi/aids/werth.html.

West, P., Sweeting, H., & Ecob, R. (1999). Family and friends' influences on the uptake of regular smoking from mid-adolescence to early adulthood. *Addiction, 97,* 1397–1411.

West, R. L., & Crook, T. H. (1990). Age differences in everyday memory: Laboratory analogues of telephone number recall. *Psychology & Aging, 5,* 520–529.

Westerhof, G., Katzko, M., Dittmann-Kohli, F., & Hayslip, B. (2001). Life contexts and health-related selves in old age: Perspectives from the United States, India and Congo/Zaire. *Journal of Aging Studies, 15,* 105–126.

Whitam, F. L., Diamond, M., & Martin, J. (1993). Homosexual orientation in twins: A report on 61 pairs and three triplet sets. *Archives of Sexual Behavior, 22,* 187–206.

Whitbeck, L. B., Simons, R. L., & Conger, R. D. (1991). The effects of early family relationships on contemporary relationships and assistance patterns between adult children and their parents. *Journals of Gerontology: Social Sciences, 46,* S330–337.

White, M., Wilson, M., Elander, G., & Persson, B. (1999). The Swedish family: Transition to parenthood. *Scandinavian Journal of Caring Sciences, 13,* 171–176.

White, W. H. (1992). G. Stanley Hall: From philosophy to developmental psychology. *Developmental Psychology, 28,* 25–34.

Whitehurst, G. J., Arnold, D. S., Epstein, J. N., Angell, A. L., Smith, M., & Fischel, J. E. (1994). A picture book reading intervention in day care and home for children from low-income families. *Developmental Psychology, 30,* 679–689.

Whitehurst, G. J., Falco, F. L., Lonigan, C. J., Fischel, J. E., DeBaryshe, B. D., Valdez-Menchaca, M. C., & Caulfield, M. (1988). Accelerating language development through picture book reading. *Developmental Psychology, 24,* 552–559.

Whitehurst, G. J., Fischel, J. E., Crone, D. A., & Nania, O. (1995, March). *First year outcomes of a clinical trial of an emergent literacy intervention in Head Start homes and classrooms.* Paper presented at the biennial meetings of the Society for Research in Child Development, Indianapolis, IN.

White-Traut, R., Nelson, M., Silvestri, J., Vasan, U., Littau, S., Meleedy-Rey, P., Gu, G., & Patel, M. (2002). Effect of auditory, tactile, visual, and vestibular intervention on length of stay, alertness, and feeding progression in preterm infants. *Developmental Medicine & Child Neurology, 44,* 91–97.

Whiting, B., & Edwards, C. (1988). *Children of different worlds.* Cambridge, MA: Harvard University Press.

Whittaker, R. (1998). Re-framing the representation of women in advertisements for hormone replacement therapy. *Nursing Inquiry, 5,* 77–86.

Whitty, M. (2003). Pushing the wrong buttons: Men's and women's attitudes toward online and offline infidelity. *CyberPsychology & Behavior, 6,* 569–579.

Wich, B. K., & Carnes, M. (1995). Menopause and the aging female reproductive system. *Endocrinology & Metabolism Clinics of North America, 24,* 273–295.

Wicki, W. (1999). The impact of family resources and satisfaction with division of labour on coping and worries after the birth of the first child. *International Journal of Behavioral Development, 23,* 431–456.

Wiederman, M., & Allgeier, E. (1992). Gender differences in mate selection criteria: Sociobiological or socioeconomic explanation? *Ethology & Sociobiology, 13,* 115–124.

Wiehe, V. (2003). Empathy and narcissism in a sample of child abuse perpetrators and a comparison sample of foster parents. *Child Abuse & Neglect, 27,* 541–555.

Wigfield, A., Eccles, J. S., MacIver, D., Reuman, D. A., & Midgley, C. (1991). Transitions during early adolescence: Changes in children's domain-specific self-perceptions and general self-esteem across the transition to junior high school. *Developmental Psychology, 27,* 552–565.

Wilcox, C., & Francis, L. (1997). The relationship between neuroticism and the perceived social desirability of feminine characteristics among 16–19-year-old females. *Social Behavior & Personality, 25,* 291–294.

Willett, W. C., Hunter, D. J., Stampfer, M. J., Colditz, G., Manson, J. E., Spiegelman, D., Rosner, B., Hennekens, C. H., & Speizer, F. E. (1992). Dietary fat and fiber in relation to risk of breast cancer: An 8-year follow-up. *Journal of the American Medical Association, 268,* 2037–2044.

Willett, W. C., Manson, J. E., Stampfer, M. J., Colditz, G. A., Rosner, B., Speizer, F. E., & Hennekens, C. H. (1995). Weight, weight change, and coronary heart disease in women: Risk within the "normal" weight range. *Journal of the American Medical Association, 273,* 461–465.

Williams, D. R. (1992). Social structure and the health behaviors of blacks. In K. W. Schaie, D. Blazer, & J. S. House (Eds.), *Aging, health behaviors, and health outcomes* (pp. 59–64). Hillsdale, NJ: Erlbaum.

Williams, J. E., & Best, D. L. (1990). *Measuring sex stereotypes: A multination study* (rev. ed.). Newbury Park, CA: Sage.

Willis, S. L. (1996). Everyday problem solving. In J. E. Birren & K. W. Schaie (Eds.), *Handbook of the psychology of aging* (4th ed., pp. 287–307). San Diego, CA: Academic Press.

Willis, S. L., Jay, G. M., Diehl, M., & Marsiske, M. (1992). Longitudinal change and prediction of everyday task competence in the elderly. *Research on Aging, 14,* 68–91.

Wilmore, J., Stanforth, P., Gagnon, J., Rice, T., Mandel, S., Leon, A., Rao, D., Skinner, J., & Bouchard, C. (2001). Cardiac output and stroke volume changes with endurance training: The HERITAGE Family Study. *Medical Science & Sports Exercise, 33,* 99–106.

Wilson, H., & Donenberg, G. (2004). Quality of parent communication about sex and its relationship to risky sexual behavior among youth in psychiatric care: A pilot study. *Journal of Child Psychology & Psychiatry & Allied Disciplines, 45,* 387–395.

Wilson, W. J. (1995). Jobless ghettos and the social outcome of youngsters. In P. Moen, G. H. Elder, Jr., & K. Lüscher (Eds.), *Examining lives in context: Perspectives on the ecology of human development* (pp. 527–543). Washington, DC: American Psychological Association.

Wimmer, H., Mayringer, H., & Landerl, K. (1998). Poor reading: A deficit in skill-automatization or a phonological deficit? *Scientific Studies of Reading, 2,* 321–340.

Winter, L., Lawton, M., Casten, R., & Sando, R. (2000). The relationship between external events and affect states in older people. *International Journal of Aging & Human Development, 50,* 85–96.

Winter, R. (1999). A Biblical and theological view of grief and bereavement. *Journal of Psychology & Christianity, 18,* 367–379.

Wintre, M., & Yaffe, M. (2000). First-year students' adjustment to university life as a function of relationships with parents. *Journal of Adolescent Research, 15,* 9–37.

Wolak, J., Mitchell, K., & Finkelhor, D. (2002). Close online relationships in a national sample of adolescents. *Adolescence, 37,* 441–455.

Wolfe, C., & Bell, M. (2004). Working memory and inhibitory control in early childhood: Contributions from physiology, temperament, and language. *Developmental Psychobiology, 44,* 68–83.

Wolfe, L., & List, J. (2004). Locus of control is fairly stable over time but does change as a result of natural events, such as the acquisition of college education. *Structural Equation Modeling, 11,* 244–260.

Wolfson, C., Handfield-Jones, R., Glass, K. C., McClaran, J., & Keyserlingk, E. (1993). Adult children's perceptions of their responsibility to provide care for dependent elderly parents. *The Gerontologist, 33,* 315–323.

Wolinsky, F. D., Stump, T. E., & Clark, D. (1995). Antecedents and consequences of physical activity and exercise among older adults. *The Gerontologist, 35,* 451–462.

Wong, C., & Tang, C. (2004). Coming out experiences and psychological distress of Chinese homosexual men in Hong Kong. *Archives of Sexual Behavior, 33,* 149–157.

Wong, D. (1993). *Whaley & Wong's essentials of pediatric nursing.* St. Louis, MO: Mosby-Yearbook, Inc.

Wong, M., Shapiro, M., Boscardin, J., & Ettner, S. (2002). Contribution of major diseases to disparities in mortality. *New England Journal of Medicine, 347,* 1585–1592.

Wood, C., & Terrell, C. (1998). Pre-school phonological awareness and subsequent literacy development. *Educational Psychology, 18,* 253–274.

Woods, N., & Mitchell, E. (1997). Pathways to depressed mood for midlife women: Observations from the Seattle Midlife Women's Health Study. *Research in Nursing & Health, 20,* 119–129.

Woodward, L., & Fergusson, D. (2000). Childhood peer relationship problems and later risks of educational under-achievement and unemployment. *Journal of Child Psychology & Psychiatry & Allied Disciplines, 41,* 191–201.

Woodward, M., & Tunstall-Pedoe, H. (1995). Alcohol consumption, diet, coronary risk factors, and prevalent coronary heart disease in men and women in the Scottish heart health study. *Journal of Epidemiology & Community Health, 49,* 354–362.

Working Group for the PEPI Trial (1995). Effects of estrogen or estrogen/progestin regimens on heart disease risk factors in postmenopausal women: The Postmenopausal Estrogen/Progestin Interventions (PEPI) Trial. *Journal of the American Medical Association, 273,* 199–208.

World Health Organization. (2000). *Violence against women.* Retrieved September 1, 2000, from http://www.who.int.

Worrell, F. (1997). Predicting successful or non-successful at-risk status using demographic risk factors. *High School Journal, 81,* 46–53.

Wortman, C. B., & Silver, R. C. (1989). The myths of coping with loss. *Journal of Consulting & Clinical Psychology, 57,* 349–357.

Wortman, C. B., & Silver, R. C. (1990). Successful mastery of bereavement and widowhood: A life course perspective. In P. B. Baltes & M. M. Baltes (Eds.), *Successful aging: Perspectives from the behavioral sciences* (pp. 225–264). New York: Cambridge University Press.

Wortman, C. B., & Silver, R. C. (1992). Reconsidering assumptions about coping with loss: An overview of current research. In L. Montada, S. Filipp, & M. J. Lerner (Eds.), *Life crises and experiences of loss in adulthood* (pp. 341–365). Hillsdale, NJ: Erlbaum.

Wortman, C. B., Silver, R. C., & Kessler, R. C. (1993). The meaning of loss and adjustment to bereavement. In M. S. Stroebe, W. Stroebe, & R. O. Hansson (Eds.), *Handbook of bereavement* (pp. 349–366). Cambridge, England: Cambridge University Press.

Wright, C., & Birks, E. (2000). Risk factors for failure to thrive: A population-based survey. *Child: Care, Health & Development, 26,* 5–16.

Wright, J., Huston, A., Murphy, K., St. Peters, M., Pinon, M., Scantlin, R., & Kotler, J. (2001). The relations of early television viewing to school readiness and vocabulary of children from low-income families: The early window project. *Child Development, 72,* 1347–1366.

Writing Group for the Women's Health Initiative Investigators. (2002). Risks and benefits of estrogen plus progestin in healthy postmenopausal women: Principal results from the Women's Health Initiative randomized controlled trial. *Journal of the American Medical Association, 288,* 321–333.

Wu, Z., & Penning, M. (1997). Marital instability after midlife. *Journal of Family Issues, 18,* 459–478.

Wyatt, G., Axelrod, J., Chin, D., Carmona, J., & Loeb, T. (2000). Examining patterns of vulnerability to domestic violence among African American women. *Violence Against Women, 6,* 495–514.

Wyatt, J., & Carlo, G. (2002). What will my parents think? Relations among adolescents' expected parental reactions, prosocial moral reasoning and prosocial and antisocial behaviors. *Journal of Adolescent Research, 17,* 646–666.

Xie, H., Cairns, R., & Cairns, B. (1999). Social networks and configurations in inner-city schools: Aggression, popularity, and implications for students with EBD. *Journal of Emotional & Behavioral Disorders, 7,* 147–155.

Yamada, A., & Singelis, T. (1999). Biculturalism and self-construal. *International Journal of Intercultural Relations, 23,* 697–709.

Yang, H., & Chandler, D. (1992). Intergenerational relations: Grievances of the elderly in rural China. *Journal of Comparative Family Studies, 23,* 431–453.

Yang, H., Lu, S., Liaw, Y., You, S., Sun, C., Wang, L., Hsiao, C., Chen, P., Chen, D., & Chen, C. (2002). Hepatitis B/e antigen and the risk of hepatocellular carcinoma. *New England Journal of Medicine, 347,* 168–174.

Yarcheski, A., Mahon, N., & Yarcheski, T. (1998). A study of introspectiveness in adolescents and young adults. *Western Journal of Nursing Research, 20,* 312–324.

Yeung, A., Chui, H., & Lau, I. (1999). Hierarchical and multidimensional academic self-concept of commercial students. *Contemporary Educational Psychology, 24,* 376–389.

Yirmiya, N., Eriel, O., Shaked, M., & Solomonica-Levi, D. (1998). Meta-analyses comparing theory of mind abilities of individuals with autism, individuals with mental retardation, and normally developing individuals. *Psychological Bulletin, 124,* 283–307.

Yirmiya, N., & Shulman, C. (1996). Seriation, conservation, and theory of mind abilities in individuals with autism, individuals with mental retardation, and normally developing children. *Child Development, 67,* 2045–2059.

Yirmiya, N., Solomonica-Levi, D., Shulman, C., & Pilowsky, T. (1996). Theory of mind abilities in individuals with autism, Down syndrome, and mental retardation of unknown etiology: The role of age and intelligence. *Journal of Child Psychology & Psychiatry & Allied Disciplines, 37,* 1003–1014.

Yonas, A., Elieff, C., & Arterberry, M. (2002). Emergence of sensitivity to pictorial depth cues: Charting development in individual infants. *Infant Behavior & Development, 25,* 495–514.

Yonas, A., & Owsley, C. (1987). Development of visual space perception. In P. Salpatek & L. Cohen (Eds.), *Handbook of infant perception, Vol. 2: From perception to cognition* (pp. 80–122). Orlando, FL: Academic Press.

Yordanova, J., Kolev, V., & Basar, E. (1998). EEG theta and frontal alpha oscillations during auditory processing change with aging. *Electroencephalography & Clinical Neurophysiology: Evoked Potentials, 108,* 497–505.

Yoshikawa, H. (1999). Welfare dynamics, support services, mothers' earnings, and child cognitive development: Implications for contemporary welfare reform. *Child Development, 70,* 779–801.

Young, A. (1997). I think, therefore I'm motivated: The relations among cognitive strategy use, motivational orientation and classroom perceptions over time. *Learning & Individual Differences, 9,* 249–283.

Young, J., & Rodgers, R. (1997). A model of radical career change in the context of psychosocial development. *Journal of Career Assessment, 5,* 167–182.

Young, K., & Nathanson, P. (2003). *Marriage a la mode: Answering the advocates of gay marriage.* Retrieved September 24, 2004, from http://www.marriageinstitute.ca/images/mmmode.pdf.

Young, M., & Bradley, M. (1998). Social withdrawal: Self-efficacy, happiness, and popularity in introverted and extroverted adolescents. *Canadian Journal of School Psychology, 14,* 21–35.

Young, S., Fox, N., & Zahn-Waxler, C. (1999). The relations between temperament and empathy in 2-year-olds. *Developmental Psychology, 35,* 1189–1197.

YouthBuild/Boston. (2000). *Program report.* Retrieved February 29, 2000, from http://www.doe.mass.edu/cs.www/cs.youthbuild.html.

Yuill, N. (1997). English children as personality theorists: Accounts of the modifiability, development, and origin of traits. *Genetic, Social & General Psychology Monographs, 123,* 5–26.

Yuji, H. (1996). Computer games and information-processing skills. *Perceptual & Motor Skills, 83,* 643–647.

Yurgelun-Todd, D., Killgore, W., & Young, A. (2002). Sex differences in cerebral tissue volume and cognitive performance during adolescence. *Psychological Reports, 91,* 743–757.

Zahn-Waxler, C., & Radke-Yarrow, M. (1982). The development of altruism: Alternative research strategies. In N. Eisenberg (Ed.), *The development of prosocial behavior* (pp. 109–138). New York: Academic Press.

Zahn-Waxler, C., Radke-Yarrow, M., & King, R. (1979). Child rearing and children's prosocial initiations toward victims of distress. *Child Development, 50,* 319–330.

Zahn-Waxler, C., Radke-Yarrow, M., Wagner, E., & Chapman, M. (1992). Development of concern for others. *Developmental Psychology, 28,* 126–136.

Zakriski, A., & Coie, J. (1996). A comparison of aggressive-rejected and nonaggressive-rejected children's interpretation of self-directed and other-directed rejection. *Child Development, 67,* 1048–1070.

Zani, B. (1993). Dating and interpersonal relationships in adolescence. In S. Jackson & H. Rodrigues-Tomé (Eds.), *Adolescence and its social worlds* (pp. 95–119). Hove, England: Erlbaum.

Zea, M., Reisen, C., Bell, C., & Caplan, R. (1997). Predicting intention to remain in college among ethnic minority and nonminority students. *Journal of Social Psychology, 137,* 149–160.

Zeanah, C., & Fox, N. (2004). Temperament and attachment disorders. *Journal of Clinical Child & Adolescent Psychology, 33,* 32–41.

Zelazo, N. A., Zelazo, P. R., Cohen, K. M., & Zelazo, P. D. (1993). Specificity of practice effects on elementary neuromotor patterns. *Developmental Psychology, 29,* 686–691.

Zelazo, P., Helwig, C., & Lau, A. (1996). Intention, act, and outcome in behavioral prediction and moral judgment. *Child Development, 67,* 2478–2492.

Zelinski, E., & Burnight, K. (1997). Sixteen-year longitudinal and time lag changes in memory and cognition in older adults. *Psychology & Aging, 12,* 503–513.

Zelinski, E. M., Gilewski, M. J., & Schaie, K. W. (1993). Individual differences in cross-sectional and 3-year longitudinal memory performance across the adult life span. *Psychology & Aging, 8,* 176–186.

Zhang, R., & Yu, Y. (2002). A study of children's coordinational ability for outcome and intention information. *Psychological Science* (China), *25,* 527–530.

Zhang, Y., Kohnstamm, G., Slotboom, A., Elphick, E., & Cheung, P. (2002). Chinese and Dutch parents' perceptions of their children's personality. *Journal of Genetic Psychology, 163,* 165–178.

Zhou, L., Dawson, M., Herr, C., & Stukas, S. (2004). American and Chinese college students' predictions of people's occupations, housework responsibilities, and hobbies as a function of cultural and gender influences. *Sex Roles, 50,* 463.

Zhou, M., Yao, L., & Xu, J. (2002). Studied the influence of Taoist education on the subjective well-being of the elderly. *Chinese Mental Health Journal, 16,* 175–176.

Zhou, Z., & Boehm, A. (2004). American and Chinese children's understanding of basic relational concepts in directions. *Psychology in the Schools, 41,* 261–272.

Zick, C., & Holden, K. (2000). An assessment of the wealth holdings of recent widows. *Journal of Gerontology, 55B,* S90–S97.

Zigler, E., & Finn-Stevenson, M. (1993). *Children in a changing world: Developmental and social issues.* Pacific Grove, CA: Brooks/Cole.

Zigler, E., & Hodapp, R. M. (1991). Behavioral functioning in individuals with mental retardation. *Annual Review of Psychology, 42,* 29–50.

Zigler, E., & Styfco, S. J. (1993). Using research and theory to justify and inform Head Start expansion. *Social Policy Report, Society for Research in Child Development, VII* (2), 1–21.

Zimmer, Z., Hickey, T., & Searle, M. S. (1995). Activity participation and well-being among older people with arthritis. *The Gerontologist, 35,* 463–471.

Zimmer-Gembeck, M. (1999). Stability, change and individual differences in involvement with friends and romantic partners among adolescent females. *Journal of Youth & Adolescence, 28,* 419–438.

Zimmerman, C. (2000). The development of scientific reasoning skills. *Developmental Review, 20,* 99–149.

Zimmerman, M., Copeland, L., Shope, J., & Dielman, T. (1997). A longitudinal study of self-esteem: Implications for adolescent development. *Journal of Youth & Adolescence, 26,* 117–141.

Zimmerman, S., Scott, A., Park, N., Hall, S., Wetherby, M., Gruber-Baldini, A., & Morgan, L. (2003). Social engagement and its relationship to service provision in residential care and assisted living. *Social Work Research, 27,* 6–18.

Zimmermann, P. (2004). Attachment representations and characteristics of friendship relations during adolescence. *Journal of Experimental Child Psychology, 88,* 83–101.

Zisook, S., Chentsova-Dutton, Y., & Shuchter, S. (1998). PTSD following bereavement. *Annals of Clinical Psychiatry, 10,* 157–163.

Zisook, S., Paulus, M., Shuchter, S., & Judd, L. (1997). The many faces of depression following spousal bereavement. *Journal of Affective Disorders, 45,* 85–94.

Zucker, A., Ostrove, J., & Stewart A. (2002). College-educated women's personality development in adulthood: Perceptions and age differences. *Psychology & Aging, 17,* 236–244.

Zunker, V. (1994). *Career Counseling.* Pacific Grove, CA: Brooks/Cole.

Zunzunegui, M., Alvarado, B., Del Ser, T., & Otero, A. (2003). Social networks, social integration, and social engagement determine cognitive decline in community-dwelling Spanish older adults. *Journals of Gerontology, Series B: Psychological Sciences & Social Sciences, 58B,* S93–S100.

Glossary

ability goals goals based on a desire to be superior to others

accommodation changing a scheme as a result of some new information

achievement test a test designed to assess specific information learned in school

activities of daily living (ADLs) self-help tasks such as bathing, dressing, and using the toilet

activity theory the idea that it is normal and healthy for older adults to try to remain as active as possible for as long as possible

adaptive reflexes reflexes, such as sucking, that help newborns survive

adolescence the transitional period between childhood and adolescence

affect dysregulation an interaction pattern in which a caregiver's emotional responses to an infant interfere with the baby's ability to learn how to regulate his or her emotions

affectional bond the emotional tie to an infant experienced by a parent

ageism a prejudicial view of older adults that characterizes them in negative ways

aging in place living in a noninstitutional environment, to which modifications have been made to accommodate an older adult's needs

aggression behavior intended to harm another person or an object

alcoholism physical and psychological dependence on alcohol

Alzheimer's disease a very severe form of dementia, the cause of which is unknown

amenity move post-retirement move away from kin to a location that has some desirable feature, such as year-round warm weather

amnion fluid-filled sac in which the fetus floats until just before it is born

analytical style a tendency to focus on the details of a task

anorexia nervosa an eating disorder characterized by self-starvation

anoxia oxygen deprivation experienced by a fetus during labor and/or delivery

assimilation the process of using a scheme to make sense of an event or experience

association areas parts of the brain where sensory, motor, and intellectual functions are linked

assortative mating (homogamy) sociologists' term for the tendency to mate with someone who has traits similar to one's own

asthma a chronic lung disease, characterized by sudden, potentially fatal attacks of breathing difficulty

atherosclerosis narrowing of the arteries caused by deposits of a fatty substance called plaque

attachment the emotional tie to a parent experienced by an infant, from which the child derives security

attachment theory the view that the ability and need to form an attachment relationship early in life are genetic characteristics of all human beings

attention-deficit hyperactivity disorder (ADHD) a mental disorder that causes children to have difficulty attending to and completing tasks

atypical development development that deviates from the typical developmental pathway in a direction that is harmful to the individual

auditory acuity how well one can hear

authoritarian parenting style a style of parenting that is low in nurturance and communication, but high in control and maturity demands

authoritative parenting style a style of parenting that is high in nurturance, maturity demands, control, and communication

automaticity the ability to recall information from long-term memory without using short-term memory capacity

avoidant couples partners who agree to disagree and who minimize conflict by avoiding each other

babbling the repetitive vocalizing of consonant-vowel combinations by an infant

Bayley Scales of Infant Development the best-known and most widely used test of infant "intelligence"

behavior genetics the study of the role of heredity in individual differences

behaviorism the view that defines development in terms of behavior changes caused by environmental influences

Big Five, the a set of five major dimensions of personality, including extraversion, agreeableness, conscientiousness, neuroticism, and openness/intellect

bilingual education an approach to second-language education in which children receive instruction in two different languages

brain death the point at which vital signs, including brain activity, are absent and resuscitation is no longer possible

bulimia an eating disorder characterized by binge eating and purging

cardiovascular disease (CVD) a set of disease processes in the heart and circulatory system

career ladder the milestones associated with a particular occupation

caregiver burden a term for the cumulative negative effects of caring for an elderly or disabled person

case study an in-depth examination of a single individual

centration the young child's tendency to think of the world in terms of one variable at a time

cephalocaudal pattern growth that proceeds from the head downward

cesarean section (c-section) delivery of an infant through incisions in the abdominal and uterine walls

chromosomes strings of genetic material in the nuclei of cells

class inclusion the understanding that subordinate classes are included in larger, superordinate classes

classical conditioning learning that results from the association of stimuli

climacteric the term used to describe the adult period during which reproductive capacity declines or is lost

clinical death a period during which vital signs are absent but resuscitation is still possible

clique four to six young people who appear to be strongly attached to one another

cognitive domain changes in thinking, memory, problem-solving, and other intellectual skills

cognitive theories theories that emphasize mental processes in development, such as logic and memory

cohort a group of individuals who share the same historical experiences at the same times in their lives

colic an infant behavior pattern involving intense daily bouts of crying totaling 3 or more hours a day

companionate relationships relationships in which grandparents have frequent contact and warm interactions with grandchildren

compensatory (kinship) migration a move to a location near family or friends that happens when an elder requires frequent help because of a disability or disease

concrete operational stage Piaget's third stage of cognitive development, during which children construct schemes that enable them to think logically about objects and events in the real world

conscience the list of "don'ts" in the superego; violation of any of these rules leads to feelings of guilt

conservation the understanding that matter can change in appearance without changing in quantity

constructivists theorists who argue that language development is a subprocess of general cognitive development

control group the group in an experiment that receives either no special treatment or a neutral treatment

conventional morality in Kohlberg's theory, the level of moral reasoning in which judgments are based on rules or norms of a group to which the person belongs

cooing making repetitive vowel sounds, particularly the uuu sound

corpus callosum the membrane that connects the right and left hemispheres of the cerebral cortex

correlation a relationship between two variables that can be expressed as a number ranging from -1.00 to $+1.00$

critical period a specific period in development when an organism is especially sensitive to the presence (or absence) of some particular kind of experience

cross-gender behavior behavior that is atypical for one's own sex but typical for the opposite sex

cross-linking the formation of undesirable bonds between proteins or fats

cross-modal transfer transfer of information from one sense to another, as happens when an infant can recognize by feel a toy he has seen but never before felt

cross-sectional design a research design in which groups of people of different ages are compared

crowd a combination of cliques, which includes both males and females

crystallized intelligence knowledge and judgment acquired through education and experience

decentration thinking that takes multiple variables into account

deductive logic a type of reasoning, based on hypothetical premises, that requires predicting a specific outcome from a general principle

defense mechanisms strategies for reducing anxiety, such as repression, denial, or projection, proposed by Freud

deferred imitation imitation that occurs in the absence of the model who first demonstrated it

delinquency antisocial behavior that includes law-breaking

dementia a neurological disorder involving problems with memory and thinking that affect an individual's emotional, social, and physical functioning

deoxyribonucleic acid (DNA) chemical material that makes up chromosomes and genes

dependent variable the characteristic or behavior that is expected to be affected by the independent variable

dialectical thought a form of thought involving recognition and acceptance of paradox and uncertainty

disengagement theory the theory that it is normal and healthy for older adults to scale down their social lives and to separate themselves from others to a certain degree

dishabituation responding to a somewhat familiar stimulus as if it were new

dominant-recessive pattern pattern of inheritance in which a single dominant gene influences a person's phenotype but two recessive genes are necessary to produce an associated trait

dyslexia problems in reading or the inability to read

eclecticism the use of multiple theoretical perspectives to explain and study human development

ecological theory Bronfenbrenner's theory that explains development in terms of relationships between individuals and their environments, or interconnected contexts

ego according to Freud, the thinking element of personality

ego ideal the list of "dos" in the superego; failure to live up to any of these leads to feelings of shame

ego integrity the feeling that one's life has been worthwhile

ego integrity versus despair stage the last of Erikson's psychosocial stages, in which older adults must achieve a sense of satisfaction with their lives

egocentrism the young child's belief that everyone sees and experiences the world the way she does

embryonic stage the second stage of prenatal development, from week 2 through week 8, during which the embryo's organ systems form

emotional regulation the ability to control emotional states and emotion-related behavior

empathy the ability to identify with another person's emotional state

empiricists theorists who argue that perceptual abilities are learned

endocrine glands glands that secrete hormones governing growth and other aspects of physical development

English-as-a-second-language (ESL) program an approach to second-language education in which children attend English classes for part of the day and receive most of their academic instruction in English

episodic memories recollections of personal events

equilibration the process of balancing assimilation and accommodation to create schemes that fit the environment

ethnic identity a sense of belonging to an ethnic group

ethnography a detailed description of a single culture or context

ethology a perspective on development that emphasizes genetically determined survival behaviors presumed to have evolved through natural selection

executive processes information-processing skills that involve devising and carrying out strategies for remembering and solving problems

experiment a study that tests a causal hypothesis

experimental group the group in an experiment that receives the treatment the experimenter thinks will produce a particular effect

expressive language the ability to use sounds, signs, or symbols to communicate meaning

expressive style a style of word learning characterized by low rates of nounlike terms and high use of personal-social words and phrases

extended family a social network of grandparents, aunts, uncles, cousins, and so on

extinction the gradual elimination of a behavior through repeated nonreinforcement

false belief principle an understanding that enables a child to look at a situation from another person's point of view and determine what kind of information will cause that person to have a false belief

fast-mapping the ability to categorically link new words to real-world referents

fetal stage the third stage of prenatal development, from week 9 to birth, during which growth and organ refinement take place

filial piety the idea that children have a duty to care for their aging parents

flexible goal adjustment a behavior pattern in which individuals adjust goals in order to enhance the likelihood of success

fluid intelligence the aspect of intelligence that reflects fundamental biological processes and does not depend on specific experiences

foreclosure in Marcia's theory, the identity status of a person who has made a commitment without having gone through a crisis; the person has simply accepted a parentally or culturally defined commitment

formal operational stage the fourth of Piaget's stages, during which adolescents learn to reason logically about abstract concepts

frail elderly older adults whose physical and/or mental impairments are so extensive that they cannot care for themselves

free radicals molecules or atoms that possess an unpaired electron

gametes cells that unite at conception (ova in females; sperm in males)

gender concept understanding of gender, gender-related behavior, and sex roles

gender constancy the understanding that gender is a component of the self that is not altered by external appearance

gender constancy theory Kohlberg's assertion that children must understand that gender is a permanent characteristic before they can adopt appropriate sex roles

gender identity the ability to correctly label oneself and others as male or female

gender schema theory an information-processing approach to gender concept development that asserts that people use a schema for each gender to process information about themselves and others

gender stability the understanding that gender is a stable, life-long characteristic

generativity a sense that one is making a valuable contribution to society by bringing up children or mentoring younger people in some way

generativity versus stagnation stage the seventh of Erikson's stages, in which middle-aged adults find meaning in contributing to the development of younger individuals

genes pieces of genetic material that control or influence traits

genital stage in Freud's theory, the period during which people reach psychosexual maturity

genotype the unique genetic blueprint of each individual

geriatric dysthymia chronic depressed mood in older adults

germinal stage the first stage of prenatal development, beginning at conception and ending at implantation (approximately 2 weeks)

gerontology the scientific study of aging

glial cells specialized cells in the brain that support neurons

gonadotrophic hormones hormones responsible for the development of the sex organs

gonads sex glands (ovaries in females; testes in males)

goodness-of-fit the degree to which an infant's temperament is adaptable to his or her environment, and vice versa

grieving the emotional response to a death

habituation a decline in attention that occurs because a stimulus has become familiar

handedness a strong preference for using one hand or the other that develops between 3 and 5 years of age

Hayflick limit the genetically programmed time limit to which each species is theoretically proposed to be subject, after which cells no longer have any capacity to replicate themselves accurately

hippocampus a brain structure that is important in learning

holophrases combinations of gestures and single words that convey more meaning than just the word alone

hospice care an approach to care for the terminally ill that emphasizes individual and family control of the process of dying

hostile aggression aggression used to hurt another person or gain an advantage

hostile/detached couples partners who fight regularly, rarely look at each other, and lack affection and support

hostile/engaged couples partners who have frequent arguments and lack the balancing effect of humor and affection

human development the scientific study of age-related changes in behavior, thinking, emotion, and personality

hypertension elevated blood pressure

hypothetico-deductive reasoning the ability to derive conclusions from hypothetical premises

id in Freud's theory, the part of the personality that comprises a person's basic sexual and aggressive impulses; it contains the libido and motivates a person to seek pleasure and avoid pain

identity an understanding of one's unique characteristics and how they have been, are, and will be manifested across ages, situations, and social roles

identity achievement in Marcia's theory, the identity status achieved by a person who has been through a crisis and reached a commitment to ideological or occupational goals

identity crisis Erikson's term for the psychological state of emotional turmoil that arises when an adolescent's sense of self becomes "unglued" so that a new, more mature sense of self can be achieved

identity diffusion in Marcia's theory, the identity status of a person who is not in the midst of a crisis and who has made no commitment

identity versus role confusion in Erikson's theory, the stage during which adolescents attain a sense of who they are

independent variable the presumed causal element in an experiment

inductive discipline a discipline strategy in which parents explain to children why a punished behavior is wrong

inductive logic a type of reasoning in which general principles are inferred from specific experiences

industry versus inferiority stage the fourth of Erikson's psychosocial stages, during which children develop a sense of their own competence through mastery of culturally defined learning tasks

infant mortality death within the first year of life

inflections additions to words that change their meaning (e.g., the s in toys, the ed in waited)

information-processing theory a theoretical perspective that uses the computer as a model to explain how the mind manages information

insecure/ambivalent attachment a pattern of attachment in which the infant shows little exploratory behavior, is greatly upset when separated from the mother, and is not reassured by her return or efforts to comfort him

insecure/avoidant attachment a pattern of attachment in which an infant avoids contact with the parent and shows no preference for the parent over other people

insecure/disorganized attachment a pattern of attachment in which an infant seems confused or apprehensive and shows contradictory behavior, such as moving toward the mother while looking away from her

institutional migration a move to an institution such as a nursing home that is necessitated by a disability

instrumental activities of daily living (IADLs) more intellectually demanding daily living tasks such as doing housework, cooking, and managing money

instrumental aggression aggression used to gain or damage an object

intelligence quotient (IQ) the ratio of mental age to chronological age; also, a general term for any kind of score derived from an intelligence test

intersensory integration coordination of information from two or more senses, as happens when an infant knows which mouth movements go with which sounds

intimacy the capacity to engage in a supportive, affectionate relationship without losing one's own sense of self

intimacy versus isolation Erikson's early adulthood stage, in which an individual must find a life partner or supportive friends in order to avoid social isolation

intimate partner abuse physical acts or other behavior intended to intimidate or harm an intimate partner

invented spelling a strategy young children with good phonological awareness skills use when they write

involved relationships relationships in which grandparents are directly involved in the everyday care of grandchildren or have close emotional ties with them

kin-keeper a family role, usually occupied by a woman, which includes responsibility for maintaining family and friendship relationships

language acquisition device (LAD) an innate language processor, theorized by Chomsky, that contains the basic grammatical structure of all human language

latency stage the fourth of Freud's psychosexual stages, during which 6- to 12-year-olds' libido is dormant while they establish relationships with same-sex peers

lateralization the process through which brain functions are divided between the two hemispheres of the cerebral cortex

learning disability a disorder in which a child has difficulty mastering a specific academic skill, even though she possesses normal intelligence and no physical or sensory handicaps

learning theories theories that assert that development results from an accumulation of experiences

libido in Freud's theory, an instinctual drive for physical pleasure present at birth and forming the motivating force behind virtually all human behavior

life structure in Levinson's theory, the underlying pattern or design of a person's life at a given time, which includes roles, relationships, and behavior patterns

lifespan perspective the current view of developmentalists that important changes occur throughout the entire human lifespan and that these changes must be interpreted in terms of the culture and context in which they occur; thus, interdisciplinary research is critical to understanding human development

limbic system the part of the brain that regulates emotional responses

locus of control a set of beliefs about the causes of events

longitudinal design a research design in which people in a single group are studied at different times in their lives

low birth weight (LBW) newborn weight below 5.5 pounds

maturation the gradual unfolding of a genetically programmed sequential pattern of change

maximum oxygen uptake (VO₂ max) a measure of the body's ability to take in and transport oxygen to various body organs

mean length of utterance (MLU) the average number of meaningful units in a sentence

means-end behavior purposeful behavior carried out in pursuit of a specific goal

memory strategies learned methods for remembering information

menarche the beginning of menstrual cycles

menopause the cessation of monthly menstrual cycles in middle-aged women

metacognition knowledge about how the mind thinks and the ability to control and reflect on one's own thought processes

metamemory knowledge about how memory works and the ability to control and reflect on one's own memory function

moral realism stage the first of Piaget's stages of moral development, in which children believe rules are inflexible)

moral relativism stage the second of Piaget's stages of moral development, in which children understand that many rules can be changed through social agreement

moratorium in Marcia's theory, the identity status of a person who is in a crisis but who has made no commitment

motherese (infant-directed speech) the simplified, higher-pitched speech that adults use with infants and young children

multi-factorial inheritance inheritance affected by both genes and the environment

multi-infarct dementia a form of dementia caused by one or more strokes

myelinization a process in neuronal development in which sheaths made of a substance called myelin gradually cover individual axons and electrically insulate them from one another to improve the conductivity of the nerve

naming explosion the period when toddlers experience rapid vocabulary growth, typically beginning between 16 and 24 months

nativism the view that human beings possess unique genetic traits that will be manifested in all members of the species, regardless of differences in environments

nativists theorists who claim that perceptual abilities are inborn

naturalistic observation the process of studying people in their normal environments

nature-nurture controversy the debate about the relative contributions of biological processes and experiential factors to development

neonate term for babies between birth and 1 month of age

neo-Piagetian theory an approach that uses information-processing principles to explain the developmental stages identified by Piaget

neurons specialized cells of the nervous system

niche-picking the process of selecting experiences on the basis of temperament

nontraditional post-secondary student a student who either attends college part-time or delays enrollment after high school graduation

norms average ages at which developmental milestones are reached

obesity body weight that is 20% or more above the normal weight for height; or a body mass index higher than that of most children of similar age

object concept an infant's understanding of the nature of objects and how they behave

object permanence the understanding that objects continue to exist when they can't be seen

objective (categorical) self the toddler's understanding that she or he is defined by various categories such as gender or qualities such as shyness

observational learning, or **modeling** learning that results from seeing a model reinforced or punished for a behavior

operant conditioning learning to repeat or stop behaviors because of their consequences

operational efficiency a neo-Piagetian term that refers to the maximum number of schemes that can be processed in working memory at one time

organogenesis process of organ development

osteoporosis loss of bone mass with age, resulting in more brittle and porous bones

overregularization attachment of regular inflections to irregular words such as the substitution of "goed" for "went"

palliative care a form of care for the terminally ill that focuses on relieving patients' pain, rather than curing their diseases

parental investment theory the theory that sex differences in mate preferences and mating behavior are based on the different amounts of time and effort men and women must invest in child-rearing

pathological grief symptoms of depression brought on by the death of a loved one

pelvic inflammatory disease an infection of the female reproductive tract that may result from a sexually transmitted disease and can lead to infertility

perimenopausal phase the stage of menopause during which estrogen and progesterone levels are erratic, menstrual cycles may be very irregular, and women begin to experience symptoms such as hot flashes

permissive parenting style a style of parenting that is high in nurturance and low in maturity demands, control, and communication

person perception the ability to classify others according to categories such as age, gender, and race

personality a pattern of responding to people and objects in the environment

personality disorder an inflexible pattern of behavior that leads to difficulty in educational, occupational, and social functioning

phenotype an individual's particular set of observed characteristics

phobia an irrational fear of an object, a person, a place, or a situation

phonological awareness children's understanding of the sound patterns of the language they are acquiring

physical domain changes in the size, shape, and characteristics of the body

pituitary gland gland that triggers other glands to release hormones

placenta specialized organ that allows substances to be transferred from mother to embryo and from embryo to mother, without their blood mixing

plasticity the ability of the brain to change in response to experience

polygenic inheritance pattern of inheritance in which many genes influence a trait

postconventional morality in Kohlberg's theory, the level of moral reasoning in which judgments are based on an integration of individual rights and the needs of society

postmenopausal phase the last stage of menopause beginning when a woman has had no menstrual periods for a year or more

post-secondary education any kind of formal educational experience that follows high school

preconventional morality in Kohlberg's theory, the level of moral reasoning in which judgments are based on authorities outside the self

preference technique a research method in which a researcher keeps track of how long a baby looks at each of two objects shown

premenopausal phase the stage of menopause during which estrogen levels fall somewhat, menstrual periods are less regular, and anovulatory cycles begin to occur

preoperational stage Piaget's second stage of cognitive development, during which children become proficient in the use of symbols in thinking and communicating but still have difficulty thinking logically

presbycusis normal loss of hearing with aging, especially of high-frequency tones

presbyopia normal loss of visual acuity with aging, especially the ability to focus the eyes on near objects

primary aging age-related physical changes that have a biological basis and are universally shared and inevitable

primary circular reactions Piaget's phrase to describe a baby's simple repetitive actions in substage 2 of the sensorimotor stage, organized around the baby's own body

primary sex characteristics the sex organs: ovaries, uterus, and vagina in the female; testes and penis in the male

primitive reflexes reflexes, controlled by "primitive" parts of the brain, that disappear during the first year of life

processing efficiency the ability to make efficient use of short-term memory capacity

programmed senescence theory the view that age-related declines are the result of species-specific genes for aging

prosocial behavior behavior intended to help another person

proximodistal pattern growth that proceeds from the middle of the body outward

pruning the process of eliminating unused synapses

psychoanalytic theories theories proposing that developmental change happens because of the influence of internal drives and emotions on behavior

psychological self an understanding of one's stable, internal traits

psychosexual stages Freud's five stages of personality development through which children move in a fixed sequence determined by maturation; the libido is centered in a different body part in each stage

psychosocial stages Erikson's eight stages, or crises, of personality development in which inner instincts interact with outer cultural and social demands to shape personality

punishment anything that follows a behavior and causes it to stop

qualitative change a change in kind or type

quantitative change a change in amount

reaction range a range between upper and lower boundaries for traits such as intelligence, which is established by one's genes; one's environment determines where, within those limits, one will be

receptive language comprehension of spoken language

referential style a style of word learning characterized by emphasis on things and people and their naming and description

reinforcement anything that follows a behavior and causes it to be repeated

relational aggression aggression aimed at damaging another person's self-esteem or peer relationships, such as by ostracism or threats of ostracism, cruel gossiping, or facial expressions of disdain

relational style a tendency to ignore the details of a task in order to focus on the "big picture"

relative right-left orientation the ability to identify right and left from multiple perspectives

religious coping the tendency to turn to religious beliefs and institutions for support in times of difficulty

reminiscence reflecting on past experience

remote relationships relationships in which grandparents do not see their grandchildren often

research ethics the guidelines researchers follow to protect the rights of animals used in research and humans who participate in studies

retaliatory aggression aggression to get back at someone who has hurt you

reticular formation the part of the brain that regulates attention

reversibility the understanding that both physical actions and mental operations can be reversed

role conflict any situation in which two or more roles are at least partially incompatible, either because they call for different behaviors or because their separate demands add up to more hours than there are in the day

role strain the strain experienced by an individual whose own qualities or skills do not measure up to the demands of some role

role-taking the ability to look at a situation from another person's perspective

satiety the feeling of fullness that follows a meal

schematic learning organization of experiences into expectancies, called schemas, which enable infants to distinguish between familiar and unfamiliar stimuli

scheme in Piaget's theory, an internal cognitive structure that provides an individual with a procedure to use in a specific circumstance

schizophrenia a serious mental disorder characterized by disturbances of thought such as delusions and hallucinations

secondary aging age-related changes that are due to environmental influences, poor health habits, or disease

secondary circular reactions repetitive actions in substage 3 of the sensorimotor period, oriented around external objects

secondary sex characteristics body parts such as breasts in females and pubic hair in both sexes

secular trend a change that occurs in developing nations when nutrition and health improve—for example, the decline in average age of menarche and the increase in average height for both children and adults that happened between the mid-18th and mid-19th centuries in Western countries

secure attachment a pattern of attachment in which an infant readily separates from the parent, seeks proximity when stressed, and uses the parent as a safe base for exploration

selective attention the ability to focus cognitive activity on the important elements of a problem or situation

self-care children children who are at home by themselves after school for an hour or more each day

self-efficacy the belief in one's capacity to cause an intended event to occur or to perform a task

self-esteem a global evaluation of one's own worth

self-regulation children's ability to conform to parental standards of behavior without direct supervision

semantic memories general knowledge

semiotic (symbolic) function the understanding that one object or behavior can represent another

senescence physical changes and declines associated with aging

sensitive period a span of months or years during which a child may be particularly responsive to specific forms of experience or particularly influenced by their absence

sensorimotor stage Piaget's first stage of development, in which infants use information from their senses and motor actions to learn about the world

separation anxiety expressions of discomfort, such as crying, when separated from an attachment figure

sequential design a research design that combines cross-sectional and longitudinal examinations of development

sex-role identity the gender-related aspects of the psychological self

sex roles behavior expected for males and females in a given culture

sex-typed behavior different patterns of behavior exhibited by boys and girls

sexual violence the use of physical coercion to force a person to engage in a sexual act against his or her will

shaping the reinforcement of intermediate steps until an individual learns a complex behavior

short-term storage space (STSS) neo-Piagetian theorist Robbie Case's term for the working memory

social-cognitive theory the theoretical perspective that asserts that social and personality development in early childhood are related to improvements in the cognitive domain

social clock a set of age norms defining a sequence of life experiences that is considered normal in a given culture and that all individuals in that culture are expected to follow

social death the point at which family members and medical personnel treat the deceased person as a corpse

social domain change in variables that are associated with the relationship of an individual to others

social referencing an infant's use of others' facial expressions as a guide to his or her own emotions

social role theory the idea that sex differences in mate preferences and mating behavior are adaptations to gender roles

social skills a set of behaviors that usually lead to being accepted as a play partner or friend by peers

social status an individual child's classification as popular, rejected, or neglected

socio-cultural theory Vygotsky's view that complex forms of thinking have their origins in social interactions rather than in an individual's private explorations

sociobiology the study of society using the methods and concepts of biology; when used by developmentalists, an approach that emphasizes genes that aid group survival

spatial cognition the ability to infer rules from and make predictions about the movement of objects in space

spatial perception the ability to identify and act on relationships between objects in space

states of consciousness different states of sleep and wakefulness in infants

stranger anxiety expressions of discomfort, such as clinging to the mother, in the presence of strangers

subjective self an infant's awareness that she or he is a separate person who endures through time and space and can act on the environment

successful aging the term gerontologists use to describe maintaining one's physical health, mental abilities, social competence, and overall satisfaction with one's life as one ages

sudden infant death syndrome (SIDS) a phenomenon in which an apparently healthy infant dies suddenly and unexpectedly

superego Freud's term for the part of personality that is the moral judge

synapses connections between neurons

synaptic plasticity the redundancy in the nervous system that ensures that it is nearly always possible for a nerve impulse to move from one neuron to another or from a neuron to another type of cell (e.g., a muscle cell)

synaptogenesis the process of synapse development

synchrony a mutual, interlocking pattern of attachment behaviors shared by a parent and child

systematic problem-solving the process of finding a solution to a problem by testing single factors

task goals goals based on a desire for self-improvement

telegraphic speech simple two-word sentences that usually include a noun and a verb

telomere a string of repetitive DNA at the tip of each chromosome in the body that appears to serve as a kind of timekeeping mechanism

temperament inborn predispositions, such as activity level, that form the foundations of personality

tenacious goal pursuit a behavior pattern in which individuals remain committed to goals that are difficult, and may be impossible, for them to achieve

teratogens substances, such as viruses and drugs, that can cause birth defects

terminal drop hypothesis the hypothesis that mental and physical functioning decline drastically only in the few years immediately preceding death

tertiary circular reactions The deliberate experimentation with variations of previous actions that occurs in substage 5 of the sensorimotor period

thanatology the scientific study of death and dying

theory of mind a set of ideas constructed by a child or adult to explain other people's ideas, beliefs, desires, and behavior

tinnitus persistent ringing in the ears

tracking the smooth movements of the eye used to follow the track of a moving object

traditional post-secondary student a student who attends college full-time immediately after graduating from high school

type A personality pattern a personality type associated with greater risk of coronary heart disease; it includes competitive achievement striving, a sense of time urgency, and, sometimes, hostility or aggressiveness

visual acuity how well one can see details at a distance

volunteerism performance of unpaid work for altruistic motives

umbilical cord organ that connects the embryo to the placenta

uninvolved parenting style a style of parenting that is low in nurturance, maturity demands, control, and communication

unique invulnerability the belief that bad things, including death, happen only to others

validating couples partners who express mutual respect, even in disagreements, and are good listeners

viability ability of the fetus to survive outside the womb

volatile couples partners who argue a lot and don't listen well, but still have more positive than negative interactions

wisdom a cognitive characteristic that includes accumulated knowledge and the ability to apply that knowledge to practical problems of living, popularly thought to be more commonly found in older adults

zygote single cell created when sperm and ovum unite

Practice Tests
CHAPTER 1 BASIC CONCEPTS AND METHODS

An Introduction to Human Development

1.1 The scientific study of age-related changes in behavior and mental processes is termed
   a. ageism.
   b. maturation.
   c. cohort effect.
   d. human development.

1.2 The philosophy that proposes that adults can mold children into whatever the adults want them to be is called
   a. morality.
   b. the blank slate.
   c. original sin.
   d. innate goodness.

1.3 Which of the following early theorists kept a baby biography of his children's development?
   a. Charles Darwin
   b. G. Stanley Hall
   c. Arnold Gesell
   d. Jean-Jacques Rousseau

1.4 During the 1950s, Dr. Benjamin Spock advocated
   a. understanding children's inborn needs.
   b. rigid sleeping and feeding schedules.
   c. openly displaying affection toward children.
   d. using tough-love parenting techniques.

1.5 One of the recent changes in the field of human development is that it has
   a. taken a more Freudian approach.
   b. increasingly focused on infancy.
   c. become more interdisciplinary.
   d. emphasized the role of the environment in determining behavior.

1.6 Plasticity refers to
   a. how many neural connections the brain has.
   b. the capacity for positive change in response to environmental demands.
   c. how long a person can live.
   d. how much a person's physical health declines in late adulthood.

Key Issues in the Study of Human Development

1.7 Which of the following is an example of an inborn bias that is charted for many infants?
   a. crying and snuggling to entice others to care for them
   b. sleeping through the night
   c. not liking solid foods
   d. being easy to sooth when they become distressed

1.8 If you regularly hear criticism in other people's comments, we might infer that you have developed an internal model of experience similar to which of the following basic assumptions?
   a. "I usually do things wrong, and that is why others criticize me."
   b. "I usually do things wrong, and people are cruel."
   c. "Apparently others do not see things in the same way that I do."
   d. "When I do things wrong, I can depend on others to help me."

1.9 The ecological approach to development emphasizes
   a. the environmental hazards of the place where a person lives.
   b. all of the different contexts in which the child is growing.
   c. how much the individual likes the outdoors.
   d. the child's temperament.

1.10 By far the most negative outcomes for a child are the result of a
   a. highly vulnerable child.
   b. poor or unsupportive environment.
   c. combination of high vulnerability and poor environment.
   d. combination of low vulnerability and unsupportive environment.

1.11 When a caterpillar changes into a butterfly, this is an example of a
   a. quantitative change.
   b. continuous change.
   c. universal change.
   d. qualitative change.

1.12 Thomas is forced to retire at age 70, even though he is physically and mentally healthy and does his job well. This is an example of

a. age norms.

b. ageism.

c. the social clock.

d. culture.

1.13 The idea that experiences occurring at the expected times for an individual's culture or cohort will pose fewer difficulties for an individual than experiences occurring at unexpected times is called the concept of

a. the critical period.

b. the historical period.

c. the sensitive period.

d. on-time and off-time events.

Research Designs and Methods

1.14 Sets of statements that propose general principles to explain development are called

a. theories.

b. the independent variables.

c. hypotheses.

d. the critical periods.

1.15 In the cross-sectional method,

a. the same group of subjects is given the same test repeatedly over a 20-year period.

b. surveys are administered to samples of people from around the country.

c. groups of subjects of different ages are studied.

d. the behaviors of subjects in a laboratory environment are compared with their behaviors in their natural setting.

1.16 How does childhood sexual abuse affect children?

a. Most children traumatized in this way show long-term effects.

b. Most children traumatized in this way commit suicide.

c. It depends on many variables, including how long the abuse lasted and at what age it began.

d. Most children traumatized in this way become child abusers themselves.

1.17 A study in which the intelligence test performance of the same group of children is assessed at different points in their lifetime is an example of which of the following designs?

a. sequential

b. longitudinal

c. cross-sectional

d. time-sampling

1.18 Which of the following is an advantage of a longitudinal study?

a. The research is completed in a short period of time.

b. The healthiest participants drop out.

c. The better-educated participants drop out.

d. It allows the researcher to compare performance by the same people at different ages.

1.19 Nicole studies parents and their children by watching them interact at the zoo. This is an example of the

a. naturalistic observation method.

b. case study method.

c. experimental method.

d. correlational method.

1.20 Which of the following is the major limitation of the correlational method?

a. Observer bias is likely.

b. It studies only single individuals.

c. It does not tell us about causal relationships.

d. Research ethics prevent its use in most developmental studies.

1.21 An experiment is testing the effects of observed violence of children's behavior. One group of children views a violent cartoon. A second group views a humorous nonviolent cartoon. A third group is not exposed to any cartoon. The first group is the

a. experimental group.

b. control group.

c. comparison group.

d. observational group.

1.22 Because developmental psychologists cannot systematically manipulate many of the variables they are most interested in, they often use

a. case studies.

b. ethnography.

c. quasi-experiments.

d. panel studies.

1.23 A detailed description of a single culture or context based on extensive observation is called

a. the cohort effect.

b. ageism.

c. maturation.

d. an ethnography.

1.24 Which of the following ethical standards for research involves the right to a written summary of a study's results?

a. knowledge of results

b. deception

c. informed consent

d. confidentiality

1.25 If you read a newspaper report that breastfeeding causes greater intelligence in childhood, you should

a. think about the breastfed children you know to determine if this statement is true.

b. consider whether it would be ethical to do an experiment comparing breastfed and bottle-fed children.

c. consider where the researchers work.

d. think about whether you were breastfed or bottle-fed.

CHAPTER 2 THEORIES OF DEVELOPMENT

Psychoanalytic Theories

2.1 Which of the following parts of personality is entirely in our unconscious?

    a. ego

    b. superego

    c. id

    d. Oedipus

2.2 Which term best describes Freud's theory of development?

    a. psychosocial stages

    b. ego development

    c. id integrity

    d. psychosexual stages

2.3 Erikson's theory differed from Freud's in that Erikson

    a. emphasized instincts more heavily than Freud.

    b. believed that our urges are primarily destructive.

    c. believed that development continued throughout the lifespan.

    d. is considered more pessimistic than Freud.

2.4 Which of the following accurately summarizes Erikson's theory?

    a. A poor interpersonal relationship can cause individuals to fixate on problems.

    b. The superego is a more powerful force than the id and drives most behavior.

    c. Without societal pressures to conform to, we would be overly destructive.

    d. Healthy development requires confronting and resolving crises throughout the lifespan.

Learning Theories

2.5 Whenever the eye doctor puffs air in your eye, you blink. Now, before she puffs the air, she says "ready"; then she puffs the air, and you blink. After doing this several times, you begin to blink as soon as she says "ready." In this example, what kind of learning has taken place?

    a. classical conditioning

    b. sensitization

    c. operant conditioning

    d. habituation

2.6 What is the unconditioned stimulus in the previous question?

    a. blinking the eye

    b. saying the word "ready"

    c. the puff of air

    d. fear of the puff of air

2.7 Which of the following is an example of shaping?

    a. paying your son for mowing the lawn

    b. praising your son for his good grades

    c. reinforcing each step of your son's behavior during toilet training

    d. withholding allowance from your son when he talks back

2.8 Bandura suggests that learning can take place without direct reinforcement. What is this type of learning called?

    a. positive reinforcement

    b. modeling

    c. instrumental conditioning

    d. classical conditioning

2.9 Together, people's beliefs about what they can and cannot do form their

    a. identity.

    b. self-efficacy.

    c. self-esteem.

    d. self-image.

2.10 Which of the following is a weakness of learning theories?

    a. They give an accurate picture of the way many behaviors are learned.

    b. They are not really developmental theories.

    c. They tend to be optimistic about the possibility of changing behavior.

    d. They can explain both consistency and change in behavior.

Cognitive Theories

2.11 Piaget felt that children develop cognitively by acquiring more complex schemes. How did he define schemes?

    a. the action of categorizing items into groups

    b. scientific theories about human development

    c. cognitive structures that provide a procedure to follow in a specific situation

    d. ideas we have about how to get what we want

2.12 You learn how to drive a car with an automatic transmission; then you try to drive a car with standard transmission. The adjustment you make is an example of the process of
   a. equilibration.
   b. assimilation.
   c. accommodation.
   d. hierarchical categorizing.

2.13 Chris is in elementary school and has learned to solve problems logically. Which of Piaget's stages best describes her level of cognitive development?
   a. concrete operational
   b. sensorimotor
   c. preoperational
   d. formal operational

2.14 Which of the following is the goal of information-processing theory?
   a. to distinguish the relative impact of nature and nurture
   b. to trace the stages of how thinking develops
   c. to uncover the hidden meaning of dreams
   d. to explain how the mind manages information

2.15 According to information-processing theory, when you are reading, you pull information about a word's meaning out of your
   a. sensory memory.
   b. short-term memory.
   c. working memory.
   d. long-term memory.

2.16 Which of the following is a weakness of Piaget's theory?
   a. He developed innovative methods of studying children's thinking.
   b. He was wrong about the ages at which children develop specific skills.
   c. His theory forced psychologists to think about child development in a new way.
   d. His findings have been replicated in virtually every culture and every cohort of children since the 1920s.

Current Trends

2.17 Which of these theories focuses on genetically determined survival behaviors that are assumed to have evolved through natural selection?
   a. ethology
   b. nativism
   c. psychoanalytic
   d. sociobiology

2.18 Individuals' behavior
   a. is completely fixed by their genetic inheritance.
   b. is based totally on their relationships with their mothers.
   c. will always be a joint product of the genetic pattern and the environment.
   d. is based on their socioeconomic status.

2.19 In Vygotsky's theory, what does scaffolding mean?
   a. building new schemes
   b. developing a firm sense of self-identity
   c. acquiring new emotional experiences through direct experience
   d. modeling and structuring a child's learning experience

2.20 Arrange the following contexts of Bronfenbrenner's ecological theory in the proper order, from the largest circle to the smallest.
   a. macrosystem, exosystem, microsystem, biological context
   b. microsystem, biological context, macrosystem, exosystem
   c. biological context, exosystem, microsystem, macrosystem
   d. macrosystem, biological context, microsystem, exosystem

2.21 A child's school is a part of her
   a. microsystem.
   b. macrosystem.
   c. exosystem.
   d. mesosystem.

Comparing Theories

2.22 In which of the following theories is a person most likely to be an active participant in his own environment?
   a. Freud's psychosexual theory
   b. classical conditioning
   c. operant conditioning
   d. Piaget's cognitive-developmental theory

2.23 In which of the following theories does development happen continuously?
   a. Erikson's psychosocial theory
   b. classical conditioning
   c. social-learning theory
   d. cognitive developmental

2.24 According to _____, a person is more likely to be influenced by nature than by nurture.
   a. Freud's psychosexual theory
   b. classical conditioning
   c. operant conditioning
   d. Piaget's cognitive developmental theory

2.25 Which of the following is *not* one of the criteria of usefulness listed in the text?
   a. Does it stimulate thinking and research?
   b. Does it explain the basic facts of development?
   c. Does it explain a person's motivation for his or her behavior?
   d. Does it generate predictions that can be tested with scientific methods?

Moral Development

2.26 Which of the following is *not* a level in the stages of moral development proposed by Lawrence Kohlberg?

a. preconventional morality

b. formal operational morality

c. conventional morality

d. postconventional morality

2.27 The civil disobedience carried out by the American civil rights movement in the 1950s and 1960s is an example of which stage of moral reasoning?

a. naïve hedonism

b. interpersonal conformity

c. social contract orientation

d. universal ethical principles

2.28 Kohlberg would say that persons who assume personal responsibility for their actions based on fundamental universal principles, such as justice and basic respect for all people, are using _____ as the basis for their moral reasoning.

a. interpersonal conformity

b. social contract

c. instrumental purpose and exchange

d. universal ethical principles

2.29 Which of the following is least important in the development of moral reasoning?

a. increased ability to see the perspective of others

b. a social environment that provides opportunities for meaningful, reciprocal dialogue about moral issues

c. parents' ability to express moral views in words that reflect a child's level of understanding

d. a foreclosure identity

2.30 Which of the following statements best describes the relationship between moral reasoning and moral behavior?

a. There is no correlation.

b. There is a perfect negative correlation.

c. There is a perfect positive correlation.

d. They are correlated, but the relationship is far from perfect.

2.31 According to Gilligan, the two distinct moral orientations involved in moral reasoning are

a. justice and empathy.

b. justice and care.

c. honesty and sincerity.

d. right and wrong.

2.32 According to researchers, what are the two forms of delinquency among adolescents?

a. vandalism and law-breaking

b. male peer-directed and female peer-directed

c. childhood-onset and adolescent-onset

d. internal and external

2.33 Which of the following is *not* a factor in the developmental pathway for childhood-onset delinquency?

a. child-specific influences, such as personality and temperament

b. parents' lack of ability to control the child

c. rejection by nonaggressive peers and gravitation toward peers with similar behavior

d. peer influence

2.34 The Fast Track Project with aggressive elementary school children has resulted in all of the following except

a. better recognition of emotions.

b. lower ratings of aggressiveness.

c. better academic performance.

d. more competence in social relationships.

CHAPTER 3   PHYSICAL AND COGNITIVE DEVELOPMENT IN EARLY ADULTHOOD

Physical Functioning

3.1   Researchers have determined that, among adults, _____ has a very powerful influence on life expectancy and quality of health.
   a. social class
   b. IQ
   c. number of children
   d. marital status

3.2   Age-related, inevitable physical changes that have a biological basis and that are shared by all human beings are known as _____ aging.
   a. normative
   b. primary
   c. secondary
   d. tertiary

3.3   Which of the following is *not* an example of primary aging?
   a. decline in ability to detect and discriminate among various smells
   b. reduction in the density of dendrites
   c. lowered fertility of women
   d. obesity

3.4   Which of the following is *not* one of the recommendations for slowing the effects of secondary aging?
   a. Get enough calcium.
   b. Stop smoking.
   c. Eat a lower-fat diet.
   d. Exercise moderately once a week.

3.5   The part of the brain that regulates emotional responses is the
   a. pituitary gland.
   b. thymus.
   c. limbic system.
   d. gray matter.

3.6   Measured in a person at rest, VO_2
   a. begins to decline gradually at about age 35.
   b. shows no change with age.
   c. increases gradually starting at age 40.
   d. declines for women and goes up for men as a function of aging.

3.7   Ovulation becomes sporadic and unpredictable in some women as early as
   a. the late 20s.
   b. the early 30s.
   c. the late 30s.
   d. the early 40s.

3.8   Infants born as a result of IVF conception are more likely to be
   a. born post-term.
   b. low-birth-weight.
   c. girls.
   d. healthy.

Health and Wellness

3.9   Blockages in the fallopian tubes caused by _____ may result in infertility in women.
   a. fatty deposits
   b. immature T cells
   c. pelvic inflammatory disease
   d. excess hormone production

3.10   According to the longitudinal Alameda County Study of health habits, the habit of _____ is not related to mortality.
   a. eating breakfast
   b. getting physical exercise
   c. smoking
   d. getting regular sleep

3.11   Which of the following is not linked with adequate social support?
   a. lower risk of depression
   b. increased stress
   c. lower risk of disease
   d. lower risk of death

3.12   Which of the following terms represents the belief in one's capacity to master tasks or control one's behavior or environment?
   a. dialectical thought
   b. external locus of control
   c. post-formal thinking
   d. self-efficacy

3.13 Which of the following is *not* a characteristic associated with abusiveness in an intimate relationship?
   a. alcohol and drug problems
   b. mental illness
   c. need for control in the relationship
   d. frequent unemployment

3.14 Intimate partner abuse may have all of the following effects on women except
   a. low self-esteem.
   b. depression.
   c. increased risk of heart disease.
   d. suicidality.

3.15 All but which one of the following might result from being a victim of sexual violence?
   a. posttraumatic stress disorder
   b. decreased intelligence
   c. physical trauma
   d. sexual dysfunction

3.16 The risk of mental health problems, such as depression or anxiety, is higher
   a. for men than for women.
   b. in early adulthood, between the ages of 25 and 44.
   c. for the elderly than for young adults.
   d. for middle-aged adults than for young adults.

3.17 Which of the following is *not* a mental disorder that is more common in young adulthood than in middle adulthood?
   a. substance abuse disorder
   b. depression
   c. alcoholism
   d. dementia

3.18 In the United States, binge drinking is particularly common among
   a. college students.
   b. those who dropped out of high school.
   c. those who have been unable to find employment.
   d. individuals who are professionally employed.

Cognitive Changes

3.19 Many researchers propose that new cognitive structures, or stages of thinking, develop in adulthood. Which of the following is *not* a structure, or stage, of thinking that develops in adulthood?
   a. contextual validity
   b. crystallized intelligence
   c. dialectical thought
   d. problem finding

3.20 Research evidence indicates that the term that best describes intellectual ability across adulthood is
   a. crystallized.
   b. declining.
   c. increasing.
   d. stable.

3.21 Which form of intelligence depends heavily on education and experience, such as the skills and knowledge learned as part of growing up in a culture?
   a. contextual
   b. crystallized
   c. dialectical
   d. fluid

Post-Secondary Education

3.22 What is the approximate percentage of U.S. high school graduates enrolling in college as full-time students immediately after graduation?
   a. 25%
   b. 33%
   c. 50%
   d. 75%

3.23 Nontraditional post-secondary students are most likely to complete their program of study when they are enrolled in _____ programs.
   a. graduate or professional
   b. bachelor's degree
   c. associate degree
   d. vocational certificate

3.24 Which of the following is a true statement about gender differences in college?
   a. Women are more likely than men to cheat.
   b. Women have higher graduation rates than men.
   c. Women score higher than men on college entrance examinations.
   d. Women are more likely than men to be admitted into honors programs.

3.25 Which of the following is *not* a true statement about the effect of race on the college experience?
   a. Native Americans have the highest drop-out rate of all the ethnic groups.
   b. African American students are more likely than students of other races or ethnicities to perceive themselves as not fitting into the college community.
   c. A strong sense of racial identity is associated with persistence and academic performance for African American students.
   d. African Americans who attend historically black colleges show more improvement in cognitive development than African Americans who attend predominantly white schools.

CHAPTER 4 SOCIAL AND PERSONALITY DEVELOPMENT IN EARLY ADULTHOOD

Theories of Social and Personality Development

4.1 According to Erikson, which of the following is an essential prerequisite to the successful resolution of the crisis of intimacy versus isolation?
   a. an identity
   b. maturity
   c. a life structure
   d. dialectical thought

4.2 According to Levinson, the first phase of a period of adjustment is called the
   a. culmination phase.
   b. beginning phase.
   c. mid-era phase.
   d. novice phase.

4.3 A woman who chose her marital partner according to the basic premises of evolutionary theory would choose
   a. another woman.
   b. a man who provided financial resources and stability.
   c. a sexually proficient partner.
   d. a healthy younger man.

4.4 Which of the following is *not* an element of social role theory explanations of mate selection?
   a. women's and men's different investments in childbearing and parenting
   b. women's and men's different gender roles
   c. choosing mates on the basis of similarity of key traits or characteristics
   d. acquiring a mate by offering one's assets, such as earning power

4.5 Which of the following is an illustration of the exchange model of mate selection?
   a. Betty is very concerned that she not be forced to raise a family as a single parent, so she proceeds cautiously when she begins a new relationship.
   b. College-educated women who anticipate earning high incomes prefer to have husbands whose earning potential is higher than their own.
   c. Men choose young, healthy women as mates in order to ensure that future children will be healthy.
   d. Men and women use their personal assets, such as sexuality or earning potential, to bargain for potential mates.

Intimate Relationships

4.6 After eight years, the probability that a couple will divorce is approximately
   a. 50%.
   b. 20%.
   c. 10%.
   d. 0%.

4.7 Which of the following factors does *not* contribute to marital satisfaction?
   a. personality characteristics of the partners
   b. sexual compatibility
   c. negative attitudes toward divorce
   d. emotional affection

4.8 Which of the following types of conflict management is associated with divorce?
   a. avoiding conflict and agreeing to disagree without rancor
   b. having disagreements that don't escalate
   c. having frequent hot arguments and little humor and affection in the relationship
   d. having frequent hot arguments but high levels of laughter and affection in the relationship

4.9 Which of the following would *not* be typical following a divorce?
   a. increase in physical illness
   b. decrease in automobile accidents
   c. higher risk of suicide
   d. increased feelings of failure

4.10 How do lesbian couples differ from heterosexual couples?
   a. Attachment is not important in predicting satisfaction in a lesbian relationship, whereas it is for heterosexual couples.
   b. Lesbian couples do not argue as much as heterosexual couples.
   c. Lesbian couples are more egalitarian than heterosexual couples.
   d. Lesbian couples do not usually expect monogamy, whereas heterosexual couples do.

4.11 Which of the following statements about the impact of marriage is true?

a. Men appear to benefit more from marriage than women do.

b. Married adults are more likely to smoke or drink to excess than singles are.

c. Men are more sensitive to negativity in their relationships than women are.

d. Married adults are less likely to exercise than single women are.

Parenthood and Other Relationships

4.12 Which of the following is a mood disorder that is likely to affect women who have recently given birth?

a. bipolar disorder

b. dysthymia

c. major depressive disorder

d. postpartum depression

4.13 What is the best predictor of postpartum depression?

a. being depressed during the pregnancy

b. giving birth to twins

c. having an unplanned and unwanted pregnancy

d. having a premature delivery

4.14 Of the following couples, which would most likely report the lowest level of marital satisfaction?

a. a recently married couple who do not have children

b. a couple who have three children in elementary school

c. a couple whose children are in college or employed

d. a retired couple who frequently take care of their grandchildren

4.15 Which of the following variables does *not* contribute to a couple's satisfaction or dissatisfaction following the birth of a child?

a. the division of labor

b. support from extended family members

c. the couple's coping strategies

d. the couple's intelligence

4.16 Which of the following statements about adult friendships appears to be true?

a. Men are generally less satisfied with their friendships than women are.

b. Men's friendships involve a lot more social support than women's friendships.

c. Women have fewer friends, but they are very close to them.

d. There tend to be no real significant differences between men's and women's friendships.

4.17 If a young man described his friendships, he would mostly speak of

a. self-disclosure and emotional support.

b. lengthy conversations.

c. shared activities.

d. the close, intimate quality of the relationships.

The Role of Worker

4.18 A young adult's choice of an occupation or a career is least likely to be influenced by

a. the social class of her/his family.

b. the family's value system and moral beliefs.

c. lifestyle habits.

d. gender.

4.19 As a scientist with a national research institute, Maria has conceived, planned, and organized a number of national research initiatives that have examined influences on the physical and mental health of adolescents. According to Holland's personality and work typology, Maria is most likely of which personality type?

a. conventional

b. enterprising

c. investigative

d. social

4.20 Which of the following statements about job satisfaction is true?

a. It stays high for men until retirement.

b. It is lowest in early adulthood.

c. It is highest in young adulthood.

d. It stays high for women until retirement.

4.21 What effects does early promotion have on the career ladder?

a. It is associated with greater advancements over one's entire career.

b. It leads to early burnout and lower job satisfaction.

c. It depends on gender and the type of promotion.

d. It creates fast track advancement for a few years, then co-worker backlash.

4.22 Donald Super proposes that the work sequence of young adulthood has two stages, the _____ stage and the _____ stage.

a. familial; external

b. investigative; realistic

c. interrupted; continuous

d. trial; establishment

4.23 Why do women feel role conflict at trying to be a worker, a parent, and a spouse, whereas men don't?

a. Employed men work more hours a week, in family work and paid employment combined, than do women.

b. Employed women work more hours a week, in family work and paid employment combined, than do men.

c. Men define themselves in terms of how caring they are, whereas women don't.

d. Women define themselves more in terms of their careers than do men.

4.24 Which of the following is the best example of role conflict?

    a. Sandra is seeking another job because she is uncomfortable with her supervisor's sexual advances.

    b. When her daughter had a high fever, Carmen had to miss an important meeting with a client.

    c. When another accountant left, Lauren agreed to take on additional clients on a temporary basis.

    d. Larry feels overwhelmed with the multiple responsibilities of his new job as a systems engineer.

4.25 Recasting or reframing a situation in a way that identifies the positive elements is called

    a. conflict management.

    b. depression.

    c. homogamy.

    d. cognitive restructuring.

CHAPTER 5 PHYSICAL AND COGNITIVE DEVELOPMENT IN MIDDLE ADULTHOOD

Physical Changes

5.1 Which of the following statements is true about the brain at mid-life?

a. The distribution of electrical activity is the same in the brains of alcoholics and those of nonalcoholics.

b. Cognitive tasks activate a larger area of brain tissue in middle-aged adults than in younger adults.

c. In middle age, more new synapses are formed than are lost.

d. Synaptic density continues to increase across adulthood.

5.2 What is the most consistent finding when neuropsychologists study how the aging brain affects cognitive functioning?

a. Dementia is the primary form of change in the aging brain.

b. Middle-aged adults have more lapses of attention and make poorer decisions than young adults.

c. Cognitive tasks activate a larger area of brain tissue in middle-aged adults than in younger adults.

d. Difficult tasks activate less brain tissue than easy tasks.

5.3 Which of the following terms refers to the time in middle or late adulthood when the reproductive capacity declines or is lost?

a. climacteric

b. genital senility

c. menopause

d. presbyopia

5.4 The term _____ means cessation of the menses.

a. menopause

b. osteoporosis

c. presbycusis

d. perimenopause

5.5 Which of the following is *not* a change typically associated with menopausal phases?

a. irregular menstrual periods

b. fluctuating hormone levels

c. thinner and less elastic vaginal tissue

d. major depression

5.6 The primary cause of menopause is

a. increasing testosterone levels.

b. decreasing estrogen levels.

c. shrinking of the uterus.

d. increased estrogen levels and decreased estradiol levels.

5.7 Which of the following is the best summary of the current research on hormone replacement therapy?

a. Hormone replacement therapy has no positive effects.

b. Hormone replacement therapy reduces the incidence of heart disease and Alzheimer's disease, but also has some negative effects.

c. Hormone replacement therapy has some positive effects, but there are ways of achieving these results without the risks associated with hormone replacement therapy.

d. Hormone replacement therapy has many benefits and no known risks.

5.8 In the condition known as _____, bone mass is reduced and bones become more brittle and porous when calcium is lost from the bones.

a. atherosclerosis

b. osteoporosis

c. presbycusis

d. Perthes' disease

5.9 Why is osteoporosis a serious health risk?

a. It causes an increased risk of coronary heart disease.

b. It is the major risk factor for diabetes.

c. It causes an increased risk of fractures and disability.

d. It lowers levels of "good" cholesterol and raises levels of "bad" cholesterol.

5.10 Which of the following statements about the incidence of osteoporosis in middle adulthood is accurate?

a. It occurs only in women.

b. The process for women is accelerated by menopause.

c. The process for men is linked to impotence.

d. It is unavoidable.

5.11 Which of the following conditions makes it necessary to use reading glasses or bifocals in order to focus on near objects?

a. cataracts

b. glaucoma

c. presbycusis

d. presbyopia

5.12 What is the central physiological process of cardiovascular disease?

a. atherosclerosis

b. an autoimmune reaction

c. hypertension

d. osteoarthritis

Health and Wellness

5.13 Which of the following statements about risk factors for heart disease is true?

    a. The risk factors are cumulative.

    b. The risk factors are completely controllable with the right effort.

    c. The only consistent controllable cause is smoking.

    d. Men are at a higher risk because they strain their hearts more than women do.

5.14 What is the type A personality characteristic that is most consistently linked to cardiovascular disease?

    a. extraversion

    b. hostility

    c. neuroticism

    d. urgency

5.15 Which of the following is *not* a known risk factor for cancer?

    a. alcohol consumption

    b. high blood pressure

    c. smoking

    d. fat consumption

5.16 What is the most significant predictor of health among middle-aged U.S. adults?

    a. degree of life satisfaction

    b. personality

    c. gender

    d. social class

Cognitive Functioning

5.17 According to Nancy Denney's model of physical and cognitive aging, the positive effects of exercise on an individual's physical or cognitive abilities will be limited by the person's

    a. age.

    b. level of life satisfaction.

    c. level of motivation.

    d. temperament.

5.18 According to the Seattle Longitudinal Study, _____ has been linked to intellectual decline.

    a. cardiovascular disease

    b. menopause

    c. obesity

    d. prostate cancer

5.19 Which of the following is research-based information that you might offer family members who sought your advice regarding what they could do to influence their longevity and help maintain their cognitive abilities in the middle adult years?

    a. Engage in cultural activities such as attending concerts.

    b. Seek new experiences.

    c. Drink a moderate amount of alcohol, especially wine.

    d. Exercise and stay physically active.

5.20 A review of the research findings on cognitive change in middle adulthood reveals that

    a. vocabularies decline.

    b. problem-solving ability is significantly impaired.

    c. mental processes get slower, but actual losses are small.

    d. performance is maintained or even slightly improved on tasks of fluid intelligence.

5.21 What aspect of memory do we utilize when we try to recall the words of a song or a poem?

    a. dialectic

    b. episodic

    c. mnemonic

    d. semantic

5.22 The cognitive structures and schematic processing of middle adulthood may lead an individual to remember

    a. material that is visually scanned better than material that is heard.

    b. episodic memories better than semantic memories.

    c. broad themes or summary information better than specific words.

    d. problem-solving strategies better than verbal skills.

5.23 According to Simonton's review of the lifetime creativity and productivity of thousands of notable scientists, people are most creative

    a. in their adolescent years.

    b. in their 20s.

    c. at about age 40.

    d. in their 60s.

CHAPTER 6 SOCIAL AND PERSONALITY DEVELOPMENT IN MIDDLE ADULTHOOD

Theories of Social and Personality Development

6.1 According to Erik Erikson, what is the developmental dilemma faced by middle-aged adults?
   a. ego integrity versus despair
   b. generativity versus stagnation
   c. inferiority versus extraversion
   d. role resolution versus identity ambivalence

6.2 Which of the following is *not* generative behavior, as described by Erikson?
   a. indulging oneself with the purchase of luxury items
   b. adopting a child
   c. teaching at the neighborhood community center
   d. serving as a leader in one's religious or faith organization

6.3 How does generativity affect later mental health?
   a. Generative people are more likely to be satisfied with their lives.
   b. Generative people are less likely to have dementia.
   c. Generative people are more likely to have attachment disorders.
   d. Generative people are less likely to commit suicide.

6.4 The research suggests that the idea of a mid-life crisis
   a. is true for men but not women.
   b. is true for women but not men.
   c. is true for most American adults.
   d. is not true.

6.5 In her job as department manager, Lois often must go to late afternoon meetings that make her unable to attend her children's extracurricular activities, such as games or concerts. What is Lois experiencing in these instances?
   a. role ambiguity
   b. role conflict
   c. role overload
   d. role strain

6.6 What is the central idea of Duvall's theory of the stages of the family life cycle?
   a. Adult development occurs as a function of the systematic and predictably changing family roles that an individual occupies.
   b. The family roles of middle adulthood are determined by the family roles an individual occupied as an infant, child, and adolescent.
   c. The success of the transition from mid-life family member to late-life solitary person is determined by the generativity versus stagnation dilemma of middle age.
   d. The family life cycle can be organized into four phases: courtship, new marriage, family, and empty nest.

6.7 Which of the following is the term used to describe transitions that are highly predictable and widely shared in any given culture or cohort, such as marrying or becoming a parent?
   a. life course markers
   b. rites of passage
   c. role evolution
   d. zones of proximal development

Changes in Relationships and Personality

6.8 Professionals label the middle adulthood cohort the _____ generation, because their family role involves giving assistance and maintaining affectional bonds in both directions in the generational chain.
   a. enabling
   b. co-dependent
   c. sandwich
   d. pipeline

6.9 Which of the following is *not* a true statement regarding the "empty nest"?
   a. Almost all women experience an identity crisis when their children leave home.
   b. Women are more likely to describe the empty nest as a positive event than a negative event.
   c. Marital satisfaction often rises among mid-life adults when their children leave home.
   d. During the empty next stage, the parental role continues, but the nature of the role is different from what it was when the children were home.

6.10 According to research on grandparent-grandchildren relationships, _____ grandparents may be everyday participants in the rearing of their grandchildren or may create unusually close emotional bonds with them.

　　a. companionate

　　b. compassionate

　　c. enmeshed

　　d. involved

6.11 The Green children see their grandparents frequently and spend time with them participating in routine, everyday activities such as watching television, visiting relatives, or preparing meals. According to the categories developed by behavioral scientists, this situation most closely resembles which type of relationship?

　　a. approximal

　　b. companionate

　　c. congenial

　　d. involved

6.12 Custodial grandparenting is more common among

　　a. white Americans than African Americans.

　　b. African Americans than white Americans.

　　c. middle-class Americans than low-income Americans.

　　d. high-income Americans than middle-class Americans.

6.13 Which of the following suggestions would *not* help a mother-in-law avoid conflict with her daughter-in-law?

　　a. Frequently drop in to see your son unexpectedly.

　　b. Don't criticize your daughter-in-law behind her back.

　　c. Don't insist on being visited every weekend or holiday.

　　d. Respect your children's wishes regarding how grandchildren are to be cared for.

6.14 When families negotiate the task of providing care to elderly parents, who is most likely to assume the caregiving role?

　　a. either the youngest or the oldest child

　　b. young adult grandchildren who do not have full-time employment or educational roles

　　c. family members who have the greatest financial resources

　　d. daughters or daughters-in-law

6.15 Which of the following terms refers to the cumulative negative effects, such as more frequent illness, experienced by caregivers who provide care to frail or demented family members?

　　a. caregiver's lament

　　b. caregiver burden

　　c. filial burden

　　d. sandwich generation effect

6.16 Which of the following does *not* characterize social networks in middle age, according to research?

　　a. more friends

　　b. less frequent interaction among friends

　　c. relationships as intimate as they were at earlier ages

　　d. less need for emotional support from individuals outside the family

6.17 Which of the following statements is true about continuity and change in personality?

　　a. Masculinity and femininity are correlated with self-esteem in adults of all ages.

　　b. The Big Five personality traits are relatively stable across adolescence and adulthood.

　　c. Personality consistently changes with age.

　　d. Traits are gained across adulthood, but traits are not lost.

Mid-Life Career Issues

6.18 Which of the following is the most accurate statement about the way middle-aged women and men experience and deal with work satisfaction?

　　a. Women and men cite similar sources of job dissatisfaction in middle age: time pressure, boring work, and difficult co-workers.

　　b. Women who are dissatisfied at work tend to communicate and negotiate with their supervisors and co-workers in order to improve unsatisfactory conditions.

　　c. Men who are dissatisfied at work tend to complain and encourage discontent among co-workers.

　　d. Men's work satisfaction is linked to their perceptions about the value and meaning of their work and the quality of relationships they formed on the job.

6.19 Which of the following is *not* a subprocess of Paul and Margaret Baltes's model of strategies that allow aging workers to maintain their job performance?

　　a. selection

　　b. maintenance

　　c. optimization

　　d. compensation

6.20 Which of the following is the best example of optimization in the "selective optimization with compensation" model of compensatory strategies for job performance?

　　a. Eric believes that one of his most effective managerial skills is to delegate important tasks and responsibilities to the junior executives in his department.

　　b. In order to remain up to date in her clinical knowledge and therapeutic techniques, Dr. Smith completes approximately 50 hours of continuing education seminars and workshops each year.

　　c. When Mrs. Washington anticipates that her busy day will trouble her arthritic knee, she wears her knee brace and takes anti-inflammatory pain medication.

　　d. Carmen has managed to lose 50 pounds by eating a low-fat, vegetarian diet and following an exercise program recommended by her physician.

6.21 Which of the following is an indirect effect of job loss?

　　a. higher levels of anxiety

　　b. financial strain

　　c. deterioration of marital relationships

　　d. higher levels of depression

6.22 Which of the following is *not* a reason for an involuntary career change?

a. An employee wishes to pursue advancement to the next career level.

b. A departmental reorganization has eliminated certain jobs.

c. New technology means that job skills are out of date.

d. Economic problems have triggered job layoffs.

6.23 Which of the following does *not* influence mental health status and ability to adjust during involuntary career transitions?

a. maintaining relationships with former co-workers

b. personality characteristics, such as neuroticism and openness to experience

c. coping skills

d. social support system

6.24 What do Baby Boomers expect from retirement?

a. They expect to work at least part-time.

b. They expect to enjoy their leisure time.

c. They expect an increase in income after retirement.

d. They expect to have only 5 years in retirement.

6.25 Many financial analysts claim that some individual Baby Boomers will be in precarious positions during retirement because of all except which one of the following?

a. They have invested in the stock market.

b. They have borrowed to achieve their financial objectives.

c. They expect to have more years in retirement.

d. They have inherited substantial wealth.

CHAPTER 7 PHYSICAL AND COGNITIVE DEVELOPMENT IN LATE ADULTHOOD

Variability in Late Adulthood

7.1 Which of the following is one of the reasons that the United States will face a demographic crisis in the near future?
   a. There were many births between 1946 and the early 1960s.
   b. Baby Boomers had more children than their parents did.
   c. Most Baby Boomers are not astute enough to manage their own finances.
   d. Americans value their autonomy.

7.2 Which of the following groups of individuals is growing most rapidly?
   a. teenagers
   b. the young old (aged 60–75)
   c. the old old (aged 75–85)
   d. the oldest old (aged 85 and over)

7.3 The most important determinant of the trajectory of an adult's mental health after age 65 is
   a. his parents' health.
   b. his parents' mental health.
   c. his family life.
   d. his health.

7.4 Which of the following is the term used by gerontologists to describe a limitation in an individual's ability to perform certain roles and tasks, such as self-care, cooking, or managing money?
   a. functional capacity
   b. independence boundary
   c. disability
   d. senility

7.5 Which of the following would *not* be considered an instrumental activity of daily living (or IADL)?
   a. bathing
   b. dressing
   c. boarding an airplane
   d. cooking

7.6 Which of the following is *not* one of the reasons that there are more women than men in nursing homes?
   a. Women live longer than men.
   b. More women than men have restricted movement because of arthritis.
   c. Women are more sociable than men.
   d. More women than men lack partners who can assist with daily living tasks.

7.7 What is the maximum lifespan for humans?
   a. 80 years for a 65-year-old man, and 90 years for an 80-year-old man
   b. 70 to 80 years, depending on race and gender
   c. 90 to 100 years
   d. 110 or 120 years

7.8 According to scientists, what is the function of telomeres?
   a. They accelerate the onset of dementia.
   b. They cause Alzheimer's disease.
   c. They facilitate synaptic plasticity.
   d. They regulate the aging process.

7.9 If you could recommend one health habit to help older family members reduce their risk of mortality and lower their risk of diseases such as diabetes, arthritis, or cancer, which of the following would be the best recommendation?
   a. Eat a diet high in antioxidants.
   b. Reduce your amount of nightly sleep.
   c. Develop and use a social support network.
   d. Get regular physical exercise.

Physical Changes

7.10 Which of the following explains why nerve impulses continue to move from neuron to neuron even when some dendrites have been lost?
   a. cross-linking
   b. geriatric dysthymia
   c. synaptic plasticity
   d. telomeres

7.11 Which of the following is *not* an age-related change to the auditory system that affects older adults?
   a. Excess ear wax is secreted.
   b. The eardrum gradually collapses.
   c. Bones of the middle ear calcify and become less elastic.
   d. Nerve pathways to the brain show some degeneration.

7.12 Age-based deterioration in the sense of _____ is least likely to have negative implications for an older adult's health or well-being.
   a. smell
   b. taste
   c. touch
   d. vision

7.13 Which of the following theories suggests that aging occurs when atoms or molecules possessing an unpaired electron enter into harmful chemical reactions within the body's cells?
   a. cross-linking
   b. DNA reparation
   c. free radicals
   d. programmed senescence

7.14 Which of the following is *not* an effect that is hypothesized to occur as a result of eating a diet high in antioxidants?
   a. enhanced sex drive
   b. somewhat increased longevity
   c. lower rates of heart disease
   d. improved vision among patients who have retinal degeneration

7.15 How do sleep patterns change in old age?
   a. Older adults go to bed later at night.
   b. Older adults wake earlier in the morning.
   c. Older adults enter "deep sleep" more easily.
   d. Older adults wake up less frequently in the middle of the night.

7.16 Which of the following is the most likely explanation for overeating and weight gain in late adulthood?
   a. Older people overeat because their taste buds are more sensitive and food tastes better.
   b. Among older people, a keener sense of smell stimulates appetite and causes overeating.
   c. As a result of age-related cognitive deficits in decision-making, older persons can no longer judge when to stop eating.
   d. The ability of the brain to regulate appetite by responding to the sense of satiety is impaired.

7.17 How does the frequency of sexual activity change across the lifespan?
   a. For men, the frequency of sexual activity increases, but for women, it decreases.
   b. The frequency of sexual activity increases with age.
   c. The frequency of sexual activity decreases with age.
   d. The frequency of sexual activity remains stable.

Mental Health

7.18 How is Alzheimer's disease diagnosed?
   a. from an autopsy
   b. from a CAT scan when symptoms occur
   c. based on behavioral observations at age 60
   d. based on memory tests done when symptoms occur

7.19 According to current estimates, what percentage of adults over age 65 in the United States are in a form of institutional care?
   a. 48%
   b. 24%
   c. 16%
   d. 4%

7.20 Which of the following is *not* an accurate statement about institutionalization among the elderly?
   a. More older men than older women are in nursing homes.
   b. Approximately 25% of those over 65 can expect to spend as long as a year in a nursing home.
   c. Approximately 40% of current older adults can expect to spend some amount of time in a nursing home before death.
   d. Although it is not inevitably so, involuntary institutionalization may be a causal factor in the rapid decline and death of older persons.

7.21 What is the strongest predictor of depression and dysthymia among older adults?
   a. family size
   b. health status
   c. marital status
   d. degree of community involvement

Cognitive Changes

7.22 According to experts, which of the following is most responsible for age-based decline in older adults' memory?
   a. disease processes, such as atherosclerosis or multi-infarct dementia
   b. depression or geriatric dysthymia
   c. physiological changes in neurons and loss of nerve conductance speed
   d. insufficient practice of metamemory skills

7.23 Which of the following is *not* one of Paul Baltes' criteria of wisdom?
   a. understanding relevance of context
   b. semantic knowledge
   c. factual knowledge
   d. procedural knowledge

7.24 According to Gene Cohen, at what age are older adults in the encore phase of creativity?
   a. 50s
   b. 60s
   c. 70s
   d. 80s

CHAPTER 8   SOCIAL AND PERSONALITY DEVELOPMENT IN LATE ADULTHOOD

Theories of Social and Personality Development

8.1 A man who accepts the way he has lived his life has developed which of the following psychological dimensions, according to Erikson?

    a. a psychological moratorium

    b. dissonance

    c. ego integrity

    d. maturation

8.2 The notion that reminiscence is a necessary and healthy aspect of aging and preparation for death is a component of which of the following theories?

    a. Erikson's stage of ego integrity versus despair

    b. disengagement theory

    c. Rowe and Kahn's successful aging paradigm

    d. Loevinger's theory of adult development

Individual Differences

8.3 The paradigm for successful aging proposed by Rowe and Kahn does *not* include which of the following dimensions?

    a. staying healthy and able

    b. retaining communication and problem-solving skills

    c. retaining cognitive abilities

    d. social engagement

8.4 Which of the following best predicts life satisfaction among older adults?

    a. high intelligence

    b. a sense of control over one's life

    c. a past history that included diverse experiences and adventures

    d. communication and problem-solving skills

8.5 Which of the following does *not* accurately describe how religious coping affects older adults?

    a. Elders who place a great deal of emphasis on religious faith worry less than those who do not.

    b. Elders who say their religious beliefs are important to them think that their lives serve an important purpose.

    c. Elders who have strong religious beliefs are more likely to commit suicide to be with God.

    d. Elders who regularly attend religious services are healthier, both physically and emotionally.

Social Relationships

8.6 What is a possible consequence when older adults experience a loss of role content or role definition?

    a. alienation or isolation

    b. a "license for eccentricity"

    c. an opportunity to assert one's individuality

    d. all of the above

8.7 Which of the following would *not* be included in the definition of aging in place?

    a. making modifications to a home in response to the changing needs of an older adult

    b. going to a nursing home

    c. hiring a home-based physical therapist

    d. living in one's home

8.8 Which of the following factors does *not* influence an older adult's decision to live with an adult child?

    a. intelligence

    b. health status

    c. income

    d. ethnicity

8.9 Who is most likely to abuse an elderly person?

    a. the person's children

    b. the person's spouse

    c. nursing home personnel or other professional caregivers

    d. strangers, such as muggers or thieves

8.10 Who is likely to provide most of the care and assistance needed by a married older adult who has a significant disability or dementia?

    a. children or other relatives

    b. professional health care providers

    c. a community or volunteer service such as a hospice

    d. the spouse

8.11 Which of the following is *not* a true statement about the family relationships of older adults?

    a Most older adults report regular contact with their adult children.

    b. The interaction between older adults and their children occurs for both social and functional purposes.

    c. Good relationships and regular contact with adult children are necessary for happiness and life satisfaction in old age.

    d. According to research, childless elders are just as happy and well adjusted as those who have children.

8.12 Contact with friends has a significant impact on all of the following except

    a. overall life satisfaction.

    b. self-esteem.

    c. likelihood that an individual will divorce.

    d. amount of loneliness.

8.13 In comparison to men's, women's

    a. friendships involve less disclosure.

    b. friendships involve less intimacy.

    c. social networks are smaller.

    d. social networks are larger.

Career Issues in Late Life

8.14 At the present time in the United States, what is the most common age for men to retire?

    a. 60

    b. 62

    c. 65

    d. 70

8.15 Which of the following is *not* an accurate statement about the factors that influence the decision to retire?

    a. Poor health lowers the average age of retirement by one to three years.

    b. Retirement-age adults who have young children at home are likely to retire early in order to rear their children.

    c. Poor health and social norms often cause working-class adults to retire earlier than individuals in the middle or upper socioeconomic groups.

    d. The most reliable predictor of retirement for a woman is whether her spouse has retired.

8.16 Which of the following does *not* play a role in older adults' decisions to retire?

    a. age

    b. religion

    c. financial support

    d. health

8.17 What is the largest source of retirement income for most older adults in the United States?

    a. financial support from children

    b. investments such as stocks, bonds, or individual retirement accounts

    c. public assistance such as food stamps

    d. Social Security

8.18 Which of the following is *not* an accurate statement about income during retirement for older adults in the United States?

    a. In 1998, only 11% of adults over age 65 were living below the poverty line.

    b. Married older adults have a higher poverty rate than single older adults.

    c. Improvements in Social Security benefits have benefited older adults more than any other age group.

    d. Compared to previous cohorts of retired adults, the current cohort of older adults had better jobs and earned more money before retirement and therefore has more savings and better benefits after retirement.

8.19 According to Charles Longino's typology of residential moves among the elderly, a/an _____ migration occurs when an older person's health deteriorates and regular nursing care is necessary.

    a. amenity

    b. compensatory

    c. familial

    d. institutional

8.20 According to Charles Longino, those who make amenity moves are likely to be

    a. in poor health.

    b. experiencing a health crisis that necessitates nursing care.

    c. married, healthy, and in possession of an adequate income.

    d. women.

8.21 Which of Longino's migrations is most likely to occur latest in adulthood?

    a. kinship

    b. amenity

    c. compensatory

    d. institutional

8.22 What is the biggest obstacle to employment for older adults who choose not to retire?

    a. poor health that interferes with job responsibilities

    b. the concerns of potential employers about older adults' ability to learn new job skills

    c. poor work habits, such as absenteeism or inability to get along with co-workers

    d. an absence of jobs or work opportunities suitable for older adults

8.23 Which of the following is *not* a reason that some men choose to continue working instead of retiring?

    a. They must continue working out of economic necessity.

    b. They want to venture into new lines of work.

    c. Their spouses do not want them at home all day.

    d. They enjoy the satisfaction that work offers.

8.24 How does skill learning in the old old compare to skill learning in younger adults?

    a. The old old take less time to learn new material than do younger adults.

    b. The old old are not able to learn new skills, whereas younger adults are.

    c. The old old take more time to learn new material than do younger adults.

    d. There is no difference in the skill learning of the old old and younger adults.

CHAPTER 9 DEATH, DYING, AND BEREAVEMENT

The Experience of Death

9.1 What form of death has an individual experienced if she has died and been resuscitated?
   a. brain death
   b. clinical death
   c. marginal death
   d. social death

9.2 What form of death has an individual experienced if he has survived on life-support systems for a number of years?
   a. brain death
   b. clinical death
   c. primitive death
   d. social death

9.3 The vast majority of people in industrialized countries die
   a. at home.
   b. in relatives' homes.
   c. in hospitals.
   d. in nursing homes.

9.4 Which of the following is *not* an element of the philosophy of hospice care?
   a. Death is normal and should be faced and accepted.
   b. Medical care should be palliative, not curative.
   c. The patient and the family should control decisions about the patient's care.
   d. Treatment should be provided by professionals trained in hospice procedures for palliative care.

The Meaning of Death across the Lifespan

9.5 When they start school, most children seem
   a. not to know anything about death.
   b. to understand the permanence of death.
   c. to engage in magical thinking about death.
   d. not to understand the universality of death.

9.6 Most young adults
   a. feel that they are invulnerable to death.
   b. underestimate the age at which they will die.
   c. feel suicidal.
   d. are not afraid of death.

9.7 According to research, how would a young adult who has just been told she has six months to live most likely want to spend her remaining time?
   a. focusing on her inner life
   b. completing unfinished projects and tying up loose ends
   c. living as she has been living, with no change in her life
   d. spending time with her loved ones

9.8 According to research, how would an older adult who has just been told she has six months to live most likely want to spend her remaining time?
   a. focusing on her inner life by praying or meditating
   b. making sure that loved ones and survivors are ready for her death
   c. completing unfinished business
   d. traveling and having exotic adventures

9.9 Which group of people is most afraid of death?
   a. young adults
   b. middle-aged adults
   c. older adults
   d. men

9.10 Feelings about death are influenced by all of the following except
   a. religious beliefs.
   b. age.
   c. people's sense of worth.
   d. intelligence.

The Process of Dying

9.11 According to Elizabeth Kübler-Ross's model of the psychological stages of dying, what is a necessary stage if an individual is to accept his death?
   a. ego integrity
   b. depression
   c. geriatric dysthymia
   d. resolution of disagreements with loved ones

9.12 An individual who says to her physician "You have made a mistake. I'm not sick!" is most likely in the _____ stage of Kübler-Ross's model of psychological preparation for death.
   a. denial
   b. defense
   c. rejection
   d. stoicism

9.13 Which of the following is *not* an accurate statement about criticisms of Kübler-Ross's model of the psychological stages of dying?

    a. The model has been criticized for failing to convey clear ideas or meaningful concepts about the process of dying.

    b. Kübler-Ross's study lacked methodological rigor, such as information on the ages of the patients studied and the frequency of the observations.

    c. Reactions to dying are culturally conditioned, and Kübler-Ross's model may not apply to other cultures.

    d. Clinicians and researchers do not agree that all dying persons exhibit the emotions Kübler-Ross identified or that the emotions are experienced in the order specified in the model.

9.14 Of the emotional responses identified in Kübler-Ross's model of the psychological stages of dying, which one is most common among Western patients?

    a. anger

    b. denial

    c. bargaining

    d. depression

9.15 Research into the relationship between an individual's emotional response to impending or probable death and the actual outcome suggests, in general, that

    a. emotional response to a condition does not affect outcome or survival rate.

    b. difficult patients who express their anger and hostility openly die sooner.

    c. individuals who question and challenge and have a fighting spirit have a more difficult recovery experience.

    d. emotional responses contribute to disease progress.

9.16 How does social support affect terminally ill patients?

    a. They experience less pain.

    b. They die sooner but more happily.

    c. They live longer.

    d. They need less medical treatment.

The Experience of Grieving

9.17 Which of the following is *not* a psychological function of death rituals?

    a. bring family members together

    b. helping the survivors understand the meaning of death itself

    c. showing others how much the survivors loved the person who died

    d. giving some transcendent meaning to death

9.18 Which of the following is *not* an accurate statement about the way widowhood affects physical and mental health?

    a. The experience of widowhood has a negative effect on immune system functioning.

    b. In the year after bereavement, the incidence of depression among widows and widowers rises significantly.

    c. Older adults who enter widowhood with a history of depression are more likely to experience depression after the death of their spouse.

    d. Depression is a universal symptom of grief that is unaffected by cultural factors.

9.19 Which of the following is *not* a suggestion for friends and family members supporting parents who have lost an infant?

    a. Don't refer to the deceased infant by name.

    b. Don't offer rationalizations that may offend the parents.

    c. Assure the grieving parents that their responses are normal.

    d. Express your own feelings of loss for the infant, if they are sincere.

Theoretical Perspectives on Grieving

9.20 Which of the following is *not* a Freudian concept that has influenced grief counseling?

    a. the idea that survivors need to talk openly about their loss in order to avoid negative long-term effects

    b. the idea that depression is an essential preparation for accepting one's death

    c. the use of defense mechanisms to cope with grief

    d. the concept of death as a trauma that will have physical or mental consequences for the survivors

9.21 Which of the following is not a pattern of grieving identified by Wortman and Silver?

    a. absent

    b. balanced

    c. chronic

    d. delayed

9.22 What form of euthanasia occurs when a physician hastens a person's death by withdrawing the life-support system?

    a. active euthanasia

    b. altruistic euthanasia

    c. assisted suicide euthanasia

    d. passive euthanasia

9.23 What form of euthanasia occurs when a physician hastens a patient's death by administering a fatal dose of a drug such as morphine?

a. active euthanasia

b. assisted suicide euthanasia

c. palliative euthanasia

d. resolved suicide

9.24 Where in the world is assisted suicide fully and explicitly legal?

a. nowhere

b. in the Netherlands

c. in Sweden

d. in the countries belonging to the European Common Market

Answers

CHAPTER 1

1.1	d
1.2	b
1.3	a
1.4	c
1.5	c
1.6	b
1.7	a
1.8	a
1.9	b
1.10	c
1.11	d
1.12	c
1.13	d
1.14	a
1.15	c
1.16	c
1.17	b
1.18	d
1.19	a
1.20	c
1.21	a
1.22	c
1.23	d
1.24	a
1.25	b

CHAPTER 2

2.1	c
2.2	d
2.3	c
2.4	d
2.5	a
2.6	c
2.7	c
2.8	b
2.9	b
2.10	b
2.11	c
2.12	c
2.13	a
2.14	d
2.15	d
2.16	b
2.17	a
2.18	c
2.19	d
2.20	a
2.21	a
2.22	d
2.23	b
2.24	a
2.25	c
2.26	b
2.27	c
2.28	d
2.29	d
2.30	d
2.31	b
2.32	c
2.33	d
2.34	c

CHAPTER 3

3.1	a
3.2	b
3.3	d
3.4	d
3.5	c
3.6	a
3.7	b
3.8	b
3.9	c
3.10	a
3.11	b
3.12	d
3.13	b
3.14	c
3.15	b
3.16	b
3.17	d
3.18	a
3.19	b
3.20	d
3.21	b
3.22	b
3.23	d
3.24	b
3.25	a

CHAPTER 4

4.1	a
4.2	d
4.3	b
4.4	a
4.5	d
4.6	d
4.7	b
4.8	c
4.9	b
4.10	c
4.11	a
4.12	d
4.13	a
4.14	b
4.15	d
4.16	a
4.17	c
4.18	c
4.19	c
4.20	b
4.21	a
4.22	d
4.23	b
4.24	b
4.25	d

CHAPTER 5

5.1	b
5.2	c
5.3	a
5.4	a
5.5	d
5.6	b
5.7	c
5.8	b
5.9	c
5.10	b
5.11	d
5.12	a
5.13	a
5.14	b
5.15	b
5.16	d
5.17	a
5.18	a
5.19	d
5.20	c
5.21	d
5.22	c
5.23	c

CHAPTER 6

6.1	b
6.2	a
6.3	a
6.4	d
6.5	b
6.6	a
6.7	a
6.8	c
6.9	b
6.10	d
6.11	b
6.12	b
6.13	a
6.14	d
6.15	b
6.16	a
6.17	b
6.18	a
6.19	b
6.20	b
6.21	c
6.22	a
6.23	a
6.24	a
6.25	d

CHAPTER 7

7.1	a
7.2	d
7.3	d
7.4	c
7.5	c
7.6	c
7.7	d
7.8	d
7.9	d
7.10	c
7.11	b
7.12	b
7.13	c
7.14	a
7.15	b
7.16	d
7.17	c
7.18	a
7.19	d
7.20	a
7.21	b
7.22	c
7.23	b
7.24	d

CHAPTER 8

8.1	c
8.2	a
8.3	b
8.4	b
8.5	c
8.6	d
8.7	b
8.8	a
8.9	b
8.10	d
8.11	c
8.12	c
8.13	d
8.14	b
8.15	b
8.16	b
8.17	d
8.18	b
8.19	d
8.20	c
8.21	d
8.22	b
8.23	c
8.24	c

CHAPTER 9

9.1	b
9.2	a
9.3	c
9.4	d
9.5	b
9.6	a
9.7	d
9.8	a
9.9	b
9.10	d
9.11	b
9.12	a
9.13	a
9.14	d
9.15	d
9.16	c
9.17	c
9.18	d
9.19	a
9.20	b
9.21	b
9.22	d
9.23	a
9.24	b